10-10-95

D1239412

*Northern English Books, Owners, and
Makers in the Late Middle Ages*

The Pilgrim meets Hagiography as a female English bookseller in her shop.
John Lydgate, *Pilgrimage of the Life of Man*. London, British Library MS
Cotton Tiberius A.vii, folio 91, ca. 1450.
Courtesy Trustees of the British Library.

Northern English Books, Owners, and Makers in the Late Middle Ages

JOHN B. FRIEDMAN

SYRACUSE UNIVERSITY PRESS

This book is published in recognition of Chancellor William P. Tolley's contributions to and continued support of education in the liberal arts and to university press publishing.

The paper used in this publication meets the minimum requirements of American National Standard for Information Sciences—Permanence of Paper for Printed Library Materials, ANSI Z39.48-1984.∞™

Library of Congress Cataloging-in-Publication Data
Friedman, John Block, 1934–
   Northern English books, owners, and makers in the late Middle Ages
/ John B. Friedman.
     p. cm.
   Includes bibliographical references (p.   ) and index.
   ISBN 0-8156-2649-5
   1. Books—England, Northern—History—1400–1600. 2. Manuscripts—
England, Northern—History. 3. Illumination of books and manuscripts,
English—England, Northern—History. 4. Book owners—England, Northern
—History. 5. Book industries and trade—England, Northern—History.
6. Manuscripts—England, Northern—Catalogs. I. Title.
Z8.G72N674 1995
745.6'7'09427—dc20   94-5288

Manufactured in the United States of America

To Bonnie

John B. Friedman, Professor of English at the University of Illinois, Urbana-Champaign, is the author of *The Monstrous Races in Medieval Art and Thought, Orpheus in the Middle Ages,* and *John de Foxton's Liber Cosmographiae (1408): An Edition and Codicological Study.*

Contents

Illustrations

Introduction

Chaucer's contemptuous treatment of northern England and its inhabitants as an area and people too remote and primitive to interest southerners is well known. Says the Summoner of northeast Yorkshire, there "as I gesse" is "a mersshy contree called Holdernesse," and the Man of Law's unfortunate Constance, set adrift off the Syrian coast, ends up "fer in Northhumberlond." The Northumbrian students John and Alan come, the Reeve says, from "fer in the north; I kan nat telle where." Their dialect is mocked, and they swear eccentrically "by Seint Cutberd." These are some of the best known but certainly not the only medieval dismissals of the supposed bleakness of northern English culture and language by southerners, going back at least to William of Malmsbury in the early twelfth century, who observed that "truely, Northumberland speech and especially that around York is so shrill and uncouth that we southerners can understand nothing of it."

Language, moreover, reflects character, for northerners, according to Ranulph Higden, a Midlands author, are "more unstable, more cruel and more unesy" than other Englishmen.[1] Even northerners recognized their linguistic isolation from the south, as we see in the mid-fifteenth century metrical life of Saint Cuthbert, composed in the "Language of the Northin lede/That can nan other Inglis rede."[2] These cultural distances, forming what Helen Jewell has termed the "great divide" between north and south, continued in English university life with constant fighting between the "nations" of northern and southern students at Oxford and Cambridge until well into the seventeenth century.[3]

Indeed, cultural distances between north and south have colored even the perceptions of some modern scholars towards the art of northern England. While the glass of York Minster is widely known and praised, and the York and Wakefield drama's literary quality everywhere admired, there has been perhaps less general awareness of the riches of northern English manuscript books and how these point to the existence of an active writing and illuminating trade serving a wide range of gentry, urban bourgeoisie, and ecclesiastical patrons in the north. I was first struck by this phenomenon when during a research trip in 1979, I was seated next to a donnish art historian at the readers' table in the Wren Library of Trinity College, Cambridge. He idly asked me, as we waited for our books to appear, what I was doing in England. When I replied that I was looking for manuscripts illuminated in York, he said pityingly, "Well, I don't suppose you'll find too many from *there.*" As I believe this book shows, I did find quite a few of them from there, but it was not an easy search.

One of the challenges in a study like this has been to locate a sufficient number of northern English manuscripts from which conclusions can be drawn, and I provide as a database a handlist in Appendix B, offering information about 236 manuscripts that most probably came from early owners in the north of England, or in many cases were made there. There has been until very recently, for instance, no catalogue of one of the most important collections of all York books, those in the York Minster Library. Though Neil Ker did not live to finish the final volume of *Medieval Manuscripts from British Libraries* containing descriptions of these manuscripts, his work has been carried on by Professor Alan J. Piper of the University of Durham.

While there are in the Prior's Kitchen Library at Durham over three hundred manuscripts of the original Priory collection, as well as several in the University Library and Ushaw College, there is no simple way except by direct examination to determine the provenance of the late medieval English books in the collection. Because of the numbers of books in them and the state of their cataloguing, the great collections in the British Library and at Oxford and Cambridge Universities pose similar problems. One must rely in large measure on the descriptive work of earlier scholars, and certainly southern decorated books have received more attention in this regard than northern ones. This paucity of attention to northern books has created, perhaps, the unavoidable impression that there are very few northern examples, and of those they were probably decorated in the south, or are in a generic "provincial" style.

For example, in an otherwise informative discussion of Thomas Chaworth, whose will was proved at York and who lived chiefly in

Nottinghamshire, at the time at the lower reaches of Yorkshire, Thorlac Turville-Petre says of his books that "the extant manuscripts owned by Chaworth are professional and costly productions, *probably made in London*," as though professionalism and *luxe* could not be found closer to Chaworth, in the Midlands or in the north. Yet one of these books, the splendid Wollaton Antiphonale, contains Chaworth's arms throughout and has a mixed Sarum and York kalendar.[4] Of the 236 northern manuscripts, many illuminated or otherwise decorated, listed in the Appendix B of the present study, only 21 also appear among the 918 manuscripts cited by the authors of the various essays in Griffiths and Pearsall's definitive *Book Production and Publishing in Britain*, whose time frame is virtually identical to that of this book. In short, northern codices, which are not as professionally and lavishly illuminated as their southern relations, have suffered a certain benign neglect quite out of keeping with their cultural and artistic interest.

For this reason, the very existence of a "northern" English manuscript raises a number of questions that call for answers. How do we know that a Latin manuscript comes from the north, if there is no dialect to localize it and no colophon to refer to a place of production? Even experts on northern book production like Ian Doyle are forced to speak tentatively: "there can be little doubt, though it cannot easily be proved, that the majority of service-books of York use were made there in the 14th and 15th centuries."[5] I began this investigation in search of these answers. Was there a distinctive northern book trade?[6] Is there a northern taste for images if the book has pictures? Or, at a more technical level, are there any regional preferences for scripts, border decoration, page size and ruling, or other aspects of *mise-en-page* on the part of the book designer? Did an illuminator from York prefer certain patterns of foliate decoration, or colors for paints and inks, to those used by a southern artist or even one from Durham?

In the broadest context, the present study seeks to answer these and larger related questions by an approach to the "archaeology," to use Delaissé's helpful term, of the handmade book produced in northern England in the century and a half before the coming of the printing press to York in 1497. In a formulation by now very well known, but nonetheless well worth repeating virtually in its entirety, the great art historian observed:

> The archaeological method demands . . . that all material techniques
> . . . be examined in each book, but particularly the secondary tech-

niques such as decoration, which, because of their consistency and their complexity, show better than the script and the miniatures the continuity and evolution in the execution of manuscripts produced by a particular group of craftsmen. The painters of the secondary decorations, less gifted than the miniaturists, did not change jobs as often, nor was it usual for them to journey from place to place as did their superior colleagues; being more stable their collaboration was more regular. Moreover, the decorations are more varied and visually more different than, for instance, the scripts. These less important decorations, which can be found in many manuscripts . . . are . . . precisely the elements of the book which, with the help of other secondary techniques . . . are most useful in individualizing a manuscript. . . . By analysing and grouping . . . the work of the human hand as it appears in book techniques, the production of manuscripts in the Middle Ages will come back to life: in other words the archaeological method will give us the possibility of writing the history of the mediaeval book.[7]

Delaissé's emphasis on border decoration is a relatively new aspect of codicological investigation, in which the whole of a manuscript and not just its text or pictures is considered. Study of minute particulars such as borders, initials, color choice, rulings, and other details of the page can yield very large returns. I have considered the border decoration of a number of northern books in detail, not so much to class them as the products of the "workshop" or "master" schools of art history, as to arrive at an understanding of "regional" style, a term I prefer to the more perjorative word "provincial." Choice of decoration and especially methods of featuring name, arms, or other identifying characteristics can be a distinct mark of a certain popular culture and a key to the book owner's idea of self, region, and class identity.

Localization is another area of manuscript study that has undergone extensive reevaluation. Though a number of valuable recent studies—most notably those of Ian Doyle, Malcolm Parkes, Michael Camille, Kathleen Scott, and Nicholas Rogers—have to varying degrees taken the "archaeological" tack, their focus has been chiefly on manuscripts produced in the southern half of England, and only Scott and Rogers, in their studies of manuscripts made at Bury St. Edmunds, have treated regional styles.[8] The idea that most elegantly ornamented books were likely to have come from southern metropolitan centers seems, from the evidence of the manuscripts I study, to be a somewhat limiting one. Royal households moved north and must have made contacts among local artisans. And a book like John de Foxton's *Liber Cosmographiae*, composed in the city of York and using sources only available in the Minster, was sent to be illuminated by an artist who had southwestern connections.[9] Many treatments of aristocratic manuscripts, especially *horae,* have concerned the relationship between the book and events in court or palace, but manuscripts of bourgeois ownership, like the Bolton *horae* (York Minster Library Additional MS 2), with an extensive program of illustration, can be seen to reflect social and religious changes and bourgeois currents that can be just as interesting for study as aristocratic ones.

Indeed, it could be said that the art of northern England in the fifteenth century has only recently come into its own through the work of cultural and art historians of what have often been considered the "minor arts," like painted glass and alabaster tomb carving. I hope in the following pages to widen the geographic and class boundaries for the study of the late medieval English handmade book and to throw some light on a broad range of handsome and fascinating books made in the north that reflect a variety of concerns, such as regional history expressing bias towards southern England, popular piety and the way it was influenced by Continental currents of thought, and the impact of gender on book commissioning.

To paraphrase Bacon, books show the man, and there are few better sources of insight into a culture than books considered as artifacts. Medieval books were repositories of all that people considered important—recipes, medical and scientific lore, history, astrology, theology, and the relations between the sexes, to name only a few subjects. They sometimes contained amateur art work added by their owners, and like old houses that go through several remodelings in different architectural styles, books had their pictures updated by later hands, and some even give evidence of changing ideologies, with "Catholic" passages mentioning the pope, Thomas of Canterbury, or references to indulgences and purgatory censored by later Protestant owners and new pages added to reflect new ideas. The books of northern England are as fascinating in these respects as the better known manuscripts of the south; upon closer examination they should have much to tell us about the society that produced them.

If nothing else then, the present study attempts to survey the range of manuscripts still surviving from the north and to indicate to the student of the handmade book the variety and often the beauty and whimsicality of books made in that region of England. Since these derive from and reflect the culture of northern England, it may be appropriate to spend a moment or two on this regional culture, which comprises for our purposes the county of Yorkshire in the center and west and the county of Durham at the east, before passing on to the overall plan of this book.

Yorkshire is the largest of the English counties, stretching north and south from the Tees to the Humber and running east and west from the east coast of England all the way to the Pennines and nearly to the Irish sea. It comprises about one-eighth of England's land. Its hub, the city of York, began as a fortress built by the Roman governor of the Britons; later historians called it Ebor after a mythical Trojan founder.[10]

English learning and literacy were early tied to Yorkshire,[11] and the history of early English Christianity centers on sites such as Whitby, founded in 675 with Northumbrian missionaries going to the Continent from England, and on York, which under Alcuin in the eighth century became a center of scholarship that rivaled or even surpassed similar centers in northern Europe.[12] This superiority in learning and culture, however, did not last into the early Middle Ages, for what might be called collectively Viking invasions by Danes and Norwegians plundered the newly established monasteries in the eighth and ninth centuries.

Many of these Danes settled in Yorkshire, especially in the west, as is attested to by place names ending in *by* and the like. Closer to the period of interest to us, Scottish invasions and continual border fighting between the English and the Scots resulted in many castles built to guard against Scottish incursions.[13] Indeed, the palatinate of Durham in the northeast, where the bishop was also a prince, developed for the same reason, and the counties of York and Durham were continuously engaged against the Scots. For example, the Battle of the Standard, where the English were victorious in 1138, showed the banners of Saints Peter of York, Cuthbert of Durham, Wilfrid of Ripon, and John of Beverly, symbolizing the union of these sees against the Scots.

In addition to the threats to social and cultural stability from across the border, there were a number of conflicts between the great magnate families like the Percys, Nevilles, and Lancasters as well as between them and the crown, culminating in the War of the Roses.[14] One need only think of the great rebellions of this period: those of Percy Hotspur in 1403, Archbishop Scrope in 1405, the earl of Northumberland in 1408, and Scrope of Masham in 1415.

It is then all the more remarkable that in spite of such constant military uncertainty, by the fourteenth century there was a rich ecclesiastical culture with about seventy Benedictine, Cistercian, and Augustinian houses in the county of York alone. The abbots and priors of these houses in many cases were very important landowners with enormous holdings. Those of York, Saint Mary's, Selby, and Guisborough stand out here. The Cistercians were in many ways the most significant order in medieval Yorkshire, with twenty houses in the fertile valleys of the highlands. Among the most prominent were Rievaulx, Byland, Fountains, Jervaulx, Meaux, Kirkstall, Roche, Furness, and Sawley.[15] More to the east, the bishop of Durham and the Benedictine priory of Saint Cuthbert, as we shall see later in this book, had vast secular holdings as well as appropriated churches. At Durham was the largest community of monks in the north.[16] All of these foundations had extensive libraries and, in many cases, scriptoria.

The diocese of York was much the largest of the twenty-two medieval dioceses of England and Wales, and almost twice as large as the county. As a result of an edict by Pope Gregory I in 601, a "Province" of York independent of that of London developed and the northern church began to take on its special identity, which the northern prelates jealously guarded.[17] The archbishop of York was next in importance to the archbishop of Canterbury, a matter that caused conflict until the end of the fourteenth century. The archbishop of York, moreover, was often at odds with the primate of Durham.[18] One other outgrowth of this independence is especially important for those interested in northern liturgical books. The various liturgical "uses" of England by the thirteenth century had been simplified, so that that of the southern part of the country was called the Salisbury or, more commonly, Sarum use or practice and that of the North was called the "use" of York. This York liturgical use is marked by certain elements and arrangements of offices in liturgical books and certain feasts in kalendars that can help to localize an otherwise anonymous missal or breviary. I have relied heavily on the York use whenever possible as a means of identifying northern books in my discussion of various manuscripts, though it should be noted that Durham diocese was an anomaly in that many books made there followed the Sarum use.[19]

The diocese of York stretched from the Soar in the Midlands to the Tees in the north and from the west coast in Cumberland to the Humber and North Sea ports in the east. Comprising Yorkshire and Nottinghamshire, the northern portions of Lancashire and portions of Westmorland and Cumberland, it contained about seventy-five religious institutions of canons, mendicants, and monks. To put this geography in more concrete terms, the southern end of the York diocese was only about one hunded miles from London.

It was divided into five archdeaconries known as York or St. Peter's, the East Riding, Richmond, Cleveland, and Nottingham, and these in turn were subdivided into around 700 parishes, of which about 504, comprising twenty-four deaneries, were actually in Yorkshire.[20] Again for the student of northern history, these ecclesiastical units are very well documented through surviving diocesan registers. York, for example, was the second earliest diocese to keep a bishop's register, beginning in 1225.[21]

This vast ecclesiastical apparatus in the north supported several types of schools. Education in the region has been well studied by Jo Ann Hoeppner Moran, who shows what an important market for the book trade it offered.[22] In the diocese of York, there was a large population[23] served by about eighty-five grammar schools with a need for books and writing materials, and many of the notables of the area, like the Roos and Percy families, had schools in their households. Within the metropolis the various grammar schools both in the cathedral and at the various churches and abbeys offered a convenient local market for an urban book trade. And the song schools of the cathedral[24] were other clients for manuscript material and the specialized services of flourishers. Admittedly, schools throughout the diocese were likely to purchase only the plainest sorts of books and the skills of workaday rubricators, scribes, and letter flourishers, but the sheer quantity of their needs could only contribute to the economic health of the book trades. Thus, aside from its more obvious need for service books, registers and the like, the ecclesiastical apparatus I have just outlined was a very important market for books, writing materials, and the services of book artisans of all kinds in less apparent ways.

Of particular importance for the consumption of books and writing materials was the burgeoning mercantile culture of the city of York, where personal wealth made through woolen manufacture and export, and shipping as well as through the provision of local goods and services developed rapidly in the fourteenth and fifteenth centuries. By this period, even after the plague of 1349 and its subsequent outbreaks,[25] the city was the material as well as the spiritual magnet of the diocese in ways that have been well described by one economic historian:

York was also an important centre for the social life of the gentry of northern England, and the luxurious foodstuffs, skilled services, and the wide variety of manufactured goods readily available . . . must have led many north countrymen to visit the city for pleasure and encouraged them to prolong their business visit[s] to the city. Country gentlemen frequently made bequests to their favourite church in York or requested burial in the Dominican and Franciscan Friaries there, and a number owned property in the city.[26]

Undoubtedly people came to York to purchase or commission books as well as to take advantage of the various services in which a pious population might be interested—such as the work of artisans engaged in making small alabaster sculptures, embroidery, or other objects for domestic devotion.[27] Book artisans would rely on specialized trades as well, such as those of parchment sellers, sewers, binders, color makers, flourishers, and the makers of cadel capitals common in music manuscripts.[28] We have seen how several markets for the services of these plainer artisans existed.

One growing market for manuscripts of a more luxurious type, however, was that supplying service books to the new private and guild chapels increasingly common in the city. In York alone there were 140 chantries.[29] Many York citizens had extensive retinues of chaplains, who all needed books and writing materials.[30] In the countryside it was fashionable for persons to have family chapels as a sign of gentrification, following the models of the Percy and FitzHugh chapels at Seamer and Ravensworth, and often these chapels were rich in service books, the Scropes, for example, having some fifty of them.

The consolidation of the York use for the northern part of England coincided with the rise of ecclesiastical legislation setting standards for clerical literacy and calling for increased instruction of the laity by means of pastoral manuals of various kinds.[31] Throughout the north, parish churches were required to provide service books of the York use and to keep them in good repair. Here was yet another market catering to private and public devotion.

Some of the parish churches had considerable libraries, which they must have acquired either through donation of books bought locally or else through commissions by their rectors. It was the custom, as we will see in chapter 1, for persons to leave money in their wills to buy books for these churches, books that would most likely have also been made locally. For example, in 1434, the library of the Parish church of St. Mary's, Scarborough, had ten antiphonals, two

portiforia or breviaries, four legendaries, eight processionals, six graduals, four manuals, two ordinals, and Huguccio of Pisa's *Magnae Derivationes*.[32] It is hard to imagine that all of these book users sent to
London for their manuscripts; it is much more probable that they
were obtained locally, in the west from York and in the east from
Durham.

Exactly where the center of this book trade in York was located
we can only guess, but based on the analogy of London, it was very
likely in the maze of small streets winding down from the cathedral.
St. Paul's, with its great need for service books and documents of all
types, had given rise to loose confederations of artisans in the streets
close to the cathedral, and it is reasonable to assume that something
similar occurred in York as well.[33] Some of the trade, particularly
that in modest paper books, may also have taken place in fairs and
markets.[34]

Durham was similarly the center of a wealthy diocese, but the
wealth was not that of an urban bourgeoisie, as there was far less
mercantile activity in Durham than in York and economic power was
not concentrated in quite the same ways because it was based largely
on agricultural, service, and extractive activity. The Durham Priory
account books, for example, contain many references to coal mining
in the region, and a Durham iron worker's account book of 1409, still
surviving, details production of iron reaching two tons a week.[35]

Durham offered several distinct sorts of markets for books and
the services of book artisans. First, there was the presence of a large
and wealthy monastery. Though many of the books used by the
monks were imported from Durham College, Oxford, or written in
their cloister, some of the decoration, binding, and preparation of
materials must have been done locally, perhaps in the area around
the present Palace Green and in Elvet, where clerks and other ecclesiastical functionaries congregated.

Durham, because of the administrative culture of the palatinate,
had an exceptional need for the materials and services of literacy—
parchment, paper, scribes, flourishers, and notaries public. The city
seemed early to have a stationers' trade, which undertook a variety of
different aspects of book creation and provision and had close ties
with the priory, catering to both the episcopal bureaucracy and to
local customers. Doyle notes, for example, that a Richard Daniel, a
Durham bookbinder, was in the service of the priory; he also made
ecclesiastical vestments.[36] And as we shall see in chapter 2, the Durham notaries public were much more involved in the copying of
books than notaries were elsewhere.

As is evident from this brief review, church and trade played very important roles in the creation of literacy and of its material appeal to religious and lay persons in the north. The books itemized in wills show that the middle classes purchased, commissioned, and displayed books, could often read and write, and felt a need for the literature of spiritual guidance associated with the names of Rolle, Hoveden, Rymington, Nassington, Love, and other northerners. The new money of the merchant classes in the fourteenth and fifteenth centuries, particularly in York, led to the commissioning of *horae* on a fairly grand scale with large programs of illustration by families in trade, if the Bolton *horae* is representative. The "ambition and upward striving," so characteristic of this class,[37] was reflected in the ownership of domestic ornament and objects hitherto associated with the aristocracy. These illustrated or, more usually, richly decorated and illuminated manuscripts of the kind often owned by a thriving merchant class for whom civic pride was a strong motive in behavior, were created, as I hope to show, not in the south of England, but locally, reflecting what might be thought of as a northern "regionalism" or nationalism. My study of northern books and their owners and makers has six parts, treating the books themselves as well as the people who wrote, decorated and commissioned them.

Chapter 1 considers the attitudes towards books exhibited in their wills by northern men and women, chiefly from the county of York, and offers some information about the practice of amateur scribes either working for others or, in several cases, about testators writing books for themselves. It lays the groundwork for our understanding of the various types of books that appealed to northerners and offers some new observations about books and gender in the region.

Chapter 2 treats the makers of these books, northern professional scribes, both religious and lay. Although the monastic houses had been the primary source of books in the earlier Middle Ages, by the fifteenth century the mendicants seem to have assumed this role in York. Three well-documented northern friar scribes are considered: William de Ellerker and Robert de Popultoun of York, and from Newcastle, John Lacy. The presence of a secular scribe, William du Stiphel, copying books for the Benedictines at Durham, indicates the existence of monastic out-workers, though the practice is not well documented in the north. Finally, the activities of the Fulloflove scribes, copyists signing their manuscripts with a given name followed by the epithet or surname *Plenus Amoris*, a translation of *Fulloflove* or *Pleindamour*, should be noticed.

Chapter 3 concerns the decorative aspects of northern manuscripts: illumination, borders, and ornamented initials, whose style indicates a distinctively northern artistic taste. Most particularly, I have noted the decorative pairing of green and purple. The latter color was made from a plant pigment called *folium*, imported to England and prepared with considerable cost and difficulty. Ten northern books contain this distinctive pigment. So too, we find the presence of an archaizing return to much older Anglo-Saxon interlace patterns that suggests a self-consciously nationalistic rejection of Franco-Flemish influence and may illustrate a civic identity and regional awareness. From a study of palette and decorative motifs, I have identified what I call the Green Canon-Page and Archaizing styles popular in or near York, which appear in at least seven surviving manuscripts.

Chapter 4 deals with a much larger group, eighteen books, which exhibit what I call the Mask Medallion and Interlace style in their border decoration. This style is equally archaizing in some respects. But it also adapts to the northern book the most current Continental fashions—especially those of Italy and Bohemia—as well as southern English fashions. The Mask Medallion and Interlace style is equaled in popularity by border styles we may call the Jutting Leaf, Italianate Leaf Wrap, and Carpel and Calyx types; of the last of these there are seventeen examples. Several of these books were decorated by the same artist, and in one case two books were written by the same scribe.

Chapter 5 is concerned with regional piety and works of spiritual guidance. It examines certain motifs in northern illuminated manuscripts that also seem to reflect a regional taste. Among these are a devotion to the wounded Sacred Heart, often presented emblematically, as in the well-known "Desert of Religion" group of Carthusian Miscellanies, as well as on shields containing the *arma Christi*, also used emblematically. Other motifs, such as the Throne of Grace style of Trinity, the IHS Holy Name monogram, and souls in a handkerchief taken up to heaven, may relate to the decorative alabaster retables and screens produced so widely in the city of York and to the south of the province.

Chapter 6 considers patronage by magnates and prelates for books in the province. Here the names of John Newton, treasurer of York Cathedral, Thomas Langley, bishop of Durham, and Thomas Rotherham, archbishop of York, stand out prominently. Knowing who paid for a book, and why, may help us to understand more about its intended audience. An observation relevant to the late fourteenth- and early fifteenth-century decorated manuscripts discussed in this chapter and, indeed, throughout the book is that of Michael Baxandall, who noted in discussing painting of the same period that

> A fifteenth-century painting is the deposit of a social relationship. On one side there was a painter who made the picture, or at least supervised its making. On the other side there was somebody else who asked him to make it, provided funds for him to make it and, after he had made it, reckoned on using it in some way or other. Both parties worked within institutions and conventions—commercial, religious, perceptual— . . . [that] influenced the forms of what they together made. . . . The pleasure of possession, an active piety, civic consciousness, . . . self-commemoration and perhaps self-advertisement, the rich man's necessary virtue and pleasure of reparation, a taste for pictures [were important]. In fact, the client need not analyse his own motives much because he generally worked through institutional forms . . . which implicitly rationalized his motives for him, usually in quite flattering ways. . . . [Such pictures] were designed for the client and people he esteemed to look at, with a view to receiving pleasing and memorable and even profitable stimulations.[38]

One interesting feature emerging from our consideration of these magnate libraries is the presence of foreign scribes and illuminators in York and Durham; Italian and probably Bohemian artists were active there in the late Ricardian period, and the Breton scribe, William du Stiphel, discussed in chapter 2, may have set a style of profuse penwork flourishing that seems to have persisted in Durham until well into the fifteenth century.

Three appendixes contain material best set off from the text of this book. The first studies the more technical aspects of the purple pigment *folium* and details the medieval recipes for its manufacture, the second briefly lists all the northern manuscripts known to me, and the third itemizes over three thousand books mentioned in wills proved in the north from 1367 to 1497.

Urbana, Illinois   John B. Friedman
March 1995

Acknowledgments

I am grateful to the Graduate College of the University of Illinois and to the American Council of Learned Societies for aid which made the research for this book possible, as well as to the librarians and staff of Arundel Castle Library; the Bibliothèque Nationale, Paris; the Boston Public Library; M. Louis Seguin, Conservateur of the Bibliothèque Municipale, Boulogne-sur-Mer; the Cambridge University Library; Bruce Barker-Benfield of the Bodleian Library; David Smith of the Borthwick Institute, York; Miss C. M. Hall of the British Library; the College of Arms, London; Roger Norris of the Dean and Chapter Library, Durham; the Durham University Library; the Grolier Club Library, New York City; the Index of Christian Art, Princeton University; the University of Leeds Library; the Rosenbach Library, Philadelphia; the John Rylands University Library, Manchester; the Library of Trinity College, Dublin; Sion College Library, London; Reverend F. J. Turner, Librarian of Stonyhurst College, Blackburn, Lancashire; the Library of Trinity College, Cambridge; and Bernard Barr of the York Minster Library. Many people over a number of years have offered advice, information, and hospitality. I should particularly like to thank Michelle Brown of the British Library; Anthony Caines, Conservation Department, Trinity College, Dublin; Madeline Caviness; Vartan Cherukian; Paul Christianson; Barrie Dobson; A. I. Doyle; Marsha Dutton; Anna F. Friedman; Anne D. Hedeman; Avril Henry; Tony Hunt; Michael Jones; A. J. Minnis of the Centre for Medieval Studies, University of York; Jay Mittenthal; Jo Ann Moran; Nigel Morgan; Dr. I. J. Pincus; A. J. Piper; Rebecca Reader; Pamela Robinson; Pauline Routh; Lucy Freeman Sandler; William Schipper; Patricia Danz Stirnemann; Lorraine Stock; Toshiyuki Takamiya; John Thompson; John Thwaites for sharing his encyclopedic acquaintance with Yorkshire geography; Linda Voigts; Brother Chrysogonus Waddell, Gethsemani Abbey,

Trappist, Kentucky; and for generous loans of her slides, and for her unrivaled knowledge of medieval English book painting, Kathleen L. Scott "fu miglior fabbro." Phillipa Hardman cast a cool and corrective eye on portions of the manuscript. The firm of Boydell and Brewer have graciously allowed me to reprint previously published material.

Northern English Books, Owners, and Makers in the Late Middle Ages

1

Northern Book-Owning Men and Women

THE EVIDENCE FROM WILLS AND EXTANT MANUSCRIPTS

Though the work of Paul Christianson has shed new light on the arts of the medieval book in the southern half of England and particularly in London,[1] very little is known about the northern English book trade, book patrons, and the reading public—especially the female reading public—before the age of print. To my knowledge, there has been no estimate of either the number of manuscript books produced in the north or the quantity of extant ones, and there has been no concerted effort to identify centers of production or patrons of decorated books among gentry and magnates of the church. What has been done is mainly the work of a liturgist, W. H. Frere, who looked at numerous surviving codices containing music,[2] and two literary scholars, George Keiser and John Thompson, who have studied the wide range of books available to the late fifteenth-century Yorkshire scribe Robert Thornton.[3]

Most recently and valuably, Jo Ann Moran's work on literacy and education in Yorkshire and Susan Cavanaugh's study of late medieval English book ownership have provided much new information about the reading public. For example, with regard to wills as sources of information on the degree of book ownership, Cavanaugh points out that a will does not always mention all of the testator's books and that wills sometimes even omitted all mention of them. So too, vernacular and paper books were often deemphasized in wills as less valuable than Latin and parchment ones, especially the liturgical books in *textura*, which had the most cash value. Nonetheless, her conclusions that "literacy was widespread, that women were among the more important consumers of vernacular literature, and above all, that books perhaps were not uncommon household items" in late medieval England will, I hope, be shown to apply to the northern half of the country as well as the southern half, from which much of her data comes.[4] Yet in spite of these "revisionists," it may not be far wrong to say that the prevalent view of books in the north is that they were few and mainly owned by men, plainly made, and chiefly of pious or practical content. Moreover, if decorated books did exist, they must have been made not locally, but in London or on the Continent.

Common sense, however, would suggest that if people loved fine books in and around London in the age of Chaucer, they would also do so in the north. And if there were ateliers capable of making such books in the south and persons with enough money to pay for them, there would be similar patrons and workshops in the thriving mercantile and ecclesiastical centers of York and Durham. Looked at purely from the viewpoint of social class, decorated books were marks of status that combined portability, durability, and sound investment value for practical and upwardly mobile people as well as for the nobility.[5] For example, between 1415 and 1419, the archbishop of York, Richard Scrope's nephew, Henry, Lord Scrope, well known from Shakespeare's *Henry V,* possessed in his private family chapel at Masham in Richmondshire some fifty service books of various sorts, many illuminated.[6] It is hard to imagine that the northern bourgeoisie, rural gentry, nobility, and ecclesiastical bureaucrats were not as taken with books as their southern counterparts and did not want to own handsome volumes, display them, and eventually bequeath them to relatives, friends, or religious or educational institutions.

York, by population England's second largest city during the Middle Ages,[7] was the obvious place to look for evidence of secular book production in the province. Not only was there a large lay and clerical book and document using public, as the following discussion of wills clearly indicates, but, as Moran's recent work has shown, there was an extensive market for student books.

Though other northern cathedral towns, such as Beverley, Ripon, and Carlisle, undoubtedly had their share of persons engaged in book production, the evidence is richest from York and Durham. From these centers there is simply a greater quantity of surviving documents.

The York Freemen's Register shows that between 1386 and 1387 fourteen scribes became freemen, as well as a color maker. One Thomas de Colton, an illuminator, became free in 1391,[8] and by the fifteenth century, there were various book artisans like binders, parchment makers and vendors, and cadel capital flourishers free of the city.[9] By 1425 the York scriveners, flourishers, and illuminators had formed themselves into a guild.[10] Undoubtedly, the increasing number of persons pursuing these crafts was the result of several factors, such as rising literacy, the value of books for social status, and the needs of schools, as well as the rise of chantries and private chapels after the first outbreak of the plague in 1349.[11] That there was a substantial amateur trade as well, which often came in conflict with the guild, we shall see. Semiprofessional copyists also made books for their own use or for their friends.[12]

One of the best sources of information about the products of these book artisans can be found in the words of the testators of late medieval wills proved in Yorkshire.[13] The wills, in conjunction with certain extant manuscripts of northern provenance, also show us that a much higher proportion of women were book owners and book commissioners than might be supposed on the basis of what is often said about the lack of female literacy in England.[14] The purpose of this chapter is to survey how the attitudes of northern book-owning men and women towards their manuscripts were revealed—chiefly, though not entirely, in their wills[15]—and to call attention to the relatively large number of amateur scribes active in the north at the close of the Middle Ages. Professional scribes or scribes who worked chiefly for others rather than for themselves will be considered in chapter 2.

The subject of wills, being very complex, calls for a few words of explanation. It should be noted that though there are a very large number of wills registered from all parts of northern England, they tend to represent the middle and upper half of society. To have a will at all, one needed to own *bona notabilia,* or goods valued at five pounds or more. This was a fairly large sum of money, about the value of two service books. Interestingly, the period when wills began to be proved in any quantity was about the time of the coming of the plague to England—an obvious response to the new awareness of mortality. As this is also the period at which professional rather than monastic manuscript production commences, we find coming together a number of interrelated factors: increased book ownership, awareness of books as valuable property for legacies, and, of course, relatively detailed references to books in these legacies.

Because wills fell under the jurisdiction of several types of ecclesiastical courts, which received both fees and portions of the estate as alms, copies were registered in a variety of ecclesiastical archives, such as those of the archbishop's Prerogative and Exchequer Courts and the Chancery Court in the metropolis. The largest collection, designated here York Probate Registry (YPR) and containing about 15,000 wills dating from 1389 onward, is housed in the Borthwick Institute for Historical Research in York; about 1,000 of these wills were recorded in the Archbishops' registers, held in the same Institute.[16] Naturally, only a relatively small proportion of these wills and inventories during the period in question, 942, or about 28 percent, make reference to book ownership, but these are of very great interest. Persons owning additional property in dioceses other than that of York had their wills registered in the Prerogative Court of Canterbury; some of these have been printed by J. W. Clay in *Northcountry Wills*. There are other collections of northern wills, especially from the various peculiars (parishes exempt from the jurisdiction of the bishop of the diocese), and from Durham, which, since they are really later than the time frame of this book, need not concern us here.[17]

Investigators of York wills owe the editor of a selection of them, Canon James Raine, an enormous debt, yet as Moran and others have well noted, Raine's *Testamenta Eboracensia* should be used with considerable care, as Raine did not list all of the books in individual wills, nor did he print in their entirety all wills containing references to books. Thus it is possible to get a somewhat distorted idea of book ownership through the wills he selected and published.

Much the same phenomenon occurred with his Durham wills as well. An extreme but not unrepresentative example of such distortion is illustrated in the will of Thomas Langley, bishop of Durham, who died in 1437, leaving a number of books. Raine's *Wills and Inventories*[18] prints only the bishop's mortuary, recording his gifts to the Library of the dean and chapter of Lyra's commentary on the Pauline Epistles, the book of Acts, and the Apocalypse (now Durham Cathedral MS A.I.4); a "dictionary," actually Pierre Bersuire's *Repertorium Biblicum* in three volumes (now Durham Cathedral MSS A.I.17–19); William of Nottingham on the Gospels (now Durham Cathedral MS A.I.1), and a *Polychronicon*.

In fact, as we shall see in chapter 6, Langley had a very impressive personal library—many of his books were attractively written and illuminated, apparently to his order—and he took considerable care to see that they were bequeathed to a variety of legatees. To John Kemp, archbishop of York, he left Augustine's *City of God;* to the bishop of Norwich he left his "very best" Gregory's *Moralia* and to Robert Rolston a less valuable copy. To John Frank he left a work called *Historiarum;* to Nicholas Wymbush, of whom we will hear more in the next chapter, a large book of *flores* from Jerome and Augustine; to his treasurer, a volume of the glossed Pauline Epistles; to John Newton a *Pupilla Oculi* (this, or another copy referred to below, may possibly be the handsomely illuminated codex now Durham Cathedral MS B.IV.33); to University College, Oxford, the *Reductorium Morale* of Bersuire; to the Cambridge University Library, Lyra in three volumes; to Durham College, Oxford, Augustine on the Psalms; to King's Hall, Augustine's *City of God;* to the Collegiate Chapel of Mary at Leicester, Durand's *Rationale,* as well as the missal with which he celebrated mass; and to the College of Maincester, which he founded, a *Flores Bernardi.* To his deacon he left Nicholas Gorran on the Psalms; to Richard Gorston, Lyra on the New Testament as well as a breviary; and to John Carbrock "a small and beautiful book" on contemplation in a case of black leather. To John Laverok he left a work called the Moralized Bestiary, perhaps that of Richard de Fournival, as well as Lyra on the Pentateuch; and to John Corby, Gregory's *Pastoral Care.* William Blackburn received a glossed Isaiah, and James Occushaugh the *Glossa Ordinaria* on Matthew and Mark. To his scribe Thomas Jobur went a large Bible, a *Decretals,* a Sext, a set of Clementines and a small breviary. To John Carleton went another *Pupilla Oculi.* To John Bonor he gave a *Speculum Judiciale* and to John Snawdon a *Corpus Juris Civilis* in five volumes. One item left to the Dean and Chapter Library but not mentioned in the mortuary was his "large Psalter, written in a large script."[19]

I have dwelt at some length on this library bequest because the two different accounts present two entirely different views of Langley. On the basis of his mortuary he seems extraordinarily limited as a book owner for a man of his station and with no presence as a bibliophile. In his will, however, he shows a love for his books, both in personalizing touches of their description and by the fact that he owned multiple copies of the same work. While there is nothing especially exotic or unusual about Langley's books, their number amounts to a very considerable sum of money and testifies to a wide circle of book-appreciating and book-using retainers, friends, and fellow prelates.

As we have seen, several of Langley's books still exist in the Durham Cathedral collection, and they show us exactly what the full list of his books and their disposition indicates—that Langley was a bibliophile who patronized northern book artisans and used the decoration in his books to express his sense of personal worth.

What follows about wills proved in York is based on the actual texts of even the most humble of these documents. York archival materials offer some very positive evidence about the taste for books at the end of the Middle Ages. The rather meager references to book ownership in the published wills from the archdeaconry of Richmond, and the dioceses of Carlisle, Beverley, and Ripon suggest that these centers were not as rich in books as was York but that books were nonetheless prized.[20] Durham, because so many of the book owners who have left evidence of their existence were monastic and did not make wills, is a somewhat anomalous diocese in this respect.

In keeping with the time frame of this book, I consider in the following discussion wills proved up to 1497, when books were first printed in York.[21] At this point, references to books in wills become increasingly infrequent, as printed books had nothing like the value of manuscripts and are often not noted in the testator's estate. I have so far recorded 3,292 books bequeathed to relatives; friends; the two universities; Jesus College and Aukland College, Rotherham; and a variety of religious institutions ranging from cathedrals to parish churches and chantry chapels.

As might be expected, service and devotional books were the most common in these bequests, amounting to 1,535 items, or almost half of the total. This ratio is maintained among the number of extant manuscripts of northern provenance, as can be seen from the handlist in Appendix B. In short, the number of extant service books seems to accord quite closely with the movement of such books in bequests during the period covered here.

Four hundred twenty-five books are of unspecified title, as when the testator says "I leave all my books to . . ." or describes them only as a "French book" or an "English book." The third largest identifiable group, however, is that of works on canon and civil law, amounting to 352 items. It attests to a very wide interest in this subject, especially, as Barrie Dobson has noted, among residentiary canons of the cathedral, who "undoubtedly possessed the largest private collections of legal works in the north of England."[22] Unfortunately, nothing like this number seems to have survived, as I have found very few legal works in my search of the major collections of English manuscripts. One possible reason, as Neil Ker has pointed out, is that when the binders of early printed books needed pastedowns, they turned their scissors to the parchment of the enormous number of law texts that had been rendered obsolete by the coming of the printing press. The binders "used chiefly the texts of the canon and civil law, taking their share of the many ponderous manuscripts, Digest, Code, 'Parvum volumen', Institutes, Decretum, Decretals, Sext and Clementines, which were turned out of the libraries during the fifty years between 1490 and 1540 and replaced by equally ponderous printed copies."[23]

It would be wrong, however, to think of the northern reading public as totally serious or pious, for the number of classical, grammatical, and literary texts, 204, is almost double the number of works of clerical and popular piety. One manuscript of Chaucer's *Canterbury Tales*, one of *Troilus and Criseyde;* one of Gower; three of *Mandeville's Travels;*[24] twelve of various works of Ovid; six of the works of Boethius; two of *Piers Plowman;* six of the works of Petrarch (one owned by Thomas Dautre, a wealthy York lawyer and bibliophile);[25] one of Boccaccio, owned by a woman; seven of romances of various types, several owned by women; one of Christine de Pisan's *Letter of Othea to Hector*, owned by a woman; and six of cycle plays demonstrate the importance of imaginative literature to those choosing to mention books in their wills. In at least one case, several "profane" works lurk within a rather pious wrapper. Sir Thomas Chaworth of Wyverthorp, Nottinghamshire, the great-grandson of Geoffrey Luttrell of the Luttrell Psalter, bequeathed in 1458 a volume titled John Lydgate's *Life of St. Albon and St. Amphibalus*, but which also contained Chaucer's *Clerk's Tale*, and the *Anelida and Arcite* as well as other works of Lydgate.[26] Oddly, not all of Chaworth's books, even his service books, were mentioned in his will.[27]

What is especially striking is evidence from the wills of clerics for an interest in drama. A clerk, William de Thorp, in 1376 left in his will a book of plays, but the contents were unspecified. Robert Lasynby, parish clerk of St. Dionysius, York, in 1455, left to the fabric of his church "ludum oreginale Sancti Dionisii." In 1464, William Downham, another chaplain of York, bequeathed to William Ball "omnes libros meos de ludo de pater noster." The most important of these "dramatic" legacies, however, is that of William Revetour, deputy town clerk, chaplain, and chantry priest of St. William's chapel, housing the shrine of Corpus Christi. Revetour, who died in 1446, left to the Corpus Christi Guild in York, of which he was Warden, "quemdam librum vocatum Le Crede Play, cum libris et vexillis eidem pertinentibus." This play appears to have been comprised of eighty-eight folios. And to the Guild of St. Christopher he also left "quemdam librum de sancto Jacobo Apostolo in sex paginis compilatum." Quite a literate man, he owned nine other Latin and vernacular books, and probably wrote the plays referred to in his will. From evidence in inventories of the property of the Corpus Christi Guild, one of 1449–1451 and one of 1465, it is clear that these "vexillis" were elaborately painted banners relating to the play, containing both visual and verbal statements of doctrine.[28] Such a concern for drama, given the guild structure of the city and what is known of the York

Cycle, is not, of course, surprising in itself, but the fact that these manuscripts were in private hands before being bequeathed to guilds may change some assumptions about the corporate performance of drama in York.

Books for choir use such as antiphonals, very tall and heavy singing books for the offices of the various canonical hours of the day, and graduals, containing music for the great feasts, are well represented, with 42 of the former and 39 of the latter. Though most of these were owned by clerics, some handsome or illuminated copies, like the Wollaton Antiphonale, were in lay hands. Though 56 Bibles, several in English, show the popularity of scripture for lay domestic reading,[29] the great majority of these books were for the public use of parishioners or priests. There were legacies of 478 breviaries, named generally by some form of the word *portiforium*, used to distinguish portable breviaries from the larger type to be read on a stand. The breviary at this period contained a kalendar, antiphons, prayers (occasionally some added in English), and hymns, besides the lessons and psalms for feasts. Noted or rubricated choral breviaries had music as well. Next in popularity are 260 missals. The missal had a kalendar, the form of the mass, the common of the saints, the *Placebo* or mass for the dead, antiphons, *gradualia*, and readings from the Epistles and the Gospels.[30] One hundred eighty-nine psalters, either containing selections for choral use or comprised of the whole book of Psalms, complete the catalogue of service books.

Among the works of pious and clerical instruction, the *Legenda Aurea* of Jacob of Voragine occurs in sixteen copies and the *Pupilla Oculi* of John de Burgh and *Pars Oculi* of William de Pagula in forty-four and fourteen copies, respectively. Burgh was a prebendary in York during Arundel's primacy and was rector of South Colingham in Nottinghamshire. Sometime between 1380 and 1385 he reworked the *Pars Oculi* for a rather more intellectual group of northern clerics.[31] Indeed, according to Hughes, York Minster was the main dissemination point for this work.[32] That Langley owned two copies of it shows something of its importance in the Durham diocese as well. Of the mendicant sermon writers and hagiographers on the Continent and in England, Jacob of Voragine was by far the most popular. There are about 350 extant manuscripts of his sermons *de tempore* alone,[33] so it is not surprising that ten copies of his sermons show his work to have been widely used in the north.

The testators speak of their books with respect, affection, and knowledge, occasionally showing a good deal of bibliophilic self-awareness, as is seen in the will of a lawyer of the court of York, John de Harwod, who died in 1406, leaving among other things "unum rubeum quarternum de papiro juxta literas alphabeti, vocatum a tabyll . . . omnium librorum meorum."[34] This concern, of course, is not evident in the impersonal inventories made by executors or by persons other than the owners, such as the compiler of the lengthy list of books given by Archbishop Thomas Rotherham to his new foundation, Jesus College,[35] but the actual wills often characterize the books with personalizing touches in the bequest, much as the testators sometimes name their horses and even their cows and drinking cups.

Many of these books appear to have been illuminated, illustrated, or sumptuously bound. By far the largest number of these is the group mentioned in the will of Walter de Skirlaw, bishop of Durham at his death in 1404. He came from Swine in Yorkshire and held both Bachelor and Doctor of Canon Law degrees from Oxford. Bishop of Coventry and of Bath and Wells before he came to Durham in 1388, Skirlaw was, like some of the other book-loving northerners we will discuss, a former Chancery clerk and Keeper of the Privy Seal, and served in various diplomatic capacities. His will describes eight books as illuminated out of a library of thirty-five volumes. These, listed as *libri capellae*, were apparently quite ornate. A missal that once belonged to John Grandisson, bishop of Exeter, is "miniatum de auro . . . habens in quolibet mense kalendarii ymagines pertinentes figuratas," suggesting a program of the labors of the months. Another missal is "miniatum de azur et vermiculo intermixtim." An "old" breviary is "miniatum per totum de azuro," while a smaller version of the same book is "miniatum cum azuro et cum litteris auri in festis principalibus," with an entry apparently added on the last folio "de littera currenti factum." Two antiphonals are "miniatum de azur per totum, excepto psalterio, quod est miniatum et intermixtum de vermiculo," while a gradual is "miniatum de azur," and another identical one has "litteras aureas in festis principalibus et dominicis."

Sir John Depeden, a knight of Healaugh, left a "primarium magnum cum litteris illuminatis." Thomas Dautre, the Chapter clerk and scribe of York mentioned earlier, owned at least two such books when he died in 1458. He left a "psalterium elomned cum auro" and a "parvum librum cum imaginis in coopertorio." The William Revetour also referred to earlier left to John Bolton, a merchant once mayor of York who owned and probably commissioned the elaborately illustrated *horae*, now York Minster Library MS Additional 2, a large Latin Bible with images in one part. This may have been the "biblia picta" given in 1486 by a York chaplain, John Lese. In the inventory of Durham Priory, 1446, reference is made to a "psalterium cum Historia Christi depicta in principio," possibly owned or commissioned by John Fosser, who was prior of Durham from 1341 to 1374. A chaplain of the parish church of Doncaster, William Barnby, gave a book which he describes as having straps, bound in red leather and containing at the beginning of the work paintings of hermits.[36] Ralph Pigot, knight of Clotherholme, left to the chapel of his manor a psalter "allomnatum."[37]

Archbishop Rotherham indicated his aesthetic judgments about his books when he gave to his collegiate foundation at Rotherham a "pulchrum missale, scriptum secundum usum . . . Eboracensis, sumptuose illuminatum," and another "pulchrum missale magni pretii . . . illuminatum," of Sarum use as well as a great antiphonal "novum et pulchrum, secundum usum Ebor." He also notes another antiphonal of identical description and use, and a gradual "novum et pulchrum, secundum usum Ebor."[38] All of these books had their second folios noted by their donor.

Other owners valued the book's contents over the pictures. William Wilmyncote, a chaplain resident in York when he wrote his own will in 1402, left to John Munkgate, a fellow chaplain, an illuminated prayer roll containing "excellent histories from the Annunciation to the day of Judgment."[39] These prayer rolls, incidentally, were not uncommon. Another one, "magnum rotulum tractatum de biblia in Latine cum ymaginibus," though the pictures are not further characterized, was left by Lasynby to John Bolton. Thomas Moragior, rector of Kirkby, bequeathed a "rotulum cum precibus secretibus," while Maria Roos left "unum rotulum de passione" to Isabella Fauconberge in her will of 1394, and Elizabeth de la River of Brandesby in 1454 left together with a primer and a psalter, "my Roulys."[40]

The Roos and de la River wills, along with a number of others made by northern women, raise the problem of female book ownership and female attitudes about books in England during the late Middle Ages. These are very fascinating questions and ones which I should like to deal with at some length because they have received rather little attention. Some recent estimates of the numbers of medieval English women who could read have resulted from applying the French "Annales" and "mentalités" styles of historiography to English cultural studies. Chief among these have been articles by Joel Rosenthal and Susan Groag Bell. The former considers primarily one social class of 435 peers and their wives; the latter, whose study is very provocative and wide-ranging, is not chiefly concerned with England in the late Middle Ages.[41]

Rosenthal in the second half of his study of "literary high culture" among these peers, examining a number of aristocratic wills, virtually all from the south of England, noted that a high proportion—some 48 percent—of the wills of aristocratic women mention books. He found that of the 251 wills he surveyed, 30 male and 41 female wills had book bequests. Bell, who had a somewhat controversial thesis to propound, looked occasionally at wills, but accepted all forms of evidence for female book ownership and use, especially that of manuscript illuminations showing women reading or receiving commissioned books. Though Bell had discussed the design of *horae* and the commissioning of translations and devotional works as areas where women's opinions mattered, she spoke rather generally and not as a student of manuscripts, accepting uncritically, for example, Margaret Deanesly's conclusions from an influential but now quite obsolete article published in 1920.[42] Bell looked chiefly at early European book ownership by 242 women living between 800 and 1500 and touched on England only in relation to Anne of Bohemia's arrival there and the impact of her bookish piety on the court of Richard II. Much of her evidence is drawn, moreover, not from books themselves, but from documents like the accounts books of Mahaut of Artois and Isabeau of Bavaria or from works of art like the Mérode altarpiece, or somewhat unrepresentative books like the *Belles Heures* of Jean de Berry and the *horae* of Mary of Burgundy. Both Rosenthal and Bell are interested, either implicitly or openly, in the way women were "empowered" by the ownership of books, especially precious ones of the type just mentioned.

The following remarks on northern English female book ownership are based on much larger statistical and broader class samplings than those of Rosenthal, for year by year there are many more medieval wills surviving from the north of England than from the south. The Maria Roos and Elizabeth de la River wills are only two of many northern legacies of books by women. There are in the wills, as well, a number of examples of women leaving money to a religious institution to purchase or repair books. On the whole, the impression is that female book ownership and presumably female literacy in the north was much higher than has traditionally been assumed. By examining middle- and upper–middle-class women's words about their books, as well as actual examples of the humbler sorts of books they owned, I hope to offer somewhat more historically and socially balanced conclusions than those of Rosenthal and Bell, especially because the latter's preoccupation with the enormously valuable illuminated manuscripts of the Continental nobility may give a somewhat skewed idea of female literacy and book ownership elsewhere.

Though my proportions of northern female to male book legacies do not match those of Rosenthal in the south, they are still very significant. Of the 942 wills mentioning books at all, 74 contain book legacies by women and an additional 13 contain legacies by women who wish either to buy a book for a church or pay for a book's repair. Since people often left money to churches for the maintenance of the buildings, the purchase of vestments, and the like, the choice of a bequest for books rather than something else is possible evidence for, if not literacy, at least a specific interest in the book rather than in some other form of pious memorial.

While a number of the wills indicate what might be called passive ownership in that the testatrix received her book originally from a father or a husband—and, as we shall see, a substantial number of these ladies were widows—there is some evidence from extant northern manuscripts that women were often actively engaged in acquiring their books. On occasion, they shaped them in various ways to fit their needs and concerns, and even chose or at least appreciated the scripts in which they were written, as we see in the case of Joan Walkyngham, a member of the gentry, who died in 1346. She shows an awareness of what must have been at the time a very new national hand when she speaks in her will of "quemdam librum scriptum littera Anglicana," and of conventional scales of script when describing a psalter "cum littera grossa."[43]

Probably the greatest opportunity for an English woman to control the arrangement and appearance of her book was in the commissioning of a *horae,* in which the gender of the Latin prayers would be hers and she could prefer the hours of the Virgin to the hours of the Cross. Her control and choice extended to the suffrages or commemorations of certain female saints, often with half-page pictures and accompanying texts of their lives. Typical prayers too, such as those to Saint Christopher or Saints Roche and Sebastian, popular plague saints, could have a strongly female emphasis, with prayers to Saint Barbara, often depicted reading, Saint Apollonia, and others. Finally, and perhaps most importantly, she could arrange that her portrait appear at several points in the book in historiated initials for prayers. Unfortunately, the ratio of surviving *horae* to other sorts of northern liturgical books is not high. Of the books called primers in

Appendix C, a term that often but not always means *horae*, only fifteen extant examples are known to me as against several times that many manuals, breviaries, psalters, and missals. The only northern *horae* clearly commissioned or adapted from Sarum use by a woman are Cambridge, Sidney Sussex College MS 37, with some York saints in the kalendar; and York Minster Library MS Additional 54; the latter will be discussed in greater detail in chapter 5. However, we may note that this volume appears to show somewhat the same sort of familial pride we will see in books owned by men like Langley and Rotherham, as the commissioner, Joan de Mountenay, a wealthy heiress of Wheatley, near Doncaster, had her arms placed in the manuscript on page 64 below a picture of Christ as the Man of Sorrows rising from the tomb. The book contains sixteen shields showing the changes in the Mountenay arms through marriage. Joan married Thomas Furnival but eventually, after her husband's death, resumed her maiden name. Interestingly, Joan had her date of birth recorded in this book: "nata est Joanna filia Thomae Mountenay militis in festum sancti Michaelis Archangeli A.D. 1321."[44] Her descendant Robert Mountenay married Isabella Wortley about 1499, the year he received the *horae;* Isabella is presumably the lady pictured reading a prayer book, perhaps even MS Additional 54, in a window in Ecclesfield church.

Though it will be discussed in detail in chapter 3, a manuscript that reflects female taste may be briefly mentioned here. A missal of the late fourteenth or early fifteenth century, now Boston Public Library MS 1576,[45] is a fairly representative example of the sort of medium-quality liturgical book produced, I believe, in the north of England, most probably in or around the city of York. Originally it belonged to the Nevilles and later to the Gascoignes of Yorkshire. Joan Neville, daughter of John, married William Gascoigne, and the *obits* of these families are in the kalendar; the earliest is 1441. The graded kalendar of York use commemorates Saint Anne, showing that the book was made after 1383, when her feast was proclaimed throughout England. Though missals were not as commonly commissioned by women for personal use as were breviaries and books of hours, Saint Anne's feast and an office for a pregnant woman on the flyleaf of the Boston volume suggest possible female ownership at some point in the book's history.

Another York missal of about the same date, now Dublin, Trinity College MS 83, comes from Patrick Brompton in Yorkshire. It was once in the possession of the Norton family, with *obits* for Alice, wife of Robert, in 1418 and for his son John in 1418/1419. This book shows early and continued female use, with a mass for a pregnant woman and a Latin prayer to St. Barbara added in a late fifteenth-century hand, followed by Middle English translations.[46]

Prayer books can also be a guide to their owner's gender. One whose internal structure suggests that it was intended for a woman is now Oxford, Bodleian Library MS Latin Liturgies e.17, a collection of prayers written about 1425–1450. This book's kalendar contains the feasts of William and Wilfrid but also has a number of southern saints, so that not too much can be concluded about the geographical location of its commissioner. Its added Middle English prayers, however, have some dialect words that tie the book to the north. These prayers seem to be of the end of the fifteenth century, to judge from a note in the hand of the additions, dated 1492. The nature of the added material would suggest that the book was owned by a nun or an anchoress. There are still unsolved questions about this book's origins and purpose. It was intended to have a series of historiated initials, and the extensive instructions in Middle English to an illuminator that remain are very like the stage directions in contemporary plays. Though they show an obsessive interest in the exact composition and realism of various scenes, they give no key to the commissioner's gender, yet the grammatical forms of the prayers in the book are feminine, and at folio 71 the owner speaks of herself by name, "I, Johanna," suggesting that the book was originally created for a woman rather than adapted at some later time. Johanna, then, may have been directly concerned with the early stages of this book's design.[47]

More closely tied to popular culture is Cambridge, Trinity College MS R.14.26, a mixed paper and parchment miscellany of political prophecy, *distinctiones,* Latin questions on music and logic, carols, and sermons from the second half of the fifteenth century. It appears to have come from the Beverley area, for on the flyleaf is a bond of Thomas Pierson, a clerk of Howden near Beverley, and portions of the book were written by a scribe named John Anlaby, a strongly northern surname. An *ex libris* at folio 11 tells us, "This booke bylonges to the good wife Sanderson at Beverley dwellynge in Weddysday merket."[48] Though Bell has stressed the tremendous importance for female literacy of the rapid increase of translations of all sorts in the fourteenth and fifteenth centuries,[49] it should be remembered that the liturgical books I have mentioned so far, as well as this miscellany, were all or mostly in Latin. And unless the good wife Sanderson had it only for its vernacular songs, MS R.14.26 also presumes some degree of female Latinity, since it is clearly a book meant to be used rather than displayed. Perhaps this woman was the wife of a scribe or worked with one and had become literate in that way. Evidence, however, for female writing skills in all classes in the north, is unfortunately scantier than that for reading ability, though at least one aristocratic northern woman was able to write, as Anne Scrope of Bolton signed her own will in 1498.[50] And as the frontispiece of this book indicates, at least one English bookseller was imagined as female.

Let us turn now to the wills themselves, considering first the pious intentions to supply or repair books for churches, which are admittedly ambiguous evidence for book possession, and then the books actually mentioned by women in their wills. The earliest examples of gifts of money in the wills are rather inconclusive. They appeared in 1395 when Katherine, wife of William of Leversham, merchant of York, left a piece of silver to buy a breviary, and when Alice, wife of John Dandson of Heden, gave an unspecified amount of money to buy books for the church of St. Augustine in that town. In the same year Johanna de Ripon of York left 3s. 4d. to provide "unum missale novum . . . to my parish church of Sampson in York." In 1426, Matilda Wright of Newark, "once a wife," bequeathed ten shillings to her parish church for a book.[51]

Later in the fifteenth century, the type of book was usually specified, and the amounts of the legacies increased, so that in 1458, Alice Hothom left four silver marks to purchase a book for the parish church of Newbald, and in 1474, Agnes Patrington of Hull, widow, left to the church of St. Mary, Hull, 3s. 4d. to buy a "legend" or collection of saints' lives.[52]

An alternative—though not necessarily a less expensive one—to the purchase of a book was a contribution to the mending of manuscript books, which, as the age of print approached, were apparently becoming increasingly tattered. These bequests come towards the end of the fifteenth century. In 1475, Cecilia Rawson gave 16s. 8d. for mending books. In 1490, Alice Presteman of Newton Grange left seven shillings to the church of St. Oswald for repair of books in the church, and in 1493, Margaret Fenton of Scardeburgh left twenty shillings, about the price of a new book, to repair a missal in the chapel of St. Sepulchre. Perhaps the most sumptuous of these legacies was that of Agnes Doncaster of York, widow, who in 1460 left the church of St. Peter the Less ten pounds for "unum missale ceterosque libros."[53]

By far the largest number of the books owned by these northern women were devotional—primers—which generally meant *horae* or other types of lay devotional books, prayer collections, psalters, and breviaries, such as are noted in the will of Agnes Bedford of Kingston-on-Hull, who in 1459 left "meum novum primarium, [and] j librum cum precibus." There were, however, some interesting exceptions to this generalization. In 1421, Maud Bowes of Dalton gave several curious books to five different women: "j romance boke . . . called *The gospelles*," "unum romance boke," "the boke with the knotts," and "j librum that is called *Trystram.*" In 1495, Margery Salvayn bequeathed a copy of Boccaccio.[54] Other women left romances, like Matilda of York, countess of Cambridge; two books in French called *Guyon le Courtois* are named in her will of 1446. Johanna Hilton, wife of Robert Hilton, a knight of Swyne in the East Riding, bequeathed a book in "romanse" that began "decem preceptis alembes" (I have been unable to identify it further). In the same legacy was a "Romanse de Septem Sages."[55] We can see from these examples that in the north women nearly rivaled men in enjoying imaginative literature, for of the codices of the literary figures—Chaucer, Boccaccio, Gower, Langland, Mandeville, and Petrarch—mentioned in the wills, two were owned by women.

Books neither liturgical nor imaginative but generally devotional make up a substantial number of the legacies. For example, Maria de Roos, mentioned earlier, the widow of John Roos and half sister of Henry Percy, at her death in 1394 left a "libro Gallico de Duce Lancastriae," most likely the devotional compendium *Livre de Seintz Medicines* written by Henry Grosmont, duke of Lancaster ca. 1300–1361 and step-uncle to Maria.[56] In 1469, Gilamote Carrek de Ebor gave a *Speculum Guidonis* or *Speculum of Guy of Warwick* in English and a French copy of *Barlaam and Josephat*.[57] Agnes Stapleton of Yorkshire, who died in 1448, as the widow of Brian Stapleton of Carlton, left an unspecified "librum de ffrensshe" as well as "meum librum vocatum Bonaventure, . . . librum meum vocatum *Prik of Conscience* et librum meum vocatum *Chastisying of Goddes Children*," and "librum meum vocatum Vice and Virtue." Probably the largest of these devotional collections was that of Elizabeth Sywardby in the East Riding, who at her death in 1468 owned a missal, a ferial psalter, a book of certain divine offices and commemorations, a book "compilato in lingua Anglic[ana] de *Revelationibus Sanctae Brigidae*," a life of Christ, probably the pseudo-Bonaventuran work, "in lingua materna," and another "compilato in Latinis," another English version of the mystery of the Passion, a meditation on the Passion "compilato per Ricardum Rolle," and a visitation of the Blessed Virgin Mary, all in all a small devotional library.[58]

Emerging clearly from the wills is another feature of the female book collections: in several cases the books were owned as much for pleasure as for use, if we can judge from the evidence offered by multiple copies of the same work. Admittedly, multiple copies were often inherited. Hawisia Aske left her five primers with carefully orchestrated descriptions: "unum primarium" to one person, "unum primarium cum uno clasp argento parato et deaurato" to another, "unum aliud primarium" to another, "unum aliud primarium luminatum cum auro cum duobus clasps argento paratis et deauratis" to another, and finally to Elisabeth Pudsay "unum parvum primarium cum uno clasp argento parato quod quondam fuit patris sui." Isabella de Emeley, who died in 1348, left not only "unum psalterium," "unum missale," and "unum missale melius," but "unam bibliothecam novam," a new bookcase in which to store her books and perhaps others belonging to the household.[59] Isabella Percy had quite a substantial collection of books, leaving besides a "parvum psalterium" psalters in French and in English.[60] Margaret Plays, the wife of William Plays, knight, spoke of "primarium meum optimum" and "omnes libros meos" in her will of 1400.[61] The Matilda of York mentioned earlier left "my big best primer."[62] Isabella Ellerker of Brandesburton, widow, had at her death in 1477 three different primers, and Eufemia Langton owned not only a missal, which she cherished because it had been Archbishop Scrope's, but a "parvum psalterium," a "psalterium," and "aliud psalterium."[63]

These were members of aristocratic families, but there is evidence of multiple ownership and decorative and devotional choice among the sorts of women who could well have been the wives of Chaucer's Five Guildsmen. That books and their use were not uncommon among women of the bourgeoisie and that such women may have had a considerable say in their composition can be inferred from the handsome *horae* made for John Bolton, merchant and mayor of York, and his wife, Alice, who was the gentlewoman of Matilda of York, receiving the enormous sum of twenty pounds from her as a legacy. Extremely pious people, the couple had papal permission to own a portable altar. This manuscript, now York Minster Library MS Additional 2, will be discussed in later chapters. It is, however, worth noting here the presence in the manuscript of a rather rare saint, Zita of Lucca—or in England, Sitha—who appears in a suffrage minia-ture, being prayed to by a woman, possibly Bolton's wife. Sitha, a domestic servant in her life, is shown in the miniature with two of her emblems, bread and a bag. A hospital in or around York was named for her.

Two other elements of the iconography of the Bolton *horae* sug-gest that a literate woman was involved in its commissioning. In a scene of St. Anne and the three Maries, the crude but vigorous illumi-nator appears to reflect popular taste by showing them holding and reading the text of books. There is, in addition to the female scenes mentioned, a rare portrait of St. Bridget writing a phrase on a bande-role, and one at folio 100v of archbishop Scrope, in his pontifical robes but not nimbused, being prayed to by a blond woman, probably Alice Bolton, wearing a golden fillet; she holds a scroll requesting of the martyred archbishop, "Sancte Ricarde Scrope ora pro nobis."

Less detailed information about bourgeois book ownership comes from the will of Agnes, widow of Robert Lockton of York, a draper who died in 1404; she speaks of her "best primer"[64] as if there were others. Margaret la Zouch, who died in 1449, the wife of John la Zouch of Totness, left "my best primer, a franssh boke, [and] my fair gret sawter,"[65] and Isabella Willoughby, who died in 1415, wife of Edmund de Willoughby of Wollaton, Nottinghamshire, which was at the lower limits of the York diocese in this period, had at least two primers, a "primarium coopertum cum nigro velvet" and "unum novum primarium."[66] The Willoughby family eventually acquired some of the books of Thomas Chaworth, including the Wollaton Antiphonale.

It is presumably such books as the Bolton *horae*, brightly bound and proudly displayed, that prompted the satirical observation of Chaucer's French contemporary, Eustache Deschamps, in his *Miroir de Mariage* on the expenses a wife could incur for a husband when she covets:

> Heures me fault de Nostre Dame,
> Si comme il appartient a fame
> Venue de noble paraige,
> Qui soient de soutil ouvraige
> D'or et d'azur, riches et cointes,
> Bien ordonneés et bien pointes,
> De fin drap d'or tresbien couvertes;

Et quant elles seront ouvertes,
Deux fermaulx d'or qui fermeront.

[A book of hours of the Virgin . . . made in suble fashion. Inside
gold and azure, rich and modish, finely painted and well ruled. I
wish it covered with fine gold cloth; then when I've opened it, two
gold clasps to close it up again.][67]

Deschamps' focus on the outward appearance of such *horae* illustrates some interesting gender differences in the way the legacies are
referred to in the wills. On the whole, the most detailed identifying
descriptions of a book's contents, such as its second folio readings
and its ornamentation, come from clerics, who were, of course, often
professionally involved with their books. Laymen, however, do seem
as well to focus on the content or interior of the volumes in slightly
more aesthetic terms than laywomen. Women tend to refer to the age
of the book or the material of the covers; that this material was more
often colored silk or velvet than leather, to judge from extant *horae*,
suggests that their books were either originally made for or perhaps
rebound for them. We recall Sir John Depeden's "primarium magnum cum litteris illuminatis," and Ralph Pigot's psalter "allomnatum."
In contrast, a woman of the same class as Depeden, Matilda, the
widow of Sir Peter de Maulay, left a "psalterium . . . coopertum cum
blodio velvett," a "psalterium . . . nigrum," and another "rubeum" at
her death in 1438, and Elizabeth Fitzhugh of Ravensworth in a will
written in English in 1427 left to her children "a sauter couered with
rede velwet," a "primer couered in rede," a "sauter couered in blew,"
a "primer couered in blew," and "a book couered in grene with
praiers thereinne."[68] Another woman of high station, Alicia Myton of
Aughton, daughter of John Aske, the seneshal of the bishop of Durham, left on her death in 1440 a "primarium cum signaculis deauratis,"[69] with the gilded clasps mentioned in Deschamp's poem. The
Maria de Roos referred to earlier left a "primarium viride,"[70] and
Agnes Stapleton, who seems to have had a large book collection,
described her "primer cum duobus clasps."[71] Johanna Grymmer of
Beverley in 1430, the widow Elena Marshall in 1490, and the Maud
Bowes mentioned earlier bequeathed books with black covers.[72] Isa-
bella Ellerker had three different primers, one distinguished from
the others by its red cover; Margaret Pigot of the same family in
Clotherholme referred to earlier, left a "red English book."[73] Anne
Scrope of Bolton bequeathed "a masse book," an "emborderd [em-

broidered] sawter," "a premer," "a Frenche book called the *Pistill of Othia*," another "frenchebook," a "white book of prayers," and "a premer clasped with silver an gylte."[74]

Of the age of books, and by inference their outmoded decoration and archaic pre-Gothic script, the wills offer some evidence. In 1444, Margaret Pudsay, the wife of Sir John Pudsay of Bolton, mentioned "uno missali veteri," and Matilda of York left an "old porto of York use" and a more fashionable "primarium viride."[75]

A considerable number of northern men left books to women, including in one case a serving maid named Agnes Celayne, who received from John Raventhorpe, a priest, a "librum Angliae de fabulis et narracionibus," with the clear intention and expectation that they should read them; primarily these were English and French works. Henry Percy in 1352 left to his daughter Isabella an intriguing "librum de natura Animalium in Gallico." In 1392 a knight, Robert Roos, of an important Yorkshire family, left a "librum de Gallico de Veteribus Historiis" to his daughter-in-law and to his daughter Eleanor a psalter in French, a Bible, possibly in English, and a French translation of Jacob of Voragine's popular standard collection of saints' lives, *Aurea Legenda*. To another daughter, Katherine, a nun, he left a psalter and to Elizabeth Stapleton a French *Sidrak and Boccas*, a curious encyclopedic collection of knowledge in dialogue form. A Thomas of the same family left in 1399 a "legendam sanctorum" to Elizabeth Redman. Thomas Hebbeden left a book in French "vocatum *Launcelote*" to an Isabella Vure or Eure. One of the most intriguing of these legacies is that of William Banks of York, who gave what seems to have been Chaucer's *Troilus* to the Elena Marshall mentioned earlier as a testatrix. Other literary and historical legacies include a copy of Gower left by John Morton of York to Joan Beaufort and a copy of the *Brut* left by Thomas Ughtred of Kexby to his wife. Alice Bolton, the pious wife who seems to have commissioned with her husband the Bolton *horae*, received a *Pricke of Conscience* from the William Revetour we spoke of earlier.[76]

Most of the female legacies, however, were to lay women or to nuns, offering an English corollary for Susan Bell's argument that Continental women were often directly involved in the promotion of reading for other women. In 1438, Eleanor Roos left four of her six Latin books to women. Matilda of York's five books were all left to women, and Constance Skelton of Cleveland, in north Yorkshire, who died in 1422, seems to have originally received a "librum matutinae de domina Isabella Stapleton." Agnes Stapleton of Yorkshire left six books to various Cistercian, Cluniac, or Benedictine nuns.[77]

What conclusions can be drawn from these wills and the few extant northern books that must have once figured among the bequests in them? In an essay rooted in the concept of culture as an instrument of power and class privilege, Rosenthal argues that book bequests were a form of female empowerment: "something in which women could and did involve themselves. Their wills may mention more books because they usually outlived their husbands and were then able to dispose of personal goods in a context of considerable personal freedom."[78] His focus here is on the exercise of choice chiefly in economic matters. Property is power, and the moment of writing a will is the one in which the dynastic impulse may be more strongly present than in earlier periods of a person's life. This economic argument, however, does not take into account other forms of choice that may be more intangible but still equally satisfying: the exercise of choice and imagination in the aesthetic realm.

What emerges from our consideration of the evidence is that not only did a much higher proportion of women in northern England in the late Middle Ages own books than has been hitherto recognized but, equally important, women mentioned books in their wills in ways that suggest that they read them, or took strong aesthetic pleasure and satisfaction from contemplating the images in them privately or displaying them to others. For example, that so many of these women did not say in their legacies "all my books" but specified them by color, content, or age and intended them to go to particular persons indicates that they had an active interest in their libraries or, in the case of legacies for purchase or repair of books, felt that the indirect creation of a book was somehow a more godly act than that of furnishing a much more visible and permanent church stall or candelabrum.

While an aesthetic response to a book is not, of course, a sign that the person can read it, it is evidence that women focused on books as a specific kind of female possession that was portable, private, could be easily taken out and examined at will as a respite from domestic cares and turmoil, and whose pages could be the occasion for contemplative and meditative, but still primarily aesthetic, activity involving fantasy, imagination, and the visual and tactile response to beauty.

Even if no female book owner mentions in her will the illumination of her book in the way that a number of the male wills do ("my new missal sumptuously illuminated" or "my breviary with a picture of a hermit and large golden letters"), the ownership of multiple copies of the same book indicates that women collected books, presumably for aesthetic reasons, and comments about their ages suggest that women responded to fashions in book script and design. When the evidence from the wills is glossed by surviving books in whose commissioning and construction women undoubtedly had a hand, we can speculate that handsome books must have been signs of imaginative freedom, personal satisfaction and status to these northern women much as the armor, the bows and peacock-feathered arrows, the cups and robes and beds so often detailed in the male wills were to their owners.

Male testators, of course, show similar forms of bibliophilic appreciation of their books and must have received much the same aesthetic gratification from owning them, for they often singled them out by their script and illumination. At his death in 1435, Thomas Hebbeden, dean of the Collegiate Church of St. Andrew, Aukland, in the Durham diocese, left to his own church "unum pulchrum psalterium subtiliter scriptum,"[79] indicating admiration for both the decoration of the book and the character of its hand. Though he did not single it out for praise, Hebbeden also owned a very handsome legal book that still survives as Durham Cathedral Library MS C.III.11, bought from Hebbeden's executors. John Gylby, rector of Knesall, Nottinghamshire, an important figure in the circle of John Newton, whose will was proved in 1434/35, speaks proudly of his "portiforium magnum et pulcrum de pleno usu Eboracensis ecclesiae," and the bibliophile John Dautre speaks of his "psalterium elomned cum auro."[80] Several testators—the William Revetour mentioned earlier; William Welwick, a vicar choral who died in 1455; William Duffield, archdeacon of Cleveland and a residentiary canon of York, who had a remarkable collection of books; and Walter Skirlaw, as well as the Joan Walkyngham mentioned in the discussion of female book ownership—even comment on the script of the books they owned. They refer indirectly to the presence in England of the newly fashionable *bâtarde* or Burgundian scripts coming to England from the commercial workshops of the Low Countries and France, for Revetour speaks of "unum primarium largum cum ymaginibus intus scriptis ad modum Flandrium"; Welwick bequeaths a "portous bastard" valued at 26s. 8d., and Duffield, who died in 1452, gives his "psalterum, scriptum manu scriptoris Franciae."[81] Skirlaw gave six of his books to University College, Oxford, and described them in the indenture he made with the master, John Appleton, as a three-volume set of Nicholas of Lyra "opere et litera parisiensi" and a repertorium, perhaps Bersuire's *Repertorium Biblicum* "de eisdem opere et litera."[82]

Even presumably unilluminated law, devotional, and grammar books were regarded warmly. Robert Manfield, canon of York, archdeacon of Cleveland, and provost of Beverley, among other important titles and benefices, lists in 1419 "preciosum librum meum Decretorum."[83] Manfield in later life became a recluse of some note. He too, like many of the northern book owners we have been discussing, had been a Chancery clerk.[84] A fellow canon of York, William Noion, speaks somewhat plaintively of "my book called *Horologium Divinae Sapientiae,* in which in life I much delighted," as he wills it to Thomas Arundel, at that time archbishop of Canterbury. Noion was a Peterhouse man and Arundel's household clerk in early life.[85] A chaplain of York, John Raventhorpe, who died in 1432, speaks of his "preciosum librum grammaticae secundum alphabetum de Catholicon."[86]

Not all of these books, of course, were given to individuals as objects of value, like a silver cup or spoon; some were left with the stipulation that they should be passed on to others. Such books formed part of "common profit" libraries. A study by Jo Ann Moran concerning William Wilmyncote's will offers a number of examples in both northern and southern English wills of books intended by the testator to be loaned to someone else by the legatee when he or she was not using them and, after the legatee died, to be passed on to other persons for the physical life of the book.[87]

Both Wilmyncote and Hebbeden left books in this way. Wilmyncote gave his small but useful library to a chaplain on the condition that when this person died, he would pass the books to the testator's clerk, who was about to take orders, and when this clerk, Richard de Swayneby died, the books were to pass to indigent priests. And to ensure compliance, the exchanges of the books should be done under official scrutiny "coram presidente Curie Ebor." Similarly, Hebbeden left a copy of the *Speculum Virtutis* to the prior of Durham for his lifetime, after which period it should become a book of "common profit" in the library.[88]

Another interesting "common profit" donation was that of the Newcastle Dominican anchorite John Lacy, who in his dual role as scribe illuminator will be considered in the next chapter. He gave a book of his own making to a chaplain named Roger Stonysdale and then to the priest of the Church of St. Nicholas of Newcastle and took the unusual precaution of putting the book's eventual destination in the work's *incipit:*

Orate pro anima fratris Iohannis Lacy anchorite de ordine fratrum predicatorum, Noui Castri super Tynam, qui hoc primarium dedit domino Rogero Stonysdale capellano ecclesie sancti Nicholai Novi Castri super Tynam ad totum tempus vite sue. Et post mortem predicti domini Rogeri volo ut tradatur alii presbitero dicte ecclesie secundum disposicionem dicti Rogeri ad terminum vite sue; & sic de presbitero in presbiterum in eadem ecclesia remanendum dummodo durauerit orandum pro anima predicti Iohannis Lacy anachorite. Anno domini millesimo CCCCmo XXXiiijto.[89]

A common pattern among men somewhat higher in the ecclesiastical structures of York and Durham than those we have just been discussing was that of leaving their books by direct donation or reversion, to their respective college libraries, where some of them still are. Many persons important in the church hierarchy of York were educated at Oxford and Cambridge colleges, like William Poteman, canon lawyer, archdeacon and residentiary canon of York; Robert Est, treasurer of York Cathedral; William Duffield, residentiary canon of York, Southwell and Beverley; William Barneby, canon of Southwell; and John Newton, Fellow of Peterhouse, Cambridge. Eventually, after taking their degrees, they returned to the north and quickly attained high administrative office in York and Durham, partly, no doubt, because of friendships they established as students. Indeed, as Dobson had noted, "it is hardly possible to exaggerate the importance of the university background of the great majority of York canons."[90]

Poteman, for example, left twelve of his books to All Souls College, Oxford, and Est gave a total of eight volumes, whose histories are documented in the records of early donations. The latter's gift consisted of five volumes of the legal work of Nicholas Tudeschis, two volumes of Dominic of San Gemigiano on the *Sext*, and a volume of Baldus on the *Code*. A list of expenses in All Souls shows that the books were very quickly transferred from York to Oxford with costs of 6s. 4d. for carriage in 1494 and 8s. for chaining the five volumes of Nicholas in the common library.[91]

William Duffield, Fellow of Merton College, Oxford, in 1398 and owner of thirty books at his death in 1453, gave a number of them to his college. His Ockham on *Sentences* is now MS G.1.3 and his Robert Cowton on the same text is MS B.1.14. His medical collection must have been quite extensive because he gave a John Gaddesden, *Rosa Medicinae* (lost), an Averroes, *Colliget* (MS N.3.8), a Constantine Africanus *Viaticum* (MS H.2.6), and two copies of Johannitius, *Isagoge* (MSS C.2.6 and N.3.4.). Another donation was an Aquinas, *Summa Theologica*, to Balliol College, Oxford (MS 43). A book quite rare in England at the time, Peter John Olivi on Matthew, was left to Merton with the wish that it be chained in the common library, but it is now lost.[92] Undoubtedly, the very large number of books with a Durham connection given to Jesus College, Cambridge, must have been donations of a similar character.[93]

This pattern of legacies to colleges can be traced among persons lower in the ecclesiastical hierarchy as well. William de Waltham, canon of York, rector of Algarkyrk, and one of John Newton's executors, in 1416 left a number of books to King's Hall, Cambridge, and Dean Richard Andrews left many books to All Souls in 1471.[94]

Though the practice I have just outlined was a common one among northern magnates, it was becoming increasingly fashionable in the fifteenth century to give books to northern foundations, especially to the newly formed York Minster Library. The person who might be called its founder was another book-owning and book-bequeathing magnate, the remarkable bibliophile John Newton, who was a Master of Peterhouse, Cambridge, and then held a variety of canonries and prebendaries. He was treasurer at York until his death in 1414 and was buried in the cathedral. Like Poteman, he gave a number of his books to his college, many of which still survive. In 1414, Newton donated some forty of the 118 volumes in his collection for the founding and development of a library at York Minster. Newton's books are extraordinary in their range of interests. Four of them are still in the Minster Library and a number at Peterhouse, Cambridge, and in other British collections. By 1418 the Minster had a new building to house Newton's books, mainly through the efforts of another of Newton's executors, Thomas Haxey. By the end of the first quarter of the century, Newton's forty books were chained on lecterns in the Minster Library and protected by horn covers.[95]

Not only was Newton a munificent giver of books but he also took an active part in disseminating their texts to others, according to Jonathan Hughes.[96] We will have occasion to treat Newton and his library in greater detail in chapters 4 and 6, where we will consider the character of his book donations and his aesthetic taste in books in so far as that can be determined from the many books surviving from his collection.

By the 1440s more modest bequests were not uncommon. Robert Alne, Fellow of Peterhouse with Newton and a key member of his circle as well as a parson of the altar of St. Nicholas and examiner-general, left a number of law books to Newton's newly founded Minster Library.[97] In 1457, John Barnygham gave his complete sermon cycle of Jacob of Voragine and his *Compendium Morale*.[98]

Well into the age of print, of course, manuscript books were still

given to the cathedral and to city churches by clerics. For example,
York Minster Library MS XVI.D.13, a thirteenth-century Bible, contains a flyleaf inscription detailing this process: "Iste liber dedit dominus Willelmus Rycherdson ad Ecclesiam Sancti Martini in
Conyngstret in Eboracum. Qui quidem Willelmus quondam fuit Per-
sona in ecclesia Cathedralis Sancti Petri. Voluit tamen ut sit Cathena-
tus in Choro sancti Martini predicti ad serviendum ibi
imperpetuum."[99] The date of this gift was 1510. Rycherdson was a
vicar choral of York Minster from 1511 to 1524.

The wills also on occasion refer to the scribes who made these
books, and what emerges from these remarks is the relatively high
proportion of amateur scribes in York. Indeed, one is reminded in
reading these wills of Curt Bühler's dictum that in the fifteenth century "the number of 'occasional' scribes, who wrote for themselves as
well as for others, could hardly have been smaller than the total of
the professional scriveners."[100] Actually, these amateur scribes left
considerably more evidence of their existence than did the professional scriveners, who remain merely names in the Freemen's
Register.[101]

The wills indicate a marked preference on the part of very
wealthy ecclesiastics for employing scribes whom they knew personally, or who were in their service, or who were simply available locally.
Let me illustrate this generalization by some examples of legacies.
The testament of John de Clifford, treasurer of York Cathedral and
chancellor of Beverley, proved in 1392, speaks of "my noted missal,
and breviary that Greneake wrote."[102] This unusual name—a form
of Greenoak—is probably that of a William Greneake, who was rector
of Scrayingham. The *Fasti Parochiales* for the deanery of Buckrose
report that on 12 May 1423, a William Greneake was presented to the
living of Scrayingham by the king. He apparently came by exchange
from the church of Rowley.[103] Greneake, who died in 1428, was a
man of some property.[104] While it would be uncommon in the south
for a beneficed priest to write books for others, it does not seem to
have been so in Yorkshire, if indeed this Greneake is the person in
question.

Another magnate, John de Scarle, Chancery and Parliamentary
clerk and later chancellor of England in 1401, who died in 1403,
refers in his will to a breviary that "dominus Roger Donk wrote" and
gives forty shillings to the said Roger.[105] This does not seem like the
act of a man who had a one-time commercial connection with his
scribe. Indeed, it suggests that Donk was not of a vastly different

status than the testator. The magnate William Poteman, among his many book bequests, made an enigmatic one of some interest in this context, "biblia mea parva" to magister Johannes Wod, who was a scrivener in York.[106]

In illustration of the relationship between commissioner and scribe, we may take the example of Robert Wolveden, also a treasurer of the cathedral, who died in 1432. He speaks in his will of a book written by master John Arston, who died in the same year. Arston's own will is extant; in it he refers to Wolveden as "my lord Treasurer" and gives the text of his own epitaph: "Here lies John Arston, one-time cleric and notary public, of German extraction, of the diocese of Mainz."[107] That Arston had a will—in which, incidentally, he leaves "meos libros" except his *Grecismus* of Eberhard of Bethune—suggests that he was a man of property.

A John Morton of York, knight and wealthy bibliophile, in 1431 returned to his brother of the same Christian name one of his own works: "unum librum scriptum manu sua propria de *Gestis Romanorum*."[108] This Morton and his wife, Juliana, were the recipients of letters of confraternity from William, prior of the York Austin Friars; the letter is contained in Oxford MS Bodley 131, which is a miscellany of devotional texts such as Nicholas Love's version of the *Mirror of the Blessed Life of Jesus*,[109] written by John Morton the scribe about 1440. The context of Morton's legacy suggests that John the scribe was a man of substance like his armigerous brother and not a scribe by trade. The writer John probably also copied another item in the book, William Flete's *de Remediis contra temptationes*.[110] This practice of making books, glosses, and tables of contents and topics for one's own use seems to have had neither social nor temporal limits in the north, lasting well into the age of print. Perhaps the most eminent of these amateur book makers was archbishop Thomas Rotherham, who copied out his own *addimenta* to certain of the works of Robert Grosseteste; we shall have more to say about his work in chapter 6. John de Feriby, subtreasurer of York Cathedral, in 1404 left his psalter with breviary "scripto de manu domini William de Feriby," his relation and a man of considerable substance himself.[111] Thomas de Farneylawe, chancellor of York, bequeathed a "kalendarium per me factum," by which he means an index of the contents of a work.[112] The will of William Waltham, canon, mentioned earlier, speaks of a certain "Interpretatione et Psalterium . . . scribi." Thomas Helton, a cleric and Prepositus of the Collegiate Church of St. Andrew at Northacastre, in a will dated 1505 bequeathed a book "manu mea propria scriptum de contentes Septem Sacramentorum" to a chaplain named Thomas Bracebrig,[113] and a John Castelay of Nottingham, occupation unspecified, gave "meum portiforum huic presenti scripto meo."[114] Master William Westerdale, a registry clerk and notary of the court of York made an interesting bequest of this type, leaving not only his "primarium de scriptura propria" but all his "prothocolla," or documents in his office, to his servant John Robinson.[115] In 1389, Richard Garton, rector of St. John's, Pikton, gave evidence of an earlier career as a clerk or notary as he left "librum meum de litteris missis que feci scribi" and "librum meum" that pertained "ad officium registratorum curia Ebor feci scribi."[116]

A somewhat similar bequest is that of a glazier, Robert Preston of York, who in 1503 left his apprentice not only his books but all his "scrolls," or glass-painting cartoons.[117] An interesting legacy in this context is a "librum de papiro non scriptum" left by William Stanes in 1435 to the use of the choir of St. Mary's Abbey, York. Even the contents of a stationer's shop could be bequeathed, as we see from the will of Thomas Gryssop. An inventory of his shop made 20 October 1446 included the following items: one book of paper valued at 8d., three paper quires valued at 9d., six books or perhaps pounds of paper valued at 9d., one ream and paper quires ready for writing valued at 3 s. 1d., and one dozen paper books valued at 18d.[118]

Only one northern bequest specifically indicates the employment of a professional scribe. In 1390 the will of Geoffrey de Cave, a clerk and notary engaged by the Chapter, left among other books a breviary, which had been started but not finished by a man called John Scrivener. A John Scriptor, yeoman, was a member of Thomas Arundel's household in 1383.[119]

Unusual scribal activity within a family can be found in the will of Robert Est, a Fellow of All Souls, Bachelor of Canon and Civil Law, and rector of Linton-in-Craven, Yorkshire. At his death in 1493, he was a Chapter clerk of York.[120] In his will he refers to a book written by his "brother, John Est"[121] containing collations from the Fathers and other tracts. This book is most probably York Minster Library MS XVI.K.16 and deserves a moment's discussion. It contains collation and Lenten sermons of York use, the *Speculum Peccatoris* of Edmund Rich, archbishop of Canterbury, Peckham's *Instructions for Parish Priests*, and Rolle's popular *Libellus de Emendatione Vitae*. The volume is a very plain one, written on parchment with two- and three-line initials and capitals in blue with red pen flourishing and quarter borders.

To judge from the various inscriptions of ownership, "Liber domini Iohannis Appilton," "Liber magistri Thomas Wencelagh Rectoris de Mydelton super Waldam," and "Liber domini Roberti Garthom capellani cantarie corporis Christi de Beverlaco," the book moved around the East Riding for a while before coming into Robert Est's hands. Its previous owners were people who would have had more of a professional interest in its contents than would Est, a notorious chopchurch.[122]

Ecclesiastical bureaucrats occasionally copied their own books at the start of their careers as clerks, to judge by the example of William Hawke, another magnate of the York diocese. Hawke, a Fellow of Pembroke Hall, Cambridge, apparently once worked as an amateur scribe, for he wrote a document for the University and King's College about 1445, and when he died in 1472, he left a book of his own making. In his will he bequeathed to Thomas Sayle, a Bachelor of Theology of the Benedictine Abbey of St. Mary's, York, "meum psalterium optimum manu mea conscriptum et glosatum per Hugonem de Vienna."[123] Hugh is Hugh of St. Cher, the famous French Dominican exegete, but commonly called Hugh of Vienna or simply Vienna.

In Gonville and Caius College, Cambridge, is a manuscript of Scotus containing questions on the third book of the *Sentences*. This volume, which was once part of a chained library, appears to be another early work by Hawke, as it bears the colophon "Hic finis est libri quod M. W. Hawke. Amen." A table of the questions was also written by him as he notes: "Explicit tabula questionum Doctoris Subtilis super tercium quod Hawke." On the last folio is a price, xxvj s. viij d., which may indicate the original cost of the volume—of which Hawke's hand makes up about a third—or of the price paid for it at some later point in its history.[124]

Similar to Hawke as a magnate yet former scribe was Thomas Greenwood, who was Doctor of Canon and Civil Law from Oxford, canon of Lincoln and York, and the holder of a number of important prebendaries at his death in 1421. Yet he had served as the scribe of the chancellor of York in 1397, the year in which he obtained his degree of Bachelor of Canon Law. Unfortunately, the inventory of Greenwood's books made after his death is defective and often illegible; he left quite a good-sized library; all of the volumes were works on law except for two service books.[125]

Though parish priests and chaplains also seem to have written books for parish use, they apparently did so from necessity rather than personal taste or preference. For example, Oxford, Bodleian

Library MS Selden Supra 40 is an ordinal of York use, very plainly made, which bears the colophon "by me, Rycharde Lostman preyst," and Richard Pees, rector of Goteham, Nottinghamshire, speaks of a breviary "quod scripsi propriis manibus meis."[126] A chaplain of York named John Bramthwaite left to the Church of All Saints a "missale cuius scribebam medietatum" in 1438.[127]

Though they do not come from wills, among the most interesting and well documented of these modest examples of northern scribal activity are those of Thomas Anlaby, who copied and illustrated the private cartulary mentioned earlier, and Edmund Norton, a Yorkshireman and presumably a younger son in the important Norton family. Norton was most probably a parish priest. Ordained in 1467 at York, he was a Fellow of Balliol College. Norton owned seventeen books, whose titles and prices he recorded on the flyleaf of a volume now MS Mullen 114 in the Catholic University of America Library, Washington, D.C., and he appears to have copied the other items in the volume, Rolle's *Emendatio Vitae,* and some Greek translations made by Leonardo Bruni. He also owned British Library MS Royal 8 A.xiii, containing William of Conches' *Moralium Dogma Philosophorum,* Petrarch's *De Contemptu Mundi,* and Alan of Lille's *Anticlaudianus;* the volume in size and character matches Mullen MS 114.[128]

It is certainly clear from our study that Norton, Hawke, Est, Anlaby, Wolveden, and others like them preferred to make their own books or to seek scribes among priests, notaries, chaplains or local semiprofessionals rather than to have books commissioned in the south or on the Continent. Perhaps they wanted greater control of the final product or simply felt more comfortable dealing with fellow northerners. It is also clear that there was a powerful clerical and ecclesiastical affinity in late fourteenth and early fifteenth century York and that it was centered around John Newton and the Minster, as certain names of book owners, book lovers and book copyists associated with him turn up repeatedly in these legacies. The wills show that a large number of books were in circulation in the north at the close of the Middle Ages; that many were owned and appreciated by women of both the middle and the upper classes; that many of these books were decorated and illuminated; and that except for the case of Durham, they were largely made outside of monasteries by amateur and professional scribes. It is to the latter class of artisans that we must now turn.

2

Northern Professional Scribes
and Scribe Families

$\mathbb{P}$erhaps the most remarkable thing about the scribes discussed in this chapter is the considerable evidence of their existence in what was in the Middle Ages usually an anonymous profession. It is clear from considering them that bookmaking had come out of the monasteries in the north by the last quarter of the fourteenth century and was largely the province of scribes who were mendicants, canons, or laymen. Three friar scribes—William de Ellerker, a Dominican; Robert de Popultoun, a Carmelite; and John Lacy, the Newcastle Dominican recluse mentioned in the last chapter—copied and oversaw and, in Lacy's case, even illuminated books. A fascinating scribe active in the northeast at Durham was a Breton named William du Stiphel, who worked for a monastery but was not a monk. A somewhat more conjectural group of professional copyists, the "Full-of-Love" family, rounds out our discussion of professional scribal activity in the north.

It appears that by the end of the Middle Ages, broadly speaking, even many monastic books were increasingly the work of lay professional scribes, as the ability to write elegant *textura* declined throughout England in the fourteenth century within many monastic houses. As we shall see in the present chapter, this decline was certainly evident in the north; so few accomplished scribes seem to have worked in monasteries that with the exception of Durham Priory, where skilled scribes and decorators were active up to the Dissolution, and Furness Abbey, where a Cistercian monk, John Stell, seems to have been both scribe and illuminator, monastic bookmaking plays a relatively minor role in our story.[1] Though the scribes were still clerics, it is now the friars—especially the Dominican, Carmelite, and Augustinian friars—who dominate the making of service books and even some secular ones.

Indeed, it is probable that some of the chronicles of various northern monastic houses were the work of professionals like the scribes we will be discussing shortly. As John Taylor has pointed out,[2] coarse examples of book hand were still written in monastic houses, of which the *Anonimalle Chronicle* at the University of Leeds is perhaps most representative; it was probably written at St. Mary's Abbey.[3] The Cistercian abbot of Meaux, William Burton, seems himself to have written two chronicles of that house, and the long version of the Kirkstall chronicle was made there. But these were the exceptions. By contrast, the *Computus* of Bolton Priory was written in York, noting that the canons had paid two shillings "pro chroniclis apud Ebor scribendis," and the shorter Kirkstall work was the product of a professional copyist writing *bâtarde* rather than *textura*, as were the various chronicles of Peter Langtoft, an Augustinian canon of Bridlington.[4] Who the scribes were who wrote such monastic books for hire is not always clear, but one possibility is that they formed part of a rapidly growing nucleus of the writing trade outside of the metropolis in the late 1370s. For example, in the West Riding villages of Scothorp "Willielmus clerke, scriptor," and Gayregrave, "Robertus Clerk escriptor" were listed in the taxation rolls with the names of all the taxpayers in a given county—called lay subsidy rolls—arranged according to trades.[5] Such persons may have been responsible for books as well as deeds, charters, wills, and the like. Other sources for large books hitherto the work of monastic copyists may have been royal clerks, some of whom were possibly active in the northwest; this is an especially important point in the case of the *Anonimalle Chronicle*. One such copyist was Richard Frampton, who between 1402 and 1410 wrote a calligraphic *Anglicana formata* of a chancery type, signing Glasgow University Library MS Hunterian T.4.1, a Latin miscellany of the fifteenth century, and who was paid the enormous sum of eighty-four pounds for copying the great "couchers," or registers of deeds, of the duchy of Lancaster, now in the London Public Records Office.[6] In short, the Ricardian and post-Ricardian periods in the north were chiefly the ages of scribes working for money or pious reasons outside of the monastery, and it is with these figures that we shall now be concerned.

Probably the earliest account of professional scribal activity in or around York is recorded in the colophon of a handsome copy of Huguccio of Pisa, *Magnae Derivationes*, which was made for the cathedral and ordered chained in the choir. In the early fifteenth century, it was removed to the newly formed Minster Library. This late thirteenth-century manuscript gives some idea of the way the cathedral obtained books. York Minster Library MS XVI.Q.15 is one of four Huguccios known to have been in the province. Now the presence of one Huguccio of Pisa in Yorkshire, let alone four, is quite a remarkable fact in itself. Manuscripts of the *Magnae Derivationes* were tall, densely written books, and even utilitarian copies were quite expensive.[7] The Minster Library example is a large double-column text with many five-line penwork initials. It has a most informative colophon. There we learn that "John le Gras, canon of York Cathedral, caused this book to be made at his own expense to be placed in a common and suitable location for the use of the priests and clerics of the choir ... where all who have questions of erudition can find in it the derivations, senses, and interpretations of words according to the order of the alphabet." A typical formulaic scribal couplet follows, concluding: "John de Gretham wrote this book and pray for me." Even the elaborate index is signed by its scribe, one William de Thornton, possibly a precursor of the famous fifteenth-century Yorkshire scribe Robert of that family name.[8] This colophon was clearly planned as part of the book and was intended to provide future readers with information about the circumstances of the book's production. Everything about this manuscript, from its layout and decoration to its colophon, is of a highly professional nature and indicates that well-developed facilities for the production of manuscripts existed in York by the third quarter of the thirteenth century and that this work seems to have been done by persons who were not monks, to judge from the makers' use of their names. John le Gras was a York canon who died shortly after 1279,[9] so this early in the history of the city we see quite an elaborate piece of bookmaking, which from the local names of the copyists, appears to have been an entirely northern endeavor, and written by secular, or at least nonmonastic, scribes in the city of York.

Needless to say, institutions the size of York Cathedral could not have relied on benefactions of the sort just discussed to ensure a steady and timely supply of service books, especially for choral use, and fortunately for the history of the northern book trade, records exist of how the cathedral officials arranged with teams of scribes, illuminators, and binders to make them. These persons participated in what Paul Christianson has aptly called "the institutional market for books and book services"[10] and what must have been only a part of the enormous demand for city services and tradesmen's labor in the cathedral cities.

The earliest surviving costing or contract from the cathedral for the making of books with which I am familiar dates from 26 August 1346 and is preserved in the Dean and Chapter Act Books. It shows in considerable detail how units from the cathedral hierarchy obtained books for liturgical use. The Act Book records an agreement between one Johannes Forbor, presumably a Minster priest, and a scribe, Robert Brekeling, concerning the writing and illuminating of a psalter. Apparently Brekeling both wrote and illuminated the text. Brekeling, called "scriptor," appeared before the Chapter and swore to provide to Forbor the book in question, a psalter with a kalendar, for the price of 5s. 6d. Joined to the psalter and in the same script was to be the Office for the Dead, with a hymnary and collectar, for an additional 4s. 3d. Thus Robert is to receive a total of 18s. 9d. for the work of copying and illuminating the book.

> Aug. 26, 1346. Comparuit Robertus Brekeling, scriptor, et jura-vit se observare condicionem factam inter ipsum et dominum Johan-nem Forbor, viz., quod idem Robertus scribet unum psalterium cum kalendario ad opus dicti domini Johannis pro 5s. et 6d.: et in eodem psalterio, de eadem litera, unum placebo et dirige cum ympnario et collectario pro 4s. 3d. Et idem Robertus luminabit omnes psalmos de grossis literis aureis positis in coloribus, et omnes grossas literas de ympnario et collectario luminabit de auro et vermilione præter grossas literas duplicium festorum, quæ erunt sicut grossæ litteræ aureæ sunt in psalterio. Et omnes literæ in principiis versuum erunt luminatæ de azuro et vermilione bonis, et omnes literæ in inceptione nocturnorum erunt grossæ literæ unciales (?) continentes v. lineas, set *beatus vir, et dixit Dominus*, continebunt vj vel vij lineas; et pro luminatione predicta dabit 5s. 6d., et ad colores, dabit pro auro 18d., et 2s. pro una cloca et furura.

[And the same Robert shall illuminate all the Psalms with large gold initials on colored grounds, and all the large initials of the hymnarius and collects he will illuminate with gold and vermillion except the initials for the double feasts, which will be done in the same style as the gold initials in the psalter. And all the versals will be illuminated with a good azure and vermillion, and all the letters at the beginning of the nocturnes will be large uncial initials of five lines except for *Beatus Vir* and *Dixit Dominus*, which open Matins and Vespers; they shall be of six or seven lines. For the aforesaid illumination Forbor ? shall give Robert five shillings, six pence and shall give Robert for gold and colors eighteen pence. Robert will also receive two shillings for a cloak and a fur robe.][11]

The last remuneration was not at all uncommon, as scribes and illuminators often received a garment in addition to their regular pay. Though nothing is said about the status of Robert Brekeling, from the absence of religious titles, we can presume he was a lay scribe. On 11 November of the same year, the Act Books record a payment, amount unspecified, to a Robert de Seleby of York, scribe. Unfortunately, in what capacity Seleby was employed by the Chapter is not mentioned, but presumably he had a relation to the officials somewhat like that of Brekeling.[12]

The teams involved in making books for the Chapter later in the century, however, seem to have included religious and secular artists. Again, the Dean and Chapter Act Books are rich sources of information. Between 1393 and 1402, two men were repeatedly employed to make service books. The records, moreover, show that the scribe often subcontracted parts of the bookmaking process and was an overseer of the entire operation.

In 1393, 41s. 8d.—a very considerable sum—was paid to "frater William de Ellerker" for the writing of two graduals for the choir and 40s. to Richard de Sterton or Stretton (the name is spelled both ways in the documents) for illuminating them. In addition, Ellerker was paid 22s. 7½d. for the purchase of parchment and 4d. for a hide for flyleaves.[13]

In 1394, William de Ellerker received a very large sum indeed from the Chapter: £11 13s. 3d. for writing and for the parchment for three books for the choir.[14]

The records for 1395 show a number of payments to artisans, presumably located by Ellerker, and indicate something of the team or atelier nature of the operation. A Robert Bookbynder was paid 10s. according to a prior agreement for sewing the gatherings of a large gradual for the choir and 20d. for three sheets of parchment for flyleaves. He also received 3s. 2d. for a deer hide for the binding. William de Ellerker also worked for the Chapter, receiving 4s. for parchment. Richard de Sterton illuminated three graduals for 40s. Two more names appear in this year: a William Selar, called "aurifaber," was paid 38s. 5d. by the Chapter to provide gold initials, and 3s. 4d. were paid to a John Brignale for seven sheets of parchment for the large gradual.[15] Selar, a prominent citizen of York, was a goldsmith, though he does not appear in the York Freemen's Register. He died 18 January 1401, and his will was proved on 28 June 1402.[16]

In 1396, Bookbynder earned 3s. for sewing a "white" psalter for the choir (so described, presumably, by its cover), and Ellerker was paid 40s. for copying two more graduals.[17]

1399 was a year in which a large and expensive gradual was made for the choir; it involved the same team of binder, scribe, and illuminator. The tying of the quires by Bookbynder cost 10s., three hides of veal for the flyleaves 2s., and the hide of a large deer to bind it 4s. To Ellerker "ex curialitate" a gratuity of 13s. 4d. was paid for writing the gradual. That this book took quite some time to make is clear from the existence of a separate debit to Sterton for illuminating one new large gradual. In 1402 a further 20s. was paid him for illuminating a large gradual, but whether it was for additional work on the one we have been discussing is not clear.[18]

While nothing more is known about the quire sewer, Sterton and the John Brignale who supplied parchment in 1395 are not so anonymous. If the illuminator's name was Stretton and not Sterton, he may be of the village of Stretton Magna in Leicestershire, from whence the illiterate Robert de Stretton, 1358–1385, bishop of Coventry and Lichfield, came.[19] John Brignale must have been a member of the same family of Brignales who were York stationers. That the craft of "stationer" was already well developed in York by John's day is evident from a reference to a Walter de Briggenhale, stationer in York during 1318–1319.[20] Oddly, however, the first reference to a stationer in the York Freemen's Register occurs in 1448, though as we saw in the example of Thomas Gryssop, the stationer, in the last chapter, at least one full-fledged stationer was active earlier.

The William de Ellerker, friar, who worked for the Chapter for so many years is such a fascinating figure that one wishes that more information was available about him. That a friar should be engaged in writing manuscripts for money is unusual, but there is a considerable amount of evidence for religious but nonmonastic involvement in various aspects of the book trade in and around York. For example, as late as 1494, a Richard Flynt, called "capellanus and tyxtwritter," was admitted to the freedom of the city as one who "desireth to be maid free of the tyxtwritters crafft and occupaccion so that he may from now furth at his libertie writte, make, bynd, note and florysche bokez and theym sell and put to sale."[21] A more specific reference to "priests" occurs in an ordinance of the guild of textwriters, luminers, noters, turners, and flourishers in 1476 stipulating that priests with benefices worth more than seven marks a year could not practice any of the crafts controlled by that guild but that a priest earning less than that could.[22] That this was still a current and irritating issue later in the century is clear from the record of an arbitration of 1487 between the scriveners and textwriters' guild and a priest, William Incecliff, about the writing and selling of books.[23]

Rather less evidence exists about mendicant scribes, but we have already noted the activities of John Lacy, Dominican. Other friars known to have worked as copyists besides Ellerker and Robert de Popultoun are Richard de Thorpe and Thomas de Cliffton, Austins of York.[24] All of these men were active at the end of the fourteenth century, though Ellerker's dates give him primacy of place here.

Ellerkers were common in the East Riding, with many persons of that name engaged in various trades, mainly cloth work,[25] but there does not seem to have been another scribe named Ellerker beside William in late fourteenth-century Yorkshire. The name originally meant "alder-marsh," and there is a village of Ellerker about seven miles southwest of Beverley, almost on the Humber. It is now in the parish of Brantingham at the apex of a triangle formed by Brough and Broomfleet.[26]

There was also an armigerous family named Ellerker; this is the more likely line for our William. The history of this family, unfortunately, is a bit unclear before the early fifteenth century, and the confusion is not helped by the family's preference for a very few Christian names. Johns had sons named William, and some Williams had sons named John. As early as 1101 a John Ellerker, son of William, built Ellerker Chapel, and Yorkshire Fines show propertied Ellerkers from a very early period, referring to Ellerkers in Brantingham parish in 1202 and to a Simon, son of a Nicholas Ellerker.[27] A writ in favor of Nicholas de Ellerker, dated York, 1298, establishes his legal existence.[28] In 1313, John and Nicholas Ellerker—the latter presumably the father of Simon—had letters patent.[29] In 1335 and 1341, a John Ellerker was spoken of in dispatches as on the king's business in Ireland.[30] This John belongs to a long and confusing line of Johns involved in royal administration, one of whom was probably the father of William de Ellerker, scribe.

J. L. Grassi has noted how a great many Yorkshiremen who were clerks in the royal administrations from Edward I through Richard II came from Howdenshire, an area on the north bank of the Humber betwen Hull and Seleby.[31] And most of them took their names from the places from which they came, such as Ellerker. A John Ellerker the elder was Keeper of Rolls and Hanaper from 1318 to 1324.[32] It appears that there were two Ellerker brothers from Howdenshire of the same name; John the elder was a Wardrobe and

Chancery clerk who was active from 1303 to 1346; and John the younger an Exchequer clerk from 1314 to 1351. Any of these John Ellerkers could have been the clerk involved in the abduction of Geoffrey Luttrell's daughter Elizabeth from the household of Walter Gloucester, a fascinating and little known story.[33] Thus the Ellerker family had a very long history of royal service and, most particularly, a service that involved writing. Undoubtedly it was this service which resulted in the line's ennoblement in the fifteenth century.

Harvey's Yorkshire Visitation of 1552 gives a pedigree for the family showing that its arms contained elements of the Risby and Delamore houses. The earliest Ellerker mentioned in this pedigree is a John, called the Judge.[34] At this period, the Ellerker seat was at Risby, a now deserted village three miles south of Beverley. This "Judge" John Ellerker had among other sons, one called William. It appears that Ellerkers already ennobled and coming from the village of that name married into the Risby family. A monument in Rowley church records a marriage between a John Ellerker "of Ellerker" and a Risby daughter in 1401, and this John Ellerker is now of Risby by 1411.[35]

He may have been the father of the John Ellerker of Rowley, whose will was proved in York in 1438. The testator appears to have been a lawyer, and his executors were wealthy and powerful citizens of York. In this will the chapel of Ellerker—dependent on Brantingham—is mentioned in a bequest. This John, calling himself "Johannes Ellerker senior," also had a son called William.[36]

The archives of beneficed clergy for the Harthill wapentake, now at the University of Hull, show several Ellerkers living just to the east of the village of that name. In 1317 a John Ellerker was presented to a benefice at Full Sutton; he may be the John referred to above as holding letters patent. A John Ellerker at Welton in 1332 was appointed overseer of the salmon fishing in the Humber and other Yorkshire rivers. He may have been the Ellerker in the service of the king. Yet another John appears to have been a cleric; he served as proctor in 1429 for the institution of John de Daleton, a canon of Lincoln, and rector of Cottingham.[37] Obviously this John must be a different person than the John who was a prebendary of Botevant between 1332 and 1339 and archdeacon of Cleveland between 1348 and 1351.[38]

To come now to our Ellerker the scribe, the only record of a William de Ellerker, mendicant, known to me, besides the costings itemized earlier, occurs in the register of Archbishop William Zouche for the year 1348. On 15 September, "apud Burton juxta Beverlacu anno 48 Willielmo de Ellerker et Willielmo Jordan ordinis predicatorum" were licensed to hear confessions in the York diocese for one year.[39] Burton is probably Bishop Burton, which is in the Harthill wapentake containing Risby and Ellerker. William Jordan was quite a famous man in later life; he would have been considerably older than Ellerker, and the younger man's appearance with him suggests that Ellerker must have been highly regarded in his order.

Admittedly, it is possible that the William Jordan of the 1348 entry is not the same man who appears for licensing in 1351 and again in 1354, but the chances are great that he is. A good deal is known about William Jordan. Originally of the Oxford convent, he was domiciled in the York convent in 1351 and 1355.[40] By 1350 he was vicar-general of the English Province[41] and by 1351 a doctor of theology.[42] He quarreled with Uthred de Boldon on mendicant poverty in 1366 and 1368[43] and disputed with John Mardisley, Franciscan, at the York Chapter in 1355.[44] He defended the mendicants before the pope at Avignon against Richard FitzRalph's attacks in 1358. Bale believed Jordan to have also written anti-Wycliffite tracts.[45] Jordan may be the friar satirized by Langland in *Piers Plowman*.

If Langland's C-text does indeed satirize Jordan, the Dominican may not have seen it, for he apparently left England in 1378. The passage in question occurs in Passus XV of the C-text and offers a magnificent description of a gluttonous choplogic friar who eats everyone else's food in the house of Conscience. The speaker wishes that the food were hot lead in the friar's mouth. Making a pun on Jordan's name and the Middle English word for chamber pot, he says that to learn what true pennance is "Y schal iangle to þis Iurdan, with his iuyste wombe."[46] So too, a scriptural text used by Uthred in his dispute with Jordan is quoted in the same passus.

If the William de Ellerker mentioned in 1348 were the same as the friar William of the costings 1395–1402, he would by medieval standards have been an elderly man while working for the Chapter at York. Yet he is the only William de Ellerker who seems to have been a scribe.

Independent testimony to his existence as a copyist in what must have been his last years comes from the colophon of a handsome manuscript of Seneca's *Declamationes* with a commentary by Nicholas Trivet, which is now London, British Library MS Royal 15.C.xii. The date and style of script are certainly consonant with the facts of Ellerker's connection with the Chapter at York. Other than the Lumley inscription on the first page,[47] a reason, though not a compelling one, to place it at some period in the north, there are no marks of provenance. There is, however, an erasure after the colophon. At one time this was interpreted to read "Liber fratrum canonicorum Sancti Augustini . . ." and the manuscript was believed to have come from Bridlington Priory in Yorkshire, an attribution rejected by Neil Ker.[48]

Unfortunately, the colophon's formulaic character does not help to delimit the scribe's specific milieu. Whatever the exact meaning of the words scraped out, the colophon above them is clear enough. It reads "et sic terminatur liber decimus declamacionum Senece ad honorem domini nostri Jesu Xristi Amen. Sum scriptor talis / monstrat mea littera qualis / quod Ellerker." As the Benedictines of Bouveret (in their collection of scribal colophons) offer numerous examples of this distich, either forming part of a larger colophon or standing alone,[49] about all the colophon tells us, then, is that Ellerker was familiar with a tag common among professional scribes.

British Library MS Royal 15.C.xii, though not a luxurious codex, shows evidence of careful design and considerable interest in decoration. It is laid out on the model of Bolognese law codices,[50] with a small block of Seneca's text surrounded by a frame of commentary by Trivet. The colophon is made ornate in a way that we shall see is common among northern manuscripts, where the resources of scribes or flourishers are preferred to paints and gold work. Set off by a paraph and red and blue capitals, the colophon in red calls attention to itself, while the minute infill work of the crossbar of the *n* in *Amen* is distinctive. The first three letters are flashed blue. Another paraph and a capital with red infill introduces the scribe's motto, while the actual name *Ellerker* is in red with blue paraph and underlining. A diminuendo of flourishes from paraph to section mark in red puts out handsome leaf and squiggle work as does the blue paraph to the side of the scribe's name.

So too, the use of simple dots as infills throughout the manuscript may be Ellerker's work, for we see it in the *S* of the colophon, and such dots form part of the work's decoration as a whole. Each book of the text is set off with a *littera partita* initial. Folio 2, for example, has a five-line initial with three-quarter chain-link border. On this page is an *S* with a three-dot infill, just as in the colophon; a similar letter decorates folio 51.

Though Ellerker is the scribe of York about whom the most varied information exists, a fellow mendicant and somewhat younger contemporary, a Carmelite named Robert de Popultoun (for so he seems to spell it), is equally important to our understanding of the compilation and manufacture of northern manuscript books. Popultoun was the compiler, overseer, partly the scribe, and possibly the decorator of Paris, Bibliothèque Nationale MS lat. 4126, usually called *Chronica et miscellanea super historiam Anglice,* though this title does not adequately describe the contents of the work.[51] Like certain other northern books, as we will see, the *Chronica* was a "recyled" manuscript, which Robert made by joining an old and a new book, and adding marginal glosses, summaries, and cross-references as well as contemporary mendicant controversial texts, in an effort to provide his house with an up-to-date work of English and mendicant history. The codex reflects a fascination with early English and Scottish history characteristic of the military situation of the fourteenth century —and, of course, Hulne's own geographical proximity to the border —as well as Carmelite preoccupations with some of the major texts of pro- and antimendicantism.[52]

Though during his later career Popultoun was the prior of Hulne Abbey on the northern outskirts of Alnwick in Northumberland in the diocese of Durham, he seems—like John de Foxton after him— to have used the resources of the York Augustinian friars' library in the compilation of his book,[53] as the codex says at one point, "ora pro Popultoun qui me compilavit Eboraci" (folio 211v). It certainly does not seem to have been compiled using the resources of the Hulne library, which, though extensive, lacked the historical material in which Popultoun was interested. The convent's collection seems not to have supplied any material in the Paris manuscript, but twelve of the items used in the compilation also appear in the catalogue of the Augustinian convent library at York. Moreover, though Popultoun gave a number of books in his personal library to his convent, these were not his historical works. He seems to have retained at least one of these, which he also used for MS lat. 4126. This volume, Henry of Huntingdon, *Historia Anglorum,* may have been commissioned by the owner. It is a well-written codex of mid-fourteenth-century date, now Trinity College, Cambridge MS R. 5.42, bearing the *ex libris* "Liber fratris Roberti de Popultoun precij 20s" on the first folio in what I take to be the prior's secretary's script.[54]

Popultoun's compilation may be dated after 1357, but probably before 1375, on the basis of internal evidence. At the opening of the manuscript is copied a papal bull, issued in 1357 in support of the mendicant orders, whose presence helps to establish a *terminus ante quem.* The actual "editor" or creator of the latest text used by Popultoun, the *Oraculum Cyrilli,* appears to have been Philippe Ribot (d. 1391), who is believed to have written it in 1370.[55]

Little is known of the friar personally. Popultoun was ordained acolyte at the church of the Carmelites in York on 18 December 1344, subdeacon in Thirsk in 1345, deacon in Ripon and priest at the Carmelite church at York some months later. He was probably born in 1326, as the customary age for ordination to subdeacon was nineteen. In 1351/52 he was licensed to hear confessions and described as of the York convent.[56] Thus he must have been only a few years younger than Ellerker, and the two men could well have known each other in York. When and where he died is unknown, but he must have lived at least until 1368. It is possible that he may have died somewhat after this date during the course of the compilation, as about half-way through the volume appears the comment written by one of his amanuenses, "anima fratris Roberti de Popultoun illa quiete perfruatur, amen, amen" (folio 155v).

Popultoun appears again in documents in 1366 and 1368, now as the prior of the Carmelite house at Hulne. The cartulary of this house still exists in London (British Library MS Harley 3897). It contains, as well as a variety of confirmatory charters, two library catalogues, which from the number and types of books, suggest that the convent had an excellent library of almost one hundred volumes. At some point in the history of MS lat. 4126, an owner or librarian recognized that Robert de Popultoun the compiler was also the prior of Hulne, as there is a cross-reference number to the Harley manuscript of the Hulne cartulary. In one catalogue of the house, dated 1366, with Popultoun then prior, eight books are described as his gifts, two of which—relatively expensive ones—were in the care of Henry Percy, earl of Northumberland and patron of Hulne, during his lifetime:

> Item unam Bibliam ex dono fratris Roberti de Populton in rubeis asseribus, precii trium marcarum cum dimedio, quem habet dominus de Percy ad terminum vite.
> Item sermones Hugonis de Sancto Victore qui incipiunt *Abiciamus* in rubeis asseribus. Roberti Populton.
> Item Summa de Virtutibus in asseribus. Roberti Populton.
> Item Bartholomeus *de proprietatibus rerum*. Roberti Populton.
> Item scriptum sermonum incipiencium *Osculatur me osculo oris sui* in nigris asseribus. Roberti Populton.
> Item vita sancti Cuthberti secundum Bedam. Ro. Populton.
> Item vita Silvestri cum aliis quindecim precii vigenti solidorum quem habet dominus de Percy ad terminum vite. Rob. Populton.
> Item Remigius super Donatum cum aliis opusculis in rubeis asseribus. Populton.[57]

These gifts amount to a substantial sum and suggest that the donor was well-to-do or came from a wealthy family.

Robert's Percy connection seems to have been beneficial to Hulne as well, for in a confirmatory charter also copied in Harley 3897 we learn that in or before 1368 the prior obtained from Percy £105 12s. 4d. for lead to roof the convent's church.[58]

Hulne is a little-known foundation.[59] Believed to be the earliest English Carmelite convent, it was also one whose buildings survived the dispossession of the religious houses almost intact. The convent was on the main road from Alnwick to Eglingham and was surrounded by a strong curtain wall. A defensive tower built by the Percy family stood adjacent. An excellent drawing of the ground plan and a minute description of the convent are given by W. H. St. John Hope.[60] Never very large, Hulne contained twenty-eight friars in 1301; there are no Suppression records.[61]

Like Ellerker, Robert seems to have been part of a large Yorkshire clerical affinity. Poppleton, which had several contemporary spellings, consists of two very small villages, both within the jurisdiction of the city of York. Nether Poppleton is four miles northwest of York and in 1831 had a population of 254. Its church of All Saints had a vicarage in the archdeaconry and diocese of York, and the patron was the archbishop of York. It was large enough to be considered a parish. Upper Poppleton, four and one-half miles northwest of York and on the south side of the Ouse, was a chapelry in the parish of St. Mary Bishops-Hill. In 1831 its population was 346. It apparently had no church and its curacy was controlled by the Dean and Chapter of York.[62]

Again as in the case of Ellerker, there was a branch of the family who were guildsmen; they appear in the registers chiefly as bow makers or weavers.[63] A larger branch, however, was in orders or held ecclesiastical positions. The Chronicle of St. Mary's abbey, York, refers to a John de Popilton at the installation and election of its abbot, Simon, in 1258, and this John was prior of the abbey's cell of St. Martin near Richmond in the same year.[64] So too, a Clement de Popilton was prior of the cell of Rumburg in 1323. In 1329 a William de Popilton was Master of the Hospital of St. Mary Magdalene, Ripon.[65] A Thomas seems to have been Master and Warden of St. Nicholas's Hospital in 1389 and canon of the Chapel of St. Mary and the Holy Angels, York, in 1397, and there was as well a York Dominican of this name.[66]

Though no Popiltons appear to have gone to Cambridge, several were educated at Oxford, at least one of whom returned to Yorkshire. An Adam was a Fellow of Balliol College, Oxford, Bachelor of Theology, and later canon of Newarke College, Leicester. He died in 1403 and gave a manuscript to his college. A John de Popilton was a student at Oxford in 1380, obtained a benefice in Hampshire, exchanged to Leicester, and then became rector of Patrick Brompton in Yorkshire in 1390 and eventually canon of the Chapel of St. Mary and the Holy Angels, dying in 1406. This John was also an executor for two members of the Ravenser family, one the archdeacon of Lincoln and the other a canon of Lincoln.[67]

What is clear from this roll call is that there were a number of fairly important Popiltons located in and around York. An interesting Northumberland connection, however, is that of a Richard de Popilton, chaplain, who was buried in York Minster in 1410 near the tomb of Henry Percy, presumably because he had some ties with that house. As we have seen, Hulne had the Percy family for a patron in the fourteenth century; thus the placement of Richard's burial spot is suggestive of a Northumberland branch of the Popilton family.[68]

Though Paris MS lat. 4126 has been described by the various scholars and editors mentioned above[69] because of the many important texts on early Scottish history it contains, most treatments deal only with this material. Moreover, as Pinkerton's virtually complete description is neither easily accessible nor entirely accurate, and because the manuscript's plan or structure is evident only when one is aware of the progression of the items, it seems worthwhile once again to devote some time to Popultoun's contributions as scribe and overseer and to an account of the book's contents.

As his name appears at the end of each of the sections that he supplied, though not necessarily in his own hand, it may be useful to present these "colophons" in tabular form and draw some inferences from them:

Folio 11 Ora pro Populton
Folio 13v Ora pro Popultoun, qui me fecit scribi
Folio 134v parce domine anime fratris Roberti de Popultoun, qui me compilavit
Folio 155 Ora pro Popultoun
Folio 155v anima fratris Roberti de Popultoun illa quiete perfruatur, amen, amen.
Folio 211v Ora pro Popiltoun qui me compilavit Eboraci
Folio 213v Ora pro fratre Roberto de Populton
Folio 252 Ora pro fratre Roberto de Populton
Folio 295 per Popultoun rescriptum

These signatures are interesting because they indicate the team nature of the volume and the idea that it is a compilation and not a work created by Popultoun himself. This notion is supported by the variety and frequent changes of hands occurring in the volume. The term "compilator" and its relatives is a heavily freighted one in the Middle Ages.[70] Typically, "qui me fecit scribi" means that the person paid another scribe to do the work, and we do see several fourteenth-century hands other than Popultoun's in the earlier part of the book, though these often sign his name at the ends of entries, as if to flatter the overseer of the project.

Popultoun's own script seems most likely to be that in which the manuscript up to the colophon at folio 13v was copied, and the phrase "qui me fecit scribi" must refer more generally to the "creation" of the book. This hand always spells the name Popultoun, which I take to be Robert's preferred spelling. It is a distinctive script, with a very prominent angled stroke to dot *i*'s and a 2-shaped *r* with a very pronounced tag. The same hand may also have made the two-line uncial initials that appear on these folios. As it is this script in which occur extensive annotations later in the Paris manuscript that show a detailed familiarity with the various historical works used in the compilation, it seems likely that it is Popultoun's own. The "Popultoun" hand stops at folio 32. At this point another scribe continues from folio 33 through the left column of folio 133v. The initials are of a different type as well, with penwork flourishing. "Popultoun" reappears at folio 211v, writing the *explicit* for the extract from Geoffrey of Monmouth, signing his name, and providing the information that he compiled the book at York. He continues to write to folio 213, but the signature for the material apparently of Robert's own composition is written by a different hand. Robert continues writing to mid-sentence on folio 246, where another scribe in a Secretary hand takes over to the end of folio 282. From there to the end of the Paris manuscript, the Joachistic extracts that conclude the work are written on two scales by yet a different hand. The penultimate text, *Prophetia Cyrilli Eremitae de monte Carmelo interprete fratre Gilberto Anglico,* was copied from an exemplar bearing the scribal colophon "I brother Peter Maymet, of the order of the Blessed Virgin of Carmel, being a student at Paris wrote this book with my own hand, copying it from a certain exceedingly old exemplar with dipthongs, at the beginning of which were curiously and marvellously depicted Cyrill in holy and priestly vestments and brother Eusebius with a barred mantle and an angel" (folio 295). Peter, a fellow Carmelite, was Bachelor of Theology in 1339 and Master of Theology when he died in 1348.[71] Presumably, this colophon was copied verbatim by one of Robert's amanuenses to honor an older Carmelite, as the comment at the bottom of the excerpt "per Popultoun r[escriptum]" is not in what I take to be Popultoun's own hand. It is difficult to know just how to interpret the rubric for the colophon "transcripta et compilavit." As this phrase does not preface the Maymet colophons in the two Cambridge manuscripts of the *Oraculum,* it probably refers to Robert de Popultoun's preliminary editorial work.

At least one of the scripts in MS Paris lat. 4126 can be associated with the prior's secretary, rubricator, and amanuensis. This writer, who has a rather uncontrolled and florid script with distinctive forms of the letters *p* and *d* is the person who signed Popultoun's name in Trinity College, Cambridge MS R.5.42. He does not seem to have served as a scribe in Popultoun's compilation—perhaps because he was not a very professional writer. He did, however, do two pieces of the *incipit* and *explicit* rubrication, where he signed Populton's name. This suggests that Popultoun must have had the book partially copied by Carmelites when he was prior of Hulne. The rubricator has a *p* with a very spiky Insular style of descender that curves forward at the tip and a *d* whose stem, instead of angling leftward, goes leftward slightly and then sharply curves back on itself to the right, making a stem like that on a piece of fruit. This scribe's hand first appears at folio 11, ending an *explicit* with a request to pray for Popultoun. It appears again in a lengthy and interesting *explicit* at folio 252:

> explicit hystoria magistri Alfridi thesaurarii Beverlacensis incipiens ad britonum et finiens in Henricum 4um annorum duorum milium ducentorum. Sequitur continuacio hystorie secundum chronica Radulphi monacho Cestrensis in suo policronicon usque ad Edwardi regis tercia. Ora pro fratre Roberto de Populton.

MS lat. 4126 has been several times foliated and paginated. As the codex once formed part of the Colbert collection before it came to the Bibliothèque Nationale and was at an earlier time in the library of William Cecil, baron Burleigh (d. 1598), who wrote his own *ex libris* at the bottom of folio 3, it is possible that the foliation was done by these owners. Popultoun himself appears to have done the pagination, some of which has been trimmed in the course of binding and rebinding. This pagination forms part of a reference system that the compiler developed to make the book easily searchable.

The pagination was done by the same person who wrote many of the annotations and historical notations in the codex—a person I take to be Popultoun himself. He was somewhat erratic and on occasion inaccurate in paginating the manuscript.

This paginator extensively annotated the margins in the later portion of the volume, using chiefly red ink. He added red headers from folio 97v onwards, as well as column references, and from folios 154v to 167r he put various dates at the tops of pages to synchronize events in sacred and secular history. The impression created by these additions is that MS lat. 4126 was to be used by other Carmelites in the Hulne library as a reference book. This impression is strengthened by a cross-referencing notation in Popultoun's red ink at folio 108, the Troy material of Dares Frigius, to "columpna 199 in libro meo." He seems also to have done some of the rubrics and ornamentation of MS lat. 4126, especially at folios 133v, 159v, and 172. For example, on the first of these folios, he has drawn and flourished eight-line blue with red hatched oakleaf infill major initials and flourished many initials violet, blue, and red.

Not only was Robert a scribe, but he served as a judicious editor as well. He sought to examine the work of Alfred of Beverly, the *Annales,* who more or less condensed Geoffrey of Monmouth's *Historia,* but went to original sources for early English history like Orosius and Eutropius. At folio 212, Robert offers what he calls a "brevis recapitulatio totius precedentie opusculi," that is, a summary of Geoffrey's *Historia* in his own words. There are additions and inserted material from Paul the Deacon, Bede, and Henry of Huntingdon. Thus he attempted to test Geoffrey's narrative against the original sources cited by Alfred of Beverley. The Paris manuscript is, then, an early example of textual criticism.

The codex shows evidence of original careful planning and the control of an overseer. It opens with a world map (not known, I believe, to most students of geography), containing the three major divisions of the world, Africa, Asia and India made by Noah among his three sons, Shem, Ham and Japhet after the flood.[72] The map's rubrics mix Latin and English, with the words for the cardinal points being given in the vernacular. This map, with its concern for division, prepares for later textual discussions of the three parts of the world. After the map comes a table of contents, giving titles and numbers of the folios on which items may be found in the book. There are twenty-six headings with five more scraped out, though the works themselves do appear. Whoever wrote the table of contents did not seem to have been the compiler, as it gives much vaguer names for works than do the very precise *incipits* of the individual sections and does not take into account all of the items. For example, the table says that item nine is the "cosmographia de quaedam grammatici," while the incipit makes clear that this *"grammaticus"* is Priscian, whose name occurs repeatedly in the section.

The overall movement of the contents of Paris MS lat. 4126 is from the universe, the divisions of the globe, and the wonders, prodigies, and marvels to be found there;[73] to a narrowing focus on world history, with Pseudo-Methodius's "Liber de initio et fine seculi"; and then to matters English, Irish, and Welsh, such as British and Scottish regnal histories. The manuscript has an apocalyptic ending, with a vision of Cyrill of Mount Carmel and some related pseudo-Joachistic texts, which among other things make extravagant claims for the mendicant orders in a new age to come.

The text proper, folios 1r–10r, opens with a collection of four papal bulls supporting all of the mendicant orders, not just the Carmelites, though two of these bulls are standard parts of Franciscan and Carmelite *bullaria* collections. The heading for this section is "decretalis contra fratres, procurata per Magistrum Ricardum Fitz Rauf, archiepiscopus Armachanum," but this is a little misleading because the bulls are actually in support of mendicancy. The first of these is Innocent VI's "Dilectis Filiis," of 1357, addressed to the abbot of Westminster and to the prior of St. Bartholomew's, Smithfield, which deals directly with FitzRalph's attack on the friars; it calls on both parties to desist in the controversy and cites several bulls that earlier had supported the friars, namely, the "Inter cunctas" of Benedict XI in 1306 on mendicant privileges, the "Super cathedram" of Boniface VIII in 1300 on the same subject, and the "Vas electionis" of John XXII against John de Poliaco in 1321. These bulls are then transcribed in full or in part through folio 10r.[74] Items one to three form a group, with "Super cathedram" breaking off abruptly, while "Vas electionis" is really item seven.

That these texts preface a miscellany concluding with a pseudo-Joachistic prophecy in which the mendicants play an important role in the Last Things can be no accident. Not only does Popultoun make these bulls conveniently available for fellow Carmelites, but by situating them as he does, he makes the orders seem part of a universal and especially English history; the work then opens with a struggle between mendicants and seculars and concludes with mendicants figuratively victorious.

Placed before the last bull, that of John XXII, at folio 9v, are some prophecies on the Welsh and the Scots,[75] manifesting a very strong dislike of the English. As is common in such collections, these verses contain material about symbolic dragons, a leopard, and lilies.[76] The next item is a brief prayer, "Te adoro creatorem," at folio 10v,[77] which may signify the compiler's wish for divine guidance.

The book now moves on to marvels and prodigies of a specifically Insular sort. Item eight, folio 11v, is a tract, "De quodam prodigio," by Stephen, a physician of York ca. 1154–1167, during the primacy of Hugh du Puiset, bishop of Durham.[78] Item nine, folio 12r, is the prologue to a verse account of various prodigies and signs in Ireland compiled by Bishop Patrick, while folios 12v–13v[79] are a portion of the text of this work entitled "de rebus Hibernie admirandis," ending at line 109 of the modern edition. Item ten, folio 14r, is the *Cosmographia* of Priscian, a Latin poem on the known world.[80] Item eleven, beginning at mid-page on folio 19r, is the supposed *Itinerarium Maritimum* of Antonius Augustus, which occurs, for example, at the bottom of the Hereford Cathedral *mappa mundi*.[81] Item twelve, folio 20r, is a short poem on the three parts of the world and the placement of mountains and rivers on the globe. Item thirteen, folio 21v, treats the measurement of the whole earth; it is probably connected with Orosius, as item fourteen, beginning mid way on folio 22v, consists of his discussion of the three parts of the earth.[82]

At folio 26v the compiler moves to Scottish geography and history. Item fifteen is the twelfth-century "De situ Albanie, que in se figuram hominis habet." The land is man-shaped because "pars namque principalis eius id est capud est in Arregarchel . . . pedes autem eius sunt supra mare Northwagie . . . corpus vero ipsius est mons qui Monid uocatur . . . brachia autem eius sunt ipsi montes qui dividunt Scociam ab Arregarchel" (folio 26v) and so on. Such an idea of the shape of Scotland derives from the fact that in some accounts the region took its name from a legendary Albanactus, who was imagined to give the land its outline.[83] Items sixteen and seventeen, extending from the middle of folio 27r to folio 29v, treat the origins of the Picts and Scots, adapted from Isidore of Seville's *Etymologiae;* in the middle of the tract, the line "sicut mihi verus relator retulit, Andreas videlicet, et venerabilis Katanensis Episcopus, natione Scotus et Dumfermelis monachus" indicates Andrew, bishop of Caithness, 1150–1185. This section to the middle of folio 31r also treats Scottish kings.[84]

Item eighteen, at folio 31r, is a narrative showing how Andrew became the patron saint of Scotland.[85] All of these gatherings form a pamphlet that at folios 32v-33, ruled but not written on, is sewn to a handsomely ornamented codex of the late thirteenth century. This contains item nineteen, at folio 33r, excerpts from the *Disciplina Clericalis* of Petrus Alphonsus,[86] and item twenty, Pseudo-Methodius's history of the world, beginning at folio 45r and ending at folio 48, whose verso is also ruled but uncompleted.[87] Next is Giraldus Cambrensis's *De Mirabilibus Hiberniae*, making up item twenty-one; it continues to folio 96v. Forming part of the Giraldus volume, in the same hand and with *littera partita* initials by the same artist, is item twenty-two, the letter of Alexander to Aristotle on the Wonders of India, which continues from folio 97r to folio 106,[88] where the Alexander text breaks off, and at this point the Giraldus letter of Alexander is sewn to the rest of the Paris manuscript. A scribe of the Popultoun compilation continues the letter of Alexander, following it with some additional Troy material.

Possibly the actual core of the compilation was a handsome but defective Peter-Giraldus-Alexander written in double columns of 36 lines. As the earlier and later portions of MS lat. 4126 are similarly ruled, though on a noticeably better grade of parchment, it is probable that these preceding and following folios were laid out to match the older materials, to which they were later sewn.

The three Troy books form a discrete group. Item twenty-three, folio 106v, is a verse recapitulation of Dictys Cretensis's *De Excidio Troiae*, and item twenty-four, folio 108r, is a précis of the *Historia Troianum* of Dares Frigius, which goes to folio 111. The twenty-fifth piece is a poetic version of Dares by Joseph Iscanus of Exeter, occupying folios 111v to 120v, mid-page.[89] Item twenty-six consists of extracts on British history drawn from Higden's *Polychronicon*;[90] it extends to folio 133r, at which point appears yet another poem on the dispersion of Troy, item twenty-seven, which goes to folio 133v.

At the second column of this page appears item twenty-eight, extracts from Isidore's *Etymologiae*, books 1, 5, and 6, written by Popultoun himself, entitled "De primis auctoribus sive scriptoribus historiarum."[91] The material is introduced with an eight-line pen-boxed initial like nothing else so far in the volume; it was probably drawn by Robert, who carries this historical material through a brief recapitulation of the six ages of the world to the middle of folio 134v.

Item twenty-nine, beginning at this folio, is a lengthy excerpt of the *Historia Britonum* of Geoffrey of Monmouth; it extends to folio 212v.[92] Midway on this folio is the thirtieth item, a treatment of Saxon kings excerpted from the twelfth-century *Historia Anglorum* of Henry of Huntingdon and the *Annales* of Alfred of Beverley.[93] At folios 242r–252 appears Alfred's *Annales*, extending to the reign of Henry IV. Item thirty-one is a continuation of Higden's *Polychronicon* to the coronation of Edward III, which ends at folio 281v. This folio marks the end of the English material. Probably the tie between the Troy matter and early British history is through the popular idea—found, for example, in the Geoffrey of Monmouth excerpt—that there is an etymological connection between the Trojan Brutus and Britain because he was the founder of the nation.

At the bottoms of various leaves in this section of the work, in a different hand and ink, are hexameter verses copied from the *Chronica* of John Beverus, or John of London, a monk of Westminster, apparently written on the bottom margins sometime after Popultoun's compilation. These classicizing verses are often used as glosses on persons from English history—Mordred and the like—who are referred to in the text.[94]

The last part of the codex is occupied by more timeless or apocalyptic matter: a series of prophecies, designed in large measure to magnify the Carmelite order. Item thirty-two at folio 282 is the *Oraculum Cyrilli*, and item thirty-three at folio 295v, in a different script, is the letter of Saint Hildegarde on the Future Tribulations of the Clergy. This work is a collection of prophetic passages from Hildegarde's writings extracted by the Monk Gebenon.[95]

The volume's penultimate text, the *Oraculum Cyrilli*, then, looks back to the opening papal bulls on mendicancy. This rather complex work in four parts begins with a preface by a friar Gilbert of England telling how he discovered the prophecy in the monastery of Cluny, written in an illuminated manuscript in Beneventan script, and how it came to be revealed to Cyrill of Mount Carmel. The work then incorporates letters purporting to be from Cyrill to Joachim of Fiore, asking him to explain the prophecy, and a reply from Joachim to Cyrill. That Joachim had long been dead by the time this series of letters was composed had no effect on the work's great popularity. The prophecy itself is followed by a commentary allegedly by Joachim, but which may have some connections with Arnold of Villanova. The original form of the *Oraculum* adapted by Ribot was probably written about 1280–1290; the work exists in fourteen manuscripts, of which Paris MS lat. 4126 is one. As it was first edited by a Carmelite, it seems to have been of great interest to the order generally. For our purposes perhaps the most important element here is that "Cyrill" used his appeal to Joachim to adapt an already existing prophecy to the history of the Carmelite order and to employ the prophecy in support of the antiquity of that history in a way that was characteristic of Carmelite propaganda in later years.

A geographical shift from the area around York to Newcastle and Durham in the northeast brings us to some of the most fascinating book-making activity in the region. A very beautiful book, apparently made in Newcastle, was the work of John Lacy, a Dominican anchorite in a *reclusorium* attached to the Dominican house of Newcastle-upon-Tyne.[96] Originally of the convent at Newcastle-under-Lyme, Staffordshire, he was ordained subdeacon in 1397 and priest the following year, when he is described as of the Shrewsbury convent.[97] Exactly when he joined the Newcastle Dominicans is uncertain, but his dates as a documented anchorite attached to that house are 1407–1434. During this period as a Newcastle recluse, he seems to have performed spiritual duties outside his cell or perhaps through a window in it, as he was very highly regarded in Newcastle and was left at least two legacies. A will of Durham diocese made by Roger Thornton, mayor of Newcastle, selects Lacy to be a celebrant of a mass for a year and leaves him six marks in payment, probably in part for his services as a confessor.[98] Another legacy to Lacy, probably for similar services, was from Cecilia Homildon. This sort of gift was customary. One member of the Chaworth family left his confessor a considerable annuity for life.[99]

To come now to Lacy's book making activities in Newcastle, his name appears in a different tonality of red ink added to the red colophon of a "Wycliffite" English New Testament given to the church of St. John, Newcastle. That he actually wrote the book, (now Bodleian MS Rawlinson C.258),[100] however, is uncertain. He appears as well to have copied a version of Deguileville's *Pèlerinage de l'âme*, or *Le Pèlerinage de la vie humaine*, which were both on occasion called *Grace Dieu*. Lacy's book was described in the catalogue of Henry Savile of Banke, Yorkshire, as written in English, and there is some confusion as to exactly what work this was. It may possibly be London, British Library MS Additional 35213. The catalogue speaks of a *Gras Dieu, Le Romance de Rose* as made by him. The English prose version of Deguileville's *Pilgrimage of Human Life* mentions the *Romance of the Rose* and has an allegorical character named Grace Dieu; perhaps Lacy had copied both of Deguileville's works in a single volume.[101]

Between 1420 and 1434, Lacy also wrote and illuminated a Latin and English volume in 151 folios containing Thoresby's *Lay Folk's Catechism*, and texts of Rolle and Hilton, as well as tracts on the Ten Commandments, the Seven Deadly Sins, and confession. Though often called a *horae*, because it begins with illustrated suffrages, a kalendar, and the Hours of the Virgin, the book (now Oxford, St. John's College MS 94) is better described as a devotional miscellany, as it also contains prayers from Augustine, Bede, and Aquinas, parts of the psalter, Jerome's *Epistola ad Demetriadem*, and sayings of the Fathers. Lacy himself called it a "primarium."[102]

The kalendar has an odd mix of saints, such as Francis and Benedict but not Dominic, and the feasts are graded in gold, green, blue, red, and black. Only Oswald and Cuthbert's feasts tie it to the northeast, while feasts for Wenefrid, Chad, and David suggest Lacy's early history in Staffordshire and Shropshire. In the kalendar, the scribe has placed *obits* for John and Tylot Lacy, "uxor eius pater frater John Lacy anachorete."

The book itself is richly decorated, with a large number of illustrated suffrages, including some for saints like Zita, which we have seen in the Bolton *horae*. There are numerous one-half, three-quarter, and full-page borders, whose stylistic elements will be noted later; suffice it to say here the borders contain large amounts of green and the Interlace and Mask Medallion motifs characteristic of the northern style discussed in the next two chapters. In addition to these decorative features, Lacy also used a good deal of gold, expertly applied, in the creation of his manuscript. This is perhaps most noticeable in the fifteen-line prayer for the maker, which is done entirely in gold letters.

Lacy's book is a production of very high quality. Though there are some idiosyncrasies in its layout and mixture of languages, scales, colors of lettering, and the like, there is nothing amateurish about the script or the illumination. Indeed, the recluse writes an ornate and professional hand, and it is rare to find so many of the talents of individual book artisans joined in one person. He can, and often does, write on two scales. His display *textura* has numerous hairlines on the *et* abbreviation, on the tag of 2-shaped *r* and on terminal *s*, as well as forking or clubbing of heads and feet of ascenders, while his smaller script is plainer, and perhaps less sure and controlled.

Like the other mendicant scribes we have discussed in this chapter, Lacy is not at all reticent about introducing himself in his work. He inserts a cartouched motto, "Lacy scripsit et illuminit," at the lower border of folio 17, and we have remarked on his armorial bearing at the bottom of folio 101v just below the gold prayer. The book ends with a request to pray for the soul "of him þat maad þis book saaf Lacy or makith it saaf" (folio 151).

Durham was, next to York, the most important market and commercial town in the north. Though records are lacking, there must have been in Durham a substantial need for writing skills, as the town had, in addition to palace and monastery, seven churches or chapels, three hospitals, and perhaps as many as two thousand residents.[103] As Dobson points out, however, there would have been a much higher emphasis on literacy in Durham than in a town like York, with its larger merchant class, because we find as untypical property holders:

> a professional hierarchy of ecclesiastical administrators and officials who served either bishop or monastery or both. . . . A very large proportion of the inhabitants of Durham must always have been committed to staffing and serving the monastery, the castle and . . . the heterogeneous collection of palatine administrative offices (chancery, exchequer, courts of law) that lay between the two.[104]

This administrative community was most probably centered in Elvet, an episcopal borough containing not only the important manor of Elvet Hall but also many tenements leased to townsmen by the convent.[105]

Owing to the peculiar administrative structure of the palatinate of Durham,[106] there was a very substantial need for scribes and notaries not only for the palace and the monastery but for the various administrative offices as well. And there was an enormous amount of administrative business conducted in the monastery during the period of interest to us by priors John Hemingburgh (1391–1416) and John Wessington (1416–1446). Wessington, whose tenure was roughly parallel to that of Thomas Langley, the bishop of Durham, employed, in addition to a private chaplain for his letters and memoranda, professional scribes and notaries like the powerful and well-educated William Doncaster, John Berelhalgh, and William Bentlay.

Doncaster and Bentlay, in fact, may show us something of the scribal relationships between the notarial community and the monastic one. Doncaster, who died in 1439, was a lawyer for Durham priory and Durham College, Oxford. In addition to his many administrative duties, he seems to have been something of a book collector and scribe as well, for in the 1395 catalogue of the Durham Priory library appears this memorandum of 1411: "Magister W. de Doncaster contulit ad communem Librariam Monachorum Dunelmi unum Inventarium sive Tabulam tocius Juris Canonici scriptum manu sua propria, post mortem suam eisdem tradendum." Originally, the document also contained a list of the second folios of the books, which is unfortunately now missing. Two of the books, glosses on the Decretals, found their way into the collection, though they apparently did not survive the Reformation.[107]

Bentlay, who lived in Elvet and was active in the 1430s and 1440s, was most likely the scribe who wrote a portion of Durham Cathedral MS C.IV.21, a table or dictionary of canon and civil law that makes up folios 251v to 276 of the volume. The *explicit* reads "tabula super sextum . . . decretalium quod Bentlay," and the colophon and text show his highly professional and graceful hand, whose flourishes and cadel work link it with the sorts of notarial hands so characteristic of Durham books. That this table to a highly technical book should have been written by a notary suggests the interrelationship between conventional monastic or commercial workshop book making and what we might think of as the administrative scribal world in Durham. As Dobson notes,

> The demand for the services of public notaries among the larger English monasteries was always considerable, but especially so at early fifteenth-century Durham. . . . The chapter sometimes used the services of notaries from York. . . . But it relied more especially on a small group of local notaries, residents of Durham and, more especially, of the convent's borough of Elvet, who staffed the upper ranks of the monastery's secretariat.[108]

Men like Bentlay and the flourishers and illuminators associated with them, moreover, appear to have been responsive to the latest Continental fashions in their trades.[109]

For example, one of the documents from the Durham Dean and Chapter Muniments collection is called 4.16.34a *Specialia*. The great fifteenth-century catalogues of the muniments, titled *Repertorium Magnum* and *Repertorium Parvum,* contain various divisions of documents of which one, *Specialia,* deals with titles and other legal evidence for monastic property rights.[110] The one of interest here must have been written by someone with a scribal training very like that of Bentlay. It shows something of the artistic embellishment of important Durham documents in the Hemingburgh and Wessington priorates, with elaborately enhanced ascenders in the first line of the page, and heavy serifing and final minim of *u* curving back to the left to make a *macron* in *um* abbreviations, as well as nicely done border decoration.

That there was a stylistic interrelationship between these professional notary scribes and decorators of the town and their monastic counterparts in Durham books as well as documents written and ornamented in the late fourteenth and early fifteenth centuries is clear. The "Durham style," as evident in those books now in the Dean and Chapter Library, which date from the beginning of the Langley period, and which may well have been made at Durham, can be broadly characterized either by notarial penwork elaboration of ascenders, cartouches, faces and grotesques growing out of the loops of ascenders at the head lines of the page, or in other large, calligraphic volumes, penwork initials containing extremely elaborate decorative infill within the bows, and swags coming off them. These features replace the more traditional gold and pigment illumination common in southern books on this scale. Such penwork initials will be considered at length in chapter 6.

Some scribes during the late Skirlaw or Langley periods who used such enhanced scripts seem to have been lay professionals. Among them were Le Borwby, who wrote two portions of Durham Cathedral MS A.I.4, signing his name at the end of each; John Wykingeston, who copied Durham Cathedral MS A.I.5; William de Kedwelly, from his name possibly a Welshman, who wrote part of *Speculum Curatorum*, Durham Cathedral MS B.IV.36; and the scribe John who wrote the first volume of Langley's Bersuire, Durham Cathedral MS A.I.17, giving his full name "codex completus hic a de fonte Johanne" as part of a cryptic colophon.

Durham monks too wrote and signed books in often equally elaborate scripts. John Lytham, 1391–1432, presumably from Lytham in Lancashire, a dependent cell of Durham,[111] wrote Durham Cathedral MS B.III.19, Grosseteste's *De Venenis*, and other works as well as a table to them, spelling his name backwards and then adding to it the formula shortly to be discussed, "nomen scriptoris Johannes plenus amoris Muhtel." Among other monastic scribes with ornate styles were Richard Sherborn, who wrote Durham Cathedral MS C.IV.28, and Richard Bell, later to be prior of Durham, who made the table to Grosseteste's *De Venenis*, Durham Cathedral MS B.III.18, signing his name in a fantastically decorated colophon at folio 227v.[112] Robert Masham, a sacristan 1391–1418, wrote in *Anglicana* a small portion of Durham Cathedral MS B.IV. 41, portions of B.IV.43 in the same collection, possibly done about 1384, and all of London, British Library MS Harley 3858, which Doyle believes may have been copied at Oxford; the book has several illuminated borders in a regional style.[113] William Seton, a bachelor of theology who also was at Durham College in the 1430s and late 1440s, is associated with the table to

Durham Cathedral MS B.III.29, written by seven different scribes, some using Secretary variants, and dated 1438. One of these writers, or possibly compilers, was a Durham monk and procurator named Thomas Stapeley (1391–1421). Seton, however, may only have arranged for its copying, for Doyle notes that the colophon "Amen quod Willelmus Seton jh" probably indicates that jh was the actual scribe of the work.[114] This "jh" may be the same scribe who copied Rolle's *Contra Amores Mundi* at folio 112v of Durham Cathedral MS B.IV.35, ending with "amen quoth jh."[115] Seton also signed with a scribal "quod" Cambridge, Sidney Sussex College MS 56 at several places but did not actually write the book,[116] whose somewhat humanistic contents link it with the work of Robert Emylton.

This copyist was one of the most unusual of the Durham monk scribes, though not for the ornateness of his script. Bachelor of Theology of Durham College, Oxford, he was active at Durham Priory between 1423 and 1448. He wrote a plain, tiny, and very distinctive hand; for a monk, he copied a striking number of literary and humanistic texts. His known production includes MS C.IV.23, a commentary on Aristotle and on Geoffrey of Vinsauf's *Poetria Nova*, as well as portions of MS A.III.29. York Minster Library MS XVI.I.1, a patristic miscellany, is also his work.[117]

One of the most interesting and enigmatic of these Durham copyists, however, was not a monk of Durham[118] but an imported lay scribe, who may have come to Durham at the behest of Uthred of Boldon, prior of the dependent cell of Finchale, four miles north of Durham on the river Wear, and stayed for a number of years, apparently as an external copyist. As Ian Doyle says, "religious houses and their members employed named and unnamed scribes in the fourteenth and fifteenth centuries, to write documents and books, both over a period and occasionally."[119] His name was William du Stiphel or le Stiphel, and he says he was a Breton[120] who worked, so far as is known, from 1381 to as late as 1407–1410, as Alan Piper and Ian Doyle have noted a cartulary of that later date, bearing the subscription "Le Stiphel."[121] From the style of the signature, which lacks the characteristic lozenge and arabesque clusters used with every other example of du Stiphel's name, it is likely that another scribe copied an earlier document written by du Stiphel, though exactly of what date and whether in *Anglicana* or *textura* is not known. From the span of his activities, it appears, according to Doyle, that the scribe "must have spent some time in the [Durham] neighborhood, and it seems he may have been many years in the employment of the priory."[122]

Nothing is known of du Stiphel's earlier life, activities, and religious status except what can be inferred from his surname and his books. In Middle Breton, the word *stiffel, styffel,* or *stivel* appears in the regional dialect of Finistère with the meaning of a stream spurting or falling from a cliff, or a washing-up spot.[123] Breton place names typically contain the syllables *plou* (parish), *loc* (holy place), *lan* (church), or *ker* (village), often joined with the name of a saint or an object, and many people bear names with the article *le* or the locative syllable *an.*

Andrew Watson believes that du Stiphel probably came from Morbihan in Brittany. In the department of Morbihan, in the diocese of Vannes, is the hamlet of Stival,[124] three and one-half kilometers from Pontivy. In Vannes, the cathedral of St. Peter, about forty-five kilometers from Stival, would have been the most likely spot for our scribe's education; though there were Franciscans at Vannes from about 1265, the convent at Pontivy was of much later date.[125] Watson's argument, however, has two weaknesses: the lack of a close phonic similarity between Stiphel and Stival and the lack of a cultural reason for his emigration.

I should like to offer two other possibilities that I believe have stronger support. First, closer to the actual spelling du Stiphel, is the name for a place on a small island, Île d'Ouessant, with a present-day population of about 1,450, about twelve kilometers from the Brest coast. On the east coast is a place called Le Stiff. A very good reason for a scribe to leave the island was the fact that it was occupied by the English during the Hundred Years' War.[126] He could have received scribal training at several convenient places on the mainland. Aside from the monastic foundations on the coast, there were Franciscan houses at Morlaix from 1236, and Franciscans, Dominicans, and Carmelites at Quimper, Quimperlé, and Saint-Pol-de-Léon from 1232.[127]

The likeliest place of origin for our scribe in my opinion, however, is the parish of Guilers, surrounding the modern town of that name, midway between Brest and St. Renan, which in 1426 had about 350 inhabitants. In this geographical setting, we have not only a perfect match for the spelling of the name but also cultural reasons that would place a person with ambitions to be more than just a country market-place scribe in precisely the setting where he could develop his talents.

The records of the sénéchaussée of Brest and Saint Renan, an inventory of seigneurial rents ordered by Francis I in 1538, show that a "Guillaume Robert tient . . . ou terrouer 'an Stiffel' " (a small village or lands surrounding a village called "le Stiffel").[128] From his name,

Robert was not a Breton but a Frenchman; he owned other land in Guilers as well.[129] The foundations of a medieval church there have been rebuilt as the present parish church of St. Valentin,[130] and a manor of Keroual still stands near Guilers.[131]

That people took their surnames from places called Stiffel is clear from a document of 1526 relating to the seigneurie of Dresnay, now in the commune of Plougras, in the Côtes-du-Nord region of Brittany, about twenty miles from Saint Brieuc, where one of the signators was named Le Stiffel. He may possibly have been an inhabitant of an Stiffel and likely a relative of William the scribe.[132] The scribe's alternate use in colophons of both *du* and *le* with his surname would be appropriate to an origin on the manor of an Stiffel in Guilers.

Certain other historical facts make Guilers the more probable origin for the scribe. Between 1342 and 1397 the castle at Brest and its surroundings were harshly garrisoned by a series of English captains, lieutenants, and receivers who exacted food, building materials, and labor from the parishes of the countryside and whose troops acted in a piratical way towards the seigneurial estates in the vicinity.[133] Because of these unsettled conditions, many clerks from the diocese of St. Pol-de-Léon sought further scribal and notarial training in Paris, the city of preference for students from this region of Brittany. For example, another Breton scribe who was quite active in Paris in the 1440s was John Run, who wrote two manuscripts now at Oxford, Bodleian Library MSS Canonic. Misc. 211 and 486. In the former book he exhibits the same pride in his origins as du Stiphel, "Iste liber completus fuit Parisius per me Johannem Run venerabilis nationis Francie provincieque laudabilis Britannie," and in the latter even names his diocese, "venerabilis Francie nacionis episcopatusque Trecorensis" (Tréguier).[134]

Thus, though it is admittedly conjectural, a possible career for the scribe may have involved early training at a Franciscan or Dominican house in St. Pol-de-Léon or at the cathedral and then a move to Paris, where he perfected his *textura*. The death of Charles V in 1380 may have caused many persons engaged in the artisanal side of Charles's numerous translating and copying projects to disperse to Avignon or even to England in spite of the Hundred Years' War.

Though the presence of a Breton like du Stiphel writing books at Durham may at first seem surprising, foreign scribes and book artisans were not unusual throughout England because of the Hundred Years' War, and it is probable that some would be in the north. We saw in chapter 1 that the fifteenth-century will of Robert Wolveden records a gift to a master John Arston, scribe and notary, who in spite of his name was from Mainz, and that the York Freemen's Register showed the presence of foreign artisans, free of the city, such as Henricus Payntour of Durdraght (1380–1381); William Smythhusen, "payntour" (1389–1390); and Peter van Rode,"colourmaker" (1400). In 1448 a Thomas Bouland practiced the trade of "scriptor,"[135] though this name may have been a form of the more English Bolland. Interestingly, Langley's own scribe and secretary had the rather un-English surname of Jobur, though he was called "alias London."[136] Certainly, contemporary French influence on the writing practices in Durham can be seen in notarial scripts and ornamentation, which show the sort of cadels we associate with Burgundian letters.[137] Another classification for certain Durham muniment documents was that of the *locellus*, a fifteenth-century variant of the *cista* or chest; a number of these documents, chiefly to do with legal and administrative business, were highly ornamented and quite ornately written.[138] Dean and Chapter Muniments Locellus 1.12 can be compared for its elaborate strap-work capitals with Jean Miélot's *Speculum Humanae Salvationis*. Indeed, several Durham books show scribal awareness of contemporary French ornate writing style. We will see in chapter 6 the possibly French character of penwork initials in Durham codices.

This French influence, however, is mainly of the mid-fifteenth century, and why there would have been a climate at Durham receptive to du Stiphel's very Continental and even rather avant garde liturgical *textura* is not clear.[139] Nor is the manner of du Stiphel's recruitment to Durham. It does not seem to have been by way of a bishop's retinue. Thomas Hatfield, bishop of Durham from 1345 to 1381, was a building-loving rather than a book-loving bishop, and although he made several trips to France with Edward, these were too early, 1346 and 1355, to have encountered our scribe. On the other hand, Walter Skirlaw, a considerable bibliophile and a north-easterner by birth and connections, was a member of several embassies to France in the early part of Richard II's reign, but he became bishop of Durham in 1388, when du Stiphel was already long established in the area.

A more likely explanation for du Stiphel's presence in the north can be found in the Continental travels of Uthred de Boldon during the period that he was prior of Finchale.[140] In 1373/74, Edward III formed a commission to discuss at Avignon papal rights to provide clergy to English churches, and Uthred was a member of it; his biographer comments "anno 73 ultra mare post pentecostem." As this seems to have been his only trip out of England, it must have been the period of his encounter with the Breton, who would perhaps have been a scribe at the papal court.[141] He was back at Finchale by 1375 and served as subprior there in 1381, when the book he had commissioned du Stiphel to write was nearly or just done. Documents show him in Finchale in 1386, the date of du Stiphel's second known work, and he stayed there until his death in 1397.

Presumably, some time on this trip to Avignon, he made contact with du Stiphel and arranged for his employment as a professional scribe in Finchale. Unfortunately, the Finchale account rolls are missing for 1380–1388, the period when the Breton's first known book was commissioned,[142] so whether Uthred paid du Stiphel for a personal copy or an additional copy for the library is uncertain. As there are, however, no references to book making of any sort in the Finchale accounts under any prior, it is likely that Uthred personally employed the Breton scribe. Doyle has noted that throughout England at this period:

> there was a widespread practice of individual religious using monetary allowances . . . for book purchases. . . . Not infrequently they employed their funds and friends to provide items direct for the communal collections, sometimes perhaps by meeting the material costs of work actually executed by themselves or their brethren.[143]

Uthred's commission was a volume of Rufinus' translation of the *Historia Ecclesiastica* of Eusebius, now British Library MS Burney 310.[144] Though the exact contents of this volume have occasioned some confusion, there is no doubt about the identity and nationality of the scribe.[145]

Du Stiphel acknowledges himself at the bottom of folio 89v: "explicit liber historie ecclesiastice secundum Eusebium. Scriptus per manum Guillelmi dicti du Stiphel de Britania pro uenerabili et religioso uiro domino Utredo Dunelmensi monacho ac sancte sacre pagine doctore. Anno domino millesimo CCCo, octuagesimo primo uicesimo sexto die mensis Augusti. In Fincal." This formula, giving the first name, followed by the word *dicti* and then the surname and place of origin is common in Continental colophons of this period.

It is odd that the scribe does not mention de Boldon's office and, however flatteringly, refers to him only as a monk. At folio 89v, the portion of the volume containing Bede's *History of the English Church and People* ends with a red signature "G. du Stiphel" with a large blue paraph. Then, at the very bottom of folio 158, some arabesque and lozenge clusters surround the words G. du Stiphel in a way characteristic of scribal signatures of this period. For example, the same curving strokes and blobs ornament the initial *H* and the name Hatton on the cartouched signature of the fifteenth-century scribe of much of National Library of Wales MS Porkington 10, folio 52v.

Certain features of du Stiphel's hand are quite distinctive, for example a high-waisted *b;* a cusp on the left side of ascenders, which appears to have required a separate movement of the pen; and, most noticeably, a billhook-like forking of the ascenders in *l* and *b,* in which the left-hand portion of the stroke bends down in a fine hairline to the left of the shaft; it is made as a separate finish with the edge of the pen tip. The script also has a pronounced leftward angle, as if the scribe were left-handed and were turning his page slightly to keep from smudging his work.

This manuscript, dated 1381, appears to be the earliest of the du Stiphel group, of which only one other is dated (1386), and seems to show the scribe at the beginning of his career, or engaged in a project in which economy and speed were paramount. The script is quite plain except for the ascenders of *l, b,* and *h,* which typically hook downward and to the right at the tops of lines. Because the main characteristics of the Breton's later style are uneconomical finishing strokes and an extremely fluent motion of the pen as it makes its way through the various strokes, the absence of these features in MS Burney 310 may indicate cost saving or perhaps the fact that the scribe was just beginning to find his style. For example, a quality of du Stiphel at his most representative is a certain amount of splaying of the pen tip at the heads of minim strokes and an evident difference between wide and narrow portions of a minim, but in Burney the minims retain more or less the same width throughout the stroke. Also, though it may be owing to poorer quality and unevenly shrinking parchment, the writing lines of what appears to be du Stiphel's first book wobble a good deal.

One common assumption in the study of much medieval artwork is that decorative mannerism is a late and even a decadent development. This is certainly true of Gothic handwriting, which follows, on the whole, the youth, maturity, and senescence of Gothic architecture.[146] If we apply this idea to du Stiphel's work, we would have to say that MS Burney 310 is the least mannered and so the earliest of the scribe's known work, dated or undated. Though there are some ornamental serifs, these are chiefly a fine vertical hairline coming from the right of the headstroke of terminal *t,* a similar but curving stroke from the left of the headstroke of the *et* abbreviation, a curving downward vertical stroke to the left of *u,* and a hairline coming from the angle of 2-shaped *r.*

A second Durham book bears du Stiphel's colophon also; it is Durham Cathedral MS A.I.3, a volume of Nicholas of Lyra's commentary on the Pentateuch and other historical books as far as the book of Job. The colophon to this volume is very similar to that of Burney MS 310: "et scripte per manum William de Stiphel ex precepto dominus Roberto Blaklaw sacre theologie bachelarii et suppriori monasterii Dunelmi anno domine 1386. 14 die mensis Aprilis, Le Stiphel."[147] Five years have passed and he seems to have become more adjusted to England, for the scribe uses an English form of his given name and does not mention that he is a Breton. The actual place the manuscript was made, however, was not, as in Burney, specified, though the details of Blaklaw's office would imply that it was written and illuminated at Durham. Unlike the earlier colophon, this one shows full awareness of his patron's office. This extremely ornate codex is much larger than Burney and more luxurious, measuring 435 × 280 mm, a tall and idiosyncratically narrow volume. Not only does the colophon indicate that the book was made for a Durham official but the title page contains an historiated initial *H* depicting a tonsured kneeling figure in Benedictine robes in what may be a donor pose, displaying a banner with the text "confessor vere / Cuthberte mei misere" and praying to St. Cuthbert, who holds a crozier and cradles the head of King Oswald in the crook of his arm. This may be a standard iconographic grouping, as it appears on the fourteenth-century octagonal font at the church of St. Cuthbert, Fishlake, eight and one-half miles northeast of Doncaster, which was controlled by the Dean and Chapter of Durham.[148] At the saint's right is a mask face of the sort we will see in the next chapter to be typical of northern manuscript illumination; from its mouth exit twisted rose and blue vines, which form the bow of the *H.* A full border in the trellis style surrounds the page at left, right, and bottom. This is a characteristic of manuscripts that are to receive little or no illumination in subsequent pages, while from archaizing dragons at lower left vines with interlace roundels and kite-shaped leaf overwrap rise to the initial. This page may be compared with the opening folio of Lambeth Palace Library MS 23, Alexander Neckham's *Super Cantica,* from Durham, which has a similar trellis border, archaizing dragons, ropy knotted vinework forming the bow of the initial, and Cuthbert also bearing Oswald's head.[149]

That the miniature indicates a presentation copy is suggested by its general similarity to what is clearly a presentation picture in the William of Nottingham codex mentioned earlier (Oxford, Bodleian Library MS Laud Misc.165, fol. 5), depicting Thomas Arundel as archbishop of Canterbury seated in a pastoral chair, surrounded by Benedictine monks and pointing to a text on the pages of a book held open before him. This miniature was made about 1396. Since the image shows that the book was a presentation to Christ Church, Canterbury, it may serve as a gloss on the Durham miniature's possibly similar purpose.[150]

Though admittedly du Stiphel could have gone for a period to work as a scribe at Durham College, Oxford, which Alan Piper thinks was a source for many Durham books,[151] and that an Oxford painter could have done the decoration, the anachronistic character of the mask face would suggest that Durham Cathedral MS A.I.3 was illuminated in the north. And there is, as well, some archival evidence that it was written there. In the Durham feretory account rolls for 1383, the sum of 3s. 4d. was contributed toward the expense of a copy of Nicholas of Lyra, presumably MS A. I.3.[152] Though Raine's comments on this codex are not completely reliable, he does observe that the work is "decidedly the best specimen of what could be done in Durham in the way of illumination at the period."[153]

Du Stiphel also wrote folios 1–76v of Durham Cathedral MS A.I.4, a companion volume of Nicholas of Lyra, completing the commentary and finished by two scribes, Le Borwby, who wrote folios 77 through the first column of 90v, and folios 157–228; and another scribe, unnamed, who continued the text from the second column of 90v through folio 156. Both of du Stiphel's collaborators were apparently professional Durham scribes contemporary with the Breton, and to judge by his name, Le Borwby was a Yorkshireman. This scribe signed with the article *le* before his name at the rulings of the bottom of the page much as had du Stiphel when he completed his stint, perhaps in imitation of the Breton's practice. This book is presumably the subject of the entry in the feretory roll for 1384–1385 showing a contribution towards its writing of another 3s. 4d.[154] As Doyle notes, MSS "A.I.3–4 were probably in progress for at least three years."[155] If then, as seems reasonable from the fact that MS A.I.4 concludes the commentary of Lyra, it was written after A.I.3, we can assume that it was actually finished about 1387 to 1388 or about one and one-half to two years after MS A.I.3. There is some reason to see it as a slightly later book stylistically as well.

A new and quite manneristic feature consonant with the assumption about Gothic art that busier is later appears in the Breton's script in the two Lyra volumes. This is the prolongation of certain finishing strokes. Now the oblique stroke that closes the bow of terminal *e* continues well out to the right of the letter and then hooks sharply down. Terminal *c*'s in words like *hoc* have a little tail coming from the top of the letter, and the bow of *h* has a similar tail at its bottom. These delicate accents are in addition to those already noted in Burney, and they seem especially profuse at the end of du Stiphel's portion of MS A.I.4.

This leaves us one undated manuscript to consider, Trinity College, Cambridge, MS B.15.30, an undecorated but still highly calligraphic topical index whose relatively small dimensions, 175 × 260 mm, arise from the fact that it was copied to be bound with a nearly contemporary but rather less well written text of the subdean of Salisbury, Thomas of Chobham's *Summa Penitentiae* or *Confessorum.* The table occupies folios 7-36v,[156] ending with the scribe's name, "Le Stiphel," surrounded by arabesque or vine pen accents around decorative lozenge clusters of the same type as in MSS Burney 310 and Durham Cathedral MS A.I.4. A similar pattern occurs in the margin of the second line of the right-hand column of folio 33v. Though there is no other information about the scribe in his colophon, the association with Finchale is still present, as the first flyleaf, a piece of a fifteenth-century account roll, contains a list of northeastern places, among them Hartlepool, Finchale, and Durham.

The script is as ornate and luxurious as MSS A.I. 3-4, but the initials are plain red Lombards, followed by a red-flashed second letter. The capitals are flashed red, with guide letters and paraph signs for the rubricator not in du Stiphel's hand, and the parchment is poor quality, with holes in some sheets. The scribe also did the rubrication—*incipits,* major text divisions, and the red Roman chapter numbers in the margins—and the black, though probably not the red, line fillers.

The elegant script shows the scribe at the height of his powers, and it is clear that he did not hurry his copying in the interest of economy, for the script of the table has even more of the serifing which we discussed in MSS A.I.3–4. For example, now both ends of *s* put out serifs, and the scribe places two horizontal bars through the shaft of the *et* abbreviation and that of the *x.* Yet there are odd signs of carelessness in other aspects of his work. His writing goes into the margin or center gutter at several points. On folio 33v at line eleven in the right column, at one point he wrote out *superbia* when he

should have left off the *s* for the initial artist and made a more ornate
u. He made several corrections by barring out words or phrases in
red and black; in some cases the errors are actually scraped out, but
poorly, going right through the parchment and making a hole. At
folio 32, for example, the rubric error *albaphatum* for *alphabetum* is
expunged; this is a curious scribal mistake, and one wonders whether
du Stiphel was elderly when he made it.

In the actual text of Chobham, done in a rather rounded, Italian-
looking or *notula*-like hand, appears more of du Stiphel's work, for
he extensively annotated the margins of Chobham's text.[157] His
lengthy "side note summaries"[158] are of several sorts, but all are delib-
erate and formal. They appear on writing lines ruled in fine ink, done
in the same pen at right angles to a vertical or gutter line added to
the margin of the text. Though there are many annotations in the
margins, only du Stiphel's are on these ruled lines. Sometimes he
gives chapter and paragraph for Chobham's patristic citations. Sometimes he epitomizes passages to allow a preacher to pick out sentences
for a sermon, as in "nichil magis naturale est hominum quam apetitus
proprii honoris" or "nullum peccatum est ita naturale sicut superbia"
(folio 44v). And sometimes the annotations direct the user through
the text, as at folio 41: "pro ista materia nota in C. 43." Thus it is clear
that du Stiphel was well acquainted with the contents of the book and
was more than a mere dutiful copyist.

In these marginalia the scribe uses the same arabesque finishing
strokes he used in MSS A.I.3–4: the tails of 2-shaped *r*, the bow of *h*,
the hairline from terminal *t*, and the lengthened minim of the second
i in *proprii*. There is, however, evidence that this was not his best
grade of *textura*, because he does not consistently use the second
stroke mentioned earlier to cusp the ascenders of *h*, *l*, and *b*.

Some conclusions emerge from the study of these five specimens
of du Stiphel's script. There is a pronounced difference in development between the hands of the two dated manuscripts of 1381 and
1386. This seems chiefly to be the addition of a second stroke to give
the characteristic cusp at the left center of minim strokes and of a
finish at the tops of ascenders. The splaying of the tops of minims also
seems to come after 1381. There appears to have been an increase in
mannerism in a book that could have been written after 1387: MS
B.15.30, a manuscript that seems clearly later than 1381 and of about
the same period as MSS A.I.3–4, contains script whose mannerism,
because of the number of different hairline finishes, places it with the
scribe's latest known *textura*.

Our possible chronology of du Stiphel's extant work might run like this. Brought to the Durham area by Uthred de Boldon at Finchale, the Breton, fairly new to England, writes MS Burney 310. (Naturally, he may also have written many other books or parts of books not now known.) By 1386 he is considered a skilled enough scribe to take on the whole of a large project, a volume of Nicholas of Lyra. He completes this book and begins MS A.I.4 about 1387, writing the first seventy-seven folios. Why does his stint break off here? Does he sign his name because he assumes that he will not be writing more of this book? Examples of his signature at several points in a manuscript suggest some relatively temporary interruption and not the quitting of the book altogether. Perhaps he was asked to do MS B.15.30, a short work written on inferior materials, and intended to return to MS A.I.4 again but never did so, and the commentary was finished by Le Borwby.

The last of our group of northern scribes may not, in fact, be a distinct group at all. There is the possibility of a family of scribes, whose work appears in southern England in the fourteenth and fifteenth centuries, having some northern members. One of the enigmatic features of late medieval English colophons is the epithet *plenus amoris* with which the scribe occasionally couples his given name.[159] I am aware of about forty such manuscripts, of which eleven are of northern origin on other evidence, and W. D. Macray has suggested that the words translate into Latin the actual surnames of Pleindamour and Fullalove. In addition to these examples, there are a score or so of scribes who call themselves John or Robert or some other name, followed by a cognomen and then the epithet *plenus amoris*. The evidence, then, is very mixed, but there are more reasons for believing in the existence of a Fulloflove scribal family than indicated, for example, by Thomas Heffernan.[160]

Let us begin with the question of a possible family of scribes called Fulloflove in England. Though originally a nickname denoting libertine ways—like "Wencher"—Fulloflove, or its variants Fullelove, Fullerlove, Fulleylove, and Fullilove, was a long-lived surname in England. An Alfred Fullalove worked as an actioner at the Purdey gun-making firm in London in 1918,[161] and at the present time variants of the name can be found in the London telephone directory.

The tendency to give nicknames to various Johns, Alices, and Walters in the period before distinct surnames to distinguish one from another was a much more popular habit in the north than in the south; accordingly, we find quite a few persons there named Fulloflove. During the early Middle English period, the English name was not always distinguished from the French *Pleindamour*. Northern lay subsidy rolls and inquisition lists, for example produce several persons with forms of these names. A Richard Playndamurs is mentioned in the Yorkshire Inquisitions Post Mortem of 1297, a John from the lay subsidy rolls of 1327, and an Agnes from the lay subsidy rolls of 1379. By 1332 the name had become Anglicized, for a William Ffuloflof appears in the lay subsidy rolls for Cumberland.[162]

In the southeast, people with this name were of sufficiently high social status to own land and to make wills. A Richard Playndamor held land at Gorleston, Suffolk, before 1317.[163] And there were Fullofloves in Norwich. A will of 1466 was proved for a John Fullolove or Fuloflove of Blickling, St. Andrew, with no occupation or estate specified. In 1479 we find a will for a Ralph Fulloflove who was rector of Westharlyng.[164]

I found no Fullofloves nor any variants of the name in the York Memorandum Books, the York Freemen's Register, or the published Yorkshire wills, but this negative evidence is not conclusive, because scribes known to be active in Yorkshire do not appear in those sources. And too, scribes as a group do not seem to have satisfied the minimum possession of five pounds of property to appear in wills, with the exception of the John Arston mentioned in the preceding chapter, who was really more a notary public than a scribe.

Whatever the significance of the nickname and later surname Fulloflove in the general population of England at the close of the Middle Ages, there is one almost certain example of its being the actual surname of a scribe who calls himself "plenus amoris" in his colophon. This man was the scribe who worked for John Gower, making that poet a handsome Sarum missal. This book, sold by Sotheby's in 1975, was probably written about 1415. The work contains an elaborate colophon of three hexameter lines, the first done in red ink and the others in black. Each line is followed by the scribal tag "quod J. Ff" and a typical pattern of ornamental dots and strokes very like those in the colophons of the Ellerker and du Stiphel codices. The colophon reads:

> Scriptor scripsisset melior bene si voluisset.
> Nomen scriptoris Iohannis plenus amoris.
> Qui scripsit carmen sit benedictus amen.[165]

The same scribe may also have written another Sarum missal for John Gower, which is now London, British Library MS Additional 59855, also with the Gower arms, where the writer says of himself "Nomen Scriptoris Johannes plenus amoris" at folio 28v.[166]

Unfortunately, as was the case with the Ellerker colophon, the formulaic nature of the scribal tag in the Gower missal sold by Sotheby's makes it difficult to conclude much about the copyist. The third line of these hexameters occurs in nineteen colophons, all but three English and all of the fourteenth and fifteenth centuries.[167] Though the unsigned sale catalogue description suggests that the initials may "very well stand for quod John Fullalove," no further evidence is offered for this idea.

Plenus amoris scribes occur in the counties of York and Durham, where codices written by persons named Peter, John, Robert, and Nicholas use the Fulloflove epithet or surname. A Peter seems to have been a scribe at Durham about 1350, writing up to folio 159v a collection of chronicles and lives of saints (now in Oxford, Bodleian Library MS Fairfax 6).[168] Independent corroboration of the existence of this Peter at Durham comes from an indenture made there in 1366, in which a copy of a *Corpus Juris Civilis* made "per manum fratris Petri de Dunelmii librarii" is mentioned.[169] It is possible—but unlikely, given the range of these dates—that he could also be the Petrus *plenus amoris* who very late in his life wrote a *Vita* of St. Catherine of Sienna now at Chantilly, a manuscript that has been dated in the first quarter of the fifteenth century.[170]

Another possible Yorkshire Fulloflove is the Johannes *plenus amoris* who wrote a text of Roger Bacon's *Perspectiva*, which makes up an article in Oxford, Bodleian MS Digby 77, from Meaux in Holderness, dating from around 1420. At the end of a text of another item in the book, the *Oculus Moralis*, is the notation "Wilflete vult quod iste liber tradatur abathie de Mews in Holdernes, quia emit eum ab uno monacho ejusdem domus pro viij. s" (folio 147v). Johannes's colophon is, unfortunately, also too conventional to localize him: "explicit expliceat ludere scriptor eat. Nomen scriptoris / Johannes plenus amoris."[171]

Aside from the Meaux provenance, there is little internally to tie MS Digby 77 to the north. The book has handsome initials and diagrams and may once have been owned by Dr. John Dee, the Elizabethan alchemist.[172] The manuscript, however, is a compilation by several scribes, of whom one signs his name "quod Wyke" (folio 191). This person appears also to have been the scribe of Oxford, Merton College MS 251 of the late fifteenth century, containing John Sharp's questions on the *De Anima*, and Antonio Andreas of Arragon's questions on the *Metaphysics*, with tables, both of which end: "Ecce finis titulacionis istarum questionum super totam methaphysicam quod

Wyke. Nunc finem feci / Da michi quid merui."[173] That this manuscript at one time contained more material is shown by the medieval
table of contents, which indicates that there was also a table to the
tract by Antonio Andreas, "secundum ordinem alphabeti secundum
Durham." Could this manuscript have had some connection with
York and Durham and indirectly point to a John Fulloflove active
there?

Some external evidence points that way. Besides the somewhat
ambiguous phrase "secundum Durham" is the fact that the Merton
College Wyke's scribal verse is identical with that of Archbishop
Thomas Rotherham's scribe, "Schaw," whose activities will be discussed in chapter 6. The verses may have been imitated by the later
professional scribe. Finally, there are three northern Wykes who may
have copied the Merton and Meaux texts. The will of Walter Bruge,
canon of York, who died in 1394, leaves among other books "unum
librum de Expositione Ewangeliorum vocatum Unum ex Quatuor" to
a Johannes Wyke.[174] Other possible identities for a northern scribe
named Wyke come from references to a William Wyke, prebendary
of Norton in 1408, and to a Geoffrey Wyke, Master of Theology,
whose presentation to the chantry of Langsole in 1422 is recorded in
the register of Bishop Thomas Langley of Durham.[175]

In the York Minster Library is a book that belonged to John
Newton, its founder. His *Super Codicem* of Cino of Pistoia (York Minster Library MS XVI. P. 8), in consequence of being Newton's gift, has
something of a Yorkshire pedigree. Though this manuscript bears no
marks of origin, the decoration is clearly regional in character and
the writing that of five English scribes. The *champ* initials and the
large initials at the opening, moreover, use a good deal of green,
which was a popular color in late medieval northern books, as we
shall see in the next chapter. The colophon to Newton's book is a very
plain one: "nomen scriptoris/ Robertus plenus amoris."[176]

Of those *plenus amoris* scribes in the north who use the phrase as
a cognomen we may note the John of Lytham mentioned earlier and
John Charke, the scribe of part of Oxford, Bodleian Library MS
Additional 106. This paper miscellany of the fifteenth century, made
in the north, contains besides John of Burgundy's plague tract, popular there, various other medical recipes and tracts written by different
hands. The fifth selection was written by a youthful scribe who signs
himself "nomen scriptoris Charke plenus amoris / totum nomen
habes / Johannum si superades / in aetate 24."[177] One possible explanation for the colophons of people like Lytham and Charke was that

having two different surnames is not uncommon in Yorkshire wills of the period. For example, a Thomas de Popiltoun was also called Kirkby; and when one cognomen is a trade name, e.g. flesshewer, the owner would often also have a place name.

Finally, one of the *plenus amoris* group is believed on other grounds to have a cognomen. This person is one of the scribes involved in the composition of the Findern Anthology (Cambridge University Library MS Ff.1.6), a commonplace book containing a very important collection of English lyrics and some romances and other texts.[178] It was made in the late fifteenth century and was for a very long time at Findern in Derbyshire. Among the scribes involved in the work was one who says of himself, "nomen scriptoris Nicholas plenus amoris," after copying the legend of Pyramus and Thisbe from Chaucer's *Legend of Good Women*.[179] It has been suggested by Ethel Seaton that this Nicholas was Nicholas Wymbush of Nocton Park and Lincoln, a King's Clerk and Master of Chancery in 1441 and 1448, dying in 1461. His benefices were all southern, but he was canon of York and prebendary of Bole from 1445 until his death. Unfortunately, the argument connecting Wymbush to this manuscript is a bit torturous.[180] It is probably best to accept Beadle and Owen's suggestion that the scribe should be classed among "estate servants of the type who acted extensively as amanuenses for the Paston family."[181]

As can be seen from considering the citations collected by the Benedictines of Bouveret in their *Colophons*, it was very common all over Europe to find scribes who call themselves *plenus amoris* and then give their surnames, often introduced in a witty or puzzling form. A fairly typical example occurs in a Bodleian Library manuscript, MS Canonic. Misc. 438 from the fifteenth century. The scribe, who also wrote another volume now Chantilly, Musée Condé MS 279 of the same date, gives in the Oxford volume the following colophon:

> Le nom de lescripvain
> est Sevestre damour plain
> Et le sein nom est Durant
> qui tousiours endure endurant.
> Aussi fault il moult endurer
> qui en cest monde veult durer.[182]

If, as Heffernan suggested, the *plenus amoris* tag is merely a jingle used for the rime of lescripvain / plain, why does the scribe take such an obvious interest in the *annominatio* of the last four lines? Sevestre, moreover, clearly distinguishes his surname "le sein" from his writing name or professional name "damour plain." How much can be extrapolated about English practice from this French example is uncertain.

Obviously, the *plenus amoris* problem is a puzzling one and not readily susceptible to interpretation. Macray's suggestion, made nearly a century ago, that "plenus amoris or fullalove seems to have been the name of a family of scribes" is no closer to being proved or disproved. If, however, there was a scribal family called Fulloflove, it appears that a branch of it was active in the north. The volumes of Peter, John, and Robert point to the possibility of Fullofloves in the north of England engaged in the writing of books.

We have seen that mendicants—and, in one case, an imported secular scribe—play a prominent role in the book-making activities in the north during the period of interest to us. Their contribution ranges from Ellerker and du Stiphel's primarily professional and commercial contracting and copywork to creation of books for collective conventual or pious individual use in the cases of Popultoun and Lacy. That there is also less well documented but still considerable evidence of professional or semiprofessional scribal activity in the north of England during this period, largely responsible for the great variety of the books that are noted in Appendix C, should by now be clear. It is likely that such persons had their counterpart in professional or at least nonmonastic artists and decorators, and it is to the artist counterparts of scribes like William de Ellerker and Robert de Popultoun, that we now turn.

3

Color and the Archaizing Style

$\mathcal{S}$ome 236 English manuscripts made between about 1375 and 1497 seem to have come from the north of England, to judge from such characteristics as feasts for regional saints, marks of ownership like coats of arms, *ex libris* inscriptions, or, in a few cases, colophons mentioning the names of scribes. Though many of these books are plain, even humble, productions, study of those that are decorated reveals certain essential differences of taste between books associated, broadly speaking, with the county of York and those associated with the county of Durham. This chapter is concerned with two aspects of decoration in the Yorkshire books that may point to a common regional taste. These are a preference for the colors green and purple in decorative borders and initials and an inclination on the part of the artists engaged in painting them to use archaizing forms deriving from Northumbrian and East Anglian manuscripts. Chapter 4 will consider a number of books whose borders incorporate medallions of Hiberno-Saxon interlace design and mask-like motifs resembling the face of a lion. Such medallions and faces appear in a wider geographic range, in manuscripts that seem to have been made in or around both York and Durham. A somewhat different form of decoration, not done with paints and brushes but with pen and ink, is common in certain Durham books made during the tenure of bishop Thomas Langley; this form will be treated separately in chapter 6.

Because most of these northern manuscripts lack sufficiently complex programs of illustration to allow several to be grouped by scene, figure, or facial type as the product of a particular workshop or artist, it is difficult to find features that two or more books share. A goodly number of even the most modest of the volumes, however, have multicolored geometrical or floral borders or floriate initials, which show distinctive palette preferences.

In examining the decoration of these books, one is struck by the considerable number of them in which there are broad areas of green used in naturalistic or non-naturalistic ways. This taste for green is shared, though not exclusively, by a group of manuscripts having very similar miniatures of the Crucifixion intended to illustrate the chief prayer in the canon of the mass, the "Te igitur."[1] Though such miniatures are, of course, widely found in missals throughout England, it is the heavy use of green in the painting that gives these northern books a common character. These volumes are Huntington Library HM 1067, Harvard, Widener MS 1, Oxford, Bodleian Library MS Gough Liturgies 5, and British Library MS Additional 43380. These four manuscripts will be called the "Green Canon-Page" group; though it is small, it is certainly possible that a number of other manuscripts now lost or simply unknown, belonged to it.

Equally small, though very distinctive, is the "Archaizing" group comprising a five-book abridgment of John of Tynemouth's *Historia Aurea,* now Cambridge University Library MS Dd.10.22, and two York missals, now Boston Public Library MS 1576 and Trinity College, Dublin MS 83. The last two of these books seem to have been done in the same workshop and show a stylistic relationship to two other Yorkshire books written by the same scribe. Besides containing a type of purple in the decoration rare in English manuscript painting of this period, two of these three manuscripts may well be the production of a group of artists who were self-consciously archaizing to the point of mannerism. The third, Trinity College, Dublin MS 83, is tied by its gold leaf work to the Boston volume. The archaizing books look much more regional in style than the Green Canon-Page group just mentioned, which follows on the whole the trends of the International Gothic Style in decoration, though in a much simplified fashion. Both of these groups exhibit colors quite unusual either in the quantities employed or in themselves, perhaps representing a northern color preference.

Because the subject of color in medieval manuscript painting is a complex and technical one, with much confusion about the names of the colors and the materials from which they were derived, and even some uncertainty as to how medieval viewers perceived hue, I will review the main characteristics of medieval green and purple pigments before approaching the decoration containing them.[2]

Late medieval English manuscript painting has a relatively uniform palette containing chiefly red, rose, blue, white lead, orange, brown, and black.[3] Two colors in the Ricardian period, however, are rather less typical of the south than of the north. The first is a purple called *folium,* or sometimes *tournesole.* Its presence in England can be traced back to Northumbrian illumination and, diachronically, to contemporary Bohemian painting. The second color is green, which in this period is not really an English color at all, but rather Bohemian. The appearance of these two colors in northern codices suggests the presence of Bohemian manuscripts in the north serving as color models, or Bohemian painters active in the region, as well as a stylistic interest in and presumably an exposure to older Northumbrian codices, like the Lindisfarne Gospels, on the part of some northern illuminators.

Amanda Simpson has argued that the illuminators who came to the court of Richard II in the retinue of Anne of Bohemia had no significant impact on English manuscript painting, observing that "there is no evidence, either documentary or stylistic, to support the view that Bohemian painting in any way influenced English painting during the second half of the fourteenth century."[4] Her claim has recently been disputed by Michael Orr, who has shown how a southwestern painter, John Siferwas, in the Sherborne Missal, borrowed from Bohemian painters their inhabited letter shafts and blue border infills with large amounts of highlighted white acanthus leaves. Nicholas Rogers has also observed the impact of Bohemian and German styles on a book painted at Bury St. Edmunds in the 1440s. And though its illuminations are missing, the presence of parallel English and Czech prayers added to a late fourteenth-century *horae* of East Anglian provenance, Boston Endowment for Biblical Research MS 13, now in the Mugar Memorial Library of Boston University, certainly suggests some contact of this manuscript with Anne's court. Given what we have seen about the book-making activities of an English Dominican friar, William de Ellerker, the fact that another Dominican, Johannes de Praga, of the York convent was ordained priest at York in 1419 is interesting.[5] On a less elaborate scale, this Bohemian influence, possibly through Baltic and Hanseatic trading contact by way of York, Beverley, and Hull,[6] is evident in a number of northern books as well.

Though the subject of Bohemian miniature painting is complex (the region designated by the term includes not only the Bohemia absorbed into Czechoslovakia, but also the art of southeastern Germany, Hungary, Rumania, and Poland), a few themes relevant to our concerns should be noted here. It has long been noticed that highly sophisticated French and Italian uses of color and treatment of foliage, as well as East Anglian interlace patterns, come to central European painting and mix there with a native tradition of a much simpler nature, producing a synthesis that has aptly been termed the International Gothic Style. This, in turn, was exported back to southern Europe.[7] That this exportation also affected English painting, as we have just seen, has been less accepted. Yet, at least for the north of England the Bohemian component, a fondness for unusual colors, and for certain forms of border decoration, seems undeniably present.

Because scriptoria and workshops in Carthusian, Cistercian, and Benedictine monasteries and in the houses of Franciscans and Dominicans in central Europe had active ties with their mother houses in France and Italy, book-making trends current in southern Europe came rapidly to the Bohemian sphere and were promptly assimilated in its art. So too the political influence of the Anjou kings in Hungary, with their tradition of beautiful illuminated court manuscripts, came to influence Czechoslovakia, and the desire of Czech nobility and upper bourgeoisie to have an armorial tradition to rival that of southern Europe produced many intricate coats of arms and armorial deeds for cities, especially in Bratislava. There, for example, the Cistercians were especially active in book production in the fifteenth century.

There is evidence that many important Bohemian painters like the Dietrichstein and Orosius Masters and the Master of the Trebon Altar had some French training, either in Paris or Avignon. Moreover, Wenceslaus IV consciously attempted to imitate at his own court the circle of scribes and painters who were supported by Charles V in France until his death in 1380. Naturally, when these painters returned home, especially to Prague, they came with recollections of the latest fashions of French art, particularly the work of the Boucicaut Master and the Limbourg brothers.

Bohemian painting drew as well, though somewhat less heavily, on Italian models, often brought by Italian merchants to the court. For example, the astronomical miniatures in roundels in manuscripts commissioned by Wenceslaus IV seem to have been derived from models from the workshop of Giovannino de Grassi. Many motifs we associate with northern Italian painting—softly flowing areas of foliage that drape as limply as cloth in borders, and thin, spaghetti-like rods with ball- or beadlike knobs and wrapped round with acanthus leaves in contrasting colors—are characteristic of Bohemian style. Hungarian painting, especially, shows the influence of Italian manuscripts, as many Hungarians studying law at Bologna brought back illuminated legal texts and Bolognese book artisans also came to Hungary. So too the Anjou king Charles I (1308–1342) and his circle commissioned Italian manuscripts and employed Italian artists. Padua Cathedral Capitular Library MS Cod.A.24, illuminated by Pseudo-Nicolo da Bologna, for example, shows scenes depicting Saint Stephen, king of Hungary. This painter also illuminated the Nekesei Bible now in the Library of Congress, Washington, D.C. During the reign of Sigismund (1387–1437), Holy Roman Emperor and brother of Wenceslaus, king of Bohemia, many Hungarians studied in Germany, and German artists started to come to Hungary as well. Hungarian scholars believe Sigismund was apparently the patron of the important illuminator "Martinus opifex," though this painter has also been claimed by the Austrians. In Budapest a new fashion of highly illuminated books containing letters patent authorizing coats of arms for individuals and cities flourished under Sigismund.[8]

Let us look for a moment at a book that was painted in Hungary in the year of Richard II's accession to the English throne in 1377. It is the Alba Julia missal MS R. II. 134.[9] in the Batthyaneum, Alba Julia, Rumania, made by a parish priest, Henry Stephen of Westfalia, working in a small town (now Malé Trnie) for a wealthy canon of Bratislava. Henry seems to say that he not only wrote and illuminated the book but also bound it (fig. 1). An example of the new interest in heraldry is the historiated initial of the Annunciation, whose bar bordering is overlaid with a loosely woven pattern of net-like interlace monochrome vine, supporting several armorial bearings in vine loops. This interlace pattern continues through the border in the form of a single vine with occasional lozenge-shaped medallions incorporated, containing various interlace motifs such as pentangles and strapwork interlace infill. At the right side of the border is a diamond-shaped medallion containing four lobes in *terre-verte* with a large *folium*-colored rectangle in the middle. *Folium*, green, and rose predominate in the arabesque sweeps of leafwork, and at the top of the page is a large daisy—obviously a borrowing from an East Anglian manuscript—with an extravagantly exaggerated carpel, or seed cone. Although we can find English manuscripts resembling the Alba Julia missal, and the individual decorative motifs just discussed can be seen in southern English painting of this period, this distinctive look in such a strong alliance with the color combination of green and purple indisputably shows Bohemian influence, and it is far more common in the north than in the south of England. In this chapter and the next, we will see how all of these motifs and colors become the dominant features of northern English book decoration.

1. Interlace and tendril border. Alba Julia Missal, Rumania, Alba Julia Batthyaneum Library MS R. II, 134, folio 11r, 1377. *Courtesy Alba Julia Batthyaneum.*

Late fourteenth- and early fifteenth-century Bohemian painting relied heavily on green pigments of three distinct compositions. *Terre-verte* was produced by crushing the minerals celadonite and glauco-nite. Quite an ancient color, it was mentioned as early as Vitruvius, who called it "green of Crete." Though considered a rather pale and neutral natural pigment, suitable chiefly for the underpainting of faces, it was used extensively by the Bohemian Master of the Die-

trichstein or Gerona Martyrology for the monochrome pictures of
the British Library *Mandeville's Travels* MS Additional 24189.[10] The
second form was *verdigris*, or "green of Greece," which was copper
acetate, made by burying copper sheets in pots of wine must and
letting them "cook" slowly in fermenting animal dung. Owing, perhaps, to the convenient presence of the wine industry, the major
source for *verdigris* seems to have been Montpellier. Unstable and
often corrosive, *verdigris* was very popular in the early Middle Ages
but declined thereafter in use because it was not chemically compati-
ble with *orpiment*, or gold pigment, or with white lead.[11] It was replaced largely by various forms of vegetable greens—made from rue,
parsley, columbine, black nightshade, the German and Florentine iris,
and ripe buckthorn or Rhamnus berries. The vegetable greens, called
in England sap-greens, were stored in hermetically sealed bladders in
a syrupy state or sometimes dried in cakes.[12] These greens were used
in both naturalistic and non-naturalistic decorative contexts, such as
costume and geometric borders.

To give a more concrete idea of the importance of green in Bohemian painting, let us consider a canon page from the missal of St.
Veit, dated 1413.[13] Crucifixion scenes were extremely popular in Bohemian and especially Hungarian art in this period,[14] and the example discussed here is quite representative. Placed on a background of
rinceaux, St. John the Evangelist, at the right of the cross, wears a
completely green robe, and the miniature is surrounded by a plain
striped green border, echoing the robe of Saint John. This type of
simple *terre-verte* border, with a contrasting stripe of darker color
within, as here, is very characteristic of Bohemian painting of the
same period; it also appears in the frames for Crucifixions in an
Hungarian missal as early as 1340 and in the city register of Kremnica, Czechoslovakia, as late as 1410.[15] From the four corners of the
St. Veit border spring arching acanthus tendrils in green, mauve, and
violet, which support and enclose at the bottom of the miniature
a large roundel of the Man of Sorrows done completely in *folium*
monochrome. The figures within the miniature, moreover, stand on
a *folium* ground. To combine these greens with the plum tones derived from *folium* as does the St. Veit decorator is characteristic of
Bohemian painting in general.

Now let us compare these images with three Crucifixion miniatures from the Green Canon-Page group of manuscripts of approxi-
mately the same date. Not only do the manuscripts contain kalendars
of York use, but the commemoration in each of the Feast of the

2. Canon page Crucifixion and interlace border. London, British Library MS Additional 43380, missal, folios 116v–117, S. XV[1]. *Courtesy Trustees of the British Library.*

Relics of York cathedral on 19 October makes it likely that these manuscripts were produced in the city of York for cathedral use.[16]

Belonging to this group of manuscripts by its relatively limited use of green is British Library MS Additional 43380, a missal originally found in a chest in the chapel of the Castle Dairy, Kendal. The book belonged to the Garnett family and contains their *obits*.[17] Heavily ornamented with full, three-quarter, and center gutter style borders, it contains numerous seven-to-ten-line *champ* initials[18] with green sprays (fig. 2).

In the canon page miniature, the figures stand on a greensward against a gold-washed ground. Groups of five red or white dots on the green represent flowers. The borders, which contain alternating rose and blue bars with gold corner pieces, put out green tendrils. This extremely common type of border, which Kathleen Scott calls the "everyman's design," is not as significant a division in the manuscript as the full border on the facing page, with an elaborate interlace medallion at bottom center;[19] we shall return to this particular motif in the next chapter.

3. Canon page Crucifixion with acanthus and rod wrap frame. San Marino, California, Huntington Library MS HM 1067, missal, folio 142v, S. XIV⁴. *Courtesy Huntington Library.*

Huntington Library MS 1067 (fig. 3) is another missal somewhat more luxurious in execution.[20] Besides the miniature considered here, there are five-to-seven-line historiated initials in full borders as well as two-to-five-line *champ* initials. The kalendar's strong interest in Cuthbert suggests ties with Durham, though one somewhat unusual feast is that of Gilbert of Sempringham, a Lincolnshire saint, on 4 February.[21]

The canon page miniature exhibits not only the green ground

but a green lining for St. John's robe. The simple highlighted rose and blue bars of London, British Library MS Additional 43380 become highlighted blue and white ones alternating with rose-colored acanthus leaf border-bar infills, where the blue acanthus leaf wraps around a vertical red rod, a feature to be discussed in the next chapter. The gold corner pieces of the Huntington manuscript are floriated, and green tendrils with gold come out from the borders into the margins. The same faint patterns of red and white floral dots on the green ground also appear. A kneeling "generic" monk,[22] to the viewer's left at the base of the cross, holds a scroll and wears a green garment beneath his black cowl. Angels by Christ's hands and side catch his blood in chalices, very much as they do in the Ebchester prayer roll and in the canon page miniatures of the Litlyngton Missal (London, Westminster Abbey MS 37), painted in 1384, and the Lapworth Missal (now Oxford, Corpus Christi College MS 394), painted in 1398.[23] The figures are all positioned against a diapered ground. The whole look of the drawing and painting is distinctly Bohemian, especially the use of green, though Dutschke speaks only of "softly modelled faces suggesting foreign influence."[24]

A much simplified form of both of these pictures occurs in miniatures in Harvard, Widener Library MS 1,[25] and Oxford, Bodley MS Gough Liturgies 5, both York manuals. In the former manuscript several hands and two different scales of *textura* are employed. With the exception of the miniature on folio 67v, the codex is quite plain, with two-line blue penwork initials flourished with red and three-to-five-line *littera partita* initials to introduce the major divisions of the book, a device characteristic of many modest northern English codices, as we shall see. Among the early owners was John Lawson of Brough Hall, Yorkshire. This manual contains some unusual paschal verses, which help to date it in 1403; these verses I have found only in Yorkshire books.[26]

The canon page miniature offers the same St. John with green robe lining and the same pattern of red floral dots in the ground (fig. 4). This motif, however, has been elaborated to serve the function of the diapering in the more expensive manuscript, for patterns of seven red dots are arrayed in groups behind the figures. The miniature is borderless and shows considerably greater economy than the other two pictures depicting the same subject. Even more simplified is the modest illumination in Gough Liturgies 5, a similar rubricated manual,[27] whose kalendar places it in southeast Yorkshire, most particularly Beverley. Close in style and size to the Widener manuscript, its

4. Canon page Crucifixion. Cambridge, Massachusetts, Harvard University Library MS Widener 1, manual, folio 67v, 1403. *Courtesy the Harry Elkins Widener Collection, The Houghton Library, Harvard University.*

decoration consists of two *litterae partitae* initials and some blue and red penwork capitals. The work's single, rather crude, Crucifixion painting at folio 15 is not otherwise distinctive except for the plain green band border around it.

All four of these northern miniatures show English illustrators' responses—though in widely varying ways—to the palette and some of the decorative features of Bohemian painting. It is likely that when the painters wished to produce their own missals or devotional books, they turned to contemporary Bohemian models, either through direct recollection, because in some cases they may have been Bohemian by training, or as is more probable, because of the presence of such books in the north.

Though these Green-Canon-Page manuscripts fall naturally together as a group because of their treatment of the Crucifixion and the prominence of the color green, a considerable number of less easily classified but still definitely northern devotional and scientific manuscripts of the late fourteenth and early fifteenth centuries show the same taste for green. Their association with York can cast light on the three books we have just discussed.

Several of these books combine private devotion and science in an unusual way. A very handsome *horae* with the astronomical kalendar of Richard de Thorpe of the Austin Convent in York,[28] now in the Pincus Collection, Beverly Hills, California, was made, I believe, at the Austin house; it too shows a marked preference for greens, even to the green ink used in the kalendar and eclipse tables. A gigantic zodiac man (fig. 5) is apparently modeled on the figure of St. Christopher, traditionally seventeen feet, eight inches tall, who in wall paintings and manuscript illumination stands in water.[29] Placed against the same sort of background patterned with *rinceaux* that we saw in the St. Veit missal, he is framed by a wide striped Bohemian-style border in two shades of green. The very fact that such *horae* were often the owner or commissioner's only book made them naturally inclusive works, often with a marked scientific and prognostic component.[30]

A zodiac man from a girdle book,[31] now MS Crouch 4, in the Ballerat Fine Art Gallery, Victoria, Australia, stands against a circular two-tone green ground, perhaps done with *terre-verte*.[32] The actual figure is placed on a darker vertical stripe of sap-green. The kalendar has a Northumberland and Benedictine emphasis: there are feasts in blue for Benedict, Chad, David, Oswin, Cuthbert; in black for the translation of Benedict and for Bede, Boisil (Cuthbert's teacher, whose body was later translated to Durham), and Hilda, all saints found in northern kalendars. The presence in the kalendar of the feast of St. Anne would place the manuscript after 1383, when the feast was established to honor Anne of Bohemia; those of David and Chad were official by 1415/16.[33] Three-line gold-on-blue *champ* initials with green sprays terminating in gold-leaf blobs in the canon and kalendar fascicules indicate regional work in the idiosyncratic

5. Zodiac man. Beverley Hills, California, Collection Dr. I. J. Pincus, kalendar of Richard de Thorpe, folio 31, ca. 1385. *Courtesy Dr. I. J. Pincus.*

proportions of the sprays. A phlebotomy miniature in the book places the "vein man" against a circular two-tone purple ground, done with *folium,* in the same vertical stripe format. In both miniatures the text occurs around the figures in roundels in the style, though much debased, of the *Très Riches Heures.*

A devotional book, the *horae* mentioned in chapter 1, commissioned and owned by a York mercer, John Bolton, and apparently written and illuminated in the city of York about 1420, also contains a considerable amount of green. Its decoration reveals that even much cruder and more popular artists showed the taste we have been discussing and may have had access to the same models, for an historiated initial of the Crowning with Thorns on folio 54v presents Christ in a very unusual green robe.[34] Besides the Feast of the Relics of the Cathedral, there are illustrated suffrages for Archbishop Richard Scrope and John of Beverley. Forty-seven full-page miniatures and six smaller miniatures in historiated six-line initials form part of full borders for the suffrages; this type of organization at the beginning of the book has been recently discussed by Kathleen Scott.[35] Capitals are done in gold, with violet ink flourishing, and gold and violet Lombardic letters alternate in the litany. There is also a suffrage for St. Bridget, who was popular in Carthusian houses like Mount Grace.[36] Well written by a scribe named John who signs his name at folio 122, the book is known as the Bolton *horae*. In 1417, John Bolton was chamberlain of York, and sheriff in 1419 and again in 1420. He was a member of Parliament in 1427 and 1428 and became mayor of York in 1431, dying in 1445.[37]

Just as green seems to dominate the work of these Green Canon-Page artists, so purple characterizes two of the three Archaizing manuscripts, and its use is widespread among northern codices that do not share other decorative details in common; ten such books survive. Unlike green, however, which was sometimes an inorganic and sometimes an organic pigment, the purple in question, called *folium* or sometimes *tournesole*,[38] is a carbon compound extracted from the juice of a plant and absorbed in cloths, dried, and stored till needed. Many scholars, following the medieval recipes for making *folium*, claim that it is red in its natural state, turning purple or blue violet after treatment with alkali, but even this chemical change is not completely agreed upon.[39] It is made from a plant which went by many names in the Middle Ages: *tournesol-en-drapeau*,[40] *tournesol de Provence, heliotropium minus tricoccum, maurelle*, and *verrucaria*[41] are only a few. The plant has been grouped with the lichen family as well. This confusion is so ubiquitous that as one scholar, Arie Wallert, who has worked with the pigment extensively, points out, "the name *tournesole* became a synonym for any clothlet color . . . [and] indicated a certain technique of extraction and preservation."[42]

Folium, then, though itself a word of very uncertain meaning, is probably the most precise and neutral of the various names for the plant pigment obtained from the juice of the seed capsules of *Chrozophora tinctoria, Juss.*, a plant of the Mediterranean littoral and a member of the family *Euphorbiaciae*, order *tricoccum*, first scientifically named in 1824 by the great French botanist Adrien de Jussieu. Information on this pigment, the plant it comes from and the process by which it was made is often incorrect or contradictory and widely dispersed; even pictures of the plant are difficult to obtain.[43] It is a

6. Seed capsule and leaves, *Chrozophora tinctoria*. Author's garden.

greyish green annual plant, with flowers about two inches in diameter, whose distinctive hairy-looking fruits contain three balls about the size of peppercorns in a trilobed capsule, whence its taxonomic name (fig. 6). It flowers from June to October. As the chemical characteristics of this pigment and the various medieval recipes by which it was manufactured are rather technical, I have confined my discussion of these matters to Appendix A.

As I suggested earlier, it is likely that northern English uses of this pigment were influenced either directly or indirectly by its appearance as a color in the miniatures and the border decoration of Bohemian manuscripts. Probably the most sophisticated medieval mixing of the tonalities afforded by this pigment was that of Bohemian painters in such books as the Boskowitzer Bible (Olomouc State Research Library MS Sign.III-3), probably painted between 1415 and 1420, whose title page, with the story of the days of the Creation in seven roundels, shows a partiality for green and violet pairings. This book takes its name from the arms of Magdalena, wife of Ladislaus Welen of Boskowitz, added at the end of the century. It shows the hand of the Master of the Dietrichstein Martyrology, who also did such books as the *Mandeville's Travels* now British Library MS Additional 24189, and whose work is widely regarded as the high point of Bohemian International Gothic style; thus his color choices in the Boskowitzer volume can be taken as representative.[44] Important not only for its paintings, this Bible also contains Jan Huss's exposition of the Decalogue. The colors in the terminals of the arabesque acanthus borderwork—whose sweeping curves tying together circular medallions are one of the dominant features of Bohemian draftsmanship in the late fourteenth and early fifteenth centuries—where various combinations of pink and rose shade into mauve and purple, presumably illustrate the admixture of white lead to the *folium* and *clarea*, or egg white binder, in the artist's paint pot to change the tonalities. These color pairings in the border foliage seem peculiarly Bohemian, as opposed to the blues, grays, and blacks in the Creation scenes, which seem to be influenced by the Italian Michelino.[45]

Even more striking is the color scheme within the miniature showing the death of Jezabel in the Bible of King Wenceslaus, 1390–1400 (Vienna, Austrian National Library MS Cod. 2759–2764), where both the ground of the picture and its frame were done in *folium* but the foliage and Jezabel's robe in green. As Josef Krása remarks of Bohemian style "indeed, we can observe a great fondness for green in this era," where whole manuscripts were painted in terreverte monochrome.[46]

Though *folium* does not occur as a major decorative feature in books known to be from Yorkshire besides the Archaizing manuscripts to be discussed in detail below, we do find it as a wash in the Crouch girdlebook mentioned earlier, and in initials and borders in several late fourteenth- and early fifteenth-century codices. These uses are relatively occasional and do not dominate the palette or seem especially integrated with the overall program of decoration.

A typically casual use of the pigment appears in a fourteenth-century breviary, New York, Grolier Club MS 3. The graded kalendar contains the Feasts of the Relics of York Cathedral, John of Beverley, Everildis, and "saint" Thomas of Hereford, who is not uncommon in northern kalendars.[47] The translation of Cuthbert is noted in red, indicating a Durham connection as well. At folio 243v appears a three-quarter border with six-line initials, some of which appear to contain *folium*, though the page is somewhat rubbed and darkened.

In this book the pigment appears to have been merely one among a number of more traditional colors employed by the painter.

A book using *folium* for major initials and borders is Sion College, London, MS Arc.L.40.2 /L.1, a fifteenth-century rubricated choir breviary of York use, coming from Skelton, near York.[48] Several of its initials have large areas of *folium* in a well-preserved state. Similar initials appear in a kalendar almanach now MS 1003/29 in the Rosenbach Library in Philadelphia.[49] Though the graded kalendar of this little known girdlebook has an odd southern and southwestern admixture of saints such as Botolph, Cuthberga, David, Chad, and Alphegius, the major York feasts for William, Wilfrid, and John of Beverley appear in red, and like the Crouch kalendar, which it strongly resembles in format, it may have had Benedictine connections, as both the feast and translation of Benedict are commemorated. The date must be after 1380, because the kalendar of John Somer[50] was employed by the maker. A number of the book's initials contain *folium*, though the violet has gone a bit mauve through age and use.

Books with more studied uses of *folium*, sometimes in conjunction with green, are York Minster Library MS Additional 69, a rubricated choir breviary, and MS XVI.K.6, the Pullein *horae*, dating from between 1405 and 1413. The former volume's graded kalendar with the Feast for the Relics of the Cathedral shows it to be of fairly late date; it was likely written after 1489, when the feasts of the Holy Name of Jesus and of the Transfiguration were promulgated in the diocese.[51] The decorative top and bottom borders employ *folium*.

MS XVI.K.6 is a finely made and elaborate parchment book with a program of six- to seven-line historiated initials. The book contains in its kalendar besides a Feast for the Relics of the Cathedral the *obit*s of the Pullein family of Pontefract and at folio 27 a suffrage to archbishop Richard Scrope, dealing in part with the five wounds he supposedly asked the executioner to give him in honor of Christ's five wounds.[52] At folio 83v, an initial showing Christ sitting on the tomb and blessing uses a large area of *folium* both plain and highlighted, for the tomb. Less well painted and dramatic, but similar in its treatment of a *folium*-colored tomb-chest, is a scene of the Man of Sorrows on folio 2 in the Lacy *horae* discussed in the previous chapter.

London, British Library MS Sloane 962 is a medical, herbal, and prognostic collection of the late fourteenth or early fifteenth century. Though this book contains no evidence of a northern connection, Linda Voigts has remarked on northern forms in its Middle English recipes,[53] and the manuscript will be more fully studied in the "Catalogue of Incipits of Scientific and Medical Writings in Old and Middle English" being prepared by Voigts and Patricia Deery Kurz. Regional in execution and inexpensive, the decoration employs inks in place of paints as much as possible. The major initial on folio 12, however, contains a *folium*-colored ground, and green ink appears prominently. Interestingly, a recipe in this manuscript on folio 141v describes how to make *folium,* called *tournesol.* If these elements are indeed features of northern taste, they may help to tie MS Sloane 962 to the north.

An especially attractive use of *folium* in decoration occurs in a more unusual book than those we have so far mentioned; it is London, British Library MS Stowe 39, the *Abbey of the Holy Ghost,* supposedly composed by John Alcock, (1430–1500) a Yorkshire contemporary of Archbishop Thomas Rotherham and supervisor of his will.[54] This work is primarily a picture book, and as it belongs to the group of illustrated devotional miscellanies to be discussed in chapter 5, we need only say here that a number of the full-page miniatures have *folium* borders and many figures wear *folium*-colored robes with green linings.

The miscellaneous group of northern manuscripts just considered employed *folium* in traditional ways as just one color among others in the palette, and there were no other features except those of geographical provenance linking the books as a group. These decorators could not be said to comprise a workshop, but merely to reveal a preference for a rather unusual color. Two manuscript painters, however, used *folium* as a major element of their decoration, where it predominates over the colors more usual in English painting of this period. And they used it so self-consciously, in conjunction with archaizing visual motifs, as to suggest that their books were made in the same location at the same time and, in the case of two of the books, painted by the same artist.

The first of these books is an unusual manuscript of John of Tynemouth's *Historia Aurea,* now Cambridge University Library MS Dd.10.22. As it does not have an obvious northern provenance, I discuss it first and at some length to set it in relation to two books connected to it stylistically and yet clearly coming from northern England. It is a five-book abridgment of the second half of the *Historia Aurea,* and it was at one time in a Cistercian house. Because John of Tynemouth and his book are little known, even to specialists in northern history, it may be helpful to present briefly the few available facts and inferences about the work and its author. This rather shadowy writer's vast and still unedited twenty-three book chronicle of world and of English history exists in eight manuscripts. Both its title and that of a companion work on English saints, *Nova Legenda*, seem adapted from the *Aurea Legenda* of Jacob of Voragine.

It is usually said that John was born about 1290, ordained at Durham, and served as vicar of Tynemouth from about 1315 to about 1325, whereupon he became an historiographer at Tynemouth's mother house of St. Albans. As his chronicle breaks off abruptly in a record of the siege of Calais in June of 1347, he may have died of the plague not long after. These dates and facts are open to interpretation. Contemporaries of the author call him sometimes John of England, John of the diocese of York, and John of York as well as John of Tynemouth. Boston of Bury even claims that John was active as late as 1366. But no mention of John occurs in the records of St. Albans, and a full text of the *Historia Aurea* was not known there until after 1420.[55]

That he was associated with the northeast, however, seems very likely, because the *Historia Aurea* was continued in the Brompton chronicles at Jervaulx and in the Hemingburgh chronicle at Guisborough. The fact, moreover, that the author's only original contributions concern events in the North and East Ridings suggests that these areas were the ones whose history he knew directly. We can conclude from an elaborately alphabetized portion of the *Nova Legenda Angliae* containing 154 saints' lives, forming folios 109-192v in York Minster Library MS XVI. G. 23, that at least one of John's two known works was of considerable interest to northerners as late as the mid-fifteenth century. The book bears a fifteenth-century subscription, "iste liber pertinet ad vestibulum Eborum."[56] So too, it is significant in this regard that one of the three chief manuscripts of the work, Lambeth Palace MS 10,11,12, came from Durham. This fourteenth-century codex bears a Durham pressmark and was by 1395 in the library there, as it is mentioned in the catalogue of that date. And it is to the third part of the Durham manuscript that MS Dd.10.22 is most closely akin in text.[57]

For all this, however, the most that can be said with certainty is that John of Tynemouth was active in the first half of the fourteenth century, that he was most probably from Northumberland, that he may have been a vicar of Tynemouth, and that in those windswept and stormy regions[58] he compiled large-scale works celebrating English secular and religious figures.

Though there is no specific codicological evidence connecting MS Dd.10.22 with the north, the codex seems likely to have originated there for two reasons: first, its extensive use of *folium* and certain features of its decoration relatively common in a number of books that originated in or around York, and second, the name William Roke faintly visible at the top of the first folio. A York merchant of that name died in 1427; unfortunately he mentioned no books in his will. A Robert Roke was also a monk of Durham about 1487–1512; his name appears in Durham Cathedral MS A.IV.29, and a Thomas Roke was a Dominican or possibly an Austin friar of the York convent in 1450.[59]

Because a date in the 1380s for this manuscript is important to my argument that the decoration is self-consciously archaic, our discussion should begin with the book's script and with some virtually identical handwriting of the same period that comes immediately after an account of a truce between the English and the French, 19 January 1342, making up the last chapter of the John of Tynemouth abridgment. The scribe of MS Dd.10.22 exhibits most of the features of *Anglicana formata* script that we might expect to find in manuscripts made between 1380 and 1410. He did not write a distinctive hand but a fairly careful and regular one. On the whole, the quality of the writing seems technically superior to that of the illustration. The initial page for book 5 (fig. 7) exhibits representative features of the script common in the late fourteenth century, such as sigmoid *s* in both initial and final position, with long *s* in the middle position, and quite long and tapered descenders of *s* and *f*.[60]

The second piece of evidence for a date in the last quarter of the fourteenth century is an additional passage copied onto the last folio immediately beneath the concluding lines of the text. Though this last page is much blurred by water damage, its content is still fairly readable. The script of the addition is much darker than the rest of the preceding text, indicating that it was written with a different batch of ink, though the hand is still the same type as that of the book itself. The format of this addition, however, differs from the rest of the manuscript, and the paragraph is not introduced by the red-flashed capitals used elsewhere.

This addition is a very interesting one, consisting of a lengthy salutation formula from an important document relating to the Great Schism. It is the opening of an encyclical letter written in the summer of 1378 by Jean du Cros, cardinal bishop of Palestrina and twelve other Frenchmen, themselves newly created cardinals by Gregory XI

7. Initial on diapered ground with polymorphs. Cambridge University Library MS Dd. 10. 22, John of Tynemouth, *Historia Aurea*, Book 5, folio 120, ca. 1380–90. *Courtesy Syndics of Cambridge University.*

just before his death in 1378. The letter violently contests the election of an Italian as Pope Urban VI. The French cardinals later that year elected Robert, bishop of Geneva, as Clement VII at Formi, who was thenceforth known as the antipope. During this period of extreme agitation by the French faction, from about May of 1378 until the election of Clement on September 20, they produced hundreds of letters attesting to the uncanonical nature of the Italian Urban's election, which they circulated to European rulers and heads of ecclesiastical bodies, warning them not to recognize Urban's authority.

This particular letter may be dated by the last line of a much blurred text which precedes it, indicating that it was written on the day of the feast of St. Benedict, 11 July 1378. Such a date agrees with the following list of schismatic cardinals in which the anti-pope Robert's name still appears. Thus the text antedates his election on 30 September.[61] For our purposes, an equally important part of the salutation formula is the closing sentence directing the letter which followed the salutation to "beloved Cistercian abbots and other abbots and all other persons of the Cistercian order."

Most likely, this formula was copied when it formed part of a contemporary document of controversy; it suggests a connection of the manuscript with a Cistercian house, of which there were twenty in northern England.[62] Thus, while this passage by no means provides a *terminus post* or *ante quem* or even identifies a particular Cistercian house, it is still useful as an indicator. Although it is true that the formula could have been written at the end of a much older book, the similarity of scripts does not suggest that this was the case, but rather that the book and formula are contemporary. Moreover, the presence of the formula points to a somewhat antiquarian cast of mind on the part of the copyist and to his connection with a Cistercian house with a sufficiently large and well organized library to contain this letter of warning about Urban VI.

That the *Historia Aurea* would have been of interest to a northern atelier and patron and also easily available for copying seems obvious. The fact, moreover, that the Cambridge volume is a plainly written abridgment of the twenty-three-book original, with initials and borders only on the opening pages of each of its five books, suggests that it was made for a patron of relatively modest means. Furthermore, this owner, or patron (if it were he who chose the format and decoration) had unconventional attitudes towards his book, since he deviated radically from what was both the standard size and pattern of decoration for this work. That the book was probably not made for monastic but rather for lay use, though it may have been among the Cistercians for a time, is suggested also by this deviation from the style apparently considered appropriate for monastic copies.

Let me illustrate this point. This is the only abridgment of the *Historia Aurea* known besides the very brief fourteenth-century summaries in British Library MSS Cotton Roll XIII.2 and Royal 13.E.ix, and indeed the only small or portable copy of the book. The three extant codices, Lambeth Palace MS 10,11,12, from Durham priory; Oxford MS Bodley 240, from Bury St. Edmunds;[63] and Cambridge, Corpus Christi College MSS 5 and 6 from St. Albans,[64] are all quite tall and similar in proportion, telling us something about contemporary expectations for large-scale historical works meant to be consulted on the reading stands of monastic libraries. The largest of the twenty-book versions measures 450 × 328 mm, the smallest 340 × 230 mm. In contrast, the abridgment is a much smaller book, measuring 222 × 150 mm.

Decorators responded to the text of the *Historia Aurea,* and the problems posed by its length, in several ways. One branch of the manuscript family, the Lambeth Palace volumes, contains representational miniatures of various historical figures—Moses, Alexander the Great, and Nero, among others—who in the style of the late antique author portraits, symbolize their particular historical epochs and introduce the books concerning the events of their reigns. Only one manuscript of this type is known.

The remaining manuscripts conform to the more common pattern for large-scale works on English history; they contain elaborate penwork initials for the successive books but no programs of illustration. Such initials reflect a decorative style considered appropriate to the chronicle form—not generally deluxe copies, but more for use than for display. With the illustrated exception just mentioned, available funds were spent on a legible text, durable writing materials, and the penwork initials, which begin the book and mark its major divisions in the other manuscripts, which range in date from 1377 to 1420. It was, then, treated by artists much as were other large-format chronicles and miscellanies containing English historical material, such as the chronicle of Rochester (now British Library MS Cotton Nero D.11).[65]

The abridgment's ornamentation differs radically from the two types of decorated full-length *Historia Aurea* manuscripts mentioned earlier. This decoration, moreover, is of a style considerably earlier than the script of the text it ornaments and, for that matter, of John of Tynemouth himself. Each of the five books of the abridgment has a major initial. These introduce the "Genealogy of the Saxon Kings," "From the nativity of Christ to the death of St. Ulstan," "On the Conquest of the Holy Land," "On King Richard," and "On King Edward." The decoration for the first pages of each of these book divisions contains several distinct historical and national components. The *mise-en-page* is contemporary with the script, showing the late fourteenth- and early fifteenth-century fashion for highly analytical lists of chapters and alternating red and blue Lombardic letters or paraph marks, as well as for rubricated *incipits* and *explicits* and other aids to reference. Such chapter lists and analytic internal divisions point to the developing interest in the book as a reference tool so ably presented by Richard and Mary Rouse, among others.[66] They allowed owners to search books quickly for material to use in sermons, literary works, and the like.

The diapered or crosshatched grounds in these five major initials, with variations in which the larger pattern is related to a similar design in a grotesque body, or where the whole ground is divided equally between colors, begin to appear in England in the early fourteenth century. An example occurs in the Tickhill Psalter from Worksop, Nottingham, in York diocese[67] (now New York Public Library MS Spencer 26), made between 1303 and 1314. Though such multipatterned diaperings become increasingly common and elaborate by the mid-century, they are, nonetheless, not very common in English manuscripts of the late fourteenth century. Their use here seems archaizing, as does the foliate border work and *rinceaux* or vine pattern with interlace and self-devouring dragon forms and trefoils.

Archaizing as well are the abridgment decorator's ropy bar borders with trefoils growing from the tails of grotesques and the interlaces of self-devouring dragons, which inhabit several of the initials. And equally old-fashioned are the anecdotal use of human-headed grotesques and parodic combats of animals and half-human forms.

That this artist was acquainted with the early fourteenth-century forms of diapering and grotesques is evident from the striking resemblance of his pages to some in Christ Church College, Oxford MS 92, *De Nobilitatibus, sapientiis et prudentiis regum,* written by Walter de Milemete, King's Clerk and Fellow of King's Hall, Cambridge, in 1327 for Edward III at his accession. In its exuberant and anecdotal use of grotesques in the borders, this book has ties with the East Anglian school of illumination. Lucy Sandler believes that the major artist of the work had four assistants; their hands appear in a number of other manuscripts.[68]

Some evidence that the "Milemete" style was not unknown in the north perhaps a generation after its period of greatest fashionability in the southeast is suggested by Cambridge, Sidney Sussex College MS 62, a mid-fourteenth-century Augustinian diurnale of York use, possibly from Kirkham Abbey. The book's geometrical borders contain at folio 7 a polymorph whose style is very much like those we

8. Women-headed polymorph on diapered ground. Oxford, Christ Church College MS 92, Walter de Milemete, *De Nobilitatibus, sapientiis et prudentiis regum,* folio 62v, 1327. *Courtesy Governing Body, Christ Church, Oxford.*

have just been talking about, as well as anecdotal animals elsewhere in the foliage within the border bars.[69]

The diapering typical of the Milemete style, in Oxford, Christ Church College MS 92, where the color pattern splits on the inhabiting figure, is very similar to that of the Cambridge abridgment's initial for book 4 (figs. 8 and 9). And the *babewyn*, or polymorphic

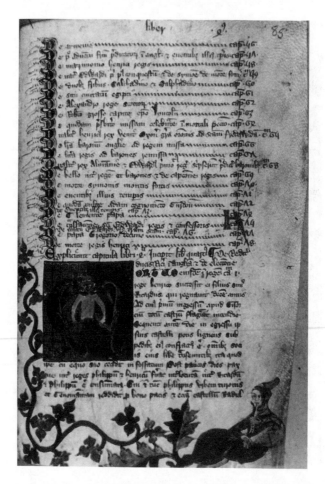

9. Initial on diapered ground with polymorphs. Cambridge University Library MS Dd. 10.22, Book 4, folio 85. *Courtesy Syndics of Cambridge University.*

grotesque, in the upper register in Milemete is very like that in the right border of the initial page of book 5 (fig. 7), but the later painter uses the more pear-shaped French Gothic facial structure with bulging, or *bombé*, forehead and wimple. Moreover, the wing treatment of the Milemete dragon at the top of the page appears to have been copied directly by the *Historia Aurea* artist when he drew his woman with headress, even to the matching number of pinions.

As can easily be seen, the abridgment painter prefers to branching foliage a more linear, ropy type of encircling border terminating in or growing from a grotesque generally human faced. This technique is very close to that of certain other East Anglian or East Anglian influenced manuscripts, such as the well-known Luttrell Psalter (British Library MS Additional MS 42130), painted ca. 1325.[70] In discussing an East Anglian *horae* in the Norwich Castle Museum, MS 158.926, Lucy Sandler has characterized this type of border as having "dynamic chains formed of numerous figural elements and only a few foliate motifs. The figures . . . are silhouetted against the parchment margin without the usual coloured background panel."[71]

In both his choice of backgrounds and in his free-standing marginal decoration, the abridgment artist seems to have been conversant with major English decoration of the first quarter of the fourteenth century. His two-color trefoils at the ends of his vines, for example, have ties with the St. Omer Psalter (now British Library MS Additional 39810), painted in East Anglia about 1333–1340,[72] while his two-color oak leaves remind us of those in the Vienna Bohun Psalter (Austrian National Library MS Cod. 1826).[73] In short, the Cambridge artist has employed a variety of "quotations" from the Milemete and Fenland workshops in his five initial pages.

Interlace patterns and dragon forms, for which the abridgment artist has a fondness, go back to the late Anglo-Saxon period. Such dragons appear in an initial of a dog-headed man with grapevines in a canon law text from Christ Church, Canterbury, made about 1120–1130 (British Library MS Cotton Claudius E.v),[74] and in the Winchester Bible.[75] *Rinceaux* like those in Cambridge University Library MS Dd.10.22, which spiral into dragon bodies either retaining the diameter of the vine or broadening into the bodies, can be found in the Winchester Bible. Later, these dragon forms, either freestanding in the margins or tenuously connected to the body of the initial, appear in the bar borders characteristic of manuscript illustration done in the first half of the thirteenth century, and often associated with the Oxford workshop directed by William de Brailes. In this style, squarish extensions of the initial grounds put out dragons with long tails that extend into the margins beyond the outmost rulings,[76] as is the case with the abridgment painter's work. Later forms of dragons in bar borders leading into initials appear, for example, in the Madresfield Hours of York use, made about 1329–1330, and the Peterborough Psalter (Brussels, Bibliothèque Royale MS 9961-62), made slightly before 1318.[77]

By the end of the fourteenth century, marginal dragons had fallen out of fashion in England, to be replaced by the architecturally realistic oratories, roundels with portrait busts, and naturalistically rendered birds and foliage so characteristic of the English phase of the International Gothic Style and so well exemplified in the work of the English painter John Siferwas and the artists of the Carmelite Missal.[78] Thus the rather anecdotal dragon, draconopede, lion, or half-clad griffon shapes that populate the margins and serve as infills in the initials of Cambridge University Library MS Dd.10.22 are quotations from or recollections of manuscripts made as much as three generations earlier. Their presence in a book of the Ricardian period allows us to think of the painter who produced it as self-consciously archaizing.

So far we have examined one highly idiosyncratic manuscript, which can be linked to northern England chiefly by an *ex libris* inscription and by the book's content. It could be a unique production. But two more manuscripts with more secure northern ties also share some of the features we have seen in MS Dd.10.22. These are missals of the later fourteenth or early fifteenth century, now Boston Public Library MS 1576, and Dublin, Trinity College MS 83. These two books appear to be related to each other because of certain other features of the decoration, such as an unusual use of gold leaf. The Boston volume, moreover, seems tied to MS Dd.10.22 because of the particular way both books use grotesques and other archaizing features of decoration. Thus in considering these three manuscripts, we can speak generally of an Archaizing style, though different artists to varying degrees may have had contact with these books, since they do not all have the same features in common.

Something of the Boston volume's early history can be inferred from its kalendar and contents. The kalendar commemorates Wilfrid, John of Beverley, and Augustine, perhaps showing a tie to Augustinian canons, and within the body of the text there are offices for Everildis and William of York. As we saw in chapter 1, St. Anne's feast and an office for a pregnant woman on the flyleaf suggest possible female ownership at some point.[79] The book originally belonged to the Neville and later the Gascoigne families of Yorkshire. Joan Neville, daughter of John, married William Gascoigne, and the *obits* of these families are in the kalendar; the earliest is 1441.

Three features of this book's handsome decoration are worthy of note. First, there is an extensive use of highlighted *folium*, both in the foliate borders and in the grotesques who appear in marginal and *bas-*

de-page contexts throughout the manuscript. Second, a typical form of decoration is a five-line *champ* initial with an extension giving rise to a highlighted *folium* bottom piece at either side of which are grotesques. The *champ* initial is made of gold leaf in unusual proportions, for the field is quite extensive in relation to the colored design it supports. We find in Trinity College, Dublin MS 83 the same technique of placing highlighted rose and blue initials on large areas of gold leaf. The gold that appears in the Boston grotesques, however, takes the form of gold powder rather than leaf. Third, the border decoration of this book employs a number of self-consciously archaizing polymorphic figures in anecdotal ways throughout the margins.[80]

Thus, Boston Public Library MS 1576 and Cambridge University Library MS Dd.10.22 share many similarities, of which the most immediately obvious is a heavy reliance on the pigment *folium*. Yet it seems unlikely that they were painted by the same artist. More likely, two different artists made them, working from the direction of a single designer and drawing on a common stock of imagery or even of cartoon or pouncing pages (sheets with pricked designs through which chalk powder was sifted to transfer outlines).

The Boston decorator achieved quite a bold dramatic effect with a more minimal use of color, primarily blue, white lead, *folium*, and gold. His *rinceaux*, moreover, are not as ropy and are much more foliate and lobate than those we saw in MS Dd.10.22. Though both artists made extensive use of white circles as a way of creating highlights, a technique of the Luttrell Psalter painter, the Boston decorator seems especially fond of ball motifs of various types. For example, the dragon-bodied figure at the bottom of folio 93 wears a ball around its neck, and its tail gives off a series of gilt balls or disks. Its rather elegant human head sports a Richard II icecream-cone-pointed beard and a dragon-shaped hat ending in a face that spits out or eats a gold ball (fig. 10). These balls recall the red and green apples used to tie the free-floating dragons to the left edge of the initial for book 2 of the *Historia Aurea* abridgment. Grotesques at folios 15v and 203 of the Boston book have gold balls under their tails in scatological parodies of the main design. Such calm, realistic human faces on polymorphic bodies seem to echo the practice of the Luttrell Psalter artist.[81]

A rubricated missal, Trinity College, Dublin MS 83, like the Boston manuscript, has a graded kalendar containing the feasts of John of Beverley and William of York as well as services and masses in the text for Yorkshire saints.[82] It also contains *obit*s of a prominent Yorkshire family, the Nortons of Patrick Brompton.

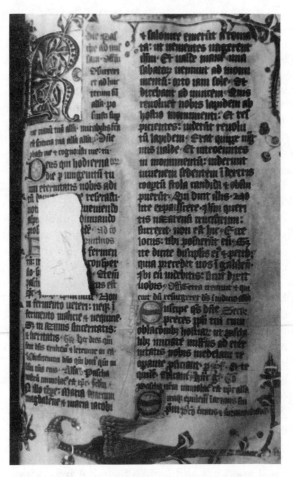

10. Floriated initial and polymorphs. Boston, Massachusetts, Boston Public Library MS 1576, folio 93r, S. XIV⁴. *Courtesy Boston Public Library.*

The book has two major forms of decoration, a miniature and floriated initials. The canon page miniature on folio 97v (fig. 11), which bears some interesting relations to Huntington Library HM 1067, discussed above, appears unfinished, with the figures merely done in ink outlines. This drawing is of high quality in a heavy-lipped Netherlandish style. A tonsured monk kneeling with a scroll is positioned to the right of the cross, on which is Christ with a large wound in his side and nails in his hands. John holds a book. The main

11. Canon page Crucifixion. Dublin, Trinity College MS 83, missal, folio 97v, S. XIV⁴. *Courtesy Trinity College.*

decorative motifs are highlighted blue and rose acanthus leaves in bar borders with gold corner pieces. Coarse diapering in horizontal gold lozenges alternates with highlighted blue and rose in similar shapes. The look of the pictures and the lozenge background is quite similar to Boulogne-sur-Mer Bibliothèque Municipale MS 93, which will be discussed in the next chapter. The full-page miniatures in that manuscript were also unfinished, with only line drawings to be filled in by the painter.

The decorator of the Dublin volume preferred center gutter bor-

ders whose bars, instead of combining rose and blue, are made entirely of gold leaf, echoing the large gold lozenges in the diapering of
the canon page miniature, with very fine ribbons of vine following
the gold and forming jutting kite-shaped leaves with stinger-like tips.
These bars branch from the floriated initial on the page and in some
cases, as at folio 85r, form a pentangle-shaped interlace medallion on
a broad area of gold leaf, which is extremely similar to the extravagant fields of gold leaf supporting paint in the Boston volume.

What conclusions can our examination of the decoration of these
manuscripts offer about the artistic climate that produced them? It
could, of course, be argued that all three books, but especially the
John of Tynemouth abridgment, were the products of artists—in
either the south or the north—who were relatively unskilled and out
of touch with fashionable London or Continental models. Yet the
Archaizing designers clearly did not work in ignorance of contemporary styles of ornamentation. On the contrary, they seem to have
looked to a number of important southern and eastern models; they
simply happen to be models made by eleventh- through early fourteenth-century artists. And what the painters who worked on these
books may have lacked in technical facility, they easily made up for in
their wide acquaintance with Anglo-Saxon, Romanesque, and East
Anglian Gothic decoration.

For example, in the case of Cambridge University Library MS
Dd.10.22, it is not the book's *mise-en-page* that is unusual for the late
fourteenth century, but rather the content of the page. The elaborate
initials for each book—with their descending hierarchy of Lombardic
letters, flourished penwork three-line chapter initials, and red-flashed
capitals—reflects, in a far more economical way, the fondness in thirteenth-century England for one-half or three-quarter page miniatures to emphasize the opening leaves of a book. So too, the blending
of such initials with decorative borders harkens back to late Gothic
registers containing grotesques, scenes of hunting and combat, and
parodic *monde renversé* anecdotes, such as we saw in the Walter de
Milemete treatise but which were more or less obsolete by 1400.

Some generalizations about the Archaizing group do emerge. For
the moment we may characterize these books by their "historicism,"
their attitude towards the past. Often remarked upon in popularizing
treatments of medieval art is the attitude to history shown in sculpture, tapestry, wall painting, and manuscript illustration. That is to
say, the historical past, which for medieval men encompassed the
mythic, the biblical, and the classical ages, as well as their own Euro-

pean or Insular past. We have all smiled at these antique heroes and heroines—Theseus, Priam, Dido, and the like—who appear in the illustrations of medieval romances wearing the armor, the clothing, and the hairstyles of fourteenth-century men and women, and who espouse contemporary values and customs. So too, Absalom, Delilah, and other Old Testament figures in picture Bibles are usually dressed in the height of contemporary fashion, and even the elephant from the adventure of Eleazar in 1 Maccabees is shown in a wall painting at the Church of St. Nicholas, Klerant, covered in fifteenth-century German plate armor except for the lower half of his trunk. Such scenes have led to the widespread view in these books that medieval people were ahistorical, with no clear conception of a past that differed in any way from the present. Perhaps this was so, yet there are many notable exceptions to the claim, among which these Archaizing artisans can be included.

It is precisely the mixture of obsolete styles and motifs that is the most interesting feature of this group, and it may be worth quoting here James D. Farquhar's remark that "decoration is more responsive to changes in taste than many other aspects of book production. Consequently, it can be a more precise indicator of date and local practice than script which, with its strong tradition, is less susceptible to changes in fashion."[83] With regard to the *Historia Aurea* abridgment, it seems likely that the artist was aware of the historical and national qualities of the work's contents and felt that English motifs drawn from various epochs during the development of the nation would aid his readers in understanding the pastness of the past that was being chronicled. Admittedly, there does not seem to have been any attempt to correlate style and particular periods or reigns; rather, the artist used his decoration only as an approximation of English history.

A pronounced archaizing tendency on the part of this decorator suggests that he may have had decidedly nationalistic and political views, or worked at the direction of a patron with them. For he apparently wished to establish a relationship between the historical content of his text and the program of decoration for the opening pages of each of the five books. For him, style had a historical implication and he had an uncharacteristically clear sense of the periodization of style.

In the case of the Boston Public Library missal, the self-consciously archaizing polymorphic figures used anecdotally throughout the margins also borrow motifs from the same pool of imagery. The painter ingeniously combines a native foliate interlace with dragons and the more Continental diapered backgrounds of court painting, blending styles and eras in a charming and highly personal way, in an apparent effort to venerate the English past and to convey the periodicity of its art.

A comparison of the decoration in the Boston missal with the five inhabited initials in the John of Tynemouth abridgment shows some striking similarities in their archaizing and anecdotal elements. And Trinity College, Dublin MS 83, though without grotesques, shows a similarly distinctive use of gold leaf and highlighting in the form of white circles and trefoils for the formal borders. These Archaizing northern books reveal their decorators' wide exposure to various styles of English manuscript painting, their fertile and whimsical imagination, their love of color, and their ability to create rich and memorable tones, especially those using *folium*. It is unlikely that these three manuscripts could have come from two different northern centers of book production, and it seems reasonable to believe that they are the products of the same group of artists.

This group, whatever else it may have had in common, was willing to invest a considerable amount of artistic energy in the acquisition and preparation of *folium*, a material that is inherently unstable and time-consuming to work with. The presence of *folium* in the pages of some of the Archaizing books points to considerable ingenuity and determination on the part of the artists employing it, especially as the material had to be imported to England. But what might be called the pigment's idiosyncrasy makes it particularly useful for identifying a northern taste, as it seems to have been too troublesome to prepare to interest the larger commercial English workshops concerned with the mass production of manuscripts, where the economic motive was more important than the aesthetic one. Quite possibly, *folium*'s chief appeal was to regional artists who were not under quite the same economic constraints as their London colleagues. It apparently had greater virtues for amateur and semiprofessional illuminators who did not have to work in stints widely separated in time and who also needed to produce tones in the painting on the last page to agree with those of the first.

Thus the choice of *folium* was a self-conscious act by the painters of these northern manuscripts. They seem to have been looking for their colors and many of their border motifs in Northumbrian and later Anglo-Saxon painting. This appeal may have been a nationalistic one, suggesting a rejection of French influence since that choice of palette and decorative motifs had been increasingly assimilated to the southern English court.[84]

Purple as the color of choice, moreover, became from a symbolic and aesthetic point of view almost as magnificent for decoration as gold, for *purpureus* often meant outlined or gilded with gold,[85] but at far less cost. With regard to Boston Public Library MS 1576 and Trinity College, Dublin MS 83, the conclusions about the combination of purple and gold—or, in the case of the latter codex, large areas of gold only—drawn by Rosamond McKitterick are especially relevant, these colors were "symbolic of great wealth, high social status and prestige."[86] Moreover, it was connected with a type of magnificent book, the *codex purpureus*, which would have been an added cachet. Thus its use can be a sign of the more limited resources of regional workshops and bourgeois patrons.

4

The Interlace and Mask Medallion Style

Besides the polymorphs, foliate vines, and diapering, which we saw as archaizing motifs in chapter 3, two other unusual decorative features occur in many northern books, especially those with distinct York associations. Taken together, they form what we might call the Interlace and Mask Medallion style. Northern decorators were fond of ropy or sometimes flat ribbon-like loosely knotted or basket weave-like interlace patterns in the corner pieces of borders or in roundels at the midpoints of side borders, or more often in a medallion-like position at the bottom of a full border. More common in late fourteenth-century Durham books than in those of York is a long run of leafless vines loosely knotted, as in macramé, and forming parts of trellis borders or of the major initials themselves.

Often giving rise to these strands of interlace from ears or mouth or sometimes incorporated within its knotting, are mask-like faces modeled, often very remotely, on the faces of lions. Naturally, several southern examples of relatively plain foliate borders with an interlace medallion in cornerpieces or center position can be found. One which comes readily to mind is the opening page of the Hengwyrt Chaucer manuscript (Aberystwyth, National Library of Wales, MS Peniarth 392 D), which has a small interlace medallion in the center of the bottom border.[1] And mask faces in conjunction with these medallions also occur in southern painting as early as the psalter of Richard of Canterbury, made about 1310–1320 (now New York, Pierpont Morgan Library MS G 53), at folio 102,[2] or throughout the borders of the Milemete manuscript (Oxford, Christ Church College MS 92), discussed in the last chapter, and as late as the Litlyngton Missal, painted 1383–1384.[3] The Richard of Canterbury artist, for example, makes use of whimsical vines tipped with daisy buds to serve as antlers for the large mask at the top right, from whose mouth issues a vine that becomes interlace medallions containing masks. A combination of interlace and mask motifs, however, used in ways that dominate the foliate border decoration, is the unique contribution of this group of northern decorators, differentiating their use of these motifs from that of southern artists of the first half of the fourteenth century.

Let us look in greater detail at the development of these two motifs in English manuscript border decoration and to their eventual appearance as part of a northern regional style. We recall that two of the figures in the decoration of Cambridge University Library MS Dd.10.22 and several in Boston Public Library MS 1576 had distorted but still recognizably human mask-like faces with protuberant reddish tongues.[4] The Cambridge artist had given these mask faces a key position in books 1 and 4 of the *Historia Aurea* abridgment, where the faces stare frontally out at the beholder, one from the initial and one from a medallion-like position at the bottom of the first page. These decorative elements go back to the Anglo-Saxon period. As we saw, the mask face in a medallion-like position—often as a boss between two *radii*—or from whose mouth or ears issue patterns of interlace, appeared in the Winchester Bible, and the type with protruding tongue is used in London, British Library MS Cotton Claudius E.v. That such boss-like masks were of interest to northern illuminators from an early period is evident from the York Psalter now MS U.3.2 in the Hunterian Museum of the University of Glasgow, where such a boss mask joins the bows of the *B* in the Beatus page.[5]

Though they are out of fashion in the south during the eleventh and twelfth centuries, such mask-like and distorted faces reappear in English manuscript painting, as Eric Millar has pointed out, by the mid thirteenth-century in such important books as the Rutland Psalter (British Library MSS Additional 62925) and the Bible of William of Devon (Royal 1.D.i.)[6] They come increasingly to populate the margins of a number of English manuscripts of the first half of the fourteenth century, taking several forms. They can be vaguely simian, as in the Bohun Psalter;[7] generic, as in the Alphonso Psalter (London, British Library MS Additional 24686);[8] or mocking, as in the Tiptoft Missal (New York, Pierpont Morgan Library MS M 107).[9] Often the mouths have long, protruding tongues, as in the borders of the St. Omer Psalter or the Tiptoft Missal. In the latter book, for example, an entire border at folio 267 contains twenty such mask faces with protruding tongues as major ornaments, and another border on folio 147 is decorated entirely with interlace motifs in the forms of quatrefoils and eight-pointed stars (figs. 12 and 13).

The Interlace and Mask Medallion artists did not draw as much

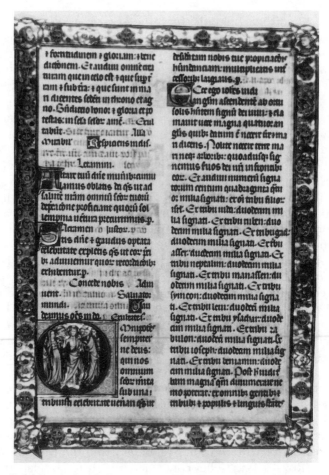

12. Gold border with lion masks. New York, Pierpont Morgan Library MS M 107, Tiptoft Missal, folio 267, S. XIV² *Courtesy Pierpont Morgan Library.*

on the Fenland style, where the interlace medallion in center position sometimes appeared, as in the Gorleston Psalter (London, British Library MS Additional 49622)[10] as did the artists we discussed in the previous chapter. Rather, they looked for many of their motifs to what has been called by Lucy Sandler, among others, the Westminster or Queen Mary Psalter style, named after London, British Library MS Royal 2.B.vii, which was painted about 1310–1320.[11] One of this

13. Gold border with interlace medallions. New York, Pierpont Morgan Library MS M 107, Tiptoft Missal, folio 147, S XIV[2]. *Courtesy Pierpont Morgan Library.*

style's many decorative features was the interlace motif, sometimes with mask faces, as we saw in the cases of the Psalter of Robert of Canterbury, painted by the Queen Mary Master, and the Litlyngton Missal.[12]

To be sure, there are mid- and late-fourteenth century southern examples in which mask faces and interlace medallions serve as major design elements. Sandler says of Oxford, Bodleian Library MS Li-

turgies 198, a psalter made about 1360, that "among [its] most striking border motifs are the masks—grotesque lion faces with long pro-
jecting tongues."[13] And of the psalter of Eleanor de Bohun (now MS
Advocates 18.6.5 in the National Library of Scotland, Edinburgh),
made between 1380 and 1392, she notes that in "the last twenty years
of the century a striking change seems to have occurred. Border
design became symmetrical, consisting of decorated bands . . . punctu-
ated by regularly placed accents of . . . interlace knots, masks, or
shields."[14] On the whole, however, most of the southern manuscripts
with these motifs do not give them a prominent position.

That the Westminster style was assimilated in the north by mid-
century is known from the M. R. James Memorial Psalter (London,
British Library MS Additional 44949), which was made, to judge from
its kalendar and litany, in the north of England, probably in the
diocese of Durham, between 1350 and 1375. Margaret Rickert believes that both the scribe and the decorator were English.[15] A typical
border occurs at folio 219v, where about two-thirds of the way down
the gold sidebars, the red and blue vines knot limply in an overhand
way. At the upper right, a dragon forms part of the vinework of
the border. Corner pieces at the bottom each contain masks of the
grotesque type we saw earlier, and between them in the middle is an
interlace medallion prominently displayed at the bottom of the page
where we might expect arms (fig. 14). As we have seen, these are not
the main elements of the Westminster or Queen Mary Psalter style,
for there they had been blended with other components—floral
work, roundels, historiated registers, armorial or heraldic motifs, and
the like. The main difference between northern and southern treatments of the interlace medallion pattern is that northern artists use it
primarily as a dominant motif within the border. However much
foliage may come out of the border elsewhere, the interlace does
not vie with other geometrical patterns or historiated registers for
prominence.

Instead, the Interlace and Mask Medallion artists appear to have
drawn on the pool of imagery found in the James Psalter, adopting
chiefly the mask faces, interlace cornerpieces and bottom medallions
of the Westminster style and making these the major features of the
decoration.[16] Possibly, such decoration can have economic and social
reasons. Masks and discrete medallion patterns could be drawn or
traced from model books or cartoons and thus done less expensively
than historiated registers filled by realistic or naturalistic types of
decoration. And for emerging gentry who did not have arms, such

14. Floriated border with interlace medallions and masks. London, British Library MS Additional 44949, M. R. James Memorial Psalter, folio 219v, 1360. *Courtesy Trustees of the British Library.*

motifs could serve a somewhat honorific role in border design by appearing in the otherwise blank space where one might expect to find armorial shields.

English interlace appears to derive from Coptic and Islamic art by way of Hiberno-Saxon metal work and was common in Insular stone carving as well.[17] Like the *folium* discussed in the last chapter, such motifs are very prominent in the carpet page decoration of much Hiberno-Saxon manuscript painting. Since interlace was such a dominant feature of earlier English painting, like the Lindisfarne Gospels, it is possible that in seizing on that element in contemporary southern painting of the Westminster style, or simply going directly to the earlier codices, these northern illuminators were expressing an archaizing and nationalistic taste much like that of the decorators discussed in the previous chapter.

Good examples of the way interlace became a major decorative element in the northern repertoire can be seen in three books with strong northern pedigrees, two quite plain and one ornate. The first was originally a single volume but is now divided into three. It seems to have have been commissioned by John Newton, the treasurer of York Cathedral and founder of the Minster Library, and we will have occasion to discuss it in chapter 6 as an illustration of his taste in book decoration. This manuscript (now Oxford, Bodleian Library MS Rawlinson C.162 and B.199, B. 200)[18] must have been separated and rebound by Rawlinson himself as three codices of works of Bede, William of Malmsbury, and Alfred of Beverley. It could not have been made much earlier than its citation in the book list appearing in Newton's will, treated in chapter 1. Typical of many such books made in the north, it is ornamented with a number of four- to five-line *champ* initials in gold. The single three-quarter border has as its focal point an interlace medallion at the bottom. Coming from the simple border are leaves, jutting out at right angles to it, which terminate in sprays putting off gold blobs with corkscrew finials. We shall discuss these "jutting leaves" shortly.

The second example is London, British Library MS Harley 2431, a breviary with the Feast of the Relics of York Cathedral. Though this book shows a close connection with York cathedral initially, the *ex libris* says that it belonged to the chapel of St. Giles by Brunton in Swaldale and to the chantry of St. Giles in the chapel of St. John the Evangelist in Ravensworth castle. Its small size suggests a book intended for private devotions, and interlace cornerpieces of modest quality dominate its border decoration.

The third of these books is the member of the Green Canon-Page group mentioned in the previous chapter, British Library MS Additional 43380, where the two elements of border design are the eight-line floriated initial at the top of the page and the large interlace medallion in center position at the bottom (fig. 2). From the handsome canon page painting on the facing page, one might expect more highly decorated borders for such a book, but the purchaser apparently was satisfied with interlace as the high point of the book's decoration elsewhere.

That on occasion late fourteenth- and early fifteenth-century northern artists with both brush and pen showed a conscious preference for these interlace medallion and mask motifs for the infill of typical floriated initials, is clear from the various initials in the Cartulary of the Cistercian abbey of Furness, Lancashire, written by John Stell, a monk of the house, in 1412. Kathleen Scott has noted a similarity of the portraits in some of the initials to those in the Beverley Cartulary (British Library MS Additional 61901).[19]

The large and handsome Furness Abbey Cartulary is now British Library MS Additional 33244, and London, Public Records Office MS D/L.42/43.[20] Though this is a high-quality volume, it is the only book known to have been produced at Furness abbey. Stell, however, seems to have been quite an experienced and self-conscious scribe; he shows himself at his desk writing—as he tells us, with a silver and not a quill pen—his own punning verse colophon "Stella, parens solis, John Stell rege, munere prolis" (fol. 2). In the British Library volume, there are several major initials containing not the usual foliate infill but mask faces or interlace medallions. A representative example of a blue mask with red mouth parts set against a gold ground appears in a four-line initial at folio 154v (fig. 15).

An example of the same taste can also be found in a more "mainstream" Durham book, discussed in chapter 2. This is Durham Cathedral Library MS A.I.3, Nicholas of Lyra written in 1386[21] by William du Stiphel. Showing the beauty of the Breton's script, it contains a *littera partita* initial *P* for one of the major divisions of the work at folio 52 (fig. 16). Within the initial is a lion mask from whose mouth and ears flows foliage. A mask face also appears as part of the historiated initial on folio 1 of the same volume. The columbines at the bottom of the first folio's trellis border—which seem to be associated with the Benedictine order—remind us of those in the Psalter of Robert of Canterbury.[22]

Let us put these generalizations to a further test in examining some manuscripts whose kalendars or contents place them in the north. As was the case with the Archaizing group discussed in chapter 3, the Interlace and Mask Medallion group includes several artists and scribes whose work can be recognized in its production. Though all the group's books have the readily recognizable characteristics I have already mentioned, several subgroups sharing specific features of decoration or script can be identified.

15. Initial with mask face. London, British Library MS Additional 33244, Furness Abbey Cartulary, folio 154v, 1412. *Courtesy Trustees of the British Library.*

The first of these I call the Jutting Leaf style. Though only a few of the eleven books in this group are clearly made by the same decorators, they share a number of stylistic features and are also linked to some other discrete groups of northern manuscripts. Books in this style have rather slim and linear two-color full-bar borders, which can to varying degrees be free of foliate medallions along the outside and gutter bars. In addition to the characteristic interlace medallions, they have numerous kite-shaped leaves jutting outward at right angles to the axis of the bar. Often, but not always, these leaves have corkscrew squiggles or finials terminating sprays of gold blobs. This last feature, of course, is not unique to the north, but can be found in various late fourteenth-century southern English manuscripts. There it may be a borrowing from the Midlands in the third quarter of the fourteenth century, as it appears, for example, in the Vernon manuscript (Oxford, Bodleian Library MS Eng. Poet. a.1). "Jutting Leaf," then, is merely a convenient label for a group of

16. *Littera partita* initial P with mask face. Durham, Dean and Chapter Library MS A. I. 3, Nicholas of Lyra, Commentary on the Bible, folio 178r, 1386. *Courtesy Durham Dean and Chapter.*

books which have a number of other elements in common as well, of which one of the most prevalent is a preference for orange tones instead of rose in conjunction with blue in foliate infills of initials.

Such books include (besides MS Rawlinson C.162, already discussed) York Minster Library MSS Additional 383, a breviary dating from about 1430; Additional 68, a mid-fourteenth-century breviary;[23] an early fifteenth-century psalter *horae*, Cambridge Trinity

College MS O.3.10;[24] two breviaries in Dublin, Trinity College MSS 85 and 87;[25] a breviary at Oxford, Bodleian Library MS Laud Misc. 84;[26] Bodleian Library MS Rawlinson Liturgies b.1, a sumptuous late fourteenth-century monastic missal from the Benedictine Abbey of St. Hilda, Whitby; British Library MS Additional 61901, the Beverley Cartulary mentioned earlier;[27] MS Stowe 12, an ordinal with Archbishop Scrope's arms on its illuminated title page; and Blackburn, Lancashire, Stonyhurst College MS 3, a missal of the late fourteenth or early fifteenth centuries.[28] Unless otherwise noted, these works are all of York use. As it would be tedious to deal with the borders in each manuscript, we may take four codices as representative of the Jutting Leaf style: the pairs Dublin, Trinity College MS 85 and Oxford, Bodleian Library MS Laud Misc. 84, and Cambridge, Trinity College MS O.3.10 and Boulogne-sur-Mer Bibliothèque Municipale MS 93. The Dublin and Oxford manuscripts are more similar to each other in small details than they are to the sister *horae* of Cambridge and Boulogne.

Bodleian MS Laud Misc. 84 and Dublin Trinity College MS 85 show the Jutting Leaf style as well as virtually identical decoration in other respects, and are more closely related to each other than to any of the others in the Jutting Leaf group just catalogued. Let us first consider the simpler jutting leaf border type of MS Laud Misc. 84,[29] a rubricated choir breviary of York use. A representative Jutting Leaf border occurs on folio 199v (fig. 17). This is a full bar border with center gutter and top, bottom, and cornerpieces. The vine or rope-like bar is quite plain, with a gilt ball of the same diameter where the bar changes from rose to blue. These vines at corners become somewhat trumpet shaped and from their hatch-marked mouths issue clusters of foliage. Blue and orange kite-shaped leaves jut out from the main bar and its branches. The seven- to eight-line initials contain in their foliate infill blue highlighted and orange highlighted kite-shaped leaves of equal size and proportion. The interlace medallion at the center bottom position has a diamond-shaped rose and blue interlace, whose blue element has a less geometrical and more macramé-like weaving. A prominent decorative feature of MS Laud Misc. 84 is the pair of sprays, ending in three gold balls with corkscrew-shaped finials, which comes from each kite-shaped leaf.

Trinity College Dublin MS 85 has a graded kalendar of York use. A representative border appears on folio 204r, a page containing one of the IHS monograms to be discussed in chapter 5 (fig. 18). Like MS Laud Misc. 84 in its sharply jutting leaves and overhand knots at the

17. Floriated border with jutting leaves and interlace medallion. Oxford, Bodleian Library MS Laud Misc. 84, folio 199v, S. XV[1] *Courtesy Bodleian Library.*

sides of the border bars, Trinity College, Dublin MS 85, however, has somewhat more dynamic ties to these knots, but they are still proportionally overlong. The leaves have rather prominent, stinger-like points. Also like MS Laud Misc. 84 is the node in its center gutter vine borders, a gold disc in which the border bars change color from rose to blue or the reverse. This book, as well, has an eight-line major initial set on a gold foil ground; at the borders are two blue kite-

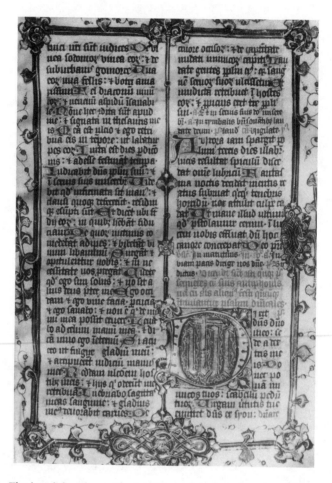

18. Floriated border with jutting leaves, interlace medallion and initial with IHS monogram. Dublin, Trinity College MS 85, breviary-psalter-missal composite, folio 204, S. XIV⁴. *Courtesy Trinity College.*

shaped leaves flanking a rose one, each highlighted with white dots and a circle. As in MS Laud Misc. 84, the high point of the decoration in Trinity College MS 85 is a large interlace medallion at the center of the bottom border, though the diamond or geometric character is not as pronounced as in MS Laud Misc. 84. This medallion is flanked by pairs of jutting leaves.

A rather rare psalter-*horae*,[30] Trinity College, Cambridge MS

O.3.10 dates from about 1410. Its kalendar of York use contains the Feast of the Relics of the Cathedral, suggesting a metropolitan connection, and the *obits* of Alice and John Rotherham in 1479 and 1492. The 159 saints and feasts noted are standard to English kalendars; of this total number, 49 saints and feasts, or roughly one-third are peculiar to the use of York. The flyleaf displays the arms of the Tunstall family of Westmorland on what appears to be a late seventeenth-century shield.[31] A signature of George Reyner of Peterborough points to yet another geographic area of ownership. Besides the Psalms, MS O.3.10 includes the matins and hours of the Passion, the office of the Holy Face, the hymn to the side-wound and related prayers, the office of the *arma Christi* or instruments of the Passion, the hymn of sorrow associated with the name of Anselm,[32] and the hymn for the Holy Name ascribed to Bernardino of Siena. The office for the Holy Face is accompanied by a striking image that appears among a number of handsome miniatures in this book; it will be discussed in the next chapter.

This manuscript has a major initial and border at folio 52 (fig. 19). At the bottom center is a medallion containing a mask face. An interlace medallion appears at the middle of the right border. Circular highlighting in white lead appears on all of the tongue-like leaves that jut out at right angles from the borders.[33] These tongues at the corners and sidepieces put out three-pronged blobs and corkscrew finials at every other tongue. Knotted clusters of vines terminate in a three-leaf group at the top or sides of the borders, in which the center leaf is much larger than those adjacent. Virtually identical patterns appear, for example, at folios 15r and 27v, where the orange mask face serves as the medallion at the bottom of the border and the vines and bars of the border come from its mouth and ears.

Particularly striking features of MS O.3.10 are the fluting of the vines that make up the borders at cornerpieces and the rendition of conic shapes in sprays, an apparent effort to imitate International Style Gothic treatments of interior space. Such hollow volumes or conic shapes in acanthus work appear with interlace medallions at several points in Rennes, Bibliothèque Municipale MS 22, the so-called York Psalter.[34] Other important examples of conic forms include folio 25 of the Carmelite Missal; folio 24 of the Bedford *horae* and psalter, London, British Library MS Additional 42131, made between 1414 and 1435; and folio 218 of Oxford, Bodleian Library MS Bodley 264, containing the Book of the Great Caan. The last of these was painted by an artist who calls himself "Johannes," whose

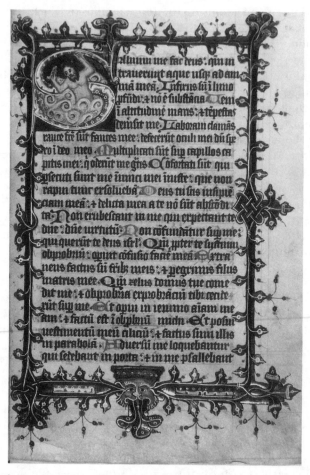

19. Floriated border with jutting leaves, mask face, interlace medallion and David in the sea in "Salvum me fac" initial. Cambridge, Trinity College MS O.3.10, psalter-hours, folio 52r, ca. 1410. *Courtesy the Master and Fellows of Trinity College, Cambridge.*

name has served as a descriptor for a style involving Italianate acanthus wrap, large carpels, and conic forms—in short, a style very like the one that we will find in a number of northern books.

Closely related to Cambridge, Trinity College MS O.3.10 is a manuscript from the same workshop, and written by the same scribe, Boulogne-sur-Mer Bibliothèque Municipale MS 93.[35] Though the book lacks the masks of the Interlace and Mask Medallion group, it has many interlace medallions and shows two major traits of the Jutting Leaf subgroup, the kite-shaped leaves with white cobra-head spotted highlighting, which protrude prominently at right angles from the borders, and the pairings of blue with orange rather than blue with rose in the painting of foliage. A representative page is folio 40v (fig. 20), which shows at the bottom center of the border the typical interlace medallion flanked by trios of jutting kite-shaped leaves. A series of white lead dots up the back of the leaf, leading to a circle highlighted by white lead, gives the leaf the appearance of a cobra head.

As the book is little known, and also because it is a very important monument in northern book painting, it deserves some discussion and detailed description of elements other than its borders. Boulogne MS 93 is a *horae* written in a very fine liturgical *textura* on two scales. Its graded kalendar, of York use, with the Feast of the Relics of the Cathedral, is quite a full one. Though it lacks the month of February, it is otherwise virtually identical to Cambridge, Trinity College MS O.3.10 in the number of saints and the proportion of those peculiar to the use of York. The presence of the Cumbrian female saint Bega (or Bees)[36] and St. Hilda does not point directly to the city of York, but more to the West Riding and to Whitby. Nothing about the kalendar suggests that the book was not written in an English atelier. The contents of the *horae* consist of Latin suffrages and prayers to saints, as well as Latin prayers to the Five Wounds, the Holy Face, and the instruments of the Passion; the Hours of the Virgin and Hours of the Cross; the Seven Penitential Psalms; the Office for the Dead; and the Commendation of Souls. Other interesting material includes a prayer, sometimes associated with Bede, in red for the Seven Last Words of Christ at 93v;[37] a prayer of St. Augustine at folios 94v-95, which should be said while elevating the host;[38] a resurrection prayer in the time of Gregory the Great in Rome from a mass celebrated in the church of Pantouras (or sometimes Pantheon); and verses on Mary Magdalene and St. George. At the end is a prayer in French for all those who are well confessed.

Up to this point, the main evidence for attributing ownership of this book has been the arms we see on the shield at folio 40v, as well as the names of "Lady Cartaret," "Lady Holland," Diana Holland, Charlotte and possibly Abigail Holland, described as spinsters, on folio 1 of the kalendar, and a monogram on folio 39. This information seems to tie the book to a northern branch of the Holland family,

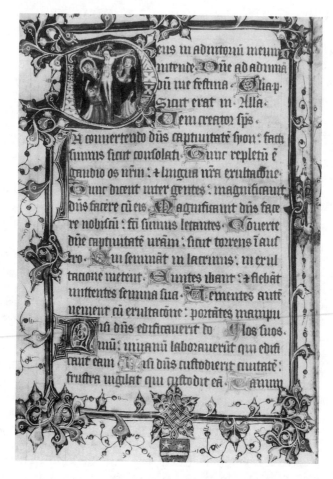

20. Floriated border with jutting leaves, interlace medallion, and historiated initial. Boulogne-sur-Mer Bibliothèque Municipale MS 93, *horae* and prayers, folio 40v, ca. 1410. *Courtesy Bibliothèque Municipale.*

prominent in the events of Thomas of Lancaster's death, to the Holmes family of Ireland, and to the Sandys family of England.

No seventeenth-century landed Hollands seem, however, to have had daughters with these names. A branch of the Carterets had a long association with the Isle of Jersey,[39] but the family had no northern branch. Nor is there any evidence in the book's kalendar of an Irish connection.

A more promising possibility for the later history of the book is that offered by Sir Thomas Strange, Chief Justice of Madras, who died in 1841 at the age of eighty-three. His wife was the daughter of an Irish baronet named Burroughs; it is unclear, however, if she was a Catholic. She may have been responsible for the crude but enthusiastic re-creation of a cut out historiated initial of Christ before Pilate and portion of script at folio 34v in 1847.[40]

Though the "O intemerata" has masculine grammatical forms, the book was possibly intended for a woman, as one of these initials contains an illustration of Anne teaching the Virgin to read, which (as we have seen earlier) was often understood as a symbol of female literacy. There is as well the presence of Bega and Hilda in the kalendar, and the full-page drawings offer two separate pictures of St. Katherine. Moreover, the Boulogne *horae* has clearly had a strong female appeal later in its life. As we saw from the names of aristocratic women, possibly recusant, in a sixteenth- or seventeenth-century hand, on the first page of the kalendar, and the repair work of Lady Strange, women have been much interested in this book.

The arms painted in the borders of Boulogne MS 93 are gules a fess argent between three mullets or, appearing in shields at the bottoms of the borders on folios 26, 40v, and 41v. Argent a fess gules appears between three crosses pommy sable on shields at 30v and 42v and these two arms are impaled on folios 39v and 45v. On folio 39v the impaled arms occur with a gold monogram in the center of a chaplet of blue and white flowers. The monogram reads EKH or perhaps ERH. Rogers, following Girard, claimed that the dexter half of these arms belonged to the Holmes of Ireland and the sinister half to branches of the Sandys family.[41]

These arms, however, are rather less certain of identification than Rogers would suggest. Gules a fess argent between three mullets or appears as an unnamed coat of arms in a manuscript called *Prince Arthur's Book*, now in London in the College of Arms. The second coat, of argent a fess gules between three crosses pommy, cannot be found at all in the Ordinaries of the College of Arms. Indeed, the only arms like those in the shields belonged to two families from Normandy, Bence de Buisson and Le Devin, who would have been unlikely to commission a book with a York kalendar and so much English material.[42] One possibility, of course, is that the shields were all very tediously and skillfully repainted at some time, though close examination of the borders did not suggest this. In spite of this seeming wealth of heraldic information, the question of the Boulogne *horae*'s original ownership cannot be resolved at the present time.

Rogers has also argued that the volume was originally planned only as a codex with ten decorative initials for the Hours of the Virgin and of the Cross, the Penitential Psalms, Office of the Dead and Commendation of Souls, and that at some point in its later history it acquired a prefatical set of devotions combined with twenty-three full-page line drawings that were apparently to be colored, perhaps with wash. It is hard to see how Rogers could have arrived at this conclusion as to the book's makeup, since it was written by a single scribe, whose hand appears in the kalendar, in the texts of the "added" devotions, and of course, in the pages with the historiated initials. Still evident, moreover, are extensive guide words for the rubrication of these devotions, in a cursive hand, presumably the scribe's, whose English origin is betrayed by his high, two-compartment *a* and long *r*, in the office for St. Michael, for example. His *textura* also seems to appear in the banderoles within the full-page drawings. The width of the writing space for all pages, moreover, is 120 mm; however, it must be said that though there is no pricking left on earlier folios, some is on folio 26, where the *horae* proper begins, as if this page may have been narrower.

The arrangement of these full-page drawings at the front of the volume is very like that of a larger group of miniatures in the Bolton *horae*, York Minster Library MS Additional 2.[43] The design seems intended to create impact early in the book, for the volume shows a gradual trailing off of funds: plain floriated major initials and simpler borders appear in the last folios, and there is a gradual reduction in flourished initials towards the end. Although a considerable amount of gold leaf was applied to these early pages, which have a heavily ruled diapered background of large diamond shapes, they were left otherwise uncompleted.

The provenance of these uncompleted drawings is uncertain. Rogers suggests that their architectural canopies reflect the practice of Bruges workshops in the 1390s, but he mentions similar examples earlier in the century from York glass.[44] Such canopies can also be found in southern manuscripts like Oxford, Bodleian Library MS Rawlinson D.939, painted in 1389, which certainly has no ties to the Netherlands, as well as in the Ebchester prayer roll from Durham, made in 1464 for John Burnby and William Ebchester, now Durham cathedral MS B.IV. 48 (fig. 21). This roll, forty-one feet long, depicting the deathbed, burial, and heavenly judgment of the former priors by St. Cuthbert and King Oswald, was commissioned in 1464 by prior Richard Bell; it traveled to some 623 religious houses whose

21. Border frames with acanthus leaves wrapped around rods, burial and ascension of a prior. Durham, Dean and Chapter Library MS B. IV.48, Ebchester mortuary prayer roll, 1464. *Courtesy Durham Dean and Chapter.*

occupants agreed to pray for the souls of the former priors John Burnby and William Ebchester. Presumably it was intended to make the fate of souls after death clear to those being solicited.[45]

Among the full-page drawings in Boulogne MS 93 is one of Saint Veronica holding the Holy Face; an office on the preceding page goes with this drawing. Though the style of this and the other drawings of the group seemed Netherlandish to Rogers, the Holy Face with angels flanking it in a quasi-liturgical manner and a kneeling soldier, unnamed in the Gospel of John but known from the *Golden Legend* of Jacob of Voragine as Longinus, is typically English. English as well is the detail of the Virgin adding her rosary to the scales, in the painting at folio 24 of Saint Michael weighing souls with the Virgin interceding.[46] Thus, there are stylistic reasons for and against considering the prefatical drawings to be of foreign manufacture.

Certainly, both the choice of subject matter for several of these drawings and their treatment show the impact of Northern European popular piety on England, especially in the eastern port cities, where contact with northern European culture was frequent. A detail not uncommon in contemporary English art but more characteristic of Netherlandish and German painting is the head of Christ on the *arma Christi* page at folio 9 represented with hands at each side yanking out his hair. This motif was a part of the apocryphal Passion cycle typically found in northern European painting.[47]

My feeling is that the artisans who produced this book made use of a set of sheets with drawings that were perhaps acquired abroad or, more probably, done by a "foreign" artist working in England to an English patron's order for a book with devotional forematter, and that these sheets were supplied to the English scribe during production. Though the sheets contain a number of high-quality prefatical drawings, these are mostly of the Annunciation, Nativity, and suffrages for saints. The devotional group of these miniatures includes the Sacred Face, the wounded Heart, and the *arma Christi*, as well as related Passion material, such as Doubting Thomas examining the side-wound and the Man of Sorrows or *Imago Pietatis* figure of Christ emerging from the tomb-chest in a frontal pose, with crossed, imploring hands.

Other evidence for an English rather than a Continental manufacture is that the figures in the full-page miniatures appear to have been painted by the same foreign or foreign-trained artist who did the Crucifixion miniature in Dublin, Trinity College 83 MS, folio 97v. Moreover, its interlace medallions and jutting, kite-shaped, orange leaves tie the Boulogne *horae* to other manuscripts in the Interlace and Mask Medallion group, which seem in all respects to be English.

Certain subjects and treatments in the full-page miniatures of Boulogne MS 93—and its historiated initials, which are English in character—moreover, have a likeness to pictures in Cambridge, Trinity College MS O.3.10, though the borders of these two books differ in that Boulogne has no mask faces and the artist does not show an interest in illusionistic hollows of the vine knotting. The size of both books, allowing for trimming of the margins, is strikingly similar, with Boulogne measuring 272 × 180 mm and Trinity 285 × 199 mm and Boulogne's writing space—a key dimension that could not be altered by rebinding—186 × 120 mm and Trinity's 185 × 120 mm. The main text boxes of twenty or twenty-four lines of script are in each book delimited by double rulings at the top, the bottom, and the outer margins. These rulings serve to define the borders. In each case, the upper or lower pair of double lines is about three lines up or down from the first or last line of the text box and a similar distance from the text box at the outer margin. Except that Boulogne has fewer writing lines per page than Trinity and so more space between the ruling lines, the pages appear to have been laid out in exactly the same way and to the same scale. Thus, it seems likely that both books were designed and ruled by the same persons.

A quick comparison will show the iconographic parallels between Cambridge, Trinity College MS O.3.10 and Boulogne MS 93. Three paintings of one-third page each open MS O.3.10. On folio 11 is Saint Veronica holding a very dark Holy Face against a sheet-like vernicle; below is a text on the Holy Face. On folio 12v is an image of the wounded Heart as an horizontal mouth-like slit with the hymn "Salve plaga lateris" directly below. This deeply cloven heart is an aspect of the Man of Sorrows iconography, in which Christ, lowered from the cross, shows his wounded heart and limbs to the beholder. In Middle English lyrics of the variety in which Christ speaks from the cross, he often says "Lo, here is my heart." The heart is on a ground of red hatch marks; intended to represent the multiplicity of Christ's wounds, such hatch marks often appear around the heart on shield-like images. Folio 13 bears an image of the *arma Christi*. Six- and seven-line historiated initials for the Psalms, with full and partial borders, complete the decoration. There is no further illumination after folio 87. The book ends with French and English prayers. This order of Holy Face, Sacred Heart, and *arma Christi* associated with an office is also followed by the Boulogne designer.

Taking these large pictures in order, both Veronica scenes contain the same basic material and the same text, but the treatment in Boulogne MS 93 shows a much more sophisticated artist and far greater visual detail. Saint Veronica's bust and head here are more in proportion to the Holy Face than in Cambridge, Trinity College MS O.3.10, where she is merely a tiny face above the frame containing the blackened face. In Boulogne, moreover, the vernicle is censed by two kneeling angels. Trinity's startlingly dark Holy Face, incidentally, reflects the influence of devotional texts and Continental works of art like the vernicle at Rome mentioned by Julian of Norwich, who in explaining why Christ's face is portrayed a morbid grayish black, speaks "of the holie vernacle of Rome, [in] which he [is] portrude with his one blessed face, when he was in his hard passion, wilfully goyng to his death, and often chaungyng of coloure, of the brownhead and the blackhead. . . . I saw the swete face . . . in browne blew, as the flessch turned more depe dede."[48]

Both pages, however, contain identical texts of the earliest form of the hymn to the Holy Face. Verbally identical four-line red rubrics introduce each office; they appear to have a common source, as they each contain the unusual poetic word *dye*, or *dia*, meaning *divinae*. The Five Wounds pages are quite similar, but again the Boulogne artist is more elaborate: a kneeling Longinus points to his eye and pierces the heart with a spear; the heart is held by an angel opposite Longinus and supported by two other angels. In contrast, MS O.3.10 merely shows a very rudimentary heart dominated by a wound. The *arma Christi* pages contain verses on the instruments of the Passion immediately following the miniature, and again the texts are identical. The drawings, however, show little similarity in iconographic treatment; for example, MS O.3.10 lacks the northern Passion detail of the yanking of Christ's hair. Though the general impression is that both books were overseen by the same designer, the Boulogne manuscript was conceived as a much more splendid production using a great deal more gold, with gold-flourished capitals; MS O.3.10, planned—at least from the decorative point of view—as an economical version of Boulogne, has alternating red and blue ink Lombardic letters.

In their content both volumes are unusual for a number of reasons, the chief one of which is that each joins prefatical material of a more private and idiosyncratic character to a fairly standard body of texts, the usual devotions of the *horae* and the seven penitential Psalms of the psalter. This prefatical material, moreover, was not an afterthought but part of the original plan.

Also, both books were copied by the same scribe. Perhaps the most immediately recognizable and striking similarities between their scripts, both of which are written on two scales, are those of the hairlines in *e* and the negative space within the bows of *q* and *o*. The peculiar short strokes in *r* joined to the shaft by a hairline are also similar in both works.

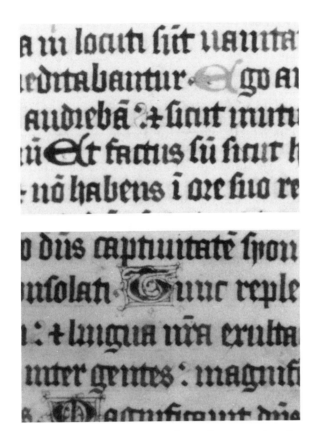

22. Specimens of script, ampersands, and punctuation from *(top)* Cambridge, Trinity College MS O.3.10 and *(bottom)* Boulogne-sur-Mer MS 93.

Punctuation and marks of abbreviation also show some striking similarities. The scribe in both books uses a distinctive colon or *punctus* made by joining two lozenges by an arabesque curve (fig. 22), and an occasional *s*-shaped stroke as a dot to indicate that a minim is an *i*. That the same scribe wrote both these books and that the same designer did the page ruling and layout and arranged the prefatical miniatures is clear. This is an incontrovertible piece of evidence for a common center of production for a pair of illuminated books in the north of England, for we are not talking about a matter of stylistic, but of quantifiable similarity.

Besides the Jutting Leaf group we can note among these north-

ern books two other categories. We might call one the Italianate Leaf
group and the other the Carpel and Calyx group, though there is
some overlap. There are six manuscripts of the leaf type. These are
York Minster Library MSS Additional 2, the Bolton *horae* and
XVI.K.6, the Pullein *horae* discussed earlier; London, British Library
MS Additional 43380, discussed in the last chapter; Cotton Augustus
A.iv, Thomas Chaworth's copy of Lydgate's *Troybook;*[49] Chicago,
Newberry Library MS +33.1, the *Polychronicon* of Ranulf Higden;
and Oxford, Bodleian MS Gough Liturgies 1, a rubricated choir breviary of the early fifteenth century.[50] The Carpel group, with four-
teen members, overlaps somewhat with the Italianate Leaf group. For
example, it contains Cambridge, Jesus College MS 45 (Vincent of
Beauvais, *Speculum Historiale*), the Newberry Library *Polychronicon,*
and London, MS Additional 43380, all of which have both motifs.
Carpel manuscripts include Cambridge, Jesus College MSS 8, Isidore
of Seville, and 48, Boethius; Cambridge, Fitzwilliam Museum MS
34, a York missal; Cambridge, Sidney Sussex College MSS 2, the
Rotherham bequest and 33, a York missal;[51] Durham University Library MS Cosin V.1.2, a York breviary from Hutton Church, Rudby
in the North Riding;[52] London, British Library MSS Royal 2.A.xvii,
horae with a York kalendar and Cotton Augustus A.iv; Oxford, Bodleian Library MSS Barlow 27[53] and Rawlinson C.142, a south Yorkshire missal;[54] York Minster Library MSS Additional 30, a missal,
Additional 69, the choir breviary mentioned earlier, XVI.K.6, the
Pullein *horae* discussed earlier, and XVI.A.9, an early fifteenth-century missal;[55] a mid-fifteenth-century rubricated missal with a partly
Sarum kalendar, but whose provenance is from Durham; Oxford,
Bodley Library MS Laud Misc. 302;[56] and, if it is indeed northern,
Pierpont Morgan Library MS M. 648.

Again, as with the Jutting Leaf group of manuscripts, several of
the Italianate Leaf wrap books are representative of the type, whose
chief feature is an attenuated acanthus leaf wrapping itself around
and rising up a thin plain spaghetti-like border bar, usually of a contrasting color. This characteristically Bohemian motif (found in the
Boskovitzer Bible, folio 1r) was also extremely popular with Italian
painters, though the precise nature of the influence is uncertain. For
example, Frinta remarks that "attenuated acanthus spiraling up
around a stalk is another example of decoration that migrated between Bohemia and western Europe in an undetermined direction."[57]
The device has also been remarked on by Margaret Rickert, who
notes that "the use of acanthus scrolls in English manuscripts . . . [in]

combination . . . with ribbon scrolls, twisted round a central rod, is found first in the Beaufort Annunciation."[58] Such rod and acanthus wrap occurs as well in its contemporary, the Wyndham Payne Crucifixion page, also by Herman Scheerre, now London, British Library MS Additional 58078.[59]

It is certainly true that the Italianate leaf wrap device is a latecomer to the north. Nearly all of the books in which I have found it seem later than the "Beaufort" volume and Wyndham Payne leaf, and a good datable example, where blue acanthus wraps itself on a red rod, is to be found in the borders of Durham Cathedral MS B.IV. 48, the Ebchester prayer roll (fig. 21). A major difference between the northern variant of the Italianate leaf wrap in this roll and the manuscripts I shall discuss, is that the prayer roll, like the two Scheerre manuscripts just mentioned, confines the wrap within the geometrical pattern of the border or, in the case of a borderless miniature, within the supporting structure of the oratory in which Gabriel and the Virgin are placed.

For the first group, Oxford, Bodleian MS Gough Liturgies 1 illustrates the least expensive form of the style. The ribbon which twists around the border rod is not a true and more time-consuming acanthus (fig. 23), and the wrap is actually made of single long leaves of alternating rose and blue, each originating from a node on the border bar indicated by two white hatch marks, as on the border bar of folio 11v, where the attenuation gives the illusion of a continuous wrap.

Much the same thing happens in MS Gough Liturgies 1 at folio 11v, where a full border of narrow gold and rose and blue bars encircles the page. The leaf makes two turns around the rod but still originates from a hatch-marked node on the bar. At the lower left is an interlace corner piece, and at the bottom center a foliate medallion. The decoration of this border varies; at the bottom and the right are the jutting kite-shaped leaves we have seen before, except that tucked into the angle where the leaf stem joins the bar is a gold ball or blob. These leaves have the cobra head-like forms with highlighting of white lead circles and dots characteristic of the leaves in Stonyhurst College MS 3. These alternate with squiggles and often give off tendrils with blobs. The left hand border, however, has a peculiarly Italianate or Bohemian vine-like wrap, which comes from the top and bottom portions of the eight-line historiated initial *E* enclosing David playing a portative organ. These broad ribbon-like forms climb randomly up and down the left border bar. The rose and blue border bars knot at this initial in an overhand manner to pro-

23. Floriated border with vine wrapped around border rod, interlace medallion, jutting leaves, and historiated initial. Oxford, Bodleian Library MS Gough Liturgies 1, breviary, folio 11v, 1390. *Courtesy Bodleian Library.*

duce a cluster of trumpet-shaped forms whose conical hollow interiors are echoed in similar forms at the interlace corner piece at lower left.

True acanthus in contrasting colors of rose and blue makes four complete wraps around the side bars at folio 15 in the Newberry *Polychronicon* (fig. 24). This manuscript shares a number of motifs in

24. Floriated border with vine and acanthus wrapped around border rod, carpel and calyx motifs. Chicago, Newberry Library MS +33.1, Ranulph Higden, *Polychronicon*, folio 15, S. XV[1]. *Courtesy Newberry Library.*

its full-page border with other books in the group, of which only one is the vine wrapping, for it also has carpel and conic forms. It is connected to York by the name of "magister Robert Bothe, once dean of York Cathedral," presumably a relative of archbishop William Bothe, and bears the date of 1489, somewhat but perhaps not too much later than the date of the book. Bothe's arms, which may have

been added—since the shield awkwardly fits its surrounding space—
appear on an armorial plaque shaped like a columbine blossom at
bottom center, which hangs from a floral hook formed from the
bottom of the center gutter border bar.[60] Extending from the six-line
initial *D* is a ribbon of highlighted blue acanthus that curls around
the narrow shaft of the border at left, while rose, green and pink
acanthus curl here and there at other points in the border. We also
saw this more expensive type of wrap in the borders of the Green
Canon-Page book, British Library MS Additional 43380 discussed in
the last chapter.

Cambridge, Jesus College MS 45 is a handsome Vincent of Beauvais, *Speculum Historiale,* with Jean Hautfuney's topical index; like
many Jesus books, this one appears to have come from the Benedictine monastery at Durham.[61] The full floral border on the first folio
and the five- to six-line floriated initials appear to be of regional
workmanship. From the six-line floriated initial at folio 1 come pink
and blue acanthus leaves that curl around one band of the two-color
bar border. This bar is striking because at the right border it is shown
weaving through itself a tapered serpent-like tail. The border artist
obviously found appealing the idea of leaves or vines wrapped
around a supporting rod, because he allows the descender of a *p* in
the last line of the page to come below the border and into the vinet
sprays below the frame, where a serpent-like pink form (with no
relationship to the border except color) wraps around the descender
like a ribbon.

The Bolton *horae* uses acanthus leaves wrapped around the two-
color narrow bar border everywhere in the book; its decoration is
perhaps the crudest technically of the books we have been examining
but is nonetheless vigorous. This motif of flowing leaf forms wrapped
around a severe geometrical bar border rod suggests the possible
presence of an Italian painter or of Italian manuscripts in the north
at the time these books were made. As we recall in connection with
John Newton's Italianate tastes, J. J. G. Alexander pointed to the
activities of an English painter imitating Italian style when illuminating certain early fourteenth-century law books at Durham,[62] and perhaps what we see in the Italianate leaf treatment is the result of some
similar activity.

Closely related to the realism and technical virtuosity of this ornamental pattern, and often occurring in the same group of books, is a
fascination with extremely realistic carpels, the central seed bearing
female organs of a flower. Though the motif is clearly related to the

25. Arabesque spray with carpel and calyx motif. Esztergom, Hungary, Bibliotheca Strigoniensis MS I.20. missal, folio 67, ca. 1400. *Courtesy Bibliotheca Metropolitana Strigoniensis.*

rise in realistic observation of all aspects of nature, birds, butterflies, and insects in the International Gothic Style down through the fifteenth century,[63] it seems to have been especially popular in a more exaggerated and extravagant form in Bohemian art. A somewhat late example is the Missal, now MS I.20, in the Bibliotheca Metropolitana Strigoniensis, Esztergom, which was made in that diocese about 1480 for a church in Bratislava[64] (fig. 25). At folio 67, vine tendrils bear two types of flowers whose emerging erect gold-colored carpels are at least as long as the body of the flower. The motif also appears in a number of southern English manuscripts of very high quality painted in the fifteenth century. These include the *horae* of Elizabeth the Queen, made about 1420, the Beauchamp Psalter, Oxford, Bodleian Library, MS Digby 277, and the Abingdon Missal, painted in 1461.[65] Many of these books show foreign influence.

The carpel motif also occurs both within the initial and in the border acanthus work in a group of northern manuscripts that mix large areas of green made from *terre-verte* with orange and blue. It was given prominence as a major design element in the Newberry Library manuscript (fig. 24), where the center gutter border met the top of the frame. There, a large orange carpel cross-hatched with yellow or gold is displayed by the blue calyx of the flower. Carpels also appear in the bottom center position in the Vincent of Beauvais manuscript just mentioned, as well as at left, right, and bottom right positions in the border. Indeed, the carpel is a long-lived decorative feature and can be found in northern manuscripts from about 1420 through about 1480.

An early use of the carpel as a major design element appears in Cambridge, Jesus College MS 8, Isidore of Seville; it is virtually identical to that in the Newberry *Polychronicon,* even to the colors and patterns used, though it must have been made at least fifty years earlier. The style of the decoration elsewhere would place the book in the early fifteenth century.[66] MS 8 has a number of five- to nine-line floriated initials and three-quarter borders. Its northern connections are two. It is among the Jesus College books, and we know this college acquired a large number of Durham manuscripts. And it was early owned by a Thomas Man, vicar of Northallerton. An initial with green, rose-pink, and orange-yellow acanthus infill sends out two blue calyx forms, whose deeply shadowed interior space is skillfully depicted. Within these cones at folios 4 and 20, for example, are pairs of dramatic conical orange carpels, cross-hatched and dotted or for variety merely dotted with yellow, which send off green sprays.

Fitzwilliam Museum, Cambridge MS 34 is a missal made for Richard and Elizabeth Fitzwilliam of Sprotborough, Yorkshire. Richard died in 1479. This missal falls somewhat towards the end of the carpel motif's popularity. A handsome large book, it has script on two scales, with numerous two-line to seven-line floriated and historiated initials, full floral borders, and at folios 2v-3r a double miniature of the patrons and their arms opposite a canon page Crucifixion.[67] A typical

26. Floriated border with carpel and calyx motifs at top and bottom center. Cambridge, Fitzwilliam Museum MS 34, missal, folio 21, between 1465 and 1479. *Courtesy Trustees of the Fitzwilliam Museum.*

full border occurs at folio 21 (fig. 26) with an initial containing a miniature of the owner offering his soul to God. At the top, bottom, and sides of the border, flower calyx forms contain orange and yellow carpels surrounded by sprays.

Evidence for a common vocabulary for the floral motifs we have been examining thus far comes from five books now in York and London. These are two York Minster Library Additional volumes,

MS 30 and MS 69, and two with the older type of press mark; MS XVI. A.9 and MS XVI. K.6, as well as British Library MS Royal 2.A.xvii. The first of these, MS Additional 30, is a missal, probably for choral use, with a York kalendar and the Feast of the Relics of the Cathedral. It seems to have been made for a man named Ralph, whose name occurs at folio 243v in offices and prayers, and perhaps copied by a York scribe named Thomas Lemyng (fol. 132). The book has numerous six- to eight-line floriated initials and full floral borders. The date of this book from its script is probably mid-fifteenth century.[68] Quite similar to it in size and decoration is Additional 69, a rubricated choir breviary with a York kalendar. It has six- to twelve-line major initials with sprays making up side and top borders. A fifteenth-century inscription indicates that the book belonged to Thomas Sherston, a chaplain.[69] Both scribes write ornate liturgical *textura* employing many hairline finishing strokes. Among the interesting similarities of the decoration in these books is the habit of outlining the major initial forms with six or eight white dots followed by a white circle and the presence of the oddly expressionistic calyx and carpel patterns to the flowers in the borders.

York Minster Library MS XVI.A.9 is another missal with a York kalendar. It has four- to seven-line initials with full floral borders and on the basis of the script is somewhat earlier in date than the three larger companion books just discussed.[70] It uses calyx and carpel motifs at the top and bottom of the bar borders as well as at points on the sides. Several two- to four-line initials contain a similar calyx and carpel combination within the initial. Similar in its decoration is MS XVI.K.6, described in the previous chapter; at folio 7v, for example, a five-line initial contains a calyx whose carpel has yellow dots. A virtually identical initial occurs on folio 10 of MS Royal 2 A.xvii, a *horae*, which has ropy interlace medallion borders and a five-line initial consisting entirely of a blue and rose calyx with a protruding powdered gold carpel (fig. 27).

Perhaps as a result of its association with Durham rather than York, Laud Misc. 302 shows some differences in how the carpel motif is used by the two decorators who worked on its borders. It is a very idiosyncratic book in other ways as well, belonging with some of the archaizing manuscripts discussed in the previous chapter in its widespread use of motifs obsolete by the period in which the manuscript was painted. For example, many of the borders have the sorts of animal parodies, bowmen shooting at animals, animal banquets, and the like, which we might find as free-standing anecdotal marginalia

27. Floriated border with interlace medallions and cornerpieces, floriated initial with carpel and calyx motif. London British Library MS Royal 2. A. xvii, *horae*, folio 10, S. XIV. *Courtesy Trustees of the British Library.*

in manuscripts of the late thirteenth to mid-fourteenth centuries such as the Luttrell Psalter, London, British Library MS Royal 10.E.iv known as the Smithfield Decretals, and similar books. Here, however, they are placed within broad strip borders often hidden in the most contemporary illusionistic foliage.

Another archaizing element in the decoration of Laud Misc. 302

28. Throne of Grace Trinity with carpels. Oxford, Bodleian Library MS Laud Misc. 302, missal, folio 142, S.XV. *Courtesy Bodleian Library.*

is the use of the mask face, which appears with protruding tongue in a border roundel at folio 8v. With this old-fashioned material, Laud Misc. 302 combines stylish Italianate acanthus leaves wrapped around a rod with conic forms and conic calyxes containing large carpels, as in borders of a page containing a Throne of Grace Trinity initial at folio 142 (fig. 28).

I should like to conclude this discussion of northern decorative border forms and motifs by examining in some detail a manuscript whose decoration epitomizes the style of the Interlace and Mask Medallion group with which we began this chapter. This book is Oxford, Bodleian Library MS Rawlinson Liturgies b.1. The book contains not only the Interlace and Mask Medallion motifs, jutting leaves, and large masses of orange and blue used in foliage, but also many archaizing elements of the type we saw in the previous chapter. This large book is written in good *textura* on two scales, showing by its wide margins a disregard for cost. The graded York kalender has feasts for the translation, octave, vigil, and relics of St. Bees.[71] The book has twenty-six full and three-quarter borders, of which a large number contain masks, interlace medallions, overhand knotting of vines and jutting leaves giving off sprays of three gold blobs with corkscrew finials.

At the opening of the manuscript, folio 12r, a mask face with a protruding tongue and mead-horn ears sits atop a full border with an interlace medallion at bottom (fig. 29). Alternatively, at some points in the manuscript, the mask is either the source of the foliage, which issues from its mouth and ears as at folio 243v, or is absorbed into the initial, serving as the source of its floriation. In its use of the mask motif, the book does not differ too much from the Bolton *horae* and York Minster Library MS Additional 383.

Two features of MS Rawlinson Liturgies b.1 that distinguish it from the typical Interlace and Mask Medallion style are the presence of large circular gold grounds behind the interlace medallions and dragons whose tails grow from the twisted bars of the border beneath them and from whose mouths the bar border emerges above them. Such a dragon, for instance, forms one leg of the letter in the initial just examined. Two similar dragons form the top and lower side of a full border at folio 121v. As we have seen from the James psalter, the dragon is quite an old-fashioned motif by the end of the fourteenth century or the beginning of the fifteenth.

These dragons link the book with several northeastern manuscripts with interlace medallions from roughly the same period that may be copies of each other. For example, the dominant decorative motifs of York Minster Library MS XVI.O.9, a fifteenth-century breviary and missal from All Saints, Pavement, York,[72] are bar borders with free-standing dragons floating in the margin and numerous six-line initials containing interlace pentangle motifs on a circular gold ground. These dragons, attenuated eagles, and pentangles are identical to, though not as skillfully done as, those found at folios 233r and

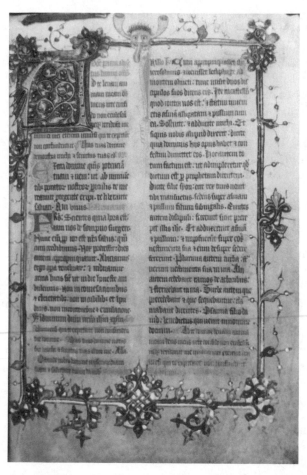

29. Floriated border with jutting leaves, interlace medallion, and mask face. Oxford, Bodleian Library MS Rawlinson Liturgies b. 1, missal, folio 12, ca. 1380. *Courtesy Bodleian Library.*

243v of MS Rawlinson Liturgies b.1. By its very idiosyncratic palette and curiously old-fashioned partial bar borders with polymorphic animals and birds, MS XVI.O.9 belongs with Cambridge University Library MS Dd.10.22 as examples of a whimsical and effective solution to the problems of decorating a manuscript of modest quality without a slavish reliance on the characteristic broad panels of sprays, vinets, and illusionistic flowers common in Franco-Flemish border

30. Floriated trellis border with interlace medallions and dragon.
London, Lambeth Palace MS 23, Bible commentary, folio 1, 1390.
Courtesy Officials of Lambeth Palace.

decoration in the south. Another book that may have been copied
from this group is the later Durham Cathedral MS B.II.30, whose
thin bar border develops into a dragon. From its mouth comes a five-
line initial in whose bow is an interlace medallion of the pentangle
variety. And finally we should mention the important Lambeth Palace
MS 23, from Durham (fig. 30). The dragon-loving artist of MS 23
drew a border-emitting creature, similar to that in Durham MS

B.II.30, at the upper right of the trellis border on the first folio; his decoration is in most other ways very similar to Durham Cathedral MS A.I.3.

These groupings indicate something about both economic strictures and aesthetic preferences in the northern English book trade during the late Middle Ages. The existence of such books suggests that some new views need to be taken about book production in this region, especially the role of foreign models. Though this Continental influence is clear, the exact form of transmission is uncertain. Indeed, the whole question of how northern artists gained access to Continental manuscripts is an intriguing one. Michael Orr in a recent paper[73] on some southern English illuminators has suggested several possibilities, such as foreign travel, the use of model books, and the collaboration in an English atelier with foreign scribes, the last of which is the most plausible explanation for our northern painters.

As to the quality of the fifteenth-century artists who created the different decorative border styles just detailed, we have seen that northern volumes are on the whole plainer than their southern and eastern counterparts, but they still show strong aesthetic preferences. The range of their border decoration runs from the rough and ready in books like York Minster Library MS XVI.A.9 to the fairly refined and elegant in Bodleian MS Rawlinson Liturgies b.1. But what these books may lack in draftsmanship, they make up for in bold and imaginative choice of decorative motifs from earlier periods in English painting and from Continental models. It seems that the artists of the Interlace and Mask medallion group usually chose simpler decoration than that being painted in the south. I have found no examples of what might be called fully developed International Gothic Style in any of the northern manuscripts I have examined, though elements of that style of drawing occur in the Boulogne *horae* and in certain other codices showing Bohemian and Netherlandish influence in the drawing or modeling of faces. An exception to this generalization is the *Liber Cosmographiae* of John de Foxton (Cambridge, Trinity College MS R.15.21), which, though written in York, had its miniatures done by the peripatetic southwestern Dominican painter John Siferwas.[74] On the whole then, the northerners do not compete stylistically with regard to borders popular in the south but were content to offer patrons adaptation of the English border art of the 1350s.

I suggest two reasons for what might be termed northern parochiality. First, there may be a parallel between the anachronistic tastes of Ricardian poets like William Langland and the poet of *Gawain and the Green Knight* and other anonymous figures of the alliterative revival and these manuscript artisans perhaps a generation later. Just as Langland and the *Gawain* poet self-consciously chose a northern or Anglo-Saxon metrical scheme and a northern or Scandinavian-influenced vocabulary, so these painters went back in time to the roots of English painting, taking Hiberno-Saxon interlace as their main decorative motif. Second, it is evident that because the quality of draftsmanship in the north was not as high as that in or around London, the sorts of portrait busts, naturalistically rendered birds, insects, and flowers, and botanically exact vinets and sprays that fill the borders of many fifteenth-century southern codices were not easy to achieve with the facilities available in the north. So grotesque masks or dragons that had no textual existence or interlace pentangles without real animals and flowers were easier to paint.

The north, then, had a regional style of considerable power and diversity, not inferior to that of the south, but simply different and responding to different sorts of constraints. And just as the border decoration in the books we have seen depicts distinctly regional taste, so the motifs filling those historiated initials and illumination in these books also display this taste. It is to these motifs that we will turn next.

5

"Hermits Painted at the Front"

IMAGES OF POPULAR PIETY IN THE NORTH

𝕿he will of William Barnby, the Yorkshire chaplain mentioned in chapter 1, contained an affecting legacy. He gave twenty shillings to the parish church of Doncaster for the repair of a gradual, and he owned only two books, both lovingly described in detail: "unum librum album parvum, cum bredis, vocatum manual sacerdotis" and another, "cum bredis, coopertum cum rubio correo, et in principio libri est pictura heremetarum et in eodem libro est de vita Christi." Barnby's small library shows two preoccupations of many fifteenth-century northern clerics. One is expressed by a book useful to a priest in his public work of caring for souls. The other is revealed by a work intended for private meditation and devotion, probably the pseudo-Bonaventuran *Meditationes Vitae Christi*, a popular devotional work. As we will soon see, books containing pictures of contemplative hermits of the Desert Fathers type, sometimes labeled Richard Rolle, or "St. Paul the first hermit," combined with visual and verbal texts illustrating events in Christ's life, especially his Passion, were important models of devotional practice and popular piety in the north, both among religious communities like the Carthusians and Benedictines and also among lay persons.[1]

The illustrated works of popular piety discussed in this chapter are similar in character to northern commonplace books and devotional works, usually compiled by clerics for their own use, or as an aid to their parish duties. Such spiritual guides began to develop in England in the hundred years before the Reformation. In most cases these clerical guides are unillustrated or contain rudimentary drawings, monograms, and the like. Indeed, it could be just such a book that Barnby refers to as a *manual sacerdotis*. These books relied heavily on exempla to capture the imagination of popular audiences, and it is such simple and often graphic stories that have their counterpart in the illustrated books in which text is subordinated to pictures.

The devotional imagery develops from what might be called a new interest in the Passion noticeable in England during the fourteenth and fifteenth centuries, and it is especially evident in the north, where it is reinforced by contact with northern European piety in the port cities of the east coast, like Hull. It is what Vincent Gillespie has called "the intense focussing on the events and images of the life and passion of Christ"[2] by the meditators, who are counseled to imagine themselves bystanders at or even participants in the events they contemplate. This attitude was common in a number of thirteenth-century Latin works, like the pseudo-Bonaventuran *Meditationes*,[3] popular with lay persons, as well as in some devotional books chiefly intended for use in the cloister, like the *Ancrene Rule*. Various meditational techniques were employed to make the Passion vivid, among which was a strong interest in the damage wrought to Christ's body before and during his Passion and the physiological changes it underwent on the Cross. Christ's torment was often expressed by various metaphors in which that body was likened to a parchment book, a scroll, a deed, or even a shield bearing a "coat of arms" that could be read by the pious meditator.[4] In the choir aisle windows of Great Malvern Priory church, Worcestershire (ca. 1430–1440), which have some similarities to the St. William Window in York Minster, for example, were great heart-like blazons with the wounds Christ received at the Crucifixion shown as long, deep slits from which issue large drops of blood. Every Sunday the parishioner would contemplate these and similar images throughout the service as an aid to feeling personally what was being talked of in the sermon.[5]

That illuminated manuscript books, like the more public arts of wall and glass painting, were often used as a devotional metaphor made them particularly suited to the context of the manuscripts treated in this chapter. One well-known expression of the need for striking graphic images to serve as an auxiliary "book" to aid in contemplation of the Passion appears in John Mirk's *Festial*: "þer ben mony þousaund of pepul þat couþ not ymagen in her hert how Crist was don on þe rood, but as þai lerne hit be syȝt of ymages and payntours." Mirk's key terms are *imagine* and *heart*. For affective piety involves two organs: the imagination, as it was considered in the Middle Ages an "organ" or front ventricle of the brain, and the heart.[6]

In some cases, small details of the Passion like the Five Wounds made by the nails and spear were imagined as the five vowels, which could be "read" and meditated upon like words, as we learn, for example, from John Whiterig, a fourteenth-century Benedictine from Durham, who explains that the words of Christ's "book" are his deeds, suffering and Passion, and the letters or characters[7] of his volume are his wounds.

Thus, the Five Wounds are the five vowels, the bases of texts that the speaker urges the pious to read. The meditator was often advised to feel sympathetically that which Christ himself felt and to let Christ metaphorically write his Passion in the book of the meditator's heart with ink made from the blood from the Five Wounds. As Gertrude of Helfta says in a particularly beautiful passage of her *Legatus Divinae Pietatis,* "write in *my* heart *your* wounds with *your* precious blood."[8]

The images of popular affective piety that will occupy us here are by no means all of those that seem to be particularly common in the north. Nor, of course, are they even peculiarly northern, for these images occur all over England. They do, however, seem especially concentrated in the north, so that a few images occur over and over again and are usually combined in ways uncommon in the south. In this regard, the Lincoln Cathedral Thornton manuscript is helpful: if (as has been suggested by Keiser, Thompson, and others) Robert Thornton exhibited a particular taste for certain Middle English imaginative works in what he chose to collect, and, of course, indicated what was readily available for him to copy, then his choice of devotional texts may also show a similar regional preference or taste. For example, Thornton copies two rather rare hymns on the *arma Christi* and the side-wound of Christ at folios 278v and 279. These hymns in turn are illustrated and occur verbatim in the two illuminated Yorkshire manuscripts discussed in chapters 3 and 4, Boulogne-sur-Mer MS 93 and Cambridge, Trinity College MS O.3.10, written by the same scribe and made in the same York workshop. It is hard to see all of this as mere coincidence. More likely, certain images appealed strongly to artists and writers in the north, and in this chapter we will see what they were and why northerners found them so attractive.

These images are the Holy Face; the Sacred Heart, bearing the side-wound Christ showed to Doubting Thomas (John 20.27); and sometimes the four other wounds from the hands and feet. Often the side-wound as a way of "reaching" Christ's heart is depicted more directly and symbolically as a heart-shaped shield bearing a face-like arrangement of wounds. Thus instead of showing the full figure of Christ with wounds in the side, hands, and feet, all of the wounds, *pars pro toto,* can be placed on the heart-shaped surface.

Equally popular are the *arma Christi*, instruments of the passion, presented heraldically, and the Throne of Grace style of Trinity, in which the crucified Christ is held outstretched on the knees of God the Father. (Sometimes combined with the latter image is one of the souls raised to God's bosom in a napkin from the office of the *commendatio animarum*, though this composite image does not, to my knowledge, occur in manuscript illumination but is confined to church sculpture.) A related visual image is that of the IHS sacred monogram, which forms part of the popular devotion to the Holy Name. Such images illustrate the general trend in the late Middle Ages to abstract or simplify long or complex verbal Passion texts and to make them as visual as possible.

In order to talk about those images most prominently featured in northern manuscripts, we will on occasion need to examine other art forms as well, such as painted glass and sculpture. Thus, some attention will be paid to the relationship between visual treatments of these images in northern manuscripts and their appearances in the alabaster panels so popular as an export throughout the York diocese in the late fourteenth and early fifteenth centuries, for there is considerable evidence that these two art forms influenced each other.

One way to understand these images is through the new fifteenth-century fascination with heraldry and personal coat-armour. The wounds or instruments of the Passion in Christ's triumph over death become analogous to the elements of an heraldic blazon representing a knight's—or a family's—past victories, like Yvain's being known as the Knight of the Lion.[9] An extreme and late statement of this idea appears in London, British Library MS Lansdowne 874:

> Why should earthes gentry make herself so good
> giuing coate armor for all the world to gaze on?
> Christ's blood alone makes gentle men of blood;
> His shamefull passion yeelds þe fairest blazon.
> For he is auncienst & of best behauiour
> whose auncestors & arms are from his savior.[10]

Michael Evans noted that "the use of shields to display the Instruments of the Passion became a convention during the later Middle Ages . . . after the establishment of the *festum lanceae et clavorum* in 1353, when devotions to the *arma Christi* became essentially a meditation on the Passion."[11] Thus the Holy Face, wounded heart, *arma Christi*, Throne of Grace, souls in the bosom of God, and IHS monogram are generally presented frontally to the viewer, often on a shield or heart-shaped background. They are the "arms" that the pious could read from afar on the armor of the Christian knight.[12]

Of the two books Barnby owned, the first, the priest's manual, is culturally related to the second, containing a painted image. Though they are not, or are only slightly illustrated, I should like to touch briefly on several of the manuals or commonplace books known to be possessed by men like Barnby, as their structure and contents may help to prepare us for some of the extensively illustrated works which will occupy us at greater length as repositories of the images of interest here.

The first is the commonplace book of John Gysborn, British Library MS Sloane 1584, which Vincent Gillespie well called "a vernacular pastoral miscellany."[13] The second is a somewhat similar miscellany of Thomas Ashbey, a Bridlington canon, now Durham University Library MS Cosin V.v.19.[14] The third is a notebook of a York priest, Robert Burton, active in the 1470s; this book, which has a kalendar of York use, is now Oxford, Bodleian Library MS Wood empt. 20.[15] These books give us a varying perspective on the intellectual and aesthetic concerns of northern regular and secular clergy in this period, as two of the books were compiled by canons and one by a priest.

Dickens believes that John Gysborn probably came from Guisborough in the North Riding and belonged to the Premonstratensian house at Coverham about two miles from Middleham, which held a number of appropriated parish churches with cure of souls.[16] Canons of the abbey served several chapels in the large parish of Middleham, among them one established by a branch of the book-owning Pigot family, mentioned in chapter 1. In the late fifteenth century, of the nineteen canons in the house, seven were vicars or parish priests in the area.[17] As an elaborately decorated prayer roll was also made at the abbey by another canon, contemporary with John, there seems to have been something of a scriptorium there as well, and Doyle notes that Premonstratensian canon scribes elsewhere in England—for example, at Sulby—worked for money.[18]

British Library MS Sloane 1584 contains on folio 12 the compiler's colophon, "scriptum per me Johannes Gysborn canonicus de Coverham." Later in his book, which was apparently put together over a long period, he calls himself a priest of Allington in Lincolnshire, a benefice controlled by the Premonstratensian house of Newbo. The compiler, who employs an *Anglicana* hand for the English excerpts and an idiosyncratic Secretary for the rest of the text, exhibits throughout the book an interest in alphabets and ornamental letter forms such as to suggest that he may have been a part-time scribe by vocation. The hand has such a mixture of forms—for example, an extremely high two-compartment a[19] of the type that appears in Oxford, Bodleian MS e Museo 160 of 1520, discussed at the end of this chapter—that it is difficult to date. On palaeographical grounds, however, Dickens's ascription of it to the 1530s seems late and a date in the 1480s might be closer because of its content as well as its script. Some of the volume deals with the arts of making manuscript books; such material would have seemed a little obsolete by the 1530s.

Memoranda, however, on 29r–32v include model letters and bonds for debt with persons from Grantham, Donnington, and Allington with dates :"the xj yer of the reyne off kynge henry the viijth (fol. 31) and "the viijth day off october in the xxijti year of the reynge of our sofferend lord kynge henry the viijth." (fol. 87v). These notes allowed Dickens to date the manuscript as he did, and Julia Boffey believes they are in Gysborn's hand.[20]

Whatever its date, the Sloane manuscript, in true medieval commonplace-book fashion, has a curious collection of texts: medical recipes for herbal drinks; recipes for engraving on iron and steel with acid; recipes for the manufacture of gold paint and powder for enameling; a treatise on colors specifically for bookmaking; recipes for glue, for preparing parchment, and for making paper shine; and an alphabet of engrossing initials. Among the pastoral items Gysborn collected are notes on the mass and the duties of deacon and subdeacon; questions for the confessor to ask; Latin and English prayers to guardian angels,[21] patriarchs, apostles and martyrs; some English prayers and lyric poems, one to the Virgin; several sermons; a treatment of the pains of hell; and a brief history of the sacrament of confession. Though the book is otherwise undecorated except that folios 1 and 28v bear large, framed strapwork medallions of the sort discussed in the last chapter, there is one drawing, presumably to satisfy the compiler's spiritual and aesthetic needs. This is a large emblematic badge of the Sacred Heart with a red bleeding sidewound, surrounded by hands and feet also with wounds, drawn in black and red ink on folio 26.[22]

The collection by Ashbey, an Augustinian canon of Bridlington active in the 1480s, focuses on the special powers conferred on this house by its saint, John of Bridlington. Ashbey has prayers to and meditations on the Virgin and St. Anne, a discussion of Gabriel's *Ave* to the Virgin,[23] and various poems on Mary and exempla illustrating her power. The compiler borrows from the Bridlington collection of miracles associated with John for many of his exempla and offers a votive office for the saint, notes on his canonization and feasts, and various works on Bridlington priory itself. The work concludes with theological and liturgical material on feasts, the symbolism of vestments, and guardian angels, for example, and quodlibets on such questions as whether men will be naked or clothed at the resurrection. Much of this compilation is in Latin, but there are English verses.[24] Ashbey was less concerned with pastoral work than either Gysborn or Robert Burton, both of whom apparently needed extracts from works about the function of the priest.

Burton's book is a very small paper volume. The Feast of the Relics of York Cathedral in red suggests that the kalendar, which is parchment and not in the same hand as the rest of the book, came from the metropolis, though the body of the book is clearly a production of its owner, who writes a good hand and signs his name at folio 44 "explicit quod R. Burton" and at folio 45 "amen quod Robertus Burtun." The priest was very much interested in the liturgical year and much of his book is really the sort of elaborated canon tables and instructions for the use of perpetual kalendars we find in York breviaries and missals. He was also interested in the sacraments and collects a variety of quodlibetal questions on them like those in the Ashbey volume. Other portions of Burton's book concern the preparation and performance of the mass, the life and character of the good priest, and technicalities for the sacrament of marriage (though this last item is balanced by a scurrilous poem on the nature of women). One area where Burton, like Gysborn, shows his interest in popular piety, is his fascination with the Five Wounds, discussion of which forms an extensive liturgical entry at folios 61 r-v. The book is undecorated save for emblematic red IHS monograms on folios 15 and 32.

Lying somewhere between these collections and several unusual illustrated miscellanies and prayer rolls designed apparently for northern Premonstratensian, Carthusian, and Benedictine houses are the various types of otherwise conventional northern office books that have interpolated a certain number of devotional images and texts that did not always form part of a typical psalter or *horae* before the late fourteenth century. Besides Boulogne-sur-Mer MS 93, the *horae* discussed in the last chapter, Trinity College, Cambridge MS O.3.10, a psalter-*horae* and hymnal, with the hours of the Passion and Office for the Dead, and Cambridge, Sidney Sussex College MS 37, a Sarum *horae* of probable northern manufacture, the *horae* now York Minster Library MS XVI. K. 6, which was briefly mentioned in chapter 3 for its use of *folium*, also offers this type of devotional picture cycle.

This book, which is sometimes called the Pullein *horae* from its *obits* of the Pullein family of Ulleskelf and Pontefract, is like Boulogne MS 93 and Trinity College, Cambridge MS O.3.10 in that it contains some twenty-four pages of six- to seven-line historiated initials throughout the text. This manuscript has been little discussed, and its pictures have never been published.[25] The Office for the Dead illustrated at folio 52v by two tonsured figures reading over a pall-draped coffin might seem at first to offer a clue to the manuscript's milieu. Though the white robes worn by these figures may be Premonstratensian or Carthusian, unfortunately the figures are not shown full-length so as to reveal the characteristic Carthusian connecting band at the lower part of the robe.

Of particular importance to us are scenes of the heart with side and limb wounds and the hymn "Salve plaga lateris" accompanying them that appear at folio 5v and a related rose with five outer and five inner petals, which follows an office for the Virgin at folio 25, where cartouches and a ring of text indicate that the flower symbolizes the *fons vitae* of blood and water issuing from the side-wound. There is a picture of God the Father with a Throne-of-Grace Trinity at folio 86v, and souls in a napkin being raised to God the Father by angels are depicted at folio 67v, illustrating the *commendatio animarum* (fig. 31).

The Holy Face that appears on folio 94 warrants some discussion. It was added by sewing a slightly later and far cruder cutting from another book to the page. This image appears in a roundel in front of a walled garden, perhaps the *hortus conclusus*, containing symbols of the Evangelists; it bears some relationship to contemporary block books. Around Christ's head, as with the rose at the beginning of the book, there is a motto taken from the opening couplet of the hymn to the Holy Face: "Salve sancta facies nostri redemptoris / in qua nitet species divini [splendoris]."[26]

Coming as it does as a seeming afterthought at the end of the codex, the Holy Face in the Pullein *horae* is less dramatically presented than it is in either of the other related manuscripts. Equally modest is the appearance of this motif in the Bolton *horae* (York Minster Library MS Additional 2), at folio 13 in a two-line historiated initial for the Pater Noster directly below another two-line initial containing the Crucifixion. Apparently, though the Holy Face was a popular motif in the north, it did not have the power there that it did on the Continent

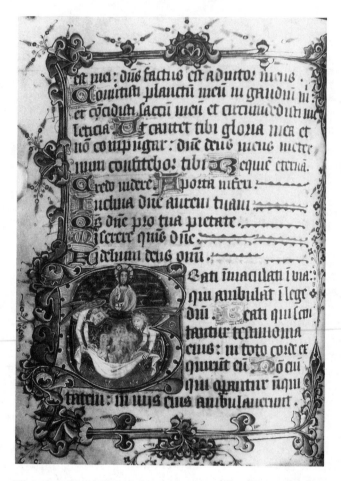

31. Historiated initial, souls in a napkin. York, Minster Library MS XVI.K.6, folio 67v, 1405–13. *Courtesy Dean and Chapter.*

and did not seem as necessary in devotional cycles as some of the other images we will be discussing. For example, Barbara Palmer, in her study and handlist of medieval art of the West Riding of Yorkshire, does not cite as many extant examples of the Holy Face as she does of other motifs of interest to us, such as the *arma Christi* and the side-wound.

The picture of the Holy Face, or vernicle, often held or displayed by Saint Veronica, was popular on lead pilgrim badges, as we recall from the portrait of Chaucer's Pardoner or from the B text of *Piers Plowman,* where a pilgrim among his other emblems carries the "vernycle bifore."[27] It also forms the subject of the hymn "Salve sancta facies," which seems to have been composed about 1330 during the papacy of John XXII.[28] It accompanies the image of the Holy Face in both the Boulogne and Trinity College, Cambridge manuscripts, introduced by an identical rubric.

Salve sancta facies nostri redemptoris,
In qua nitet species divini splendoris,
Impressa panniculo nivei candoris
Dataque verniculo signum ob amoris.

Salve decus seculi speculum sanctorum,
Quod videre cupiunt spiritus celorum:
Nos ab omni macula purga viciorum
Atque nos consorcio iunge beatorum.

Salve nostra gloria in hac vita dura,
Labili et fragili cito transitura;
Nos perduc ad patriam o felix figura,
Ad videndam faciem que est Christi pura.

Esto nobis quesumus tutum adiuuamen,
Dulce refrigerium atque consolamen,
Ut nobis non noceat hostile grauamen,
Sed fruamur requie omnis dicant, amen.

Hail, holy face of our redeemer,
in which shines the semblance of divine splendor,
impressing the linen white as snow,
and giving to the vernicle the sign of His love.

Hail, ornament and mirror of the saints in eternity,
that desire to see the spirit of the heavens:
cleanse us from all spot of vice,
and join us to the community of the blessed.

Hail, our glory in this harsh life,
weak and fragile, so quickly shifting—
O happy countenance, lead us to our Father,
to the sight of that face which is Christ's cleanness.

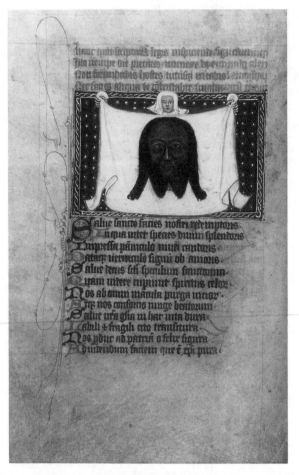

32. Holy Face. Cambridge, Trinity College MS O. 3.10, folio 11v.
Courtesy Master and Fellows of Trinity College, Cambridge.

O face, be to us the support and succor we seek,
our sweet refreshment and our consolation,
in order that no trouble annoy or perplex us—
but that we enjoy your rest. Let all say amen.[29]

While there are several different ways the head could be presented—for example, nimbused, or crowned with thorns—it is

33. Holy Face. Boulogne-sur-Mer MS 93, folio 6v. *Courtesy Bibliothèque Municipale.*

usually displayed on a *sudarium,* or sheet of linen, held by St. Veronica, the "veronice ymaginem tuam sudario impressam" of the prayer for the office in the Boulogne and Trinity, Cambridge manuscripts.[30] The style and proportions of the face presented on the *sudarium* suggest a Netherlandish model for the artist of MS Trinity College, Cambridge O.3.10.[31] In both of these scenes, as in the Trinity College, Cambridge manuscript, folio 11v (fig. 32), the face is darkened, and it might have been that way in Boulogne, folio 6v (fig. 33) had the images been completed. We recall from the last chapter that Julian of Norwich explained why Christ's face in the imagery of popular piety is of changing color, blackened, or morbidly gray-black.[32]

Like the Holy Face, the material on the side and limb wounds comes from the Continent, entering the English liturgy in the early fifteenth century,[33] though it was chiefly a votive mass in England, and we do not find the actual festival as we do in Continental works. The supposed origin of this mass is presented in the York priest Robert Burton's notebook.

Burton tells how Pope Boniface II (in some accounts Boniface VIII, or Innocent VI, or Giles the Great) on his deathbed prayed to God to prolong his life, and God responded by sending the archangel Raphael with the office and mass of the Five Wounds, which had originally been composed by John the Evangelist. Advising the pope to get up from his sickbed and write out the office and repeat it five times, the archangel stood by while Boniface was duly cured. By the fifteenth century, were a priest to say the office five times for a sick or dead person, he or she would be freed from much of the pain of purgatory.[34] The northern variant of this office in the York missal contains the full account of the Crucifixion in John 19, but concentrates on the side-wound more than on the wounds in the hands and feet. Extremely popular in the north among all classes, an image of the Five Wounds appeared on a badge used by the rebels during the Pilgrimage of Grace rebellion against Henry VIII in 1536–1537 and by the Norton family as late as the Rising of the North in 1569.[35]

Pfaff has noted the popularity of the cult of the Five Wounds in private devotions and votive masses, and we are all familiar with its appearance in *Gawain and the Green Knight*, where we are told of the hero that "alle his afyaunce vpon folde watz in þe fyue woundez."[36] Pfaff claims that its earliest appearance in England seems to have been at Durham, in the mid-fifteenth-century missal now Oxford, Bodleian MS Laud Misc. 302,[37] discussed in the previous chapter. However, Trinity College, Dublin MS 83, folios 189v-191; Cambridge, Trinity College MS O.3.10; Cambridge, Sidney Sussex MS 37; Boulogne-sur-Mer MS 93; and the slightly later Bolton *horae*, York Minster Library MS Additional 2, folio 175v are other northern rivals of comparable or even slightly earlier date. The hymn from the Boulogne *horae* is representative. Its rubric shows a slight variation on the Boniface-Gregory pattern: "Hanc oracionem composuit Egidius magnus et dominus papa Johannes XXII dedicavit eam C. dierum indulgencie. Et beatus Leo papa adiunxit quadraginta dies cotidie devote dicentibus." The concrete visual imagery of the actual hymn, however, focuses entirely on the side-wound and the other *plagae* are more abstractly handled.

Salve plaga lateris nostri redemptoris
ex te enim profluit fons rosei coloris
et vera medicina tocius doloris,
et eterna requies humani laboris.

Salve plaga domini, salus peccatorum:
tu es consolacio perfecta iustorum.
Et grata refectio tu es beatorum.
Et pacis fruitio portaque celorum.

Salve plaga domini, recens et fecunda,
emanavit nam ex te salutaris unda:
per quam liberabimur a morte secunda
cuncti servientes hic tibi mente munda.

Salve plaga domini, domus requiei.
Tu tutum refugium, ancora fidei.
Per te iam a crimine nos purgemur rei.
Et post introibimus in conspectu dei. Amen.

Hail, wound in our savior's side—
a fountain of rosy color flows forth from you,
and true medicine of all pain
and eternal rest from human toil.

Hail, wound of our lord, salvation of sinners—
thou art a consolation for those perfected in righteousness,
and thou art a pleasing refection of the blessed,
and fruit of peace and gate of heaven.

Hail, o wound, so fresh and fecund,
for from you flows a wave of salvation
that will free from a second death
all of clean mind who serve you.

Hail, wound of the lord, house of rest—
thou art a refuge from cares, an anchor of faith.
By you, we are washed clean of sinful things
and afterward we will enter into the presence of God. Amen.[38]

As the rubric indicated, often a certain number of days were remitted from purgatory for the person contemplating these wounds

in images on a regular basis—perhaps having these images in the
home or wearing them on finger rings that could be regularly kissed.
Such indulgences were often "authorized" by various popes in a
rather fabulous way,[39] as shown in an indulgence scroll in the
Beinecke Library, Yale, MS 410, which reads "Innocent hath grauntid
to What man or Woman þat dayly Worshyppeth deuoutly the .v.
principall Woundes of our lorde . . . the vij partes of there penance
relesid in þe paynes of purgatory."[40]

Putting a large, striking image of the heart alone or of the Man
of Sorrows with wounds into a *horae* or prayer roll would make such
contemplation very practical. York Minster Library MS Additional
54, the Mountenay *horae* discussed in chapter 1, contains a single
image for contemplation. This volume is especially interesting because not only does the will of one of its later owners describe its
iconography, but we also have the actual book. Additional 54 is a
horae of Sarum use adapted to York use with Wilfrid's and John of
Beverley's feasts written into the kalendar in a contemporary script.
A small, portable book, its decoration is very plain, but the work
contains at page 64 a one-half-page drawing in the Italian style of
Christ as a Man of Sorrows rising from the tomb, with the lower half
of the body still within it. Just below the tomb-chest are arms of
the Mountenay family.[41] A red inscription, now much rubbed, below
the image of Christ offers this indulgence: "Summa omnium indul-
genciarum istarum viginti sex milia annorum et XXXa de vera
indulgencia."

A picture of the heart with a wound like an eye and drops of
blood as the lashes appears in the office for the Sacred Heart in the
Sidney Sussex College *horae*, MS 37 at folio 130v. A similar seven-
line image of the wounded heart occurs in York Minster Library MS
XVI.K.6 just before the hymn to the Holy Face (fig. 34); the position-
ing of the wounds on the heart gives it something of the appearance
of a human face. In the Pullein *horae*, alternating gold, violet, and
blue and red uncials flank the heart, making up a text: "fili michi da
cor tuum," which seems to echo the invocation of a presumably well-
known prayer referred to by Gertrude of Helfta in her *Legatus:*
"Domine Jesu Christe, Fili Dei vivi, da mihi toto corde."[42]

The many drops of blood that often appear around the wounds
on these shield-like images were imagined to have both an abstract
magical or apotropaic power and, as the *fons vitae* described in a
related series of metaphors, to serve to quench the thirst of the devout
contemplator. For example, in the illustrated Carthusian miscellany,

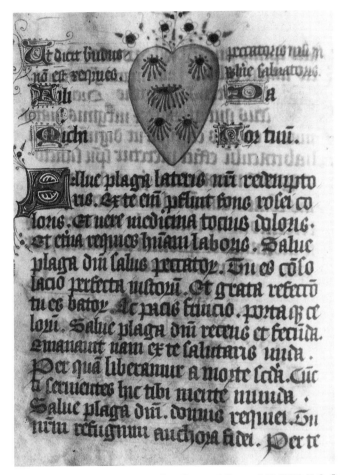

34. Sacred Heart as a face. York, Minster Library MS XVI.K.6, folio 25v. *Courtesy Dean and Chapter.*

London, British Library MS Additional 37049, a large picture of a heart bears the inscription "M CCCC LCX XV woundes," and underneath the large, slit-like wound in the middle of the heart is another numerical formula, M CCCCC M XLVij C V, and the word "drops." What should be 5,475 wounds and 547,500 drops of blood are the numbers that come from saying fifteen Pater Nosters and Aves each day for a year, multiplying the five wounds in a formula of 15×365; an analogous formula produces the large number of drops of blood.

A similar idea, setting the number of the drops at 5,409, occurs in the Wakefield Resurrection play.[43]

The *fons vitae* idea, on the other hand, combines several metaphors that are well seen in a Middle English lyric from London, British Library MS Arundel 286, involving both shelter in and refreshment from the heart:

> Ihesus woundes so wide
> Ben welles of lif to þe goode,
> Namely þe stronde of hys syde,
> þat ran ful breme on þe rode.
> . . . .
> ჳif þee liste to drinke,
> to fle þe fendes of helle,
> Bowe þu doun to þe brinke
> & mekely taste of þe welle.[44]

It is to this tradition that Archbishop Thomas Rotherham's will pays homage when he refers to himself as one "born again by the holy bath flowing from the side of Jesus."[45]

Undoubtedly the broad, deep slits dominating the hearts in both Cambridge, Trinity College MS O.3.10, and Oxford Bodleian MS Latin Liturgies f. 2 (figs. 35 and 36) derive from this idea of the devout actually entering into the heart to find a spiritual home. Indeed, in the former miniature the wound in the side as it is transferred to its more heraldic place on the heart-shield is not only lozenge-shaped to distinguish it from the nail holes but also a great deal larger, as if to suggest an entrance to the heart of Christ. The wound appears directly and symbolically as a sort of steaming chasm with what seem to be wisps of vapor coming forth from the aperture. In the latter miniature, discussed in greater detail below, the heart shape opens to reveal an actual heart within. The idea probably has German origins, and we find it in a hymn to the side-wound that calls it "porta patens et profunda," presumably referring to the mysteries within.[46] The rather striking view of the opening in the Trinity College miniature, however, suggests Mechtild of Hackeborn's allegory of Anima the soul and its visit within Christ's heart in the *Liber Specialis Gratiae:* "Anima, coming to the wound in the heart, saw the opening emitting, as in a similitude, great burning flames and vapor."[47]

Such imagery seems to follow Christ's remark to Thomas, "put out your hand and place it in my side" (John 21:27), where it is clear

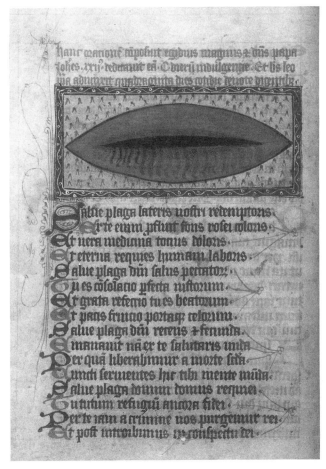

35. Sacred Heart with wound. Cambridge, Trinity College MS
O.3.10, folio 12v. *Courtesy Master and Fellows of Trinity College,
Cambridge.*

that the wound is to be understood as hand-sized and hence much
larger than the nail holes. The side-wound, then, is imagined as a
physical refuge in which the devout seek shelter and into which they
actually enter and become one with the figure of the crucified Christ,
as when Julian of Norwich says of her vision of it, "and ther he
shewyd a feyer and delectable place, and large jnow for alle man-
kynde that shalle be savyd and rest in pees and in loue."[48]

36. Side wound with wounded heart within. Oxford, Bodleian Library MS Latin Liturgies f. 2, *horae*, folio 4v, 1405–13. *Courtesy Bodleian Library.*

Though Jeffrey Hamburger's observations about the devotional importance of such side wounds over those of the hands and feet focus chiefly on German or Northern European examples, his remarks are nonetheless useful here: "whereas the other *arma* function as symbols, standing pars pro toto for the torment of the Passion, the side-wound confronts us as if we could see it directly. The miniature aspires to the immediacy of a vision; the visual has become a simulacrum of the visionary."[49]

These spatial associations of the side-wound, moreover, are graphically portrayed in various formulae for making measurements from it, and the wound is generally portrayed as tall, sometimes depicted the height of the whole miniature, as if it did actually serve a measurement function for the manuscript's owner.[50] Though these formulae appear in other forms of art, they are most common in prayer rolls of the type given as legacies in the wills discussed in chapter 1. However, the only surviving example of such an illustrated northern prayer roll, to my knowledge, is one now in the Pierpont Morgan Library, MS Glazier 39.[51] This was written by a contemporary and fellow canon of John Gysborn, a Canon Perceval at Coverham Abbey, who is otherwise unknown.[52] Perceval tells us that he came from Rudby, in Cleveland near Stokesley, Yorkshire, and Curt Bühler suggests that the maker's references to Pope Innocent VIII and King Charles VIII of France point to a date of composition about 1484. The roll, measuring nineteen and one-half feet long and about seven inches wide, was sewn together of nine parchment strips of varying length and decorated in black and red ink, presumably by the writer, with texts in both colors. It may have been made for the use of the abbey, as other works in roll form on a similar scale were extant at Durham Priory. About similar rolls Rossell Hope Robbins argued that they were intended to be unrolled before the congregations in churches as an aid to devotion.[53] The entire roll has a continuous border with a spiraling floral pattern that looks Coptic or Celtic. This motif also establishes vertical divisions of the roll to form registers containing pictures and offices for various saints.

Like some of the books we have already looked at, Perceval's roll opens with Passion images: the crown of thorns; the nails, whose length is described in a rubric; the wounded heart. After these opening emblems appears a scene of St. Roche; it and one of St. Sebastian later suggest that the scroll was of interest as a practical protection against the plague.[54] The image of Roche is followed by one of an angel holding a reliquary and then by one of an obscure Breton saint, Armel, accompanied by a verse prayer. The image of this saint, who became of interest in England with the accession of King Henry VII, helps to suggest a date for the scroll of perhaps 1485. A scene of a *Pietà* with a woman's prayer, "Ego misera peccatrix," suggests that Perceval was copying an exemplar possibly like the "rotula de passione" mentioned in the will of Maria de Roos, obtained from a woman of a local family. The fifth picture is that of the wounded heart (fig. 37) with a transliterated macaronic, chiefly Greek, inscription: "Agyos otheos sancte deus agyos iskiros sancte fortis agyos athanatos elyison

37. Sacred Heart. New York, Pierpont Morgan Library MS Glazier 39, Canon Perceval prayer roll, unfoliated, 1485. *Courtesy Pierpont Morgan Library.*

. . . pater noster ave maria." This is a refrain for the Reproaches in the liturgy for Good Friday. The use of Greek here reminds us of the second of the two pictures of obvious Byzantine inspiration that open British Library MS Additional 37049: one of Christ, entitled in passable Greek characters "isous o basilous ioudon ton christos," echoing Matthew 27:37 ("Jesus Christ, the king of the Jews").[55]

In Perceval's roll the wounded heart is followed by a representation of the pelican in its piety, which belongs to the *arma Christi* tradition to be considered shortly. The next image is another crown of thorns hanging on a cross, whose shaft contains a wounded heart. A text below on the apotropaic properties of the length of the cross shaft follows. Antony is the next saint depicted. Then there is a large representation of Henry VI accompanied by a chained antelope, and a shield bearing the arms of England. Next to Henry is John the Baptist in the desert, surrounded by various animals, followed by John the Evangelist, St. George and the dragon, St. Christopher (also popularly a plague saint, and called upon in this way here), Mary Magdalene, St. Michael, and the martyrdoms of Saints Erasmus, Lawrence, Margaret, and Katherine, all accompanied by various texts in red highlighted with black.

The scroll concludes with some words of its maker to the users:

Noghte to lyke þow me to lake
for this schrowyll by-hynd my bake
but whare þe fynde that I offende
I pray þow mekeley it amende
for ilk a sere man has a wyte
and thare-by he shal wyrke it
for vnto powre erudicione
I make thys symple formacione.
Chanon in Couerham withowten le
in þe ordere of Premonstre
þat tyme þis schrowyll I dyd wryte
whare-fore I pray þou me not wyte
in haste done so trewle
thare-fore it apperyth full symple.
In Rudby towne of my moder fre
I was borne wyth-owtyn le
Schawyn I was to þe order clene
the vigill of All Haloes evyn.
My name it was Percevall
Ihesu to þe blys he bryng vs all.

From the contents of this roll, it can be seen that it exhibits the same concerns as the other northern books we have been considering, combining the standard suffrages of the liturgy with the images of the wounded heart, *arma Christi*, and Throne of Grace. Perceval's roll, however, like most prayer rolls, has a somewhat more immediate and practical application than the *horae*, offering direct benefits both spiritual and secular to the user.

A Middle English text in the Glazier roll explains that the cross on which the wounded heart rests "XV tymes is þe trew lenth of our Lorde Ihesu Criste. And þat day that þou lokes on it er beris it apone the, that day sall no wekid sprete haue pouer to hurte þe. . . . This is registrede at Rome in Seynt John Laternence." Besides this general promise of help, specific claims are that these measurements will protect one in battle and will aid women in childbirth.

The nails of the first image in the roll, which are seven inches long, have much the same magical powers.[56] As with the cross shaft, a text in red explains "Theis er the veray trew lenth of the thre nailis of our lorde Jhesu Criste to whame pape Innocent sent this same lenth un to Kyng Charls and granted to hym al so to every man and woman þat with devocon worshippis þaim dayly and bereth þame a pone thaim with v pater noster v ave maria and a crede that [they] shall have vii peticions grauntede þame." These petitions are similar to the promises made in the earlier "length" prayer and add the medical detail of protection from pestilences and fevers. Amulets promising various benefits, using measurements based on the height of Christ or on the length of various implements—especially the nails in the Passion—as well as the measurements of the side-wound, have been well studied by Bühler[57] and need little discussion here.

The image of the wounds forming a metaphorical or even actual rose, such as we saw at the opening of the Pullein *horae*, and which is hinted at by the imagery of the first stanza of the hymn "Salve plaga lateris" is a fairly common one in affective or devotional texts.[58] And in Mechtild's *Liber specialis gratiae*, the side-wound is compared to the flower: "et ecce rosa pulcherrima habens quinque folia exivit de Corde Dei totum pectus ejus cooperiens."[59] A fourteenth-century French *horae* glosses a picture of the cross with *arma Christi* and five roses "les v roses signifient le v plaies," while the distinctively medita-tive character of the image is made clear in John Lydgate's "A Seying of the Nightingale": "Make of þees fyve, in þyn hert a roose / And let it þeer contynuelly abyde . . . Gadre on heepe þees rosen floures fyve, / In þy memorye enprynt hem al þy lyve."[60]

The rose image of the Pullein *horae* is a bit more complex because it combines Marian symbolism with the *fons vitae* idea. The flower, tinted a lovely Marian blue, appears on folio 25v at the end of a prayer to the Virgin to protect the speaker from evil and from a sudden and improvident death. It is surrounded by a motto: "Hic fons ortorum: puteus et aqua vivorum. Hic jubilus morum: hic lotrix criminorum." At the left top and bottom, two other scrolls read "Hic sanguis," and at the right two more say "Hec aqua."

Perceval's prayer roll gave special prominence to the *arma Christi*, which in a great many medieval works of art are literally the blazon of Christ, like the various heraldic elements in coat-armour. The *arma* were supposedly numbered by St. Peter and sanctioned by Pope In-nocent IV in 1246, or at least many texts containing them so claim, such as the influential mid-fourteenth-century *Omne Bonum* of Jacob le Palmer.[61] Sometimes accompanying verses promise a pardon from some of the pains of purgatory to one who meditates daily on the *arma Christi*.

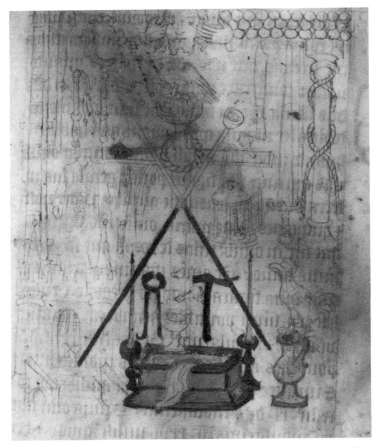

38. *Arma Christi.* Boulogne-sur-Mer MS 93, folio 9. *Courtesy Bibliothèque Municipale.*

The uncompleted painting of the *arma Christi* in Boulogne-sur-Mer MS 93, folio 9 (fig. 38) and the completed one in Cambridge, Trinity College MS O.3.10, folio 13r (fig. 39) are of this type, where the actual office is preceded by a rubric: "a summary of the number of years of indulgence gained by venerating the Passion of our lord Jesus Christ. Look on this image every day for a year and you will get six thousand seven hundred and fifty-five years and a half and three days," and so on.[62] The number of the *arma* in such pictures and offices varies from as few as twenty-four to as many as thirty-three in

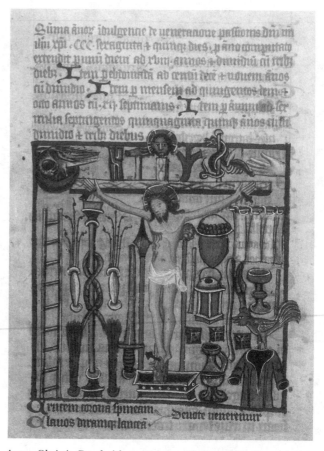

39. *Arma Christi.* Cambridge, Trinity College MS O.3.10, folio 13.
Courtesy Master and Fellows of Trinity College, Cambridge.

the Boulogne and Trinity College, Cambridge manuscripts, where
the offices list identical instruments:

Crucem, coronam, spineam
Clavos, diramque lanceam   devote veneremur
Acetum, fel, veronicam
Virgam, sputa, & spongeam   jugiter meditemur

Velum, lanternam nobilem   arundines pungentes
Pelicanum et calicem
Tunicam inconsutilem   et funes urgentes
Columpnam minime fragilem

Flagella, fustes innumerabiles   denarios ter denos
Enses latronum horribiles
Manus cedentes dissimules   urceos amenos
Cultellos duros & forcipes

Serpentem, scalam & malleum   corditer recolamus
Sepulcrum, lumen, candelabrum
Faciunt hec nam regium   perpetuum speramus
Vexillum, per quod gaudium.

Cross, crown, thorns,
nails, and probing lance—(Devoutly we revere thee)
vinegar, gall, veronica,
rod, spittle and sponge—(Perpetually we meditate on thee)

Veil, lordly lantern, (Striking reeds)
Pelican and chalice,
Seamless tunic, (Deadly crowding near)
Column exceedingly fragile

Scourge with thongs, blows uncountable, (Thruppence thrice ten)
horribly strained shoulders of the thieves,
Traitorous hands yielding him up, (A lovely ewer)
harsh knife and forceps,

Snake, ladder and hammer, (With heartfelt feeling we recollect it)
tomb, light, candelabrum—
all make here those royal arms and ensign (We trust in it perpetually)
by which we praise Him.[63]

Though these instruments may vary in order and may be depicted differently in different manuscripts, they are typically the
cross, crown of thorns, nails, spear and sword, knife of the circumci-
sion, the pelican, the lantern, the "manus" (often called "depillans"
when influenced by the northern Passion cycle), the seamless tunic,
the three dice, the veil of the temple, the flagella or scourges with five
lashes, the column of the scourging wrapped round with a cord, a

ladder of nine rungs, the nails and hammer, flagons of vinegar and gall, the reed with a sponge, smith's tongs or forceps, bundles of rods, spittle as drops or coming from faces, a tomb, a vine spouting blood, the brass serpent on a pole, a fist in a buffeting position, the traitor's purse with thirty coins, a chalice, the cock which crowed thrice, a club, and a lantern.

The tradition we are concerned with here can vary in concreteness. Sometimes the wounds or the instruments of the Passion will be rendered in great detail, and sometimes they are abstracted to the point that they are only wounds with no body. In the nave of Silkstone church in Yorkshire, for example, is a fifteenth-century roof boss that shows angels holding shields with the Five Wounds or with the instruments of the Passion, and on a late fourteenth-century roof boss at Methley church, the heart-shield is accompanied by two hands and two feet; occasionally the hands and feet have individual verses associated with them.[64]

Such shields were very common supporters of the *arma* and the wounds. The older metaphor of the shield of faith, deriving from the Epistle to the Ephesians 6, was often represented as a more or less triangular image reproducing the tapered shields of the thirteenth century, wide at the wedge of Christ's outstretched arms and narrow where the feet would be crossed; it was designed symbolically to picture the shield of faith, often with Trinitarian elements.

In more elaborate versions, as at Silkstone, these shields with the *arma Christi* were often held by or presented to the viewer by a pair of standing or kneeling angels, as in Boulogne-sur-Mer MS 93, an idea going back to William de Brailes, the influential thirteenth-century Oxford illuminator; in his Last Judgement miniature in a psalter, Cambridge, Fitzwilliam Museum MS 330, the angels hold instruments of the Passion.[65] These representations occur widely throughout the north, one example in Aberdeenshire appearing in a stone panel set in the wall of Castle Fraser, in which an angel carries a shield and a banderole below reads *arma Christi*. Closer to the area of concern to us, a particularly handsome and striking scene of the *arma Christi* in glass appears in a shield formerly in St. Saviour, York, and now in the West Window, All Saints, Pavement, York.[66] Such angelic shield bearers often occur contemporaneously in secular contexts in Yorkshire as well, for example on the Gascoigne-Mowbray (1419) and Redman-Aldburgh (1426) tomb-chests at Harewood a few miles to the north of Leeds.[67]

Another enormously important image of affective piety in late medieval northern England is that of the Trinity. Its representation, popular in stained glass, alabaster carving, tomb sculpture, and manuscript illumination, seems to reflect a devotion amounting to a cult in the north. The rather obscure order of Trinitarian friars had an important house, that of Saint Robert at Knaresboro near York, glorifying a local saint, Robert Flower, whose cave hermitage is still visible below a bank of the river Nid. Many northern men and women, especially those in and around the city of York, left substantial offerings in their wills to the Trinitarians. And there were guilds and fraternities dedicated to the Trinity or invoking it as a patron. The image of the Trinity appeared on even the most modest of domestic and ecclesiastical utensils. For example, Archbishop Thomas Rotherham gave as legacies a chalice and a paxbread both bearing images of the Trinity, and such gifts are very common in other wills.[68]

There are several ways this image was typically represented in the north. Relatively uncommon was a simple grouping of three persons. The Bolton *horae* offers both this type (fig. 40) and, as we shall see shortly, an alternative representation. In the Bolton triune type, God the Father crowned, and slightly older, sits opposite the Son, and an angel personifying the Holy Spirit flutters between them.[69] An example of this figure group also appears on an alabaster panel in the Yorkshire Museum, discovered in the foundations of a house of chantry priests in York. A standing Christ in the center of the group is supported by the seated Father and a personified Holy Spirit at either side; there may have been some confusion on the carver's part with the imagery of the Deposition from the Cross.[70] Presumably, the triune group Trinity was less successful as a devotional image because, as the Bolton *horae* shows, it was difficult to distinguish among the three persons of the Trinity in size and importance, and presumably the artist or the owner felt it necessary to include a more recognizable scene at a later point in the codex[71] (fig. 41).

By far more common on the Continent and in England is the image of God the Father holding on his knees an outstretched figure of the crucified Son, with dove overhead. This grouping is usually called the Throne of Grace. The figure type, which borrows from *Maiestas Domini* and Crucifixion scenes, occurs in place of the sorts of canon page Crucifixions we saw in chapter 3.[72] Though perhaps in theory heretical because the proportions of God the Father are exaggerated with respect to those of the Son, it is an image of considerable dramatic impact. These Trinities appear widely in the north in stone and glasswork, as well as in manuscript painting. Examples in architec-

40. Trinity as three persons. York, Minster Library MS Additional 2, Bolton *horae* folio 37v, after 1405 and before 1445. *Courtesy Dean and Chapter.*

tural media can be found on the south face of the west tower at the Church of St. Mary, Tickhill[73] and in painted glass in York Minster in the nineteenth bay of the north transept, in the windows of the church of St. Michael, Spurrier Gate, All Saints, Pavement, York, formerly in Saint Saviour, ca. 1370,[74] and in All Saints Church, North Street, York, to name only a few of the more famous examples.[75]

Similar images of probable or certain northern provenance also occur in sculpture. Throne of Grace Trinities are depicted in a small alabaster carving at Ampleforth Abbey, Yorkshire,[76] and in monumental Yorkshire tomb sculpture in some alabaster panels at Methley

41. Throne of Grace Trinity. York, Minster Library MS Additional 2, folio 33. *Courtesy Dean and Chapter.*

Church at Sheriff Hutton and in the parish church of Harewood near Leeds.[77] As alabaster carving seems to show some interesting relationships to manuscript illustration in the north, it may be worth saying something about the material itself and the trade in objects manufactured from it in the north of England before proceeding to the images themselves.

Alabaster, a crystalline calcium sulphate ocurring in England in large amounts in Staffordshire and in Derbyshire, is soft and quickly carved. In the late Middle Ages, a significant amount of it was quarried in Buttercrame near York.[78] Apparently, an equally large alabaster quarry was worked at Fairborne near Leeds.[79]

Some evidence exists for a York city school of alabaster carving. The York Freemen's Register lists eight persons practicing the trade of alabaster carving, but, unfortunately, the earliest of these references dates from 1457.[80] That these people were of moderate wealth and some prominence in city life is suggested in the will of a late fifteenth-century "Johannes Ropar civis et alabaste civitatis Ebor."[81] Some of these alabaster workers must also have been marble workers, and here the evidence is earlier, for there is a reference in the Freemen's Register to "Thomas Neuton marbler filius Johannis Neuton, marbler" free of the City of York in 1428.[82] John Jacob has spoken of this problem: "It is generally assumed that York was a probable centre for the manufacture of at least one type of panel, . . . the likeness of some of the tables to the panel of 'the Trinity' on the tomb at Sheriff Hutton suggests that the York tables, at any rate, may have come from the same workshop as the tombs."[83] Francis Cheetham also suggests that "the discovery in 1957 of several late medieval panels of an unusually large size, originally forming an alabaster altarpiece of the life of St. William of York, may point to the carving of altarpieces, as well as tombs, in York."[84] In short, though much of the information about alabaster working in York is fragmentary, most of it suggests a trade in the material there and solely lay artisans who worked it. Thus Hughes's idea that possibly "recluses were responsible for carving the alabaster tablets depicting scenes from the Passion that were so common in York"[85] seems rather speculative.

It has long been known since the work of W.L. Hildburgh[86] that there is a very close relation between medieval English carved alabasters and the staging of the medieval English cycle plays, with carvers possibly representing the sets they saw in these plays, or persons in the guilds responsible for staging these plays looking to alabasters for the details of certain scenes. And current scholarship has seen the influence of the plays on the carvings. Pauline Routh, an authority on alabasters, has noted that "there is little doubt that the source of many of these [panels] was the mystery plays."[87] Yet the relation between manuscript painting and alabasters has been less explored.

Evidence, however, that there is such a relation and that it may be relevant to the study of northern manuscript imagery comes from a simple comparison of two works of art. An alabaster and wood triptych made about 1400 (now in the Victoria and Albert Museum)

42. Trinity-Annunciation, alabaster triptych panel. London, Victoria and Albert Museum, accession number A193-1946, ca. 1400. *Courtesy Victoria and Albert Museum.*

depicts an Annunciation and a Trinity interestingly combined in a single image: the lily "tree" of the Annunciation in the lower part becomes the wood of the cross on which Christ is crucified in the upper (fig. 42). The Annunciation panel has a raised relief decoration in which the whole of the background is painted gold, and small dots in a fence-like pattern with a center dot in the square lattice give something of the effect of the raised dots on Celtic metal work or

Hiberno-Saxon manuscript painting. The pattern of dots continues as border stripes into the upper Trinity register. We need only compare this background with that in the second of the Trinities in the Bolton *horae* (fig. 41) to see the strong likelihood of influence from alabaster to miniature. The *horae,* painted in the first quarter of the fifteenth century, employs for most of the full- and half-page miniatures a gold background containing raised dots in similar patterns. We shall have occasion to see other examples of background pattern influence from alabaster to illumination shortly.

Let us return now to the alabaster Trinities. At Methley[88] is an alabaster tomb-chest of Sir Robert Waterton and his wife, ca. 1424, whose center panel depicts a Throne of Grace Trinity beneath an elaborate canopy. At either side angels hold heraldic shields. In the Church of St. Helen and the Holy Cross in Sheriff Hutton in the North Riding is a similar tomb-chest commissioned by Sir Richard Redman and his wife, Elizabeth Aldburgh. Carved around 1426, its south face contains representations of angels holding shields now defaced. At each side of a canopied Trinity, donors pray at the base of the cross.[89] Its costume, armor, and many details of funeral iconography are very like those on the Waterton tomb. The Methley panel in turn appears to have been copied in a now much defaced sculpture at Ripon Minster on the west face of the choir screen entrance.[90] According to Pauline Routh and Richard Knowles, these monuments may have been produced by a short-lived workshop in York.[91]

Some scholars, in dating extant alabaster carvings, have divided them into various classes according to the form of the canopy over the figure group. As Philip Nelson points out, a type "surmounted by a canted and embattled canopy, worked upon the same piece of alabaster," apparently produced in a York workshop between 1380 and 1420, can be distinguished from the later forms chiefly of Nottingham origin, in which the canopies are on separate pieces of stone.[92]

The crenellated character of many of these alabaster canopies and other architectural details, which has been used by Hildburgh to show ties with the staging of medieval drama, also appears in northern manuscript illumination. For example the *transi* tomb that illustrates the curious "Debate Between the Body and the Worms" in London, British Library MS Additional 37049 has heraldic shields and arcades possibly intended to contain Trinities, like some of the tomb-chests we have just been considering. And it also has a crenellated railing around the effigy on the lid. So too, the Man of Sorrows emerges from a rather squarish arcaded tomb in York Minster Library MS Additional 54, very like the alabaster examples.

We have seen that there is a stylistic relationship between the Throne of Grace Trinities occurring in these media and some of those in northern manuscript painting, though the precise form and direction of the transmission is uncertain. Six examples of the image occur in programs of illustration for books certainly or possibly made in the north. These are the full-page representation in the Bolton *horae*, York Minster Library Additional 2, already mentioned; historiated miniatures in York Minster Library MS XVI.K.6, the Pullein *horae* (fig. 43); in the Fitzwilliam Missal, Cambridge, Fitzwilliam Museum MS 34, folio 210; in Oxford, Bodleian Library MS Laud Misc. 302, folio 142 (fig. 28), the Durham missal discussed in the previous chapter; New York, Pierpont Morgan MS Glazier 39, the Perceval prayer roll discussed earlier; and finally, in the same collection, MS M 648, Nicholas Love's version of the *Meditations on the Life of Christ*. The first five of these, conventional representations for the most part, do not differ from their southern counterparts. Though the last manuscript does not have obvious northern ties, there is some reason to place its fabrication in the north, and it offers an interesting variant of the Throne of Grace idea.

The contents of this manuscript, in part the *Meditations* and in part an extract of the *Revelations* of St. Bridget, certainly suggest a Carthusian house and possibly a northern one. The manuscript, painted in a regional style—the cataloguer calls it "mediocre work of the early XVth century"—contains sixteen miniatures; on folio 5v there is a large and dramatic Trinity of the Throne of Grace type. The Morgan catalogue associates the miniature with an atelier from the Low Countries. Though the painting, the border decoration, and the look of the volume seem English, the artist does betray some Netherlandish training or influence. As we shall see, there are in its miniatures at least two features that tie it to northern English work.[93]

The border decoration of Pierpont Morgan MS M 648 shows several motifs common in northern books, most particularly a fondness for the large floral carpel and calyx forms discussed in the previous chapter. This motif, of course, is not in itself a sure sign of a northern atelier. And it is accompanied in the Nicholas Love manuscript by elaborate sprays, which are quite uncharacteristic of northern books, though these sprays are not integrated into the border decoration and may have been added later. Two other details however, are unusual. The miniature of the otherwise conventional An-

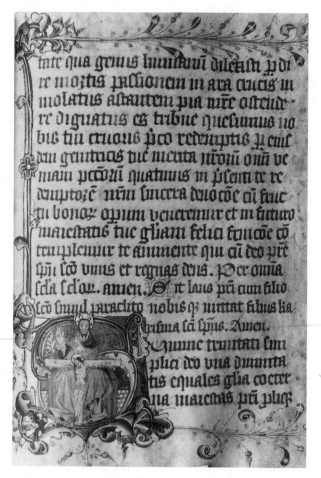

43. Historiated initial with Throne of Grace. York, Minster Library
MS XVI.K.6, folio 86. *Courtesy Dean and Chapter.*

nunciation on folio 10 shows the angel on a curious tiled floor with a
black ground on which appears a pattern of green isosceles triangles
with ornamental circles, and this device appears elsewhere in the
manuscript. Just such a pattern appears in the foreground of the
Holy Face miniature of unknown origins added at the end of
the Pullein *horae;* though the green shapes are diamonds rather than
isoscelean, the pattern in that color combination is uncommon
enough to be provocative.[94] Also, God the Father wears a voluminous

blue mantle, whose heavily fluted folds open to reveal a red lining. The edges of the fluting are outlined with a series of white lead dots. Though much more crudely painted, the Trinity scene in the Bolton *horae*, executed in York at about the same time as the Love volume, shows God the Father in a fluted two-color robe with a similar pattern of outlining dots.

A third type of Trinity representation, which appears in alabasters but not in any known English manuscript illumination, combines the Throne of Grace idea with the motif of the napkin—supported by angels at each side—containing images of the souls of the saved. The napkin of souls seems to come from the *commendatio animarum*, a specific set of Psalms combined with a prayer, common in *horae* in the fourteenth and fifteenth centuries and illustrates in part the Gospel of Luke 16.22. There are four alabaster freestanding and seven panel representations—probably for altarpieces—of this composition known; it does not appear in Continental art.[95] One of these alabasters seems to have influenced the style of miniature that combines the Throne of Grace with the napkin.

An excellent reproduction of an English example, probably from Nottingham, is published in an essay by Pamela Sheingorn. The motif also occurs in several alabasters now in northern locations, though whether they were made in York or further south cannot be determined. The earliest, from the 1370s or early 1380s, is in the Burrell Collection of the Glasgow Museum and Art Gallery. This freestanding figure of God the Father, with Throne of Grace Trinity on his knees, holds the napkin containing souls.[96]

A late fifteenth-century alabaster example whose polychrome treatment more decidedly suggests a northern workshop is in the Victoria and Albert Museum (fig. 44). It shows a crowned God the Father blessing with his right hand three souls in a napkin directly above a Throne of Grace Trinity supported by two angels. Four angels, two upper and two lower, catch the sacred blood in chalices. The background of the carving has two forms of decoration; one is a gold ground which has a pattern of small circles cut with a flat-tipped drill bit. The depressions below the surface of the ground were then colored. Elsewhere on the carving, there is a ground of dark paint with patterns of flowers made of six white dots with a red dot in the center. This floral design we have seen in the Green Canon-Page group of Crucifixion miniatures discussed in chapter 3. At least two other alabasters with a possible provenance in Yorkshire, those at Byland Abbey and at Ripon Minster, have this pattern, though in the

44. Drillwork and polychrome flower pattern background to souls in a napkin and Throne of Grace Trinity, alabaster panel. London, Victoria and Albert Museum, accession number 901-1945, ca. 1480. *Courtesy Victoria and Albert Museum.*

first instance there is no direct evidence of a medieval connection with the abbey.[97]

While there is no known manuscript representation of the *commendatio animarum* combined with a Trinity,[98] there are some interesting variants of the idea in northern, or possibly northern, painting. Sheingorn has shown how the old idea of souls brought to the bosom of Abraham[99] in a napkin as an image of paradise forming part of the liturgy for the dead was combined with the Throne of Grace Trinity to make a representation of All Saints, and serves to magnify the feast of All Saints. Breviary texts of the Office for the Dead offer a prayer, the Subvenite, for the soul of the dead person, asking that he or she be received by Christ and conducted by a chorus of angels into Abraham's bosom.[100] And as we saw, souls are often raised there in the napkin, which was associated with martyrdoms and the deaths of saints.[101]

In time, the Bosom of Abraham was replaced by a "home," visually identified as God the Father or the Son, where the receiving figure sits on the rainbow of the Last Judgment, or is nimbused with a cross, or wears a triune crown, or is censed by angels. In the *commendatio animae* miniature of the Pullein *horae*, for example, God the Father wears a nimbus and also holds an orb (fig. 31). Directions for the unpainted miniature of the same subject at folio 95v in Bodley MS Latin Liturgies e. 17 describe Christ appearing from a cloud as two angels bear souls up to him in a napkin. An interesting example of the idea is the finial of the south side of the Percy tomb in Beverley Minster, which shows Christ as the recipient of the souls seated on the tomb-chest and holding a soul who stands in a napkin supported at the ends by two angels. A similar finial on the north side of the tomb shows Christ with a large ogival side-wound. The sculptor of the Percy tomb was widely influential in the northwest, and the tomb indicates clearly the well-developed character of some of the iconographic elements we have been discussing.[102]

The Throne of Grace Trinity was increasingly associated with the feast of All Saints and by the late Middle Ages replaced the Adoration of the Lamb in representations of and hymns for the feast. This feast was commonly celebrated with that of All Souls, which had a liturgical program of the Office for the Dead, requiem masses, and appropriate prayers. Such scenes and texts imagined the blessed souls in heaven gazing at the Trinity, an experience in which living worshipers prayed to participate. In short, the idea of the bosom of Abraham as a resting place, whether connected with the patriarch or more usually with God the Father in the period of interest to us, is a common image for a paradise populated by All Souls. Moreover, it usually symbolizes the avoidance of the torments of limbo through the effect of prayers said to the Trinity and All Saints by the living. And many churches dedicated to All Saints or All Souls used a representation of the Bosom of Abraham style of Trinity as a principle image of worship, which was simpler and more effective as a focus than a more miscellaneous representation of a group of saints or souls. Sheingorn notes that "by showing a group of anonymous souls in a cloth, the Bosom of Abraham Trinity refers to both the blessedness of the dead who died in the Lord and to the rescue of souls from purgatory through the intercession of the living."[103]

Two interesting embodiments of some of these ideas are the Throne of Grace Trinity scene from Pierpont Morgan MS M 648 mentioned earlier in this chapter and the scene of the raising of the soul of prior William Ebchester in the Durham prayer roll we discussed in chapter 4. Though I must agree with Sheingorn that no manuscript painting conflates the napkin of souls raised to the Bosom of Abraham and the Throne of Grace Trinity (at least among the northern books I have studied), there is a conscious allusion to the idea in the Trinity scene of the Nicholas Love volume. In the miniature a throng of crowned or patriarchal figures stretches behind the enthroned God the Father, who holds a crucified Christ with a very prominent side-wound. The dove flutters above the head of Christ, whose nimbus echoes the pattern of that of God the Father. The question here is the nature of this throng. I suggest that these are the blessed: the figures of All Saints and All Souls, who are more usually shown in *commendatio animarum* miniatures being lifted to God in the napkin.[104] The prominent crowns on male and female figures and the presence of an important "gatekeeper" at God's right hand recall the great Last Judgment miniature in the Bolton *horae* (fig. 45). Here, at the bottom of the scene, some of the naked but otherwise crowned or tiara-wearing figures turn into the hellmouth, and others turn away from it to stand before St. Peter, who holds a large key.[105] In Morgan M 648, the souls and saints are now in heaven, and the prominent figure is probably St. Peter, often shown bald.[106]

An interesting variant of some of these motifs appears in the Ebchester prayer roll. The prior's naked soul is being censed by angels while being raised in a napkin to a heaven filled with crowned and tiara-wearing figures. Below, a choir of the Benedictines of Durham pray (fig. 21).

The last of the isolated images to occupy us here is that of the letters of the Holy Name, most usually found in the form of a monogram reading IHS, with the ascender of the minuscule *H* represented as a cross, sometimes bearing the figure of Christ. Like the devotions to the Holy Face, the Five Wounds, and the Trinity we have examined thus far, the cult of the Holy Name was very popular in the north,

45. Christ at Last Judgment. York, Minster Library MS Additional 2, folio 208. *Courtesy Dean and Chapter.*

especially during the late fourteenth and early fifteenth centuries, and it is embodied in many forms of popular piety, ranging from the simple appearance of the letters of the monogram, such as those that occur at several points in the notebook of the York priest, Robert Burton, to very elaborate meditational images borne on shields in manuscripts like British Library MS Additional 37049.

The IHS image embodies and expresses the symbolism of the feast and offices of the Holy Name, which the Convocation of York, in accord with the desire of Archbishop Thomas Rotherham, on 27 February 1489 had ordained to be celebrated throughout the Province of York on 7 August.[107] Richard Pfaff traces several currents in its development from a popular devotional cult to its actual incorporation into the liturgy in the late fifteenth century. Of these, the most important to us are "in Italy, the emotional, hortatory, and eirenic use of the Name in the preaching of Bernardino of Siena . . . [and] in Germany and the Low Countries, a devotion . . . to the Holy Name as the Eternal Wisdom of God, propagated chiefly by Heinrich Suso."[108] The votive mass for the Holy Name was often found in manuscripts as early as 1388 together with a similar mass for the Five Wounds, as we saw in the Durham missal, Oxford, Bodleian Laud Misc. 302, folio 232v, mentioned earlier in connection with the *humiliavit* mass for the Five Wounds.[109] There was, moreover, a tradition of hymns and indulgences similar to those associated with the images examined earlier.[110] So too, as we found with the Five Wounds, three thousand years of indulgence was guaranteed by Boniface for each mass celebrated.

Besides the most famous northern foundation to the Holy Name —Jesus College, Rotherham, endowed by the archbishop in his will— there were smaller foundations like the chantry chapel with an altar to the Holy Name that was established by Richard Scrope when he was bishop at Lichfield in 1388.[111]

Venerations of the Holy Name occur in a variety of northern manuscripts, such as Trinity College, Cambridge MS O.3.10; York Minster Library MS Additional 2, the Bolton *horae;* and a closely related York *horae* associated with the shop of Herman Scheerre, Oxford, Bodley MS Latin Liturgies f.2, made possibly for the Scropes of Bolton. All three contain a poem addressing Christ directly: "O bone Jesu, O dulcissime Jesu," based on a supposed Bernardine prayer, "O bone Jesu,"of which the operative part reads "O nomen Jesu nomen dulce, nomen Jesu nomen dilectabile, nomen Jesu nomen comfortans. Quid est Jesu nisi salvator? Ergo Jesu, propter nomen tuum salva me."[112] The text in MS Latin Liturgies f.2 ends with several repetitions of the holy name: "Jesu, Jesu, O dulcissime Jesu."[113]

The Scrope *horae* is an interesting manuscript in its own right. Though it is of Sarum use, it has commemorations of John of Bridlington and archbishop Scrope at folios 143 and 147 and a picture of Scrope's beheading at folio 146v. There is a portrait of the owners, presumably Scropes of Bolton, at folio 29. The kalendar, at least, must have been made in the low countries or by a scribe using a Netherlandish model, as there are Flemish saints like Gudule, Dympha, and Waletrude, who would not normally form part of a Sarum kalendar. Its full-page miniatures are by two artists, one of them Herman Scheerre. Perhaps what Ian Doyle has said about English books and Flemish scribes could also be applied to Flemish artists, for he has pointed out that "earlier in the fifteenth century, and increasingly, there were professional scribes and artists from the Low Countries and Germany working in England, some on ME texts, and many books of hours, some containing ME devotions while also incorporating Continental matter, seem to have been made abroad, especially in Flanders."[114] The borders, however, contain several motifs such as the interlace medallions and overhand knotting we examined as northern features in the last chapter and were most probably made locally, while the pictures were purchased abroad or made by foreign artists working in England. The image on folio 4v, mentioned earlier (fig. 36), is particularly relevant to our concerns here. This large sidewound is in the form of a vertical slit against a green background of *rinceaux* framed by a much-rubbed Bohemian-style band border. Within the wound is a smaller three-dimensional heart bearing five wounds. Around the edge of the image is written a motto: "Hec plage Christi sint adveniam michi [custi?]. Quinque vulnera dei sint medicina mei." ["May Christ's wounds protect me, and the Lord's five wounds be my medicine."][115]

To come now to visual representations of this devotion to the Holy Name, we see that like the Trinity, it was a popular image in domestic and ecclesiastical contexts, where it was typically a monogram made of the majescule letters *I* or sometimes *J*, and minuscule *h* and majescule *S*. As we have seen, the ascender of the *h* was often given a crossbar and so elaborated into a crucifix. These northern English monograms seem to have Continental and ultimately Bohemian origins.

A good Continental illustration of how the Holy Name could be made into a motif to be venerated on a shield appears in Paris, Bibliothèque Nationale MS fr. 1175, Philippe de Mézières, *Livre au la vertue du sacrement de mariage*. This work was composed between 1385 and 1389, and the manuscript in question must have been illuminated close to this latter date as it contains a presentation miniature described by one scholar "as a work of political propaganda to favor a royal marriage."[116] Philippe himself was directly responsible for the iconography of this miniature, which must have seemed to him conventional and acceptable in court circles. The picture on folio 1 shows the author garbed as a Celestine of Paris, holding out his book and kneeling at the base of a column which bears a very large rose inclosing an IHS monogram, actually a YHS, against a background of *rinceaux*. At the other side of the column, a kneeling husband and wife donor couple with an open book on a stand venerate the image. The shaft of the *h* is cruciform and bears the crucified figure of Christ. Other strokes contain representations of the Virgin, Longinus, and St. John. Here the Holy Name and the actual figure are combined, spread out for display. As Joan Williamson explains this image: "Philippe invites the donors to share in the redemptive fruit of the Passion by the meditation provided."[117]

The inhabited letter shafts of the Mézières monogram are related to similar inhabited and animated letter shafts in Giovannino de Grassi's Bergamo sketchbook,[118] which in turn have been traced in origin to the inhabited letter shafts of Bohemian illumination. For example, there is an animated capital of this type in the portable breviary of Bishop Jan Stredy, chancellor of Charles IV, made between 1360 and 1364 and now in the National Museum of Prague.[119]

Another line in the monogram's development is the long tradition in which letters like *alpha* and *omega, chi* and *rho* and the *T* in the "Te igitur" of the mass become images in their own right, sometimes even acquiring pictures within the letter forms. In Hiberno-Saxon painting, letters of this sort were often extremely large, or done in purple and gold.[120] Such "special" letters also combine with a somewhat different pictorial tradition, that of the *carmina figurata,* or poems in the shapes of things, like the famous "Easter Wings" poem of George Herbert, or the *Calligrames* of Guillaume Apollinaire.

Holy Name monograms, which occur in several northern manuscripts, reflect a wide general interest in this motif for decorative and meditational purposes. Such, for example, was probably the form of the embroidery on an ecclesiastical vestment bequeathed in a will of 1483 made by the Pontefract chaplain Thomas Rawson, who records a legacy of a red surplice "figuratem cum nomine Jhesu."[121] In the York breviary, Trinity College, Dublin MS 85, an eight-line major initial containing such a monogram introduces a Psalm (fig. 18). The ascender of *h* is crossed to suggest the Crucifixion, though it bears no actual image. Similar to this monogram is one from early in the Bolton *horae,* where a lovely white Marian rose, whose five petals recall the Five Wounds, introduces a prayer: "Benedictum sit nomen domini nostri Jhesu Xhristi dei et gloriose virginis Marie matris eius" (fol. 4v). On the petals are the letters *I e s u s* and in the inner portion *M a r i a*. At the very center of the flower are the letters *Ihc* with the ascender of *h* surmounted by a crown. It is possible that this rose may also represent a Yorkist political badge. And we will see a similar monogram in the final group of northern books to be discussed.

These monograms serve as a major motif in the group of Carthusian or Benedictine miscellanies containing the *Desert of Religion*. The group brings together a great many of the images that we have examined piecemeal in various northern manuscripts in this chapter in a specifically devotional and eremitic context which seems to develop from the work of the German mystic Henry Suso, originally intended for the use of nuns, but in these English books adapted for both male and female religious.[122] In one of these books, British Library MS Additional 37049, the IHS monogram occurs five times in emblematic contexts, as in a drawing of an oratory showing Richard Rolle within and seated under an honorific canopy. He bears the cruciform IHS monogram on his chest.

Though several aspects of this manuscript and the two similar books related to it have been studied, no one work integrates the devotional iconography with the many texts contained in these volumes.[123] It would take us far afield to examine all three manuscripts in detail, but to place them as a context for certain of the images we have been considering may be helpful here.

Recent scholarship agrees that MS Additional 37049 is a northern book. Ian Doyle speaks of "its strongly northern English" and places it in a Carthusian milieu, possibly Mount Grace, because it contains verses on the founding of that order among its 70 different items and 145 wash drawings of varying quality, many to do with the Passion and the Five Wounds.[124] Mountgrace, near Northallerton, was founded in 1398.[125] Another possibility is the house at Kingston-upon-Hull, founded in 1377. As Carthusian writers migrated from one house to another, they disseminated their work, and so it is difficult to know precisely where a particular Carthusian text may have originated.[126]

That MS Additional 37049 seems to have influenced a somewhat similar miscellany—of known Carthusian provenance, meditative in purpose, and partially illustrated—may be a piece of evidence in support of the earlier book's Carthusian genesis. This is Oxford, Bodleian Library MS e.museo 160, a verse chronicle in a manuscript well known as an important repository of plays.[127] The last event in the verse chronicle is 1520, and it can be presumed to have been compiled

in that year. The language of the work has been variously characterized as north Midlands and southern Yorkshire, or possibly northeast
Nottinghamshire or northwest Lincolnshire.[128] The verse chronicle
also mentions historical events of a very local character at Beverley.

Though the book is too late to warrant extended discussion here,
C. B. Rowntree, its editor, who sees it as a product of a northern
Charterhouse like Mount Grace or Hull, points out its many similarit-
ies to British Library MS Additional 37049. Both works contain mate-
rial on the founding of the Carthusian order, abridgments of
Mandeville's Travels, and portions of Henry Suso's *Horologium
Sapientiae*.[129]

Even less is known for certain about other aspects of MS Additional 37049 than its provenance, and there is even sharp disagree-
ment about the number of copyists involved in its composition. Doyle
believed it was written by a single scribe, while James Hogg, following
Brant Doty's study of the manuscript, sees as many as four.[130]

The first two pages of the book are vellum, the rest much-
trimmed and otherwise damaged paper. The remaining ninety-six
folios must have formed part of some other book, since folio 1 now is
marked 94; moreover, not only do the two vellum leaves seem to have
come from another volume, but the leaves of even the paper text may
originally have had a different order. Stains, smudges, and grease
suggest that this rebinding occurred relatively long after the book was
in use.[131] In short, the earlier state and intention of this manuscript
remains tantalizingly obscure, and it is difficult to generalize about it.

That its iconography is strongly regional, however, is clear. Virtually all the miniatures depicting Christ in MS Additional 37049 emphasize the Sacred Heart, Five Wounds, and Holy Name for
meditative purposes in ways now familiar to us. These images are
placed on the page in what Kathleen Scott has called an "unusual two-
column layout,"[132] which ties them closely to the texts they illustrate.
As these miniatures have been published by Hogg, we need touch
here only on those that bear some iconographic relationship to the
traditions we have outlined.

These northern emphases range from a simple, outsized side-
wound with many drops of blood, at folio 20r, to a standing figure of
Christ cupping the side-wound with the left hand, while dripping
blood from his wounded right hand upon a curious face-like, heart-
shaped shield. The large, horizontal lozenge-like wound at the middle
of the heart and the four smaller wounds at the corners with drops
of blood like eyelashes make the shield resemble a human face, as we

saw in similar pictures from the Sidney Sussex MS 37 and Pullein *horae*. At folio 23v a crucified Christ holds his "charter" surrounded by the *arma Christi* and at the base of the cross is the wounded heart surmounted by the IHS monogram enclosed in a roundel. Folio 24v shows a smaller figure of Christ holding outstretched the wounded heart labeled with the formulae for calculating the numbers of the drops, with cruciform IHS monograms at either side. On folio 46r is an angel holding a large IHS cruciform monogram set on a shield and at the verso an angel holds a similar shield bearing the same lozenge-like wound with eye-like smaller wounds akin to that at folio 20. This shield is worshiped by a leaf-covered St. Paul, "the first hermit," in a desert oratory below. Other angels display shields with the *arma Christi* and the actual Crucifixion on them; at folio 61v an angel holds a shield with a lance piercing the heart in the center and disembodied wounded hands and feet at the corners. It should be evident that what we saw as a northern preoccupation with certain images earlier in this chapter comes out strongly in British Library MS Additional 37049.

At Folio 36v of this manuscript also appears the first of several pictures containing the motto "Jesus est amor meus," the first line of a vernacular translation of a very popular meditative poem in Rolle's *Incendiarium Amoris*. The motto often seems to have been used with the full meditational power of the whole text behind it: Margery Kempe had a ring made bearing this motto, and it begins an ownership poem on folio 147 in a Scrope prayerbook now Cambridge, CUL MS Kk.3.5, "Ihesus est amor meus / ho that lust for to loke / rede on this boke, / be he of cyte toun or thrope / pray he for my lady Scrope."[133]

This is one of the most dramatic and well drawn of the manuscript's images (fig. 46). A monk in a green landscape worships a red heart pierced by a banderole bearing the motto "est amor meus." From the heart grows a plant whose tendrils support an acanthus scroll IHS motto. The acanthus leaves wrap around the tendrils of the plant and clearly show the internal volumes of the leaves in the way that we have seen was common in northern book decoration. The subject of both verb and motto, the crucified Christ himself, makes up the ascender with the cross stroke of the *H*. As the tendrils emerge from the wrap, they bear small rosettes with the word "luf." The viewer is then compelled, in order to make sense of the illustration, to supply the noun *Jesus* as the subject of the motto and the verb. This IHS monogram used emblematically is very common through-

46. Monks worship Sacred Heart. London, British Library MS Additional 37049, devotional miscellany, folio 36v, S. XV². *Courtesy Trustees of the British Library.*

out MS Additional 37049. An elaborate strap-work IHS monogram in a frame occurs at folio 67r. At folio 81 the apostles tow a cart of the faithful, bearing a large banner with cruciform IHS monogram towards heaven; the whole image seems to have been taken from a dramatic representation, perhaps that of a Corpus Christi celebration.[134]

The motif of souls in a napkin also appears, with the artist's treatment of it relying heavily on the Trinitarian iconography discussed earlier. At folio 37v is a drawing labeled "the mounte of perfection," in which Christ in a cloud holds a napkin full of souls, and folio 71v contains a *commendatio animarum* image, depicting Christ with a cloud or furled cloth full of souls.

Two other books in the same collection also show some relationship to British Library MS Additional 37049. These are MSS Cotton Faustina B. vi, part ii, and Stowe 39, both of which date from the mid-fifteenth century.[135] These two manuscripts, however, seem on the whole more unified, containing fewer miscellaneous meditative texts and material of a nonmeditative character (such as the abridged *Mandeville's Travels* of MS Additional 37049). Doyle attributes them to a Benedictine monastery and a nunnery, probably Benedictine, in the North Riding of Yorkshire because MS Cotton Faustina B.vi contains a picture of Saint Hilda of Whitby.[136]

Though all three books present versions of the *Desert of Religion*[137] —in MS Cotton Faustina B.vi at folios 1-23 and in MS Stowe 39 at folios 11-32—the illustrations in MSS Faustina B.vi and Stowe 39 are of a much higher artistic quality than those in British Library MS Additional 37049. MS Stowe 39 also contains the *Abbey of the Holy Ghost*, perhaps composed by John Alcock, to whom Emden attributes the work on the basis of such an ascription in another manuscript of the work, from Rievaulx, in Corpus Christi College, Oxford MS 155, folio 258.[138] This book once formed part of London, British Library MSS Cotton Vespasian D.xiii and Vitellius D.v.

Alcock was born in Beverley, Yorkshire, and educated at Cambridge. He was a contemporary of Rotherham and had a similar career, though chiefly in the south. Doctor of Law before 1461, he held mostly London benefices. He became bishop of Rochester in 1472, of Worcester in 1476, and of Ely in 1486, dying in that see in 1500. He founded Jesus College, Cambridge, had an important influence on architecture, and translated or wrote a number of devotional allegorical books in his earlier period.[139] Alcock was fond of puzzle pictures containing his name and seems to have commissioned fourteen pairs of stained glass cocks for the Old Library of Jesus College, which pun on his name.[140] Besides the cock as a rebus, he may also have been connected with the pig. When he was bishop of Worcester, a donor portrait once appeared in the glass of the south clerestory window, associating him with Antony's pig, wearing a bell. This saint, often presented as the founder of monasticism, appears with a pig in the illustrations of the miscellanies discussed here.[141]

MS Stowe 39 consists chiefly of pictures; both they and the border decoration seem clearly regional work, with green and *folium* having major roles in the artist's palette.[142] At folio 12v, for example, Mary, wearing a robe of green and *folium*, intercedes with God for mankind. Other aspects of the book's decorative scheme help to tie it to the north. Its initials are highlighted with white lead dots very like those in manuscripts painted at Durham. The artist, moreover, shows a preference for a blue darker than that typically found in southern manuscripts. Finally, at folio 21r in one of the tree diagrams that make up the rectos of the codex is a blue single columbine of a type we have seen in Durham books often symbolizing the Benedictine order. Both this detail and the depiction of Benedictine nuns in British Library MS Cotton Faustina B.vi, part ii, suggest possible Benedictine milieux for the books. This is more evident in Cotton Faustina: at folio 17v, a woman in a black habit over white robes prays to the *arma Christi* on a shield entitled "scutum passionis," held by an angel, and at folio 21v a woman (probably Saint Hilda of Whitby) in white with black and dark blue over garment holds a crozier, a book, and a halo.

In all three of these devotional picture books, there is a strong emphasis on the eremitic life, and numerous pictures of hermits and material associated with the *Vitae Patrum* appear. This material seems to go back to Jacob of Voragine's *Aurea Legenda* and to Henry Suso, whose Life reports that for the purposes of personal meditation and for the teaching of nuns, the walls of his chapel depicted such scenes as well as texts from this work.[143] One of his most important manuscripts, the *Exemplar* of about 1370, which has illustrative programs of images scattered about on the full page, accompanied by small narrative or symbolic text blocks or cartouches, is very likely the inspiration for the illustrative programs in our three northern devotional books.[144] His *Horologium Sapientiae*, moreover, a work popular in the north, with six copies bequeathed in wills, and excerpted in British Library MS Additional 37049, had praised the Desert Fathers as Christian knights and philosophers.[145] In northern England this material had also been recommended for nuns and anchoresses from an early period, as we find the mid-twelfth-century Cistercian, Aelred of Rievaulx, including reading from the *Vitae Patrum* as a prescription for the woman he addresses as his sister in the *De Institutione Inclusarum*.[146] The great interest, moreover, in anchorites and anchoresses as well as desert monasticism in the period considered here is especially evident among the Cistercian and Carthusian houses in the wilds of Yorkshire.[147]

Suso was particularly attracted to two of these desert saints, Paul and his follower Antony, both of whom are also very popular in the northern books of interest here. In British Library MS Additional 37049, St. Paul, labeled the first hermit, is dressed in leaves and, in an odd mix of devotional styles, prays to the side-wound and limb wounds depicted on a shield held by an angel. The two related manuscripts, Stowe and Cotton Faustina, use an elaborate program of allegorical trees on the rectos to illustrate and heighten what is going on in the multiple miniatures scattered on the versos.

The books all feature Antony, Paul, John the Baptist, and the two Marys, Mary Magdalene and Mary of Egypt, who are sometimes confused on the basis of a story in the *Aurea Legenda*. Paul, John, and the Marys, moreover, wear unusually colored or exotic garments of hair, animal skins, or leaves. Particularly striking in this regard is MS Stowe 39: at folio 32v, St. Antony wears a *folium* and blue robe (fig. 47); at folio 14v, a scene shows either Mary Magdalene or Mary of Egypt dressed in a hair garment,[148] the composition framed by a *folium* border with a strongly violet cast.

The figure of St. John the Baptist as an early hermit is more clearly stressed in MSS Cotton Faustina B.vi and Stowe 39 than in MS Additional 37049. The character of the illuminations for MS Cotton Faustina B.vi, part ii, is very similar to those of MS Stowe 39; it too is a vellum manuscript and, like MS Stowe 39, has twenty tree diagrams.[149] In the two more elegant books, John wears a camel skin whose head and legs hang down strikingly below an outer robe. As the Gospel of Mark 1.6 mentions only a garment of camel's hair, "vestitus pilis cameli," the use of the skin of the whole animal is an artist's imaginative addition, presumably to heighten the eremitic and exotically "eastern" character of the saint. It also serves to tie these two books firmly to the north. One scholar has suggested that this camel skin is a distinctive mark of York glass painters,[150] and although southern examples of the motif can be found, there are a rather large number of fifteenth-century representations of John the Baptist so dressed, in and around York.

The camel skin beneath the robe appears in the south aisle, second window from the east, of Holy Trinity church, Goodramgate; in the south transept of York Minster; in the east aisle of St. Michael, Spurriergate; in the east window of the north aisle of St. Michaelle Belfrey; and in the east window glass at Methley Church in the West Riding. The camel skin also appears in sculpture and other manuscript illuminations: for example, on the Gascoigne-Percy Monument at Harewood;[151] on the Perceval Roll; at folio 183v of Oxford,

47. Saint Antony with pig. London, British Library MS Stowe 39, devotional miscellany, folio 20v, S. XV² *Courtesy Trustees of the British Library.*

Bodleian Library MS Laud Misc. 302; and in the Bolton *horae* in York Minster Library, folio 39, where a rather savage-looking camel's head forms the hem of John the Baptist's robe.

One of the aphorisms of the Desert Fathers in the text called *Verba Seniorum* seems to lie behind the northern artist's picture of the leaf-covered Paul.[152] The passage in question compares man to a tree: "the covering and ornamentation of the tree, its leaves, are like the body's labors."[153] Thus the idea that the hermit's good deeds are the leaves that cover his body is taken literally in the illustration. Though the presence of the allegorical trees in the other two books may come in part from allegorical works like the *Speculum Virginum*, which also has strongly German associations,[154] the most likely source of influence is *Vitae Patrum* material. In Paul's iconography there is probably also an admixture of the leafy garments found on the "naked" Indian philosopher Dindymus and his followers the Bragmanii in illustrated Alexander legends.[155]

Another story from the *Vitae Patrum* depicted in MS Additional 37049 at folio 19v is that of a young man who eats honey, while below him wait a unicorn and a Leviathan-like hellmouth. The story from the *Barlaam and Josephat* section of the *Vitae Patrum* seems to have come to the illustrator from the *Gesta Romanorum* C. 114.

MS Faustina B.vi, part ii, contains a somewhat larger number of the motifs discussed in this chapter than does MS Stowe 39, and in this respect it is much closer in illustrative character to British Library MS Additional 37049. For example, in MS Faustina B.vi, part ii, an angel holds a shield bearing an IHS monogram (fig. 48). At folio 8v, Richard Rolle in a white habit with a Richard II beard (somewhat archaic by this period) holds on his chest an IHS gold monogram with a crucifix-shaped ascender. Above him are three angels whose faces suggest the Netherlandish style of drawing in Boulogne-sur-Mer MS 93. At folio 12v a very well-painted John the Baptist stands on a green ground; his camel skin robe is visible at hem and wrist.

One feature of MS Cotton Faustina B.vi that may help to explain the intention of the work is that on folio 23v a person in a long robe with an oddly shaped red hat on which is written the letter *u* or *v* contemplates Christ on the cross. As the parallel figure at the same place in British Library MS Additional 37049 is of a monk, the hatted man may represent a type of meditative guide to the material being depicted, illustrating Jeffrey Hamburger's view that the various hermits in these three books "become exemplars not only of virtue, but also of viewing. They set an example for the reader, guiding his attention back from the text to the symbolic diagram."[156] Though the exact manner in which these three books were intended to be used and their precise audience may not now be determined, the general outlines of their meditative purpose and its dependence on the motifs examined in this chapter are evident.

How many of the manuscripts we have discussed have a particular meditative focus, and how they employ the same devotional imagery for their owners to contemplate immediately upon opening the books, is also clear. In the case of Boulogne-sur-Mer MS 93 and Trinity College, Cambridge MS O.3.10, the picture of Christ's face, his wounds, and the instruments of the Passion are all readily accessible for meditation, with accompanying texts that would help the process but are not absolutely necessary to it.

From the order of these images in each manuscript, it can be seen that the designer placed them programmatically, moving the owner's

48. Angel holds IHS monogram on shield. London, British Library MS Cotton Faustina B.vi, pt ii, devotional miscellany, folio 3, S. XV² *Courtesy Trustees of the British Library.*

imagination from the general Holy Face, to the more specific Sacred Heart, and finally to the overall suffering of all parts of Christ's body inflicted by the *arma* during the Passion. Unlike the three *Desert of Religion* devotional miscellanies just discussed, in which the Virgin plays a key role as an explainer of the scene and as a repository for the beholders' sorrow, the prefatical miniatures of the two manuscripts focus on Christ alone and the physical changes wrought upon his body and complexion through the Passion.

Several writers like Rolle had talked familiarly of Christ's color and appearance in their lyrics, often in color contrasts of ruddy and white. This imagery was reminiscent of similar color contrasts in contemporary love lyrics. Though the Gospels had not specified color changes during the Passion, such details were quickly supplied, and the pallor of the crucified Christ became a standard feature of devotional iconography.

The development and popularization of the rood screen in parish church architecture, the polychrome alabaster Crucifixion panels made in the north and in Nottinghamshire, and the polychrome limewood crucifixes often imported from northern Europe, which became common in English monastic and parish churches and private chapels, had important effects. Through such decorative elements, Christ's changing skin coloration and realistically rendered wounds could become part of every parishioner's visual vocabulary. In manuscript painting, the increasing standardization of the Crucifixion scene placed before the canon of the mass in the missal made Christ's pathos familiar in a more miniaturized way, as we have seen in the Green Canon-Page illumination style discussed in chapter 3.

Adjurations of many sorts in the imperative to regard Christ's face become institutionalized through the enormously influential *Aurea Legenda* of Jacob of Voragine, with its supposedly Bernardine "respice in faciem Christi."[157] The Holy Face with its blackened countenance in the Trinity College, Cambridge volume, and, we presume, the companion image in the Boulogne hours, which may have been intended for a similar treatment, must have made a poignant statement about death. Moreover, the image made Christ's suffering concrete in the way that the suffering of many plague victims was depicted or described through the color changes that were part of the medieval tradition of affective physiognomy. Such imagery—and the allied images of the wounded heart and the Christ adorning the crucifixes of IHS monograms—in the late Middle Ages in England as elsewhere, shows not the calm, idealized beauty of Christ's face but the decomposition of death, giving a concrete power to the Passion texts not otherwise easily gained.

The owners or viewers of the books, the glass, and the alabasters were then not simply spectators each time they regarded them but were intensely engaged by the event as depicted or symbolized there —ranging from the practical and beneficial in the form of rubrics in the manuscripts and scrolls promising remission of punishment, to matters more abstract and spiritual. Through these pictures these spectators were emotionally involved in what they beheld. They saw faces like their own and imagined hearts like their own, as well as the various pains that the different tools in the *arma Christi* representations could bring to their own bodies and limbs. The bright colors of many of the drawings in these books, or in the glass in the churches of York and other places, moreover, aided in memorizing the scenes and they illustrated in the same way the fact that striking and unusual color combinations had long been used in treatises on the arts of memory to aid the meditator to recall specific events and fix them in memory.[158]

Thus the temporal and geographical distances between the actual events of the Passion and the situation of fifteenth-century northern English book owners like William Barnby and the other persons who meditated on them could be narrowed through contemplation. That this style of meditation, using a certain group of images appearing in media as various as the manuscript book, the glass window, and the domestic alabaster, has been convincingly established as distinctively northern should now be clear.

6

Three Northern Magnates as Book Patrons

JOHN NEWTON, THOMAS LANGLEY, THOMAS ROTHERHAM,

AND THEIR MANUSCRIPTS

*T*he number of impressive personal libraries in the counties of York and Durham during the late Middle Ages, and the range of interests they reveal, suggest extensive bibliophilic activity involving the wealthy and often learned higher ecclesiastical administrators[1] and prelates of the northern church. Though much is known about the influence of such persons on the development of the illuminated book in the southern part of England during the late Middle Ages— for example, the roles of Richard Mitford, bishop of Salisbury, and Robert Brunyng, abbot of Sherborne, as the patrons of the Sherborne Missal illuminated by John Siferwas—their influence in the north has not been studied.[2]

The books of three important figures in the northern church can show us much not only about their owners' patronage of artists and scribes but also about their predilections in decorative styles, which may have helped to create something of a regional taste. John Newton, at his death in 1414, was treasurer of York Cathedral and responsible for the creation of the cathedral library. Thomas Langley, bishop of Durham, 1406–1436, though less of a bibliophile than the other two, owned an impressive book collection and may have fostered an idiosyncratic Durham style in book decoration. Archbishop Thomas Rotherham, who died in 1500, founded Jesus College, Rotherham, with his own book collection. Diplomats and statesmen as well as ecclesiastical dignitaries, these men were also active in supporting education with regard to books: Newton's library endowment and gift of books to Peterhouse, Cambridge, and Rotherham's educational work are well known; but Langley too endowed a college, and he was involved in the founding of Sion Abbey.[3]

Though these magnates gratified their book-loving tastes on a larger scale than other northerners,[4] it is unquestionable that books of all sorts were very much in fashion in the north at the end of the Middle Ages and that many wealthy men and women felt it was their civic and social duty to commission books.[5] As is suggested by the types of volumes listed in Appendix C, the book-owning impulse was expressed somewhat differently in the north than in the south, as it led to more to legal, pious, and meditational books than to works of imaginative literature, but the desire to commission, to ornament, and to display large copies—and to use them to convey one's social status, as, for instance, by armorial bearings on title pages—was very much the same. Thus instead of Chaucer, Gower, Hoccleve, and Lydgate, our northern magnates commissioned texts of mystical and devotional writers, works of canon and civil law, and scriptural commentaries and collections of biblical *distinctiones.*

The earliest of the three magnates to concern us, John Newton, was born in the diocese of York, "probably the son or grandson of a substantial York mercer, John Newton,"[6] and studied at Peterhouse, Cambridge, where he became Bachelor of Civil Law by 1375, Doctor of Canon Law by 1378, and was elected Master of the College in 1382. He held this post until 1397.[7] Among his contemporaries were two men who would be instrumental in his later ecclesiastical success, Thomas Arundel and Richard Scrope. Apparently recommended to Arundel by Scrope, who became the new bishop's official at Ely, Newton held a number of administrative offices at Ely, as Arundel, who was provided to this see at the age of twenty, needed men with legal training. He was advocate of the Consistory Court at Ely in 1376 and in the same year was commissary-general. As early as 1377, Newton, in company with Scrope, appears in Arundel's register in a legal capacity. From 1379 to 1388 he succeeded Scrope as Arundel's official, and later, John Fordham's, Arundel's successor at Ely. This role was an extremely demanding one and carried extensive powers, for the official heard and often settled cases brought to the court by persons in the diocese as well as proceeding against persons guilty of crimes. He also proved and administered wills and convoked synods.[8]

Being presented to the rectory of Rattlesden in the Norwich diocese, Newton took orders and was ordained a priest by Arundel in 1380. He then followed the usual path of ecclesiastical careerism with five exchanges in Staffordshire, Northamptonshire, and Lincolnshire, apparently under the patronage of Arundel. In 1393 he served the bishop of Durham as a diplomat in France. When Arundel became archbishop of York in 1388, he reunited many of his Ely administrators, and Newton flourished in the north just as much as he had in the south, becoming official of York in 1398 and serving as vicar-general from 1390 to 1396. Later, under Richard Scrope, from 1398 until his death he held similar offices.[9] Even after he had moved to York, Newton retained his ties with his college, keeping the Mastership of Peterhouse for four more years, and in 1411 making a large and important gift of books to the college.

Newton became a residentiary canon of the York Chapter perhaps as early as 1388, and treasurer of York cathedral in 1393, an office he also held till the end of his life. At the time of his death in 1414, he was the center of a circle of gentry and clerics with a strong interest in northern devotional writers. Though Hughes tantalizingly claims that this John Newton apparently owned or possessed for a period of time Cambridge, Emmanuel College MS 35, containing various texts of Rolle and Bonaventure, as well as Honorius of Autun's *Cognitio Vitae*, to which he contributed marginal glosses and some editing of the Rolle material, as well as a brief table "tabula huius libri additur per magistrum Johannem de Neuton," this view has not been accepted by other scholars. In any case, Newton was in the habit of making tables and indices, as in his will he mentions a Seneca given to Peterhouse with "tabulas eiusdem in quaternis." He may also have been engaged in other amateur scribal projects, as the Peterhouse compotus rolls during his mastership in 1380–1381 show a charge of ten pence "pro papiro et pergameno pro rotulis et quaternis."[10]

From his various stalls, prebends, and livings, Newton became very wealthy, traveling in a private barge on the Ouse, which he left to St. Mary's abbey, York, and describing himself in his will as "deliciis affluens." He also maintained men in livery, as the will of John Harwod, the advocate of the Court of York mentioned in chapter 1, left to his clerk "a green furred gown, of the livery of our treasurer."[11]

Newton owned 118 books. Of these the Peterhouse bequest disposed of about two-thirds, chiefly literary, historical, and grammatical; the cartage from York to Cambridge alone costing 6s. 8d.[12] A number of service books, along with altar cloths and priestly vestments, went to various northern parish churches. For example, he left to the church of Alne in the North Riding "unum missale novum, et unum antiphonar minus ac unum graduale melius," while another antiphonal "melius" went to Wilton in the same area. Seventy books, forty on law and the rest theology, scriptural commentaries, and the didactic works of northerners like Hoveden, Rolle, and Rymington, were given to found the York Minster Library. This work was carried out by his executors, Thomas Haxey, King's Clerk and a residentiary canon, who became treasurer in 1418, and John Gylby, another Scrope protégé,[13] who were Newton's friends from his Cambridge and Ely period[14] and members of Arundel's and Scrope's household retinue. Many of John Newton's books are still at the Minster, and at Oxford and Cambridge, and it is some of these that will concern us now.

Of the books given to Peterhouse and other institutions outside of York, thirty-one still exist. They show a discerning taste on Newton's part, both for the books that he bought ready-made, as in the case of several twelfth- and thirteenth-century codices, and those that he probably commissioned. Indeed, one of his books, a sermon collection, he describes in his will as a "librum pulcrum" [*sic*], presumably referring to its ornamentation.[15] Of the twenty fourteenth- and fifteenth-century books whose provenance can be tentatively identified, twelve are English and the rest Italian.[16] A number of these have handsome penwork ornamentation, and several have illuminated initials. To mention only the more expensive of these, Peterhouse 275, a Boethius, *Consolation of Philosophy* with Trivet commentary, has fine *litterae partitae* initials and two scales of script, a large, vigorous *textura* for the text and a smaller cursive used for the commentary. Similarly, MS Peterhouse 36, Bartholomew de Saxo Ferrato's *Super Infortiatum*, had many large historiated initials, now mostly cut out. On the whole, Newton's books tend to be working copies, often finely decorated but still of a practical character, rather than intended chiefly for display.

Three items in his library may fairly represent his taste. The first, Oxford, Bodleian Library MS Rawlinson B. 199, is the collection of English historical writers once forming part of Rawlinson C. 162, discussed in chapter 4, whose large margins and plain though well-written text show that it was originally an expensive and luxurious book, of English workmanship and presumably made for Newton.[17] York Minster Library MS XVI.P.7 is one of a group of Italian law books—MS XVI.P.5, Bartholomew de Saxo Ferrato, *Lectura Codicis;* MS XVI.P.6, Bartholomew de Saxo Ferrato on the New Digest; MS XVI.P.7, Bartholomew de Saxo Ferrato on the Old Digest; and MS XVI.P.8, Cino of Pistoia, *Super Codicem.*[18] The three Bartholomews seem to have been produced by the same Italian scribe and workshop and are dated 1401. York Minster Library MS XVI.P.7, containing Bartholomew on the New Digest, is a tall, handsome paper volume ornamented by both illumination and ornate penwork Lombardic initials reeded with blue and red. Characteristically Italian red and blue acanthus in drapery-like forms ornaments the volume for major initials. These books Newton apparently bought readymade or perhaps obtained on a trip abroad. Indeed, Hughes claims that "Newton . . . may have been in touch with Italian scholars."[19] He seems, however, to have commissioned York Minster Library MS XVI.P.8, which is the work of an English scribe and presumably an English illuminator. The book appears to be late fourteenth century.

The scribe, as we recall from chapter 2, signs his name "Robertus plenus amoris," which gives no clue to his nationality, but his *a* (characteristically higher than the other letters in the line) reveals at least an English scribal training. The decoration of the major initial on the first folio and the *champ* initials throughout have a regional character. These books show something of Newton's taste even in the fairly utilitarian genres of the law book and the historical treatise.

Thomas Langley was another northerner, born about 1360 around Middleton, just north of Manchester,[20] apparently from his arms the third son in a family of the minor nobility.[21] Becoming a member of John of Gaunt's retinue, he was named one of his executors. He served as King's Clerk to Henry IV and soon Keeper of the Privy Seal, in consequence becoming one of the king's closest advisors and eventually chancellor of England. He was consecrated bishop of Durham in 1406 and was engaged in diplomatic service under Henry IV and Henry V, serving as executor for both royal wills. Interestingly, in the light of Langley's bookish interests, he received for his royal service a gift of a missal and breviary rather than the plate or other domestic valuables we might expect.

Langley became in time one of the five richest landholders in England, and much of his wealth was expressed by his books. Oddly, this side of his character is minimized by Robin Storey, his biographer, who devoted only a paragraph to the bishop's library.[22] While, admittedly, Langley was much away from his diocese until his last years, as we saw earlier from his will, he seems to have amassed a considerable number of books, and to have been rewarded with books in a bequest, and so may have had a greater involvement with books and their making in Durham than his registers or life records would indicate. As we noted in chapter 1, thirty-three books were left to various members of his entourage and to institutions. Moreover, some of these books were very expensive; for example, a set of Bersuire in three beautifully illuminated volumes left to Durham priory cost sixty pounds, or was valued at this sum, for the difference is not clear in the document. Langley's William of Nottingham, Concordance to the Gospels—the largest volume in the modern Dean and Chapter Library and the dread of book fetchers—was worth twenty pounds.[23] It seems, then, that Langley owned a number of books that appear to be related by their decorative style as well as by their pressmarks, making up the earliest numbers in the Durham cataloguing system. Thus MS A.I.1 was seen by the early cataloguer as of a piece with and stylistically related to MS A.I.6, which bears Langley's arms. Though there is no specific decorative feature except the extremely elaborate penwork initials to tie MS A.I.1 to others known to be his, it is mentioned in his will. When Langley was installed as bishop of Durham in 1406, there was already under his predecessor Walter Skirlaw a well-developed civic tradition of very ornate and beautiful notarial writing, as well as book making in both the town and the monastery. And, as we saw in chapter 1, Skirlaw was a literate and book-loving bishop, who may well have been the patron for some of the book artisans we shall soon be discussing.

The flourisher associated with Langley's books is an interesting and enigmatic figure. This artist, who certainly worked very closely with the scribe, for his lattice-work infilling even appears in the bows of William du Stiphel's capitals in MS A.I.3, drew an ornate *littera partita* major initial, which gives off elaborate penwork oak-leaf outlines with fine lattice work. Whether he was monastic or secular is a puzzling question. As Doyle notes:

> In the last century and a half of the middle ages in England . . . monastic book production cannot be considered as operating independently of book production by other hands and outside the monasteries. Apart from the writing, and possibly much of the flourishing, some illumination may have been done by monks . . . and for both flourishing and illumination there are possibilities of careful research revealing peculiarities so constantly accompanying scribal hands which can be identified firmly as monastic that the likelihood that decoration is by outside specialists (as I suspect it often was) may be reduced.[24]

The Durham feretory rolls for roughly the period of Thomas Langley's bishopric give somewhat mixed evidence for monastic and secular bookmaking and ornamenting. During the office of William Pocklington, in 1402–1403, the sum of five shillings was paid to a

William Durham for writing a gradual. William does not have the title *dominus*, which generally implies a monk, so he was most likely a secular scribe. In 1413–1414, during the office of Robert Crayk, another five shillings was paid to a *dominus* Richard Fereby towards the illumination of a book, and in 1447–1448, during the office of William Dalton, a *dominus* John Palman was paid ten pence for writing and illuminating four tablets about saint Cuthbert.[25]

This last entry also occurs in the Durham Priory account roll for 1447–1448: "domino Johanni Palman scriptura 4or tabularum cum oracionibus de Sct. Cuthberto, et cum illuminacione earundem 10d," where Palman is also called *dominus*. Yet in the following year the account rolls show that considerable sums were paid to Palman for combined services that suggest more the stationer or book entrepreneur than a monk: "domino Johannis Palman pro ligatura et coopertura portophorem ac pro diversis quaternis pergameni de vitiis et historiis quorundam sanctorum in eiusdem omissi, per ipsum de novo scriptis et inseretis, 13s. 8d. Eidem pro consimilibus scriptura, ligatura et coopertura cuiusdam libri de officiis mortuorum 2s.6d. In pergameno empto [of or by Palman?] pro scriptura dictorum librorum 2s. 6d."[26] These entries suggest that some people engaged in scribal and decorative activities for the priory may have been indiscriminately called *dominus* as much for respect as for a precise indication of their status as monks or laymen. It was, however, common in the fifteenth century for money payments to be made to monks for various tasks within the monastery.[27] By contrast, the fabric rolls of Selby abbey, Yorkshire, for 1447 show a substantial payment for the noting of a gradual to an Oliver Writ, who seems clearly to have been a lay artisan.[28] There is no incontrovertible evidence, then, that Durham flourishers were monks rather than lay artists.

Though it must remain tentative, an hypothesis that would help to explain the presence of such a gifted artist at Durham, as well as the fairly constant association of his work with that of the William du Stiphel discussed in chapter 2, is that the Breton scribe was also a flourisher. Thus the extremely large filigree or ornately flourished *littera partita* letters occurring in books written by du Stiphel, as well as in books contemporary with him but by other hands, such as MS A.I.1, need not necessarily be the production of a penwork specialist. Perhaps du Stiphel was a full-time scribe and a part-time flourisher, writing and ornamenting some Durham books and only ornamenting others. Perhaps too, his distinctive way of making flourished initials set a style occurring in a number of other Durham books that have no connection with him. Admittedly, the idea that du Stiphel was both scribe and flourisher seems to run counter to scribal conventions, for these two tasks were normally the province of different persons.

The widely held idea that scribes and flourishers or painters were always different people has been expressed by Ian Doyle in a study of the scribe William Ebesham: "The flourishing of initial letters in blue and red was normally a specialist's job and would have been charged separately by number and size," but more recently he suggested that "it is probable that [flourishing] was a common accomplishment of scribes of various sorts, amateur as well as professional."[29] There are, however, exceptions to this general belief. Sonia Scott-Fleming has noted that "pen flourishing . . . [is] no more difficult than writing, and is therefore allied with it. A scribe, copying a text, could have drawn the pen flourishing also."[30] Thus, for example, the scribe of Cologne Diocezanbibliothek MS I B, dated 1289, states in his colophon "ego frater Johannes de Valkenburg scripsi et notavi et illuminavi istud graduale." And the Henry Stephen of Westfalia, mentioned in chapter 3, who wrote the Alba Julia missal tells us in his colophon of 1377 "finitus est iste liber per manus Heinrici dicti Stephani de Westfalia . . . cum scriptura, illuminatura, ligatura."[31] Nor should we forget that du Stiphel got his training in France, where we have the example of Jacques Maci or Mathey, a remarkable scribe-flourisher. François Avril, in his extensive study of Maci,[32] notes that from the twelfth century on, specialized artists did red and blue running titles, paraphs, and line fillers, but their major task was the *litterae magnae* of the type we will be discussing, *litterae parvae*, and *versiculi*, or small letters that do not rise above the ascender line of the text.[33] Though, typically, fees were paid separately to the scribe and to the letter maker, as we see in MS Vat. Lat. 6443, folio 204v, a manuscript made between 1338 and 1342[34] "solvi pro scriptura VII lib. VIs . . . item pro illuminando: XIXs. videlicet pro VIIIc litteris parvis et LIV litteris partitis." Maci, however, seems to have been the scribe and letter ornamenter of Bernard Gui's *Flores Chronicorum*, Paris, Bibliothèque Nationale MS lat. 4975, where at folio 177 appears his costing "XIVcx paraffs, IIIc et L versets, IIIIc lettres, VII moins II lettres partities." In England, there is late fifteenth-century evidence for a single person being a scribe, flourisher, and cadel capital maker. Edward Botiller, leaving the Benedictine house at Westminster in April 1489 to enter the Cluniac priory of St. Millburghe at Wenlock, received from his prior, John Estrey, a letter dimissory to the Cluniac prior Richard Synger, which contained this testimonial: "the same Edward [is] a faire writer, a fflorissher and maker of Capitall letters."[35]

Let us then turn to the flourisher whose work appears in three of the du Stiphel manuscripts and elsewhere in Durham books of the same period. His *littera partita* initials are of two general sorts, each of which is associated with du Stiphel manuscripts as well as with other Durham codices. The MS A.I.3 type uses the standard scalloped white parchment area which separates the red and blue ink filling the left and right sides of the bows in letters like *o* or *p*, as well as the bar of an I/J border. The initial *P* with mask face infill discussed in chapter 4 is representative of the technique (fig. 16). Within the blue areas are white circles made from the parchment ground; in these are small red dots. White foliage with violet hatch-mark highlights set on a ground of red hatch-work infill comes from the mouth and ears of the mask face.

MS A.I.4 in this group does not use purple dots in the red area of the *littera partita*, but leaves the white circles blank. Otherwise the technique is similar to that we have outlined. There are also two other books not written by du Stiphel, MSS C.IV.20b and A.I.6. The latter has the white circles with red dots only in the blue portion. The MS Burney 310 group does not rely on such dots for decorative accents but instead uses a more graceful and carefully worked-out pattern, where blue intrudes into red in the bows, comprising a blue *v*, a blue circular bulb, almost enclosed by red, and another blue *v*. As befits this relatively modest manuscript, however, there are only eight *litterae partitae*, though all of the major filigree initials use combinations of red, blue, and violet inks for outline and accent. Though the numbers of bulbs and *v*'s may vary depending on letter size, this pattern is the same in the du Stiphel book and in MS A.I.1, MS C.III,11, and MS 4.16.34a *Specialia*, a document.

There is less variation in the infill of the initials. Typically, the Durham master—if, indeed, there is only one—uses as infill for his *littera partita* initials *rinceaux* whose parallel dark lines outline and enclose the white parchment and terminate in oak-leaf or acanthus patterns. These are often entwined to form the visual center of an interlace medallion or the mask face so characteristic of northern decoration. The main leaf pattern within the initial is often repeated in roundels containing a single leaf with an acorn, which are attached to cornerpieces or I/J borders. Small dots, circles, or sometimes horizontal strokes on the leaves give accents. At the tops and bottoms of chainwork red and blue borders in the left margins, or developing from the tops of the initials themselves, there are headpieces and tailpieces, swags sometimes straight and sometimes curved, which resemble the bill of a sawfish. Between the foliate "teeth" along the edges of these forms is more of the red latticework[36] found elsewhere in the initial. These headpieces, a distinctive part of the artist's work, branch off the chain-link bordering or the initial at a slight angle or lie parallel to the top of the text column, or shoot straight up from the initial following the long axis of the page, or at their fanciest, branch in arabesque or sinuous forms at about a 30 degree angle to the long axis. Around these swags are frogspawn, or patterns resembling an elongated bunch of grapes, terminating in five tendrils.

In the main forms of the actual initials, small white circles or circles containing a colored dot are often used. Purple ink in three of the du Stiphel manuscripts adds an accent to the red and blue pen decoration. In some initials in other Durham books, purple ink is employed for additional work around the body of the initial, or in the swag, or to form the two slashes used as decorative accents on the leaves. Where the leaves are purple, red makes the slashes. In some cases, red alternates with blue in grounds within the infill rather as paints in these colors do in the more luxurious *champ* initial.

These chainwork bar or *baguette* borders vary considerably from manuscript to manuscript. Though comprised of a series of segments of alternating red and blue tooth- and bulb-like shapes, the number or size of these forms, as well as the squiggles that come off at right angles to the axis of the chainwork bars, show no obvious relationships, except that the penwork borders of MSS A.I.1 and Burney 310 seem to have been drawn by the same hand, for they have the same tooth and bulb pattern, which as it changes color puts out a squiggle consisting of a hairspring-like spiral with three slashes and a finial stroke that hangs rather limply downward.[37] This form of decoration as a tail or development of a *littera partita* was a fairly common one, especially in the north.

The type of initial that appears in these Durham books as well as in a number of northern codices of the fourteenth and fifteenth centuries has an interesting history. It developed from an English taste, common in the early fourteenth century, for using *litterae partitae* with red latticework. The idea traveled to France later in the century and became popular in the late fourteenth and early fifteenth centuries throughout northern Europe. Then, it would seem, the idea returned from France to northern England, especially during the late fourteenth and early fifteenth centuries.[38]

At the risk of complicating the flourishing process unduly, we may conclude that there is a possibility that several hands flourished letters in Durham during the end of the fourteenth and the beginning of the fifteenth century. We may posit artists who drew the chainwork borders and possibly the *littera partita* forms, leaving the infill and the swags to a master hand—perhaps that of du Stiphel. This would account for the greater similarity among the filigree decorations in the manuscripts of interest to us and also for the variety in the less linear decorative elements in the books. It also seems more economical for a delicate pen to do tracery throughout a manuscript than for the artist to change pens and inks, concerning himself with broad or painterly shapes for a time and then returning to the filigree.

The most dominant single characteristic of the Durham master's work, and the chief way in which he differs from most other makers of the *littera partita* initial in northern England, however, is his characteristic placement of the various decorative patterns of his infill on a background of fine red latticework, patterns of a sort we noticed in the bows of the *diminuendo* letters after the initial in Cambridge University Library MS Dd.10.22 (fig. 7). Though there is rather little known about contemporary terms for various forms of page decoration in England in the late Middle Ages, some recent studies of French designers' directions to painters and flourishers may throw light on English practice.[39] The type of decoration we note in the work of the Durham flourisher, whoever he may have been, is, as we have seen, decidedly French in inspiration, and one component of it bears the name *rouge hache*. A manuscript of the *Grandes Chroniques de France*, now Paris, Bibliothèque Nationale MS fr. 2613, must have been written after 1347, to judge by the arms of a branch of the Chatillon family it contains, and the style of the script would suggest a date of about 1380–1390.[40] On folio 145v is a seven-line initial at the side of which can still be read instructions to the illuminator to supply a *rouge hache* background for the infill. Though the flourisher actually chose to do this work predominately in blue ink, it is apparent that this phrase signifies a "chiseled" ground of ivy leaves and *rinceaux* on red latticework, which fills the center of the *littera partita* initial, the outside of which is surrounded by typical red and blue ink penwork.

The technique was a popular one elsewhere on the Continent in the early part of the fifteenth century as well. A Bible from Cologne, now Brussels, Bibliothèque Royale MSS 383 and 384, from 1423 contains a number of *littera partita* initials with *rouge hache* both in the infill in the center and as a rectangular background for the initial itself, though the swags are nowhere near as exuberant as those in the Durham volumes.[41] The *rouge hache* in these Continental examples suggests that the type of initials popular in France and Germany at about the end of the fourteenth and the first half of the fifteenth centuries could well have formed part of du Stiphel's stylistic vocabulary.

Apparently, this French *rouge hache* style was not confined to manuscripts written by du Stiphel, and the flourisher's production includes several volumes bearing the Langley arms or name or noted as his in his will. Among the manuscripts with *rouge hache* decoration giving evidence of this connection are Durham MS A.I.1, William of Nottingham's Gospel concordance. Another, MS A.I.5, Nicholas of Lyra's commentary on the Pauline Epistles and the Apocalypse, shows Langley's name on folio 2: "Liber Sancti Cuthberti de communi libraria monachorum Dunelmi, ex dono domini Thomae Langley episcopi ejusdem." And MS A.I.6, Nicholas of Gorran on the Pentateuch, bears Langley's arms on the title page.

As to the identity of the scribe of MS A.I.1, there is no evidence except that he was nearly the equal of du Stiphel in craftsmanship and working at about the same date, roughly late fourteenth century. That the chainwork borders in this manuscript seem to have been done by the same artist as the one who worked on MS Burney 310 could place some of the decoration as early as 1381. This scribe's descenders, however, show clubbing or forking at the foot, and he wrote a less fluent and more angular hand than the Breton. The flourisher's work in the letter *P* (fig. 49) here shows clearly the *rouge hache* ground on which the tracery of the infill in the bow is laid; hatchwork continues outside the letter both in the swags and in the blue decoration to the left of the *P*'s stem. The five tendrils of the swags end in three tiny balls which put out hairlines. The quality of these initials in MS A.I.1 is the finest in the group of books with this type of decoration, as befits the book's size and probable expense.

Durham Cathedral MS A.I.5, written by a John Wykingeston at the end of the fourteenth century, agrees in scale (400 × 270 mm) with the other large volumes of commentaries and preaching aids to which Langley was partial. This manuscript differs a bit from the others in the Langley group in that it contains two distinct forms of decoration, one of which seems quite likely to have been done by the scribe. Wykingeston's practice here may help to support our hypothesis that scribe's and flourisher's roles could be combined in one person

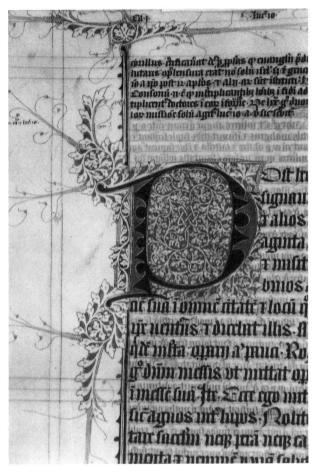

49. Penwork flourished initial. Durham, Dean and Chapter Library
MS A.I.1, William of Nottingham, Concordance of the Gospels, folio
170v, S. XV[1] *Courtesy Durham Dean and Chapter.*

in certain of the Durham books. On the one hand, there is the typical
large-scale penwork we have been discussing and on the other, some
highly idiosyncratic work, which seems to be that of Wykingeston
himself.

The penwork flourished nine-line *litterae partitae* in MS A.I.5 are
similar to the decoration we have just seen, though in this manuscript
the initials are not as regular and luxurious as in some of the codices

mentioned earlier. It certainly does not seem to be by the hand of du Stiphel and points to a not too skilled and somewhat perfunctory imitator of the best of these Durham letters. Throughout this manuscript, however, the ascenders of letters at the top of the line are extended, and handsomely drawn grotesques and animals are perched on them; these drawings are by the same hand that did the dragon and vine work at the *explicit* and *incipit* on folio 91v and so are presumably Wykingeston's work. On folio 44r, faces ending in leafy bodies adorn the ascender; hanging down from a horn on one of these heads is an interlace medallion whose form imitates a notary's mark. When notaries public had copied a document, they attested to this act by a brief paragraph at the bottom of the page. This attestation was accompanied by a mark peculiar to the notary in question, consisting of his initials or sign, often wittily signifying the name; a notary named Fishwick, for example, might have a mark comprised of a fish with a candlewick. Such a medallion in MS A.I.5 is further evidence for the interrelationship between the professional worlds of textwriters and notaries public in Durham, mentioned earlier.[42]

Durham Cathedral MS A.I.6 not only contains the *rouge hache* style of flourishing but also has a highly ornamented first folio, the style of whose full-page trellis border has some interesting resemblances to the border of A.I.3. The shield containing a mullet or spur-like rowel with five points indicates the cadency (variant of arms) for a third son in Langley's armorial bearing; it occurs at the cornerpieces as well as at top and bottom of the center gutter in the border. This manuscript, though large and luxurious, is written in a Secretary hand of a more crowded and less controlled character than any hand appearing in the books we have so far discussed. It contains a great many twelve-line major *littera partita* initials done in red and blue.

The last manuscript in this group, a table to the works of Aristotle from the end of the fourteenth century, Durham MS C.IV.20b, is altogether a cruder book than those we have been examining—less ornate and written in a cursive script. Its *rouge hache* work is contained in more modest *littera partita* initials of seven lines, but the decoration shows the same swagging, resembling the bill of a sawfish, and the horizontal accent lines on the white leaves filling the *littera partita* initial.

The "Durham flourisher" seems to have fostered a style that influenced a large number of books and even documents in Durham. Based on an examination of all the manuscripts in the Dean and Chapter Library covering the Skirlaw-Langley episcopates, I have found seven such books and documents, of varying quality. In all but two of these flourishings, the decoration is associated with a *littera partita* initial. Besides the notarial document Dean and Chapter Muniments MS 4.16.34a Specialia, the style of this flourisher occurs in Durham MSS A.III.27, Holkot on Wisdom, late fourteenth century; A.IV.5, Peter of Herenthal on Psalms, fourteenth century; B.II.4, works of Chrysostom, fourteenth century; B.III.6, sermons of Augustine, end of the fourteenth century; B.III.29, table to various authors and dated 1438; and C.III.11, *Casus* of Bartholomew of Sancto Concordio of Pisa, fourteenth century. The last of these manuscripts came to Durham as a purchase from the executors of Thomas Hebbeden, another book-owning northern magnate, who was dean of the Collegiate Church of St. Andrew, Aukland, and Langley's Spiritual Chancellor. Hebbeden's will was recorded in Langley's register.[43] The work in all of these books is sufficiently crude—with the exception of MS 4.16.34a Specialia—to suggest that the decoration was done in the style of but not by the pen of the Durham latticework master.

Perhaps the most that can be concluded from this examination of the evidence is that the *rouge hache* infills and swags, work of a very high order and often suggesting in the larger manuscripts considerable financial resources for the artist, show a French influence and could by period and skill have been done by du Stiphel. If one artist did these filigree letters at Durham in the last quarter of the fourteenth century, he seems to have influenced other artists or assistants who worked on lesser books, establishing a distinct "Durham" style of penwork decoration.

We come now to the last of our three magnates, Archbishop Thomas Rotherham. He had a well-documented career, which falls, like John Newton's, into three phases as scholar and library builder, statesman, and cleric.[44] He was a Yorkshireman, born to an armigerous family in 1423 in Rotherham, a largish mining and iron-working town of about three thousand, on the site of what was to become Jesus College. By 1443, he was at King's College, Cambridge, where he stayed about fourteen years, becoming Doctor of Theology by 1463.

He also held increasingly important positions in the royal administration, presumably through these appointments amassing the money necessary to indulge his taste for fine books. He was chaplain to John Vere, earl of Oxford, before 1461 and King's Chaplain in 1461. In 1467 he was made Keeper of the Privy Seal and chaplain to

Edward IV. By 1474 he was chancellor of England. Partly as a result of this household and royal service, he was made bishop of Rochester and ambassador to France in 1465, provost of Beverley in 1465, bishop of Lincoln in 1472, and in 1480 archbishop of York. This last position, which he held until his death in 1500, had a yearly income of over two thousand pounds.

Yet his later career was not entirely an ecclesiastical one, for in 1469 he was elected chancellor of Cambridge, and he was Master of Pembroke Hall from 1480 to 1488. To house the large number of books he gave to the university he built and outfitted in 1482 the original *Bibliotheca Minor,* which later became part of Cambridge University Library.[45] The size of this bequest has been variously estimated; four manuscripts and thirty-four printed books from it still survive.[46] A similar gift to Pembroke College shows some of his humanistic interests: MS 168, Aulus Gellus's *Attic Nights,* which Rotherham apparently commissioned or purchased, as it is a fifteenth-century book written in a fine humanistic hand. He also played a very important role in the development of Lincoln College, Oxford.[47]

For our purposes, his most important act as a bibliophile was to found Jesus College, Rotherham, in 1483 and to prepare a charter listing all the books he gave, which is now Cambridge, Sidney Sussex College MS 2. Indeed, he began to prepare his will, with careful attention to his library, twenty-five years before his death, making, as he tells us, several versions, in his own hand, complete with book inventory.[48]

Rotherham gave to the college 105 books, all of them manuscripts. As each of these books had a second folio reference in the bequest, these references have helped in several cases to identify surviving examples. These books are detailed at the end of the charter and again more elaborately itemized in his registered will and roll copy of 1498. As we saw in chapter 1, his will lists his books often with aesthetic or laudatory comments; for example, five volumes, missals, antiphonals and graduals, are called "sumptuously illuminated," "of great price," or "new and beautiful."

Four books from the Rotherham Jesus College bequest still survive. Besides Cambridge, Sidney Sussex College MS 2, the charter for the college, there are York Minster Library, MS XVI.A.6; Cambridge, Trinity College MS O.4.40; and Cambridge, University Library MS Ff.3.15,[49] all dating from the end of the fifteenth century. As all of these volumes but the first contain works of Robert Grosseteste, bishop of Lincoln, and so duplicate each other, this author may have appealed especially to Rotherham because of their common Lincoln connection.

Two of these books, York Minster Library MS XVI.A.6 and Cambridge University Library MS Ff.3.15, were written by the same scribe, "Schaw," who may have been Rotherham's personal scribe. He concluded them with the same scribal verses: "Hunc finem feci / Da michi quod merui quod Schaw."[50] Whatever his precise relationship to Rotherham, he sought to curry favor and was a highly accomplished text writer with notarial training. He wrote the text and the rubrics of both manuscripts in a beautiful engrossing hand. Schaw was a very decorative scribe, often ornamenting his page with cadel ascenders at the top line and prolonged descenders at the bottom. His style was to have a very handsome nine-line capital—in black in the York MS and in blue in the Cambridge one—to begin new sections of text. In addition, he drew faces within top-line letter bows in both books.

The Cambridge volume, written on fine parchment with large margins, has five-line capitals with guide letters. Though such letters are normally the directions of the scribe for a flourisher, it is likely that Schaw himself did the capitals, since the extremely fluent character of the flourishing of occasional descenders at the bottoms of lines extending well into the lower margin and of the flourished strokes of ascenders at headlines seems very like the work of the capitals (fig. 50).

In both the York Minster Library and Cambridge books, Schaw inserts Rotherham's own glosses on Grosseteste's text, incorporating these *addimenta* into the text as though they were of an equal authorial status, and indicating this by a special colophon. Thus in MS XVI.A.6, after some material from Pseudo-Jerome, Schaw concludes "quod M. T. Rotherham" at folio 102v; and in MS Ff.3.15, after similar additions at folio 115, he writes "quod M.T. Rotherham," and at folio 194 at the end of the work "quod M.T. Rotherham." Schaw also provided a table to the contents of the Cambridge volume, which ends at folio 205 *"explicit* Schaw."

We can gain an idea of Rotherham's artistic taste from York Minster Library MS XVI.A.6 and from Sidney Sussex College MS 2. Each book has a major initial but no other painted decoration. The illumination of the major initial in the York volume, an eagle and a mask face with Schaw's comment "assit principio sancta Maria meo" above it with its sprays and teasels, is of somewhat higher quality than the work in Sidney Sussex. It is possible that these were both work-

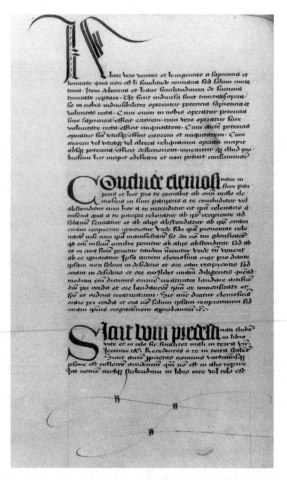

50. Script with enhanced ascenders and descenders. Cambridge University Library MS Ff. 3.15, *Dicta* of Robert Grosseteste, folio 73v, after 1489. *Courtesy Syndics of Cambridge University.*

shop initials, and though the motifs may be heraldic in some way, they may also be workshop model book motifs—especially the mask face, which, as we have seen, was extremely common in northern codices of this period.

The Sidney Sussex volume is a large parchment book (425 × 225 mm); the inventory occurs on folios 10-12v. It was written by several scribes. Its title page (fig. 51) has a major initial containing on a gold

51. Spray-work border and arms. Cambridge, Sidney Sussex College MS 2, Archbishop Thomas Rotherham's charter for Jesus College, Rotherham, folio 1, after 1489. *By permission of the Master and Fellows of Sidney Sussex College, Cambridge.*

ground a portrait of Rotherham in his archbishop's regalia, holding a cross. There are two coats of arms. Rotherham's arms are at the top margin: three stags vert or roebucks trippant argent impale the arms of the see of York, a now tarnished silver pall with the bend of the cross between the pall's branches. At the side margin are the Rotherham arms again, and at the bottom of the page the arms of York.

The motto "Da te deo" appears with each set of arms. Rotherham's arms are what are called canting, where the heraldic devices play on the owner's name or some component of it, such as the syllable *ro* in Rotherham.[51]

Another of Rotherham's college endowment books to survive is the *Dicta* of Grosseteste, Cambridge, Trinity College MS O.4.40, which has red, blue, and gold flourished initials and a handsome border and initial of English provenance on the first folio. Like some of the other manuscripts of ecclesiastical magnates we have discussed, it has aristocratic pretensions, with a much-rubbed shield at the bottom of the first page, bearing an argent cross moline in sable.

Certain conclusions emerge about the manuscripts owned by or associated with these three northern magnates and about the scribes and decorators who appear to have worked on their books. At Durham, at least, there seems to have been much more cooperation between commercial and administrative notaries and monastic scribes in the making of books than one might expect. Moreover, as has been noted by other scholars,[52] one of the main activities of these fifteenth-century scribes was the making of tables as reference aids to the searching of older books, an activity that also occurred at York.[53] Many of the monks at Durham made these tables, and it is the type of work that we associate with the rote copying that went on in many monasteries, yet we also find such reference aids made by both William Bentlay and William du Stiphel, who were scribes of a very different order.

Naturally, these conclusions can be based only on the surviving codices, which may not give completely representative pictures of their owners' tastes. Six manuscripts, however, use some form of armorial, heraldic, or pseudoheraldic decoration on the first folio only, designed to indicate and glorify the owners' social, ecclesiastical, and intellectual status. In one Rotherham book the commissioner's views of the text were added as of equal authority with the work of the original author. In the case of Durham Cathedral Library MS A.I.3, the picture of Cuthbert as a bishop may reflect in some way Bishop Skirlaw's own office, if indeed, that is the manuscript's commissioner. If, however, we place the book in the first decade of the fifteenth century, the picture could relate to Langley himself. These books by their decoration, whether of penwork or of illuminator—and in the case of the volumes associated with Langley, by their grand scale— attest to their owners' power and importance but do it without the elaborate programs of illumination that we see so often in southern books. Though there is no reason to assume that these magnates lacked the money to purchase such decorative skills, it may be possible that the artists capable of doing such work were not as readily available in the north as they were in the south and that the work of local artists like the Durham latticework master was used as a substitute.

Probably much of what we said about the social function of books with regard to these three magnates applies generally to the bulk of the manuscripts we have discussed. On the whole, northern manuscript art in both its decorative and figurative aspects reflected certain social attitudes of the new class of bourgeois and gentrified book owners. These owners appear showy but skeptical, a bit flamboyant, but often with a strong satiric side, to judge from some of the more ornate manuscripts, such as the *Historia Aurea* abridgment CUL Dd. 10.22, Bodleian Library MS Laud. Misc. 302, with its *monde renversé* and comic parodic elements; and Boston Public Library MS 1576, with similar comic and parodic decoration.

In their self-consciously unfashionable decoration, many of these books are deeply subversive. Northern decorated books differ from southern ones in cheapness and simplicity. Their decorators show little interest in producing poor copies of southern Franco-Flemish or Anglo-Flemish styles and more enthusiasm for archaizing as an answer to the problem of style. Where contemporary elements are used, as in the cases of the carpel and calyx, they are often exaggerated and strange. Rarely dull, surviving northern books are vigorous, innovative, idiosyncratic, popular, and fascinating reflections of the region from which they come.

Appendixes
Abbreviations
Notes
Glossary
Bibliography
Index

Appendix A

THE PIGMENT *FOLIUM*

For those who may be interested in the more technical aspects of the pigment *folium*, we should note that even the origin of the name is uncertain. Mary Philadelphia Merrifield claims, following British Library MS Sloane 416, fol. 132, that linen rags soaked in the juice of *Chrozophora tinctoria* were dried or preserved between sheets, or *folia*, in blotter books, and that this practice was the source of the word.[1] This theory, however, is not supported by contemporary evidence; indeed, such recipes typically mention air drying of rags and preservation in boxes or glass jars. One possible explanation for the word *folium* is a paleographical one. If we assume that from a very early period, *torna-ad-solem* as a name for plants which give a blue-purple pigment was common, it is possible that the descenders of *f* and long *s*, especially in Carolingian minuscule, could have been confused and a plant name *solium* or *folium* could have developed from this confusion in the later Middle Ages. Some support for this is the common spelling for the word *biffus*—the word for blue-violet—as *bissus* in several medieval Italian color treatises.[2]

Chrozophora tinctoria has received little attention in modern times. With the notable exception of the study by Arie Wallert, whose focus is primarily chromatographic, and some research in progress by Cheryl Porter of the University of London, in some ways the earliest scholarship, done when the plant had an economic significance as a dye material in the town of Grand-Gallargues in southern France, is still the most informative.[3] The only detailed account of the harvest, manufacture, and storage of the juice of *Chrozophora tinctoria*, to my knowledge, appears in an article written in 1842 by N. Joly, and remains to this day, like the nearly contemporary discussion by Merrifield, an extremely informative piece of scholarship. The chief virtue of Joly's discussion is that he is describing the color changes of the material caused by the primitive methods used six hundred years earlier by medieval artisans and that he treats the plant as of economic importance to the region, which it must also have been in the Middle Ages as a source for illuminators' pigment.

The commune of Grand-Gallargues is in the department of Gard, in the

227

arrondissement of Nîmes, about seven miles northwest of the city, and in the canton of Vauvert on the river Vidourle. This river forms the boundary between the departments of Gard and Hérault. Grand-Gallargues, which has a present-day population of about two thousand,[4] seems to have been the center for the cultivation and commercial processing of *Chrozophora tinctoria*. This countryside, made famous in the autobiography of Marcel Pagnol, is a dry and mountainous one. Though the guild records of the town begin only about 1600, the manufacture of the pigment is mentioned at that time and there is every reason to believe that Grand-Gallargues was probably the center of export for *folium* elsewhere on the Continent and to England during the Middle Ages.

Apparently the industry was so central to the town's economic life that there were local regulations which prohibited gathering the plant before the twenty-fifth of August, when it would have been completely mature, and the whole town was seasonally involved with the harvest of what was called *maurelle*. Joly quotes a Huguenot antiquary, who makes a prophetically accurate observation about the *maurelliers:* "Few trades are as mysterious. Those who do the work don't know the destination of their products; those who profit don't know its preparation, and those who have described it have transmitted only lies."[5]

Joly visited Grand-Gallargues to see the industry in August 1839. On the morning that *Chrozophora tinctoria* is gathered, the plants are placed in a horse-driven press, very like an olive oil mill, macerated, and the juice—at this point a dark green, nearly blue, and very viscous—is run off through brush strainers into large wooden tubs. The pressings on the strainers are then mixed with urine, which apparently serves as a solvent, and again milled. Once the juice is obtained, it is drawn into long tubs, and pieces of a sort of heavy clean cheesecloth are dipped in it, removed, and immediately dried in sun and wind. The drying must take place on a good day, for if the weather is stormy, the cloths never turn blue.

At this point the dry cloths undergo an exposure to *aluminiadou,* a layer of horse or mule dung about a half meter thick. The dung must be recent and just beginning to ferment, becoming hot in consequence and releasing ammonia vapor. Over this dung bed are strewn handfuls of fresh straw, and the cheesecloths placed on this are covered over with more straw and a light coating of dung or sometimes a large sheet to concentrate the fumes of the *aluminiadou.* The dyer checks periodically to see that the two surfaces of the cloths are equally colored and that overlong exposure does not ruin the blue tint, which when it leaves, never comes again (instead, the cloth goes yellow). This process continues for about an hour and a half.

Everything at this point hinges on the character of the *aluminiadou,* which Joly remarked "est la pierre de touche du veritable maurellier."[6] The cloths are then dried a second time, soaked in plant pressings mixed with urine, and put on the dung, to be taken off only when they have turned a dark purple.

A version he mentions of the process used in the late eighteenth century seems more like that given in the medieval artists' recipes for preparing *folium*. Here fermented urine was combined with quicklime, calcium hydroxide, in proportions of ten pounds of quicklime to twelve gallons of urine and a little alum added as a mordant. Calcined alum was often used as a solvent to extract colors, such as that from brazilwood. This is probably the origin of the word *aluminiadou*. The cheesecloths were suspended about a foot above tubs containing this mixture and were covered with a sheet. One to two days later the cloths became a beautiful blue. Though a slower process than that involving the dung bed, this was also a safer method, since one left the cloth exposed till the desired color was achieved.

After the cloths were properly dyed, they were baled and exported to Holland for dying cheese. The rags were steeped in water, the cheese dipped in the water and immediately dried off; the action of the lactic and butyric acids made the outer layer of the cheese go red.[7] This local industry apparently continued into the 1870s, when the coming of aniline dyes rendered it obsolete.[8] Other uses of these cloths were for coloring jams and jellies, sugar-wrapping paper, and wine; indeed, Gerard in his *Herbal* speaks of this practice as common in the sixteenth century, mentioning cloths of "a perfect purple colour" made from plants called "tornsole" that grow "about Montpelier in Languedock, where it is had in great vse to staine and die clouts . . . and are strangers in England as yet;" with these cloths the French "cookes and confectioners doe colour iellies, wines, meates, and sundry confectures."[9]

Joly's contemporary, Mary Philadelphia Merrifield, claims that in the Middle Ages *Chrozophora tinctoria* was primarily a plant growing in marshy areas around Montpellier in southern France, basing this belief on some remarks made by Jean le Bègue in his treatise on artists' colors, circa 1431, and on a brief discussion in a recipe manuscript of the fourteenth-century, *Liber de Coloribus Illuminatorum siue Pictorum*, which occupies folios 142v–149r in British Library MS Sloane 1754: "The morel is a kind of plant which grows in the land of St. Giles. And from this plant three grains go out in the seed, and with these three grains cloths are dyed, and so yield up a splendid color called folium."[10] Her topographic data more or less agree with Joly's direct observation, as St. Giles is about thirteen miles from Nîmes, but modern botanists show the plant as more characteristic of the fallow slopes of the many small mountains and hillsides studded with vineyards in the departments of Gard and Hérault, departments slightly out of the area of Montpellier.[11]

The plant, however, is not confined to Provence, as it can be found also in Italy (especially Sicily and Sardinia), Portugal, Turkey, Cyprus, northern Greece, Hungary, Albania, Bulgaria, Russia, Spain, Egypt, Tunisia, Algeria, Morocco, modern-day Israel, and Syria, on the slopes of Mount Cassius, near Antioch, where as recently as the mid-1920s it was still gathered by young women as a fingernail coloring and as an aphrodisiac.[12] It is also said to grow in India, but what was studied there seems to have been a subspecies of *Chrozophora tinctoria* called *Hierosolmitana*, which does not occur in Europe.[13]

Let us next consider the chemistry of this obscure pigment, in so far as that is known. To judge by Joly's observations, as well as by the medieval recipes describing the manufacture of *folium*, the juice of *Chrozophora tinctoria* belongs to the large class of acid-base indicators like litmus whose hues change as their pH or concentration of hydrogen ions in solution shifts from acid to alkaline. Without going into the chemistry of indicators in detail, we may note that an indicator is generally a carbon-containing chemical that changes color depending on the number of hydrogens attached to it. In a solution, some of the hydrogens remain bound to the indicator molecules, while others are released into the liquid. Acid liquids contain many free hydrogen ions. In such a solution most of the indicator molecules will be covered with bound hydrogens. Basic solutions have very few free hydrogen ions and tend to pull the hydrogens away from indicator molecules, changing their shapes and therefore their color.

Various indicators differ in how tightly they retain hydrogens and in their shape changes after the removal of a hydrogen. For some types, a very basic liquid is required to remove the ions and change the color; others are dissociated almost all of the time, binding hydrogens only in the most acidic situations. At a pH specific for the indicator, each molecule in solution will have exactly half of its hydrogens bound and half free. Small shifts to either side of this point will change the color of the solution and are termed "within the range" of the indicator. Typically, indicators may be shifted back and forth from one color to the other simply by decreasing or increasing the liquid's number of hydrogen ions within this range. For some indicators, however, including *folium*, the color change is virtually irreversible.

Remembering that a low pH value corresponds to a high concentration of free hydrogens, and therefore an acidic solution, while a high pH describes a basic solution, let us look at the pH's of some of the important solutions used in *folium* pigment preparation. Water, which has a pH of 7, is called neutral and is the set point in the middle of the scale. Urine, widely used in the medieval recipes for the preparation of *folium*, is initially acidic, with a pH of 4.8 to 7.5, but is converted to a base (pH higher than 7) after prolonged exposure to air. Vinegar in wine must, which is also used in medieval recipes, has a very acidic pH of 3. Litmus, the best known of the acid-base indicators, has a pH of 4.7 to 8.2, red at the lower end, blue at the higher end. This is similar enough to *folium*'s range and color change, to raise the question of whether *folium* may actually be a litmus-related compound.

Though the *folium* colorant has never been synthesized, suggestions about its chemical components have been offered by Heinz Roosen-Runge and by Françoise Flieder, and its infrared spectrum is known. Their identifications, however, have been disputed recently by Wallert. Roosen-Runge believed that anthocyanin formed the colorant,[14] and Flieder claimed that one of its four components is the chief coloring agent of litmus, azolithmin;

the others are erythrolithmin, also in litmus, erythrolein, and a compound she calls spaniolithmin, but which I have been unable to find in any chemical handbook. Nor has correspondence with Flieder clarified what she meant by the term.[15]

Wallert notes that ultraviolet, visible and mass spectra show considerable differences between the *folium* colorant and that found in common anthocyanin colorants.[16] Moreover, with respect to the connection with the lichen colorants, according to *Conn's Biological Stains*, the precise chemical composition of azolithmin is not known, and it is not even clear if it is a single compound.[17] Azolithmin's pH shift, according to *Long's Biochemists' Handbook*, is 5.0 for red and 8.0 for blue, and according to the *Merck Index* 4.5 for red and 8.3 for blue,[18] which seems to agree more or less with what is known about the shift points for *folium*, but though both are color indicators, as Wallert notes, the colors of *folium* and lichens behave very differently chemically, and indeed, "the [chemical] structure of the real turnsole still has not been established."[19]

The medieval recipes for making *folium* and for changing its pH fall into two groups. In the oldest ones, the material is called *folium*, and the recipe seems to involve the direct introduction to the pigment of urine, quicklime, lye made from beech, oak or artemisia, and vine wood ashes. The basicity in this case comes from the potassium carbonate or potash obtained from the calcining process.[20] Such a recipe first appears in the *De Diversis Artibus*. The second type, generally associated with the word *tornesol*, prescribes the use of ammonia vapors obtained from urine or dung. Such recipes begin to appear in the fourteenth century, and the cheesecloth manufacture at Grand-Gallargues belongs to this category.

The *De Diversis Artibus*, a treatise by the German Benedictine Theophilus, possibly Roger of Helmarshausen, dates from the tenth century. In book 1, in a section on materials for manuscript painting, the author says:

> There are three kinds of folium—one red, another purple, the third blue [violet], and you mix them in this way.
> Take some ashes . . . [and] put them in a fire until they are white hot. . . . Pour on some urine and stir. . . . When the preparation has settled and become clear, pour it on some red folium . . . and add to it a fourth part of quicklime. . . . If you wish [to obtain] purple folium, use this preparation without adding lime.[21]

Theophilus suggests that purple and blue-violet *folium* are obtained by the direct addition of urine and quicklime, but the purple form needs less basicity. Moreover, the implication of this recipe is that one begins with red *folium* and then achieves the other colors in succession.

Theophilus's recipe is very ambiguous. It is quite unclear if the alkaline matter is added to the juice of the plant as it comes from seeds during the manufacture of the pigment or when the artist is ready to prepare it for illuminating and is choosing his tonalities. The real question, then, is the means by which this "purplish" color was varied according to the artist's needs.

The *Mappae Clavicula*, a recipe collection from about the same period, suggests that the pigment so produced is less a stain than a substance remaining on the surface of the parchment, and needing a binder, for the *Mappae* author notes that pigments that are opaque or translucent—depending on the thickness of the layer—on parchment include *folium*, which is tempered with *clarea* or egg white as a binder. It could also be mixed with white lead to obtain a pink or could be applied as a transparent glaze over other colors, such as ultramarine or *verdigris*.[22]

Recent attempts to make *folium* according to these medieval recipes have been inconclusive. The fullest published account of such experiments is that of Roosen-Runge,[23] who studied all the pigments of the Lindisfarne Gospels, comparing areas of the miniatures with samples of the same colors manufactured according to the recipes offered in *De Diversis Artibus*, the *Mappae Clavicula*, and the Lucca manuscript. By means of polarized and ultraviolet light, he compared pigments to samples under high magnification and took photomicrographs under both reflected and transmitted light, creating a series of color plates for all of the materials known to have been used by the Lindisfarne painters. It is these plates, containing the only modern published examples of the pigment, which must be used for comparison with medieval manuscript miniatures.[24]

Although Roosen-Runge devoted several pages of his pigment catalogue to his experiments with *folium*, his attempts to bring about a shift from *folium rubeum* to *saphireum* by altering the pH through the "direct application" method had inconsistent results. He noted, moreover, that with lemon juice he could obtain both *rubeum* and *saphireum* as well as by using the methods in the recipe books. Also, apparently exposure to light might be involved in the color shifts as well.

Perhaps the most useful of his findings was that the juice as it came from the seeds of *Chrozophora tinctoria* had a pH of 4, which is somewhat less acidic than vinegar, moving to neutrality and purple at a pH of 7 and blue and alkalinity at a pH of 12.[25] The pigment could be destroyed by mold, for the juice developed a brownish or oxblood tone apparently related to the acids created when the material grew mold. This reaction may explain why the *folium* employed in some medieval manuscripts has a brownish cast to the purple, perhaps the result of an acidic environment.

Arie Wallert, in a letter to me, enclosing a reddish clothlet, describes his own attempt to make *folium* in 1988. The juice, coming directly from the seeds of *Chrozophora tinctoria* plants obtained from southern France

> was a deep, inky blue; this colour only remains blue if it is immediately stored in a dry alkaline environment. For instance in clothlets that have been pretreated with unslaked lime, potassium carbonate

and the like. If the colorant remains in solution for some time or if pH is too low (pH 7 already is) the colour irreversibly turns to red. It is impossible then to make it blue again. And even blue clothlets that are dry and have been stored in a stable environment, show a tendency to change into a purplish red.

The conclusion reached was that "the recipe is meant to start with the blue and not to end with it."[26] Yet Theophilus's recipe certainly suggests a progression from red to blue to blue-violet; and Joly, while not speaking of red, indicates that the shift from blue though alkalinization was a shift from blue juice to dark purple cloths.

Thus, it appears that there is an essential defect in the "direct alkalinization" method. Either some key ingredient or process was omitted from works like the *De Diversis Artibus* and its later medieval copies, or the recipe never worked at all. But since *folium* is known to exist, it is likely that something happened to the original recipe in the course of its early medieval transmission and that later medieval recipes of the "vapor" type were the ones by which the material was actually produced.

Let us turn to the second method now. These *tournesole* recipes all have in common exposure to ammonia vapors. The clearly Mediterranean setting of the late fourteenth-century Neopolitan *De Arte Illuminandi* makes it seem likely that the compiler had an actual acquaintance with *Chrozophora tinctoria*. His recipe speaks of "a blue made from the plant which is called turnsole [que vocatur torna-ad-solem] and it remains azure blue for a year, after which it is converted into a violet color." There is, moreover, a clear distinction between the color phases of the process. The description of the plant in question and the directions for manufacture are quite detailed and practical; indeed, they sound very like the process described by Joly.

Now this is the way to make the color from this plant. Take the seeds which are collected from the middle of July until the middle of September. And the plant has grey [flowers] and its fruits or seeds are three joined in one. And they should be gathered in good weather. And without bruising the seeds, they should be detached from the stems from which they hang, and lain on an old clean linen cloth. Fold up the cloth and squeeze until the juice runs into a vitreous pot, and continue the process until you have enough. Then take other pieces of clean used linen cloths which have been soaked first several times with a lye made from water and quicklime, and then thoroughly wash them with clear water and dry them. They can even be prepared without the lime. And when they are dry, saturate them in this juice a day and a night. Then in a dark, damp place, put some rich garden soil on a tray and let a healthy man who has been been drinking wine copiously urinate on the earth. And over it, furthermore, you erect a rack of canes or rods, so that the soaked cloths can be spread out above the urine vapor, without touching the earth, for three or four days, until they dry. Then put these cloths under books and put them in a box, or in a glass jar, close it up and put it in quicklime in a dry, out of the way spot, and so preserve them.[27]

The instructions given here clearly indicate *Chrozophora tinctoria*, which does indeed have a trilobate seed capsule and a pale, flat, gray-green color of leaf. Possibly the difference in date of harvest, September rather than late August, merely indicates a slightly different geography from that of southern France. The tendency of the material to change color over time agrees with Wallert's own experience, though the change in the modern material was to a reddish purple. Presumably the storage in a jar surrounded by quicklime was to create an alkaline rather than acid environment in case the seal of the jar was poor.

That such unstable blue-purple pigments quickly changing to red were known in England is clear from a recipe "to make turnesolle" added in a sixteenth-century hand to a fifteenth-century manuscript associated with Blythe near Nottingham, whose present whereabouts are uncertain; it was once the property of Reginald Rawdon Hastings, many of whose books were sold to the Huntington Library. It is a paper commonplace book containing recipes for alchemical, medical, and artists' materials as well as a treatise on coinage. The recipe involves red wine, brazilwood, ceruce and "a nowunce of whede flowres." Though "whede" flowers maybe *Chrozophora tinctoria*, it is more likely that this recipe uses native cornflowers or possibly woad. Then take, the Middle English writer continues, "fayre lynen clothe that is olde and cleyn wasshen and putt them into the wyne and dyppe it welle therin and then wrynge it uppe a lyttyle and then henge it to dry in a place frome sone or wynde. . . . And when thi clothe is drye . . . ley it owt of the eyre or elles it wylle turne owt of blew into red."[28]

As can be seen from the English example just given, both the vapor and direct alkalinization methods have the same system of preparing the clothlets. This system can also be found in the Strasburg manuscript, a fifteenth-century German treatise formerly Strasburg Municipal Library MS Cod. A.VI.19, destroyed in the war of 1870, but whose contents were preserved through a transcription. As with the previous recipe, though the blue rags mentioned in this work were probably prepared with cornflower juice, the process must have been the same for *folium*.

Take some clean pieces of old linen that have been well bleached and washed white and steep the rags in the colour. Then turn them over so that they get thoroughly saturated and are evenly coloured on both sides, the colour quite soaked up yet the rags not dripping.

Then taking them out carefully, hang them up in the open air on a line or on a clothes-horse and leave them to dry. . . . The blue rags must be wrapped in paper and be laid in a clean wooden box and must then be kept on some high shelf where it smells sweet and clean and where the colour will not be affected by mould. If the rags are kept in this way, they will remain fresh and lovely for as long as twenty years without fading.[29]

When the artist was ready to paint with *folium*, according to a fifteenth-century Middle English treatise found in Aberystwyth National Library MS Porkington 10, he should "take gum water, and put hit into a schelle of an oystere; then take a pece of tornesole, and ley hit in the water of gum, and let hit ly awhyle therein, and then wrynge it throɔe a clothe to thou se the water be welle colouryd, and then florysche bokys therewith."[30] A similar recipe in the same manuscript uses glair or *clarea*.[31]

The detailed character of the urine vapor methods of producing *folium* in the Sloane and *De Arte Illuminandi* recipes suggest that these were the methods actually followed, rather than the rather vague and alchemical-sounding direct alkalinization system described by Theophilus. To achieve several different tonalities would then have required that clothlets storing the appropriate tones be on hand. The artist then need not have been a color maker or a chemist; he need only have chosen the colors he wished and soaked the clothlets in the binder. Thus three clothlets could contain the major shades of *folium*, which could in turn have been varied slightly with white lead or other additives that we know were used. For example, the Naples manuscript says that to make clear violet, "misce folium cum albo; incide de folio; matiza de albo plumbo."[32]

As an English artist would be dependent on his clothlets for the tones from which he would mix his own *folium*, and these could vary considerably, depending on the acidity or alkalinity of the preparation at the time it reached him; consequently, it would seem that the pigment would be very difficult to produce in uniform batches. Indeed, its color variants seem to have been created for the occasion and even for the stint; their uniqueness gives a special charm to the books in which they appear, and anyone who has examined Oxford, Bodleian MS Rawlinson D. 939 will recall the child-like character of the various purple washes applied to the parchment.

Folium must have been known to the English as early as the Gospels of St. Augustine, Cambridge, Corpus Christi College MS 286,[33] a manuscript that dates from the sixth century. It was ostensibly sent from Rome by Gregory to Augustine of Canterbury and was in England by the end of the seventh century. By about the eighth century, the pigment must have been in general use among Hiberno-Saxon artists, as can be seen from the Book of Kells, the St. Chad Gospels, and particularly the Lindisfarne Gospels.[34] All three types of *folium*—*rubeum*, *purpureum*, and *saphireum*—are used by the Lindisfarne artist, presumably Eadfrith, bishop of Lindisfarne from 698 to 721;[35] it is generally believed that the Gospels were painted between 687 and 698.[36] The outer frame of an Evangelist portrait at folio 25v is a shade midway between *rubeum* and *purpureum*, while the color of the tunic is between *purpureum* and *saphireum*. A reddish or acid form appears in the outer frame of the portrait of Luke on folio 137v, while the plum color in Mark's cloak on 93v is the pure form of the purple color. Luke's pallium is the pure *saphireum*.[37]

As a considerable amount of research is going on with regard to all the pigments used in medieval painting, it is likely that more information will soon become available about this fascinating plant and its colorant. For the moment, this account of what is generally known about *folium* may serve to indicate something of its importance in medieval illumination both on the Continent and in England.

Appendix B

A HANDLIST OF EXTANT NORTHERN MANUSCRIPTS

Manuscripts are described by location, pressmark, date, type, kalendar if present, overall dimensions, writing material, number of folios, number of lines per page or column, decoration, and reason for assuming a northern provenance.

1. Aberystwyth, Wales, National Library MS 9852C, S. XIV², Beverley kalendar, 250 × 165 mm, parchment, 6 folios, 1 × 30–31, undecorated, Collegiate Church of St. John of Beverley.

2. ———, MS Brogyntyn II.5 (formerly MS Porkington 19), 1419, English translation of Suso's *Horologium Sapientiae*, 230 × 150 mm, parchment, 184 pages, 1 × 27, undecorated, written at Mountgrace Carthusian Priory, Yorkshire.

3. Arundel Castle, West Sussex, unnumbered, S. XV, antiphonal, York use, 410 × 280 mm, parchment, vii + 257 folios, 2 × 50, red and blue flourished initials, Collegiate Chapel of St. Mary and the Holy Angels, York.

4. ———, unnumbered, 1425, *Pricke of Conscience*, 225 × 145 mm, parchment, 141 folios, 1 × 32, red and blue flourished initials, York Franciscans, northeast Midlands dialect.

5. Beverly Hills, California, Collection I. J. Pincus, 1385, Richard de Thorpe, York kalendar and almanach, 170 × 110 mm, parchment, 118 folios, 1 × 25, gold, blue, rose initials, astronomical drawings, and paintings.

6. Blackburn, Lancashire, Stonyhurst College MS 2, S. XIV, Cistercian missal, 410 × 292 mm, parchment, 190 folios, 2 × 30, penwork initials, historiated initial, province of York.

7. ———, MS 3, S.XV¹, missal, York kalendar with the Feast of the Relics of the Cathedral, 374 × 253 mm, parchment, i + 225 folios, 2 × 36, gold and violet initials, full gold and blue borders, Tetham Church, Richmond Archdeaconry.

8. Boston, Massachusetts, Boston Public Library MS 1576, S. XIV⁴, missal, York kalendar, 230 × 340 mm, parchment, 227 folios, 2 × 34, gold initials, bar borders with polymorphs, Neville and Gascoigne *obits*.

238 Appendix B

9. Boulogne-sur-Mer, Bibliothèque Municipale MS 93, S.XV[1], prayers and *horae*, York kalendar, 272 × 180 mm, parchment, 96 folios, 1 × 20, historiated initials, 23 full-page drawings, full and partial borders.

10. Cambrai, Bibliothèque Municipale MS 255, 1419, Middle English translation of Suso's *Horologium Sapientiae*, 218 × 150 mm, parchment, 63 folios, 1 × 30–33, colored initials, Mount Grace colophon.

11. Cambridge, England, Cambridge University Library MS Additional 3110, S.XV, breviary, York saints in sanctorale, 182 × 127 mm, parchment, ii + 245 folios, 2 × 34, gold-blue-violet initials.

12. ———, MS Dd.10.22, ca. 1380–1390, John of Tynemouth, *Historia Aurea*, abridgment, 222 × 150 mm, parchment, ii + 159 folios, 1 × 36, floriated initials, name William Roke on folio 1, York merchant, died 1427.

13. ———, MS Ee.4.19, S.XIV[4], manual, York, 283 × 188 mm, parchment, 96 folios, 1 × 27–28, red and blue flourished initials, *litterae partitae*, colophon, John Castleford, William Bramelay, chaplains of York, Hospital of St. Leonard, York.

14. ———, MS Ff.1.14, S.XV, William Flete, *Remedia* and other tracts, 200 × 140 mm, paper, 208 folios, 1 × 28, undecorated, written by Robert Wasselyn, chaplain of York.

15. ———, MS Ff.3.15, before 1498, *Dicta* of Robert Grosseteste with *addimenta* of Thomas Rotherham, 300 × 200 mm, parchment, iv + 205 + iii folios, 1 × 42, colored capitals.

16. ———, MS Kk.3.5 (formerly Clare College MS 5) S.XV, prayers, 217 × 147 mm, parchment, 148 folios, 1 × 19, illuminations now cut out, initials and borders, owned by a Yorkshire house honoring St. Honoratus and by a Lady Scrope.

17. ———, Corpus Christi College, MS 96, 1425, Chronicle of Jervaulx Abbey, 360 × 230 mm, parchment, ii + 239 folios, 1 × 48, blue penwork initials, colophon of Jervaulx.

18. ———, Emmanuel College MS 35, S. XV, Rolle tracts, 215 × 140 mm, paper, iii + 235 + ii, 1 × 30, penwork initials, table by John Newton.

19. ———, Fitzwilliam Museum MS 34, between 1465 and 1479, missal, York kalendar, 388 × 245 mm, parchment, i + 232 + i folios, 2 × 35, gold initials, historiated initials and full floral borders, two full-page miniatures, made for Fitzwilliams of Sprotborough, Yorkshire.

20. ———, MS 329, the Anlaby Cartulary, ca. 1450, 285 × 180 mm, parchment, 152 folios, 1 × 41–45, colored initials and coats of arms, written by Thomas Anlaby.

21. ———, McClean MS 169, S.XV, Pseudo-Boethius, *De Disciplina Scolarum* and other tracts, 184 × 126 mm, parchment, 283 + iii folios, 1 × 31, undecorated, written by Robert Emylton, monk of Durham Priory.

22. ———, Jesus College MS 8, S.XV, Isidore of Seville, 285 × 190 mm, parchment, i + 200 + ii folios, 1 × 40, floriated initials, 3/4 borders, owned by Thomas Man, vicar of Northallerton.

23. ———, MS 22, S. XIV[4], gradual, 294 × 173 mm, parchment, 39 + iii folios, 8 staves of music per page, undecorated, feasts for Cuthbert and for his translation.

24. ———, MS 41, S.XIV[4], *Speculum Religiosum* and tract of Uthred of Boldon, 217 × 147 mm, parchment, 176 folios, 1 × 37, undecorated, belonged to Durham Priory.

25. ———, MS 45, S. XV, Vincent of Beauvais, *Speculum Historiale* with Jean Hautfuney's topical index, 197 × 125 mm, parchment, iii + 264 folios, 1 × 32, floriated initials, full floral border, belonged to Durham Priory.

26. ———, MS 48, S.XV, Boethius, *De Consolatione Philosophiae* with Trivet commentary, 180 × 122 mm, parchment, iv + 354 + iv folios, 1 × 27–36, floriated initials, full floral border, belonged to Durham Priory.

27. ———, MS 55, S.XV[4], Premonstratensian ordinal, 205 × 141 mm, paper, 143 folios, 1 × 30, undecorated, Premonstratensian house of St. Agatha, Easby, near Richmond, Yorkshire.

28. ———, MS 61, S. XIV[4], rule of St. Benedict, 205 × 133 mm, parchment, 105 folios, 1 × 33, undecorated, *obit* of John Fishbourn, monk of Durham Priory, d. 1434, and other Durham inscriptions.

29. ———, MS 67, S.XIV, Thomas Walleys, *Communiloquium*, 181 × 141 mm, parchment, 228 folios, 1 × 33, undecorated, belonged to Durham Priory.

30. ———, MS 70, S.XV, Pseudo-Robert Grosseteste, commentary on Boethius, *De Consolatione Philosophiae*, works of Ambrose, Ovid, Seneca, 175 × 120 mm, parchment, ii + 122 + ii folios, 1 × 52, flourished initals, 3/4 border, written by Robert Emylton, monk of Durham Priory.

31. ———, MS 77, S.XV[4], Augustinian diurnale, York kalendar with the Feast of the Relics of the Cathedral, 102 × 70 mm, paper, iii + 234 + viii folios, 1 × 22, red pen initials, possibly Austin canons of Bridlington.

32. ———, Pembroke College MS 248, S.XV, William of Pagula, *Oculus Sacerdotalis*, 301 × 192 mm, parchment, 140 + vi folios, 2 × 44, red penwork flourished initials, owned by William Hobbyses, rector of Hye Mansell, Heregh, Yorkshire, 1457–1465, second folio corresponds to item 444 of York Austin catalogue.

33. ———, St. John's College MS 59,1472, *Tractatus de Sacramentis*, 152 × 148 mm, paper, 15 folios, 1 × 29, undecorated, written by Richard Lepar, chaplain of Foston, Yorkshire.

34. ———, MS 74, S.XIV[1], Bible, 378 × 235 mm, parchment, 482 + ii folios, 2 × 48, red with green and blue with red initials, arms and floriated major initials, full borders, polymorphs, Guisborough Priory.

35. ———, MS 102, between 1398 and 1405, consuetudinary, York, 223 × 147 mm, parchment, ii + 275 + iii folios, 1 × 30, penwork initials, and 3/4 border, St. Mary's Abbey, York.

36. ———, King's College MS 31, S.XV, missal, York kalendar, 180 × 128 mm, parchment, iii + 191 + ii folios, 2 × 36, gold initials, full floral borders.

37. ———, Sidney Sussex College MS 2, before 1498, Rotherham Charter, 425 × 225 mm, 18 folios, 1 × 43, historiated initial, spray borders, coats of arms.

38. ———, MS 33, 1460–1480, missal, York kalendar with the Feast of the Relics of the Cathedral, 280 × 178 mm, parchment, vii + 291 + v folios, 2 × 36, historiated initials, center and bottom borders, from York Cathedral.

39. ———, MS 36, S. XIV¹, prayers, York, 155 × 115 mm, parchment, 198 folios, single and double columns, painting for the office of the Holy Face cut out, Kirkham Abbey.

40. ———, MS 37, *horae*, 1440–1450, Sarum use, 141 × 89 mm, parchment, 152 + v folios, 1 × 18, illuminations and borders, belonged to Churche family, John of Beverley, William, and Cuthbert in kalendar.

41. ———, MS 62, S.XIV², Augustinian diurnale, York kalendar with the Feast of the Relics of the Cathedral, 75 × 48 mm, parchment, iv + 210 + v folios, 1 × 20, gold and historiated initials, gold diapered borders, possibly Kirkham Abbey.

42. ———, Trinity College MS B.15.30, ca. 1390, table to Thomas of Chobham, *Summa Penitentiae*, 260 × 175 mm, parchment, 37 folios, 2 × 27, undecorated, written by William du Stiphel, Durham Priory.

43. ———, MS O.3.10, ca. 1410, psalter-*horae*, York kalendar, Feast of the Relics of the Cathedral, 285 × 199 mm, parchment, i + 144 + i folios, 1 × 24, gold-blue-red initials, historiated initials, full and ¾ borders, Tunstall of Westmorland arms.

44. ———, MS O.4.40, before 1489, Robert Grosseteste, *Dicta*, 318 × 217 mm, parchment, viii + 168 + i folios, 2 × 42, red-blue-gold initials, full floral border and arms, second folio reading shows it was given by Thomas Rotherham to Jesus College.

45. ———, MS R.5.42, S.XIV², Henry of Huntingdon, *Historia Anglorum*, 250 × 179 mm, parchment, 171 + i folios, 1 × 31, red and blue penwork initials, belonged to Robert de Poultoun, O.Carm., Hulne, Alnwick, Northumberland.

46. ———, MS R.7.9, S. XIV, Chronicle of Guisborough, 211 × 145 mm, parchment, 107 folios, 1 × 36, red and blue initials.

47. ———, MS R.14.26, S.XV⁴, Latin questions on music, carols, sermon, logical treatises, 147 × 107 mm, paper and parchment, 150 folios, 1 × 25, undecorated, folio 1 S.XV⁴ bond of Thomas Pierson of Howden, folio 11, *ex libris*, Sanderson of Beverley, written by John Anlaby.

48. ———, MS R.15.21, 1408, John de Foxton, *Liber Cosmographiae*, York kalendar, 254 × 175 mm, parchment, 119 folios, 2 × 39–40, 12 full-page paintings, astrological and prognostic drawings, Trinitarian house of St. Robert, Knaresboro, Yorkshire.

49. Cambridge, Massachusetts, Harvard University MS Widener 1, 1403, manual, York kalendar with the Feast of the Relics of the Cathedral, 267 × 177 mm, parchment, iv + 175 + iii folios, 1 × 21, pen *litterae partitae* initials, ¼ page Crucifixion miniature.

50. Chicago, Illinois, Newberry Library MS + 33.1, S.XV⁴, Ranulph Higden, *Polychronicon*, 380 × 260 mm, parchment, 142 folios, 2 × 54, gold dentelle floriated initials, full floral borders, arms of Bothe family and inscription, Robert Bothe, dean of York Cathedral.

51. Dublin, Trinity College MS 83, S.XIV⁴, rubricated missal, York kalendar, 295 × 202 mm, parchment, 192 folios, 2 × 39–40, *champ* initials, floral borders, ¹/₂ page miniature of Crucifixion, *obit*s of Nortons of Patrick Brompton, Yorkshire.

52. ———, MS 85, S.XIV⁴, breviary, psalter, part of York missal, York kalendar, 228 × 157 mm, parchment, ii + 393 + vi + i folios, 2 × 37–39, red and blue flourished initials, floral borders.

53. ———, MS 87, S.XV, breviary, York kalendar, 214 × 141 mm, parchment, 132 folios, 2 × 42, gold and colored initials, floral borders, references to practices of York Cathedral.

54. ———, MS 207, S.XV, Robert Grosseteste, *De Lingua*, 250 × 175 mm, parchment, 57 folios, 2 × 48–50, *champ* initials, full borders, *ex libris*, St. Mary's Abbey, York.

55. ———, MS 359, 1372–1425, York Augustinian Friars' library catalogue, 291 × 186 mm, parchment, iv + 44 + iii folios, 1 × 30.

56. ———, MS 516, S.XV², John of Bridlington, *Prophetia*, 210 × 141 mm, parchment and paper, 223 folios, 1 × 32, undecorated, Neville inscription.

57. Durham Cathedral, Dean and Chapter Library MS A.I.1, S.XV¹, William of Nottingham, Concordance to the Gospels, 530 × 360 mm, parchment, i + 361 + i folios, 2 × 62, blue-violet-red *litterae partitae* initials, a Thomas Langley book.

58. ———, MS A.I.3, 1386, Nicholas of Lyra, Bible commentary, 430 × 270 mm, parchment, 310 folios, 2 × 60, blue-violet-red *litterae partitae* and flourished initials, full floral border with historiated initial, written by William du Stiphel at Durham Priory.

59. ———, MS A.I.4, 1388–1390, Nicholas of Lyra, Bible commentary, 435 × 280 mm, parchment, i + 228 folios, 2 × 60, *litterae partitae* initials and partial penwork borders, written by William de Stiphel, Le Borwby, and an unnamed scribe at Durham Priory.

60. ———, MS A.I.5, S.XV¹, Nicholas of Lyra, Bible commentary, 400 × 270 mm, parchment, ii + 156 + iii folios, 2 × 56, *litterae partitae* initials, written by John Wykingeston, a Thomas Langley book.

61. ———, MS A.I.6, S.XV¹, Nicholas Gorran, Bible commentary, 455 × 280 mm, parchment, ii + 273 + i folios, 2 × 64, full floral border, *litterae partitae* initials and full trellis border, Thomas Langley arms at folio 1.

62. ———, MS A.III.27, S.XIV⁴, Robert Holkot on Wisdom, 300 × 195 mm, parchment, 227 folios, 2 × 54, red and blue flourished penwork initials, from Durham Priory.

63. ———, MS A.IV.5, S.XIV⁴, Peter of Herenthal, on Psalms, 262 × 180 mm, parchment, ii + 223 folios, 1 × 52, red and blue flourished initials,

from Durham Priory, *ex libris*, William Dalton and Stephen Howden, monks of Durham Priory.

64. ———, MS B.II.29, ca. 1350, works of St. Augustine, 330 × 210 mm, parchment, 412 + i folios, 2 × 44, red-violet penwork initials, borders, from Durham Priory.

65. ———, MS B.III.6, S.XIV⁴, sermons of St. Augustine, 295 × 200 mm, parchment, 263 + i folios, 2 × 50, blue-red-gold initials, *litterae partitae* initials, *ex libris*, Thomas Rome, monk of Durham Priory.

66. ———, MS B.III.18, S.XIV⁴, works of Bernard, Innocent, and Robert Grosseteste, 315 × 220 mm, parchment, 292 folios, 2 × 32–48, gold and blue *litterae partitae* initials, large brushwork Lombardic capitals, Grosseteste portion written by Richard Bell, prior of Durham.

67. ———, MS B.III.19, S.XV, works of Robert Grosseteste, 315 × 220 mm, paper, 258 folios, 2 × 44, gold initials, full penwork border, written by John Lytham, monk of Durham Priory.

68. ———, MS B.III.22, S.XIV, Pseudo-Bonaventure, *Meditations* and other tracts, 340 × 215 mm, parchment, iii + 154 + 1 folios, 2 × 58, blue and red penwork initials, *ex libris*, William Kybbyll, monk of Durham Priory.

69. ———, B.III.27, 1438, table to St. Augustine, *De Civitate Dei*, 330 × 210 mm, parchment, iii + 89 + i folios, 2 × 53, red and blue penwork initials, acquired by Thomas Lund, monk of Durham Priory.

70. ———, MS B.III.29, 1438, table to various authors, 375 × 250 mm, parchment, i + 373 + iii folios, 2 × 58, *litterae partitae* initials, penwork border, partly written by Thomas Stapeley (1391–1421) and J. H., monks of Durham Priory.

71. ———, MS B.IV.36, S.XIV⁴, *Speculum Curatorum*, 280 × 180 mm, parchment, 195 + ii folios, 1 × 41, *litterae partitae* initials, violet penwork capitals, written by William Kedwelly, monk of Durham Priory.

72. ———, MS B.IV.42, S.XV², table to works of the fathers, 255 × 180 mm, parchment, iii + 257 + iii folios, 1 × 44, red and blue penwork initials, partly written by Robert Moreby (1410–1447), monk of Durham Priory.

73. ———, MS B.IV.48, 1464, Ebchester obituary prayer roll, 13 meters × 225 mm, parchment, illuminated with full-page paintings of the death and burial of John Burnby and William Ebchester, priors of Durham.

74. ———, MS C.III.11, 1400, 308 × 192 mm, parchment, 230 folios, 2 × 39, red and blue initals and *litterae partitae*, owned by Thomas Hebbeden, from Durham Priory.

75. ———, MS C.IV.20b, S. XIV⁴, table to Aristotle, 270 × 185 mm, parchment, 198 folios, 2 × 43, red and blue penwork initials, red and violet *littera partita* initial, from Durham Priory.

76. ———, MS C.IV.21, S.XV, table to the Sext, 290 × 215 mm, parchment, 240 folios, 1 × 39, blue Lombardic capitals, partly written by William Bentlay, notary of Durham.

77. ———, MS C.IV.23, S.XV, miscellany, Walter Burley, Geoffrey of Vinsauf, 215 × 145 mm, parchment, 129 folios, 1 × 15, undecorated, written by John Fishborne (d. 1434), and Robert Emylton, monks of Durham Priory.

78. ———, University Library, MS Cosin V.I.2, before 1456, breviary, York kalendar, 475 × 345 mm, parchment, 106 folios, 2 × 26, floriated initials and borders, Church of Hutton, Rudby, north Yorkshire.

79. ———, MS V.IV.23, 1477, *Fasciculus Morum*, 1477, 207 × 145 mm, paper, ii + 172 + i folios, 1 × 25–30, red ink Lombardic letters, written by Thomas Olyphant, a Cumbrian or Nottinghamshire scribe.

80. ———, MS V.v.19, ca. 1480–1520, miscellany of Thomas Ashbey, canon of Bridlington, 145 × 100 mm, paper, 82 folios, 1 × 15–19, undecorated.

81. Glasgow University, Hunterian Collection MS General 1130, 1430–1440, Pseudo-Bonaventure, *Meditationes,* and other works, 294 × 202 mm, parchment, i + 145 + i folios, 1 × 30, armorial initials, 3/4 spraywork borders, borders by the same artist as that of York Minster Library MS XVI.K.6, arms of Robert Willoughby of Eresby, Nottinghamshire.

82. Göttingen, Universitätsbibliothek MS theol. 107r, 1375–1400, *Cursor Mundi,* 270 × 180 mm, parchment, 206 folios, 2 × 36, 88 decorated initials with pictures, full borders, coat of arms, Lopton of Yorkshire inscription and Yorkshire dialect.

83. Kew, Public Records Office MPC 56, ex DL 31/61, 1405–1408, map of Inclesmoor, near York, parchment, 225 × 90 mm, fine red and black letters, St. Mary's Abbey, York.

84. Leeds, University Library MS Ripon 8, 1418, psalter and hymnal, York kalendar, 310 × 215 mm, parchment, iii + 188 + v folios, 2 × 24, blue and red penwork initials, Kendale family *obits,* Ripon Minster.

85. ———, Brotherton Library MS 16, S.XV[1], Beverley Prayer Book, 131 × 84 mm, parchment, 131 folios, 1 × 13, painted armorial initials, full floral borders, Habtreholme *obits,* Collegiate Church of St. John of Beverley.

86. ———, Brotherton Library MS 29, 1350–1400, *Anonimalle Chronicle,* 240 × 150 mm, parchment, i + 353 folios, 1 × 41, *litterae partitae* initials, written at St. Mary's Abbey, York.

87. ———, Brotherton Library MS Dean and Chapter 432, S.XV[1], ordinal, York kalendar with the Feast of the Relics of the Cathedral, 380 × 278 mm, parchment and paper, 94 folios, 2 × 38, red and blue penwork initials, *obit* of Thomas Barrow, rector of Cottingham, Yorkshire, 1493.

88. ———, Brotherton Library MS Dean and Chapter 434, S.XV[2], missal of York use, 200 mm (fragmentary) parchment, blue penwork initials, owned by William Wraye of Ripon.

89. Lincoln Cathedral MS C.4.3, S.XIV[4], manual, York kalendar, 240 × 165mm, parchment, 97 folios, 2 × 37, green-red-blue penwork initials.

90. ———, MS 66, S.XV[1], priest's manual, 215 × 140 mm, paper, 144 folios, 1 × 35, red initials, contains certificate of Robert Ben, priest of Pontefract, Yorkshire.

91. ——, MS 87, S.XIV¹, manual, York kalendar, 245 × 170 mm, parchment, 97 folios, 2 × 37, spaces for initials.

92. ——, MS 91, 1430–1450, poetic miscellany, 210 × 130 mm irregular, paper, 322 folios, 1 × 36–39, 2 × 36–39, blue-pink-green floriate initials written by and for Robert Thornton, East Newton, Yorkshire.

93. ——, MS 228, S.XV, Pseudo-Bonaventure, *Meditationes*, 170 × 120 mm, parchment, 188 folios, 1 × 26, red and blue penwork initials, apparently belonged to Christopher Braystanes, monk of St. Mary's Abbey, York.

94. ——, MS 298A, item 12, S.XV, leaf of York kalendar from breviary or missal, 300 × 190 mm, parchment, 1 × 26, blue and red kalends.

95. London, British Library MS Additional 24361, S.XV, miscellany, 175 × 70 mm, parchment, 89 folios, 1 × 43, undecorated, *ex libris*, Walter Hotham, monk of St. Mary's Abbey, York.

96. ——, MS 31042, S.XV², miscellany with *Cursor Mundi* and other texts, 271 × 192 mm, parchment and paper, 183 folios, 1–2 × 36–43, green and red Lombardic letters, written by and for Robert Thornton, East Newton, Yorkshire.

97. ——, MS 32578, 1405, *Pricke of Conscience*, 210 × 140 mm, paper, 103 folios, 1 × 35–36, colored pen initials, written by Robert Farneylaw, chaplain of Bolton.

98. ——, MS 33244, 1412, cartulary of Furness Abbey, 385 × 255 mm, parchment, 227 folios, 2 × 33–35, decorated initials, full-page border and illumination, written by John Stell, monk of Furness.

99. ——, MS 37049, S.XV², *Desert of Religion* and other devotional texts, 275 × 200 mm, paper, 96 folios, 2 × 42–45, many full-page wash drawings, from a Carthusian house in Yorkshire.

100. ——, MS 37511, S. XIV⁴, breviary, with York feasts, 93 × 70 mm, parchment, i + 85 folios, 1 × 21, red penwork initials.

101. ——, MS 39676, S.XIV, diurnale, York kalendar, 85 × 55 mm, parchment, i + 198 folios, 1 × 17, blue with red penwork initials, St. Mary's, Beverley.

102. ——, MS 43380, S.XV¹, missal, York kalendar with the Feast of the Relics of the Cathedral, 190 × 227 mm, parchment, 221 folios, 2 × 39–40, *champ* initials, full-page borders, Crucifixion miniature.

103. ——, MS 44949, 1360, psalter, northern kalendar, 260 × 170 mm, parchment, 305 folios, 1 × 22, historiated initials, full borders.

104. ——, MS 61901, 1390–1410, Beverley cartulary, 370 × 255 mm, parchment, 90 folios, 2 × 28, floriated and historiated initials, full border, Beverley, Hull, or York, *ex libris*, William Wraye of Ripon.

105. ——, MS 62450, S.XV², homilary, 265 × 185 mm, paper, v + 173 + iii folios, 1 × 33, gold-blue-red initials, written by John Awne, monk of Mount Grace Priory, Yorkshire, bookplate of Lord Herries of Terregles, Everingham Park, Yorkshire.

106. ——, Arundel MS 231, S.XIV⁴, John of Abbeville, *Morales Exposi-*

tiones, 265 × 170 mm, parchment, 243 folios, 1 × 37, penwork initials with ½ border, written by John Munkgate, monk of Fountains Abbey, Yorkshire.

107. ———, MS Arundel 507, ca. 1397, collection of proverbial Latin poetry, Rolle, parchment and paper, 260 × 170 mm, 100 folios, 1 × 50, undecorated, compiled by John Segbruck, monk of Durham Priory.

108. ———, MS Burney 310, 1381, Eusebius, *Historia Ecclesiastica*, 350 × 230 mm, parchment, 176 folios, 2 × 46, *litterae partitae* initials, written by William du Stiphel at Finchale, Durham diocese.

109. ———, MS 335, S. XIV², breviary with York kalendar, 140 × 95 mm, parchment, ii + 342 folios, 1 × 24, gold-rose-blue initials, partial borders.

110. ———, MS Cotton Augustus A.iv, ca. 1450, John Lydgate, *Troy Book*, 350 × 150 mm, parchment, 154 folios, 2 × 49, rose and gold initials, ¼ and ½ page miniatures, partial and full borders, with arms of Thomas Chaworth.

111. ———, MS Cotton Faustina B.vi, part ii, S. XV², *Desert of Religion* and other devotional treatises, 520 × 200 mm, parchment, 36 folios, 1 × 40, borders, drawings, and paintings.

112. ———, MS Cotton Vespasian B. xxiii, S. XIV², miscellany, 252 × 110 mm, parchment, iv + 126 + iii folios, 1 × 43–59, owned by John Erghome, prior of the Augustinian Friars, York.

113. ———, MS Egerton 1982, S XIV⁴, *Mandeville's Travels*, 215 × 145 mm, parchment, 132 folios, 1 × 30, red and blue penwork initials, *champ* initial, northern dialect forms.

114. ———, MSS 2025, 34190, S.XV, breviary of these two fragments, York kalendar, 170 × 115 mm, parchment, i + 37 + iii and i + 63 + i folios, 2 × 34, gold-blue-purple initials, partial borders.

115. ———, MS 2572, S.XV–XVIII, York kalendar, guild book of York Barber Surgeons, 274 × 193 mm, parchment and paper, i + 144 folios, 1 × 30, drawings in blue, red, yellow, and green inks. See G. A. Auden, The Guild of Barber Surgeons of the City of York, *Proceedings of the Royal Society of Medicine* 21 (1928): 70–76.

116. ———, MS Harley 1663, S.XIV–XV, *horae*, York kalendar, 135 × 100 mm, parchment, 148 folios, 1 × 15, blue major initials,

117. ———, MS 1804, S. XV², *horae* and kalendar, diocese of Durham, 140 × 80 mm, parchment, 38 folios, 1 × 18, blue and red penwork initials, *littera partita* initial, *obits* for priors and bishops of Durham.

118. ———, MS 2332, 1399, kalendar almanach, York, 140 × 112 mm, parchment, iii + 24 + iii folios, many drawings.

119. ———, MS 2369, 1450–1500, scientific miscellany, York feasts and dedication for All Saints, Pavement, in kalendar, 124 × 92 mm, parchment, 92 folios, 1 × 27, red and blue penwork initials.

120. ———, MS 2431, 1425–1430, breviary, York kalendar, 167 × 110 mm, parchment, 142 folios, 1 × 18, pink and blue initials, full-page borders, Chapel of St. Giles, by Brunton in Swaldale.

121. ———, MS 2394, S.XV, *Pricke of Conscience*, 210 × 140 mm, paper and parchment, 129 folios, 1 × 35–40, undecorated, northern dialect.

122. ———, 2431, 1425–1430, breviary, York kalendar with the Feast of the Relics of the Cathedral, 167 × 110 mm, parchment, 142 folios, 1 × 18, gold-blue-red-green initials, full borders, from the Chapel of Brompton on Swale, Yorkshire and then the chantry of St. Giles in the Chapel of St. John Evangelist, Ravensworth, Yorkshire.

123. ———, MS 2885, S.XIV, breviary, York kalendar, 122 × 90 mm, parchment, 80 folios, 2 × 38, blue and gold initials and partial borders.

124. ———, MS 3585, S.XV, *Dicta* of Robert Grosseteste and other texts, 265 × 190 mm, parchment, 155 folios, 2 × 55, *litterae partitae* initials, ¾ spray borders, written by Robert Masham, monk of Durham Priory, 1391–1418.

125. ———, MS Landsdowne 403, 1408, York Corpus Christi Guild confraternity book, 278 × 182 mm, parchment, 9 folios, 1 × 34, gold initials.

126. ———, MS Royal 2.A. xvii, S.XIV, votive hours, York kalendar, 208 × 125 mm, parchment, i + 149 folios, 1 × 14, gold initials, borders.

127. ———, MS 15.C.xii, ca. 1380, Seneca, *Declamationes* with commentary by Nicholas Trivet, 310 × 210 mm, parchment, ii + 147 + ii folios, 2 × 41, red and blue penwork initials, *litterae partitae*, ¾ border, written by William Ellerker, O.P., of York.

128. ———, MS 17.A.xvi, 1420, kalendar almanach, York, 140 × 112 mm, parchment, 31 folios, 1 × 21, many drawings.

129. ———, MS Sloane 480, S.XV, medical-alchemical miscellany and York kalendar, 135 × 85 mm, parchment and paper, 162 folios, 1 × 18, undecorated, inscription by Thomas and John Postylthwait of Pomfret in the county of York.

130. ———, MS 1584, S.XV[4], miscellany of John Gysborn, Premonstratensian canon of Coverham, Yorkshire, 140 × 95 mm, paper and parchment, 96 folios, 1 × 21-22, initials, drawings.

131. ———, Stowe MS 12, folios 358–395, before 1383, ordinal, 180 × 290 mm, parchment, 2 × 32, illuminated border, arms of archbishop Richard Scrope. See *Catalogue of the Stowe Manuscripts in the British Museum* (London: British Museum, 1895), 1:9.

132. ———, MS 39, S.XV[2], *Abbey of the Holy Ghost* and other devotional texts, 265 × 190 mm, parchment, 33 folios, 1 × 37, decorative borders, many full-page paintings, from a Benedictine house in Yorkshire.

133. ———, College of Arms, MS Arundel 6, S.XIV[4], historical miscellany, 350 × 220 mm, parchment, i + 146 + i folios, 2 × 40–50, 1 × 61, red and blue penwork initials, belonged to John Erghome, prior of the Augustinian friars, York.

134. ———, Lambeth Palace MS 23, XIV[4], Alexander Neckham, on Canticles; Voragine, sermons; Wyclif, sermons; Bromyard, *Distinctiones;* 397 × 282 mm, parchment, 284 folios, 2 × 66, historiated major initial, 2 full trellis borders.

135. ———, Sion College MS Arc. L.40.2/L. 1, S. XIV-XV, rubricated

choir breviary with York kalendar, 288 × 190 mm, parchment, ix + 453 + xi folios, 2 × 33–51, gold-blue-pink initials, *litterae partitae* initials, border, Skelton, near York.

136. ———, MS Arc. L 40.2/L.41, S.XV, sequentiae of York use, 220 × 150 mm, paper, ii + 39 + iii folios, 1 × 24, red initials.

137. ———, Society of Antiquaries MSS 285 and 718, S.XV, manual fragments, York Cathedral excommunication formula, 215 × 180 mm, parchment, 8 folios, 1 × 24, blue with red penwork initials.

138. ———, MS 101, before 1459, miscellany of Thomas Wardon of Westmorland, 300 × 210 mm, paper, 101 folios, varying numbers of columns and lines per page, undecorated.

139. ———, St. Paul's Cathedral Library MS 13, S.XV, Peter de Crescentiis, *Liber Ruralium Commodorum,* 290 × 200 mm, paper, ii + 101 + ii folios, 2 × 51–57, red penwork initials, came from York Minster Library.

140. ———, Westminister Abbey MS 10, S. XV, marriage service of York use, 215 × 177 mm, parchment, 12 folios, 1 × 24, major penwork initials.

141. Manchester University, John Rylands Library MS Lat. 186, S.XII–XV, missal with York kalendar, 291 × 199 mm, parchment, 185 folios, 2 × 24, blue and red initials, *litterae partitae,* possibly Beverley Minster and Roche Abbey.

142. ———, MS Lat. 219, 1388–1396, Meaux chronicle, 288 × 217 mm, paper, 177 + vi folios, 1 × 36, undecorated.

143. ———, MS Lat. 224, S.XIV, cartulary of Fountains Abbey, 310 × 221 mm, paper, 420 + iii folios, 1 × 25, black and white initial.

144. ———, MS Lat. 365, S.XIV, mariale, 240 × 158 mm, parchment, 343 + iii folios, 2 × 49, blue and red penwork and *litterae partitae* initials, *ex libris,* John de Kirkeby, monk of Fountains Abbey, Yorkshire.

145. New York, Columbia University Butler Library MS Plimpton 263, 1440, Trevisa's translation of Bartholomeus Anglicus, *De Proprietatibus Rerum, Charter of the Abbey of the Holy Ghost,* Middle English meditations on the mass, 550 × 390 mm, parchment, 379 folios, 2 × 45, painted initials, full and partial borders, with arms of Thomas Chaworth.

146. ———, Grolier Club MS 3, S.XIV, breviary, York kalendar with the Feast of the Relics of the Cathedral, 110 × 60 mm, parchment, 461 folios, 1 × 33–37, blue-pink-orange-purple initials, *littera partita* initial, full and partial borders.

147. ———, Pierpont Morgan Library MS M 766, after 1401, *Speculum Humanae Salvationis,* 330 × 240 mm, parchment, 71 folios, 2 × 25, red penwork initials, border, small colored drawings, office of John of Bridlington and arms of Thirkill and Colville families, Yorkshire.

148. ———, MS Glazier 39, ca. 1485, prayer roll with York kalendar, 6 meters × 192 mm, parchment, brushwork borders and miniatures, written and illuminated by Canon Perceval, Coverham Abbey, Yorkshire.

149. University of Nottingham Library MS 250, ca. 1425, Wollaton an-

tiphonal, 580 × 390 mm, parchment, 412 folios, 2 × 39, painted initials and full borders and initials, arms of Thomas Chaworth.

150. Oslo/London: The Schøyen Collection, MS 1581, 1425, kalendar almanach of York use, 147 × 106 mm, parchment, 29 folios, 1 × 14 average, brown, red, green, purple, yellow, blue, and burnished gold drawings. See *Western Manuscripts and Miniatures, Sotheby's Catalogue, Tuesday, 24 June 1986,* lot 68, pp. 72–75.

151. Oxford, Bodleian Library MS Additional A.106, SC 29003, S.XV², Middle English medical recipes, 204 × 144 mm, paper with parchment fly-leaves, iii + 290 + ii folios, 1 × 22–32, red initials, northern dialect, written by John Charke, *Plenus Amoris.*

152. ———, MS Ashmole 42, 1350–1375, paraphrase of Sunday lessons on the Gospels, 220 × 130 mm, parchment, i + 257 folios, 1 × 38, red and blue penwork initials, written by WS, northern dialect.

153. ———, MS 1152, S.XV¹, statutes, 205 × 140 mm, parchment, 292 folios, 1 × 29, blue-red-gold-violet penwork initials, ¼ borders, major gold-blue-pink *champ* initial, inscription of Swillyngton family, Yorkshire.

154. ———, MS 1504, S.XIV⁴, missal fragment, York use, 410 × 280 mm, parchment, 2 × 29, red and blue penwork initials, *littera partita* initial.

155. ———, MS Barlow 27, SC 6466, 1480, history of the archbishops of York, 225 × 156 mm, parchment, ii + 62 folios, 1 × 31, gold-rose-blue painted initials, full border on first folio.

156. ———, MS Bodley 68, S.XV, York kalendar and astronomical tracts, 172 × 120 mm, parchment, ii + 50 folios, 1 × 36, undecorated.

157. ———, MS 78b (University College MS 78b), S.XIV², rubricated missal, York use, 337 × 225 mm, parchment, i + 184 +i folios, 2 × 42, red-blue-gold initials, ¾ floriated border, Church of St. Mary, Norton-Cuckney, Nottinghamshire.

158. ———, MS 131, SC 1999, 1438, letter of confraternity from William, prior of the York Augustinians to John and Juliana Morton; William Nassington, *Speculum Vite,* 208 × 140 mm, paper and parchment, ii + 150 folios, 1 × 10 (letter), red penwork initials.

159. ———, MS 842, SC 2575, before 1477, Theinred of Dover, musical treatises, 220 × 140 mm, parchment, ii + 78 folios, 1 × 32, red penwork initials, from Byland Abbey, Yorkshire, and possibly given by John Erghome to the York Augustinian Convent library.

160. ———, MS Bodley Liturgies 132, S.XIV⁴, *horae,* diocese of York, 112 × 80 mm, parchment, 1 × 133 folios, 1 × 16, illuminated initials and borders.

161. ———, MS Digby 77, SC 1678, S.XIV², Roger Bacon, *De Perspectiva,* and other scientific and moral tracts, 210 × 135 mm, parchment, 197 folios, 2 × 40, gold-red-blue initials, partly written by John *Plenus Amoris,* from Meaux Abbey, Holderness, Yorkshire.

162. ———, MS Douce 114, SC 21688, after 1411, saints' lives, 221 × 155 mm, parchment, ii + 150 + ii folios, 1 × 31, red and blue penwork

initials and partial border, *litterae partitae*, from the Carthusian house of Beauvale, Nottinghamshire.

163. ———, MS 225, 1410, pontifical, York Cathedral, 120 × 85 mm,
parchment, 152 folios, 1 × 16–18, undecorated.

164. ———, MS Fairfax 6, S.XIV², chronicle and lives of saints of Durham priory, 329 × 209 mm, parchment, vi + 299 folios, 2 × 48, flourished
red and blue initials, written by Petrus *Plenus Amoris* at Durham Priory.

165. ———, MS 7, S.XV⁴, cartulary of Augustinian Priory of Kirkham,
288 × 212 mm, parchment, ii + 105 folios, 1 × 40–52, undecorated.

166. ———, MS 9, S.XV, cartulary of Augustinian Priory of Warter,
with deeds, 317 × 216 mm, parchment, i + 107 folios, 1 × 43, red and blue
initials.

167. ———, MS Gough Liturgies 1, SC 18328, 1390, rubricated choir
breviary, York kalendar, 490 × 345 mm, parchment, i + 200 + i folios, 2 ×
51, red and blue penwork initials, historiated initial, full floriated border.

168. ———, MS 5, SC 18341 S.XV², rubricated manual, kalendar of
York use, 225 × 150 mm, parchment, iii + 45 + iii folios, 2 × 24, red and
blue penwork initials, painting of a crucifix.

169. ———, MS 18, SC 18332, S.XIV¹–XV, psalter, kalendar for Tynemouth priory, Northumberland, 88 × 60 mm, parchment, 198 folios, 1 ×
18, historiated initials with ¾ borders.

170. ———, MS Hatton, 12, SC 4127, S.XV⁴, Rolle, commentary on
Psalms, 355 × 245 mm, parchment, 213 folios, 2 × 40, red and blue penwork
initials and partial border, large black ink drawing of cross, northern dialect,
Hesketh family, Lancashire.

171. ———, MS Lat. Liturgies b.5, S.XV², gradual, York diocese, 461
× 279 mm, parchment, ii + 135 + ii folios, 12 staves of four lines, red and
blue penwork initials, *litterae partitae* initials, from the Church of St. Peter and
St. Paul, East Drayton, Nottinghamshire.

172. ———, MS e.17,1425, prayers, York diocese, 215 × 155 mm,
parchment, 108 folios, 1 × 21, gold-green-blue-rose initials, partial borders,
extremely detailed instructions for illuminations never completed, texts in
northern English, owned by a woman named Johanna.

173. ———, MS f.2, SC 29741, 1405–1413, *horae*, Sarum use, Flemish
saints, but commemorations for Bridlington and Scrope, 142 × 107 mm,
parchment, i + 171 + ii folios, 1 × 22–24, historiated initials, full-page
miniatures and fullborders by two artists, one Herman Scheerre, possibly
owned by Scrope family.

174. ———, MS g.1, SC 31379, S.XV, psalter, kalendar similar to York,
116 × 80 mm, parchment, i + 214 folios, 1 × 21, red and blue penwork
initials, gold initials with side and top borders, St. Mary's Abbey, York.

175. ———, Laud Miscellanies 84 (g.54), SC 1219, S.XV¹, rubricated
choir breviary from York Cathedral porch, 260 × 176 mm, parchment, 386
folios, 2 × 46, red and blue penwork initials, gold-orange-pink initials, full
borders, *obits* of Wilkinson and Young families.

176. ———, MS 302, S.XV, noted missal from Durham, Sarum use, with York and Durham saints, 385 × 257 mm, parchment, 266 folios, 2 × 41, illuminated initials and borders.

177. ———, MS Lyell 17, S.XIV², Martin Polonus, 292 × 195 mm, parchment, iv + 125 folios, 2 × 43, undecorated, *ex libris*, St. Mary's abbey, York.

178. ———, MS e. musaeo 126, S.XIV⁴, processional, York kalendar, 225 × 150 mm, parchment, ii + 80 + i folios, 1 × 27, red and blue penwork initials, Church of Everingham, Nether Poppleton near York. Made for Robert Bawdwyn, chaplain for a church of St. Oswald.

179. ———, New College MS B.90, S.XV, sermons of Richard Fitz-Ralph, 388 × 250 mm, parchment, 276 folios, 2 × 60, painted initials, full borders, Scrope arms.

180. ———, MS Rawlinson Liturgies b.1, SC 15850, ca. 1380, missal, York kalendar, 375 × 250 mm, parchment, 281 folios, 2 × 31, floriate initials and full floriate borders, Benedictine Abbey of Saints Peter and Hilda, Whitby, Yorkshire.

181. ———, MS b. 455, SC 11802–5, S.XV¹, cartulary of the hospitals of St. Peter or St. Leonard, York, 420 × 290 mm, parchment, 232 folios, 1 × 47, gold Lombardic letters on blue-rose ground with green and gold sprays.

182. ———, MS c. 142, S.XV³ missal, Sarum use, 309 × 203 mm, parchment, 284 folios, 2 × 31, red and blue penwork initials, gold capitals with violet flourishing, full-page miniature of Jesus and three Marys with evangelists, floriated borders, mass for John of Bridlington, probably south Yorkshire.

183. ———, MS c. 162, S.XV¹, Bede, *Historia Ecclesiastica*, makes one volume with Rawlinson MS B.199–200, 310 × 210 mm, parchment, 102 folios, 2 × 44, red and blue Lombardic letters, floriated initials, ¾ gold and rose floral border, probable John Newton book.

184. ———, MS c. 258, 1400, Middle English translation of the New Testament, 156 × 150 mm, parchment, 182 folios, 2 × 40, red and blue penwork initials, *ex libris*, John Lacy, O.P., Newcastle-upon-Tyne.

185. ———, MS. c. 553, S.XV, *horae*, York kalendar, with the Feast of the Relics of the Cathedral, 176 × 126 mm, parchment, i + 148 + i folios, 1 × 18, major red and blue initials, drawings of large cross, *arma Christi*, busts of bishop and monk, St.Mary's Abbey, York.

186. ———, MS d. 938, S.XIV, belt kalendar of York use, 190 × 140 mm, parchment, i + 12 folios, 1 × 33, undecorated, used by Trinitarians at Knaresboro.

187. ———, MS d. 984, S.XIV, missal fragment, York use, 298 × 198 mm, parchment, 2 × 36, red and blue penwork initials.

188. ———, MS d. 1218, S.XV¹, kalendar, adapted to York use, 208 × 145 mm, paper and parchment, iii + 45 + iv folios, 1 × 44, red capitals and initials, possibly written by William Wrythe.

189. ———, MS g. 170, SC 14893, S.XIV², psalter with kalendar altered from York to Sarum use, 294 × 192 mm, parchment, i + 229 + i folios, 1 × 17, major initials, full border, red and green line fillers, *litterae partitae* initials, *obits* of Henry and Agnes Wynquike.

190. ———, MS Selden Supra 40, S.XV, ordinal, York use, 211 × 145 mm, paper, i + 133 + iv folios, 1 × 40, undecorated, written by Richard Lostman, priest.

191. ———, University College MS 6, S.XIV, patristic and classical miscellany, 190× 139 mm, parchment, xl + 588 folios, 1–2 × 27–56, undecorated, belonged to Dominicans of Beverley.

192. ———, MS 76, S.XIV, extracts of works of St. Augustine, 300 × 205 mm, paper, ii + 308 + ii folios, 1 × 45, undecorated, made by John Castell, residentiary canon of York.

193. ———, MS 82, S.XV, Beverley cartulary, 345 × 260 mm, parchment, 133 folios, 1 × 40, colored initials, full-page drawings.

194. ———, MS Wood empt. 20, SC 8608, S.XV, notebook of Robert Burton, York priest, York kalendar, 148 × 116 mm, parchment and paper, ii + 99 folios, 1 × 21 pen drawings.

195. ———, Balliol College MS 33, S.XIV², William of Nottingham, concordance to the Gospels, 410 × 250 mm, parchment, 356 folios, 2 × 63, *champ* initials, major initials, full border, gift of a York parson.

196. ———, MS 50,1424, Hugh Ripelin, *Compendium Theologiae*, and other tracts, 295 × 200 mm, parchment, 112 folios, 2 × 47, gold-blue-rose *champ* initials, owned by Robert Pollam, vicar of Penistone, Yorkshire.

197. ———, Corpus Christi College MS 161, S.XV¹, *Speculum Humanae Salvationis*, 298 × 215 mm, parchment, xiv + 224 pages, 1 × 33, 192 tinted drawings. Kathleen Scott believes this manuscript was copied in Yorkshire.

198. ———, MS 225, S.XIV, Pseudo-Aquinas, Questions, 205 × 145 mm, parchment, 251 folios, 2 × 40, blue with red penwork flourished initials, belonged to Dominicans of Beverley and also to Robert Stanniforth, O.P., of Beverley.

199. ———, MS 489, fragment no. 56, S.XIV, page of a missal, York use, 253 × 162 mm, parchment, 2 × 29, undecorated.

200. ———, Merton College MS 102, S.XV, *Distinctiones Mauricii* and preaching tract by Dominican Jacob Fusignani, 333 × 230 mm, parchment, 288 folios, 2 × 52, owned by Thomas Farneylow or Farneylawe, chancellor of York.

201. ———, MS 265, 1410, Roger of Waltham, *Compendium Morale*, 210 × 150 mm, parchment, 112 folios, 1 × 33, blue with red penwork initials, violet *littera partita* initial, owned by Thomas Bloxham, canon of Beverley (d. 1478).

202. ———, MS 320, 1350–1375, Henry de Bracton, *Opus de Legibus et consuetudinibus Angliae*, 345 × 245 mm, parchment, 194 + i folios, 2 × 70, red and blue penwork initials, *champ* initial, ¼ border, owned by Thomas Farneylawe, chancellor of York.

203. ———, St. John's College MS 94, 1420–1434, *horae* and prayers, 270 × 170 mm, parchment, i + 151 + i folios, 1 × 20–43, 2 × 16–53, historiated initials, gold letters, floriated borders, written and illuminated by John Lacy, O.P., of Newcastle-upon-Tyne.

204. Paris, Bibliothèque Nationale, MS lat. 4126, S.XIV¹–1364, miscellany, 310 × 178 mm, parchment, 296 leaves, foliated and paginated, 2 × 34, world map, red and blue colored initials, compiled and partly written by Robert de Popultoun, O.Carm., in York.

205. Philadelphia, Rosenbach Museum and Library MS 1004/29, after 1380, portable York kalendar and tables, 360 × 154 mm, parchment, 10 folded leaves, 3 × 36, red and blue penwork initials, vinet border, several drawings, vein man.

206. Formerly Pleasington Hall, near Blackburn, Lancashire, collection of W. Butler-Bowden, present whereabouts unknown, S.XV¹, missal, York use, 298 × 198 mm, parchment, 270 folios, 2 × 34, gold initials, Crucifixion scene cut out, floriated borders, Church of Broughton-in-Amounderness, archdeaconry of Richmond, York diocese. See F. C. Eaeles, "On a Fifteenth-Century York Missal Formerly Used in the Church of Broughton-in-Amounderness," *Chetham Miscellanies* 6, n.s. 94 (Manchester: Chetham Society, 1935), 1–11.

207. San Marino, Calif., Huntington Museum MS HM 1067, S.XIV⁴, missal, York kalendar, 265 × 175 mm, parchment, ii + iii + 297 + ii folios, 2 × 36, gold and historiated initials, full borders, Crucifixion scene, Langdale bookplate, Houghton Hall, Yorkshire.

208. ———, MS HM 140, S.XV³, Lydgate and Chaucer poetic miscellany, 288 × 204 mm, paper, 170 + ii folios, 1 × 28–38, red initials, owned by Thomas Chaworth.

209. Tokyo, collection of Toshiyuki Takamiya, S.XIV³, Bede, *Historia Ecclesiastica*, 320 × 230 mm, parchment, ii + 88 folios, 1 × 42, gold initials, accounts of Robert of Staynford, Idoine Percy's steward ca. 1365.

210. ———, S.XV², Middle English abridgment of *Mandeville's Travels*, medical texts, list of 44 archbishops of York to 1342, notes on life of St. Wilfrid, 170 × 125 mm, parchment, vi + 116 folios, 1 × 21–22, rose-blue-gold initials, ¾ border with arms of Norton family, Yorkshire.

211. ———, ca. 1450, Nicholas Love, *Meditations on the Life of Christ*, 275 × 180 mm, parchment, 129 folios, 1 × 32, red and blue penwork initial, possibly from Mount Grace Priory, Yorkshire, owned by Joan Holand.

212. Trowbridge, Wiltshire, Steeple Ashton Vicarage, ca. 1450, *horae*, York portion has William and Wilfrid in litany, 158 × 115 mm, parchment, ii + 156 + ii folios, 2 × 14, red and blue penwork initials; Samuel Hay, a former owner, came from Pudsey, Yorkshire. See William Smith, "The Fifteenth-Century-Manuscript *Horae* in the Parochial Library of Steeple Ashton," *Manuscripta* 25 (1981): 151–63.

213. Urbana, Illinois, University of Illinois, De Ricci MS 130, ca. 1390, breviary, York kalendar, 175 × 120 mm, parchment, iv + 271 + iv folios, 2 × 35, red and violet penwork initials, *litterae partitae* initials, drawing of

zodiac man, bookplate of Lord Herries of Terregles, Everingham Park, Yorkshire.

214. Victoria, Australia, Ballerat Fine Art Gallery MS Crouch 4, S.XV, portable kalendar, York use, 160 × 41 mm, parchment, 2 × 23, kalendar has feathered sprays, drawings of vein and zodiac men.

215. Washington, D.C., Catholic University of America Library, MS Mullen 114, 1470, patristic and classical miscellany, 180 × 120 mm, parchment, 211 folios, 1 × 24–35, undecorated, compiled by Edmund Norton, Yorkshire.

216. York, Minster Library, MS Additional 2, after 1405 and before 1445, *horae*, York kalendar, with the Feast of the Relics of the Cathedral, 150 × 100 mm, parchment, iv + 210 + iv folios, 1 × 16, blue penwork initials, historiated initials, full floral borders, 47 full-page miniatures, written by a scribe called John, *obit* of John Bolton, merchant and mayor of York, 1445.

217. ———, MS 30, S.XV², missal, York kalendar with the Feast of the Relics of the Cathedral, 418 × 292 mm, parchment, iv + 235 + iv folios, 2 × 36, gold with blue initials, full floral borders, written for a man named Ralph.

218. ———, MS 54, ca. 1390, *horae*, Sarum kalendar adapted to York, 200 × 130 mm, parchment, 127 folios, 1 × 21, red and blue penwork initials, gold and blue initials, miniature of Christ as Man of Sorrows, arms and *obits* of Mountenay family, Wheatley, near Doncaster, Yorkshire.

219. ———, MS 67, after 1405, *horae*, York kalendar, 200 × 130 mm, parchment, vi + 125 folios, 1 × 14, red and blue penwork initials, gold and blue initials, *ex libris*, Richard Redman of Kirkby Overblow, near Wetherby, Yorkshire.

220. ———, MS 68, S.XIV², breviary, York kalendar, 145 × 87 mm, parchment, ii + 374 + ii folios, 2 × 36, red and blue penwork initials, gold initials and partial borders, miniature for feast of St. Andrew.

221. ———, MS 69, after 1489, rubricated choir breviary, York kalendar with the Feast of the Relics of the Cathedral, 492 × 350 mm, parchment, 356 folios, 2 × 54, floriated initials, partial floral border, *ex libris*, Thomas Sherston, chaplain.

222. ———, MS 70, S.XV¹, breviary, York kalendar, 420 × 278 mm, parchment, 335 folios, 2 × 41, red and blue penwork initials, *littera partita* initial.

223. ———, MS 115, S.XV², breviary, York kalendar, 157 × 110 mm, parchment, vii + 371 + vii folios, 2 × 37, gold initials with partial borders.

224. ———, MS 383, ca. 1430, breviary, York kalendar, 170 × 118 mm, parchment, ii + 368 + ii folios, 2 × 35, blue and gold initials, full-page borders.

225. ———, MS XVI.A.6, before April 1483, sermons of Robert Grosseteste, 310 × 220 mm, parchment, ii + 184 + iii folios, 1 × 42, blue Lombardic letters, painted major initial, written by Schaw for Thomas Rotherham, archbishop of York.

226. ———, MS XVI.A.9, S.XV¹, missal, York kalendar, 300 × 210

mm, parchment, i + 215 + i folios, 2 × 35, red and blue penwork initials, gold-blue-green initials, full floriated borders.

227. ———, MS XVI.D.9, S.XIV–XV, sermons of William Peraldus, 262 × 185 mm, parchment, iii + 217 + iii folios, 2 × 50, red and violet penwork initials, drawing, from Durham priory, inscriptions of Stephen Howden, prior of Durham (d. 1444), and Thomas Swalwell, monk of Durham Priory.

228. ———, MS XVI.I.1, S.XV[2], patristic miscellany, 290 × 110 mm, paper, vi + 214 + vii folios, 1 × 79–92, undecorated, written by Robert Emylton, monk of Durham priory, inscription Robert Weardale, monk of Durham Priory.

229. ———, MS XVI.I.3, S.XV[2], missal, York kalendar with the Feast of the Relics of the Cathedral, 285 × 202 mm, parchment, iii + 173 + iii folios, 2 × 41, blue with red and blue penwork initials.

230. ———, MS XVI.I.9, S.XV[1], *Speculum Spiritualium*, 277 × 200 mm, parchment, vi + 224 folios, 1 × 31–36, red and blue penwork initials, written at Mount Grace Priory, Yorkshire.

231. ———, MS XVI.K.6 (formerly called MS XVI.G.5), between 1405 and 1413, *horae*, York kalendar with the Feast of the Relics of the Cathedral, 215 × 162 mm, parchment, iv + 113 + iv folios, 1 × 19, many gold historiated initials, floriated borders, *obits* of Pullein family of Pontefract, written by a scribe named Cawod for a parishioner of All Saints, Pavement, York.

232. ———, MS XVI.K.16, S.XV[1], collation book and devotional tracts, York diocese, 196 × 124 mm, parchment, v + 197 + iii folios, 1 × 23, red and blue penwork initials and ¼ borders, belonged to John Appleton, vicar choral of York, 1425, and later to Robert Gorthom of Beverley.

233. ———, MS XVI.M.4, S.XV[1], manual, York use, 255 × 170 mm, parchment, iv + 18 + iv + 71 + v folios, 1 × 24, red and blue penwork initials, gold with blue major initials, Yorkist rose on folio 47.

234. ———, MS XVI.O.9, breviary, S.XIV[2]–XV, York kalendar, 160 × 108 mm, parchment, ii + 308 folios, 2 × 39, red with blue penwork initials, gold major initials with floriated borders, used at All Saints, Pavement, York, in the fifteenth century.

235. ———, MS XVI.O.23, S.XV[1], breviary, York kalendar, 125 × 85 mm, parchment, ii + 465 + ii folios, 2 × 28, gold with blue initials, ¾ border, belonged to Robert Rycherson of Molescrofte, near Beverley.

236. ———, MS XVI.P.8, S.XIV[4], Cino of Pistoia, *Super Codicem*, 437 × 296 mm, parchment, i + 313 + i folios, 2 × 79–83, gold-blue-pink initials with vines, trefoils, and gold sprays, written by Robertus *Plenus Amoris*, and belonged to John Newton.

Appendix C

BOOK OWNERSHIP IN THE NORTH

A CENSUS FROM WILLS

Service and Devotional Books

Antiphonals or "couchers" 42
Bibles 56
Breviaries 478
Collects 4
Commemorations 1
Confessionals 1
Creed, 2
Devotions 7
Dirge Books 32
Gospels (Latin) 15
Gospels (English) 2
Graduals 39
Hymnals 18
Invitationals 3
Journals 19
Manuals 48
Martyrologies 5
Mass for John of Bridlington 1
Matutinals 3
Missals 260

New Testament (individual books) 2
Old Testament (individual books) 12
Orations 12
Ordinals 25
Paternosters 5
Pauline Epistles 14
Penitentials 2
Pyes 9
Pontificals 6
Prayers 6
Prefaces to the Mass 1
Primers 148
Processionals 56
Psalters 189
Sacramentaries 4
Sanctorales 1
Troparia 6
Vespers 1

Total: 1,535

Northern English Book Ownership as evidenced by published and unpublished wills 1369–1497 proved in the Province of York, by published wills of the dioceses of Beverley, Durham, Ripon, and Carlisle and by the inventories of Auckland College and Jesus College, Rotherham. Total: 3,292

Books: Classical, Literary, Grammatical

Aesop 2
Alan of Lille, *De Planctu Naturae*[1] 2
Alexander of Villadei, *Doctrinale de
    Grammatica* 2
Ars dictandi 1
Ars memorativa 1
Barlaam and Josephat (French) 1
Barlaam and Josephat (English) 1
Boccaccio 1
Boethius, *De Consolatione
    Philosophiae,* with Aquinas
    commentary 1
————, Table of topics 2
————, with Trivet commentary[2]
    1
————, with Tumbacus
    commentary 1
————, with unspecified
    commentary 1
————, unspecified 1
Ps.-Boethius, *De Disciplina
    Scolarum,* with commentary 1
————, *De Trinitate* 1
Brachiolini, Poggio, *Epistolae* 1
Cato, 1
Cato, *Disticha* 2
Chaucer, *Canterbury Tales* 1
————, *Troilus and Criseyde* 1
Chrétien de Troyes, Lancelot 1
Cicero, *De Officiis,* with
    commentary of Peter Marcus
    1
————, *Epistolae,* with
    commentary 2
————, *Orations* 1
Claudian 1
"Decem Preceptis Alembes"
    (French) 1
Dictionary in three parts[3] 1
Donatus, *Ars Grammatica* 2
Eberhard of Bethune, *Grecisimus* 2
Gesta Alexandri 3
Gesta Romanorum 4

Gesta Troiae 1
Gower, John 1
Grammars 43
Guido de Columna, *Bellum
    Trojanum*[4] 6
Guyon le Courtois 2
Horace, *Ars Poeticae* 2
————, *Epistolae* 1
————, unspecified 1
Huguccio, *Magnae Derivationes*
    3
Isidore, *Etymologiae* 4
John of Garland, *Multorum
    Vocabulorum Equivocorum
    Interpretatio* 2
————, grammar 1
John Balbus of Genoa, *Catholicon*
    12
John of Salisbury, *Polycraticon* 1
Josephus, *De Bello Judaico* 1
Langland, William, *Piers Plowman*
    2
Letter formularies 3
Letter formulary of papal curia
    1
Letter formularies, table to 1
Liber Vocabulorum 1
Lucan, *De Bello Punico* 1
————, unspecified 1
Macrobius, *Saturnalia*[5] 1
Mandeville's Travels 3
Martianus Capella, *De Nuptiis
    Mercurii et Philologiae,* with
    commentary of Remigius of
    Auxerre 1
Medulla Grammatice 6
Modo dictandi 1
Ovid, *Ars Amatoria* 3
————, *Epistolae ex Ponto* 3
————, *Ibis* 1
————, *Metamorphosis* with
    commentary by "Theodolus" 1
————, *Remedia Amoris* 2

———, *Tristia* 1
———, unspecified 1
Papias, *Elementarium* 1
Ps.-Peter of Blois, *Libellus de Arte Dictandi* 3
Petrarch, *De Remediis Utriusque Fortune*[6] 4
———, *De Vita Solitaria* 1
———, unspecified 1
Plays (unspecified) 6
Pliny, *Historia Naturalis* 1
Promptuarius 1
Roman de la Rose 1
Romance book 1
Romance book called *The Gospels* 1
Sallust, *Bellum Catilinae* 1
———, *Bellum Jugurthinum* 1
———, *Invectivus in Ciceronem* 1
———, *Vita* 1
Seven Sages of Rome (French) 1

Seneca, *Declamationes*, with Trivet commentary[7] 2
Seneca, *Epistles*[8] 1
Seneca (table of topics) 1
Sextus Julius Frontinus, *Strategematon*[9] 1
Silius Italicus, *Punica* 1
Speculum Regiminis (Cato moralized) 4
Summa dictaminis 1
Terence, Comedies 1
Terence, glosses 1
Tibullus, *Vita* 1
Titus and Vespasian 1
Tristan 1
Liber Valerius Maximus[10] 1
Vegetius Renatus, Favius, *De Rei Militari*[11] 1

Total: 204

Books: Historical

Aimonius of Fleury, *De Abbreviatione Historiarum*[12] 1
Alfred of Beverley[13] 1
Bede, *Ecclesiastical History* 4
Chronicles 4
Chronicles (English) 1
Chronicon[14] 2
Higden, Ranulph, *Polychronicon* 10
Historiarum 1
History books 2
Layamon, *Brut* 3
Liber cronicarum 1

Polonus, Martin, *Chronicon Imperatorum* 1
Middle English translation of the *Polychronicon* by John Trevisa 2
Trivet, Nicholas 1
Veteris historiis (French) 1
Vincent of Beauvais, *Speculum Historiale* 2
Walter of Gysburn, Chronicle 1
William of Malmsbury, *De Gestis Pontificum Anglorum*[15] 1

Total: 39

Books: Philosophy and Logic

Abelard, Peter, *Sentences* 2
———, Bonaventure on[16] 2
———, Codeton on 1
———, Cowton, Robert, O.F.M., on 1
Aristotle, *De Anima* 1

———, *De Caelo et Mundi* 1
———, *De Generatione Animalium* 1
———, *Ethica* 1
———, *Metaphysica*, unspecified commentator on 1
———, *Meteorologia* 2

———, *Physica* 2
———, *Liber de Problematibus* 1
Duns Scotus, on IV Sentences 1
———, Logic 1
Franciscus, *Super Tribus Libris*
    Sententiarum 1
Giles, on Sentences 1
Horsehead 1
Karneby, Commentary on
    Metaphysics 1
Logic books 2
Lombard, Peter, *Liber Sententiarum*
    9
Peter of Blois on Sentences 1
Praepositivus, *Summa super*
    Sententiis Petris Lombardi 2

Sentences, table to 1
Summa, unspecified 1
Thomas Aquinas, *Articulis Fidei* 1
———, *Contra Errores Grecorum* 1
———, *De Sacramentis Ecclesie* 1
———, *Quaestiones de Malo* 1
———, *Summa Theologiae* 6
Vetus Logicae Expositio 1
William of Ockham, on Sentences
    1
Ysoderus Episcopus, *Super Tribus*
    Libris Sententiarum 1
                                    Total: 51

Books: Miscellaneous or Unclassifiable

Apostrophe ad summum
    Pontificem Bonifacium
    Octavum 1
Augustine of Anchona 1
Ballad, Motet, Prick-song, and
    Song books, 11
Blank books and quires 38
Books, unspecified 311
Contra dicta Reginald Peacock 1
Defensorium Fidei 1
English books, unspecified 13
French books, unspecified 14
Gallus, abbot of Konigsaal,
    Malogranatum[17] 1
Giles of Rome, *De Regimine*
    Principum[18] 6
Liber de Canticis 1
Liber Contemplacionis (possibly
    Hilton or Rolle) 1

Liber originalium 1
De Ligna (Grosseteste?)1
Maulde boke[19] 1
Narrationes, unspecified 1
Personal library catalogue 1
Regula Benedicti 1
———, St. Francis 1
Record books 1
Registers 2
Rolls 8
Sanctu spiritu 1
Sgdonis doctorum (?) 1
Theologie 1
Tractates 26
Virginal (so-called) 1
Vision of Tundale 1
                                    Total: 452

Books: Patristic

Ambrose, *Hexameron* 1
———, *De Trinitate* 1
Augustine, *De Agone Christiano* 1
———, *Civitate Dei* 4

———, *De Consensu Evangelistarum*
    1
———, *De Ieiunio Sabbati* 1
———, *De Mendacio* 1

———, *De Sermone Domine in Monte*
1
———, *De Trinitate*[20] 4
———, *De Utilitate Agendi*
Penitentiam 1
———, *De Verbis Domini et Apostoli*
1
———, *Flores* 1
———, *Summa* 1
———, *Super Genesim ad Litteram* 1
———, unspecified[21] 3
Ps.-Augustine, *De Conflictu Vitiorum*
et Virtutum 1
———, *De Partibus Fide* 1
———, *De Singularitate Clericorum* 1
———, *De Spiritu et Anima* 2
———, *De Vita Christiana ad*
Sororem Suam 1
———, *Quinquageni* 1
———, *Regula de Vita Clericorum* 1
———, *Sermones ad Fratres in Eremo*
1
———, *Super Exodum ad Litteram* 1
Bede, *Omelia* 2
Cassiodorus, *Historia Ecclesiastica*
Tripartita[22] 1
———, *Variae* 1
Gregory, on Canticles 1

———, *Dialogues* 4
———, *Omelia* 8
———, *Moralia* 4
Moralia (table to) 1
———, *Pastoral Care* 6
———, *Super Ezechielem* 3
———, *Trentals* 1
Hugh of St. Victor, *De Institutione*
Noviciorum 1
———, *De Sacramentis* 3
———, *De Claustro Animae* 1
———, *Super Ezechielem* 1
Isidore of Seville, *Summum Bonum*
1
Jerome, *Interpretationes Hebraicorum*
Nominum[23] 1
———, *Vitae Patrum* 6
———, Middle English version of
Vitae Patrum 1
John Chrysostom, *De Compunctione*
1
Lactantius, *Divine Institutiones* 2
Rabanus Maurus, *De Universo* 1
Remigius of Auxerre, exposition of
the mass 1
———, *Omelia* 1
Richard of St. Victor, *De Trinitate* 1
Total: 87

Books: Miscellaneous, of Clerical and Popular Piety

ABC of Divinity, English 1
Abingdon, Edmund, *Speculum*
Ecclesie[24] 5
Ps.-Alcuin, *Speculum Moralium* 1
Almachutus, Saint, vita 1
Alphabet of Tales 1
Alphonsus de Spina, *Fortalicium*
Fidei 1
Anthony of Forciglioni, *Summa*
Confessionale 3
Ars moriendi 2
Attestatione fidei 1
Bartholomew of Parma,
Breviloquium 1

Becket, Thomas, *Vita* 3
Beleth, John, *Summa de Ecclesiasticis*
Officiis 3
Bernard, *Epistolae*[25] 1
———, Life, 1
———, *Meditationes* 4
———, unspecified 1
Bonaventure, unspecified 3
Bridget, Saint, *Revelations*[26] 6
Burgh, John de, *Pupilla Oculi* 44
Cassian, John, *Collationes Patrum* 2
Caulibus, John de, *Speculum Vitae*
Christi 10
Chastising of God's Children[27] 1

Comestor, Peter, *Historia Scholastica*
    6
Compendium morale 1
David of Augsburg, *De Exterioris et
    Interioris Hominis compositione*[28]
    1
Durand, William, *Rationale
    Divinorum* 4
Egidius, *De Peccato Originali* 1
Epistola Lilii, or *Correctoria* 1
Exempla scripturae 1
Gerard of Liège (Hugh of St.
    Cher), *De Doctrina Cordis*[29] 2
Gilbert Crispin, *Disputatio Judaei
    cum Christiano*[30] 1
Gilbert of Tournai or William de la
    Fourmenterie, O.F.M.,
    Pharetra Doctorum 3
Gorran, Nicholas, *Fundamentum
    Aureum* 1
Grace Dieu (Middle English prose
    version of Deguileville,
    Pélerinage)[31] 2
Grace Dieu, French translation? 1
Grosseteste, Robert, unspecified 2
——, *Dicta*[32] 1
Guido of Mount Rocher, *Manipulus
    Curatorum* 3
Helen, Saint, Festial 1
Hilton, Walter 2
Homilies, unspecified 3
Honorius of Autun, *Gemma
    Ecclesiae* 2
Innocent III, *De Contemptu Mundi* 2
——, *Miseria Conditionis Hominis*
    1
Jacob of Voragine, *Legenda Aurea*
    16
James of Milan, *Stimulus Amoris*[33] 2
John of Hoveden, *Philomela* 1
John of Tynemouth, *Sanctilogium* 1
Katherine, Saint, English life 1
——, *Vita* 1
Lecturem moralem 1
Legenda Sanctorum 46

Liber de potentia dei 1
Liber de distributione vitiorum 1
Liber de laudibus beate Marie 1
Lydgate, John(?), *St. Albon and St
    Amphibalus*[34] 1
Magister Summarum 1
Marcus of Orvieto(?), *De
    Moralitatibus* 1
Mechtild of Hackeborn,
    Revelationes,[35] (possibly
      Middle English *Book of
    Ghostly Grace*) 1
Meditations 3
Miracles of BVM 4
Mystery of Passion 4
Narrationes et Fabulis in English
    1
Nider, John, O.P., *Preceptorium
    Divine Legis* 1
Oracione Dominica 2
Parvum Pilgrim (Middle English
    verse version of Pélerinage) 1
William Peraldus (Parisiensis), *De
    Vitiis et Virtutibus* 6
——, *Speculum Beatorum* 1
Peter of Limoges, *Oculus Morale* 2
Peter of Riga, *Aurora* 4
Poul, William, of Pagula, *Ocula
    Sacerdotis*[36] 7
——, *Pars Oculi* 1
Pricke of Conscience 5
Raymond of Penneforte, *Summa
    Penitentiae*[37] 8
Regimen animarum 1
Riall, (possibly *Somme le Roi* or
    Caxton's *Ryal Book* [1484][38] 1
Rolle, Richard, *Expositio super
    Judica me Deus* 1
——, *Incendiarium Amoris* 1
——, *Liber de Emendatio Vitae* 1
——, *Melos Amoris* 1
——, *Septem Donis* 2
——, works unspecified 7
Rymington, William, *Stimulus
    Peccatoris*[39] 1

Solempnia Pharonis 1
Speculum Christiani[40] 2
Speculum Conscientiae 1
Speculum Exemplorum 2
Speculum Humanae Salvationis
    1
Speculum Prelatorum 1
Speculum Procuratoris 1
Speculum Sacerdotale[41] 2
Speculum Virtutis 1
Spiritu Guidonis (treatise on
    Purgatory) 1
Spiser, John, or Robert Silk,
    Fasciculus Morum[42] 1
Suso, Henry, *Horologium Divinae*
    Sapientiae 6

———, Middle English *Seven Points*
    of True Love and Everlasting
    Wisdom 1
Theologia Naturalis 1
Thomas of Chobham, *Summa*
    Confessorum 10
Tractatus Officie Misse 1
Visitatio BVM (John Waldeby?) 1
William de Lanicia, O.F.M., *Diaeta*
    Salutis[43] 2
William of Waddington, *Manuel des*
    péchés 2
William of Auvergne, *De Fide et*
    Legibus 1
                        Total: 319

Books: Canon and Civil Law[44]

Andreas, John, *In Collectario* 1
———, *Jeronianum* 1
———, *Lectura* 3
———, *Super Sextum Librum* 10
———, *Super Regulis Juris* 2
———, *Super Clementinas* 3
———, *In Novellam* 3
Astaraxus 1
Aver, John 1
Azzo, Johannes of Bologna, *Summa*
    Institutionem Justinianum 4
Barnardi, Casimarius, *Super*
    Decretales 1
Bartholomew Sancto Concordia of
    Pisa, glosses on *Decretals*[45] 1
Bartolo de Saxoferrato, *De Casibus*
    Conscientiae 4
———, *De Reprisalibus et Armis* 1
———, *Super Codicem*[46] 2
———, *Super Digestum Novum*[47] 2
———, *Super Digestum Vetus*[48] 2
———, *Super Infortiatum*[49] 1
Beaumont, Lewis, (bishop of
    Durham), *Synodial Constitutions*
    1
Berengarius Fredolis, *Summa* 1

Bowyk, H., *Super Decretales* 1
Bracton, Henry, *Liber de Jure Terre*
    4
Brocardus, *Liber Juris Civilis* or
    Summa Brocardica[50] 1
Bromyard, John, *Tractatus Iuris*
    Civilis et Canonici ad Moralem
    Materiem Applicati[51] 2
Calderinus, John, of Bologna,
    Tabula Auctoritatum. In Libris
    Decretorum 1
Cardinal in Regulis (probably
    Henry of Segusia, cardinal-
    bishop of Ostia) 2
Casuarius juris canonici 1
Casus Decretalium 1
Casus Infortiati 1
Casus Novum 1
Casus Vetus 1
Causa of Thomas of Canterbury 1
"Chri' " *Super Codicem* (perhaps
    Christopher?) 1
Cino da Pistoia, *Super Codicem*[52] 1
Codex 8
Compostellanus, Bernard 1
Conclusiones super Clementinum 1

Conclusionibus Rotae 2
Concordantiae Bibliae et Totius Juris Canonici 1
Constitutiones Cantuariensis Provinciae 2
Constitutiones Clementinas 13
Constitutiones of Otto and Othobonus 10
Corpus Juris Canonicis 2
Corpus Juris Civilis 10
Digestum Infortiatum 1
Digestum Novum 5
Digestum Vetus 5
Dinus de Rossionibus de Mugello, *Regulis Juris* 2
———, *Super Novum* 1
Dominic of San Gimignano, *Lectura super Extravagantes* 1
Durand, William, *Super Sextum* 1
———, *Speculum Judiciale*[53] 9
———, *Speculator super Reportorium Aureum* 4
Ecclesiasticis Metrodorus 1
Executione de diversiis sententiarum 1
Galcotti, Albert, *Margarita* 1
Gascoigne, William, *Registrum* 10
Gesselinus, *Super Clementinas* 4
———, *Super Extravagantes* 1
Goffredus de Trano, *Summa super Titulis Decretalium* 1
Gratian, *Decretals* 21
Gregory IX, *Liber Decretorum* 26
Guido de Baisio, *Rosarium* 4
———, *Super Sextum* 1
Henry of Segusia (Hostiensis), *Summa Aurea* 6
———, *In Summa Roffredi* 3
Infortiatum 6
Innocent IV, *Abbreviatum* 1
———, *Apparatus in Quinque Libros Decretalium* 5
Jacob de Belviso, *Super Authentica* 1[54]
Jacob of Theramo, *Belial* or *Peccatorum Consolatio* 2

Johannes de Atona, Glosses on *Constitutiones* of Otto and Othobonus 2
John of Legnano, *De Bello* 4
———, *Super Clementinas* 4
———, *Super Decretales* 1
———, *Super Mandagout* 1
John XXII, *Extravagantes* 2
Law, unspecified 11
Lectura Abbatis super Decretales 3
Lyndwood, William, *Constitutiones Provinciales* 3
Notes of Fines 1
Parvum Volumen 7
Paulus, *Super Clementinas*[55] 4
Peraldus, William, *De Prebendis* 2
Peter de Bella Pertica, *Super Codicem*[56] 1
Peter de Brescia, *Repertorium utriusque Juris* 1
Peter de Sampson, *Lectura super Decretales* 1
Placentius, *Super Institutionum* 1
Polonus, Martin, *Tabula in Decretalium et Decretales*[57] 2
Poul, William, of Pagula, *Summa Summarum* 11
Practica Juris 1
Roffred of Benevento, *De Jure Canonico*[58] 2
———, *De Jure Civili* 1
———, *Summa de Ordine Judiciario* 1
Scriptura Trangavera 1
Sext 13
Sherwood, William, Glosses on Canterbury Constitutions 1
Statuta Angliae 6
Summa Juris 1
Summa Justicie 1
Tabula, juris civilis et canonicis 1
Tancred, *Liber de Judiciis*[59] 1
Textus 2

Tudeschus, Nicholas
  (Panormitanus) *Practica de
  Modo Procedendi in Judicio* 1
Ubaldi, Baldo, *Super Codicem* 1
Vetus 6
Vocabularium Juris 1

William, *In Rosario super Decretales*
  1
———, *Super Clementinas* 5
William of Mandagout, *Super
  Electionibus* 3
                          Total: 352

Books: Medical

Averroes, *Colliget* 1
Antidotarium Nicholai 3
Bernard of Gordon, *Practica Dicta
  Lilum Medicinae* 1
Constantine Africanus, *Viaticum* 1
De Veneno 1
Ferrarius, Johannes, *De Febribus* 1
Hortus Sanitatis 1
Isaac Judaeus, *De Urinis* 1
Johannitius, *Isagoge* 2

John of Gaddesden, *Rosa Medicinae*
  1
Liber de Medicinis 1
Liber Fisica 2
Platearius, Johannes, *Circa Instans
  (De Simplicibus medicini)* 1
Richard of Wendover, *Libri de
  Practici* 1
Sextus, *de Urinis* 1
                          Total: 19

Books: Exegetical, Collections of Distinctiones

Ps.-Alcuin, *De Divinis Officiis* 1
Anselm, *Cur Deus Homo* 2
———, *Meditations* 1
———, *Tractatus super Apocalypsim* 1
———, unspecified 1
Anthony of Padua, on the Gospels
  1
Aquinas, Thomas, *De Passione
  Christi* 1
———, *De Veritate* 1
———, *De Visiositatibus* 1
Aureoli, Peter, *Compendium Literali
  Totius Scripturae* 1
Bartholomei theologiae 1
Benedict, *Flores* 1
Bernard, *Super Canticis* 3
Bersuire, Pierre, *Repertorium
  Biblicum* 1
Bible Vocabulary 1
Bonaventure, unspecified 9
Brito, William, *Expositio
  Vocabulorum Bibliae*[60] 8
———, *Liber Prologos super
  Bibliae* 1

Bromyard, John, *Summa
  Praedicantium* 2
Cassiodorus, on Psalms 1
Collectarium super Psalterum 1
Concordanciarum biblicae liber
  magnus (Hugh of St. Cher?) 3
De Difficilibus Vocabilibus Bibliae
  1
Ps.-Dionysius, *Ordo Angelicae* 3
Distinctiones 1
Dubia scripturae 4
English Exposition of Gospels 1
English Bible commentary 1
Exposition of the Mass 1
Exposition of the Psalter [Rolle?] 1
Gilbert of Hoyland, *Super Canticis*
  1
Glossa, on Apocalypse 2
———, on Canticles 1
———, on New Testament 1
———, on Old Testament 1
Glossa Ordinaria, on Acts of
  Apostles 1
———, on Job 1

————, on Prophets 1
————, on Psalms 1
Glossa (Wycliffite) on Ave Maria
Stella Maris 2
Gorran, Nicholas, on Psalms 1
————, Postilla on Luke 1
————, Themes for Sunday
Sermons 1
Haymo of Auxerre, *Super Epistolas
Pauli* 3
Herenthal, Peter, or Floriacensis,
Expositio Psalmorum 1
Holkot, Robert, *Convertimini* 1
Intentiones Biblicae 1
Interpretationes 1
Johannes Parisiensis (Surdus), *De
Universo Corporali et Spirituali* 1
————, on Gospels 2
Johannes de Abbatis Villa, *Postillae
super Epistolas et Evangelia
Dominicalia* 1
Ps.-John Chrysostom, *Opus
Imperfectum super Mattheum*[61] 8
John of Wales, *Communilquium*[62] 1
*Liber Historiarum cum morali
expositione Veteris Testamenti et
guttis Evangeliorum* 1
Liber Vocabulorum 1
Malachias de Hibernia, *De Venenis*
1
Maurice, O.F.M., *Distinctiones Fratri
Mauricii* (circa abiectionem)[63]
1
Maurice of Sanuta, *De sancta
Salome* 1
Mirfeld, John, *Floriarum
Bartholomei*[64] 2
Ps.-Nicholas de Pergamenus,
Dialogus Creaturarum[65] 2

Nicholas of Lyra, on Maccabees 1
————, on Major and Minor
Prophets 1
————, on Pauline Epistles 1
————, on Psalter 1
————, on the whole Bible 13
Tables to Lyra on the whole Bible
1
Odo, on the Gospels 2
————, unspecified 2
Patrell, on Numbers and Ruth 1
Olivi, Peter John, on Matthew 1
Peter of Blois, *Super Job* 2
Peter of Riga, *Aurora* 2
Prophet, John, on the Gospels 1
Ripelin, Hugh, of Strassbourg,
Compendium Vertitatis Theologiae
8
Roger of Waltham, *Remediarium
Conversorum*[66] 1
Rolle, Richard, glosses on the
Office for the Dead 3
————, *Expositio Psalterium* 2
————, *Duodecim Capitulis* 1
Rosarium Theologiae[67] 1
Stephen of Canterbury, on
Genesis[68] 1
Summa angelicae 1
Summa Biblicae 1
Thomas of Ireland, *Manipulus
Florum* 1
Tractate on the mass 1
William of Nottingham, *Concordia
Evangelistarum*[69] 5
William of Tournai, *Flores Bernardi*
3

Total: 158

Collections of Sermons

Albert of Padua, Sermons 1
Calin, Sermons 1
Cotys, Sermons 1

Grosseteste, Robert, Sermons 1
Holkot, Robert, Sermones
dominicales 1

Jacob of Voragine, Sermons 10
Johannes de Abbatis Villa,
   Sermons 1
Liber Sermonizandi 2
Leonard of Utino, Sermons 1
Michael of Milan, O.F.M., Sermons
   2
Odo, abbot of Morimond, Sermons
   1
Robert, O.F.M., episcopus
   Aquensis, Sermons 1

Robert de Licio, Sermones de
   laudibus sanctorum 2
Roger of Salisbury, Sermons 1
Sermons, unspecified 15
Sermons, on Mary Magdalene 3
Table to sermons 1
William of Lanicia, Abiciamus of
   Sermon Themes 1
               Total: 46

Books: Scientific

Albertus Magnus, *De Homine in
   Principio* 1
Avicenna, Philosophia prima 1
Bartholomaeus Anglicus, *De
   Proprietatibus Rerum* 3
Bestiary 1
Calendar 6
De Arte Kalendarium 1
Gerard of Cremona, *Liber
   Theoricam Planetarum* 1
Honorius, *Imago Mundi* 3
———, *Lucidarius* 3
———, *Lucidarius* (French) 1

John of Sacrobosco, *Computus* 2
Lapidary 1
Liber de Compositione
   Instrumentum Astronomiae 1
Ptolemy, *Quadripartitum* 1
Scot, Michael, on Aristotle, 1
Sidrak and Boccus (French) 1
Tollitan (possibly Arzachel of
   Toledo), *De Prognosticatione
   Futuri Saeculi*[70] 1
William of Conches, *Dogma
   Moralium Philosophorum* 1
               Total: 30

Abbreviations

In order to avoid repetition and for greater readability of the notes, journal and series titles of more than one word are given in abbreviated form.

AA	*Archaeologia Aeliana*
AArc	*Art and Archaeology*
AB	*Art Bulletin*
ABG	*Archiv für Buchgewerbe und Gebrauchsgraphik*
ABSHF	*Annuaire-Bulletin de la Société de l 'Histoire de France*
AC	*Analecta Cartusiana*
AFP	*Archivum Fratrum Praedicatorum*
AH	*Art History*
AHDLMA	*Archives d'histoire doctrinale et littéraire du moyen âge*
AHR	*American Historical Review*
AJ	*Antiquaries Journal*
AmpJ	*Ampleforth Journal*
AnB	*Analecta Bollandiana*
AnBr	*Annales de Bretagne*
AnH	Guido M. Dreves and C. Blume, eds., *Analecta Hymnica Medii Aevi*
ArcJ	*Archaeological Journal*
AV	*Antichita vivà*
BBCS	*Bulletin of the Board of Celtic Studies*
BC	*Book Collector*
BEC	*Bibliothèque de l'école des Chartes*
BEP	*Bulletin des Études Portugaises*
BIHR	Borthwick Institute for Historical Research, York
	Register 10, Zouche, 1342–1352
	Register 11, Thoresby, 1352–1373
	Registers 12–13, Neville, 1374–1388
	Register 14, Arundel, 1388–1396
	Register 15, Waldby, 1396–1398

	Register 16, Scrope, 1398–1405
	Registers 17–18, Bowet, 1407–1416, 1416–1426
	Register 19, Kemp 1426–1452
	Register 20, Booth, 1452–1464
	Register 23, Rotherham, 1480–1500
	Register 25, Savage, 1501–1507
BJP	*Ben Johnson Papers*
BJRL	*Bulletin of the John Rylands University Library*
BLJ	*British Library Journal*
BLR	*Bodleian Library Record*
BM	*Burlington Magazine*
BML	Walter Howard Frere, *Bibliotheca Musico-Liturgica. A Descriptive Handlist of the Musical and Latin-Liturgical Manuscripts of the Middle Ages Preserved in the Libraries of Great Britain and Ireland*
BMQ	*British Museum Quarterly*
BPLQ	*Boston Public Library Quarterly*
BPPB	Derek Pearsall and Jeremy Griffiths, eds., *Book Production and Publishing in Britain 1375–1475*
BQR	*Bodleian Quarterly Record*
BRUC	A.B. Emden, *A Biographical Register of the University of Cambridge to 1500*
BRUO	A.B. Emden, *A Biographical Register of the University of Oxford to A.D. 1500*, 3 vols.
BSAF	*Bulletin de la société archéologique du Finistère*
BullIHR	*Bulletin of the Institute of Historical Research*
BullM	*Bulletin Monumentale*
CA	*Critica d'Arte*
CAHME	T.F. Tout, *Chapters in the Administrative History of Mediaeval England: The Wardrobe, The Chamber and the Small Seals*
CEPR	William Henry Bliss, C. Johnson, and Jessie A. Twemlow, eds., *Calendar of Entries in the Papal Registers Relating to Great Britain and Ireland: Papal Letters*
CLC	*Columbia Library Columns*
CM	*Clio Medica*
CSM	*Camden Society Miscellany*
CV	*Les Cahiers Vernonnais*
DCAB	Dean and Chapter Act Book, York Minster Library
DCP	Dean and Chapter Peculiar, York Minster Library

DUJ	*Durham University Journal*
EcHR	*Economic History Review*
EETS	Early English Text Society
EGM	Nigel Morgan, *Early Gothic Manuscripts* (1) *1190–1250* and (2) *1250–1285*
EHR	*English Historical Review*
EL	*Ephemerides Liturgicae*
EMS	*English Manuscript Studies 1100–1700*
FS	*Franciscan Studies*
GBA	*Gazette des beaux-arts*
GM	Lucy Freeman Sandler, *Gothic Manuscripts 1285–1385*
HT	*History Today*
HTR	*Harvard Theological Review*
IMBL	Otto Pächt and J.J.G. Alexander, *Illuminated Manuscripts in the Bodleian Library Oxford 3: British, Irish, and Icelandic Schools*
IMOC	J.J.G. Alexander and Elżbieta Temple, *Illuminated Manuscripts in Oxford College Libraries, the University Archives and the Taylor Institution*
IMU	*Italia medievale e umanistica*
IR	*Innes Review*
James, *Clare*	M. R. James, *A Descriptive Catalogue of the Western Manuscripts in the Library of Clare College*
James, *Corpus*	M. R. James, *A Descriptive Catalogue of the Manuscripts in the Library of Corpus Christi College, Cambridge*, 2 vols.
James, *Emmanuel*	M. R. James, *A Descriptive Catalogue of the Western Manuscripts in the Library of Emmanuel College*
James, *Fitzwilliam*	M. R. James, *A Descriptive Catalogue of the Manuscripts in the Fitzwilliam Museum*
James, *Gonville*	M. R. James, *A Descriptive Catalogue of the Manuscripts in the Library of Gonville and Caius College*, 3 vols.
James, *Jesus*	M. R. James, *A Descriptive Catalogue of the Manuscripts in the Library of Jesus College, Cambridge*
James, *Kings*	M. R. James, *A Descriptive Catalogue of the Manuscripts in King's College*
James, *Lambeth Palace*	M. R. James and Claude Jenkins, *A Descriptive Catalogue of the Manuscripts in the Library of Lambeth Palace*, 5 vols.
James, *McClean*	M. R. James, *A Descriptive Catalogue of the*

	McClean Collection of Manuscripts in the Fitzwilliam Museum, Cambridge
James, *Pembroke*	M. R. James, *A Descriptive Catalogue of the Manuscripts in the Library of Pembroke College, Cambridge*
James, *Peterhouse*	M. R. James, *A Descriptive Catalogue of the Manuscripts in the Library of Peterhouse*
James, *Sidney Sussex*	M. R. James, *A Descriptive Catalogue of the Manuscripts in the Library of Sidney Sussex College, Cambridge*
James, *Trinity*	M. R. James, *A Descriptive Catalogue of the Western Manuscripts in the Library of Trinity College, Cambridge*, 4 vols.
James, *Trinity Hall*	M. R. James, *A Descriptive Catalogue of the Manuscripts in the Library of Trinity Hall*
JBAA	*Journal of the British Archaeological Association*
JBSMGP	*Journal of the British Society of Master Glass Painters*
JEGP	*Journal of English and Germanic Philology*
JEH	*Journal of Ecclesiastical History*
JHG	*Journal of the History of Geography*
JKSAK	*Jahrbuch der Kunsthistorischen Sammlungen des allerhöchsten Kaiserhauses*
JPGMJ	*J. Paul Getty Museum Journal*
JPK	*Jahrbuch der preussischen Kunstsammlungen*
JRMMRA	*Journal of the Rocky Mountain Medieval and Renaissance Association*
JWCI	*Journal of the Warburg and Courtauld Institutes*
LPS	*Local Population Studies*
LQ	*Library Quarterly*
LS	*Life of the Spirit*
LSE	*Leeds Studies in English*
LVS	*La Vie Spirituelle*
MAe	*Medium Aevum*
MAHEFR	*Mélanges d'archéologie et d'histoire de l'école française de Rome*
MGH	*Monumenta Germaniae Historiae*
MH	*Mediaevalia et Humanistica*
MJ	*Museums Journal*
MJK	*Marburger Jahrbuch für Kunstwissenschaft*
ML	*Medioevo Latino*
MLGB	Neil Ker, *Medieval Libraries of Great Britain: A List of Surviving Books*
MLGB, Watson	Neil Ker and Andrew Watson, *Medieval Libraries of Great Britain, Supplement*

MLQ	*Modern Language Quarterly*
MLR	*Modern Language Review*
MMBL	Neil Ker, *Medieval Manuscripts in British Libraries*, Vols. 1–3
MMBL, Piper	Neil Ker and Alan J. Piper, *Medieval Manuscripts in British Libraries*, vol. 4: Paisley-York
MRS	*Mediaeval and Renaissance Studies*
MS	*Mediaeval Studies*
MSHAB	*Mémoires de la société d'histoire et d'archéologie de Bretagne*
MSKB	*Museen der Stadt Köln Bulletin*
N&Q	*Notes & Queries*
NH	*Northern History*
NLWJ	*National Library of Wales Journal*
NMS	*Nottingham Medieval Studies*
PL	*Patrologia Latina*
PMLA	*Publications of the Modern Language Association*
PP	*Past and Present*
PQ	*Philological Quarterly*
PRO	Public Records Office, London
PRSM	*Proceedings of the Royal Society of Medicine*
PSAL	*Proceedings of the Society of Antiquaries of London*
PSAS	*Proceedings of the Society of Antiquaries of Scotland*
PULC	*Princeton University Library Chronicle*
RA	*Revue de l'art*
RB	*Revue Bénédictine*
RES	*Review of English Studies*
RFCY	Francis C. Collins ed., *Register of the Freemen of the City of York* (Surtees Society, vols. 96, 102)
RHF	*Revue d'histoire franciscaine*
RLR	*Revue des langues romanes*
RM	C. M. Kauffmann, *Romanesque Manuscripts 1066–1190*
Robinson, *Cambridge*	Pamela R. Robinson, *Catalogue of Dated and Datable Manuscripts c. 737–1600 in Cambridge Libraries*, 2 vols.
RSSHN	*Revue des sociétés savantes de Haute-Normandie*
RTL	Robin L. Storey, ed., *The Registers of Thomas Langley, Bishop of Durham* (Surtees Society, vols. 164, 166, 169, 170)
SA	*Studia Anselmiana*
SAC	*Studies in the Age of Chaucer*
SB	*Studies in Bibliography*
SC	Falconer Madan and H. H. E. Craster, eds., *A*

	Summary Catalogue of Western Manuscripts in the Bodleian Library in Oxford
ScrC	Scrittura e Civiltà
SG	Studia Gratiana
SHR	Scottish Historical Review
SN	Studia Neophilologica
SP	Studies in Philology
SS	Studia Senesi
SSHMB	Society for the Social History of Medicine Bulletin
StC	Studies in Conservation
TAASDN	Transactions of the Architectural and Archaeological Society of Durham and Northumberland
TAPS	Transactions of the American Philosophical Society
TCBS	Transactions of the Cambridge Bibliographical Society
TCD	Marvin L. Colker, Trinity College Library Dublin: Descriptive Catalogue of the Mediaeval and Renaissance Latin Manuscripts
TCWAAS	Transactions of the Cumberland and Westmorland Antiquarian and Archaeological Society
TE	James Raine ed., Testamenta Eboracensia (Surtees Society, vols. 4, 30, 45, 53, 79, 106)
TEAS	Transactions of the Essex Archaeological Society
TEBS	Transactions of the Edinburgh Bibliographical Society
TLCAS	Transactions of the Lancashire and Cheshire Antiquarian Society
TPAPA	Transactions and Proceedings of the American Philological Association
TRHS	Transactions of the Royal Historical Society
TRSL	Transactions of the Royal Society of Literature
TSCPP	Transactions and Studies of the College of Physicians of Philadelphia
TSM	Thoresby Society Miscellanea
TTS	Transactions of the Thoroton Society
UISLL	University of Illinois Studies in Language and Literature
VCH: Durham	William Page, ed., Victoria County History, County of Durham
VCH: York	William Page, ed., Victoria County History, County of York
Watson, London	Andrew Watson, Catalogue of Dated and Datable Manuscripts c. 700–1600 in the British Library, 2 vols.
Watson, Oxford	Andrew Watson, Catalogue of Dated and Datable

	Manuscripts c. 435–1600 in Oxford Libraries, 2 vols.
WI	*Word and Image*
WRJ	*Wallraf-Richartz Jahrbuch*
WS	Walpole Society
YAJ	*Yorkshire Archaeological Journal*
YASRS	Yorkshire Archaeological Society Record Series
YMB	Maud Sellers and Joyce W. Percy, eds., *York Memorandum Book* (Surtees Society, vols. 120, 125, 186)
YULG	*Yale University Library Gazette*
ZDADL	*Zeitschrift für deutsches Altertum und deutsche Literatur*

Notes

Introduction

1. See Geoffrey Chaucer, *The Summoner's Tale* (ll. 1709–10), *The Man of Law's Tale* (l. 508), and *The Reeves' Tale* (ll. 4015, 4127), in Larry Benson, ed., *The Riverside Chaucer* (Boston: Houghton Mifflin, 1987), and J. R. R. Tolkien, "Chaucer as a Philologist: *The Reeve's Tale*," *Transactions of the Philological Society* (1934), 3–5, 55–59. The passage from William of Malmsbury occurs in N. E. S. A. Hamilton, ed., *De Gestis Pontificum Anglorum Libri Quinque* (Rolls Series, no. 52; reprint, Millwood, N.Y., Kraus, 1967), book 3: 209. On William, see R. M. Thomson, "William of Malmsbury as Historian and Man of Letters," *JEH* 29 (1978): 387–413. William's remark is adapted by Ranulph Higden in the *Polychronicon;* see Churchill Babington, ed., *Polychronicon Ranulphi Higden Monachi Cestrensis* (Rolls Series no. 41; reprint, Millwood, N.Y.: Kraus, 1964), vol. 2, book 1: 167.

2. See J. T. Fowler, ed., *Life of St. Cuthbert in English Verse* (Surtees Society Vol. 87, Durham; Surtees Society, 1889), xiv. The *Cursor Mundi*, ed. Richard Morris, EETS, o.s., 66 (London: Kegan Paul, Trench, Trübner, 1877–1892), vol. 3, ll. 20061–20064, p. 1148, has virtually the same passage; the narrator says of his text, "in sotherin englis was it draun, / And turnd it haue i till our aun / Langage of northrin lede, / þat can nan oiþer englis rede."

3. An excellent study of this question is that of Helen M. Jewell, "North and South: The Antiquity of the Great Divide," *NH* 27 (1991): 1–25.

4. Thorlac Turville-Petre, "Some Medieval English Manuscripts in the North-East Midlands," in Derek Pearsall, ed., *Manuscripts and Readers in Fifteenth-Century England* (Woodbridge, Suffolk: D. S. Brewer, 1983), 133, my emphasis. It must be noted that Arthur Du Boulay Hill, "The Wollaton Antiphonale," *TTS* 36 (1932), says that "the internal evidence of the book, following the Sarum rather than the York Use, is entirely against any Yorkshire source" (p. 48), but there is too much evidence for Sarum kalendars adapted to northern service books—such as the example of York Minster Library MS Additional 54, discussed in chapters 1 and 5—and for book patrons like Robert Willoughby going to York for his books to discount a Nottinghamshire or more northern manufacture for the antiphonal. See the excellent discussion on altering *horae* by Janet Backhouse, *The Madresfield Hours: A Fourteenth-Century Manuscript in the Library of Earl Beauchamp* (Oxford: Oxford Univ. Press, 1975), 11–13.

5. A. I. Doyle, "The English Provincial Book Trade before Printing," in P. Isaac, ed., *Six Centuries of the Provincial Book Trade in Britain* (Winchester: St. Paul's Bibliographies, 1990), 19.

6. On the more usual groupings of production centers, see Michael A. Michael, "Oxford, Cambridge and London: Towards a Theory for 'Grouping' of English Gothic Manuscripts," *BM* 130 (1988): 107–15.

7. L. M. J. Delaissé, "Towards a History of the Mediaeval Book," in Antonio Piolanti, ed., *Miscellanea André Combes* (Rome: Pont. Università Lateranense, 1967–68), 1: 33–34, 35. See, somewhat more recently, A. Gruys, "Codicology or Archaeology of the Book? A False Dilemma," *Ouaerendo* 2 (1972): 87–108; Albert Derolez, "Codicologie ou archéologie du livre? Quelques observations sur la leçon inaugurale de M. Albert Gruys à l 'Université catholique de Nimègue," *Scriptorium* 27 (1973): 47–49.

8. Work by Doyle and Scott will be cited throughout this study. Kathleen Scott's *Later Gothic Manuscripts* (London: Harvey Miller) is forthcoming. For the Bury St. Edmunds style, see Kathleen Scott, "Lydgate's Lives of Saints Edmund and Fremund: A Newly-located Manuscript in Arundel Castle," *Viator* 13 (1982): 335–66, and Nicholas J. Rogers, "Fitzwilliam Museum MS 3–1979: A Bury St. Edmunds Book of Hours and the Origins of the Bury Style," in Daniel Williams, ed., *England in the Fifteenth Century: Proceedings of the 1986 Harlaxton Symposium* (Woodbridge, Suffolk: Boydell Press, 1987), 229–43.

9. See John B. Friedman, "John Siferwas and the Mythological Illustrations in the *Liber Cosmographiae* of John de Foxton," *Speculum* 58 (1983): 391–418. On literary patronage of manuscripts generally, see P. J. Lucas, "The Growth and Development of English Literary Patronage in the Later Middle Ages and Early Renaissance," *The Library*, 6th ser., 4 (1982): 219–48.

10. See Angelo Raine, *Mediaeval York* (London: John Murray, 1955). See also David Hey, *Yorkshire from A. D. 1000* (London and New York: Longman, 1986); and Frank Musgrove, *The North of England: A History from Roman Times to the Present* (Oxford: Blackwell, 1990).

11. See for example, Benjamin Wade, *Yorkshire Ruined Abbeys* (London: E. J. Burrow, 1938).

12. See generally, Rosamond McKitterick, ed., *The Uses of Literacy in Early Mediaeval Europe* (Cambridge: Cambridge Univ. Press, 1990); Michael Clanchy, *From Memory to Written Record. England, 1066–1307* (Cambridge, Mass.: Harvard Univ. Press, 1979); Carlo M. Cipolla, *Literacy and Development in the West* (Harmondsworth, Eng.: Penguin, 1969); and Harvey J. Graff, *Literacy in History: An Interdisciplinary Research Bibliography* (New York: Garland, 1981).

13. See E. Miller, *War in the North: The Anglo-Scottish Wars of the Middle Ages* (Hull: Univ. of Hull Publ., 1960).

14. See, for example, Ralph A. Griffiths, "Local Rivalries and National Politics: The Percies, the Nevilles, and the Duke of Exeter, 1452–55," *Speculum* 43 (1968): 589–632; Robin L. Storey, *The End of the House of Lancaster* (London: Barrie and Rockliff, 1966); Robert Somerville, *The History of the Duchy of Lancaster* (London: Chancellor and Council of the Duchy of Lancaster, 1953); and John M. W. Bean, *The Estates of the Percy Family 1416–1537* (London: Oxford Univ. Press, 1958). See generally, T. B. Pugh, "The Magnates, Knights and Gentry," in Stanley B. Chrimes et al., eds., *Fifteenth-Century England 1399–1509: Studies in Politics and History* (Manchester: Manchester Univ. Press, 1972), 86–128; Robin L. Storey, "The North of England," in the same collection, 129–44; and M. E. James, "The First Earl of Cumberland (1493–1542) and the Decline of Northern Feudalism," *NH* 1 (1966): 43–69. An excellent recent study focusing on the northeast is A. J. Pollard, *North-Eastern England During the Wars of the Roses: Lay Society, War, and Politics 1450–1500* (Oxford: Clarendon, 1990).

15. See David Knowles and R. Neville Hadcock, *Medieval Religious Houses: England*

and Wales (London: Longman, 1971), 110–28, and the earlier studies of J. S. Fletcher, *The Cistercians in Yorkshire* (London: Society for the Promotion of Christian Knowledge, 1919), and Francis A. Mullin, *A History of the Work of the Cistercians in Yorkshire 1131–1300* (Washington, D.C.: Catholic Univ. of America Press, 1932), as well as more recently, R. A. Donkin, *The Cistercians: Studies in the Geography of Medieval England and Wales* (Toronto: Pontifical Institute, 1978).

16. Robert Surtees, *The History and Antiquities of the County Palatine of Durham* (London: Surtees Society, 1816–1840), 4 vols.; *A History of Northumberland Issued under the Direction of the Northumberland County History Committee* (Newcastle: A. Reid Sons, 1893–1940); Bryan Waites, "The Monastic Settlement of North-East Yorkshire," *YAJ* 140 (1961): 478–95; R. A. Lomas, "The Priory of Durham and Its Demesnes in the Fourteenth and Fifteenth Centuries," *EcHR*, 2d ser., 31 (1978): 339–53; and M. Bonney, *Lordship and the Urban Community: Durham and Its Overlords 1250–1540* (Cambridge: Cambridge Univ. Press, 1990). For good photographs of Durham Priory, see Anne Boyd, *Life in a Medieval Monastery: Durham Priory in the Fifteenth Century* (Cambridge: Cambridge Univ. Press, 1987).

17. See F. M. Stenton, *Anglo-Saxon England* (Oxford: Clarendon, 1943), and Geoffry Hill, *English Dioceses, a History of their Limits from the Earliest Times to the Present Day* (London: E. Stock, 1900), for discussion of the northern ecclesiastical divisions. For the later period, see Robin L. Storey, *Diocesan Administration in Fifteenth-Century England* (York: St. Anthony's Press, 1972).

18. Jean Scammell, "The Origin and Limitations of the Liberty of Durham," *EHR* 81 (1966): 449–73.

19. On the use of York, see Backhouse, *The Madresfield Hours*, introduction. For some standard studies of "use," see Falconer Madan, "Hours of the Virgin Mary: Tests for Localization," *BQR* 3 (1920): 40–44; M. R. James, "Points to be observed in the description and collation of Manuscripts, particularly Books of Hours," in James, *Fitzwilliam*, xxiii–xxxviii; and John Plummer, " 'Use' and 'Beyond Use'," in Roger S. Wieck et al., *Time Sanctified: The Book of Hours in Medieval Art and Life* (Baltimore: Walters Art Gallery, 1988), 149–156. One saint, for example, whose presence in a kalendar or in commemorations helps in identifying a Yorkshire book is Everildis; for her "history" see James, *Sidney Sussex*, 22–23.

20. *VCH: York* 3: 80–88.

21. Clanchy, *From Memory to Written Record*, 55.

22. Jo Ann Hoeppner Moran, *The Growth of English Schooling 1340–1548: Learning, Literacy, and Laicization in Pre-Reformation York Diocese* (Princeton, N.J.: Princeton Univ. Press, 1985), which updates the discussion in her doctoral dissertation, "Educational Development and Social Change in York Diocese from the Fourteenth Century to 1548," Brandeis University, 1975.

23. Moran, *The Growth*, 95–98; a convenient list of these schools is given in Appendix B (237–79), with locations and dates of foundation where known. To give a precise idea of medieval populations is difficult, but according to Moran, the diocese of York had a population of about 275,000 *(The Growth,* 180).

24. *The Growth*, 112–21.

25. See A. H. Thompson, "The Pestilences of the Fourteenth Century in the Diocese of York," *ArcJ* 71 (1914): 97–154; and more recently John M. W. Bean, "Plague, Population and Economic Decline in England in the Later Middle Ages," *EcHR*, 2d ser., 15 (1963): 423–37, and P. J. P. Goldberg, "Mortality and Economic Change in the Diocese of York, 1390–1514," *NH* 24 (1988): 38–55.

26. J. N. Bartlett, "The Expansion and Decline of York in the Later Middle

Ages," *EcHr*, 2d ser., 12 (1959): 19. See generally, C. Dyer, *Standards of Living in the Later Middle Ages: Social Change in England c. 1200–1520* (Cambridge: Cambridge Univ. Press, 1989); M. Stanley, "The Geographical Distribution of Wealth in Medieval England," *JHG* 6 (1980): 315–20; H. C. Darby et al., "The Changing Geographical Distribution of Wealth in England, 1086–1334–1525," *JHG* 5 (1979): 247–62, especially p. 260; and R. S. Schofield, "The Geographical Distribution of Wealth in England, 1334–1649," *EcHR*, 2d ser., 18 (1965): 483–510, especially p. 504, Table 2. See also Herbert Heaton, *The Yorkshire Woollen and Worsted Industries* (Oxford: Oxford Univ. Press, 1965). Other useful studies are E. B. Fryde, *The Wool Accounts of William de la Pole: A Study of Some Aspects of the English Wool Trade at the Start of the Hundred Years' War* (York: St. Anthony's Press, 1964); Fryde, *Some Business Transactions of the York Merchants: John Goldbeter, William Acastre and Partners 1336–49* (York: St. Anthony's Press, 1966); and Jennifer I. Kermode, "The Merchants of Three Northern English Towns," in Cecil H. Clough, ed., *Profession, Vocation, and Culture in Later Medieval England: Essays Dedicated to the Memory of A. R. Meyers* (Liverpool: Liverpool Univ. Press, 1982), 7–48. On towns like York, Beverley, and Hull, see Colin Platt, *The English Medieval Town* (London: Secker and Warburg, 1976) and Susan Reynolds, *An Introduction to the History of English Medieval Towns* (Oxford and New York: Clarendon, 1982).

27. On York art generally, see the discussion by R. Barrie Dobson in Boris Ford, ed., *The Cambridge Guide to the Arts in Britain*, vol. 2, *The Middle Ages* (Cambridge: Cambridge Univ. Press, 1988), 200–13.

28. E. Gordon Duff, *The English Provincial Printers, Stationers and Bookbinders to 1557* (Cambridge: Cambridge Univ. Press, 1912), 42–65.

29. See generally, K. L. Wood-Legh, *Perpetual Chantries in Britain* (Cambridge: Cambridge Univ. Press, 1965); R. B. Dobson, "The Foundation of Perpetual Chantries by the Citizens of Medieval York," in G. J. Cuming, ed., *Studies in Church History* 4 (Leiden: Brill, 1967), 22–38; and E. A. Gee, "The Topography of Altars, Chantries and Shrines in York Minster," *AJ* 64 (1984): 347–48. See also Thomas Percy, ed., *The Regulations and Establishment of the Household of Henry Algernon Percy* (London: A. Brown, 1905) and for oratories in private homes, A. H. Thompson, "The Register of the Archdeacons of Richmond, 1442–1477, pt. i," *YAJ* 30 (1931): 38. For areas outside the city or further north and to the west, see M. A. Riley, "The Foundation of Chantries in the Counties of Nottingham and York, 1350–1400," *YAJ* 33 (1937): 159–60, and to the west, Robin L. Storey, "The Chantries of Cumberland and Westmorland," *TCWAAS*, n. s., 60 (1960): 66–96, and 62 (1962): 145–70.

30. See James Raine, ed., *Wills and Inventories Illustrative of the History, Manners, Language, Statistics &c. of the Northern Counties of England from the Eleventh Century Downwards* (1853; Durham: G. Andrew, reprint, 1967), 50, and *YMB* 2: 223. See generally, Peter Mackie, "Chaplains in the Diocese of York, 1480–1530: The Testamentary Evidence," *YAJ* 58 (1986): 123–33.

31. J. R. H. Moorman, *Church Life in England in the Thirteenth Century* (Cambridge: Cambridge Univ. Press, 1945), 90–109. See on these manuals, William Pantin, *The English Church in the Fourteenth Century* (Cambridge: Cambridge Univ. Press, 1955), and as an example, T. F. Simmons and H. E. Nolloth, eds., *Archbishop Thoresby's The Lay Folks Catechism*, EETS, o.s., 118 (1901; reprint, Millwood, N.Y: Kraus, 1975).

32. W. H. St. John Hope, "Inventory of the Parish Church of St. Mary, Scarborough, 1434; and that of the White Friars or Carmelites of Newcastle-on-Tyne, 1538," *Archaeologia* 51, pt.i (1888): 61–72.

33. See on the neighborhood around St. Paul's, C. Paul Christianson, "A Commu-

nity of Book Artisans in Chaucer's London," *Viator* 20 (1989): 209, and his "Evidence for the Study of London's Late Medieval Manuscript-Book Trade," in *BPPB*, 89–90. For the bookmaking quarter of Paris, differently situated because of the presence of the university, see Richard H. and Mary A. Rouse, "The Commercial Production of Manuscript Books, Late-Thirteenth-Century and Early-Fourteenth-Century Paris," in Linda Brownrigg, ed., *Medieval Book Production: Assessing the Evidence* (Los Altos Hills, Calif.: Red Gull Press, 1990), especially 104–107.

34. See K. L. McCutcheon, *Yorkshire Fairs and Markets to the End of the Eighteenth Century* (Leeds: Thoresby Society, 1940), and more generally, Ellen W. Moore, *The Fairs of Medieval England: An Introductory Study* (Toronto: Pontifical Institute, 1985).

35. See generally, J. L. Bolton, *The Medieval English Economy 1150–1500* (Totowa, N.J.: Rowman and Littlefield, 1980); on shipping, see G. V. Scammell, "English Merchant Shipping at the End of the Middle Ages: Some East Coast Evidence," *EcHR*, 2d ser., 13 (1961): 327–41; J. B. Blake, "The Medieval Coal Trade of Northeast England: Some Fourteenth Century Evidence," *NH* 2 (1967): 1–26; Bryan Waites, "Medieval Iron Working in Northeast Yorkshire," *Geography* 49 (1964): 33–43; and for mining in the northeast, though slightly later than the period covered here, I. S. W. Blanchard, "Commercial Crisis and Change: Trade and the Industrial Economy of the North-East, 1509–1532," *NH* 8 (1973): 64–85. The ironworker's account book is discussed by Gaillard T. Lapsley, "The Account Roll of a Fifteenth-Century Iron Master," *EHR* 14 (1899): 509–29.

36. Ian Doyle, "The English Provincial Book Trade before Printing," 22n.

37. F. R. H. Du Boulay, *An Age of Ambition: English Society in the Late Middle Ages* (New York: Viking, 1970), 79.

38. Michael Baxandall, *Painting and Experience in Fifteenth-Century Italy: A Primer in the Social History of Pictorial Style* (Oxford: Oxford Univ. Press, 1988), 1, 3.

1. Northern Book-owning Men and Women: The Evidence from Wills and Extant Manuscripts

1. See, for example, his "Evidence for the Study of London's Late Medieval Manuscript-Book Trade," in *BPPB*, 87–108; *A Directory of London Stationers and Book Artisans 1300–1500* (New York: Bibliographical Soc. of America, 1990); *Memorials of the Book Trade in Medieval London: The Archives of Old London Bridge* (Cambridge: D.S. Brewer, 1987); "Early London Bookbinders and Parchmeners," *Book Collector* 34 (1985): 41–54; and "A Century of the Manuscript-Book Trade in Late Medieval London," *MH*, n.s., 12 (1984): 143–65.

2. See *BML*, passim.

3. George Keiser, " 'To Knawe God Almyghtyn': Robert Thornton's Devotional Book," in James Hogg, ed., *Spätmittelalterliche Geistliche Literatur in der Nationalsprache* (Salzburg: Institut für Anglistik und Amerikanistik, 1984) 2: 103–29; "More Light on the Life and Milieu of Robert Thornton," *SB* 36 (1983): 111–19; "Þe Holy Boke Gratia Dei," *Viator* 12 (1981): 289–317; and "Lincoln Cathedral Library MS 91: Life and Milieu of the Scribe," *SB* 32 (1979): 158–79. See also John J. Thompson, *Robert Thornton and the London Thornton Manuscript* (Cambridge: D.S. Brewer, 1987), and D. S. Brewer and A. E. B. Owen, eds., *The Thornton Manuscript, Lincoln Cathedral MS 91* (London: Scolar Press, 1975).

4. See Moran, *The Growth*, as well as her earlier work mentioned in this book. I am greatly indebted to Professor Moran for help and information for the present

chapter. Though we cover very much the same ground, our studies have very different emphases; I consider a more limited time period and am chiefly concerned in this chapter with the aesthetic and codicological aspects of these legacies; she is principally interested in what they say about education and literacy. Valuable too is Susan H. Cavanaugh's "A Study of Books Privately Owned in England 1300–1450" (Ph.D. diss. University of Pennsylvania, 1980), 9, 11, 19. Cavanaugh's material on York wills, however, is based on the often defective or partial texts published by Raine in *Testamenta Eboracensia* rather than on direct consultation of the wills themselves; nor does her study extend beyond 1450. Kermode, "The Merchants of Three Northern English Towns," in Clough, ed., *Profession, Vocation and Culture*, devotes only a paragraph to book ownership among the merchants of Hull, Beverley, and York; following Deanesly and Vale (see below), she concludes that "very few of the wills read contained bequests of books, and without exception those books were religious: psalters, missals, primers" (36). Jonathan Hughes, *Pastors and Visionaries: Religion and Secular Life in Late Medieval Yorkshire* (Woodbridge, Suffolk: Boydell Press, 1988) does not treat books and literacy in a systematic way. On English literacy and book ownership in the period covered here, see Joel Rosenthal, *Late Medieval England 1377–1485: A Bibliography of Historical Scholarship 1975–1989* (Kalamazoo, Mich.: Medieval Institute, 1992).

5. See M. G. A. Vale, *Piety, Charity and Literacy among the Yorkshire Gentry, 1370–1480*, Borthwick Paper no. 50 (York: St. Anthony's Press, 1976), 29, who applies uncritically to Yorkshire Margaret Deanesly's generalizations in "Vernacular Books in England in the Fourteenth and Fifteenth Centuries," *MLR* 15 (1920): 349–58 for all of England. Vale speaks of "the extreme booklessness of the population as a whole, the rarity of vernacular books as opposed to Latin, and the preponderance, among vernacular books, of works of piety or devotion over secular books, such as romances or chronicles" on the basis of a very small sample of wills: "this conclusion would, at first sight, seem to be borne out by a study of the wills of the Yorkshire gentry." Vale, however, is useful on the number of wills written in English or by the testators themselves (5–6). See also Malcolm Parkes, "The Literacy of the Laity," in David Daiches and Anthony Thorlby, eds., *Literature and Western Civilization*, vol. 2, *The Mediaeval World* (London: Aldus, 1973), 555–57; R. H. Bartle, "A Study of Private Book Collections in England Between c. 1200 and the Early Years of the Sixteenth Century, with Special Reference to Books Belonging to Ecclesiastical Dignitaries" (B.Litt. thesis, Oxford University, 1956), and Sylvia Thrupp, *The Merchant Class of Medieval London 1300–1500* (1948; reprint, Ann Arbor: Univ. of Michigan Press, 1989), 161–62.

6. On the Scrope books, see Charles L. Kingsford, "Two Forfeitures in the Year of Agincourt," *Archaeologia* 70 (1920): 91.

7. Josiah Cox Russell, *British Medieval Population* (Albuquerque, N.M.: Univ. of New Mexico press, 1948), 142; Bartlett, "The Expansion and Decline of York," 17–33; and more recently, Moran, *The Growth*, 127.

8. See *RFCY*, 1: 90.

9. See *YMB*, 1: 56–57, and Moran, *The Growth*, 52.

10. See *YMB*, 1, loc. cit. A readable but undocumented study is that of Richard York Hawkin, *A History of the Freemen of the City of York* (York: James L. Burdekin, 1955), 13, 32. For some cautions about conclusions drawn from the Freemen's registers, see R. Barrie Dobson, "Admissions to the Freedom of the City of York in the Later Middle Ages," *EcHR*, 2d ser., 26 (1973): 1–21.

11. The Scrope books at Masham, for example, would have given employment to a very large number of book artisans.

12. See *YMB*, 3: 193–97, 206–11, and chapter 5 of the present study.

13. Kate Harris, "Patrons, Buyers and Owners: The Evidence for Ownership and the Rôle of Book Owners in Book Production and the Book Trade," in *BPPB*, 163–65.

14. Women hardly figure in Clanchy's *From Memory to Written Record*, though admittedly, his cutoff date is several generations earlier than the starting point of the present study.

15. See generally, Michael Sheehan, *The Will in Medieval England from the Conversion of the Anglo-Saxons to the End of the Thirteenth Century* (Toronto: Pontifical Institute, 1963); Peter Walne, *English Wills* (Richmond: Virginia State Library Publ., 1964); Michael L. Zell, "Fifteenth-and Sixteenth-Century Wills as Historical Sources," *Archives* 14 (1979): 67–74, as well as Moran, *The Growth*, 227–36.

16. Though he treats a later time period than I do, Ronald A. Marchant, *The Church under the Law: Justice, Administration and Discipline in the Diocese of York, 1560–1640* (Cambridge: Cambridge Univ. Press, 1969) provides a good overview of wills, which, strictly speaking, should be distinguished from testaments, dealing with goods, while wills deal with land. I use wills in the broadest sense. About 2,500 wills, a great many of clerics, fell under the jurisdiction of the Peculiar Court of the Dean and Chapter; they are located in the York Minster Library. See Sandra Brown, *The Medieval Courts of the York Minster Peculiar*, Borthwick Paper no. 66 (York: St. Anthony's Press, 1984). The archbishops' registers are available on microfilm in the following form: *Church Authority and Power in Medieval and Early Modern Britain Microform: The Episcopal Registers 1215–1650, Part One. Registers of the Archbishops of York, 1215–1650* (Brighton, Sussex: Harvester Press, 1983).

17. A list of the various probate courts of Yorkshire, most of which are from the sixteenth and later centuries, can be found in Francis Collins, ed., *Index of Wills in the York Registry 1389–1514*, YASRS 6 (Worksop, Eng.: Yorkshire Archaeological Soc., 1889) as Appendix III. See generally, C. I. A. Ritchie, *The Ecclesiastical Courts of York* (Arbroath, Eng.: Herald Press, 1956), and for the Borthwick Institute, David M. Smith, *A Guide to the Archive Collections in the Borthwick Institute of Historical Research* (York, 1973); N. Gurney, "The Borthwick Institute of Historical Research," *Archives* 7 (1966): 157–62; and J. S. Purvis, "The Archives of York," in Cuming, ed., *Studies in Church History* 4: 1–14, and *The Archives of the York Diocesan Registry* (York: St. Anthony's Press, 1952; reprint, London, 1967).

18. Raine, ed., *Wills and Inventories*, part 1: 88. The actual text of the will is in BIHR Reg. 19, Kemp, folios 501–503.

19. James Raine, ed., *Historiae Dunelmensis Scriptores Tres, Gaufridus de Coldingham, Robertus de Graystanes, et Willielmus de Chambre*, Surtees Society vol. 9 (London and Edinburgh: Surtees Society, 1834), Appendix, ccxli–ccxlvii. For other contrasts between what books a person seems to have left from the evidence of an inventory or mortuary and what he actually left, see Moran, *The Growth*, 209, and Cavanaugh, "A Study of Books Privately Owned," 15–17, which shows an example of a reverse difference between the incomplete will and complete inventory of John de Scardeburgh. See also A. I. Doyle, who remarks that "many medieval wills . . . fail to record books almost certainly in the testators' possession at the time of their deaths, even when others are precisely listed and no general phrase (such as 'all my books') covers the whole," "Books Connected with the Vere Family and Barking Abbey," *TEAS*, n. s., 25 (1958): 138.

20. Partly, this is owing to the lack of surviving documents. The registers from the archdeaconry of Richmond, published by Thompson as "The Registers of the Archdeaconry of Richmond, 1361–1442," *YAJ* 25 (1920): 129–268, are a case in point,

for the earliest register exists only as an abstract of collations to benefices and the like made from the lost originals by the seventeenth-century antiquarian Matthew Hutton, while the later original manuscript at Manchester contains very few wills. The paucity of Carlisle wills is mentioned briefly by R. B. Dobson, "Cathedral Chapters and Cathedral Cities: York, Durham and Carlisle in the Fifteenth Century," *NH* 19 (1983): 38 and n. 65. Though a series of fourteenth and fifteenth-century wills from Leeds and the district are published in the Thoresby Society *Miscellanea* (vols. 2: 98–110, 205–214; 4: 1–16, 139–147; 9: 81–96, 161–192, 246–277; 11: 37–68, 289–320; 15: 10–25; and 19), they contain very few references to books.

21. A few wills of particular interest are drawn from the early years of the sixteenth century. For printing in York, see William K. and E. Margaret Sessions, *Printing in York from the 1490's to the Present Day* (York: William Sessions, 1976), 2, and, more recently, Paul Morgan, "Early Printing and Binding in York, Some New Facts," *BC* 30 (1981): 216–224. Probably the most important study in recent years of the impact of printing is that of Elizabeth Eisenstein, *The Printing Press as an Agent of Change: Communications and Cultural Transformations in Early Modern Europe* (Cambridge: Cambridge Univ. Press, 1979-80) though all of her conclusions should not be accepted uncritically, especially for England.

22. R. Barrie Dobson, "The Residentiary Canons of York in the Fifteenth Century," *JEH* 30 (1979): 157.

23. *Pastedowns in Oxford Bindings*, Oxford Bibliographical Society, n. s., 5 (Oxford: Clarendon, 1954), ix.

24. The sources for these legacies are as follows: *Canterbury Tales*, John Preston, merchant, YPR vol. 4, fol. 220; *Troilus and Criseyde*, William Banks, a member of the gentry, DCP L 2/4, fol. 288; Gower, called "Glover," John Morton of York, YPR, vol. 2, fol. 653v; Boccaccio, Marjory Salvayn, YPR, vol. 5, fol. 480, and *TE* 4:116; *Piers Plowman*, John Wyndhill, rector of Arncliffe, Yorkshire, DCP, L 2/4, fol. 115v, and YPR, vol. 3, fols. 369v–370, and *TE* 2:32–35; Walter Bruge, canon of York, YPR, vol. 2, fols. 369v–370 and *TE* 1:209; Petrarch, Thomas Dautre, Chancery Clerk of York, YPR, vol. 3, fol. 493v; and John Newton, *Remedia Fortunae*, YPR, vol. 1, fols. 168–171, and *TE* 1:366. See Moran, *The Growth*, 205, for discussion, and J. A. Burrow, "The Audience of *Piers Plowman*," *Anglia* 75 (1957): 373–84, for northern interest in this poem. For Mandeville, see John de Scardeburgh, York Minster Library, Dean and Chapter Inventory, membrane 2 "Maundevile in paupiro, et gallico," Thomas Roos, YPR, vol. 3, fols. 23v, 355v, 598, and George Darell of Sessay, Yorkshire (d. 1432), *TE* 2:28. On the possible identity of these codices, see M. C. Seymour, "The English Manuscripts of *Mandeville's Travels*," *TEBS* 4, pt. 5 (1966), who mentions the connection of this work with the north of England (p. 174) and lists the following as probably being written there: Manchester, Chetham's Library MS 6711; Dublin, Trinity College MS 604; London, British Library MSS Egerton 1982 and Additional 37049, the very important Carthusian miscellany to be discussed in chapter 5; and Oxford, Bodleian Library MS Ashmole 751. To this list should be added a codex in the Tokyo, Takamiya, collection, which has strong Yorkshire ties. This is formerly Bradfer-Lawrence MS 7, an early fifteenth-century Middle English abridgment on vellum. Its northern connection is suggested by lists of forty-four archbishops of York to 1342 on flyleaves and notes on the life of St. Wilfrid at the end of the book. The arms are those of the Norton family of Yorkshire. See Phyllis M. Giles, "A Handlist of the Bradfer-Lawrence Manuscripts Deposited on Loan at the Fitzwilliam Museum," *TCBS* 6 (1973): 88. At least two Mandevilles were also at Durham. One is now Cambridge, Jesus College, MS

35; see James, *Jesus*, 56–57. The other, a French version, Durham Cathedral Library MS B.III. 3, may have been written in England and could possibly be one of these books.

25. It is easy to confuse the two Dautres of York. One was John, a lawyer and bibliophile, who on the death of his father Thomas in 1437, inherited many of his fifteen books, most of them literary. See YPR, vol. 2, fols. 413–414, and *TE*. 2:230–32. John died in 1458, leaving the books to others. Thomas Dautre was a Chapter Clerk at York. He appears in *RFCY*, 1:86, for 1387 as a clerk and in *TE* 3:20–21, as a writer, signator, and registrar of a will with the Chapter. This was the testament of Thomas Dalby, archdeacon of Richmond, made in 1400. Thomas Dautre's own will in YPR, vol. 3, fols. 493v-494 describes him as "clericus," and he apparently served the archbishop of York as a scribe.

26. This manuscript is probably now San Marino, Calif. Huntington Museum MS HM 140. See C. W. Dutschke et al., *Guide to Medieval and Renaissance Manuscripts in the Huntington Library* (San Marino, Calif.: Huntington Library, 1989), 1:185–90. See John M. Manly and Edith Rickert, eds., *The Text of the Canterbury Tales Studied on the Basis of All Known Manuscripts* (Chicago: Univ. of Chicago Press, 1940), 1:609–10. MS HM 140, formerly Phillipps 8299, is in a northeast Midlands dialect consonant with Chaworth's area of activity. It is briefly discussed by Daniel S. Silvia, "Some Fifteenth-Century Manuscripts of the *Canterbury Tales*," in Beryl Rowland, ed., *Chaucer and Middle English Studies in Honour of Rossell Hope Robbins* (Kent, Ohio: Kent State Univ. Press, 1974), 158–59.

27. See BIHR Reg. 20, Booth, fols. 275–276, and *TE* 2:220–29. See Harris, "The Role of Owners," in *BPPB*, 164. Other devotional books in Chaworth's will were an English version of the *Horologium Sapientiae* and a *Grace Dieu*. See below, n. 53 and A. I. Doyle, "A Survey of the Origins and Circulation of Theological Writings in English in the 14th, 15th and Early 16th Centuries with Special Consideration of the Part of the Clergy Therein" (Ph.D. diss., Cambridge University #2301–2, 1953), vol. 1:200–206, and vol. 2:267; and Hughes, *Pastors and Visionaries*, 105. Chaworth is discussed by Turville-Petre, "Some Medieval English Manuscripts," 132–33. Chaworth owned at least three very fine books not mentioned in the will, all bearing his arms, as if commissioned by him. These were John Lydgate's *Troybook*, now London, British Library MS Cotton Augustus A.iv; John of Trevisa's translation of Bartholomaeus Anglicus, *De Proprietatibus Rerum*, now New York, Columbia University, Butler Library MS Plimpton 263, which was apparently written for Chaworth by Roger Motram, whose name appears in the colophon; and the Wollaton Antiphonale, now in the University of Nottingham Library, MS 250. On the first book see H. L. D. Ward, *Catalogue of Romances in the Department of Manuscripts in the British Museum* (London: British Library, 1883; reprint, 1961), 75; on the second, see G. A. Plimpton, *The Education of Chaucer* (London: Oxford Univ. Press, 1935), who publishes a page of it as pl. 5; Bertha M. Frick, "Columbia's Giant Encyclopedia: Plimpton ms.no.263," *CLC* 2.3 (1953): 8–15; and, on the third, Hill, "The Wollaton Antiphonal," 42–50.

28. Thorp, DCP, vol. 1, fol. 63. For Lasynby, see YPR, vol. 2, fol. 342v; for Downham, YPR, vol. 2, fols. 487–487v, *TE* 2:268. For Revetour see YPR vol. 2, fol. 138v, and *TE* 2:117. A thorough discussion of Revetour's play in its dramatic context is that of Alexandra Johnston, "The Plays of the Religious Guilds of York: The Creed Play and the Pater Noster Play," *Speculum* 50 (1975): 55–90. The Guild of St. Christopher is discussed by Eileen White, *The St. Christopher and St. George Guild of York*, Borthwick Paper no. 72 (York: St. Anthony's Press, 1987), especially, p. 11. See also

Alexandra Johnston and Margaret Rogerson, eds., *Records of Early English Drama: York* (Toronto: Pontifical Institute, 1979) 10–11, and Allan H. Nelson, *The Medieval English Stage: Corpus Christi Pageants and Plays* (Chicago: Univ. of Chicago Press, 1974), 52. References to the continuing importance of Revetour's legacy made in the York City Archive House Books are printed from the originals by Johnston, "The Plays of the Religious Guilds of York," appendix, 81–83. The acquisition of social status from the production of these plays is discussed by Mervyn James, "Ritual, Drama and Social Body in the Late Medieval English Town," *PP* 98 (1983): 3–29.

29. As Ralph Hanna points out in *"Compilatio* and the Wife of Bath: Latin Backgrounds, Ricardian Texts," in A. J. Minnis, ed., *Latin and Vernacular. Studies in Late-Medieval Texts and Manuscripts* (Cambridge: D. S. Brewer, 1989), "the possibility of free reading, and of concomitant free interpretation, is a major worry of opponents of Wycliffite biblical translation" (11, n. 26). In the north, documented Lollard activity at the beginning of the fifteenth century appears to have centered in a small community in Newcastle and around several priests in Durham diocese. See M. G. Snape, "Some Evidence of Lollard Activity in the Diocese of Durham in the Early Fifteenth Century," *AA*, 4th ser., 39 (1961): 355–61. Moran, *The Growth,* minimizes Lollardry in the north (193–219). See also Arthur G. Dickens, *Lollards and Protestants in the Diocese of York* (Oxford: Oxford Univ. Press for Univ. of Hull, 1959), and Anne Hudson, "The Debate on Bible Translation, Oxford 1401," in Anne Hudson, ed., *Lollards and Their Books* (London: Hambledon, 1985), 67–84.

30. On this nomenclature, see Elizabeth Brunskill, "Missals, Portifers and Pyes," *BJP* 2 (1974): 1–34.

31. See L. E. Boyle, "The *Oculus Sacerdotis* and Some Other Works of William of Pagula," *TRHS,* 5th ser., 5 (1955): 81–110, and on John de Burgh, see *BRUC,* 107.

32. Hughes, *Pastors and Visionaries,* 193–94.

33. J. B. Schneyer, *Repertorium der lateinischen Sermones des Mittelalters für die Zeit von 1150–1350* (Münster: Aschendorff, 1969–1980), vol. 3, s.v. Jacobus de Voragine.

34. Harwod, YPR, vol. 1, fol. 142, and *TE* 1:341–42. See also *BRUO* 2:882. Harwod had a close relationship with John Newton, calling him "my special lord" and leaving him his choice of the testator's books. See also Hughes, *Pastors and Visonaries,* 201.

35. Now Cambridge, Sidney Sussex College MS 2. See James, *Sidney Sussex,* 5–8. On Thomas Rotherham, see chap. 6 below.

36. For Skirlaw, see *TE* 1:306–25; *BRUO* 3:1708–1710; and Arthur Francis Leach, "Wykeham's Books at New College," *Collectanea* 3, Oxford Historical Society 32 (Oxford: Clarendon, 1896), 230. For Depeden, see YPR, vol. 3, fols. 88v–89v; Dautre, YPR, vol. 2, fols. 413–414; Lese, YPR, vol. 5, fol. 284; Fosser, *Wills and Inventories,* 91, and R. Barrie Dobson, *Durham Priory, 1400–1450* (Cambridge: Cambridge Univ. Press, 1973), s.v. Fossor; Barnby, BIHR Reg. 23, Rotherham, fol. 324, and cited in *TE* 4:115.

37. Pigot, YPR, vol. 4, fols. 23v–24, and *TE* 3:157.

38. DCP vol. 2, fols. 23–26, and *TE* 4:143.

39. YPR vol. 3, fols. 226v–227. See Jo Ann Moran, "A 'Common Profit' Library in Fifteenth-Century England and Other Books for Chaplains," *Manuscripta* 28 (1984): 17–25.

40. Moragior, YPR, vol. 4, fol. 93v; Roos, BIHR Reg. 14, Arundel, fol. 47v, *TE* 1:203; de la River, *TE* 2:174. On the question of female wills, most usually made by widows, see Doris Stenton, *The English Woman in History* (London: Allen and Unwin, 1957), 31–33.

41. Joel T. Rosenthal, "Aristocratic Cultural Patronage and Book Bequests, 1350–1500," *BJRL* 64 (1981–1982): 522–48, and Susan Groag Bell, "Medieval Women Book Owners: Arbiters of Lay Piety and Ambassadors of Culture," reprinted in Mary Erler and Maryanne Kowaleski, eds., *Women and Power in the Middle Ages* (Athens: Univ. of Georgia, 1988), 149–87. See more recently for England, P. J. P. Goldberg, *Women, Work, and Life Cycle in a Medieval Economy: Women in York and Yorkshire, c. 1300–1520* (New York: Oxford Univ. Press, 1992); Judith M. Bennett, "Medieval Women, Modern Women: Across the Great Divide," in David Aers, ed., *Culture and History 1350–1600: Essays on English Communities, Identities and Writing* (Detroit: Wayne State Univ. Press, 1992), 147–75; Josephine Koster Tarvers, " 'Thys ys my mystrys boke': English Women as Readers and Writers in Late Medieval England," in Charlotte Morse et al., eds. *The Uses of Manuscripts in Literary Studies: Essays in Memory of Judson Boyce Allen* (Kalamazoo, Mich.: Medieval Institute, 1992), 305–27; Janet S. Loengard, " 'Legal History and the Medieval Englishwoman' Revisited: Some New Directions," in Joel T. Rosenthal, ed., *Medieval Women and the Sources of Medieval History* (Athens: Univ. of Georgia Press, 1990), 210–36; and George Keiser, "Patronage and Piety in Fifteenth-Century England: Margaret, Duchess of Clarence, Symon Wynter and Beinecke MS 317," *YULG* 60 (1985): 32–46, though none treats northern books or female owners specifically. Carol M. Meale's article, " '. . . all the bokes that I haue of latyn, englisch, and frensch': Laywomen and Their Books in Late Medieval England," deals with some of the same book legacies discussed in my chapter (in *Women and Literature in Britain 1150–1500* [Cambridge Studies in Medieval Literature], ed. Carol M. Meale [Cambridge: Cambridge Univ. Press, 1993], 128–58). See also for the idea that the Yorkshire scribe-anthologist Robert Thornton got texts from nuns at Nunmunkton, Keiser's "More light on the Life and Milieu of Robert Thornton," cited above, 111–19.

42. See Deanesly, "Vernacular Books in England in the Fourteenth and Fifteenth Centuries."

43. For Walkyngham, see *TE* 1:17.

44. See Paul Saenger, "Books of Hours and the Reading Habits of the Later Middle Ages," *ScrC* 9 (1985): 239–69. An excellent discussion of the *horae* from a feminist perspective appears in Claire Donovan, *The de Brailes Hours. Shaping the Book of Hours in Thirteenth-Century Oxford* (London: The British Library, 1991) where the owner's portraits are discussed on pp. 23–24 and 152–55. Presumably, much the same things could be said of arms. In a will of June 6, 1499, a knight, Nicholas Mountenay, left to Robert Mountenay a book that the testator described as follows: "uno primarium cum armis meis pictis." BIHR Reg. 25, Savage, fol. 369. Bedford, YPR, vol. 2, fols. 418–419. Joseph Hunter, *Hallamshire: The History and Topography of the Parish of Sheffield in the County of York* (London: Virtue, 1875), 391, erroneously called this book a missal, as he had not seen it. Hughes, *Pastors and Visionaries*, 31, identifies the miniature as "the Descent from the Cross." The manuscript is fully described in *MMBL*, Piper, 809–811.

45. The manuscript is little known. See Z. Haraszti, "Additions to the Rare Book Department," *BPLQ* 9 (1957): 60–61.

46. See *TCD.* 1:147–50. See also Claudio Leonardi, "Patricius Hibernorum ep.," *ML* 5 (1982), no. 2790, p. 346, where the manuscript is erroneously called MS 85 instead of 83. On Barbara and other female saints with a particular appeal to women, see Ellen Muller, "Saintly Virgins: The Veneration of Virgin Saints in Religious Women's Communities," in *Saints and She-Devils: Images of Women in the Fifteenth and Sixteenth Centuries*, ed. Lène Dresen-Coenders (London: Rubicon Press, 1987), 83–100 and for Barbara particularly, 90, 91.

47. *IMBL* 3, item 809. This manuscript is discussed by Ian Doyle, "A Text Attributed to Ruusbroec Circulating in England," in A. Ampe, ed., *Dr. L. Reypens-Album* (Antwerp: Ruusbroec Genootschap, 1964), 158, who cautions about the instructions for the pictures "that neither these nor the language of the other ME items are clearly northern" (158, n. 25). On the matter of instructions to illuminators, see C. E. Pickford, "An Arthurian Manuscript in the John Rylands Library," *BJRL* 31 (1948): 330–44; and Sandra L. Hindman, "The Roles of Author and Artist in the Procedure of Illustrating Late Medieval Texts," in David Burchmore, ed., *Text and Image*, ACTA, vol. 10 (Binghamton, N.Y.: Center for Medieval and Early Renaissance Studies, 1983), 27–62.

48. See James, *Trinity* 2:307–309. Anlabys of the town of Anlaby near Beverley formed a clerical affinity around Beverley and York at this period, and one or possibly two well-to-do women of this name were buried in the Dominican convent at Beverley. See C. F. R. Palmer, "The Friars Preachers, or Black Friars of Beverley," *YAJ* 7 (1882): 37. The book gifts of Thomas Anlaby are mentioned in detail on folios 1v and xxviijv of the Anlaby Cartulary of ca. 1450, now Cambridge, Fitzwilliam Museum MS 329. The pious and learned Anlaby not only wrote the cartulary but drew and illuminated several pictures for it, one of which shows himself in tonsure and his wife in the habit of a Benedictine lay nun as donors worshiping at the foot of a Crucifixion scene. His relative Katherine was a prioress of Nunkeeling in the East Riding. See M. R. James, "The Anlaby Cartulary," *YAJ* 31 (1934): 337–47, especially p. 343, for a description of the miniatures and a transcription of much of this fascinating private cartulary. See, more recently, F. Wormald and P. M. Giles, *A Descriptive Catalogue of the Additional Illuminated Manuscripts in the Fitzwilliam Museum Acquired between 1895 and 1979 (Excluding the McClean Collection)* (Cambridge: Cambridge Univ. Press, 1982), vol. 2, pl. 85, and Robinson, *Cambridge*, vol. 1, no. 204: 67, and vol. 2:254. I am indebted to Pamela Robinson for bringing the Anlaby volume to my attention. Another Thomas Anlaby was a rector of Everingham; he left five books in 1476, YPR vol. V, folio 9. See *BRUC*, 13.

49. Bell, "Medieval Women Book Owners," 150.

50. Prerogative Court of Canterbury, Register Horne, fol. 26, Public Records Office Prob. 11/11, in J. Challenor and C. Smith, *Index of Wills Proved in the Prerogative Court of Canterbury 1383–1558, and now Preserved in the Principal Probate Registry, Somerset House, London* (British Record Society Limited, Index Library 10, London, 1893–1895) 2 vols., s.v. Scrope, and *TE* 4:149–54. On the question of Continental female writing and reading skills, from which some conclusions might be drawn about English practice, see generally, Joan Ferrante, "The Education of Women in the Middle Ages in Theory, Fact, and Fantasy," in P. H. Labalme, ed., *Beyond their Sex: Learned Women of the European Past* (New York: New York Univ. Press, 1980), 9–42.

51. Leversham, Lambeth Palace wills, Reg. Chichele, 1, fol. 94; Dandson, YPR, vol. 3, fol. 15; Ripon, YPR, vol. 3, fol. 25; Wright, YPR, vol. 2, fol. 510v.

52. Hothom, DCP L 2/4, fol. 288v; Patrington, YPR, vol. 5, fol. 65.

53. Rawson, YPR, vol. 4, fol. 107; Presteman, YPR, vol. 5, fol. 393; Fenton, YPR, vol. 5, fol. 436; Doncaster, YPR, vol. 2, fol. 434.

54. For Bowes, see Raine, ed., *Wills and Inventories*, 65. A better text appears in *RTL* 2:196. Boccaccio, Marjory Salvayn, see above, n 24.

55. Matilda of York, BIHR 19 Reg. Kemp, fol. 192, *TE* 2:118–24. This will is listed in Raine's Index as no. 37, when it is actually no. 97. Johanna Hilton (d. 1432), wife of Robert Hilton, knight of Swyne, East Riding, owned "Romanse incipit cum decem preceptis alembes, romanse de septem sages." YPR, vol. 3, fol. 347, *TE* 2:23–25.

56. *TE* 1:201–203. See E. J. Arnould, ed., *Henry of Lancaster, Le Livre des seyntz médicines* (Oxford: Blackwell, 1940), and the same author's *Étude sur le livre des Saintes Médicines du Duc Henri de Lancastre* (Paris: M. Didier, 1948), and more recently, Kenneth Fowler, *The King's Lieutenant: Henry of Grosmont, First Duke of Lancaster, 1310–1361* (London: Elek, 1969), 193–96.

57. YPR, vol. 2, fol. 585v, *TE* 1:352.

58. For Stapleton, see H. E. Chetwynd-Stapylton, "The Stapletons of Yorkshire," *YAJ* 8 (1883–1884): 65–116, 223–258, 381–423, 427–74. Prerogative Court of Canterbury, Register Luffenam, fol. 35, Public Records Office, Probate 11/3, *Index of Wills Proved in the Prerogative Court of Canterbury 1383–1558*, s.v. Sywardby, *TE* 3:163, and J. W. Clay, ed., *North Country Wills: Abstracts of Wills at Somerset House and Lambeth Palace, 1383–1558*, Surtees Society vol. 116 (Durham: Surtees Society 1908), 48–49.

59. Aske, DCP L 2/4, folio 264v, *TE* 2:143; Emeley, *TE* 1:50–52.

60. YPR, vol. 3, fol. 63v; *TE* 1:270–72.

61. YPR, vol. 3, fol. 44; *TE* 1:258.

62. n. 55.

63. Ellerker, YPR, vol. 5, fol. 127; Langton, YPR, vol. 2, fols. 597v–598, and *TE* 2:258–60.

64. YPR, vol. 3, fol. 227.

65. BIHR Reg. 19, Kemp, fol. 56.

66. BIHR Reg. 18, Bowet, fol. 362, *TE* 1:381–383.

67. See Gaston Raynaud, ed., *Oeuvres complètes d'Eustache Deschamps* (Paris: SATF, 1894), 9:45–46; 15:ll. 1311–1319. Translation mine.

68. Mauley, YPR, vol. 3, fols. 546v–547, and *TE* 2:66–68; Fitzhugh, Raine, ed., *Wills and Inventories*, 74–75, and *RTL*, 3:63.

69. Myton, YPR, vol. 2, fols. 672v–673, *TE* 2:76.

70. See above, n. 40.

71. *TE* 2:302.

72. Bowes, loc. cit.; Marshall, DCP L 2/4, vol. 1, fol. 376; Grymmer, YPR, 2, fols. 633v–634.

73. Ellerker, YPR, vol. 5, fol. 127; Pigot, YPR, vol. 5, fol. 267, and *TE* 4:6.

74. See note 50 above. These books were not noted by Raine in *TE*.

75. Pudsay, YPR, vol. 2, fol. 97, and *TE* 2:108.

76. The servant was Agnes Celayne; she was left the book by a priest, John Raventhorpe, in 1432, YPR, vol. 3, fol. 358, *TE* 2:28–29; Percy, *TE* 1:59; Robert Roos, YPR, vol. 1, fol. 51, *TE* 1:178–80; Thomas Roos, YPR, vol. 3, fol. 23v–24, *TE* 1:252; Hebbeden, loc. cit.; Banks, YPR, vol. 2, 653v; Morton, *TE* 2:13–15; Ughtred, *TE* 1:241–45, 243; Revetour, YPR, vol. 2, 238r, and *TE* 2:117. Also interesting in this context is the book list with anathema, itemizing ten Latin manuscripts and a printed book left by a Peter, vicar of Swine, to the nuns of Swine in the East Riding. Aside from Mechtild's *Book of Spiritual Grace* and a work of St. Bridget, which we might expect to find, the list included several surprising items, like Isidore's *Etymologiae* and Peter Comestor's *Historia Scholastica*. See James, *King's College*, MS 18, 34–35, and David Bell, *The Libraries of the Cistercians, Gilbertines and Premonstratensians*, Corpus of British Medieval Library Catalogues 3 (London: British Library and British Academy, 1992).

77. Roos, YPR, vol. 3, fol. 529, and *TE* 2:65–66; Stapleton, loc. cit.

78. Rosenthal, "Aristocratic Cultural Patronage," p. 536.

79. Raine, ed., *Wills and Inventories*, pt. 1:83. A much more accurate text of Hebbeden's will is published in *RTL* 4:159–62. On Hebbeden, see *BRUO* 3:2182.

80. YPR, vol. 3, fols. 419v–420, and *TE* 2:51; Dautre, *TE* 2:232.

81. Welwick, DCP, vol. 1, fol. 353; Duffield, BIHR Reg. 20, Booth, fols. 272–74. On this subject see J. van den Gheyn, *Album belge de paléographie. Recueil de spécimens d'écritures d'auteurs et de manuscrits belges* (Brussels: Jette, 1908); Gerard Isaac Lieftinck, *Manuscrits datés conservés dans les Pays-Bas: Catalogue paléographique des manuscrits en écriture latine portant des indications de date* (Amsterdam: North Holland Publishing Co., and Leiden: Brill, 1964–1988), 2 vols.; and Pierre Cockshaw, "Mentions d'auteurs, de copistes, d'enlumineurs et de libraires dans les comptes généraux de l'État Bourguignon (1384–1419)," *Scriptorium* 23 (1969): 122–44.

82. For the indenture between Skirlaw and Appleton, see W. C. Trevelyan, "The Copy of an Indenture Preserved Amongst the Records of University College, Oxford, dated 1404, Between Walter Bishop of Durham and the Master of that College," *AA*, 1st ser., 2 (1832): 99; also printed in B. Botfield, ed., *Catalogi Veteres Librorum Ecclesiae Cathedralis Dunelmi*, Surtees Society, vol. 7 (London: Surtees Society, 1838), 127–28.

83. See J. W. Clay, ed., *North Country Wills*, 20. This item is omitted from the list of Manfield's books published by Cavanaugh, "A Study of Books Privately Owned," 555.

84. See *BRUO* 2:1213–1214. Thomas Rymer, ed., *Foedera* (London, 1704–1735), 9:275, notes a legacy to Robert, recluse of Beverley.

85. DCAB L 2 (4), fol. 139 and *TE* 3:29. See also *BRUO* 2:1213–1214, and Hughes, *Pastors and Visionaries*, 179. A good account of Noion can be found in Margaret Aston, *Thomas Arundel, A Study of Church Life in the Reign of Richard II* (Oxford: Clarendon, 1967), 244–45, 313–15.

86. YPR, vol. 3, fol. 358.

87. Moran, "A 'Common Profit' Library," 25, and see also Anne Hudson, "Some Aspects of Lollard Book Production," in Derek Baker, ed., *Schism, Heresy and Religious Protest* (Cambridge: Cambridge Univ. Press, 1972), 147–57, and Vincent Gillespie, "Vernacular Books of Religion," in *BPPB*, 319–20.

88. Moran, "A 'Common Profit' Library," 25.

89. Oxford, St. John's College MS 94, fol. 1.

90. Dobson, "The Residentiary Canons," 158, and generally, Joel Rosenthal, "The Fifteenth-Century Episcopate: Careers and Bequests," in Derek Baker, ed., *Sanctity and Secularity: The Church and the World* (Oxford: Blackwell, 1973), 117–27.

91. On Poteman, see *BRUO* 3:1506–1507. See also Neil Ker, *Records of All Souls College Library 1437–1600* (Oxford: Oxford Univ. Press, 1971), 124, 107, 133. On Est, see *BRUO* 1:648.

92. On Duffield, see *BRUO* 1:602, and Ker, *Records of All Souls College Library 1437–1600*, 173 n. 1.

93. See James, *Jesus.*

94. Waltham, *TE* 3:59; Andrews, *TE* 3:234; and *BRUO* 1:81.

95. The phrase is that of C. T. Allmand, "The Civil Lawyers," In Clough, ed., *Profession, Vocation, and Culture*, 168. See YPR, loc. cit. See also *BRUC*, 421–22; Thomas Alfred Walker, *A Biographical Register of Peterhouse Men* (Cambridge: Cambridge Univ. Press, 1927–29), 1:19–20, and the excellent study by C. B. L. Barr, "The Minster Library," in G. E. Aylmer and Reginald Cant, eds., *A History of York Minster* (Oxford: Clarendon, 1977), 494–95, as well as Thomas Kelly, *Early Public Libraries: A History of Public Libraries in Great Britain Before 1850* (London: Library Association, 1966), 25. On the practice of chaining reference books, see B. H. Streeter, *The Chained Library* (London: Macmillan, 1931).

96. *Pastors and Visionaries*, 22–23. Hughes's argument is not compelling.

97. YPR, vol. 2, fol. 682, and *TE* 2:78, 206. See, on Alne, *BRUC*, 10–11. He also left several classical, patristic, and humanistic texts to his college library through reversion. For five books, including Rolle's *Melos Contemplativum*, left to the Cambridge University Library by Alne, see Henry Bradshaw, "Two Lists of Books in the University Library," in *The Collected Papers of Henry Bradshaw*, ed. J.H. Jenkinson (Cambridge: Cambridge Univ. Press, 1889), 25, 29, 34. Alne also gave his Augustine's *De Trinitate* to Peterhouse, where it is now MS 78. See James, *Peterhouse*, 8, 96. See also Hughes, *Pastors and Visionaries*, 200–201.

98. YPR, vol. 2, fol. 348, and *TE* 2:206.

99. See *MMBL*, Piper, 700–701.

100. Curt Bühler, *The Fifteenth-Century Book* (Philadelphia: Univ. of Pennsylvania Press, 1960), 20.

101. Of the fifteen scriveners or *scriptores* listed in the York Freemen's Register between 1377 and 1450, none appears in connection with any extant manuscripts with which I am acquainted.

102. DCP, vol. 1, fol. 104, and *TE* 1:171. See also *BRUO* 3:2162.

103. N. A. H. Lawrance, ed., *Fasti Parochiales V: Deanery of Buckrose*, YASRS 143 (Leeds: Yorkshire Archaeological Soc., 1983), 38. In the environs of York in Thorp Arch lived a carpenter, Richard Greneake. See George T. Clark, "Rolls of the Collectors in the West-Riding of the Lay-Subsidy Poll Tax, 2 Richard II," *YAJ* 7 (1882): 175.

104. YPR, vol. 2, fol. 544.

105. John de Scarle, DCP, vol. 1, fol. 133v, and *TE* 3:22–25. See also *CAHME* 3:432 n. 1, 448 n. 2, 450, 488, 492 n. 2; 4:3–4, 8–9, 62; 6:17.

106. William Poteman, DCP, vol. 2, fol. 1.

107. Wolveden, DCP, vol. 1, fol. 235v, and *TE* 3:92. Arston, loc. cit., fols. 234v–235. Interestingly, Wolveden was himself bequeathed a devotional book, Bodleian Library MS Rawlinson 8c, by an anchorite of Litchfield "librum devotum cujus copiam habui de anachorita Lichfeld"; see Doyle, "A Survey of the Origins," 2:135.

108. YPR, vol. 2, fol. 654, and *TE* 2:15. Because of the fact that both brothers were named John, there is some confusion about the books they owned and who wrote them. For example, Cavanaugh, "A Study of Books Privately Owned," 597, takes John Morton's brother John for John Alne, a Cistercian of London and Robert Alne's brother, as the recipient of the *Gesta Romanorum*. Though the time period treated is rather earlier than Morton's, Ralph V. Turner's "The *Miles Literatus* in Twelfth- and Thirteenth-Century England: How Rare a Phenomenon?" *AHR* 83 (1978): 928–45, is of interest.

109. See Elizabeth Salter, *Nicholas Love's Myrrour of the Blessed Lyf of Jesu Christ*, AC 10 (Salzburg: Institut für Anglistik und Amerikanistik, 1974), 3.

110. See Doyle, "A Survey of the Origins," 2:68–69, and M. B. Hackett, "William Flete and the *De Remediis Contra Temptaciones*," in J. A. Watt et al., eds., *Medieval Studies Presented to Aubrey Gwynn, S.J.* (Dublin: O. Lochlainn, 1961), 337–38, and 347, where Hackett, not unreasonably, confuses John Morton the scribe with his brother of the same name.

111. On John de Feriby, see DCP, vol. 1, fol. 136. William de Feriby may be the person of that name who died in 1379 and was fellow of Balliol College, Oxford, proctor of the University, canon of York, and archdeacon of Cleveland, as William gave his breviary to a John de Feriby of Bolton, who may also have been his brother; see DCP, vol. 1, fol. 68. Another possibility is the William de Feriby, King's Clerk and rector of Middleton in Shelfordshire, who died in 1394 (DCP, vol. 1, fol. 111). Ian

Doyle, "Book Production by the Monastic Orders in England (c. 1375–1530): Assessing the Evidence," in Brownrigg, ed., *Medieval Book Production*, 1–19, mentions a scribe, John de Feriby, who died in 1444 (13–14). I am grateful to the publisher for letting me see this article at an early stage of publication.

112. For Farneylawe, see DCP, vol. 1, fol. 69, and *TE* 1:101–103, as well as *BRUO* 2:668. Two of his books are still extant at Merton College, Oxford, a *Distinctiones Mauricii*, MS I.3.7 and a Henry de Bracton, *Opus de Legibus et Consuetudinibus Angliae*, MS O.3.9. See F. M. Powicke, *The Medieval Books of Merton College* (Oxford: Clarendon, 1931), p. 161, no. 528 and no. 527. This person may be related to the chaplain-scribe who copied folios 1–103 of a *Pricke of Conscience*, now London, British Library MS Additional 32578, which bears the colophon: "With outyn any misse, Mary thou pray / that we may come to blisse, amen, quod Farnelay. / Laus tibi rex Christi quoniam liber explicit iste. 1405 secundum manum Roberti Ffarnelay capellani manentis in Bolton. Finito libro sit laus et gloria Christo. Amen." See Watson, *London*, 1: no. 356, p. 75, and 2: pl. 311.

113. For Helton, see BIHR Reg. 25, Savage, fol. 164.

114. For Castelay, see YPR, vol. 4, fol. 201.

115. For Westerdale, see YPR, vol. 4, fol. 219.

116. For Garton, see DCP, vol. 1, fol. 95. Richard seems to have come from a family of clerical scribes, for it is likely that he was related to Robert and Thomas Garton. The former was a rector of Kirklington in 1396, a prebendary of Newton in Durham diocese, and King's Clerk in 1399. The latter was rector of the church of St. John the Baptist and archbishop Scrope's penitentiary in 1399 as well as an administrator in the Newton circle, being appointed chamberlain and later sub-treasurer as well as one of the keepers of Newton's library; he died in 1418. A manuscript of the *Cibus Anime*, a devotional work associated with York Minster, now Cambridge, Trinity Hall MS 16, requests in red in its colophon: "orate pro animabus Roberti et Thomae et pro anima Henrici Garton," fol. 91v. See James, *Trinity Hall*, 34; Vincent Gillespie, "Cura Pastoralis in Deserto," in Michael Sargent, ed., *De Cella in Seculum* (Woodbridge, Suffolk: D. S. Brewer, 1989), 180, and "The *Cibus Anime* Book 3: A Guide for Contemplatives?" in *Spiritualität Heute und Gestern*, AC 35 (Salzburg: Institut für Anglistik und Amerikanistik, 1983), 3: 90–119.

117. For Preston, see YPR, vol. 6, fol. 71.

118. For Stanes, see YPR, vol. 3, fol. 435v; for Gryssop, see YPR, vol. 1, fol. 260v.

119. For Geoffrey de Cave's will, see YPR, vol. 1, fol. 12. On John Scriptor, see Aston, *Thomas Arundel*, Appendix 6, p. 412. It is possible that this man and the writer of portions of the Vernon manuscript, a scribe of Litchfield named John Scrivein, active in the 1390s, may be the same. See on this point A. I. Doyle, ed., *The Vernon Manuscript, A Facsimile of Bodleian Library, Oxford, MS. Eng. Poet. a.1* (Cambridge: Boydell and Brewer, 1986), 13–14. Perhaps in spite of his name, John Scrivener may have later become a chaplain, as in 1432 a cleric of this name was presented to a chantry in the church of St. Mary, Scurveton. See Thompson ed., "The Registers," 369, p. 219.

120. *BRUO* 1:648.

121. DCP, vol. 1, fol. 331v, and *TE* 3:160.

122. MS XVI.K.16 is described in *MMBL*, Piper, 733–34. Though he notes the presence of a fifteenth century inscription "ex dono domini Roberti," Piper does not make the connection with Est.

123. YPR, vol. 4, fol. 171, and cited in *TE* 3:220. On Sayle, see *BRUO* 3:1650.

124. James, *Gonville and Caius*, 1:343, MS 296/690, fol. 77.
125. *BRUO* 3:2179, and *TE* 3:61–65.
126. Pees, YPR, vol. 2, fol. 678.
127. Bramthwaite, YPR, vol. 3, fol. 566.
128. For Norton, see *BRUO* 2:1372. For a description of this manuscript, see Seymour De Ricci, *A Census of Medieval and Renaissance Manuscripts in the United States and Canada* (New York, H. W. Wilson, 1935–40), 1:454–55, and Albinia de la Mare, *Duke Humfrey's Library and the Divinity School 1488–1988: An Exhibition at the Bodleian Library June-August 1988* (Oxford: Bodleian Library, 1988), item 77, p. 92. MS Royal 8.A.xiii is discussed by G. F. Warner and J. P. Gilson, *Catalogue of Western Manuscripts in the Old Royal and King's Collections*, vol. 1 (London: British Museum, 1921), 213. Leonard E. Boyle and Richard H. Rouse, "A Fifteenth-Century List of the Books of Edmund Norton," *Speculum* 50 (1975): 284–88, offer a study of Norton's book list.

2. Northern Professional Scribes and Scribe Families

1. See on this subject, Doyle, "Book Production," 1–19. There are, of course, colophons in some northern books by monastic scribes. Two such scribes were active at Fountains abbey. About 1350, a native of the city of York, John de Munkgate, who was procurator, copied British Library MS Arundel 231. British Library MS Additional 24203, a fourteenth-century copy of the *Pricke of Conscience*, is signed "per fratrem Johannes de Bageby commonachum monasterii beate Marie de Fontibus" (fol. 150v). And a John Awne, of the Carthusian house of Mount Grace near Northallerton, wrote British Library MS Additional 62450 in 1450. The famous North Riding copyist Robert Thornton was neither a religious, nor strictly speaking, a lay professional scribe. He has, moreover, been so much studied that he hardly needs discussion here, especially since his manuscripts are of a very utilitarian cast, interesting mainly for their contents. For a bibliography on Thornton, see chap. 1, n. 3.
2. J. Taylor, *Medieval Historical Writing In Yorkshire*, Borthwick Papers no. 19 (York: St. Anthony's Press, 1961), 28.
3. See Wendy R. Childs and John Taylor, eds., *The Anonimalle Chronicle 1307–1334*, YASRS (Leeds: Yorkshire Archaeological Soc., 1991).
4. See for background, I. Kershaw, *Bolton Priory: The Economy of a Northern Monastery, 1286–1325* (Oxford: Oxford Univ. Press, 1973). For the Kirkstall chronicles and Peter Langtoft, see N. Denholm-Young, *Handwriting in England and Wales* (Cardiff: Univ. of Wales Press, 1954), 46–47, and generally, John Taylor, *English Historical Literature in the Fourteenth Century* (Oxford: Clarendon Press, 1987), 16–17, 19, 150–51; M. V. Clarke and Noel Denholm-Young, "The Kirkstall Chronicle 1355–1400," reprinted in L.S. Sutherland and M. McKisack, eds., *Fourteenth Century Studies by M. V. Clarke* (Oxford: Clarendon, 1937), 99–114; and John Taylor, *The Kirkstall Abbey Chronicles* (Leeds: Thoresby Soc., 1952).
5. See George T. Clark, "The West-Riding Poll Tax and Lay-Subsidy Rolls, 2d Richard II," 150, 165. See also Margaret Spufford, "Wills and their Scribes," *LPS* 8 (1972): 55–57.
6. That a "chancery clerk or clerks with York connections" had a hand in this chronicle is noted by Taylor, *English Historical Literature*, 142–43, and for Yorkshire ties with the Chancery, see J. L. Grassi, "Royal Clerks from the Archdiocese of York in the Fourteenth Century," *NH* 5 (1970): 12–33. On Frampton and the Hunterian volume, see John Young and P. Henderson Aitken, *A Catalogue of the Manuscripts in the*

Library of the Hunterian Museum in the University of Glasgow (Glasgow: J. Maclehose and Sons, 1908), 89–91. The Duchy of Lancaster books are MSS D.L. 42/1 and 2. See Robert Somerville, "The Cowcher Books of the Duchy of Lancaster," *EHR* 51 (1936): 598–615, and *History of the Duchy of Lancaster*, 1: pl. 1, facing p. 22, and pl. 7, facing p. 140. See Christianson, "A Community," 214. Frampton also appears to have copied a book of royal statutes, Huntington Library MS HM 19920. See Dutschke et al., *Guide to Medieval and Renaissance Manuscripts*, 2:608–18, and fig. 82, which shows a representative miniature and specimen of Frampton's script. This is a collection of Yorkshire statutes with historiated initials related to the Carmelite Missal Dutch master. It has Yorkshire feasts in the kalendar, such as the translations of Wilfrid, William, and John of Beverley, and a decree of archbishop Grey, fols. 93–98. It was written about 1413.

7. For an annotated bibliography of Huguccio's life and works, see Giuseppe Cremascoli, "Uguccione da Pisa: Saggio bibliografico," *Aevum* 42 (1968): 123–68. The major studies are Claus Riessner, *Die "Magnae Derivationes" des Uguccione da Pisa und ihre Bedeutung für die romanische Philologie* (Rome: Edizioni di Storia e Letteratura, 1965); Corrado Leonardi, "La vita e l'opera di Uguccione da Pisa decretista," *SG* 4 (1956–1957): 37–120; and Jean Holzworth, "Hugutio's 'Derivationes' and Arnulfus' Commentary on Ovid's *Fasti*," *TPAPA* 73 (1942): 259–76. On the manuscript tradition, see G. L. Bursill-Hall, *A Census of Medieval Latin Grammatical Manuscripts* (Stuttgart: Frommann-Holzboog, 1981), and A. Marigo, *I Codici manoscritti delle "Derivationes" di Uguccione Pisano* (Rome: Istituto di Studi Romani, 1936). See, most recently, Wolfgang P. Müller, "Huguccio of Pisa: Canonist, Bishop, and Grammarian?" *Viator* 22 (1991): 121–52, who throws substantial new light on the authorship of the *Magnae Derivationes*, 137–40, and his *Huguccio* (Washington, D.C.: Catholic Univ. of America, 1994).

8. The manuscript is fully described and the Latin text of the colophon is given in *MMBL*, Piper, 783–84.

9. On Le Gras, see Charles Travis Clay, ed., *York Minster Fasti*, YASRS 124, (Leeds, 1958), 2:16–17; Barr, "The Minster Library," 491, 494; Kelly, *Early Public Libraries*, 25, and *BRUO* 2:1127.

10. Christianson, "A Community," 214.

11. The Latin text is published by James Raine, ed., *Fabric Rolls of York Minster*, Surtees Society, vol. 35 (Durham: Surtees Society, 1859), 165–66. See on the Brekeling contract, Michael A. Michael, "English Illuminators c. 1190–1450: A Survey from Documentary Sources," *EMS* 4(1993): 62–113. He discusses Brekeling on p. 75 and in Appendix I, p. 77. For an interesting discussion of the way such letters were itemized and specific colors were mentioned in contracts and instructions to artists, see Patricia Stirnemann and Marie-Thérèse Gousset, "Marques, Mots, Pratiques: Leur Signification et leurs liens dans le Travail des Enlumineurs," in Olga Weijers, ed., *Vocabulaire du Livre et de l'écriture au moyen âge* (Turnhout: Brepols, 1989), 35–55. More information exists about Continental artists' contracts than about English scribal contracts. See Martin Wackernagel, *The World of the Florentine Renaissance Artist*, trans. A. Luchs (Princeton, N.J.: Princeton Univ. Press, 1981); H. Glasser, *Artists' Contracts of the Early Renaissance* (New York: Garland, 1977); D. S. Chambers, *Patrons and Artists in the Italian Renaissance* (London: Macmillan, 1970); and G. de Carné; "Contrat pour la copie d'un missel au XVᵉ Siècle," in X. Barral i Altet et al. eds., *Artistes, Artisans et Production Artistique en Bretagne au Moyen Âge* (Rennes, 1983), 127.

12. DCAB, 1343–1368 H i (2), fol. 30: "Xi die mensis November anno domini xlvi comparavit Robertus de Seleby de Eborum scriptor." Two persons called "scriptor," a Henry Scriptor in 1456 and a John Kele in 1451, are mentioned as having been summoned to the court of York in the Court Act Book, now York Diocesan Registry

MS R. As.55, published in part by J. S. Purvis as *A Mediaeval Act Book with Some Account of Ecclesiastical Jurisdiction at York* (York: Herald Printing Works, 1943) Appendix 5, trades, p. 74, but in what capacity is not stated.

13. DCAB, Roll Ei/18,130/1393: "De 41s 8d solutis hoc anno fratri Willielmo Ellerker pro scriptura duorum gradualium pro choro [et] de 40s solutis domino Richard de Styrt[t]on pro eluminacione dictorum duorum gradualium [et] de 22s 7 1/2d [ob] solutis dicto Willielmo pro pergameno empto per ipsum Willielmum [et] pro super pellicio pro custodiendis quaternis 4d."

14. Ibid., "Pars secunda de 11 L 13s 3d solutis fratri Willielmo Ellerker in plenam solucionem pro scriptura et pergameno pro iii libros pro choro."

15. "Pars secunda Roberto Bukebynder pro ligatura unius magni gradualis pro choro, ex convencione facta 10s eidem pro iii pellibus pergameni pro eodem custodiendo 20d eidem pro 1 pelle cervi pro coopertura dicti libri 3s 2d fratri Willielmo Ellerker pro pergameno 4s domino Ricardo de Styrton in plenam solucionem pro alumpnyng trium gradualium 40s. De 38s 5d solutis Willielmo Selar aurifabro pro sua operacione. De 3s 4d solutis domino Johanni Brignale pro vii pellibus pergameni emptis pro magno graduali predicto" (fol. 131).

16. See Collins, ed., *Index of the Wills in the York Registry*, 147. See Dobson, "Admissions to the Freedom of the City of York in the Later Middle Ages."

17. In 1396 "et de 3s solutis Roberto Bukebynder pro ligatura albi psalteri in choro. Fratri Willielmo de Ellerker pro scriptura duorum gradalium in choro 40s."

18. In 1399 "pars prima Roberto Bukebynder pro ligatura unius magni gradualis pro choro 10s. Pro iii pellibus vitulinis pro custodia dicti gradualis 2s pro corio magni cervi pro dicto graduali cooperiendo 4s fratri Willielmo Ellerker pro scriptura gradualis in choro, ex curialitate 13s 4d." In 1399 "pars secunda domino Richardo de Styrton pro alumnacione unius magni gradualis novi in choro 20s." In 1402 "pars prima in expensis in alumpnacione magni gradualis in choro per dominum Richard de Stretton 20s."

19. See Ronald A. Wilson, ed., *The First [and Second] Register of Bishop Robert de Stretton 1358–1385: An Abstract of the Contents*, William Salt Archaeological Society, n.s., 8 and 10, pt. 2 (London: Harrison, 1905–7), introduction.

20. See British Library MS Add. 17362, fol. 8.

21. *YMB*, 3:195 and William K. and Margaret Sessions, *Printing in York*, 2.

22. *YMB*, 3:195.

23. *YMB*, 3:196–97. For the terms *textwriter* and *luminer* or *lymnour*, see Christianson, "A Community," 208.

24. See John B. Friedman, "Richard de Thorpe's Astronomical Kalendar and the Luxury Book Trade at York," *SAC* 7 (1985): 137–60. Unfortunately, K. W. Humphreys, "Scribes and the Medieval Friars," in Peter Schweigler, ed., *Bibliothekswelt und Kulturgeschichte. Eine internationale Festgabe für Joachim Wieder zum 65. Geburtstag* (Munich: Verlag Dokumentation, 1977), 213–20, deals only with Continental mendicant scribes.

25. *RFCY*, 1:16, 30, 77, 93, for Ellerkers in the cloth trades. Ellerkers were also guildspeople. See Robert A. Skaife, ed., *The Register of the Guild of Corpus Christi*, Surtees Society, vol. 57 (Durham: Surtees Society, 1872), 59, 78, for a Johanna Ellerker in 1455 and 1470.

26. See John George Hall, *A History of South Cave* (Hull: E. Ombler, 1892), 201.

27. James Raine, ed., *Yorkshire Fines*, Surtees Society, vol. 94 (Durham: Surtees Society, 1897), 48–49.

28. British Library MS Royal 10.A.x, fol. 187.

29. PRO/Rot. Pat. 7 Edward III, memb. 15.

30. PRO/Rot. Scot. 9 Edward III, memb. 36.

31. See Grassi, "Royal Clerks from the Archdiocese of York," 12–13. See also *CAHME* 2:306, and 3:5, 86, 215–16.

32. Grassi, "Royal Clerks," 21.

33. Loc. cit. For the account of the abduction, see John Bernard Burke, *Burke's Complete Peerage*, vol. 8 (London: Burke's Peerage, 1932), 287.

34. See George Oliver, *The History and Antiquities of the Town and Minster of Beverley* (Beverley: Eng.: M. Turner, 1829), 506–508; Hall, *A History of South Cave*, 11, 201–205, and F. W. Dendy, ed., *Visitations of the North*, Surtees Society, vol. 122 (Durham: Surtees Society, 1912), 1:5.

35. *VCH: York*, 4:147 n. 55.

36. R. B. Dobson, ed., *York City Chamberlains' Account Rolls 1396–1500*, Surtees Society, vol. 192 (Durham: Surtees Society, 1980), 12, mentions a John Ellerker as Sergeaunt of the Law in 1434; another of this name and rank or perhaps the same one appears in *YMB* 3:68, 151.

37. The records of institutions to benefices for the Harthill Wapentake are in the Brynmor Jones Library of the University of Hull. I am grateful to the university archivist, Brian Dyson, for supplying me with this information.

38. See B. Jones, ed., *John Le Neve, Fasti Ecclesiae Anglicanae 1300–1541*, vol. 6: *Northern Province* (London: Athlone, 1963), 19, 37.

39. BIHR, Reg. 10, Zouche, fol. 278v. See also fol. 280 and BIHR Reg. 11, Thoresby, fol. 25v. See also A. B. Emden, "Dominican Confessors and Preachers Licensed by Medieval English Bishops," *AFP* 32 (1962): 209. Emden, *A Survey of Dominicans in England Based on the Ordination Lists in Episcopal Registers (1268 to 1538)* (Rome: S. Sabina, 1967), does not record Ellerker's ordination.

40. BIHR, Reg. 10, loc. cit.

41. BIHR, Reg. 10, fol. 279.

42. *BRUO* 2:1022.

43. See W. A. Pantin, *Documents Illustrating the Activities of the General and Provincial Chapters of the English Black Monks, 1215–1540*, Camden Series, 3d ser., 45, (London: Royal Historical Soc., 1931–37), 3:309. See also Mildred Marcett, *Uhtred de Boldon, Friar William Jordan and Piers Plowman* (New York: Mildred Marcett, 1938), 49–56.

44. See Andrew G. Little, *Grey Friars in Oxford* (Oxford, 1892), 242, and generally, L. M. Goldthorp, "The Franciscans and Dominicans in Yorkshire Part II. The Black Friars," *YAJ* 32 (1936): 422.

45. See John Bale, *Scriptorum Illustrium Maioris Brytanniae Catalogus* (1557–59; reprint, Farnborough, Hants.: Gregg Press, 1971), 1:483.

46. Derek Pearsall, ed., *Piers Plowman by William Langland, an Edition of the C-Text* (Berkeley: Univ. of California Press, 1978), passus 15, l. 92, p. 250. See also A. Gwynn, "The Date of the B-Text of *Piers Plowman*," *RES* 19 (1943), who discusses William Jordan's career on 2–4.

47. Sears Jayne and Francis R. Johnson, eds., *The Lumley Library: The Catalogue of 1609* (London: The British Museum, 1956), item 2085, p. 238.

48. See Warner and Gilson, *Catalogue of Western Manuscripts in the Old Royal and King's Collections*, 2:169. Even with the aid of the remarkable video spectrometer at the British Library, the inscription remains unreadable. See *MLGB*, 13. In a letter to me of 10 Oct. 1986, Kenneth Humphreys, who has worked extensively with medieval English book catalogues, nonetheless believes the MS to come from Bridlington Priory.

49. Bénédictines du Bouveret, *Colophons du manuscrits occidentaux des origines au XVIᵉ siècle*, Spicilegii Friburgensis Subsidia, 7 (Fribourg, 1965–1982), 3: item 23609, p. 517. The somewhat enigmatic continuation of the colophon published in this work; "quoth Ellerker, quod Latine sonat: respondet Ellerker," seems to have existed only in the imagination of one of the sources used in the compilation of *Colophons*, according to François Huot, O.S.B., in a letter to me of 5 May 1988.

50. For examples of such page layouts, see A. Melnikas, *The Corpus of the Miniatures in the Manuscripts of Decretum Gratiani* (Rome: Libreria Ateneo Salesiano, 1975), and more recently, F. Ebel, et al., *Römisches Rechtsleben im Mittelalter Miniaturen aus den Handschriften des Corpus Juris Civilis* (Heidelberg: C.F. Müller Juristicher Verlag, 1988).

51. MS lat. 4126 has been discussed on the basis of a description of its contents made by Joseph Stevenson by Thomas D. Hardy, *Descriptive Catalogue of Materials Relating to the History of Great Britain and Ireland*, Rolls Series, no. 26; reprint, Millwood, N.Y.: Kraus, 1967), 2:170–71; Jacob Hammer, "Note on a Manuscript of Geoffrey of Monmouth's *Historia Regum Britanniae*," *PQ* 12 (1933): 225–34, and "A Commentary on the *Prophetia Merlini* (Geoffrey of Monmouth's *Historia Regum Britanniae*) Book VII," *Speculum* 10 (1935): 5; Charles Samaran et al., *Catalogue des manuscrits en écriture latine datés* (Paris, 1962), 2: 488, where Popultoun's scribal contributions are listed as fols. 10–32, 133v–134, 246–252, and 282–295, and François Avril and Patricia Danz Stirnemann, *Manuscrits enluminés d'origine insulaire VIIᵉ–XXᵉ Siècle* (Paris: Bibliothèque Nationale, 1987), no. 204: 163–165. A good brief account occurs in W. Levison's review of Neil Ker's *Medieval Libraries of Great Britain: A List of Surviving Books* in *MAe* 11 (1942): 112–114. See more recently, Marjorie O. Anderson, "The Scottish Materials in the Paris Manuscript, Bibliothèque Nationale Latin 4126," *SHR* 28 (1949): 37–39, and *Kings and Kingship in Early Scotland* (Edinburgh: Chatto and Windus, 1973), 235 and 240–60, for editions of the Scottish texts included by Popultoun. The only relatively complete list of its contents that I know of is that published by John Pinkerton, *An Enquiry into the History of Scotland* (Edinburgh: Bell and Bradfute, 1814), 1:471–76.

52. See for example, Robert W. Hanning, *The Vision of History in Early Britain from Gildas to Geoffrey of Monmouth* (New York: Columbia Univ. Press, 1966); J.A. Tuck, "Northumbrian Society in the Fourteenth Century," *NH* 6 (1971): 22–39; Stanley G. Mendyk, *Speculum Britanniae: Regional Study, Antiquarianism, and Science in Britain to 1700* (Toronto: Univ. of Toronto Press, 1989); Lionel Stones, "English Chroniclers and the Affairs of Scotland, 1286–1296," in R. H. C. Davis et al., eds., *The Writing of History in the Middle Ages: Essays Presented to Richard William Southern* (Oxford: Clarendon Press, 1981), 323–48; and most recently, David Dumville, *Histories and Pseudo-Histories of the Insular Middle Ages* (Aldershot, Hampshire: Variorum, 1990).

53. This catalogue has recently been published by K. W. Humphreys, ed., *The Friars' Libraries*, Corpus of British Medieval Library Catalogues (London: The British Library, 1990), 11–154, whose work replaces the edition by M.R. James. Humphreys emends the list of items that occur in both Popultoun's compilation and in the Austin Friars' library offered by E. J. Cowan, "The Scottish Chronicle in the Poppleton Manuscript," *IR* 32 (1961): 3–21, on p. xxxiv. On the Yorkshire compiler John de Foxton and his book, see John B. Friedman, ed., *John de Foxton's Liber Cosmographiae (1408): An Edition and Codicological Study* (Leiden: Brill, 1988). As Popultoun also seems to have used for the *Cronica de origine antiquorum Pictorum* at folio 27 two Geoffrey of Monmouth manuscripts, Cambridge, Corpus Christi College, MS 139 and Cambridge University Library MS Ff.1.27, which were at one time in the Cistercian house of Sawley not far from York, he may have traveled outside the city in search of books too. See

here Anderson, *Kings and Kingship in Early Scotland*, p. 237; *MLGB* 177; and Kenneth Jackson et al., *Celtic and Saxon: Studies in the Early British Border* (Cambridge: Cambridge Univ. Press, 1964), 118.

54. James, *Trinity*, 2:210–11. The twenty shillings was the price paid by Robert either for the book secondhand or to have it written.

55. See Paul Chandler, "Philippe Ribot," *Dictionnaire de Spiritualité Ascétique et Mystique*, vol. 13 (Paris: Beauchesne, 1987), 537–39.

56. BIHR Reg. Zouche 10, fols. 9v, 11, 13, 13v, and 28o. Emden, *A Survey of Dominicans in England*, 226, lists Robert de Popultoun's ordination to acolyte, though he was not a Dominican, but does not mention his subsequent ordinations at Thirsk, Ripon, and York. On ages at ordination in England, see Peter Heath, *The English Parish Clergy on the Eve of the Reformation* (London: Routledge and Kegan Paul, 1969), 15.

57. Fols. 52, 54v, 55, 55v. This catalogue has recently been published by Humphreys, ed., *The Friars' Libraries*, with a facsimile of the first page, pp. 168, 171, 172–73, 174 and pl. 5. Humphreys' work, which replaces that of earlier scholars, offers on p. 160 the date of 1366 for the catalogue. See also G. R. C. Davis, *Medieval Cartularies of Great Britain* (London: Longmans, Green, 1958), no. 11, p. 3; W. H. St. John Hope, "On the Whitefriars or Carmelites of Hulne, Northumberland," *ArcJ* 47 (1890): 116–17; W. Dickson, "Contents of the Cartulary of Hulne Abbey," *AA*, 1st ser., 3 (1844): 46–47; George Tate, *The History of the Borough, Castle and Barony of Alnwick* (Alnwick: H.H. Blair, 1867–1869), 2:49, 51–53; and Charles Henry Hartshorne, *Feudal and Military Antiquities of Northumberland and the Scottish Borders* (London: Bell and Daldy, 1858), appendix, cii.

58. Hartshorne, *Feudal and Military Antiquities*, 268 and appendix, xcv. See John M. W. Bean, "The Percies' Acquisition of Alnwick," *AA*, 4th ser., 32 (1954): 318–19.

59. The convent is discussed briefly by Colin Platt, *The Abbeys and Priories of Medieval England* (London: Secker and Warburg, 1984), 189, with good aerial photographs of the ruins, figs. 134 and 135, and pp. 192–93. Another photograph is given in David Knowles and J.K.S. St. Joseph, *Monastic Sites from the Air* (Cambridge: Cambridge Univ. Press, 1952), 256–57. See also Knowles and Hadcock, *Medieval Religious Houses: England and Wales*, 197, and Keith J. Egan, O. Carm., "Medieval Carmelite Houses, England and Wales," *Carmelus* 16 (1969): 179–80, with excellent bibliography.

60. "On the WhiteFriars or Carmelites of Hulne," 107–13.

61. See Egan, "Medieval Carmelite Houses," 179 n.2.

62. See Samuel Lewis, *A Topographical Dictionary of England* (London: S. Lewis, 1831), 3:555.

63. See *RFCY*, 1: index, s.v. Poppleton.

64. See H. H. E. Craster and M. E. Thornton, eds., *The Chronicle of St. Mary's Abbey, York*, Surtees Society, vol.148, (York: Surtees Society, 1934), 3, 4, 78, and *VCH: York*, 3:112, 325.

65. See generally, Rotha Mary Clay, *The Medieval Hospitals of England* (London: Methuen, 1909).

66. *VCH: York*, 3:349, and A. Hamilton Thompson, "The Chapel of St. Mary and the Holy Angels, Otherwise Known as St. Sepulchre's Chapel, at York, pt. ii," *YAJ* 36 (1945): 226. Emden, *A Survey of Dominicans in England*, 230, records the ordination to acolyte of a Thomas de Popilton at York in 1363.

67. See *BRUO* 3:1500, and Thompson, "The Chapel," loc. cit.

68. See n. 56 above.

69. See n. 50 above.

70. See the study by Neil Hathaway, "Compilatio: from Plagiarism to Compiling," *Viator* 20 (1989): 19–44.

71. The last two "Cyrill" texts of MS lat. 4126 also appear with Maymet's name in Gonville and Caius College MS 388, James, *Gonville*, 8:449; and Cambridge, Corpus Christi College MS 404, James, *Corpus*, 2:274. The former is a collection of Joachistic material with *vaticinia* and drawings, the latter a miscellany not obviously mendicant and with only the last two itmes of a Joachistic character. On Maymet, see the brief, nearly contemporary, account of him offered by Johannes Trisse, published by Bartholomaeus Maria Xiberta, *De Scriptoribus Scholasticis Saeculi XIV ex Ordine Carmelitarum* (Louvain: Bureaux de la Revue, 1931), 33.

72. This map is discussed at some length in John B. Friedman, "Cultural Conflicts in Medieval World Maps," in Stuart Schwartz, ed., *Implicit Understandings: Observing, Reporting, and Reflecting on the Encounters between Europeans and Other Peoples in the Early Modern Era* (Cambridge: Cambridge Univ. Press, 1994), 64–95.

73. On this tradition, see John B. Friedman, *The Monstrous Races in Medieval Art and Thought* (Cambridge, Mass.: Harvard Univ. Press, 1981), 100–110.

74. See Katherine Walsh, *A Fourteenth-Century Scholar and Primate: Richard Fitz-Ralph in Oxford, Avignon and Armagh* (Oxford: Clarendon, 1981); Penn Szittya, *The Antifraternal Tradition in Medieval Literature* (Princeton, N.J.: Princeton Univ. Press, 1986) and Louis L. Hammerich, *The Beginning of the Strife between Richard FitzRalph and the Mendicants, with an Edition of his Autobiographical Prayer and his Proposition 'Unusquisque'* (Copenhagen: Levin and Munksgaard, 1938). For the texts of these bulls in a controversial setting, see Eliseus Monsignano, *Bullarium Carmelitanum* (Rome: G. Plachi, 1715), 97–99, and John Baptist Constant, *Bullarium Franciscanum* (Rome: Sacrae Congregationis, 1759), 305. "Inter cunctas" is printed by Constant, 11–14, but not by Monsignano, while "Super cathedram" occurs in Constant, 498, but not in Monsignano. "Vas electionis" is found in Constant, 208–9, and "Dilectis filiis" appears in both Constant, 305, and Monsignano, 98. See on the first three bulls, Szittya, 74, 80 n, and 298.

75. See J. S. P. Tatlock, "Geoffrey of Monmouth and the Date of *Regnum Scotorum*," *Speculum* 9 (1934): 135–39. The prophecy is published by William F. Skene, *Chronicles of the Picts and Chronicles of the Scots* (Edinburgh: H. M. General Register House, 1867), 117–18, and by Pinkerton, *An Enquiry*, 1:501–2.

76. These belong among the stock imagery of Merlin prophecies, drawn from Geoffrey of Monmouth's *Historia*, with the dragons referring to the Saxons and Britons, the leopard to the English royal arms, and the lillies to France. This material is discussed by Anderson, "Scottish Materials," 33–34; and Tatlock, "Geoffrey of Monmouth and the Date of *Regnum Scotorum*," 136–37. See, generally, on this work, Caroline D. Eckhardt, *The Prophetia Merlini of Geoffrey of Monmouth: A Fifteenth-Century English Commentary* (Cambridge, Mass.: Medieval Academy of America, 1982), and Rupert Taylor, *The Political Prophecy in England* (New York: Columbia Univ. Press, 1911). A set of marginal glosses in MS lat. 4126, deal with the *Prophetia Merlini*; as they were apparently added as an afterthought, I do not mention them as a separate item in the makeup of the codex.

77. This item is omitted in the list of contents published by Pinkerton.

78. See C. H. Talbot and E. A. Hammond, *The Medical Practitioners in Medieval England* (London: Wellcome Historical Medical Library, 1965), 326. Stephen witnessed a grant by Hugh to the Cistercians of Rivaulx. I am grateful to Linda Voigts for this reference.

79. See Aubrey Gwynn, ed., *The Writings of Bishop Patrick 1074–1084*, Scriptores

Latini Hiberniae, vol. 1 (Dublin: Dublin Institute for Advanced Studies, 1955), 56–58. Paris MS lat. 4126 is discussed briefly on p. 47.

80. See P. van de Woestijne, ed., *La Périégèse de Priscien* (Bruges: Rijksuniversiteit te Gent, 1953).

81. For recent discussion, see Peter Barber, "Visual Encyclopedias: The Hereford and other Mappae Mundi," *The Map Collector* 48 (1989): 2–8; Meryl Jancey, *Mappa Mundi: The Map of the World in Hereford Cathedral: A Brief Guide* (Hereford: Friends of Hereford Cathedral, 1987); and Peter Wiseman, "Julius Caesar and the Hereford World Map," *HT* 37 (1987): 53–57.

82. This material is adapted from Pliny, *Natural History*, book 5, chaps. 1–3.

83. This text is briefly discussed by Anderson, "Scottish Materials," 34, and the full text is printed by Anderson, *Kings and Kingship in Early Scotland*, 240–45.

84. These two texts are published by Pinkerton, *An Enquiry*, 1:490–97.

85. This text is published by Pinkerton, op. cit., 498–500.

86. See Joseph R. Jones and John E. Keller, eds. and trans., *The Scholar's Guide: A Translation of the Twelfth-Century Disciplina Clericalis of Pedro Alfonso* (Toronto: Pontifical Institute, 1969).

87. Ernst Sackur, ed., *Sibyllinische Texte und Forschungen* (Halle: M. Niemeyer, 1898).

88. Anderson, in both of her studies of the manuscript's contents, seems to have been unaware that its construction involved the joining of two books. She apparently ordered photographs of only a portion of the manuscript and so did not realize that much of the book is of thirteenth-century date, saying "the whole volume from 3 to 295 recto was apparently written at one time" ("Scottish Materials," 31). On Giraldus, see E. A. Williams, "A Bibliography of Giraldus Cambrensis," *NLWJ* 12 (1961): 97–140. For the Alexander material, see M. Feldbusch, ed., *Epistola Alexandri ad Aristotelem* (Meisenheim am Glam: Hain, 1976).

89. See Werner Eisenhut, ed., *Dictys Cretensis Ephemeridos Belli Troiani Libri* (Leipzig: Teubner 1973), and Ferdinand Meister, ed., *Daretis Phyrgii De Exidio Troiae Historia* (Leipzig: Teubner 1873). For the verse versions, see Ludwig Gompf, ed., *Werke und Briefe von Joseph Iscanus* (Leiden: Brill, 1970), and Jürgen Stohlmann, ed., *Anonymi Historia Troyana Daretis Frigii* (Düsseldorf: Henn, 1968). On these two writers, see Margaret J. Ehrhart, *The Judgment of the Trojan Prince Paris in Medieval Literature* (Philadelphia: Univ. of Pennsylvania Press, 1987), 31–32 and notes.

90. See John Taylor, *The Universal Chronicle of Ranulf Higden* (Oxford: Clarendon, 1966).

91. This material is discussed by Hammer, "Note on a Manuscript," 225.

92. See Acton Griscom, *The Historia Regum Britanniae of Geoffrey of Monmouth* (London: Longmans, Green, 1929); Hammer, "Note on a Manuscript," loc. cit.; Antonia Gransden, *Historical Writing in England c. 550 to c. 1307* (Ithaca, N.Y.: Cornell Univ. Press, 1974), 1:200–208; and more recently, Julia C. Crick, *The Historia Regum Britannie of Geoffrey of Monmouh*, vol. 4: *Dissemination and Reception in the Later Middle Ages* (Woodbridge, Suffolk: D. S. Brewer, 1991).

93. On Alfred, see Gransden, *Historical Writing in England*, 1: 186, 195, 212, and 249 n. On Henry, see Thomas Arnold, ed., *Henry of Huntingdon, Historia Anglorum*, (Rolls Series, no. 74; reprint, Millwood, N.Y.: Kraus, 1964).

94. On John of London or John Beverus, the author of a Lamentation on the Death of Edward I, see Beryl Smalley, *English Friars and Antiquity in the Early Fourteenth Century* (Oxford: Blackwell, 1960), 11–12; Gransden, *Historical Writing in England*,

1:459–60 and notes, and 2:17 n. 83, and her "The Continuations of the *Flores Histori-arum* from 1265 to 1327," *MS* 36 (1974): 472–80. Hammer, "Note on a Manuscript," 231–34, also mentions John Beverus, and quotes some of the classicizing tags used as glosses by Popultoun. A John Beverus also commissioned London, British Library MS Royal 2.F.vii for St. Albans; presumably he is the same person as John of London. The *Chronica* of John Beverus is Lambeth Palace MS 419 (James, *Lambeth Palace*, 4:577–79).

95. On Hildegarde's "Letter to the Clergy of Cologne," *PL* 197, 244–53, see Kathryn Kerby-Fulton, "Hildegard of Bingen and Anti-Mendicant Propaganda," *Traditio* 43 (1987): 391–93. See the edition of the *Oraculum Cyrilli* by P. Piur in Konrad Burdach, *Vom Mittelalter zur Reformation*, part. 2 iv (Berlin: Weidmann, 1912), appendix 241–327; Marjorie Reeves, *The Influence of Prophecy in the Later Middle Ages, A Study in Joachimism* (Oxford: Clarendon, 1969), 57 and Appendix A, 522–23; and Jeanne Bignami-Odier, *Études sur Jean de Roquetaillade (Johannes de Rupescissa)* (Paris: J. Vrin, 1952), 53–112.

96. On Lacy, see most recently, Doyle, "The English Provincial Book Trade," 22–23; Ann K. Warren, *Anchorites and Their Patrons in Medieval England* (Berkeley: Univ. of California Press, 1985), 24, 69, 252, 259; and in fuller detail, Rotha Mary Clay, "Further Studies on Medieval Recluses," *JBAA*, 3d ser., 16 (1953): 75–78, and "Some Northern Anchorites," *AA*, 4th ser., 33 (1955): 210–12. Conrad Pepler's study, "John Lacy: A Dominican Contemplative," *LS* 5 (1951): 397–400, is brief but helpful. On recluses generally, see Francis D. Darwin, *The English Mediaeval Recluse* (London: Society for the Promotion of Christian Knowledge, 1944), and W.J. Sheils, ed., *Monks, Hermits and the Ascetic Tradition* (Oxford: Blackwell, 1985).

97. See Emden, *A Survey of Dominicans in England*, 76. From his arms, Lacy was probably a member of the Pontefract branch of the famous family of that name. See W. E. Wightman, *The Lacy Family in England and Normandy, 1066–1194* (Oxford: Clarendon, 1966), 17–86.

98. See *RTL* 3:165. Thornton does not actually name Lacy but refers to the "recluse of Newcastell."

99. See Hughes, *Pastors and Visionaries*,12. An excellent account of this sort of relation between wealthy citizens of York and the mendicant orders there is given by Barrie Dobson, "Mendicant Ideal and Practice in Late Medieval York," in P. V. Addyman and V. E. Black, eds., *Archaeological Papers from York Presented to M. W. Barley* (York: York Archaeological Trust, 1984), 109–22. Friars also served as executors of bourgeois wills. See a case of 1400 relating to the Austin friars of York cited in W.P. Baildon, "Notes on the Religious and Secular Houses of Yorkshire," *YASRS*, 81 (1931): 94.

100. See on this subject generally, Conrad Lindberg, "The Manuscripts and Versions of the Wycliffite Bible: A Preliminary Survey," *SN* 42 (1970): 333–47.

101. See Andrew Watson, *The Manuscripts of Henry Savile of Banke* (London: The Bibliographical Society, 1969), 30, and A. I. Doyle and George B. Pace, "Further Texts of Chaucer's Minor Poems," *SB* 28 (1975): 43. I owe this latter reference to Kathleen Scott. The Thomas Chaworth mentioned in chap. 1 leaves an "Englisshe boke called Grace de Dieu," but the issue is complicated by the fact that there was a Middle English devotional work—of Yorkshire origins—called the Holy Book of Grace Dieu, so that it is not certain precisely what such references mean. Turville-Petre, "Some Medieval English manuscripts," 133, seems certain that the work referred to by Chaworth is the prose translation of Deguileville. See on this subject, Keiser, "þe Holy Boke Gratia Dei," 289–93.

102. See on this manuscript, Deanesly, "Vernacular Books in England," 357, and Clay, "Further Studies," 77. The contents of the manuscript are briefly described by James Finch Royster, "A Middle English Treatise on the Ten Commandments," *SP* 6 (1910): 6–7. See more recently, Anne Hudson, "A New Look at the Lay Folks' Catechism," *Viator* 16 (1985): 243–58. See also Henry O. Coxe, *Catalogus Codicum Manuscriptorum qui in Collegiis Aulisque Oxoniensibus Hodie Adservantur* (Oxford: Clarendon, 1852), vol. 2, St. John Baptist's College, item, no. 94, pp. 26–27; and *IMOC*, item 418, p. 42.

103. See A. E. Smailes, *North England* (London: Nelson, 1968): 109–126 and Maurice Beresford, *New Towns of the Middle Ages* (London: Lutterworth Press, 1967), 430–32 as well as Russell, *British Medieval Population*, 145. A good ecclesiastical map of the county of Durham and its deaneries appears in *VCH: Durham*, 2:76.

104. Dobson, *Durham Priory, 1400–1450*, 140–141, and Doyle, "The English Provincial Book Trade before Printing," 22.

105. See R. A. Lomas," A Northern Farm at the end of the Middle Ages: Elvethall Manor, Durham 1443/44–1513/14," *NH* 18 (1982): 26–53. For good maps and views of the area, see R. Neville Hadcock, "A Map of Mediaeval Northumberland and Durham," *AA* 4th ser., 16 (1939): 148–218, pls. 23 and 24, facing p. 218; and Norman McCord, ed., *Durham History from the Air* (Newcastle-on-Tyne: Graham, 1971), 30–31, pls. 23a and 23b.

106. See Gaillard T. Lapsley, *The County Palatine of Durham*, Harvard Historical Studies, 8 (New York: Longmans, Green, 1900).

107. See Botfield, ed., *Catalogi Veteres*, 48–49, 112–13. Durham Cathedral MS B.IV.3, Ps.-Chrysostom, *Opus Imperfectum in Mattheum* and other works, was also given by Doncaster. Botfield says that MS C.IV.21 may be Doncaster's book (p. li), but as Bentlay signed this table, this seems unlikely. See on Doncaster, *BRUO* 1:585, and Dobson, *Durham Priory, 1400–1450*, 134–35, 139–40, and for men very like Doncaster in York, David Dasef, "The Lawyers of the York Curia, 1400–1435" (M.A. thesis, University of York, 1977).

108. Dobson, *Durham Priory, 1400–1450*, 140–41.

109. See, for Durham documentation on Bentlay, the letter books of the Prior and Chapter, Durham Dean and Chapter Muniments Registrum Parvum II, fol. 52v, 183v–184, 194. I am grateful to Alan J. Piper for this information. Some useful analogies may be drawn between the idea that notaries copied books in Durham and the more documented examples of this practice in Scotland. See here R. J. Lyall, "Books and Book Owners in Fifteenth-Century Scotland," in *BPPB*, 244–46 for examples. See generally on notaries, C. R. Cheney, *Notaries Public in England in the Thirteenth and Fourteenth Centuries* (Oxford: Clarendon, 1972) and his "Notaries Public in Italy and England in the Late Middle Ages," *SS* 92 (1980): 173–88.

110. For a good working account of this very complex and sometimes baffling collection, see W. A. Pantin, *Report on the Muniments of the Dean and Chapter of Durham* (n.p., 1939) and for *Specialia*, 11, 16, and J. Conway-Davies, "The Muniments of the Dean and Chapter of Durham," *DUJ* 44 (1951–52): 77–87.

111. H. Fishwick, *The History of the Parish of Lytham in the County of Lancaster*, Chetham Society, vol. 60 (Manchester: Chetham Society, 1974), 65–93. This person is listed as a monk of Durham (*RTL*, 1:68), as cellarer in 1416, (*RTL*, 2:118), and as the *socius* of the *feretrarius* John Durham in 1418. See James Raine, *Saint Cuthbert* (Durham: G. Andrews, 1828), 114.

112. See *MLGB*, Watson, 86. The signature "Ric Bell" contains a dot over the *c*,

suggesting a contraction of Richard, but the *R* does not have an angled leg but rather a horizontal tie to the *i*. On Bell, see Barrie Dobson, "Richard Bell, Prior of Durham (1464–1478) and Bishop of Carlisle (1478–1495)," *TCWAAS*, n.s., 65 (1965): 182–221.

113. On Masham, see *MLGB*, Watson, 94. Doyle notes that Masham may have obtained some of the indices which form MS B.IV.43 when he was at Durham College Oxford in the 1390s ("Book Production," 8–9).

114. "Book Production," 9. Stapeley is mentioned in the list of monks present at the election of Wessington in 1416 (*RTL*, 2:117).

115. Discussed by Margaret Deanesly, ed., *The Incendium Amoris of Richard Rolle of Hampole* (reprint, Folcroft, Pa.: Folcroft Library Edition, 1974), 31.

116. On Seton, see *BRUO*, 3:1671–72, and Doyle, "Book Production," 9.

117. For Emylton, see *BRUO*, 1:642, and as the *socius* of the *feretrarii* John Burnby and Richard Kellow in 1439, see Raine, *Saint Cuthbert*, 115. A miscellany he copied, now Cambridge, Fitzwilliam Museum MS McClean 169 is remarkably various. It contains the pseudo-Boethian *De Disciplina Scolarum* with Trivet's commentary, Boethius' *De Natura dei, De Trinitate, Contra Eutychen, De Fide,* and *De Ebdomadibus;* Clement's *De Fide,* Plato's *Timaeus,* with Chalcidius' commentary; the commentary of "Trismegistus" on Asclepius; Cicero, *Tusculan Disputations;* Apuleius' *De Deo Socratis;* Isaac on Urines; Alpharabius' *De Divisione Scientiarum;* Grosseteste's *De Ortu Philosophorum;* the Sybilline Prophecies; Bradwardine on Artificial Memory; Campanus' Geometry, the Practice of Geometry, and Philosophical Propositions; Selections from Ralph of Diceto; and the *Mythologia* of Fulgentius. See on this manuscript, James, *McClean*, 323–27. He also copied Cambridge, Jesus College MS 70, containing William of Conches' commentary on Boethius' *Consolation of Philosophy;* a tract on the *metra* of the *Consolation;* Ambrose, *De Bono Mortis;* Pseudo-Hugh of St. Victor on Virtues and Vices, and another tract on conscience; Seneca's *De Remediis Fortunae;* Ovid's *De Vetula,* with Emylton's own annotations; and some tracts on Ovid. On this manuscript, see James, *Jesus*, 106–108. York Minster Library MS XVI.I.1 is fully described in *MMBL*, Piper, 706–709. Doyle, "Book Production," 9–10, discusses Emylton and reproduces specimens of his hand in figs. 4–5. Another plain script in this group is that of Robert Moreby, monk of Durham 1410–1447, Bachelor of Theology by 1425 and Master of Wearmouth by 1430, who was a Yorkshireman, to judge by his name. He copied folios 1–104v of MS B.IV.42. See *MLGB*, Watson, 95; Dobson, *Durham Priory, 1400–1450,* 354, and *VCH: Durham,* 2:85.

118. Raine, *Saint Cuthbert,* in describing an initial in Durham Cathedral MS A.I.3 showing Cuthbert being prayed to by a Benedictine monk, claims that this scene depicts "Stiphel the writer . . . uttering the following unscriptural prayer 'Confessor vere, Cuthberte mei miserere' " (131) but gives no evidence to support his suggestion. Watson, *London,* lists du Stiphel in the index, vol. 1:179, as O.S.B., also without evidence. In his colophons, du Stiphel does not use the titles "Frater" or "Dominus," often associated with monastic scribes, and names himself in his books repeatedly and proudly. Though Emylton writes "deo gratias quod R. Emylton" at seven places in Cambridge, Jesus College MS 70, du Stiphel never uses such religious formulae in his books.

119. Doyle, "Book Production," 2, and "The English Provincial Book Trade," 22. On Finchale, see C. R. Peers, "Finchale Priory," *AA*, 4th ser., 4 (1927): 193–220, and Dobson, *Durham Priory, 1400–1450,* 310–11. A good view of the archaeological remains of Finchale can be found in McCord, ed., *Durham History from the Air,* 28 and pl. 22.

120. As nearly all the monks of Durham were local men and there is no evidence of any other Frenchman in the monastery during the period of interest to us, the presumption must be that du Stiphel was a foreign scribe, whose rather proud and elaborate way of identifying himself is unusual in an Englishman, for as the example of John Run (see below) indicates, Continental scribes much more frequently gave their names, religious affiliations, and dates of completing the work than did English ones. On the reasons why scribes of any nation signed their books, see the interesting discussion by Robinson, *Cambridge,* 1:10–12. Though it is possible that the scribe's reference to his country could mean Britain, this seems extremely unlikely for several reasons. If du Stiphel were English, writing in England, he would not be likely to mention the fact. So too, as R. J. Mitchell, "English Law Students at Bologna in the Fifteenth Century," *EHR* 51 (1936): 270, points out, though in Bolognese records, " 'Britannia' is used for both England and Brittany without discrimination . . . in nine cases out of ten Brittany is indicated." As we will see shortly, John Run, another French scribe, gives his "nation" in France as "Britannia," and finally, Brittany provides several place names offering excellent matches for the scribe's quite un-English name.

121. Durham, Dean and Chapter Muniments Cart. I, fol. 58v, written in a cursive *Anglicana.* See Doyle, "Book Production," 8. The cartulary is of fifteenth-century date (Pantin, *Report on the Muniments,* 11–12).

122. "Book Production," 8.

123. Émile Ernault, *Glossaire Moyen-Breton (1895–96; reprint,* Marseille: Lafitte, 1976), 655. See also Grégoire de Rostrenen, *Dictionnaire Français-Celtique, ou français-Breton* (Guingamp, France, 1834); J. F. M. M. A. Le Gonidec, *Dictionnaire Breton-français* (Saint Brieuc, France: L Prudhomme, 1850); François Vallée, *Grand Dictionnaire Français-Breton* (Saint Brieuc: Les Presses Bretonnes, 1980). See also Bernard Tanguy, *Les noms de lieux Bretons I. Toponymie descriptive* (Rennes: CRDP, 1975), 94.

124. Watson, *London,* 99. See L. Rosenzweig, *Dictionnaire topographique du département du Morbihan* (Paris: Imprimerie Nationale, 1870). See also Stivel, at Lannilis in Finistère, mentioned by Tanguy, *Les noms de lieux bretons,* 94. Somewhat farther from the spelling of the scribe's name is Stiffelou, in the commune of Lambézellec, Finistère, which had 77 inhabitants in 1894. See Paul Joanne, *Dictionnaire géographique et administratif de la France* (Paris: Rachette, 1905), 7: 4737.

125. See Hervé Martin, *Les Ordres mendiants en Bretagne (vers 1230–vers 1530)* (Paris: C. Klineksieck, 1975); and Richard W. Emery, *The Friars in Medieval France, A Catalogue of French Mendicant Convents 1200–1550* (New York: Columbia Univ. Press, 1962), 94, to which should be added Adrian Staring, "Notes on a List of Carmelite Houses in Medieval France," *Carmelus* 11 (1964): 150–60. For a good historical overview, see Michael Jones, "L'Histoire du bas moyen âge breton (1200–1500)," *MSHAB* 56 (1979): 207–20, and for the possibilities of municipal and abbey schools, his "L'Enseignement en Bretagne à la fin du moyen âge: quelque terrains de recherche," *MSHAB* 53 (1975–76): 33–49, and a fuller English version, "Education in Brittany during the Later Middle Ages: A Survey," *NMS* 22 (1978): 58–77; he discusses clerics providing education at Vannes in the fourteenth century on p. 38 of the French version. For the diocese of Vannes and Stival in particular, see G. Duhem, *Les églises de France: Morbihan* (Paris: Librairie Letouzey et Ané, 1932), 150–51, 206–209.

126. See Michel de Mauny, *Le Pays de Léon* (Rennes: Armor, 1977), 219–20, and for the church and chapels there, R. Couffon and A. Le Bars, *Répertoire des églises et chapelles du diocèse de Quimper et de Léon* (Saint-Brieuc, France: Les Presses Bretonnes, 1959), 146–47.

127. For mendicant sites in Finistère, see Emery, *The Friars in Medieval France*. 56.
128. See J. Kerhervé, A–F. Peres, and B. Tanguy, eds., *Les Biens de la couronne dans la sénéchaussée de Brest et Saint-Renan* (Brest: Institut Culturel de Bretagne, 1984), 237. I am indebted to Michael Jones of the University of Nottingham for this reference. The Guilers discussed by Conen de Saint-Luc, "Guilers," *BSAF* 43 (1916): 320–29, is the town rather than the parish.
129. Kerhervé et al., eds., *Les Biens de la couronne*, 168.
130. See Couffon and Le Bars, *Répertoire des églises et chapelles du diocèse de Quimper et de Léon*, 132, for a discussion of this church.
131. Kerhervé et al., eds., *Les Biens de la couronne*, fig. 28.
132. See M. Lamaré, ed., *Inventaire-sommaire des archives départementales antérieures à 1790: Côtes-du-Nord*, (Saint-Brieuc, France: Imprimerie et Librairie de Guyon, 1896), tôme second, première partie, série E, p. 85, liasse E.1747, côtes 1070–1097. For Plougras, see Joanne, *Dictionnaire* (1899), 5:3564.
133. See Michael Jones, *Ducal Brittany 1364–1399* (Oxford: Oxford Univ. Press, 1970), 143–71 and Appendixes C and D, and, more generally, Kenneth Fowler, "Les finances et la discipline dans les armées anglaises en France au XIVᶜ siècle," *CV* 4 (1966): 55–84.
134. Fols. 144 and 115. See Watson, *Oxford*, item 311, pp. 50–51 and item 361, p.58, and *Colophons*, 4: items 11287 and 11286, p. 476. See generally, A. Chédeville, "L'Immigration bretonne dans la royaume de France du XIᶜ début du XIVᶜ siècle," *AnBr* 81 (1974): 301–43, and Jones, "L'enseignement en Bretagne à la fin du moyen âge," 35, 39, 41 especially the tables at pp. 48–49. Jones notes that Bibliothèque Nationale MS lat. 8685 contains an advertisement for a writing master at Nantes, Robert de Turribus, offering courses lasting one or two months; he was active 1435–1465 (36 n. 11). He is discussed and facsimiles of his advertisement sheets published by S. H. Steinberg, "Medieval Writing-Masters," *The Library*, 4th ser., 22 (1941): 1–24. See, generally, on the teaching of writing at this period, Françoise Gasparri, "L'Enseignement de l'écriture à la fin du moyen âge: A propos du 'Tractatus in omnem modum scribendi,' ms.76 de l'abbaye de Kremsmünster," *ScrC* 3 (1979): 243–65. On private libraries in late medieval Brittany, see A. de la Borderie, "Notes sur les livres et les bibliothèques au Moyen Âge en Bretagne," *BEC* 23 (1862): 39–53. On a workshop near Nantes that must have offered opportunities for scribal employment and even training, see Eberhard König, "Un atelier d'enluminure à Nantes et l'art du temps de Fouquet," *RA* 35 (1977): 64–75.
135. *RFCY*, 1:78, 88, 105, 168.
136. For Jobur's career, see *RTL*, 1:xxii–xxiii, which does not, however, indicate his actual birthplace. Jobur was one of Langley's four most favored scribes or registrars, Thomas Lyes, Robert Berall, and Lawrence Stafford. Whether these men also wrote books, for Langley or for others, is unknown.
137. See Adrian Wilson and Joyce Lancaster Wilson, *A Medieval Mirror: Speculum Humanae Salvationis 1324–1500* (Berkeley: Univ. of California Press, 1984), 49–85.
138. Pantin, *Report on the Muniments*, 5, 18–20, and J. Conway-Davies, "The Muniments of the Dean and Chapter, 85–86.
139. For cusping of ascenders, otiose hairlines, and double hairlines on the abbreviation of *et*, we might compare the Sherborne Missal, written about 1400–1406 by a Dominican scribe, John Was or Whas. See Richard Marks and Nigel Morgan, *The Golden Age of English Manuscript Painting, 1200–1500* (New York: Harvey Miller, 1981) p. 94. The closest example of script offered by Watson, *London*, at all similar to du

Stiphel's in its forking of the tops of ascenders is that of British Library MS Add. 17440, a missal written in Belgium in 1483, vol. 1:51; vol. 2: pl. 834.

140. Prior John Wessington's very brief life of Uthred in British Library MS Add. 6162, fol. 31v, is only a list of dates and places; an unsigned transcription has been published as "A Mediaeval Biography," in *BullIHR* 3 (1925–26): 46. See also R. B. Hepple, "Uthred of Boldon," *AA*, 3d ser., 17 (1920): 153–68, which has generally been superceded by *BRUO*, 1:212–13; David Knowles, *Saints and Scholars* (Cambridge: Cambridge Univ. Press, 1962), 134–41; and Dobson, *Durham Priory, 1400–1450*, 345–46.

141. See *CEPR*, 4:125, 127. For Bretons at Avignon at about this period, see Jacques Verger, "Le recrutement géographique des universités françaises au début du XVᵉ siècle d'après les *Suppliques* de 1403," *MAHEFR* 82 (1970): 879. I have not found a record of du Stiphel in Karl H. Shäfer, *Die Ausgaben der apostolischen Kammer unter Johann XXII Nebst den Jahresbilanzen von 1316–1375*, Vatikanische Quellen zur Geschichte der päpstlichen Hof-und Finanzverwaltung (Paderborn: F. Schoningh, 1911), vol. 2; or *Die Ausgaben unter Benedikt XII., Klemens VI., und Innocenz VI.* (Paderborn: F. Schoningh, 1914) vol. 3; or Ludwig Mohler, ed., *Die Einnahmen der apostolichen Kammer . . .*(Paderborn: F. Schoningh, 1931), vol. 5. Another, though also undocumented possibility, is that of an encounter with the scribe in Bruges in this period. See Edouard Perroy, "The Anglo-French Negotiations at Bruges 1374–77," *CM* 19, Camden Society, 3rd ser., 80 (1952): v–xix.

142. See James Raine, ed., *The Priory of Finchale, The Charters of Endowment, Inventories, and Account Rolls of the Priory of Finchale*, Surtees Society, vol. 6 (Durham: Surtees Society, 1837). The accounts for the Uthred de Boldon period occur on pp. xcvi–cxix. Raine briefly mentions du Stiphel on p. xxiii.

143. Doyle, "Book Production," 1.

144. See Watson, *London*, 1:99, no. 511, and 2: no. 270.

145. Hepple implies erroneously in "Uthred de Boldon," 166 that this book is actually two volumes, one of Bede and one of Eusebius. The volume contains ten different items: the *Historia* of Eusebius, to fol. 147; *Historia Ecclesiastica*, to fol. 179; Bede, *Historia Ecclesiastica*, to fol. 315; Nennius, *Eulogium Brittonum Insule*, to fol. 316; Nennius, *Historia Brittonum* on the same page; his *Miribilibus Brittonum Insule* to fol. 328; a *Vita Gildae* to fol. 330, followed by a *Vita Bedae*, and fragments of letters of Sergius and Abbot Ceolfrid to fol. 342, and then lives of various saints, such as Benedict and Ceolfrid, to the end.

146. For a fuller, computer-assisted analysis of du Stiphel's script, see John B. Friedman, "Cluster Analysis and the Manuscript Chronology of William du Stiphel, a Fourteenth-Century Scribe at Durham," in *History and Computing* 4 (1992): 14–38. See the comparison of the arch tracery in early and late Gothic windows to Gothic script and *lettre bourguignonne* made by the great French palaeographer Robert Marichal, "l'Ecriture Latine et la civilisation occidentale du 1ᵉʳ au XVIᵉ siècle," in Marcel Cohen and Jean Sainte Fare Garnot, eds., *L'Écriture et la psychologie des peuples* (Paris: Armand Colin, 1963), 233–42, and figs. 38 and 43. Elements of this comparison have recently been criticized by Michael Camille, "The Book of Signs: Writing and Visual Difference in Gothic Manuscript Illumination," *WI* 1 (1985): 137.

147. For older discussion, see Raine, *The Priory of Finchale*, xxiii, Raine, *Saint Cuthbert*, 131–32 and Botfield, ed., *Catalogi Veteres*, 192, who both follow Thomas Rud, *Codicum Manuscriptorum Ecclesiae Cathedralis Dunelmensis Catalogus Classicus*, ed. J. Raine (Durham: G. Andrews, 1825) in giving the name as "Willielmi Blaklaw." See also Dobson, *Durham Priory, 1400–1450*, 377.

148. For the background of this story, see David Hugh Farmer, *The Oxford Diction-ary of the Saints* (Oxford: Clarendon, 1978), 304–305, and more fully, Robert Folz, "St. Oswald roi de Northumbrie, étude d'hagiographie royale," *AnB* 98 (1980): 49–74. A good recent collection is Gerald Bonner et al., eds., *St. Cuthbert: His Cult and his Commu-nity to AD 1200* (Woodbridge, Suffolk, and Wolfeboro, N.H.: Boydell Press, 1989). For the font, see Barbara Palmer, *The Early Art of the West Riding of Yorkshire* (Kalamazoo, Mich.: Medieval Institute, 1990), 199. The image without kneeling figure also appears on the exterior of the west tower of Fishlake church. In the Bolton *horae*, York Minster Library MS Add. 2, the suffrage for St. Cuthbert presents the saint holding Oswald's head outstretched towards the viewer in his hand rather than in the crook of the arm (fol. 40v).

149. MS A.I.3 has been noted as an example of the "trellis" style of border by Kathleen Scott, "Design, Decoration, and Illustration," in *BPPB*, 50 and n. 108. For a description of Lambeth Palace MS 23, see James, *Lambeth Palace*, 1:37–39. On the general similiarity of the miniature to that in Lambeth Palace MS 23, see Doyle, "Book Production," 18 n. 45.

150. See generally, *GM*, 2: no. 125, pp. 138–40; and *IMBL*, 3: no.739, p. 66. The book is also discussed by Raine, *Saint Cuthbert*, 131–32.

151. See A. J. Piper, "The Libraries of the Monks of Durham," in M. B. Parkes and Andrew G. Watson, eds., *Medieval Scribes, Manuscripts, and Libraries: Essays Presented to N. R. Ker* (London: Scolar, 1978), 244–48. A good study of Durham college is that of Herbert E. D. Blakiston, "Some Durham College Rolls," *Collectanea* 3, vol. 32 (Ox-ford: Oxford Historical Society, 1896), 1–76, and more recently, Dobson, *Durham Priory, 1400–1450*, 343–59.

152. J. T. Fowler, ed., *Extracts from the Account Rolls of the Abbey of Durham*, Surtees Society, vol. 99 (Durham: Surtees Society, 1898), 131.

153. Raine, *St. Cuthbert*, 132.

154. Fowler, *Extracts*, 132.

155. Doyle, "Book Production," 18 n. 45.

156. See James, *Trinity*, 1:494–96, and F. Broomfield, ed., Thomas of Chobam, *Summa Confessorum*, Analecta Mediaevalia Namurcensia 25 (Louvain: Éditions Nauwe-laerts, 1968).

157. James does not note that du Stiphel's hand appears extensively in the Chob-ham section of the codex.

158. This is Ian Doyle's description of them in a letter to me of 16 Oct. 1990.

159. A discussion of the *"plenus amoris"* question appears in W. D. Macray, *Annals of the Bodleian Library, Oxford* (1890; reprint, Oxford: Clarendon, 1984), 21 n. 1, who believes that "Plenus-Amoris or Fullaflove, seems to have been the name of a family of scribes. But the expression seems often also to have been used for the mere sake of rhyme." Thomas Heffernan, "The Use of the Phrase *Plenus Amoris* in Scribal Colo-phons," *N&Q*, 226 (Dec. 1981): 493–94, suggests that the "phrase is more likely a rhetorical tag than a name."

160. As I do not believe that the known English *plenus amoris* (PA) scribes have ever been listed in one place, it may be worth doing so here to show the wide popularity of the epithet or name, extending, in the case of Thomas Olston, to 1521. I am indebted to Kathleen Scott for bringing some of these scribes to my attention. In addition to the ones mentioned in the text, the examples known to me are: Cambridge University Library MS Ff.1.6, Nicholaus PA, fol. 67v; MS Gg.1.6, Willelmus PA, fol. 2; MS Gg.1.34, John Fermore PA, fol. 109v; MS Kk.1.6, Walterus PA, fol. 179v; Cam-bridge, Trinity College MS B.11.24, Johannes PA, fol. 96r; MS O.1.57, William PA,

fol. 125r; Cambridge, Gonville and and Caius College MS 128/166, Richard PA, p. 386; Gonville and Caius College MS 383/603, Johannes PA, fol. 119; Gonville and Caius College MS 417/447, Willemus Berdon PA, fol. 90; Cambridge, Jesus College MS 29, Thomas PA, fol. 64; Cambridge, St. John's College MS 147, Iohannes PA, fol. 119; MS 137, Richardus PA, fol. 113v; Cambridge, Peterhouse MS 177, Willelmus PA, fol. 191; Glasgow Hunterian Museum MS T. 4.1, Ricardus Frampton PA, fol. 126; Holkham Hall MS 668, Johannes PA, fol. 159v; London, British Library MS Royal VII. F.11, Johannes PA, fol. 121; MS Sloane 513, Galfridus PA, fol. 155; MS Stowe 16, Ricardus Wanton PA, fol. 2r; London, Westminster Abbey MS 26, Christo PA, fol. 128r; MS 27, Thomas PA, fol. 1r; Manchester, John Rylands University Library MS 176, John Freryng PA, fol. 194; Minneapolis, University of Minnesota Library MS Z 822 N81, fol. 185r, Richardus PA; Oxford, Bodleian Library MS Add. A.106, John Charke PA, fol. 267; MS Bodley 264, Thomas Smyth PA, fol. 215v; MS Bodley 643, John Esteby PA, fol. 134; MS Bodley 493, Robertus PA, fol. 55v; MS Digby 77, John PA, art. 1 and 2, fol. 56v; MS Fairfax 6, Petrus PA, fol. 159v; MS Hatton 19, Thomas Doule PA, fol. 94v; MS Rawlinson B.214, Jhon Wilde PA, fol. 233r; MS Rawlinson Liturgies g.12, Thomas Olston PA, fol. 295; MS Rawlinson Poet. 137, Tilot PA, fol. 41; All Souls College MS 51, Guilelmus PA, fol. 279; Oxford, University College MS 142, Thomas PA, fol. 121; and Rome, Vatican Library MS Ottoboniani Lat. 116, John Wenaston PA, fol. 170v. This last scribe is mentioned by Charles Samaran and André Vernet in "Les Livres de Thomas Basin (1412–1490)," in Guy Cambier, ed. *Hommages à André Boutemy* (Brussels: Collections Latomus 145, 1976), 331 n. 12. I am grateful to Charles J. Ermatinger of St. Louis University for bringing this reference to my attention.

161. See Jan Jönsjö, *Studies on Middle English Nicknames I. Compounds*, Lund Studies in English, 55 (Lund: Liber Laromedel/C.W.K. Gleerup, 1979), s.v. Fuloflove, Playndamurs. P. H. Reaney, *A Dictionary of British Surnames* (London: Routledge and Kegan Paul, 1977), p. 127, and C. M. Matthews, *English Surnames* (New York: Scribner, 1967), mention Emma, Richard, and Matilda Pleindamurs in Lancashire, 28–29, 154–55. See also Gustav Fransson, *Middle English Surnames of Occupation 1100–1350*, Lund Studies in English 3 (Lund: C.W.K. Gleerup, 1935). For Alfred Fullalove, see Richard Beaumont, *Purdey's: The Guns and the Family* (North Pomfret, Vt.: David and Charles, 1984), 132.

162. See for Richard, the assize rolls for Lancashire, *Lancaster Records Society* 47, 49 (1904–1905), and for William, J. P. Steel, ed., *Subsidy: Being the Account of a Fifteenth and Tenth Collected 6th Edward III* (Kendal: T. Wilson, 1912). See generally G. L. Harris, *King, Parliament and Public Finance in Medieval England to 1369* (Oxford: Clarendon, 1975)

163. Muniments of Magdalene College, Oxford, Spitlings, nos. 27 and 106.

164. For John and Ralph, see M. A. Farrow, *Index of Wills Proved in the Consistory Court of Norwich 1370–1550*, 1, (London: Norfolk Record Society, 1943–1945), 160.

165. Folio 280v. *Sotheby's Auction Catalogue, Tuesday, 25th March, 1975*, item 2956, pp. 56–59. Both of Gower's "Johannes plenus amoris" books have been mentioned by Cavanaugh, "A Study of Books Privately Owned in England," 368–70.

166. See typescript " 'Rough Register' of Acquisitions of the Department of Manuscripts, British Library 1976–1980," 31, and Margaret Annie Eugenie Nickson, *The British Library, Guide to the Catalogues and Indexes of the Department of Manuscripts* (London: The British Library Board, 1982).

167. *Colophons* 3:125–26.

168. SC 3886.

169. Botfield, ed., *Catalogi Veteres,* item viii, p. 122.

170. Chantilly, Musée Condé MS 741 (738) "nomen scriptoris petrus plenus amoris," fol. 200. I am indebted to Kathleen Scott for this reference. See Samaran, *Catalogue de manuscrits datés,* 1:393, and *Colophons* 5:item 15250, p. 51.

171. Fol. 56v. See *Colophons,* 3: item 8428, p. 125.

172. See M. R. James, *Lists of Manuscripts Formerly Owned by Dr. John Dee* (Cambridge: Cambridge Univ. Press, 1921), 22, and A. G. Watson and R. J. Roberts, *John Dee's Library Catalogue* (London: Bibliographical Society, 1990). For a fifteenth-century catalogue of the library of this house, see Edward A. Bond, ed., *Chronica Monasterii de Melsa* III (Rolls Series, no. 43, 1886; reprint, Millwood, N.Y.: Kraus, 1967), appendix, lxxxiii–c.

173. See Powicke, *The Medieval Books of Merton College,* no. 1202, p. 231.

174. See chap. 1, n. 24.

175. William Wyke, *RTL,* 1:42–43; Geoffrey, *RTL,* 3:14.

176. *MMBL,* Piper, 770–771.

177. SC 29003.

178. See Richard Beadle and A. E. B. Owen, eds., *The Findern Manuscript: Cambridge University Library MS Ff.1.6* (London: Scolar Press, 1977), and more recently, Kate Harris, "The Origins and Make-up of Cambridge University Library MS Ff.1.6," *TCBS* 8, pt. 3 (1983), 303. Sarah McNamer, "Female Authors, Provincial Setting: The Re-Versing of Courtly Love in the Findern Manuscript," *Viator* 22 (1991): 278–310, does not mention Nicholas. It is possible that the scribe signing himself "Joly Jankyn plenus amoris," who appears to have copied the anonymous *Libel of English Policy* in the commonplace book of Thomas Wardon of Westmorland appendix 2, item 138, had a similar role as an estate servant. The colophon appears on fol. 50. I am grateful to Karen Mura for calling this scribe to my attention.

179. Nicholas is scribe 14, writing fol. 67v.

180. Ethel Seaton, *Sir Richard Roos c. 1410–1482 Lancastrian Poet* (London: Rupert Hart-Davis, 1961), 85, 152.

181. Beadle and Owen, eds., *The Findern Manuscript,* xvi, 19 n.

182. See *Colophons* 5: item 17157, p. 309, and for the Chantilly volume, Samaran, *Catalogue de manuscrits datés,* 1:390.

3. Color and the Archaizing Style

1. See Rudolf Suntrup, *"Te igitur*—Initialen und Kanonbilder in mittelalterlichen Sakramentarschriften," in Christel Meier and Uwe Ruberg, eds., *Text und Bild: Aspekte des Zusammen-wirkens Zweier Künste im Mittelalter und früher Neuzeit* (Wiesbaden: Reichert, 1980), 278–382, for the historical development of these pictures.

2. See, generally, for tastes in color during the Middle Ages, Gottfried Haupt, *Die Farbensymbolik in der sakralen Kunst des abendländischen Mittelalters* (Dresden: Dittert, 1941); and John Gage, "Colour in History: Relative and Absolute," *AH* 1 (1978): 104–30, esp. 109–12. Recent studies are Régine Pernoud, *Couleurs du moyen âge,* Images du Monde I (Geneva: Éditions Claire Fontaine, 1987), and Josef Riederer, "Pigment-untersuchung bei Buchmalereien," *Restaurator* 5 (1981): 151–55.

3. No single study treats this subject in detail, though there is some discussion in *EGM* (1) where the author notes that in the early Gothic period in England "in particular . . . purple is seldom used" (1:31–32), and in *GM,* 1:42, 45, and color plates. See

also François Avril, "La technique de l'enluminure d'après les textes médiévaux: essai de bibliographie," typescript, Réunion du Comité de l'Icom pour les laboratoires de Musées et de Sous-Comité de l'Icom pour le traitement des peintures, Paris, 1967. The bibliographies of early color treatises given in Charles Cailhol, "Sources bibliographiques pour l'étude des pigments utilisés en peinture jusqu'au XVᶜ siècle," *RSSHN: Histoire de l'Art* 20 (1960): 23–53, and S. M. Alexander, "Towards a History of Art Materials—A Survey of Published Technical Literature in the Arts: Part I From Antiquity to 1599," *Art and Archaeology Technical Abstracts Supplement* 7, no 3 (1969): 123–48 are also helpful. To be added to them are D. Bommarito, "Il ms 25 della Newberry Library: la tradizione dei ricettari e trattati sui colori nel Medioevo e Rinascimento veneto e toscano," *La Bibliofilia* 87 (1985): 1–38 and V. Trost," Tinte und Farben. Zum Erhaltungszustand der Manesseschen Liederhandschrift," in E. Mittler et al., eds. *Codex Manesse. Die Grosse Heidelburger Leiderhandschrift. Texte. Bilder. Sachen* (Heidelberg: Braus, 1988), 440–45. See more recently on pigments, Louisa J. V. Dunlop, "The Use of Colour in Parisian Manuscript Illumination c. 1320–1420 with Special Reference to the Availability of Pigments and their Commerce at that Period," unpublished diss., University of Manchester, 1988, which is more accessible as Louisa Dunlop, "Pigments and Painting Materials in Fourteenth- and Early Fifteenth-Century Parisian Manuscript Illumination," in Xavier Barral i Altet, ed., *Artistes, artisans et production artistique au moyen âge, 3: Fabrication et consomation de l'oeuvre* (Paris: Picard, 1990), 272–93. In spite of its promising title, pigments are not discussed in Doris H. Banks, *Medieval Manuscript Bookmaking: A Bibliographic Guide* (Metuchen, N.J.: Scarecrow Press, 1989). The most useful general study of the subject is J. J. G. Alexander, *Medieval Illuminators and their Methods of Work* (New Haven: Yale Univ. Press, 1992).

4. Amanda Simpson, *The Connections between English and Bohemian Painting during the Second Half of the Fourteenth Century* (New York: Garland, 1984), 184–86. See generally, Gervase Mathew, *The Court of Richard II* (London: John Murray, 1968). Margaret Rickert, *The Reconstructed Carmelite Missal* (London: Faber and Faber, 1952), 76–80, has spoken of the *Liber Regalis* as the work of Bohemian artists, but Nigel Morgan and Lucy Freeman Sandler, "Manuscript Illumination of the Thirteenth and Fourteenth Centuries," in Jonathan Alexander and Paul Binski, eds., *Age of Chivalry: Art in Plantagenet England 1200–1400* (London: Royal Academy of Arts, 1987), have suggested that there is no clear stylistic evidence of foreign illuminators working in England until the appearance of the so-called Dutch artist of the Carmelite Missal in 1395–1400 (156). In the same volume, J. J. G. Alexander speaks of a manuscript, Cambridge, Magdalene College, Pepys MS 1916, ca. 1370–1390, as having "stylistic links with Bohemian art" (402). See M. R. James, "An English Medieval Sketch-Book, No. 1916 in the Pepysian Library, Magdalene College, Cambridge," *WS* 13 (1924–1925): 1–17.

5. Michael Orr, "Bohemian Influences on English Manuscripts from around 1400," an unpublished paper presented at the 21st International Congress on Medieval Studies, Kalamazoo, Mich., May 9, 1986. On MS 13, see Judith Oliver, ed., *Manuscripts Sacred and Secular from the Collections of the Endowment for Biblical Research and Boston University* (Boston: Endowment for Biblical Research, 1985), item no. 86, pp. 50–52, and Rogers, "Fitzwilliam Museum MS 3–1979," 243. Praga's ordination is listed by Emden, *A Survey of Dominicans in England*, 239, who discusses the presence of Continental Dominicans in England on p. 25.

6. See R. A. Pelham, "Medieval Foreign Trade: Eastern Ports," in H. C. Darby, ed., *An Historical Geography of England before A. D. 1800* (1936; reprint, Cambridge: Cambridge Univ. Press, 1986), 324–27, who mentions English imports of litmus and madder coming from the Baltic, and M. M. Postan, "The Economic and Political

Relations of England and the Hanse (1400 to 1475)," in E. Power and M. M. Postan, eds., *Studies in English Trade in the Fifteenth Century* (1933; reprint, London: Routledge and Kegan Paul, 1966), 91–153. See generally, Johannes Schildhauer, *The Hansa: History and Culture*, trans. K. Vanovitch (n.p.: Dorset Press, 1988) and A. D'Haenens, *Europe of the North Sea and the Baltic: The World of the Hanse* (Antwerp: Fonds Mercator, 1984).

7. See, generally, on Bohemian International Gothic Style painting, Otto Kletzel, "Studien zur böhmischen Buchmalerei," *MJK* 7 (1933): 1–76; Antonin Matějcěk and Jaroslav Pěsina, *Czech Gothic Painting 1350–1450* (Prague: Melantrich, 1950); Albert Kutal, *Gothic Art in Bohemia and Moravia* (London: Hamlyn, 1972); Meta Harrsen, *Medieval and Renaissance Manuscripts in the Pierpont Morgan Library*, vol. 2, *Central European Manuscripts* (New York: Pierpont Morgan Library, 1958); Gerhardt Schmidt, "Malerei bis 1450: Tafelmalerei-Wandmalerei-Buchmalerei," in Karl M. Swoboda, ed., *Gotik in Böhmen* (Munich: Prestel-Verlag, 1969), 167–321; Erich Bachmann, ed., *Gothic Art in Bohemia: Architecture, Sculpture and Painting* (Oxford: Phaidon, 1977), updates Swoboda. For the idea that East Anglian painting influenced Bohemian artists, see Jan Květ, *Illuminované Rukopisy Královny Rejčky* (Prague: Céske Akademie ved a Uméni, 1931).

8. A good account of the development of Hungarian miniature painting is offered in Ilona Berkovits, *Illuminated Manuscripts in Hungary: XI–XVI Centuries*, trans. Zsuzsanna Horn (Shannon: Irish University Press, 1969), 25–62. On Italian influence, especially in the floral border motifs, see Mojmir Frinta, "The Master of the Gerona Martyrology and Bohemian Illumination," *AB* 46 (1964): 283–306, esp. 288–289.

9. Miniatures from this missal are published and briefly discussed by Alzbeta Güntherová, *Illuminierte handschriften aus der Slowakei* (Prague: Artia, 1962), item 9, pp. 20–21. The colors discussed here may be seen in the illustration of folio 11r in this volume. See also Berkovits, *Illuminated Manuscripts in Hungary*, 36. Similar combinations of green and *folium* occur in the borders to the missal of George Pálóczy, archbishop of Esztergom, National Library of Budapest, MS CLM 359, fol. 91, 1423–1439. This book is discussed by Berkovits, *Illuminated Manuscripts in Hungary*, 52–53.

10. See Josef Krása, *The Travels of Sir John Mandeville: A Manuscript in the British Library* (New York: Braziller, 1983). The best study of *terre-verte* is that of Carol A. Grissom, "Green Earth," in Robert L. Feller, ed., *Artists' Pigments: A Handbook of Their History and Characterization* (Washington, D. C.: National Gallery of Art, 1986), 141–67. Green, of course, was very common for grassy grounds in late Continental manuscripts such as the hunting book of Gaston Phoebus and the *Belles* and *Très Riches Heures* of Jean de Berry. English artists attempting a representational treatment of grass, on occasion, use it as well, as in the Litlyngton Missal, London, Westminster Abbey MS 37, made in 1383–1384, where it appears in the main Crucifixion scene and in small scenes such as the nailing to the cross. See on this manuscript *GM*, 2, no. 150, pp. 172–75, and Alexander and Binski, eds., *Age of Chivalry*, who offer a brief discussion and reproduction of the Litlyngton Missal canon page (518–19, figure 714). For a full set of recipes for the greens made from mineral earths, see Mary Philadelphia Merrifield, ed., *William of St. Omer, De Coloribus Faciendis*, in *Original Treatises Dating from the XII to XVIIIth Centuries on the Arts of Painting* (1849; reprint, New York: Dover, 1967), 1:116–27.

11. See Hermann Kühn, "Verdigris and Copper Resinate," *StC* 15 (1970): 12–36, and on the destructive character of the material, Gerhard Banik, "Discoloration of Green Copper Pigments in Manuscripts and Works of Graphic Art," *Restaurator* 10 (1989): 61–73.

12. For the process of making some of these vegetable greens, see Daniel Varney Thompson, Jr., and George Heard Hamilton, eds., *An Anonymous Fourteenth-Century Treatise De Arte Illuminandi* (New Haven: Yale Univ. Press, 1933), 6–7 and notes, 29, 43–44, as well as Thompson, "Artificial Vermillion in the Middle Ages," *Technical Studies in the Field of the Fine Arts* 2 (1933): 64–65; and *The Materials of Medieval Painting* (1936; reprint, New York: Dover, 1956), 170–73. The most recent study of these vegetable greens is that of Heinz Roosen-Runge, *Farbgebung und Technik frühmittelalterlicher Buchmalerei. Studien zu den Traktaten "Mappae Clavicula" und "Heraclius"* (Munich: Deutscher Verlag, 1967), 2:99–102, microphotographs 236–43. A late fourteenth-century English manuscript where this green is used in an expressionistic way is Oxford, Bodleian Library MS Rawlinson D.939. See on this manuscript John B. Friedman, "Harry the Haywarde and Talbat his Dog: An Illustrated Girdlebook from Worcestershire," in Carol Fisher and Kathleen Scott, eds., *Art into Life: Collected Papers from the Kresge Art Museum Medieval Symposia* (East Lansing, Mich.: Michigan State Univ. Press, 1995), 115–53.

13. Czechslovakia, Brno State Archive MS St. Jacob 8/10, folio 161r. For other examples, see the canon pages of the missals of Nicholas of Nissa, 1410–1415, Wroclaw Museum of Fine Arts Inv. 7564, fol. 141v; and R 165, workshop of John of Zittau, fol. 150v. See Ernst Kloss, *Die Schlesische Buchmalerei des Mittelalters* (Berlin: Deutscher Verein für Kunstwissenschaft, 1942), 108–38, 222. I am indebted to Dr. Stefan Kubow, director of the Wroclaw University Library, for information about the latter manuscript. A virtually identical picture, made by a Czech artist working in Austria, Nicholas of Brno, was published by H.P. Kraus, *Fifty Mediaeval and Renaissance Manuscripts, Catalogue 88* (New York: H.P.Kraus, n.d), no. 16, p. 39, a missal of the use of Passau, made about 1450; the page has a green border and ground and John's robe is all green with a blue lining while that of the Virgin is blue with a green one.

14. See Kloss, *Die Schlesische Buchmalerei*, 94–104, and Berkovits, *Illuminated Manuscripts in Hungary*, 40.

15. Missal, Budapest National Library CLM 220, fol. 144v, and Kremnica, City Archive, fol. 8. The first of these is published by Berkovits, *Illuminated Manuscripts in Hungary*, pl. 8, and the second discussed by her on p. 40.

16. See generally R. W. Pfaff, *New Liturgical Feasts in Later Medieval England* (Oxford: Clarendon, 1970).

17. See John F. Curwen, "The Castle Dairy, Kendal," *TCWAAS*, n.s., 16 (1916): 106–107; Archdale A. King, *Liturgies of the Past* (London: Longmans, Green, 1959), 326–47; and "A.J.C.","A Missal of the Use of York," *BMO* 7 (1932–1933): 107–109.

18. For a good study of this type of initial, see Stirnemann and Gousset, "Marques, mots, pratiques," 34–55.

19. Kathleen Scott, "Design, Decoration and Illustration," in *BPPB*, 48–49.

20. This manuscript has been fully described by Dutschke et al., *Guide to Medieval and Renaissance Manuscripts*, 1:337–39. She notes that "the borders [share] some similar stylistic features with London, Brit. Lib. Add. 43380" (339).

21. See Archdale A. King, *Liturgies of the Religious Orders* (London: Longmans, Green, 1955) 396–409, and R. M. Woolley, ed., *The Gilbertine Rite* (London: Henry Bradshaw Soc., 1921), 1:xi–xxxv.

22. See on such figures Kathleen Scott, "*Caveat Lector:* Ownership and Standardization in the Illustration of Fifteenth-Century English Manuscripts," *EMS* 1 (1989): 42–43, and n. 53.

23. See Alexander and Binski, eds., *Age of Chivalry*, who offer a brief discussion and reproduction of the Lapworth Missal (520–21, fig. 717).

24. See Dutschke et al., *Guide to Medieval and Renaissance Manuscripts*, 1:339.

25. See Roger S. Wieck, *Late Medieval and Renaissance Illuminated Manuscripts 1350–1525 in the Houghton Library* (Cambridge, Mass.: Harvard College Library, 1983), 137.

26. See Friedman, ed., *John de Foxton's Liber Cosmographiae*, xxv. To be added to the discussion there is Dublin, Trinity College MS 85, another northern book with a York kalendar, which has the "Aprilis flectit ab alto" verses at fol. 155. These are briefly mentioned in *TCD*, 1:153.

27. See SC 18341 and *BML*, vol. 1:111, item 321.

28. See Friedman, "Richard de Thorpe's Astronomical Kalendar," 137–60.

29. A well-known example in a good state of preservation occurs in Haddon Hall chapel, Derbyshire. See generally, H. C. Whaite, *St. Christopher in English Mediaeval Wallpainting* (London: University College, 1929); E.C. Stahl, *Die Legende vom heiligen Riesen Christophorus in der Graphik des 15. und 16. Jahrhunderts* (Munich: J.J. Lentner, 1920); John Salmon, "St. Christopher in English Medieval Art and Life," *JBAA*, n.s., 2 41 (1936): 76–115, and Douglas Gray, *Themes and Images in the Medieval Religious Lyric* (London: Routledge and Kegan Paul, 1972), 157–58, 279. For Christopher's height, see the poem on "The Height of Christ" in London, Lambeth Palace MS 306, in Frederick J. Furnivall, ed., *Political, Religious, and Love Poems*, EETS: o.s. 15 (Oxford: Oxford Univ. Press, 1965), 61.

30. See on this point Charles W. Clark, "The Zodiac Man in Medieval Medical Astrology," *JRMMRA* 3 (1982): 13–38; Harry Bober, "The Zodiacal Miniature of the *Très Riches Heures* of the Duke of Berry—Its Sources and Meaning," *JWCI* 11 (1948): 1–34; and O. Neugebauer, "Astronomical and Calendrical Data in the *Très Riches Heures*," in Millard Meiss, *The Limbourgs and their Contemporaries* (New York: Pierpont Morgan Library, 1974), 421–31. Natural history was also often incorporated in the margins of *horae* pages as well.

31. On such books, see Otto Glauning, "Der Buchbeutel in der Bildenden Kunst," *ABG* 63 (1926): 124–52, who prints on p. 125 a fifteenth-century woodcut showing a man wearing one at his belt; Lisl and Hugo Alker, *Das Beutelbuch in der bildenden Kunst. Ein beschreibendes Verzeichnis. Zusammengestellt von Lisl und Hugo Alker*, (Mainz: Gutenberg, 1966) and Supplement, *Gutenberg-Jahrbuch* (1978), 302–308; M.-C. Garand, "Livres de poche médiévaux à Dijon et à Rome," *Scriptorium* 25 (1971): 18–24; and Linda E. Voigts, "Scientific and Medical Books," in *BPPB*, 356, who gives some examples, fig. 37 and n. 40, and offers further discussion of the Pincus *horae* mentioned above. For a survey of recent bibliography, see J. A. Szirmai, "The Girdle-book of the Museum Meermanno-Westreenianum," *Quaerendo* 18 (1988): 18 n. 7. Other belt books of this type are Harvard, MS Houghton Typ. 287H; New York, Pierpont Morgan Library M. 941; and Oxford, Bodleian Library MS Douce 71.

32. Folio 5r. See K.V. Sinclair, *Medieval and Renaissance Treasures of the Ballerat Art Gallery, The Crouch Manuscripts* (Sydney: Wentworth, 1968), 36, pl. xii, and his *Descriptive Catalogue of the Medieval and Renaissance Western Manuscripts in Australia* (Sydney: Wentworth, 1969), 274–75. See also Margaret M. Manion and Vera F. Vines, *Medieval and Renaissance Illuminated Manuscripts in Australian Collections* (Sydney: Sydney Univ. Press, 1984), no. 44, pp. 109–110, pl. 27, and figs. 94–95. Another York manuscript with a pronounced use of green is Archbishop Thomas Rotherham's charter for Jesus College, Rotherham, Yorkshire, now Cambridge, Sidney Sussex College MS 2, which we shall consider more fully in chap. 6; green appears in the ground of the initial, the lining of the archbishop's cloak, the border decoration, and the coats of arms. Similarly, the Lacy *horae*, Oxford, St. John's College MS 94, which we discussed in chap. 2, uses

green frequently in the decoration. For example, a miniature on fol. 16v shows Lacy in his cell praying to the Virgin and John the Evangelist, who flank a now destroyed crucified Christ. The figures are placed on a green ground, and St. John wears the green robe we saw in the canon pages earlier. Even the Virgin's blue gown has a green lining. So too, green makes up one wall of Lacy's cell.

33. See Pfaff, *New Liturgical Feasts*, 2–3.

34. The book has been described and discussed in *MMBL*, Piper, 786–91. The possibility of a Continental connection for the scribe John about whom nothing but his name is known should be noted. He offered a pious colophon: "Qui scripsit scribat / semper cum domino ivvat. Vivat in celis Iohannes nomine felix." Though this distich is formulaic, it is worth remarking here that Austrian National Library MS Theol. Lat. 16 (53), a fifteenth-century Bible, bears a virtually identical formula. "Qui scripsit semper cum domino vivat / Vivat in celis. Iohannes nomine felix" (fol. 522). Kermode, "The Merchants of Three Northern English Towns," gives a Bolton pedigree (49).

35. "Design, Decoration and Illustration," in *BPPB*, 35.

36. See James Hogg, "Mount Grace Charter House and late Medieval English Spirituality," *Collectanea Cartusiensia* 3: *AC* 82.3 (Salzburg: Institut für Anglistik und Amerikanistik, 1980), 18–21.

37. See E. Milner White and Frederick Harrison, "A Medieval Hours of York Use," *Friends of the Minster: Seventeenth Annual Report* (1945): 14–18, 27–29.

38. See Arie Wallert, "*Chrozophora tinctoria Juss.*, Problems in Identifying an Illumination Colorant," *Restaurator* 11 (1990); 141–55: Franco Brunello, *De Arte Illuminandi e altri trattati sulla tecnica della miniatura medievale* (Vicenza: Nieri Pozza, 1975), 219–20; Merrifield, *Original Treatises*, 1: clxxxviii–cxcvi; Thompson and Hamilton, eds., *An Anonymous Fourteenth-Century Treatise De Arte Illuminandi*, 41–43; and Thompson, *The Materials*, 126, 142–43. See generally, John Christopher Willis, *A Dictionary of the Flowering Plants and Ferns* (Cambridge: Cambridge Univ. Press, 1957), 143–44, where it is still associated with *tournesol;* Immanuel Löw, "Semitische Farberpflanzen," in *Zeitschrift . . . in die Flora der Juden* (Vienna: G. Olms, 1924–34), 115–22; S. Zuriel et al., "Controlling Weeds in Peanuts with Dinitramine," *Phytoparasitica* 4, no.2 (Aug. 1976): 151; Gustav Hegi, *Illustrierte Flora von Mittel-Europa* (Berlin: P. Parey, 1979), vol.5, 1:120; Roosen-Runge, *Farbgebung*, 2:34–35; H. Roosen-Runge and A. E. A. Werner, "The Pictorial Technique of the Lindisfarne Gospels," in T.D. Kendrick et al., eds., *Evangeliorum Quattuor Codex Lindisfarnensis* (Olten and New York: Urs Graf and Philip C. Duschenes, 1960), 1, 5:263–76; and *"folium,"* in Hermann Kühn et al. eds., *Farbmittel, Buchmalerei, Tafel- und Leinwandmalerei* (Stuttgart: Reclam, 1984), 81. Indeed, *tournesole* seems to have been a generic name for a variety of plants giving a blue or purple color, and *Chrozophora tinctoria* figures under this name in several medieval recipe collections and artist's handbooks as well as modern studies of them. For example, see R. D. Harley, *Artists' Pigments c. 1600–1835* (London: Butterworths, 1970), 57–58, who refers to it under the heading *tournesol* and does not mention the word *folium* at all in her discussion, though she is aware of the plant's botanical name, erroneously calling it *"Croton tinctorium"* (57). In spite of its promising title, neither the word *folium* nor, indeed, purples produced from plants are treated in M. E. Chevreul, ed., *Pigments et colorants de l'antiquité et du moyen âge, teinture, peinture, enluminure: études historiques et physico-chimiques* (Paris: CNRS, 1990). *The Colour Index* (Bradford, Yorkshire: Soc. of Dyers and Colourists, 1976) calls *folium tournesole,* lumping it with lichens: C.I.28, "Natural red," though it is neither red nor a lichen.

39. Wallert, in a letter to me of 7 Feb. 1991. In *"Chrozophora,"* 146, citing G. A.

Swan, "Isolation, structure, and synthesis of hermidin, a chromogen from Mercurialis perennis L.," *Journal of the Chemical Society, Perkin Transactions* 1 (1985): 1757–1766, Wallert feels that the connection of the *folium* colorant with hermidin is the most promising of the chemical comparisons made so far.

40. See Franco Brunello, *L'Arte della Tintura nella storia dell'umanità* (Vicenza: N. Pozza, 1968), 136.

41. See H. L. Gerth van Wijk, *A Dictionary of Plant Names* (1911–16; reprint, Vaals, Holland: A. Asher, 1971), 302. One of these less common names, *verrucaria*, because of its supposed power to cure warts, is helpful in identifying the plant. A medieval recipe for the manufacture of *folium* occurs in a late fourteenth-century medical and alchemical collection that also treats artists' materials. This is British Library MS Sloane 1754, where the plant recommended to make *folium* or *tournesole* is called *verrucaria*. The author helpfully notes that "the difference between the larger and the smaller verrucaria is that the flowers of the large species have buds which look like warts and the small species has neither flowers nor buds" (fol. 235v). The wart-like nature of the buds must have suggested its supposed medical properties. Tony Hunt, *Plant Names of Medieval England* (Cambridge: Boydell and Brewer, 1989), 260, notes that *verrucaria* in England meant *Cichorium intybus* L. and in a letter of 19 Aug. 1989 suggested that the author of the recipe in MS Sloane 1754 meant chickory, which was occasionally used as a blue dye, and cornflowers. John Parkinson, *Theatrum Botanicum, The Theater of Plantes or an Universal and Compleate Herball* (London: Thomas Cotes, 1640), 439–440, whose engraving clearly shows *Chrozophora tinctoria*, called the plant "Heliotropium tricoccum. The colouring or dying Turnsole" and gave a number of examples of its being called *verrucaria*, indicating that it was used to remove "warts, swollen wens, and other hard kernels or excrescences, in the face, eye-lids, or any other part of the body."

42. Wallert, "*Chrozophora*," 143; see 144–45 for various confusions of *Chrozophora tinctoria* with members of the litmus family. See also, for the relation between *tournesole*" as a name for *Chrozophora tinctoria* and as a name for the pigment made from lichens, E.G. Loeber, "Tournesol-Lappen," *IPH* (International Association of Paper Historians) *Information* 19, nos.3–4 (1985): 103–108.

43. To my knowledge, the only conveniently accessible published pictures of an entire *Chrozophora tinctoria* plant are the engraving printed by John Gerard, *The Herball or Generall Historie of Plantes* (London: Islip, Norton, and Whitakers, 1633), 334, and reproduced by John Parkinson, *Theatrum Botanicum,* 439, where it is called *tornesole,* and the drawing in Zohary, *Flora Palaestina,* pl. 385, (see my Appendix A). Gerard's engraving is published by Wallert, "*Chrozophora*," fig. 1, p. 145. A drawing showing the three-seeded capsule occurs in a fifteenth-century Venetian recipe collection, now British Library MS Sloane 416, fol. 132r, and an actual photograph of the seed capsules is published by Marcel Thomas and Françoise Flieder, "La composition des parchemins pourprés démystifié par la chromatographie en phase gazeuse,"in Madeleine Hours, ed., *La Vie mystérieuse des chefs-d'oeuvre: La science au service de l'art* (Paris: Denöel / Gonthier, 1980), p.233.

44. A survey of the literature and an argument for a date of 1414–1417 is given by Zoroslava Drobná, "Kresba problematice bible Boskovské," *Uměni* 13 (1965); 127–38, in Czech with a German summary. In a seminal article, Otto Pächt, "A Bohemian Martyrology," *BM* 73 (1938): 192–204, suggests a date of 1400, and gives an excellent study of the Master artist's style, but does not discuss the colors. See also Frinta, "The Master of the Gerona *Martyrology*," 296, and Jaroslav Pěsina, "Desková Malba Katalog

Descové Knižní," in Frantisek Kavka et al., *Ceské uměni Gotické 1350–1420* (Prague: Academia Praha, 1970), 295–96. There was a thriving scriptorium and illumination workshop in Olomouc at this period. See M. Flodr, *Skriptorium olomoucké* (Prague, 1960) and Josef Krása, "Olomoucké iluminované rukopisy," *Uměni* 16 (1968): 413–16. Krása dates the Boskowitzer Bible 1417 (414) and more recently, in *The Travels of Sir John Mandeville* (36) gives the dating offered above.

45. Frinta, "The Master of the Gerona *Martyrology*," 285 speaks of this painter's "unusual color harmonies," mentioning "black, cocoa, aubergine, mauve, and Venetian red" as well as "salmon, old rose, pale buff, and creamy raspberry" and "lilac." Frinta, of course, was not primarily interested in the palette of the MSS he discusses, but it should be noted that five of the colors he rather impressionistically names were actually tonalities of *folium*.

46. See Krása, *The Travels of Sir John Mandeville*, 26–29, for a discussion of color in the Boskowitzer Bible and other works of the Dietrichstein Master. A convenient color reproduction of the Jezabel miniature is published in Marcel Thomas, *The Golden Age: Manuscript Painting at the Time of Jean, Duke of Berry* (New York: Braziller, 1979), pl. 11 and discussion. See Josef Krása, *Die Handschriften König Wenzels IV* (Prague: Odeon, 1971), and Julius von Schlosser, "Die Bilderhandschriften Königs Wenzel I," *JKSAK* 14 (1893): 214–317. *Folium*, of course, occurs occasionally in French and Flemish painting in the International Gothic Style but is not common. An instance, presumably to magnify Christ's nobility, occurs in a manuscript of the Yprès school from the workshop of Melchior Broederlam, made about 1400–1410, where in a resurrection scene, Christ rises from the tomb wearing a beautiful purple robe (fol. 73v), published by H.P. Kraus, *Fifty Mediaeval and Renaissance Manuscripts*, no. 26, p. 58, and discussed on pp. 57–59.

47. See generally, J. R. Maddicott, *Thomas of Lancaster, 1307–1322: A Study in the Reign of Edward II* (Oxford: Oxford Univ. Press, 1970), 329–30; and more recently, Christopher Page, "The Rhymed Office for St. Thomas of Lancaster: Poetry, Politics and Liturgy in Fourteenth-Century England," in Derek Pearsall, ed., *Essays in Memory of Elizabeth Salter*, Leeds Studies in English 14 (Leeds: Univ. of Leeds School of English, 1983), 134–51.

48. *MMBL*, 1:264–65.

49. A partial description has been given by Y. O'Neill in David Anderson, ed., *Sixty Bokes Olde and Newe. Manuscripts and Early Printed Books from Libraries in or near Philadelphia Illustrating Chaucer's Sources, His Works and Their Influence* (Knoxville: Univ. of Tennessee Press, 1986), no. 49, pp. 92–95. I am grateful to the officials of the Rosenbach Library for allowing me to consult and photograph this manuscript.

50. A convenient discussion of Somer's work and a list of manuscripts containing it may be found in Sigmund Eisner, ed., *The Kalendarium of Nicholas of Lynn* (London: Scolar Press, 1980), 8–9. An edition of Somer's kalendar made by Lynn Mooney is forthcoming from the same press.

51. See for MS Additional 69, *MMBL*, Piper, 816–18, and also Pfaff, *New Liturgical Feasts*, 3–4, 13–39.

52. MS XVI.K.6 is described in *MMBL*, Piper, 727–30, and mentioned by Hughes, *Pastors and Visionaries*, 31. The border sprays in this manuscript, as Kathleen Scott has noted, were done by the artist who did the sprays on folio 142r of Glasgow University Library, MS General 1130, a Nicholas Love *Meditations on the Life of Christ* of 1430–1440 bearing the Willoughby arms. See on this manuscript, Nigel Thorp, *The Glory of the Page, Medieval and Renaissance Illuminated Manuscripts from Glasgow University*

Library (London: Harvey Miller, 1987), no. 33, p. 85 and fig. The suffrage for Scrope, with three others from *horae* of York use, is printed by Christopher Wordsworth, ed., *Horae Eboracenses: The Prymer or Hours of the Blessed Virgin Mary, according to the Use of the Illustrious Church of York*, Surtees Society, vol. 132 (Durham: Surtees Society, 1920), Appendix 4, pp. 181–83. To these should be added a hymn for Scrope and a painting of him being revered by a woman, presumably Alice, wife of John Bolton, in the Bolton *horae*, YML Add. 2, fol. 100v. In the same manuscript, at fol. 202v, is a picture of Scrope holding a windmill, which signifies the place of his martyrdom; the figure is titled "S. Ricardus." For the last phase of Scrope's career, see E.F. Jacob, *The Fifteenth Century, 1399–1485* (Oxford: Clarendon, 1961), 58–62; and P. McNiven, "The Betrayal of Archbishop Scrope," *BJRL* 54 (1971): 173–213. On the rise of new cults in Yorkshire generally and on that of Scrope in particular, see Hughes, *Pastors and Visionaries*, 298–299, 306–11, and more thoroughly, J. W. McKenna, "Popular Canonization as Political Propaganda: the Cult of Archbishop Scrope," *Speculum* 45 (1970): 608–23. An interesting study of Scrope's tomb and tomb cult is that of T. W. French, "The Tomb of Archbishop Scrope in York Minster," *YAJ* 61 (1989): 95–102, with illustrations. Mentions of Scrope in glass painting occur in Richard Marks, "The Glazing of Fotheringhay Church and College," *JBAA* 130 (1977): 96–97.

53. Letter of 29 Aug. 1991. The manuscript is mentioned by Linda E. Voigts and Robert P. Hudson, "A drynke þat men callen dwale to make a man to slepe whyle men kerven him. A Surgical Anesthetic from Late Medieval England," in Sheila Campbell et al., eds., *Health, Disease and Healing in Medieval Culture* (New York: St. Martin's, 1992), 49. See also E.J.L. Scott, *Index to the Sloane Manuscripts in the British Museum* (reprint London: Trustees of the British Museum, 1971).

54. *BRUC*, 5–6, and John Guest in a pamphlet, *Thomas de Rotherham Archbishop of York and his College of Jesus at Rotherham. A Paper read before the Rotherham Literary and Scientific Society 18th November, 1867* (Rotherham: A. Gilling, 1869), 38. A definite connection between Alcock and York comes from the fact that his canting arms: shield argent a fess between three cocks' heads sable a mitre or occurs in the western light of All Saints Church, North Street, York.

55. The most important studies of John of Tynemouth are by Carl Horstman, ed., *Nova Legenda Anglie* (Oxford: Clarendon, 1901), 1:xii–lvii; Vivian Hunter Galbraith, "The *Historia Aurea* of John, Vicar of Tynemouth, and the Sources of the St. Albans Chronicle (1327–1377)," in H. W. C. Davis, ed., *Essays in History Presented to Reginald Lane Poole* (reprint, Freeport, N.Y.: Books for Libraries Press, 1967), 379–98, who essentially repeats the description of Cambridge University Library MS Dd.10.22 from the University Library catalogue: Galbraith, "Extracts from the *Historia Aurea* and a French 'Brut' (1317–1347)," *EHR* 43 (1928): 203–17; Gransden, *Historical Writing in England: c. 1307-to the Early Sixteenth Century* (Ithaca, N.Y.: Cornell Univ. Press, 1982), 2:56, 344–45, n. 7; and Taylor, *English Historical Literature*, 103–105.

56. Fol. 193v. See *MMBL*, Piper, 705–706.

57. See James, *Lambeth Palace*, 1:22–26, and Botfield, ed., *Catalogi Veteres*, 56.

58. William S. Gibson, *The History of the Monastery Founded at Tynemouth, in the Diocese of Durham*, 2 vols. (London: William S. Gibson, 1846–1847).

59. The manuscript is briefly described in C. Hardwick and H. R. Luard, *A Catalogue of the Manuscripts Preserved in the Library of the University of Cambridge* (reprint, Millwood, N.J.: Kraus, 1980), vol. 1, no. 581, pp. 418–19. For Rokes at Durham, see *MLGB*, Watson, 96. On Thomas Roke, see Emden, *A Survey of Dominicans in England*, 247.

60. See M. B. Parkes, *English Cursive Book Hands 1250–1500* (1969; reprint, London: Scolar Press, 1979), xvii–xviii, pl. 2.i (1381) and 23.i (1412–13). I am grateful to Ian Doyle for suggestions concerning the date of this manuscript.

61. See Augustin Theiner, ed., Caesar Baronius, *Annales Ecclesiastici* (Paris: Barri-Ducis, 1864–83), 26:316, and A. Ciaconius, *Vitae et res gestae pontificum Romanorum et S. R. E. Cardinalium* (Paris: P. and A. de Rubeis, 1687), vol. 3, col. 601. I am greatly indebted for information on this formula to Brother Chrysogonus Waddell of the Abbey of Gethsemani, Trappist, Kentucky.

62. See introduction, n. 15. See also, C. H. Talbot, "A List of Cistercian Manuscripts in Great Britain," *Traditio* 8 (1952): 402–18.

63. See SC 2469, pp. 384–385. The manuscript is briefly discussed in William A. Pantin, "Some Medieval English Treatises on the Origins of Monasticism," in Veronica Ruffer and A. J. Taylor, eds., *Medieval Studies Presented to Rose Graham* (Oxford: Oxford Univ. Press, 1950), 189–215. Doyle, in speaking of this book, observes that the *Historia Aurea* was "bulky, . . . slow and costly to copy" ("Book Production," 6).

64. See James, *Corpus Christi*, 1:14–17.

65. For a brief discussion of this decorative style, see Friedman, ed., *John de Foxton's Liber Cosmographiae*, li.

66. See generally, Richard H. Rouse and Mary A. Rouse, *Preachers, Florilegia and Sermons: Studies on the Manipulus Florum of Thomas of Ireland*, Studies and Texts 47 (Toronto: Pontifical Institute, 1979), 11–26, 34–36, 233–35; L. W. Daly, *Contributions to a History of Alphabetization in Antiquity and the Middle Ages* (Brussels: Latomus, 1967); and F. J. Witty, "Early Indexing Techniques: A Study of Several Book Indexes of the Fourteenth, Fifteenth, and early sixteenth Centuries," *LQ* 35 (1965): 141–48, and more recently, J. P. Gumbert, "La Page intelligible: quelques remarques," in Weijers, ed., *Vocabulaire du livre et de l'écriture au moyen âge*, 111–19.

67. On this manuscript see *GM*, vol.2, no. 26, pp. 32–33, for discussion and bibliography.

68. On this and two related manuscripts, see J. J. G. Alexander, "Painting and Manuscript Illumination for Royal Patrons in the Later Middle Ages," in V. J. Scattergood and J. W. Sherborne, eds., *English Court Culture in the Later Middle Ages* (London: Duckworth, 1983), 141–42; *GM*, vol.2, no. 84, pp. 91–93, for discussion and bibliography; and more recently, Michael A. Michael, "The Artists of the Walter de Milemete Treatise" (Ph.D. diss. University of London, 1987).

69. See James, *Sidney Sussex*, 44–45.

70. See Eric George Millar, *The Luttrell Psalter* (London: British Museum, 1932), who calls the work the last phase of the East Anglian school, 15–16, and more recently, Michael Camille, "Labouring for the Lord: The Ploughman and the Social Order in the Luttrell Psalter," *AH* 10 (1987): 423–54, who focuses chiefly on the economic currents exemplified in the decoration.

71. *GM*, vol. 2, no. 47, pp. 53–55.

72. Ibid., vol. 2, no. 104, pp. 113–15.

73. Ibid., vol. 2, no. 133, pp. 147–49, for discussion and bibliography.

74. *RM*, no. 21, pp. 63–64, fig. 51.

75. *RM*, no. 83, pp. 108–111. See generally, Francis Wormald, "Decorated Initials in English MSS from 900 to 1100," *Archaeologia* 91 (1945): 107–35.

76. See *EGM* (1), 1:114–123, for discussion.

77. See *GM*, vol. 2, no. 37, pp. 42–43, and Backhouse, *The Madresfield Hours* for examples. For the Peterborough Psalter, see *GM*, vol. 1, no. 40, pp. 45–47, and Lucy

Freeman Sandler's *The Peterborough Psalter in Brussels and Other Fenland Manuscripts* London: Harvey Miller, 1974).

78. See Derek Turner, *English Book Illustration 966–1846*, I, *Illuminated Manuscripts* (London: British Museum, 1965) and Rickert, *The Reconstructed Carmelite Missal*.

79. St. Anne was often used as a symbol for female literacy. See on this point Kathleen Ashley and Pamela Sheingorn, eds., *Interpreting Cultural Symbols: Saint Anne in Late Medieval Society* (Athens: Univ. of Georgia Press, 1990), introduction, 27, and Myra D. Orth, "Madame Sainte Anne," 204, in the same collection. As an illustration of the idea that Anne may appear prominently in books owned by women, see the Lady Scrope prayer book, made for a Yorkshire house honoring St. Honoratus, Cambridge University Library MS Kk.3.5, where there are two commemorations for St. Anne (James, *Clare*, 7).

80. See Lucy Freeman Sandler, "Reflections on the Construction of Hybrids in English Gothic Marginal Illustration," in Moshe Barasch et al., eds., *Art the Ape of Nature: Essays in Honor of H. W. Janson* (New York and Englewood Cliffs, N.J.: Abrams and Prentice-Hall, 1981), 51–65.

81. See Millar, *the Luttrell Psalter*, 15–16.

82. See chapter 1, n. 46.

83. Sandra Hindman and James D. Farquhar, *Pen to Press: Illustrated Manuscripts and Printed Books in the First Century of Printing* (College Park: Univ. of Maryland Press, 1977), 68.

84. Some useful parallels here may be drawn from V. H. Galbraith, "Nationality and Language in Medieval England," *TRHS*, 4th ser., 23 (1941): 113–28.

85. Gage, "Colour in History," 109–10.

86. Rosamond McKitterick, *The Carolingians and the Written Word* (Cambridge: Cambridge Univ. Press, 1989), 143. Though the author is acquainted with the term *folium*, she still speaks of it as of a "a pigment prepared from the juice of the fruits and flowers of the *tournesol* or *morella* plant," and does not question the Theophilus recipe which—oddly, considering the period covered by her own book—she dates in the twelfth century. Gold and purple also had a long association in alchemical writing and practice; see, for example, A. Wallert, "Alchemy and Medieval Art Technology," in Z.R.W.M. von Martels, ed., *Alchemy Revisited: Proceedings of the International Conference on the History of Alchemy at the University of Gröningen 17–19 April 1989* (Leiden: E.J. Brill, 1990), 159–60.

4. The Interlace and Mask Medallion Style

1. Paul Ruggiers, ed., *The Canterbury Tales: A Facsimile and Transcription of the Hengwrt Manuscript* (Norman: Univ. of Oklahoma Press, 1979), fol. 2, frontispiece.

2. See *GM*, vol. 2, no. 57, pp. 66–67 and fig. 143.

3. See *GM*, vol. 2, no. 150, pp. 172–75, and Alexander and Binski, eds., *Age of Chivalry*, fig. 714, pp. 518–19. A reproduction of fol. 286v is published by Eric G. Millar, *English Illuminated Manuscripts from the XIVth to the XVth Centuries* (Paris: G. van Oest, 1928), pl. 72.

4. See Millar, *The Luttrell Psalter*, 15–16 for a discussion of mask faces.

5. The manuscript, painted about 1170, is published and discussed by T.S.R. Boase, *The York Psalter* (New York: Thomas Yoseloff, 1962), 30–31, pl. 8.

6. Millar, *The Luttrell Psalter*, 15, and see *EGM* (2), vol. 1, no. 112, no. 159.

7. Fol. 85v.

8. Fol. 11, *GM*, vol. 2, no. 1, pp. 13–14, and see G. Evelyn Hutchinson, "Attitudes toward Nature in Medieval England: The Alphonso and Bird Psalters," *Isis* 65 (1974): 5–37.

9. *GM*, vol. 2, no. 78, pp. 84–86.

10. *GM*, vol. 2, no. 50, pp. 56–58, fig. 118.

11. *GM*, vol. 2, no. 56, pp. 64–66, and Lynda Dennison, "An Illuminator of the Queen Mary Psalter Group: The Ancient 6 Master," *AJ* 66 (1986): 287–314.

12. From about 1410 and generally believed to show Bohemian influence is the Bible of Richard II, London, British Library MS Royal 1.E.ix. The manuscript has also been connected with the shop of Herman Scheerre. A page with interlace medallions in the borders, though these do not form the main element of decoration, is published by Millar, *English Illuminated Manuscripts*, as pl. 74. It is now believed that the book has no connection with Richard II. See J.J.G. Alexander, "Painting and Manuscript Illumination," in Scattergood and Sherborne, eds., *English Court Culture in the Later Middle Ages*, 147 n. 22.

13. *GM*, vol. 2, no. 121, p. 135. It is worth noting that lion-like or diabolical masks were of interest to Bohemian painters too, appearing in the Boskowitzer Bible discussed in the previous chapter and in the work of the illuminator Nicholas of Brno, who was active in Vienna and in Klosterneuburg between 1410 and 1430. See Karl Oettinger, "Der Illuminator Nikolaus," *JPK* 45 (1933): 221–38. For a list of Bohemian manuscripts in which this motif occurs, see Frinta, "The Master of the Gerona *Martyrology*," 296 n. 30. Mask faces of the lion-headed type with protruding tongues also appear as wooden ceiling boss decoration in English churches. See, for example Christopher Brighton, *Lincoln Cathedral Cloister Bosses*, (Lincoln: Honywood Press, 1985) fig. 77, p. 29.

14. *GM*, vol. 2, no. 142, pp. 163–65. See particularly fols. 9 and 48.

15. *GM*, vol. 2, no. 127, p. 141; Eric G. Millar, "The Egerton Genesis and the M. R. James Memorial Manuscript," *Archaeologia* 87 (1938): 1–5; and Margaret Rickert, *Painting in Britain: The Middle Ages* (Harmondsworth, Eng.: Penguin, 1965), 167–68.

16. Two other features of the James Psalter were also used by the group: overhand knotting of vines at various points within the border, not just in the corner pieces or medallions, and small gold blobs with spiral hairline finials, often made with several corkscrew-like strokes, placed at the very bottom of the page.

17. Douglas R. Hudson, "Keltic Metalwork and Manuscript Illumination," *"Metallurgia* 31 (1945): 283–90; William Y. Adams, "Celtic Interlace and Coptic Interlace," *Antiquity* 49 (1975): 301–303; Iain Bain, *Celtic Knotwork* (London: Constable, 1986); and generally, Martin Werner, *Insular Art: An Annotated Bibliography* (Boston: G.K. Hall, 1984).

18. See for discussion William D. Macray, *Catalogi Codicum Manuscriptorum Bibliothecae Bodleianae Pars V. fasciculus I Viri . . . Ricardi Rawlinson* (Oxford: Clarendon, 1878), 529–30; *IMBL*, 3: nos. 845, 846, p. 74, and Rudolf Brotanek, "Nachlese zu den Hss. der *Epistola Cuthberti* und des *Sterbespruches Bedas*," *Anglia* 64 (1940): 178–79.

19. Cited by Ian Doyle, Appendix 1, in Richard Morris and Eric Cambridge, "Beverley Minster before the Early Thirteenth Century," in *Medieval Art and Architecture in the East Riding of Yorkshire*, ed. Christopher Wilson (London: British Archaeological Association, 1989), 21. A representative full border from this manuscript is published by Morris and Cambridge as Plate 3; it shows interlace medallions at top, middle, and bottom as well as the jutting leaf style.

20. See S.B. Gaythorpe, "Richard Esk's Metrical Account of Furness Abbey,"

TCWAAS 53 (1953): 98–109; Watson, *London*, vol. 1, item 357, p. 76, and Davis, *Medieval Cartularies of Great Britain*, nos. 428–29. See also J. C. Atkinson, ed., *The Coucher Book of Furness Abbey*, Chetham Society, n.s., 9, 11, 14 (Manchester: Chetham Society, 1886–1888). The manuscript is mentioned by Doyle ("Book Production," 12), who thinks that the initials are "by a peripatetic craftsman . . . in touch with more southerly centers."

21. See chap. 2, nn. 146–52, for discussion and bibliography.

22. There is some uncertainty about the exact significance of these flowers. They appear, for example, in the Vernon Manuscript, *Pricke of Conscience*, fol. 265r, and the editor, A.I. Doyle, remarks "the columbines which hang from the vinet at this point . . . are not so much evidence of provenance as of artistic school and period. They also occur on single pages in two manuscripts probably made for Benedictines of Norwich Cathedral Priory (Bodley 316 and Canon. Misc. 1120) c. 1394–1400 and one certainly made for those of Durham now Chapter Library A.I.3, in 1386, in the first and last with pictures of monks. . . . It is therefore tempting to wonder if the columbines could have had some sort of association with monasticism if not Benedictines for blue is the colour sometimes employed (rather than pure black) for their habit in miniatures" (9). This motif also occurs at the bottom of the major border in a late fourteenth-century Ranulph Higden, *Polychronicon* from Norwich cathedral priory, now Paris, Bibliothèque Nationale MS. lat. 4922, fol. 11. See Avril and Stirnemann, *Manuscrits enluminés d'origine insulaire*, no. 207, pp. 165–66 and pl. 90. The preponderance of the evidence seems to suggest that the flowers symbolized the Benedictine order.

23. MSS Additional 68 and 383 are described in *MMBL*, Piper, 813–15 and 822–24.

24. For full description, see James, *Trinity*, 3:192–94. Extracts from the manuscript are printed and some of its illuminations discussed by Wordsworth, ed., *Horae Eboracenses*, Appendix 3, 168–180.

25. See *TCD*, 152–54, 156. See also Andrew Hughes, *Medieval Manuscripts for Mass and Office* (Toronto: Pontifical Institute, 1982), p. 375, no. 43, p. 398; and *BML*, vol. II.1.2, items 723 and 722, p. 64.

26. SC 1219, *BML*, vol. I.2, p. 14, item 31, and Michel Hugo, *Les Tonaires*, publications de la société français de musicologie, 3d ser., 2 (Paris: Société français de Musicologie, 1971), 22. This book has a kalendar containing the Feast of the relics of York Cathedral and a number of full-page borders with overhand knotting and interlace medallions or interlace side pieces. It seems to have come from York Cathedral.

27. See Doyle, Appendix 1, 20–21, and Appendix 2 for a synopsis of the contents.

28. See *BML*, vol. II.1.2, item 628, p. 32.

29. *IMBL*, 3: item 810, p. 72, and pl. 78. See also *BML* vol. I.1.2, item 31, p. 14.

30. See for a discussion of the type, Adelaide Bennett, "A Late Thirteenth-Century Psalter-Hours from London," in W.M. Ormrod, ed., *England in the Thirteenth Century: Proceedings of the 1984 Harlaxton Symposium* (Woodbridge, Suffolk: Boydell, 1986), 15–30.

31. See chap. six for discussion of Thomas Rotherham. See *BML*, vol. II.1.2, item 954, p. 151. On the Tunstalls, see W.H. Chippindall, "Tunstall of Thurland Castle," *TCWAAS*, n.s., 28 (1928): 292–313.

32. A number of texts of this type are associated with Anselm's name. See André Wilmart, *Auteurs spirituels et textes dévots du moyen âge latin* (1932; reprint, Paris; Études Augustiniennes, 1971), 147–216 and 482, and Wilmart, "La Tradition des prières de

Saint Anselm: Tables et notes," _RB_ 36 (1924): 52–71. See also F. S. Schmitt, ed., _Sancti Anselmi Cantuariensis Archiepiscopi opera omnia_ (Edinburgh: T. Nelson, 1938–1961), vol. 3. For a visual witness, see Otto Pächt, "The Illustration of St. Anselm's Prayers and Meditations," _JWCI_ 19 (1956): 68–83.

33. Ian Doyle has noted that these white dots were popular not only in Yorkshire but also in the west Midlands, citing _IMBL_ 3: no. 810, York Breviary; British Library MS Harley 4196; the Vernon manuscript and Bodley MS Ashmole 41 as examples (Appendix, nn. 124, 125).

34. See Rickert, _The Reconstructed Carmelite Missal,_ and Millar, _English Illuminated Manuscripts,_ pls. 81, figure (d), 85 and 86. The Rennes psalter once formed part of London, British Library MS Royal 2. A.xviii, the Beauchamp _horae._ Though the kalendar is Sarum, Margaret Rickert in her discussion of the interrelation of the two manuscripts, has noted that the feasts for St. Cuthbert and the _memoria_ and portrait of St. John of Bridlington point towards York. See "The So-called Beaufort Hours and York Psalter," _BM_ 104 (1962): 238–46; these borders appear in fig. 9 and 10 and are discussed on p. 244. There is some evidence that York Minster Library MS Add. 383 was decorated by the artist who did the borders of Trinity College, Cambridge MS O.3.10, as both border artists employed similar fluting and conic forms. Like MS O.3.10, MS Add. 383 (fol. 113) shows at the top of the border an orange mask face from whose ears and mouth come the full and center gutter of the foliate borders highlighted by white dots and circles. As the face in MS Add. 383 contains the largest area of a single color in the page's decoration, both this fact and its position allow it to dominate the border. Like MS O.3.10, the jutting leaf forms of MS Add. 383 put off three-pronged blobs and corkscrew finials, while the more luxurious MS O.3.10 uses this device at every tongue, and both manuscripts employ three-leaf groups at top and bottom border in which the center leaf is much larger than those adjacent. In the borders of both manuscripts, the vines become a flower-like rose-colored cone, lined with blue and highlighted with two white circles, deeply notched back in the center, containing a gold leaf stamen-shaped cone; from it come three tendrils ending in green blobs and corkscrew finials. There is also a linear white highlighting along the rose or blue vines that ends on the kite-shaped leaves in a circle. So too, each portion of the border vine in both books where it shifts from rose to blue or the reverse has a discrete piece of vine in contrasting color knotted to it.

35. The book is actually catalogued as MS 93 (101), as there are several volumes bearing the pressmark 93. The description by Alexandre Gérard, _Catalogue des livres manuscrits et imprimés composant la bibliothèque de la ville de Boulogne-sur-Mer_ (Boulogne-sur-Mer: Imprimerie de C. Aigne, 1844) is inadequate. See on this manuscript, Nicholas Rogers, "The Boulogne Hours: An Addition to York Art, "_The EDAM Newsletter_ 6 (1984): 35–41. I am indebted to Kathleen Scott for this reference, and for originally bringing this manuscript to my attention. See also _Catalogue Général des Manuscrits des Bibliothèques Publiques des Départements, IV Arras-Avranches-Boulogne_ (Paris: Imprimerie Nationale, 1872), 628–29, and Ulrike Jenni, _Das Skizzenbuch der internationalen Gotik in den Uffizien: der Übergang vom Musterbuch zum Skizzenbuch_ (Vienna: Holzhausen, 1976). Janet Backhouse, _The Madresfield Hours_ (9 n. 1) said that she was preparing a study of the Boulogne _horae._ I am most grateful to the Conservateur, M. Louis Seguin, who kindly allowed me to photograph this fascinating volume, and to the very welcoming staff of this library.

36. See John M. Todd, "Saint Bega: Cult, Fact and Legend," _TCWAAS_ 80 (1980): 23–35.

37. See V. Leroquais, *Les livres d'heures, manuscrits de la Bibliothèque nationale* (Paris: Protat Frères, 1927–43), 3:342.

38. See for some Middle English examples, Rossell Hope Robbins, "Private Prayers in Middle English Verse," *SP* 36 (1939): 472.

39. John Burke, *A Genealogical and Heraldic History of the Extinct and Dormant Baronetcies of England* (London: J.R. Smith, 1844), *s.v.* Cartaret. Good introductions to English heraldry are those of A. R. Wagner, *Heralds and Heraldry in the Middle Ages* (London: Oxford Univ. Press, 1956) and Richard Marks and F. Anne Payne, *British Heraldry* (London: British Museum, 1982).

40. "Lady Strange restituit, 1847" is written above the miniature. The form of the eight is a little ambiguous, and it is read as a six by Rogers. It was common in municipal libraries in France just after the Revolution for the new curators to cut out miniatures from the manuscripts in their care and send albums containing them as greeting cards. See generally, A. N. L. Munby, *Connoisseurs and Medieval Miniatures 1750–1850* (Oxford: Clarendon, 1972). As the book was already in the Municipal Library by 1847, it is likely that Lady Strange was an English Catholic with an interest in calligraphy and miniature painting living in Boulogne, who arranged to have the page repaired or who may have done the work herself. Rogers also identifies the confession scene in an initial at fol. 45v as that of a priest absolving a kneeling woman and thinks on this basis the Boulogne *horae* was intended for a woman, but it is clear from comparing the hair style with that of the women in the miniature of the Education of the Virgin that the penitent is a man, especially as the figure appears to be bearded.

41. John W. Papworth, *An Alphabetical Dictionary of about 50,000 Coats of Arms belonging to Families in Great Britain and Ireland* (1857; reprint, Baltimore: Genealogical Publishing Co., 1965) following Thomas Robson, *The British Herald*, 3 vols. (Sunderland, Eng.: Thomas Robson, 1830) and Joseph Edmondson, *A Complete Body of Heraldry* (London: T. Spilsbury, 1780). The arms argent a fess gules between three crosses pommy sable are, in fact, not associated with the Sandys family, whose arms were similar but clearly not the arms of Boulogne. Interestingly, however, in light of the presence of St. Bees in the kalendar, the register of the priory of St. Bees, Cumbria, a cell of St. Mary's, York, contains a memorandum about a controversy in 1496 between the prior, Edmund Thornton, and a Christopher Sandes, about the rights to some hawks, the priory being in a rocky area famed as breeding grounds for the birds. The Sandes had bought the nearby manor of Rottington early in the fifteenth century. See James Wilson, ed., *The Register of the Priory of St. Bees*, Surtees Society, vol. 126 (Durham: Surtees Society, 1915), 193, and Cumberland Feet of Fines, 9 Henry V. no. 8.

42. The Prince Arthur manuscript is now London, College of Arms, PAB Vin 152, p. 123. For the Norman arms, see Jean Louis Renesse, *Dictionnaire de Figures Héraldiques* (Brussels: Société belge de Librairie, 1892–1903), 3:322. I am very grateful to Thomas Woodcock, Somerest Herald, College of Arms, London, for help with these identifications.

43. Rogers, "Fitzwilliam Museum MS 3–1979," p. 232, compares a similar group of prefatical full-page miniatures in the Bury St. Edmunds book to those in Boulogne MS 93.

44. Rogers, "The Boulogne Hours," 36.

45. The roll was edited and discussed by James Raine, *The Obituary Roll of William Ebchester and John Burnby, Priors of Durham*, Surtees Society, vol. 31 (Durham: Surtees

Society, 1856). Some not very accurate engravings of it appear as plates I, II, III to face p.18. For later discussion of similar Continental obituary rolls sent by messenger upon the death of an abbot from monastery to monastery in a region, on which an increasing number of obituaries were recorded, see Léopold Delisle "Rouleaux des Morts du IXᵉ au XVᵉ siècle," *Annuaire-Bulletin de la Société de l'histoire de France* 135 (1866): 177–279, and Clanchy, *From Memory to Written Record*, 109.

46. See John Jacob, *English Medieval Alabaster Carvings, A Catalogue* (York: City of York Art Gallery, 1954), item 79. See, for discussion, W. L. Hildburgh, "An English Alabaster Carving of *St. Michael Weighing a Soul*," *BM* 89 (1947): 129–31, fig. C. Hildburgh lists eight wall paintings, a stone panel, and five other alabasters, all English, of this scene, and knows of no Continental examples. See more recently, Francis Cheetham, *English Medieval Alabasters* (Oxford: Phaidon, Christie's, 1984), 133.

47. See, for the yanking of the hair, John B. Friedman, "Bald Jonah and the Exegesis of 4 Kings 2.23," *Traditio* 44 (1988): 125–44.

48. Edmund Colledge and James Walsh, eds., *A Book of Showings to the Anchoress Julian of Norwich*, Studies and Texts 35 (Toronto: Pontifical Institute, 1978), pt. 2, Revelation 2, ch. 10, p. 328; Revelation 8, ch. 16, p. 357. Julian's remark here may bear some relationship to the well-known passage by Richard of Saint Victor who made out of the ripening green fig becoming black an allegory of Christ's Passion, "qui in fine vitae suae temporalis niger et discolor jacuit in sepulchro." See A. and E. Borgnet, eds., *De Laudibus Beatae Mariae Virginis* in *B. Alberti Magni . . . Opera Omnia* (Paris: Vivès, 1898), vol. 36, bk. XII, cap. 6, sec. xxii, p. 811.

49. Cotton Augustus A.iv is the Lydgate Troybook mentioned in chapter 1. See Turville-Petre, "Some Medieval English Manuscripts," 132–33 and pl. 1, for discussion and reproduction. At the upper left cornerpiece on fol. 1 is a large carpel and calyx.

50. SC 18328, and *BML*, vol. I.1.2, item 30, p. 14.

51. James, *Sidney Sussex*, 2–9, 16–18.

52. A full typescript description of this volume has been made by Ian Doyle, who kindly let me see it in advance of publication.

53. SC 6466 and *IMBL*, 3, no.1119, p.97. See fol. 1, which has a number of characteristically northern elements, such as acanthus leaves wrapped around a severe border bar, an interlace medallion, an unusual use of green, and flower carpels in a dominant center medallion position in the border, as well as a specific regional content, a history of the archbishops of York.

54. SC 12007, and *BML*, vol. I.1.2, item 260, p.91.

55. *MMBL*; Piper, 693–95.

56. SC 903. On this manuscript, see *IMBL*, 3, no. 1011, p.87 and plate 94 (b-c), though little idea of the book's magnificence and whimsy is conveyed. See also *BML*, vol. I.1.2, item 261, p.92. The kalendar of this book contains a feast for the translation of Cuthbert, as well as feasts for John of Beverley and Oswin, and Oswin is mentioned in the text at fol. 174. I am very grateful to Kathleen Scott for information on this manuscript.

57. M. Frinta, "The Master of the Gerona *Martyrology*," 305 n. 63.

58. *Painting in Britain*, 184. The Beaufort Annunciation is fol. 23v of London, British Library MS Royal 2.A.xviii, now usually called the Beauchamp *horae*, painted about 1415.

59. Both the Beauchaump painting and the Wyndham Payne leaf are reproduced by D. H. Turner in "the Wyndham Payne Crucifixion," *BLJ* 2 (1976): 8–26, figs. 1 and 3.

60. See Paul Saenger, *A Catalogue of the Pre-1500 Western Manuscript Books at the*

Newberry Library (Chicago: Univ. of Chicago Press, 1989), 59–60, and Scott, "Caveat Lector: Ownership and Standardization," 21 nn. 7–9, 53–54.

61. See James, *Jesus*, 69.

62. "An English Illuminator's Work in Some Fourteenth-Century Italian Law-books at Durham," *Medieval Art and Architecture at Durham Cathedral*, British Archeological Association Conference Transactions 3 (London: British Archeological Assoc., 1980), 151, for a discussion of borders and miniatures added to manuscripts made in Italy, but brought back to Durham, possibly unbound.

63. Thomas Da Costa Kaufmann and Virginia Roehrig Kaufmann, "The Sanctification of Nature: Observations on the Origins of Trompe l'Oeil in Netherlandish Book Painting of the Fifteenth and Sixteenth Centuries," *JPGMJ* 19 (1991): esp. 47–60.

64. This miniature is reproduced in color in Berkovits, *Illuminated Manuscripts in Hungary*, pl. 23, and black and white, fig. 27, and briefly mentioned on p. 58. I am grateful to Dr. Paul Cséfalvay for information on the missal's present location.

65. See Millar, *English Illuminated Manuscripts, horae* of Elizabeth the Queen, fols. 17, 24v, pl. 90; Beauchaump *horae* and Psalter, fol. 23v, pl. 91; Abingdon Missal, fol. 113v, pl. 100.

66. See James, *Jesus*, 6. A variant of the calyx pattern, but merely offering a cone without realistic botanic detail and with no or only rudimentary carpels, occurs in manuscripts from Newcastle and Beverley, the Lacy *horae*, Oxford, St. John's College 94, for example, fols. 1v–2, which has been discussed in previous chapters, and the Beverley prayer book now in the Brotherton collection of the University of Leeds. Lacy's book contains several mask faces as well as a number of interlace medallions at fols. 29r, 36v, and 39r. On fol. 2, Christ rises from a *folium*-painted tomb-chest. On the Beverley prayer book, see D. Cox, *The Brotherton Collection, University of Leeds. Its Contents Described with Illustrations of Fifty Books and Manuscripts* (Leeds: Leeds Univ. Library, 1986), 4.

67. See James, *Fitzwilliam*, 87–88, *BML*, vol. I.1.2, item 1008, p.164, and more recently, Robinson, *Cambridge*, 1, no. 193, p.65. See for reproduction, Kathleen Scott, "Caveat Lector: Ownership and Standardization," 34–35, pl. 10. Cambridge, Jesus College MS 48, a Boethius, *Consolation of Philosophy* with Trivet commentary, may have come from Durham and was written by an English scribe. The Trivet portion dates from the early fifteenth century and contains a full floral border and six-line floriated initials. The border of fol. 188 is very similar in character to that of MS Fitzwilliam 34, though it is earlier by a good forty years. There is the same Italianate acanthus wrap, and except for teasels and large, illusionistic English daisy buds, the Boethius has similar orange carpels with yellow seed dots and sprays. For description, see James, *Jesus*, 78.

68. See *MMBL*, Piper, 800–802.

69. Ibid., 816–18.

70. Ibid., 693–95.

71. SC 15850 and *BML*, vol. I.2, item 271, p.95. This manuscript is not mentioned by Todd, "Saint Bega."

72. See *MMBL*, Piper, 756–59.

73. "The Work of a Foreign-Trained Artist in the Hours of Elizabeth the Queen," given at the 27th International Congress of Medieval Studies, Kalamazoo, Mich., May 7, 1992. See also Nicholas J. Rogers, "Books of Hours Produced in the Low Countries for the English Market in the Fifteenth Century" (M. Litt. thesis, Cambridge University, 1982).

74. See Friedman, ed., *John de Foxton's Liber Cosmographiae*, liii–lxii.

5. "Hermits Painted at the Front":
Images of Popular Piety in the North

1. BIHR Reg. 23, Rotherham, fol. 324. A similar will by another York chaplain, John Burns, leaves "j librum vocatum Bonaventura in Meditat. in papiro," *TE*, 3:199 n. See Michael Sargent, "Bonaventura English: A Survey of the Middle English Prose Translations of Early Franciscan Literature," *Spätmittelalterliche Geistliche Literatur in der Nationalsprache* 2 (*AC* 106, 1984), 145–76 for the range of this material. Both Rolle and St. Paul were believed in the fifteenth century to have established "rules" for hermits. Rolle's was called the "regula heremitarum." See Virginia Davis, "The Rule of St. Paul, the First Hermit, in late Medieval England," in W. J. Sheils, ed., *Monks, Hermits and the Ascetic Tradition* (Oxford: Blackwell, 1985), 203–14. A portrait of Rolle in this capacity appears in London, British Library MS Cotton Faustina B. vi, pt. ii, to be discussed below. The portrait is mentioned briefly by C. Horstman, ed., *Yorkshire Writers, Richard Rolle of Hampole an English Father of the Church and his Followers* (London: Swan, Sonnenschein and Co., 1895–1896), 2:xxxiv.

2. Vincent Gillespie, "Strange Images of Death: The Passion in Later Medieval English Devotional and Mystical Writing," in Erwin A. Stürzl et al., eds., *Zeit, Tod und Ewigkeit in der Renaissance Literatur* (*AC,* Salzburg, 1987), 3: 111–59, and Gillespie's "Vernacular Books of Religion," in *BPPB*, 317–44. See R. Kieckhefer, "Major Currents in Late Medieval Devotion," in Jill Raitt et al., *Christian Spirituality: High Middle Ages and Reformation,* World Spirituality 17 (New York: Crossroad, 1989), 75–108; Étienne Gilson, "Saint Bonaventure et L'Iconographie de la Passion," *RHF* 1 (1924): 405–24; M. R. Miles, *Image as Insight: Visual Understanding in Western Christianity and Secular Culture* (Boston: Beacon Press, 1985); Margaret Aston, "Devotional Literacy," in her *Lollards and Reformers: Images and Literacy in Late Medieval Religion* (London: Hambledon, 1984); Valerie Lagorio and Ritamary Bradley, eds., *The 14th-Century English Mystics: A Comprehensive Annotated Bibliography* (New York: Garland, 1981); and Nicholas Watson, *Richard Rolle and the Invention of Authority* (Cambridge: Cambridge Univ. Press, 1991), and Flora Lewis, "From Image to Illustration: The Place of Devotional Images in the Book of Hours," in Gaston Duchet-Suchaux, ed., *Iconographie Médiévale* (Paris: CNRS, 1990), 36–42 and 39n. 28 (without evidence).

3. Elizabeth Salter, "Ludolphus of Saxony and his English Translators, "*MAe* 33 (1964): 26–35, and Elizabeth Zeeman, "Nicholas Love: A Fifteenth-Century Translator," *RES*, n.s., 6, 22 (1955): 113–27. See the new edition of Love's *Mirror* by Michael Sargent, *Nicholas Love's Mirror of the Blessed Life of Jesus Christ: A Critical Edition* (New York: Garland, 1993).

4. See Hope Emily Allen, ed., *The English Writings of Richard Rolle* (Oxford: Clarendon, 1931; reprint, St. Clair Shores, Mich.: Scholarly Press, 1971), 36, and more recently, Vincent Gillespie, "Mystics' Foot: Rolle and Affectivity," in Marion Glasscoe, ed., *The Medieval Mystical Tradition in England* Exeter: Univ. of Exeter, 1982, 199–230.

5. See Gordon M. Rushforth, *Medieval Christian Imagery* (Oxford: Clarendon Press, 1936). This similarity is chiefly one of style rather than subject, and suggests that the windows were done by the same workshop, possibly that of John Thornton (50–55). Rushforth discusses the remains of this passion shield (367). See more recently L. A. Hamand, *The Ancient Windows of Great Malvern Priory Church* (St. Albans, Eng.: Campfield Press, 1978), 22.

6. Theodor Erbe, ed., *John Mirk, Festial: A Collection of Homilies by Johannes Mirkus (John Mirk)*, EETS: e.s. 96 (1905; reprint, Millwood, N.Y.: Kraus, 1975), 171. This is a

late restatement of Gregory the Great's famous remark that pictures serve as the literature of the uneducated, "delighting our minds with the Resurrection and stroking them with the Passion." See *Epistola ad Serenum, MGH Epp.* 2:270.13 and 271.1, p. 195. On the theory of the ventricles and for imagination as contained in the front ventricle, see Edwin Clarke and Kenneth Dewhurst, *An Illustrated History of Brain Function* (Berkeley: Univ. of California Press, 1972, 10–48; Clarke, "The Early History of the Cerebral Ventricles," *TSCPP* 30 (1962); 85–89; and most recently, Simon Kemp, *Medieval Psychology* (Westport, Conn.: Greenwood, 1990), 54–56.

7. See Hugh Farmer, ed., "Meditaciones Cuisdam Monachi Apud Farneland Quondam Solitarii," *SA* 41 (1957): 141–245. See p. 191, "verba uoluminis huius sunt actas Christi, dolores et passiones eius . . . littere seu caracteres uoluminis huius uulnera eius sunt, quorum quinque plage quinque sunt uocales, cetere uero consonantes libri tui: disce ergo legere." An English version of this interesting northern writer appears by the same editor as *The Monk of Farne* (Baltimore: Helicon, 1961). See also William A. Pantin, "The Monk-Solitary of Farne: A Fourteenth-Century English Mystic," *EHR* 59 (1944): 162–86. An earlier development of the metaphor appears in a sermon of Odo of Cheriton, London, British Library MS Egerton, 2890, fol. 163r, published by Bernhard Bischoff, "Elementarunterricht und 'Probationes Pennae' in der ersten Hälfte des Mittelalters," *Mittelalterliche Studien* 1 (Stuttgart: Anton Hiersemann, 1966), p. 75: "Sicut enim carta, in qua scribitur doctrina parvulorum, quatuor clauis affigitur in poste, sic caro Christi extensa est in cruce . . . cuius quinque vulnera quasi quinque vocales pro nobis ad Patrem per se sonant. Cetere circumstances sunt consonantes et sicut abecedarium viam aperit in omnem facultatem." For a discussion of the late medieval sense of *caracteres*, see John B. Friedman, " 'Dies boni et mali, obitus, et contra hec remedium': Remedies for Fortune in Some Late Medieval English Manuscripts," *JEGP* 90 (1991): 311–26.

8. Pierre Doyère, ed. and trans., *Gertrude D'Helfta, Oeuvres Spirituelles*, Sources Chrétiennes 139 (Paris: Les Éditions du Cerf, 1968), bk. 2, ch. iv, p.242, my emphasis. For a convenient English version of some of this fascinating work, see Alexandra Barratt, trans., *The Herald of God's Loving-Kindness: Books One and Two*, Cistercian Fathers Series 35 (Kalamazoo, Mich.: Medieval Institute, 1991), 109. A related metaphor is well expressed by Chaucer in his *ABC*, ed. Benson, "with his precious blood he wrot the bille / Upon the crois" (ll. 59–60); this metaphor ultimately goes back to the letter to the Colossians 2.14, where Christ is the "charter" or "chirographum" placed on the cross to refute Satan's power over mankind. See generally, M. C. Spalding, *The Middle English Charters of Christ* (Bryn Mawr, Pa.: Bryn Mawr College, 1914), and Peter Revell, *Fifteenth-Century English Prayers and Meditations: A Descriptive List of Manuscripts in the British Library* (New York: Garland, 1975), 7–10. See on the chirographum idea, Bernhard Bischoff, "Zur Frühgeschichte des mittelalterlichen Chirographum," loc. cit., 118–22, and R. W. Hunt, ed., *Umbrae Codicum Occidentalium* 4 (Amsterdam: North-Holland, 1961), ix. I owe these references to my colleague Charles Wright.

9. This subject is provocatively treated by Hughes, *Pastors and Visionaries*, 31–32.

10. Fol. 72.

11. Michael Evans, "An Illustrated Fragment of Peraldus's *Summa* of Vice: Harleian MS 3244," *JWCI* 45 (1982): 25.

12. A later development of this Pauline idea appears in Dürer's well-known engraving of the Christian warrior, published by Erwin Panofsky, *The Life and Art of Albrecht Dürer* (Princeton, N.J.: Princeton Univ. Press, 1955), pl. 207.

13. Gillespie, "Vernacular Books of Religion," in *BPPB*, 336 n.8. See on MS

Sloane 1584, *MLGB*, 55. Gysborn is briefly discussed by A. G. Dickens, *The English Reformation* (New York: Peter Bedrick, 1990), 27. Dickens's list of the contents of this work is not complete. Fols. 1–4 treat administration of deacons and subdeacons after the Premonstratensian rule; 5 explains ministration at the altar; 6 treats *medica;* 7–12 discuss confessional questions; 13 contains verses on the vanity of the world; 14–17 contain verses on the Virgin; 18 contains St. Bernard's fast; 19 offers directions for the sacrament of confession; 21 contains Innocent the IV's vision; 23 gives directions for prayers; 25, 41, 43, 45, 62 contain medica; 27–34, 36v offer letter formularies; 34 treats the pains of hell; 35, 39–41 contain directions for color and glue making, parchment sizing and smoothing, enameling and etching; 37–39 discuss the plague in England; 42 and 84 present more *medica;* 46–50 contain an Easter exhortation; 50v–62 contain a confessional formulary; 63–80 contain a treatise on confession; 85–87 present several Middle English poems; and 89–95 give a life of an hermit. The Middle English poem on the Virgin contained in this manuscript has been discussed by Robbins, "Private Prayers," 471. An excellent though brief recent discussion of the commonplace book as an English genre is that of Julia Boffey and John J. Thompson, "Anthologies and Miscellanies: Production and Choice of Texts," in *BPPB*, 292–95.

14. An unsigned typescript folio-by-folio description of the contents of MS Cosin V.v. 19 is available in the Durham University Library. I am grateful to Dr. Jan Rhodes of that library for information about this codex.

15. SC 8608. See Roy Martin Haines, "A York Priest's Notebook" in his *Ecclesia Anglicana: Studies in the English Church of the Late Middle Ages* (Toronto: Pontifical Institute, 1989), 156–79, who publishes lengthy excerpts from the notebook, and Watson, *Oxford*, no. 711, p. 118, and pl. 708, where it is dated 1471.

16. See William M. Anson, "Coverham Abbey," *YAJ* 25 (1923): 271–301, and L. H. Cottineau, *Répertoire topo-bibliographique des abbayes et prieurés* (Mâcon, France: Protat Frères, 1939), 1:906–907.

17. L'Anson, 282. Gysborn's name does not appear in the list of members of the community between 1475 and 1500.

18. Doyle, "Book Production," 13.

19. See Parkes, *English Cursive Book Hands*, pl. 12 (ii), c. 1470.

20. Professor Julia Boffey most kindly provided me with a transcription of these notes in a letter of 23 July 1991. Though he does not call himself a canon of Coverham, a John Gysburgh copied, also over a long period, Oxford, Merton College MS 204, *Speculum Humane Vite*, containing the following colophon, "Inceptus et scriptus est liber iste . . . anno domini millesimo CCCCmo quadragesimo sexto" at fol. 2 and at fol. 181v "et sic finitur totus liber . . . scriptus atque completus per manus domini Johannis Gisburgh" with a date thirteen years later. At the end of the book appears the name "Gisburgh" at fol. 208. See Watson, *Oxford*, no. 841, p. 140, pl. 443; and Powicke, *The Medieval Books of Merton College*, no. 1253, p. 244. Perhaps he was the John Gisburgh who served as the archbishop of York's household clerk in 1453 when he became a canon of the Chapel of St. Mary and the Holy Angels. His career is detailed in Thompson, "The Chapel of St. Mary and the Holy Angels," 237. Yet a different John Gysburgh was a residentiary canon of York in the 1480s. See the York Diocesan Registry MS R. As.55, fol. 186, in Purvis, ed., *A Medieval Act Book*, 21, and Appendix 3, p. 65. The residentiary canon John Gysburgh left a will, DCP 1, fols. 350–51.

21. For similar prayers, see Wilmart, *Auteurs spirituels*.

22. On the Sacred Heart generally, see Jean Vincent Bainvel, *Devotion to the Sacred Heart: The Doctrine and Its History*, trans. E. Leahy (London: Burns and Oates, 1924),

and Louis Gougaud, *Devotional and Ascetic Practices in the Middle Ages* (London: Burns, Oates and Washborne, 1927), 75–130.

23. This material may be related to the *Salutatio Angelica* of the York Austin friar John Waldeby. See *BRUO*, 3: 1958, for a list of MSS. There were copies in the York Austins's Library (Humphreys, *The Friars' Libraries*, item 574, p. 142), and among the books given by Rotherham to Jesus College. Waldeby's tract is published by M. J. Morrin, *John Waldeby, OSA, c. 1315–c. 1372, English Augustinian Preacher and Writer*, Studia Augustiniana Historia 2 (Rome: Analecta Augustiniana, 1975).

24. See Dickens, *The English Reformation*, 25–27.

25. The listing of the pictures in *MMBL*, Piper 729–30, does not make clear the number and elaborateness of these historiated initials. At fol. 31, Christ at the resurrection appears. At fol. 77 commence suffrages to Peter and Paul; fol. 77, Andrew and James; fol. 77v, John; fol. 78, St. Thomas of India; fol. 78v, Phillip; fol. 79, Bartholomew and Matthew; fol. 79v, Simon and Jude; fols. 80–80v, and Agnes and Christopher, fol. 81. At fol. 81 also begins a brief life of Christ, with a Crucifixion of the foreign canon page type discussed in chap. 3. Christ standing with a *patibulum* appears at fol. 82, and there is a *Pietà* at fol. 84. At fol. 85v begins a brief life of the Virgin with the Annunciation. The Virgin and Child appear at fol. 87, Mary queen of heaven at fol. 90, and a "Noli me tangere" at fol. 91. Margaret at fol. 91v, Dionysius at fol. 92v, and Katherine at fol. 93 conclude the sequence.

26. It is hard to see why Hughes, *Pastors and Visionaries*, translated the motto as "Constancy in our Lord and redeemer" (31). Similar offices for the Holy Face occur on fol. 111 in MS Sidney Sussex 37, a *horae* of Sarum use but with John of Beverley, William, and Cuthbert in the kalendar, apparently owned by a woman, and in MS 36 a York prayer book in the same collection. A picture for the office seems to have been cut out of the latter book. See James, *Sidney Sussex*, 19–25 and 44–45.

27. George Kane and E. Talbot Donaldson, eds., *Piers Plowman: The B Version* (London: Athlone, 1988), passus 5, l. 523, p. 339.

28. *AnH*, vols. XXIII.32, p. 27, and XXIV.4, pp. 20–23.

29. Boulogne, fol. 6; Trinity, fol. 11. See F. J. Mone, ed., *Lateinische Hymnen des Mittelalters* (1853–55; reprint, Aalen, Germ.: Scientia, 1964), vol. 1, item 119, p. 155 for the hymn. Translation mine. See S. Courbin, "Les Offices de la Sainte Face." *BEP*, n.s. 11 (1947): 32–38.

30. On the Veronica and related matters, see Karl Pearson, *Die Fronika, Ein Beitrag zur Geschichte des Christusbildes in Mittelalters* (Strassburg: K. J. Trübner, 1887), where the hymn is discussed on p. 22, and P. Perdrizet, "De la Véronique et de sainte Véronique," *Seminarium Kondakovianum* 5 (1932): 1–15. See more recently, Flora Lewis, "The Veronica: Image, Legend and Viewer," in Ormrod, ed., *England in the Thirteenth Century*, 100–106; A. Chastel, "La Véronique," *RA* 40–41 (1978): 71–82; and Carlo Bertelli, "The *Image of Pity* in Santa Croce in Gerusalemme," in D. Fraser et al., eds., *Essays in the History of Art presented to Rudolf Wittkower* (London: Phaidon, 1967), 40–55. On medieval interest in the Holy Face generally, see E. von Dobschütz, *Christusbilder: Untersuchungen zur christlichen Legende* (Leipzig: J.C. Hinrichs, 1899), and R. H. Bowers, "Middle-English Verses on the Appearance of Christ," *Anglia* 70 (1951): 430–33. Two good Netherlandish examples of *horae* with Veronica displaying Holy Faces on white sheets or towels can be found in Anne S. Korteweg, ed., *Kriezels, aubergines en takkenbossen. Randversiering in Noordnederlandse handschriften uit de vijftiende eeuw* ('s-Gravenhage: Rijksmuseum Meermano-Westreenianum/Kroninklijke Bibliotheek, 1992), p. 39, fig. 4, and p. 81, fig. 53.

31. A virtually identical scene appears in the Hague, Royal Library MS 76 G 13, fol. 39, a Dutch *horae* of 1470. See A. W. Byvanck and G. J. Hoogewerff, *Noord-Nederlandische Miniaturen* (The Hague: Martin Nijhoff, 1925), 3, no. 113, pl. 20, fig. 91, and p. 48.

32. See generally, Paul Pieper, "Zum Werk des Meisters der Heiligen Veronika," in Rudolf Hillebrecht, ed., *Festschrift für Gert von der Osten* (Cologne: M. DuMont Schauberg, 1970), 85–99, and Frank Günther Zehnder, "Salve sancta facies. Zu Christusbildern in der Kölner gotischen Malerei," *MSKB* 3 (1986): 41–44. Another darkened Holy Face from 1400, by an anonymous master, is now in the Wallraf-Richartz Museum. See Isolde Lübbeke, *Early German Painting 1350–1550* (London: Sotheby's Publications, 1991), 307, fig. 2.

33. An excellent overview of the subject with copious documentation from patristic sources is Ignazio Bonetti, *Le Stimate della Passione* (Rovigo, Italy: Istituto padano de Arti Grafiche, 1952) See also William E. A. Axon, "The Symbolism of the 'Five Wounds of Christ,'" *TLCAS* 10 (1892): 67–77; Gougaud, *Devotional and Ascetic Practices of the Middle Ages*, 82; Douglas Gray, "The Five Wounds of Our Lord," *N&Q* 208 (1963): I, pp. 50–51, II, pp. 82–89, III, pp. 127–34, IV, pp. 163–68; and A. Q. Breeze, "The Number of Christ's Wounds," *BBCS* 32 (1985): 84–91.

34. Burton, fols. 61r-v; the actual mass occupies folios 61v–64. See Pfaff, *New Liturgical Feasts*, 84–97.

35. See O. M. Dalton, "Coventry Finger Rings," *PSAL*, 2d ser., 23 (1911): 343; and unsigned, "A Relic of the Pilgrimage of Grace," *YAJ* 21 (1911): 107–109. See also Gougaud, *Devotional and Ascetic Practices in the Middle Ages*, p. 91 and notes. On the Pilgrimage of Grace generally, see Arthur G. Dickens, "Secular and Religious Motivation in the Pilgrimage of Grace," in Cuming, ed., *Studies in Church History*, 4:39–64.

36. Norman Davis, ed., *Sir Gawain and the Green Knight* (Oxford: Clarendon, 1968), 642, p. 18.

37. *New Liturgical Feasts*, 86.

38. Fol. 8v. Translation mine. On this rubric, see Gougaud, *Devotional and Ascetic Practices in the Middle Ages*, 102. See also the metrical offices for the wounds in *AnH* vol. XXXI. items 66, 67, pp. 85–87. Robert Thornton, the Yorkshire scribe and compiler, copied the hymns on the Five Wounds and that on the *arma Christi* discussed below in Lincoln Cathedral MS 91, fol. 278. See R. M. Thomson, *Catalogue of the MSS of Lincoln Cathedral Chapter Library* (Cambridge: D. S. Brewer, 1989), 68. They are published by Horstman, ed., *Yorkshire Writers* 1: Appendix 1, p. 410, no. 23.

39. For an idea of the popularity of such material, see Revell, *Fifteenth-Century English Prayers and Meditations.* On the origins of the prayer, see Gougaud, *Devotional and Ascetic Practices in the Middle Ages*, 86.

40. Barbara Shailor, *Catalogue of Medieval and Renaissance Manuscripts in the Beinecke Rare Book Room and Manuscript Library, Yale University* (Binghamton, N.Y.; MRTS, 1987), 2:309. Shailor, in *The Medieval Book, Illustrated from the Beinecke Rare Book and Manuscript Library* (Toronto: Univ. of Toronto Press and Medieval Academy of America, 1991) publishes the handsome illumination of the *arma Christi* from this roll as fig. 83, p. 87.

41. On this image, see Erwin Panofsky, "'Imago Pietatis.' Ein Beitrag zur Typengeschichte des 'Schmerzensmanns' und der 'Maria Mediatrix',," in Gustav Kirstein, ed., *Festschrift für Max J. Friedländer zum 60 Geburstage* (Leipzig: E. A. Seemann, 1927), 261–308; J. W. Robinson, "The Late Medieval Cult of Jesus and the Mystery Plays," *PMLA* 80 (1965): 508–14; James H. Stubblebine, "Segna di Buonaventura and the

Image of the Man of Sorrows," *Gesta* 8 (1969): 3–13, and Hans Belting, *Das Bild und sein Publikum im Mittelalter: Form und Funktion früher Bildtafeln der Passion* (Berlin: Geebr. Mann, 1981).

42. Doyère, ed. and trans., *Oeuvres Spirituelles,* loc. cit.; Barratt, *The Herald,* loc. cit.

43. This formula is discussed by Thomas W. Ross, "Five Fifteenth-Century 'Emblem' Verses from Brit. Mus. Addit. MS 37049," *Speculum* 32 (1957): 275, and more recently by Marjorie M. Malvern, "An Ernest 'Monyscyon' and 'þinge Delectabyll' Realized Verbally and Visually in a 'Disputacion Betwyx þe Body and Wormes', A Middle English Poem Inspired by Tomb Art and Northern Spirituality," *Viator* 13 (1982): 423 n. 19. See also Carleton Brown and Rossell Hope Robbins, eds., *Index of Middle English Verse* (New York: Columbia Univ. Press, 1943), no. 3443, p. 550, as well as Oxford, Bodleian MS Douce 1, and London, British Library MS Harley 1706, fol. 210, where a rubric for a lyric notes "as clerkes seyne and specyally Seynt Anselme þere were vppon þe . . . body of . . . Jhesu Cryste open woundes by nombre v. þousand iiij hundred seuenty and fyue." See on this "authentication," Revell, *Fifteenth-Century English Prayers and Meditations,* 13. This number is arrived at by saying fifteen Pater Nosters and Aves daily for one year. On the motif in the Wakefield Resurrection play, see George England and Alfred W. Pollard, eds., *The Towneley Plays,* EETS: e.s., 71 (1897; reprint, Millwood, N.Y.: Kraus, 1978), p. 314, ll. 282–84. On this sort of devotional piety in the drama, see generally, Clifford Davidson, "Northern Spirituality and the Late Medieval Drama of York," in E. Rozanne Elder, ed., *The Spirituality of Western Christendom* (Kalamazoo, Mich.: Medieval Institute, 1976), 125–51.

44. This poem is published by Carleton Brown, ed., *Religious Lyrics of the XVth Century* (Oxford: Clarendon, 1939), no. 100, p. 149, and its context discussed by Gray, *Themes and Images,* 134. The *fons vitae* idea of the blood from the wounds as a source of spiritual nourishment is studied by W. A. Reybekiel, *Fons Vitae* (Bremen, 1934) and with a number of Continental illustrations by Maj-Britt Wadell, *Fons Pietatis. Eine ikonographische Studie* (Göteborg: Akademisk avhandling, 1969). An excellent treatment relating the theme to the northern miscellanies is that of Karl Josef Höltgren, "Arbor, Scala und Fons Vitae. Vorformen devotionaler Embleme in einer mittelenglischen Handschrift (B.M. Add. MS. 37049)," in Arno Esch, ed., *Chaucer und Seine Zeit, Symposion für Walter F. Schirmer* (Tübingen: Max Niemeyer Verlag, 1968), 355–91, esp. 384–89. For the background of affective piety in lyrics such as these, see David L. Jeffrey, *The Early English Lyric and Franciscan Spirituality* (Lincoln: Univ. of Nebraska Press, 1975); Siegfried Wenzel, *Preachers, Poets and the Early English Lyric* (Princeton, N.J.: Princeton Univ. Press, 1986); Thomas H. Bestul, "Chaucer's *Parson's Tale* and the Late-Medieval Tradition of Religious Meditation," *Speculum* 64 (1989): 600–19; and John V. Fleming, *An Introduction to the Franciscan Literature of the Middle Ages* (Chicago: Franciscan Herald Press, 1977).

45. A translation of Rotherham's entire will is given by Guest, *Thomas de Rotherham,* 24.

46. *AnH* vol. L, item 369, p. 537, and Mone, ed., *Lateinische Hymnen,* vol. 1, item 126, p. 166, from a fifteenth-century German manuscript. The best study of this material is J. Szövérffy, *Latin Hymns,* Typologie des Sources du Moyen Âge Occidental 55 (Turnhout, Belgium: Brepols, 1989).

47. See [Louis Paquelin] ed., *Sanctae Mechtildis . . . Liber Specialis Gratiae . . . Solesmensium OSB Monachorum cura et opera* (Poitiers and Paris: H. Oudin Frères, 1877), vol. 2, pars 1, lib. 2, c. 19, p. 70. A Middle English version of this work was called *The Book of Ghostly Grace.* See Appendix 3, below, for a bequest of a manuscript containing it.

For a recent study of Mechtild and her milieu, see Mary Jeremy Finnegan, *The Women of Helfta, Scholars and Mystics* (Athens: Univ. of Georgia Press, 1991), 44–61.

48. Colledge and Walsh, eds., *A Book of Showings*, part 2, Revelation 10, ch. 24, pp. 394–95. On the elliptical, diamond, or lozenge shape of the wound, see Gougaud, *Devotional and Ascetic Practices in the Middle Ages*, 101.

49. Jeffrey Hamburger, "The Visual and the Visionary: The Image in Late Medieval Monastic Devotions," *Viator* 20 (1989): 176.

50. See W. Sparrow-Simpson, "On the Pilgrimage to Bromholm in Norfolk," and "On the Measure of the Wound in the Side of the Redeemer, Worn Anciently as a Charm," *JBAA* 30 (1874): 52–61 and 357–74.

51. This manuscript has been discussed by W. Heneage Legge, "A Decorated Mediaeval Roll of Prayers," *The Reliquary* n.s., 10 (1904): 99–112, and by Curt F. Bühler, "Prayers and Charms in Certain Middle English Scrolls," *Speculum* 39 (1964): 275, 277–78.

52. Like Gysborn, Perceval does not appear in L'Anson's list of members of the house in the late fifteenth century.

53. See Rossell Hope Robbins, "The 'Arma Christi' Rolls," *MLR* 34 (1939): 415–21. The claim is questioned by Evans, "An Illustrated Fragment of Peraldus's *Summa* of Vice," 25–26, n. 76, on the grounds that though such rolls are long, they are too narrow to have any visual impact at a distance of more than a few feet.

54. On this subject, see John B. Friedman, " 'He hath a thousand slayn this pestilence': Iconography of the Plague in the Late Middle Ages," in F. X. Newman, ed., *Social Unrest in the Late Middle Ages* (Binghamton, N.Y.: MRTS, 1986), 75–112. On similar prayers to saints, both female and male, for medical help, see E. F. Frey, "Saints in Medical History," *CM* 14 (1979): 35–70.

55. Bertelli, "The Image of Pity," 48nn.

56. Nails of a similar length occur in the illustrations of the prayer roll now Yale University, Beinecke MS 410, discussed above.

57. Bühler, "Prayers and Charms," 276–77, and see Joseph W. Hewitt, "The Use of Nails in the Crucifixion," *HTR* 5 (1932): 29–45.

58. See, for example, St. Bonaventure: "vide ergo, quomodo hoc flore rosae floruit rubicundus Jesus! vide totum corpus; ubi rosae florem non invenies?" *Vitis Mystica seu tractatus de passione Domini*, cap. 22, 2, in *Decem Opuscula ad Theologiam Mysticam Spectantia . . . a PP Collegii S. Bonaventurae* (Quaracchi, Italy: Typographia Collegii, 1949), 503.

59. See [Paquelin] ed., *Sanctae Mechtildis . . . Liber Specialis Gratiae*, 2:198. See also the lost fifteenth-century poem on the Five Wounds, which compares the wound in the right hand to a red rose (l. 10). This poem, perhaps written or merely copied by a William Billyng, was originally in an illuminated parchment prayer roll about eight feet long; it now exists only in a facsimile made by the editor W. Bateman, *The Five Wounds of Christ* (Manchester, 1814). This edition is difficult to obtain, but the poem itself, which shows the "aureate diction" of the Scottish Chaucerians, has been printed in the article by William Axon mentioned earlier in this chapter, n. 33.

60. Paris, Arsenal MS fr. 28, fol. 15r. See on this manuscript, H. Martin, *Catalogue de manuscrits de la bibliothèque de l'arsenal*, 1 (Paris: Imprimerie Nationale, 1885), 173. See Henry N. MacCracken, ed., *The Minor Poems of John Lydgate* EETS: e.s., (London and Oxford: Kegan Paul and Henry Frowde, 1911), ll. 115–16, 118–19, p. 225. In the anonymous *Testamentum Christi* Christ brings God (["cotearmour"]) *semé* with five red roses, F. J. Furnivall, ed., *The Minor Poems of the Vernon MS*, part 2, EETS: o.s., 117

(1892; reprint, Millwood, N.Y.:, Kraus, 1987), p. 656, ll. 215–22. Metaphoric uses of the blossom pattern to figure the Virgin are common in Middle English. See, for example, Israel Gollancz and Magdalene Weale, eds., *The Quatrefoil of Love*, EETS; o.s., 195 (London: Oxford Univ. Press, 1935).

61. London, British Library MS Royal 6 E.vi, fol. 15r. See Lucy Freeman Sandler, "Omne bonum: *Compilatio* and *Ordinatio* in an English Illustrated Encyclopedia of the Fourteenth Century," in Brownrigg, ed., *Medieval Book Production*, 183–200, and "Notes for the Illuminator: The Case of the *Omne Bonum*," *AB* 71 (1989), 551–64. For the supposed Petrine authority, see British Library MS Royal 17 A. xxvii, fol. 80, "þese armus of crist boþ god & man / Sent Petur þe pop discriuet hem." For other examples, see Revell, *Fifteenth-Century English Prayers and Meditations*, 15.

62. "Summa annorum indulgencie de veneracione passionis domini nostri Jesu Christi: ccc sexaginta et quinque dies. Pro anno computato, extendit per unum diem ad xviii annos et dimidium cum tribus diebus. Item per ebdomadam, ad centum decem et novem annos cum dimidio. Item per mensem, ad quingentos deni, et octo annos cum xij septimanis. Item per annum, ad sex milia septigentos quinquaginta quinque annos cum dimidio et tribus diebus" (fol. 8v).

63. See *AnH*, Vol. XV, item 27, pp. 47–48. The hymn is published by Horstman, ed., *Yorkshire Writers* 1, Appendix 1, p. 410, no. 22. Translation mine. Interesting Middle English treatments of this material are given in London, British Library MSS Royal 17.A.27 and Additional 22029. The former begins with a picture of a vernicle held by two angels as does Boulogne-sur-Mer MS 93, and the latter opens with the face on the sheet held by Saint Veronica as in Trinity College, Cambridge MS O.3.10. Reproductions of the pictures, and texts of the poems from each manuscript are published by Richard Morris, ed., *Legends of the Holy Rood: Symbols of the Passion and Cross-Poems* EETS: o.s., 46 (1871; reprint, New York: Greenwood, 1969), 170–93. The bibliography on the *arma Christi* is large. See, for example, H. M. Gillett, *The Story of the Relics of the Passion* (Oxford: Blackwell, 1935) who treats the various legendary locations of the spear, the crown of thorns, pieces of the wood of the cross and the like; and R. Berliner, *"Arma Christi,"* in *MJBK* 6 (1955): 35–152. In 1987, I saw an example of the *arma* surmounting a roadside cross outside a house on Île d'Orléans in the St. Lawrence river just east of Québec City.

64. See particularly, for examples of hands and feet with verses, Gray, "The Five Wounds of our Lord," II 88–89.

65. On this painter, see Donovan, *The de brailes Hours*.

66. Published by Charles Carter, "The *Arma Christi* in Scotland," *PSAS* 90 (1956–7): 120, pl. 10, fig. a. The St. Saviour shield is published by Davidson, "Northern Spirituality," (pl. 3, p. 149). A good assortment of northern *arma Christi* representations appears in Palmer, *The Early Art of the West Riding*, 108.

67. See Pauline Routh and Richard Knowles, *The Medieval Monuments of Harewood* (Wakefield, Yorkshire: Wakefield Historical Soc., 1983), 15, 17. Angels holding shields of various kinds were very common on Yorkshire tomb-chests. See Arthur Gardner, *Alabaster Tombs of the Pre-Reformation Period in England* (Cambridge: Cambridge Univ. Press, 1940), appendix, for a chart; they are discussed on pp. 17–18.

68. Two examples of letters of confraternity between the House of St. Robert and certain Yorkshire magnates, containing considerable incidental information about Trinitarian practices, are published by Christopher Wordsworth, "Yorkshire Pardons and Indulgences," *YAJ* 16 (1902): 399–418. On late medieval religious cults generally and social groups invoking the Trinity, see Christopher Brooke, "Reflections on Late

Medieval Cults and Devotions," in Robert G. Benson and Eric W. Naylor, eds., *Essays in Honor of Edward B. King* (Sewanee, Tenn.: Univ. of the South Press, 1991), 33–45; Barbara Hanawalt, "Keepers of the Lights: Late Medieval English Parish Guilds," *JMRS* 14 (1984): 21–37; J. J. Scarisbrick, *The Reformation and the English People* (Oxford: Blackwell, 1984), 19–39; M. Rubin, "*Corpus Christi* Fraternities and Late Medieval Piety," in W. J. Sheils and D. Wood, eds., *Voluntary Religion* (Oxford: Blackwell, 1986), 97–109; W. R. Jones, "English Religious Brotherhoods and Medieval Lay Piety," *The Historian* 36 (1974): 646–59; and Herbert Francis Westlake, *Parish Guilds of Mediaeval England* (New York: Macmillan, 1919). For Rotherham's vessals, see Guest, *Thomas de Rotherham*, 28, 29. For the whole question of bequests of works of art such as those left by Rotherham and magnates like him, see Joel T. Rosenthal, *The Purchase of Paradise: Gift Giving and the Aristocracy 1307–1485* (London: Routledge and Kegan Paul, 1972).

69. Fol. 37v. See, on this way of representing the Trinity, the London Carmelite, Thomas Netter, *De Sacramentalibus*, 19, c. 155, in Bonaventura Blanciotti, ed., Thomas Netter, *Doctrinale Fidei Ecclesiae Catholicae contra Wiclevistae et Hussitas* (1757; reprint, Farnborough, Hants., Eng.: Gregg Press, 1967).

70. This is discussed in G. F. Willmot, "A Discovery at York," *MJ* 57 (1957): 35–36, and fig. 13, and mentioned by Cheetham, *English Medieval Alabasters*, 296.

71. Fol. 33. Trinities in which Christ as the Son stands in front of God the Father and is about as tall appear at Holy Trinity church, Goodramgate, east window, and at the church of St. John Micklegate, York, now moved to the north transept of York Minster, window 45; they have no parallels in manuscript illumination. On the former see Pauline Sheppard Routh, "A Gift and its Giver: John Walker and the East Window of Holy Trinity, Goodramgate, York," *YAJ* 58 (1986): 109–21. There were, of course, many imaginative ways in which the Trinity idea was made visually appealing, as, for example, the three rabbits each with two ears but with only three ears between them in the window of Holy Trinity Church at Long Melford, Suffolk. On the Trinity motif generally, see A. Heimann, "Trinitas Creator Mundi," *JWCI* 2 (1938): 42–52 and P. Springer, " 'Trinitäts-Creator-Annus': Beiträge zur mittelalterlichen Trinitätsikono-graphie," *WRJ* 38 (1976): 17–46.

72. See Sara Jane Pearman, "The Iconographic Development of the Cruciform Throne of Grace from the Twelfth Century to the Sixteenth Century" (Ph.D. diss., Case Western Reserve University, 1974), which supplements Rickert's discussion in *The Reconstructed Carmelite Missal*, 45–49.

73. Palmer, *The Early Art of the West Riding*, 162, fig. 50.

74. See Clifford Davidson, *York Art: A Subject List of Extant and Lost Art Including Items Relevant to Early Drama* (Kalamazoo, Mich.: Medieval Institute, 1978), 120.

75. See E. A. Gee, "The Painted Glass of All Saints' Church, North Street, York," *Archaeologia*, 2d ser., nos. 52, 102 (1969), 156 and pl. 19.

76. Philip Nelson, "The Byland Trinity Preserved at Ampleforth Abbey," *AmpJ* 23 (1918): 100. Cheetham, *English Medieval Alabasters*, discusses Trinities on pp. 296–310, pointing out that the motif is one of the most popular subjects for carvers, and defines four main types of figure groupings on p. 296.

77. See Pauline Routh, *Medieval Effigial Alabaster Tombs in Yorkshire* (Ipswich, Eng.: Boydell Press, 1976).

78. Nelson, "The Byland Trinity," 99.

79. K. A. Esdaile, "Sculptors and Sculpture in Yorkshire," *YAJ* 35 (1943): 365; Jacob, *English Medieval Alabaster Carvings: Catalogue*, 2; and W. H. St. John Hope, "On the Early Workings of Alabaster in England," in W. H. St. John Hope and Edward

Prior, eds., *Illustrated Catalogue of the Exhibition of English Medieval Alabaster Work* (Oxford: Horace Hart, 1913), 1–15. See most recently, Nigel Ramsay, "La production et exportation des albâtres anglais médiévaux," in Xavier Barral i Altet, ed., *Artistes, artisan*, 609–19.

80. *RFCY* 1: 177.

81. *YPR*, vol. 4, fol. 87. See on this new and important class, Heather Swanson, *Medieval Artisans: An Urban Class in Late Medieval England* (Oxford: Blackwell, 1989).

82. *RFCY*, 1:142.

83. Jacob, *English Medieval Alabaster Carvings: Catalogue*, 2.

84. Cheetham, *English Medieval Alabasters*, 15.

85. Hughes, *Pastors and Visionaries*, 109.

86. W. L. Hildburgh, "English Alabaster Carvings as Records of the Medieval Religious Drama," *Archaeologia* 93 (1949): 51–101.

87. Letter of 23 Jan. 1987.

88. H. Stanley Darbyshire and George D. Lumb, eds., *The History of Methley*, Thoresby Society, vol. 35 (Leeds: Thoresby Society, 1937).

89. See Pauline Routh and Richard Knowles, *The Sheriff Hutton Alabaster: A Reassessment* (Wakefield, Yorkshire: Rosalba Press, 1981), 20, 24, who date it 1436.

90. See Routh and Knowles, *The Medieval Monuments at Harewood*, 18, for a reproduction of the Waterton tomb and above it for comparison the much more damaged Redman-Aldburgh tomb. The stylistic similarities are discussed on p. 24. On Ripon, see Palmer, *The Early Art of the West Riding of Yorkshire*, 162. Pauline Routh, in her interesting article " 'Full of Imageis': The Ripon Alabasters," *YAJ* 57 (1985): 93–100, does not mention this carving, but in a letter of 14 December 1991 says that its polychrome decoration appears to have been in the white daisy with red center style.

91. Routh and Knowles, *The Sheriff Hutton Alabaster*, 18.

92. See Philip Nelson, "English Alabasters of the Embattled Type," *ArcJ* 75 (1918): 310–34. E. S. Prior and Arthur Gardner, *An Account of Medieval Figure Sculpture in England* (Cambridge: Cambridge Univ. Press, 1912), 44, is the source of these categories and for the idea of a York workshop. A recent revision of some of the older theories on dating by Lynda Rollason, "English Alabasters in the Fifteenth Century," in Williams, ed., *England in the Fifteenth Century*, 245–54, does not really concern the issues discussed here. See also Palmer, *The Early Art of the West Riding*, 161. Excellent examples of these integral embattled canopies can be seen in pls. 2 and 3 of Routh, " 'Full of Imageis'," 95, 97.

93. Unsigned typescript catalogue entry, p. 1. Ian Doyle, "Reflections on Some Manuscripts of Nicholas Love's *Myrrour of the Blessed Lyf of Jesu Christ*," *LSE*, n.s., 14 (1983): 82–93, has some important observations on the possibly metropolitan milieux in which many of these MSS were copied. I have not included this manuscript in the handlist of Appendix B because its northern connection is rather conjectural.

94. Floors with ivory and black square tiles are common in manuscript painting of Netherlandish influence. See, for example, the Throne of Grace Trinity miniature in the *horae* of Catherine of Cleves, John Plummer, ed., *The Hours of Catherine of Cleves* (New York: George Braziller, 1966), pl. 38. That the motif was certainly exported to England or used by Netherlandish illuminators working in England is clear from a *horae*, Durham, Ushaw College MS 10, written in Bruges by John Heinemann in 1408 and discussed and reproduced by Edmund Colledge, "South Netherlands Books of Hours Made for England," *Scriptorium* 32 (1978): 55–57 and pl. 11a. They may be referred to in Criseyde's "paved parlour" in Chaucer's *Troilus and Criseyde* II, 82, as

well. See also Christopher F. R. de Hamel, "Reflections on the Trade in Books of Hours at Ghent and Bruges," in J. B. Trapp, ed., *Manuscripts in the Fifty Years after the Invention of Printing* (London: Warburg Institute, 1983), 29–33. Excellent studies of Flemish illumination and the book trade in this period are to be found in Alain Arnould and Elisabeth Leedham-Green, eds., *Fifteenth-Century Flemish Manuscripts in Cambridge Collections* (*TCBS* 10, pt. 2) (Cambridge: Cambridge Univ. Press, 1992), with an extensive bibliography.

95. See Cheetham, *English Medieval Alabasters*, 296, and more fully, Pamela Sheingorn, "The Bosom of Abraham Trinity: A Late Medieval All Saints Image," in Williams, ed., *England in the Fifteenth Century*, 273–95. A plate with this image appears on p. 296.

96. This carving has been published by Alexander and Binski, *Age of Chivalry*, fig. 707 and pp. 514–15, and is discussed and dated by Richard Marks, *The Burrell Collection* (London: Collins, 1983), fig. 10, p. 92.

97. Cheetham, *English Medieval Alabasters*, 302, refers to the "usual daisy pattern" on this panel.

98. Francis Cheetham, "A Fifteenth-Century English Alabaster Altar-Piece in Norwich Castle Museum," *BM* 125 (1983): 359, is corrected by Sheingorn, 275 n. 7, in this matter.

99. Sheingorn gives an excellent account of the Bosom of Abraham idea's development on pp. 275–78.

100. See on this point Louis Gougaud, "Étude sur les 'Ordines Commendationis Animae'," *EL* 49 (1935): 17, and Henry Littlehales, ed., *The Prymer or Lay Folk's Prayer Book* (1895; reprint, Millwood, N.Y.: Kraus, 1981), 69–70.

101. On this point see Deborah Markow, "The Iconography of the Soul in Medieval Art" (Ph.D. diss., New York University, 1983).

102. See for reproductions, Nicholas Dawson, "The Percy Tomb at Beverley Minster: The Style of the Sculpture," in F. H. Thompson, ed., *Studies in Medieval Sculpture* (London: Society of Antiquaries, 1983), pl. 47 and pp. 125–28, 145–46.

103. Sheingorn, 295. For the points earlier in the paragraph, see Sheingorn, 287–92.

104. The Pierpont Morgan Library typescript catalogue description, 1, speaks of "the Blessed within a mandorla supported by four angels."

105. The possibility that the mercer John Bolton was influenced in his choice of imagery by the Mercers' Judgment plays should not be discounted. See Alexandra F. Johnston and Margaret Dorrell, "The Doomsday Pageant of the York Mercers, 1433," *LSE*, n. s., 5 (1971): 29–34, and "The York Mercers and their Pageant of Doomsday, 1433–1526," in *LSE*, n.s., 6 (1972): 10–35.

106. See Gertrud Schiller, *Ikonographie der christlichen kunst* (Gütersloh: Güterslohen Verlagshaus Gerd Mohn, 1966–1976), vols. 1 and 2, *s.v.*

107. See Pfaff, *New Liturgical Feasts*, 62–83, esp. 74–75. See BIHR Reg. 23, Rotherham, fol. 246. The importance of this act for Rotherham is evident in his will.

108. Ibid., 62. Rolle was given the authorship of the Suso mass for the Holy Name in Cambridge University Library MS Kk.6.20. See André Wilmart, "Le 'Jubilus' sur le nom de Jésus dit de Saint Bernard," *EL* (1943): 1–285, and more recently, Lisa Esposito, "Orationes Excerpte de Diversis Tractatibus quos Composuit Beatus Ricardus Heremita ad Honorem Nominis Ihesu, Edited from Cambridge University Library MS Kk.6.20" (Ph.D. diss., University of York, 1982). The English version appears in Horstman ed., *Yorkshire Writers*, 1:186–91. Bernardine of Sienna, born in 1380, made

a famous preaching tour in 1417; his vernacular sermons did much to develop the cult of the Holy Name. See *S. Bernardini Senensis ordinis fratrum minorum opera omnia* 5 (Florence: Quarrachi, 1956), and Bernardine Mazzarella's pious but useful survey "St. Bernardine of Siena, A Model Preacher," *FS*, n.s., 4, 25 (1944): 309–27.

109. Another York missal containing the Holy Name mass is Oxford, University College MS 78b, fol. 154v.

110. A hymn to the Holy Name appears, for example, in *AnH* Vol. XI, item 12, p. 16. See also Oxford, Bodleian MS Laud misc. 302, fol. 232v. See generally André Cabussut, "La dévotion au Nom de Jésus dans l'Église d'Occident," *LVS* 86 (1952): 46–69.

111. See Pfaff, *New Liturgical Feasts*, 79 n. 3.

112. Though the English prayer roll with painting of a Throne of Grace Trinity with donor, now Princeton University Library MS 126, has no obvious features pointing to northern production, the focus on the Throne of Grace Trinity with donor and the Holy Name prayer suggest a possible connection with the Bolton *horae*, where both of these features appear. On this roll, see Jeanne E. Krochalis, "God and Mammon: Prayers and Rents in Princeton MS 126," *PULC* 44 (1983): 209–22; Krochalis translates the prayer but does not tie it to the tradition of the Holy Name.

113. MS Latin Liturgies f.2, fols. 111–112. Hughes, at 267 n. 34 of *Pastors and Visionaries*, confuses this manuscript with the prayer book in the Bodleian Library, Oxford, MS Bodley Latin Liturgies e. 17, discussed in chap. 1. A Middle English version of the veneration exists in London, British Library MS Harley 2339, fol. 8 (see Revell, *Fifteenth-Century English Prayers and Meditations*, 88).

114. A. I. Doyle, "A Text Attributed to Ruusbroec," 164. Robert A. Caldwell, "The Scribe of the Chaucer MS, Cambridge University Library Gg.4.27," *MLQ* 5 (1944): 33–44, argues that a Flemish scribe copied this Chaucer manuscript. See also Colledge, "South Netherlands Books of Hours," 56, and J.-F. Bense, *The Anglo-Dutch Relations from Earliest Times to the Death of William the Third* ('s-Gravenhage: Martinus Nijhoff, 1924).

115. SC 29741. On this manuscript, see S. Van Dijk, "Books of Hours," Bodleian Library typescript, vol. 4, pp. 2145–2146, and *IMBL* 3, no. 795, pp. 70–71, and figs. a–d of pl. 77. The manuscript is also noted by Charles L. Kuhn, "Herman Scheerre and English Illumination of the Early Fifteenth Century," *AB* 22 (1940): who remarks that "the book . . . was probably intended for a York patron" (141). A more recent discussion is that of Turner, "The Wyndham Payne Crucifixion," 15–16.

116. Reproduction in Joan B. Williamson, "Paris B.N. MS fr. 1175: A Collaboration Between Author and Artist," in Burchmore, ed., *Text and Image*, 77–92. The miniature is published as fig. 1 on p. 79.

117. Williamson, "Paris B.N. MS fr. 1175," 82.

118. See Janet Backhouse, "An Illuminator's Sketchbook," *BLJ* 1 (1975): 3–14, for the mid-fifteenth-century English letter book, British Library MS Sloane 1448A, figs. v–vi, for figure-inhabited alphabets. For recent studies of Giovannino's alphabets, see Antonio Cadei, "Giovannino de Grassi nel Taccuino di Bergamo," *CA* 17 (1970): 17–36, and more recently, his *Studi di miniatura Lombarda: Giovannino de Grassi, Belbello da Pavia* (Rome: Viella, 1984), 41–83.

119. See Cadei, "Giovannino de Grassi," p. 23 and fig. 9, p. 27.

120. An excellent study of this idea in a period rather earlier than ours is that of Rosamond McKitterick, "Text and Image in the Carolingian World," in her *Uses of Literacy*, esp. 304–11.

121. Robert B. Cook, "Wills of Leeds and District," *TSM* 26 (1924): 314.

122. I am much indebted to the recent study by Jeffrey Hamburger, "The Use of Images in the Pastoral Care of Nuns: the case of Heinrich Suso and the Dominicans," *AB* 71 (1989): 20–46, in my analysis of these manuscripts. See also, more generally, S. Ringbom, "Devotional Images and Imaginative Devotions: Notes on the Place of Art in Late Medieval Piety," *GBA*, 6th ser., 73 (1969): 159–170.

123. A helpful brief summary of the poem was published by the late Marjorie Malvern in her somewhat neglected piece on one of the items in this miscellany. The manuscript has been generally discussed by Erwin Panofsky, *Tomb Sculpture* (London: Thames and Hudson, 1964), 65, and Hope Emily Allen, *Writings Ascribed to Richard Rolle, Hermit of Hampole, and Materials for His Biography*, MLA Monograph Series 3 (reprint, Millwood N.Y.: Kraus, 1966), 307. In spite of his often expressed contempt for the other scholars who have studied British Museum MS Additional 37049, James Hogg, who has written in bulk, at least, the most about this manuscript, contributes little to our knowledge of it, since much of his work is a mere restatement of the description offered in Falconer Madan et al., *Catalogue of the Additions to the Manuscripts in the British Museum 1900–1905* (1905; reprint, London: British Library, 1969), 324–32. Transcriptions of the ME texts and reproductions of the pictures from the codex appear in James Hogg, "A Morbid Preoccupation with Mortality? The Carthusian London British Library MS Add. 37049," in Erwin Stürzl et al., eds., *Zeit, Tod*, vol. 2, 139–89; "Unpublished Texts in the Carthusian Northern Middle English Religious Miscellany British Library MS Add. 37049," in James Hogg, ed. *Essays in Honour of Erwin Stürzl . . .* (Salzburg, 1984), 241–84, and *An Illustrated Yorkshire Carthusian Religious Miscellany . . . MS 37049 (AC*, Salzburg, 1981). For studies of these drawings on a more limited scale, see Francis Wormald, "Some Popular Miniatures and their Rich Relations," in Peter Bloch and Joseph Hoster, eds., *Miscellanea Pro Arte. Zur Vollendung des 60. Lebensjahres am 13. Januar 1965.* (Düsseldorf: Schriften des Pro Arte Medii Aevi, 1965), 279–85; H. Mellick, "A Study of Texts and Drawings in B.M. Additional MS 37049," (Ph.D. diss., Centre for Medieval Studies, University of York, 1972); Höltgren, "Arbor, Scala und Fons Vitae," 355–91; and most recently, Hamburger, "The Use of Images," 43–44. Alan Fletcher of Trinity College, Dublin is preparing a facsimile of the manuscript.

124. See Doyle, "A Survey of the Origins," 2:191, who discusses the pictures on the first two vellum folios; Hogg, "Unpublished Texts," 243; and R. H. Bowers, "Middle English Verses on the Founding of the Carthusian Order," *Speculum* 42 (1967): 710–13. For a helpful treatment of English Carthusianism, see E. Margaret Thompson, *The Carthusian Order in England* (London: Macmillan, 1930; reprint, New York, n.d).

125. Good pictures of Mount Grace's remains appear in James Hogg, "Surviving English Carthusian Remains: Beauvale, Coventry, Mountgrace: Album," *AC* 36 (1976).

126. Michael Sargent, "The Transmission by the English Carthusians of some Late Medieval Spiritual Writings," *JEH* 27 (1976): 225–40. Hughes, *Pastors and Visionaries*, includes without evidence MS Additional 37049 among books copied at Mount Grace, 109 n. 153. For library catalogues of the houses at Hull and Mount Grace, see Thompson, *The Carthusian Order in England*, 324–26 and 330–31.

127. SC 3962. The manuscript has been studied by C. B. Rowntree, *A Carthusian World View: Bodleian MS e Museo 160 (AC* 35.9, Salzburg: Institut für Anglistik und Amerikanistik, 1990), and D. C. Baker, J. L. Murphy, and L. B. Hall, eds., *The Late Medieval Religious Plays of Bodleian MS Digby 133 and e Museo 160*, EETS: o.s., 283 (Oxford: Oxford Univ. Press, 1982), lxxvi, n. 2, say it, like MS Additional 37049, is

"Carthusian and northern." An edition by Professor Laveice Ward of Hofstra College is forthcoming. I have not included this manuscript in the handlist in Appendix B because its date really places it outside the time frame of the present book.

128. Rowntree, *A Carthusian World View*, 13, 23.
129. Ibid., 15–16, 27.
130. Doyle, "A Survey of the Origins," 2:244; Hogg, "Unpublished Texts," 249–52.
131. Hogg, "Unpublished Texts," 247–48.
132. "Design, Decoration and Illustration," in *BPPB:* 59 n. 52. It is worth noting that in the Cain and Abel miniature illustrating the Creation and Temptation at the beginning of the manuscript, Cain has the short doublet and parti-colored hose of Anger in the marginal illustration for *Piers Plowman* in MS Douce 104. See Derek Pearsall and Kathleen Scott, *The Illustrations of Bodleian Library, Oxford, MS Douce 104* (Cambridge: D. S. Brewer, 1992).
133. See Sanford B. Meech and Hope Emily Allen, eds., *The Book of Margery Kempe*, EETS: o.s. 212 (London: H. Milford and Oxford Univ. Press, 1940), 78, and Hughes, *Pastors and Visionaries*, 267. See on the motto and poem, Revell, *Fifteenth-Century English Prayers and Meditations*, 39–40. An accurate text of the "Jesus est amor meus" poem in MS Additional 37049, fol. 36v, is published by Höltgren, "Arbor, Scala und Fons Vitae," 362–65. For the Scrope prayer book, formerly Cambridge Clare College MS 5, see James, *Clare*, 7 and Appendix 2.
134. See Höltgren, 366–67, for a discussion of the IHS monogram in these texts.
135. Doyle, "A Survey of the Origins," 2:192. For the parallels between some of the texts, see Karl Brünner, "Mittelenglische Todesgedichte," *Archiv* n.s., 67, 167 (1935): 20–35. On their Carthusian character, see Höltgren, "Arbor, Scala und Fons Vitae," 357–59.
136. See generally on this subject, D. H. Turner, et al., eds., *The Benedictines in Britain* (London: Braziller, 1980).
137. See, for an edition of the Middle English text of this work, Walter Hübner, "The Desert of Religion," *Archiv*, n.s., 26, 126 (1911): 58–74, and Hope Emily Allen, "The Desert of Religion: Addendum," *Archiv*, n.s., 27, 127 (1911): 388–90, who notes that it is mostly an adaptation of William of Nassington's *Speculum Vitae*.
138. See Peter S. Jolliffe, *A Check-List of Middle English Prose Writings of Spiritual Guidance* (Toronto: Pontifical Institute, 1974), 98–99, and David Bell, *An Index of Authors and Works in Cistercian Libraries in Great Britain* Cistercian Publications 130 (Kalamazoo, Mich.: Medieval Institute, 1992), who discusses Alcock's authorship on p. 86.
139. See *BRUC*, 5–6. A recent study by Julie A. Smith, "An Image of a Preaching Bishop in Late Medieval England: The 1498 Woodcut Portrait of Bishop John Alcock," *Viator* 21 (1990): 301–22, does not mention the Abbey of the Holy Ghost or Alcock's devotion to St. Antony.
140. Reproduced by Smith as fig. 6.
141. Rushforth, 243–45. See also Rose Graham, ed., *A Picture Book of the Life of Saint Anthony the Abbot. A Reproduction in full of a Manuscript of the Year 1426 in the Malta Public Library at Valetta* (Oxford: Roxburgh Club, 1937).
142. It is possible that the artist's repetitive use of these two colors may have had a mnemonic function, as Hugh of St. Victor in his *De Arca Noe Mystica* uses them in this way in an association with a cross and a symbolic lamb (*PL* 176, 681–702). Hugh's text was in the Austin Library at York (Humphreys, *The Friars' Libraries*, item 289 f., p. 69).

143. See Hamburger, "The Use of Images," 29–30.

144. See Edmund Colledge and J. C. Marler, " 'Mystical Pictures' in the Suso 'Exemplar', MS Strasbourg 2929," *AFP* 54 (1984): 293–354.

145. Pius Künzle, ed., *Heinrich Seuses Horologium Sapientiae*, Spicilegium Friburgense 23, (Freiburg: Universitätsverlag, 1977), 94, 484, 546–47. See Roger Lovatt, "Henry Suso and the Medieval Mystical Tradition in England" in Glasscoe, ed., *The Medieval Mystical Tradition in England*, 47–62, and Wiltrud Wichgraf, "Suso's 'Horologium Sapientiae' in England. Nach Handschriften des 15.Jahrhunderts," *Anglia* 53 (1929): 123–133, 269–87; and *Anglia* 54 (1930), 351–52. The material also had some currency in Carthusian circles. See the illustrated *Vitae Patrum* texts in Brussels, Bibliothèque Royale MS 9229–30, discussed by M. Smeyers and B. Cardon, "Brabant of Parijs: Aantekeningen bij een handschrift met vrome legenden, afkomstig uit het kartuizerklooster te Zelem bij Diest," *Handschriften uit Dietse Kerken en Kloosters* (Diest: Vrienden van het Stedelijk Museum en Archief Diest, 1983), 31–99. An early fifteenth-century cycle of frescoes showing scenes from the lives of the Desert Fathers intended for an order modeling itself on the Fathers appears at the Augustinian Convent of San Marta in Siena. See Ellen Callmann, "Thebaid Studies," *AV* 14 (1975); 6–7, figs. 3–7.

146. A. Hoste and C. H. Talbot, eds., *Aelredi Rivallensis Opera Omnia*, Corpus Christianorum: Continuatio Medievalis 1, (Turnhout, Belgium: Brepols, 1971), sec. 56. See also Alexandra Barratt, "The *De Institutione Inclusarum* of Aelred of Rievaulx and the Carthusian Order," *JTS* 23 (1977): 528–36.

147. See generally, B. Ward, "The Desert Myth: Reflections on the Desert Ideal in Early Cistercian Monasticism," in Basil Pennington, *One Yet Two: Monastic Tradition East and West* (Kalamazoo, Mich.: Medieval Institute, 1976), 183–99; Constance L. Rosenthal, *The Vitae Patrum in Old and Middle English Literature* (Philadelphia: Univ. of Pennsylvania, 1936); and more recently, the late Alison Goddard Elliott, *Roads to Paradise: Reading the Lives of the Early Saints* (Hanover, N.H.: Univ. Press of New England, 1987).

148. On hairy figures see Charles A. Williams, "Oriental Affinities of the Legend of the Hairy Anchorite, Part I: Pre-Christian," *UISLL* 10 (1925): 187–242; "Oriental Affinities of the Legend of the Hairy Anchorite Part II: Christian," ibid., 11 (1926); 429–509, and "The German Legends of the Hairy Anchorite," ibid., 18 (1935): 1–140. For Mary of Egypt, see Rosenthal, *The Vitae Patrum*, 42–43, and A. T. Baker, "La Vie de Sainte Marie l'Egyptienne," *RLR* 59 (1916–1917): 145–400.

149. See Rickert, *Painting in Britain*, 198–99.

150. John Alder Knowles, "A History of the York School of Glass-Painting, VII" *JBSMGP* 3 (1929): 39.

151. See Routh and Knowles, *The Medieval Monuments of Harewood*, 33–40. On Methley glass, see James Fowler, "On the Painted Glass at Methley." *YAJ* 1 (1870): 215–20.

152. See Columba M. Batlle, *Die "Adhortationes sanctorum patrum" ("verba seniorum") in lateinischen Mittelalter: Überlieferung, Fortleben und Wirkung* (Münster: Aschendorff, 1972), and B. A. O'Connor, *Henri d'Arci's Vitas Patrum: A Thirteenth Century Anglo-Norman Rimed Translation of the Verba Seniorum* (Washington, D.C.: Catholic Univ. of America Press, 1949).

153. *PL* 73, 913–14.

154. See M. Bernards, *Speculum Virginum: Geistigkeit und Seelenleben der Frau im Hochmittelalter* (Cologne: Böhlau, 1982), and more particularly on the tree drawings,

E. Greenhill, *Die Stellung der Handschrift British Museum Arundel 44 in der Überlieferung des Speculum Virginum* (Munich: Hueber, 1966).

155. See Friedman, *The Monstrous Races*, fig. 16.

156. Hamburger, "The Use of Images," 43.

157. Theodor Graesse, ed., *Jacobi a Voragine Legend aurea vulgo historia lombardica dicta* (1846; reprint, Osnabrück: Zeller, 1969), Cap. 53, 226.

158. See here Davidson, "Northern Spirituality," 127, and on color in memory treatises, Mary Carruthers, *The Book of Memory: A Study of Memory in Medieval Culture* (Cambridge: Cambridge Univ. Press, 1990), 8–9, 133, and, generally, her provocative chapter on "Memory and the Book," 221–57.

6. Three Northern Magnates as Book Patrons Before the Age of Print: John Newton, Thomas Langley, Thomas Rotherham, and Their Manuscripts

1. See *CAHME*, 3:11–24, 51–54, for a list of Chancellors, Treasurers, and Keepers of the Seal during the reigns of Edward III through Richard II, many of whom were churchmen, and Stanley B. Chrimes, *An Introduction to the Administrative History of Mediaeval England* (Oxford: Blackwell, 1966). See more recently, R. E. Rodes, Jr., *Ecclesiastical Administration in Medieval England: The Anglo Saxons to the Reformation* (Notre Dame, Ind.: Univ. of Notre Dame Press, 1977), 100–51.

2. The name of John Erghome naturally suggests itself as one of the most important of such magnates, but he is not discussed here for two reasons. I have already talked about him and his books at some length in *John de Foxtons's Liber Cosmographiae*, xvii–xxi, and also because, though he was an ardent book collector, all of the known manuscripts associated with his name are rather earlier than the time frame of this study; indeed, the only book we can say that Erghome may have commissioned is the *Liber Cosmographiae*. So too, John Shirwood, bishop of Durham, who died in 1493, was certainly a book collector and bibliophile, but as most of his books were humanistic and printed, and as he seems to have purchased his few manuscripts in Italy, he falls somewhat outside the scope of the present study. See P. S. Allen, "Bishop Shirwood of Durham and his Library," *EHR* 25 (1910): 445–56.

3. See Robin L. Storey, *Thomas Langley and the Bishopric of Durham, 1406–1437* (London: Soc. for the Promotion of Christian Knowledge, 1961), 7–8, 45, and more fully, Deanesly, ed., *The Incendium Amoris*, 78–79, 98.

4. The opulent side of Newton's character is discussed by Hughes, *Pastors and Visionaries*, 9.

5. For southern generalizations that may also apply in the north, see Thrupp, *The Merchant Class of Medieval London*, 161–63, 247–48.

6. See Deanesly, ed., *The Incendium Amoris*, 64–65.

7. Thomas Alfred Walker, *A Biographical Register of Peterhouse Men* (Cambridge: Cambridge Univ. Press, 1927–1929), 1: 19–20, as well as Aston, *Thomas Arundel*, 39, 294–95, 298, 315–16, and Jacob, *The Fifteenth Century*, 286–87.

8. The documents from the Arundel registers and records of the Consistory Court relating to Newton's legal activities are conveniently printed in Aston, *Thomas Arundel*, Appendices 3 and 5, 394, 408. Those for Newton's various appointments as an ecclesiastical administrator are printed by Deansley ed., *The Incendium Amoris*, 62–73.

9. See *BRUC*, 421–22, and Aston, *Thomas Arundel*, 294–95, 297–98.

10. See Hughes, *Pastors and Visionaries*, 199–203. His conclusion that "the first indication of the emergence of York Minster as a centre of scholarship coincides with Newton's arrival as the cathedral of the early 1390's" (201) should also be accepted cautiously. On Newton's role in Emmanuel College MS 35, see A. I. Doyle, "The Work of a Late Fifteenth-Century English Scribe, William Ebesham," *BJRL* 39 (1957): 310–11, and Michael Sargent, *James Grenehalgh as Textual Critic* (AC 85, Salzburg: Institut für Anglistik und Amerikanistik, 1984), 2:479 n. 5. Emmanuel College MS 35 is described by Deanesly, ed., *The Incendium Amoris*, 12–15.

11. *TE*, 1:364, 341. On the custom of granting robes as an indication of livery, and its abuses, see *CAHME*, 1:194; 3:440; 4:414–15, and the Wakefield *Second Shepherds' Play*, ll 28–36.

12. Peterhouse, Compotus roll 1411–1412, printed in Deanesly, ed., *The Incendium Amoris*, 67 n. 2.

13. See *BRUC*, 258, and Aston, *Thomas Arundel*, 311.

14. As Hughes, *Pastors and Visionaries*, 186–87; points out: "by the beginning of the fifteenth century nearly all of Arundel's leading Ely clerks, their kinsmen and servants, had been reunited in the service of the church of York."

15. Chap. 1, nn. 95–96.

16. Helpful on the Italianate context for Newton's book purchases is Mitchell, "English Law Students," 270–87; she notes that a number of Yorkshiremen were resident at Bologna, including William Shirwood, Ralph Makerell, "William" of York, and Everard Strangeways. Bolognese records of English residents begin in 1423. See more recently, George B. Parks, *The English Traveler in Italy. The Middle Ages (to 1525)* (Palo Alto, Calif.: Stanford Univ. Press, 1954), who publishes lists of Englishmen at Italian universities other than Bologna. Several northerners are mentioned. For an earlier example of a northerner's response to Italian decorative style, see Alexander, "An English Illuminator's Work in some Fourteenth-Century Italian Law Books at Durham," 149–52.

17. See on this book *MLGB*, 216 and for description, Macray, *Catalogi Codicum Fasciculus* 2:72. *Fasciculus* 1:529–30, and *IMBL*, nos. 845, 846, pp. 74–75.

18. See for description *MMBL*, Piper, 768–71.

19. Hughes, *Pastors and Visionaries*, 200.

20. The three major studies of Langley are A. Hamilton Thompson, "Thomas Langley, Bishop of Durham, 1406–1437," *DUJ* 38 (1945): 1–16; Storey, *Thomas Langley and the Bishopric of Durham, 1406–1437*, chiefly administrative in focus; and Dobson, *Durham Priory, 1400–1450*.

21. On Langley's arms, see C. H. Hunter Blair, "The Armorials of the County Palatine of Durham," *AA*, 4th ser., 4 (1927): 13–14.

22. Storey, *Thomas Langley*, 95–96.

23. Hughes's claim about this book, that "Thomas Arundel owned the . . . Nottingham which descended into the hands of Thomas Langley" (*Pastors and Visionaries*, 229), is based on a misreading of Beryl Smalley, "which William of Nottingham ?" *MRS* 3 (1954), who actually says (212) that another William of Nottingham, Oxford, MS Bodleian Laud Misc. 165, was owned by Arundel. For some idea of the value of the Bersuire and Nottingham in nearly contemporary terms, see H. E. Bell, "The Price of Books in Medieval England," *The Library*, 4th ser., 17 (1936): 312–32, and Thrupp, *The Merchant Class*, 162.

24. Doyle, "Book Production," 15. There is a brief account of book production at the priory in *VCH: Durham*, 2:88.

25. Fowler, ed., *Extracts*, 141, 158.

26. Fowler, ed., *Extracts*, 473, 275–76. Palman apparently was not alone in doing a variety of tasks associated with the book trade. The Richard Daniel of Durham, book binder (mentioned above in the introduction), also made church vestments for Finchale in 1450.

27. See R. H. Snape, *English Monastic Finances in the Later Middle Ages* (Cambridge: Cambridge Univ. Press, 1926), chap. 6.

28. See John H. Tillotson, ed., *Monastery and Society in the Late Middle Ages, Selected Account Rolls from Selby Abbey, Yorkshire, 1398–1537* (Woodbridge, Suffolk: Boydell and Brewer, 1988), 225.

29. Doyle, "The Work of a Late Fifteenth-Century English Scribe," 303, and a talk "Dating the Development of the Style of Penwork Flourishing of Initials in Later Fourteenth-Century England," Comte-International de Paléographie Latine, Vatican City, Rome, September 1990. The author most graciously provided me with a typescript in advance of publication.

30. *The Analysis of Pen Flourishing in Thirteenth-Century Manuscripts* (Leiden: Brill, 1989), 10. See also J. J. G. Alexander, "Scribes as Artists: the Arabesque Initial in Twelfth-Century English Manuscripts," in Parkes and Watson, eds., *Medieval Scribes*, 87–116, and Alexander, *The Decorated Letter* (London: Thames and Hudson, 1978).

31. See Judith Oliver, "The Mosan Origins of Johannes von Valkenburg," *WRJ* 40 (1978): 23–27. For this reference I am indebted to Joan Holladay, who in a letter of 13 Nov. 1990 noted that the inscription could as easily be by the patron as the scribe. Von Valkenburg also seems to have written, noted, and illuminated Bonn, Universitätsbibliothek Cod. 384, fol. 2. Similarly, the colophon of MS Ludwig VI.1 (now in the J. Paul Getty Museum, Malibu) notes: "Ego Jacobellus dictus muriolus de Salerno hunc librum scripsi, notavi et minavi." The red colophon of Henry Stephen occurs on fol. 246v of the Alba Julia missal. See chap. 3, n. 9.

32. François Avril, "Un Enlumineur ornemaniste parisien de la première moitié du XIVe siècle: Jacobus Mathey (Jacquet Maci?)," *BullM* 129 (1971): 249–64. John Lacy, the Newcastle recluse whom we discussed in chap. 2, also both wrote and painted books, and presumably made the initials as well.

33. See generally Ellen Beer, *Beiträge zur oberrheinischen Buchmalerei in der ersten Hälfte des 14, Jahrhunderts, unter besonderer Berücksichtigung der Initialornamentik* (Basel: Birkhäuser, 1959).

34. See Albert Poncelet, *Catalogus Codicum Hagiographicorum Latinorum Bibliothecae Vaticanae* (Brussels: Apud Socios Bollandianos, 1910), 183.

35. See J. Armitage Robinson and M. R. James, *The Manuscripts of Westminster Abbey* (Cambridge: Cambridge Univ. Press, 1909), 12. The letter appears in Westminster Abbey Register A, fol. 30v. See also Sonia Scott-Fleming, *The Analysis*, 10 n. 4.

36. In describing certain aspects of these initials, I have adopted for consistency Sonia Scott-Fleming's terminology wherever applicable. Her discussion of "latticework" appears on p. 69.

37. Doyle, in "Dating the Development of Penwork Flourishing," refers to the flourishing of both of these manuscripts, noting the two- and three-lobed leaf work with hatching.

38. I am grateful to Patricia Stirnemann for information on this point in a letter of 19 Jan. 1991. See also Avril and Stirnemann, eds., *Manuscrits enluminés d'origine insulaire*, pl. 67.

39. See Stirnemann and Gousset, "Marques, Mots, Pratiques," 34–55.

40. This heraldic information was provided by Mme. Hélène Loyau, Section Co-dicologique, Institut de la Recherches et de l'histoire des Textes, Paris, and kindly made available to me by Anne D. Hedeman, who describes and reproduces some of the manuscript in her recent study, *The Royal Image: Illustrations from the Grandes Chroniques de France, 1274–1422* (Berkeley: Univ. of California Press, 1991).

41. A number of these initials are published in F. Masai and Martin Wittek, eds., *Manuscrits Datés Conservés en Belgique, 1401–1450* (Brussels: Éditions scientifiques E. Story-Scientia, 1968–   ) 2:32, item 149, and pl. 283–85. See also Korteweg, ed., *Kriezels, aubergines en takkenbossen,* for examples of extremely elaborate penwork flourished initials in Netherlandish MSS of the same period.

42. See J. S. Purvis, *Notarial Signs from the York Archiepiscopal Records* (London and York: St. Anthony's Press, 1957) for a discussion of notarial signs. A good example of a Durham notary's mark, that of John de Herle, drawn from BIHR Reg. 1, Neville, fol. 95, appears as fig. 35.

43. See *RTL,* 1:xv–xvi, for an account of Hebbeden's clerical career. The college of Aukland contained an extensive library somewhat after Hebbenden's tenure. See Durham Episcopal Registers, Fox, fol. 26, for an inventory.

44. See Helen Jewell, "English Bishops as Educational Benefactors in the Later Fifteenth Century," in Barrie Dobson, ed., *The Church, Politics and Patronage in the Fifteenth Century* (Gloucester: Sutton, 1984), 156–57.

45. For general biographical details, see Arthur Francis Leach, *Early Yorkshire Schools,* YASRS 33 (Leeds: Yorkshire Archaeological Society, 1899), 2:xxiii–xxvi; *BRUC,* 1593–1596; John Guest, *Thomas de Rotherham, Archbishop of York,* 5–13; and more accessibly, Henry Leigh Bennett, *Archbishop Thomas Rotherham* (Lincoln: J. W. Ruddock, 1901). Nicholas Orme's remarks on Rotherham, *English Schools in the Middle Ages* (London, 1973), 78, 126, and 137, recapitulate material in Leach. See also John N. Miner, *The Grammar Schools of Medieval England: A. F. Leach in Historiographical Perspectives* (Montreal: McGill-Queen's Univ. Press, 1990); and Astrik Gabriel, "Motivations of the Founders of Medieval Colleges," in Astrik L. Gabriel, ed., *Garlandia. Studies in the History of the Mediaeval University* (Notre Dame, Ind.: Univ. of Notre Dame Press, 1969), 211–23. The book gift is discussed by Bennett, 62–63. A reevaluation of Rotherham's munificence as a book donor appears in N. R. Ker, "Medieval Manuscripts from Norwich Cathedral Priory," *TCBS* 1 (1949–1953): 1–2. A seventeenth-century donor's book, now Cambridge University Library MS Oo.7.52, contains a list "ex dono Reverendi Patris in Christo Tho. Rotherami Episcopi Lincolniensis et Cancellarii Angliae" of some 200 volumes, but Ker doubts whether they were all given by Rotherham. On this issue see J. C. T. Oates and H. L. Pink, "Three Sixteenth- Century Catalogues of the University Library," *TCBS* 1 (1949–1953): 310–11.

46. The manuscripts are Cambridge University Library MS Dd. 1.31, *Catholicon* (Oates and Pink, p. 321); Cambridge University Library MS Ff.3.5, Apuleius, *De Deo Socratis,* and Macrobius, *Saturnalia;* Cambridge University Library MS Ff.4.38, tables to theological treatises; and Cambridge University Library MS Gg.4 .5, Alexandrides and Lucan (Oates and Pink, pp. 316, 337). Why Ker did not include Cambridge University Library MS Ff. 3.15, discussed below, is not clear.

47. See Bennett, *Archbishop Rotherham,* 64–70, and James, *Pembroke,* 166–67.

48. His final will is York DCAB II.23, with a roll copy also containing the book inventory now Cambridge, Sidney Sussex College, MS 3. The will of 1475 is published by Guest, *Thomas Rotherham,* 135. See James, *Sidney Sussex,* 2–9, for description of MSS 2 and 3. The foundation and the archbishop's will are discussed by Bennett, *Archbishop Rotherham,* pp. 137–62, who, however, devotes only a few sentences to the books.

49. York Minster Library MS XVI.A.6 is described in *MMBL*, Piper, 691–92, and mentioned by S. Harrison Thomson, *The Writings of Robert Grosseteste Bishop of Lincoln 1235–1253* (1940; reprint, New York: Kraus, 1971), 160–61. On the Cambridge University Library volume, see Oates and Pink, 324. MS Ff. 3.15 is item 118 of the catalogue of 1556–57 "Compendium Morale" or item 125 "dicta Lincoln'," and appears to have been item 186 of Rotherham's donation. For a list in the catalogue of 1573 headed "ex dono Tho. Rotherham," see ibid., 330–32, comprising sixty-six items of which a Livy (105); a Liber Theologicus (112); the "dicta Lincoln'" already referred to; a tractatus de occupacione cordis (114); a Egesippus (115); a Franciscus Accursus (116); a four-volume Scotus (117); a Thomas Aquinas (118); a "Pars," probably canon law (120); a liber distinctionum (127); a Bartholomew, *super Lecturas Dominic Abbatis* (128); a Pars Iuris (129); a Plautus (130); and a Bible (163) are specifically called manuscripts. Trinity College Cambridge MS O.4.40 is described by James, *Trinity*, 3:288. Sidney Sussex MS 2 gives on fol. 12v the second folio reading "tibus," which allows this codex to be identified as one of the books of the Rotherham bequest.

50. These colophons occur in York Minster Library MS XVI.A.6, on fol. 183v, and in Cambridge University Library MS Ff.3.15, on fols. 184r–v. As can be seen from this foliation, Schaw wrote each manuscript with the same number of long lines on the same scale to produce virtually identical texts. A Perceval Schaw was admitted fellow of Peterhouse in 1447 (Walker, *A Biographical Register*, 1:46).

51. See for other examples, Hunter Blair, "The Armorials," 7–8. Bennett, *Archbishop Rotherham*, 165, discusses the arms as well, giving three variants.

52. See S. L. Greenslade, "The Contents of the Library of Durham Cathedral Priory," *TAASDN* (1965): 367, and Dobson, *Durham Priory, 1400–1450*, 370.

53. See Friedman, ed., *John de Foxton's Liber Cosmographiae*, xli–xlii.

Appendix A: The Pigment *Folium*

1. See Merrifield, cxcii.

2. See Brunello, ed., *De Arte Illuminandi*, 177, 208.

3. N. Joly, "Recherches sur la fabrication du tournésol en drapeaux, et sur le principe colorant du *Chrozophora tinctoria* employé à cette fabrication," *Annales de Chemie et de Physique*, 3d ser., 6 (1842): 111–26.

4. On Grand-Gallargues, see Joanne, *Dictionnaire géographique et administratif de la France*, 4:1759. Eugène Germer-Durand, *Dictionnaire Topographique du département du Gard* (Paris: Imprimarie Imperiale, 1868), 94, said the town had thirty households in 1384 and was still of fairly good size in 1434. For a present-day population figure of 9,103 for the whole canton of Vauvert, see Dominique Lacroix, *Paroisses et communes de France: Dictionnaire d'histoire administrative et démographique* (Paris: CNRS, 1986), 462. See also René Maruejol, *Le Gard à travers l'histoire* (Nîmes: Assoc. . . . du Gard, 1973).

5. J. Hughes, *Une Excursion dans la Commune de Grand-Gallargues* (Nîmes: J. Hughes, 1836), 145.

6. Joly, 118. He also experimented on his own with *Chrozophora tinctoria*. Grinding up roots, stems, leaves, and flowers, Joly found the juice to have a green suspension from which a violet supernatant rose to the surface. Evaporating the juice to an azur-colored resin that could be used as a watercolor paint, he found that treated with acid, the resin became irreversibly red, going to yellow. Other experiments that he performed with the cloths of Grand-Gallargues steeped in cold water produced a blue-tinted liquid. This too would turn irreversibly red by contact with acid. The liquid from

these cloths changed color quickly, going from blue to red in several days, as did the dry cloths themselves in air and humidity (121–26). This behavior is in keeping with the general instability of the color as noted by Wallert.

7. *Colour Index*, 3241.

8. Brunello, *L'arte della Tintura*, 284–87, 304–305, discusses the invention and development of these dyes in detail.

9. Gerard, *The Herball*. 335–336.

10. Loc. cit. This portion of the manuscript has been published, translated, and dated by Daniel V. Thompson, Jr., *"Liber de coloribus Illuminatorum siue Pictorum* from *Sloane MS. No. 1754," Speculum* 1 (1926): 299.

11. See H. Loret and A. Barrandon, *Flore de Montpellier* (Montpellier: C. Coulet, 1876), 2:597.

12. On geographic distribution, see D. Prain, "The Genus *Chrozophora," Kew Bulletin* (1918); 103–109; Marcel Guinochet and Roger de Vilmorin, *Flore de France* (Paris: CNRS, 1973), fasc. 2, p. 767; G. Kuhnholtz-Lordat and G. Blanchet, *Flore des environs immédiats de Montpellier* (Paris: P. Lechevalier, 1948), 2:157; Thomas G. Tutin et al., eds., *Flora Europaea* (Cambridge: Cambridge Univ. Press, 1968), 2:211; Pietro Zanghieri, *Flora Italica* (Padua: CEDAM, 1976), 1:360, item 388; H. S. Thompson, *Flowering Plants of the Riviera* (London: Longmans, 1914), 189; Joaquin Más y Guindal, *Plantas Tintóreas, Taniferas y Cauchiferas* (Madrid: Ministerio de Agricultura, 1943), 44–45; Michael Zohary, *Flora Palaestina* (Jerusalem: Academy of Sciences and Humanities, 1972), pt. 2, p. 267 and pl. 385; George E. Post, *Flora of Syria, Palestine and Sinai* (Beirut: Amer. Univ. of Beirut Press, 1933), 2: 507, and A. Radcliffe-Smith, "Chrozophora A. Juss," in P. H. Davis ed., *Flora of Turkey and the East Aegean Islands* (Edinburgh Univ. Press, 1982), 7:567–69. The information about *Chrozophora tinctoria*'s occurrence in Greece was provided in a letter of 5 Mar. 1989 by Professor O. H. Volk of the Institute for Pharmacy and Botany of the University of Würzburg, and about its use in Syria through discussions with Dr. G. M. Churukian, of Paris, Illinois.

13. See V. K. Kapoor et al., "Studies on some Indian Seed Oils," *Fitoterapia* 57 (1986): 188–90, who call the plant *Chrozophora indica*. See also Wallert, "*Chrozophora*," n. 15.

14. Roosen-Runge, *Farbgebung*, 2:35.

15. See Françoise Flieder, "Mise au point des techniques d'identification des pigments et des liants inclus dans la couche picturales de enluminures de manuscrits," *StC* 13 (1968): 69. Thomas and Flieder, "La composition des parchemins pourprés," find that the "codex purpureus" manuscripts Bibliothèque Nationale MS suppl. grèc. 1286, Sinope Gospels, second half of the sixth century, and Bibliothèque Municipale de Reims MS 11, Gospels of the Cathedral of Reims, second half of the ninth century, were prepared with *folium* rather than, as one might expect, with a purple extracted from the shellfish *murex brandaris*, or orseille, a colorant made from a lichen. Only *folium* contains, according to Thomas and Flieder, an "aliphatic" colorant, whose characteristics appeared in chromatographic analyses of the two manuscripts (232–33).

16. Wallert, "*Chrozophora*," 146.

17. *Conn's Biological Stains*, 339.

18. C. Long, *Biochemist's Handbook* (London: Spon, 1961) and *The Merck Index*, 11th ed. (Rahway, N.J.: Merck, 1989), no. 5426. On azolithmin, see Kolthoff, *Acid Base Indicators*, 160–62, 174, 208, 355, 361, 365–66, 373, 377, 387.

19. Wallert, "*Chrozophora*," 146–47.

20. Thompson, ed., *De Arte Illuminandi*, n. 47.

21. C. R. Dodwell, ed. and trans. *Theophilus, The Various Arts, De Diversis Artibus* (reprint, Oxford, 1986), chap. 33, pp. 30–31.

22. Cyril S. Smith and John G. Hawthorne, eds. and trans., *Mappae Clavicula: A Little Key to the World of Medieval Techniques*, in *TAPS*, n.s., 64, 4 (Philadelphia: Amer. Philosophical Soc., 1974) *s.v. folium, clarea*. For more recent studies of this work, see Robert Halleux and Paul Meyvaert, "les origines de la Mappa Clavicula," *AHDLMA* 54 (1987): 7–58; Eckhard Freise, "Zur Person des Theophilus und seiner monastichen Umwelt," in Anton Legner, ed., *Ornamenta Ecclesiae: Kunst und Kunstler der Romanik* (Cologne: Schnütgen Museum, 1985), 1:357–62; and Birgit Bänsch and Susanne Linscheid-Burdich, "Theophilus, Schedula diversarum artium: Textauszüge," in the same volume, 363–84.

23. Roosen-Runge, *Farbgebung*, 2:34–36.

24. It is to be hoped that studies on various medieval painters' pigments now being conducted by the Forschungstelle für Technik mittelalterlicher Buchmalerei in Göttingen, established by Heinz Roosen-Runge and now directed by Robert Fuchs and Doris Oltrögge, will soon be published.

25. Slightly different figures are given by Wallert. "*Chrozophora*," 146.

26. Wallert, "*Chrozophora*," 145, follows this reversed order: "the juice squeezed out of the seed capsules of *Chrozophora tinctoria* is of a deep, inky blue with a considerable coloring strength. Nevertheless, when the raw extract is treated with acids, the color changes via a much weaker violet to the red."

27. Brunello, ed., *De Arte Illuminandi*, 62–66. The reading of the scribal abbreviation for *inter* or *infra* may have to do with Merrifield's idea of the name *folium* coming from the drying of the cloths "among" the leaves of a blotter book.

28. John Harley and Francis Bickley, eds., *Report on the Manuscripts of the Late Reginald Rawdon Hastings, Esq., of the Manor House, Ashby de la Zouche*, London: Historical Manuscripts Commission, H. M. Stationery Office, 1928), 1:417–30. The passage in question comes from p. 428. This and other recipes from the book were also published, with minor errors in spelling, by J. R. Clemens, "Fifteenth Century English Recipes for the Making of Pigments," *AArc* 34 (1933): 208–209, who does not appear to have consulted the manuscript, since what he offers as foliation is actually the page numbers from Harley and Bickley, whose work, however, goes unmentioned in his article.

29. Viola and Rosamund Borradaile, eds. and trans., *The Strasburg Manuscript: A Medieval Painters' Handbook* (London: Scopas, 1966), 39.

30. See J. O. Halliwell, ed., *Early English Miscellanies in Prose and Verse* (1855; reprint, New York: AMS, 1966), 77. In addition to *clarea* or glair, other binders were sometimes used for *folium*, such as gum Arabic, isinglass, or a fishglue called *icthycolleon* made from sturgeon bladders cooked for a long time over low heat.

31. The *Liber de Coloribus* says much the same thing, with the difference that the clothlet is cut into fine shreds and then skimmed from the glair after it has released its pigment (Thompson, ed., *Liber de Coloribus*, 287). Treatments of this binder are by D. V. Thompson, Jr., "The *De Clarea* of the so-called 'Anonymous Bernensis'," *Technical Studies in the Field of the Fine Arts* 1 (1932): 8–19 and 69–81, and, more recently, Rolf E. Straub, ed., " 'De Clarea' in der Burgerbibliothek Berne. Eine Anleitung für Buchmalerei aus dem Hochmittelalter," *Jahresbericht 1964* (Zurich: Schweizerisches Institut für Kunstwissenschaft, 1965), 89–114.

32. Brunello, ed., *De Arte Illuminandi*, p. 186. See also Hellmut Lehmann-Haupt, ed., *The Göttingen Model Book* (1972; reprint Columbia, Mo.: Univ. of Missouri Press, 1978), fol. 6r, p. 45.

33. See Roosen-Runge, *Farbgebung,* 1:42–43; James, *Corpus,* 2:52–56; and F. Wormald, *The Miniatures in the Gospels of St. Augustine (Corpus Christi College, Ms 286)* (Cambridge: Cambridge Univ. Press, 1954), 1. See also E. A. Lowe, *Codices Latini Antiquiores* (Oxford: Clarendon, 1935), vol. 2, no. 126.

34. For a convenient assortment of the different tones of *folium,* see Carl Nordenfalk, *Celtic and Anglo-Saxon Painting* (New York: Braziller, 1977), pls. 9, 18, 37, 44, and 48. In a letter of 24 Aug. 1989, and in "The Pigments and Organic Colours," in Peter Fox, ed., *The Book of Kells Ms. 58 Trinity College Library, Dublin: Commentary* (Lucerne: Faksimile-Verlag, 1990), 215–17, Anthony Caines suggests that the manuscript used a purple made from madder or a lichen called cudbear rather than *folium.*

35. For a good recent discussion, see Janet Backhouse, *The Lindisfarne Gospels* (Oxford: Phaidon and British Library, 1981).

36. See Kendrick, ed., *Evangelium Quattuor,* 2:5.

37. These identifications were made by Roosen-Runge and Werner, "The Pictorial Technique," 268–71. See also Alexander, "Some Aesthetic Principles," 145–54.

Appendix C: Book Ownership in the North: A Census from Wills

1. A possible Newton book, once in Cambridge, Peterhouse MS no. 165. See James, *Peterhouse,* 12.

2. A Newton manuscript, now Cambridge, Peterhouse MS no. 275. This English book dates from the fourteenth century. It has very fine *litterae partitae* initials and two scales of script, a large *textura* for the text and a smaller cursive commentary. See James, *Peterhouse,* 348.

3. This legacy is probably Bishop Thomas Langley's copy of Pierre Bersuire, *Reductorium Morale,* now Durham Cathedral Library MS A.I.17,18,19.

4. A Newton manuscript, now Cambridge, Peterhouse MS no. 173. This Italian book has very handsome initials and dates from the late fourteenth or early fifteenth century. See James, *Peterhouse,* 200, and more recently, Colin N. Mann, *Petrarch Manuscripts in the British Isles* (Padua: Editrice Antenore, 1975).

5. A Newton manuscript, now Cambridge, Peterhouse MS no. 249. This book was made in England in the fifteenth century, James, *Peterhouse,* 303–4.

6. Rudolf Schottlander, ed., *Francesco Petrarcha De remediis utriusque Fortune* (Munich: Fink, 1988).

7. A Newton manuscript, now Cambridge, Peterhouse MS no. 162. This fourteenth-century book bears Newton's name as the giver, and the catch words use English long *r.* See James, *Peterhouse,* 190.

8. A Newton book, once in Cambridge, Peterhouse MS no. 164. See James, *Peterhouse,* 12.

9. A Newton manuscript, now Cambridge, Peterhouse MS no. 196. On this fifteenth-century English book, see n. 11, below, and James, *Peterhouse,* 230.

10. A Newton manuscript, now Cambridge, Peterhouse MS no. 258. This well-written fifteenth-century English book has fine *champ* initials. See James, *Peterhouse,* 323–24.

11. A Newton manuscript, now Cambridge, Peterhouse MS no. 196. This book appears to be English. See James, *Peterhouse,* 230n. 8, and C. R. Schrader, "A Handlist of Extant Manuscripts Containing the *De Re Militari* of Favius Vegetius Renatus," *Scriptorium* 33 (1979): 280–305.

12. A Newton manuscript, now Cambridge, Peterhouse MS no. 196. See note 9, above.

13. A Newton manuscript, now Oxford, Bodleian Library MS Rawlinson C. 162.

14. Possibly Peter of Poitiers, *Compendium veteris testamenti,* now York Minster Library MS Additional 256, a roll.

15. A Newton manuscript, now Oxford, Bodleian Library MS Rawlinson C.162.

16. This book is now Pembroke College MS 216. It was left by Thomas Anlaby.

17. See B. Haage, "Zur Überlieferung des 'Malogranatum,' " *ZDADL* 108 (1979): 407–14.

18. A Newton manuscript, Cambridge, Peterhouse MS no. 233. This book is in an Italian hand. See James, *Peterhouse,* 285.

19. This legacy may possibly be British Library MS Harley 2409, William Flete, *Remedia contra temptationes,* owned by Mald or Maud Wade, prioress of Swine, East Yorkshire, before 1482.

20. A Newton Manuscript, now Oxford, Bodleian Library MS Laud Misc. 140, fol. 1, "iste liber est de thesauraria Ebor ecclesie."

21. A Newton book, Cambridge, Trinity College, MS R.5.40. See *MLGB,* 216.

22. A Newton manuscript, now Cambridge, Peterhouse MS no. 167. This handsome thirteenth-century book bears Newton's name in a near contemporary script. See James, *Peterhouse,* 194.

23. A Newton manuscript, now Cambridge, Peterhouse MS no. 149. This elegantly produced book dates from the twelfth and thirteenth centuries. See James, *Peterhouse,* 177–78.

24. Helen P. Forshaw, ed., *Edmund of Abingdon's Speculum Religiosorum* and *Speculum Ecclesie,* Auctores Britannici Medii Aevi 3 (Oxford: Oxford Univ. Press, 1973). See 11.

25. A Newton manuscript, now Cambridge, Peterhouse MS no. 133. This large, handsome English book dates from the late fourteenth or early fifteenth century. See James, *Peterhouse,* 160–61.

26. See Roger Ellis, "Flores ad Fabricandam . . . Coronam: An Investigation into the Uses of the *Revelations* of St. Bridget of Sweden in Fifteenth-Century England," *MAe* 51 (1982): 163–86.

27. Perhaps an Agnes Stapleton manuscript. See J. Bazire and E. Colledge, eds., *The Chastising of God's Children and the Treatise of Perfection of the Sons of God* (Oxford: Blackwell, 1957).

28. Ps.-Bonaventure in *Opera omnia edita Collegii a S. Bonaventurae* (Quarrachi, Italy: Collegium S. Bonaventurae, 1899). See P. S. Jolliffe, "Middle English Translations of the *De Exterioris et Interioris Hominis Compositione,*" *MS* 36 (1974): 259–77.

29. Mary Patrick Candon, "An Edition of the 15th-Century Middle English Translation of Gerard of Liège's *De Doctrina Cordis*" (Ph.D. diss., Fordham University, 1963). See G. Hendrix, "Hugh of St. Cher, O. P., Author of Two Texts Attributed to the Thirteenth-Century Cistercian Gerard of Liège," *Studia Cisterciensia R.P. Edmondo Mikkers Oblata, Studie Cistercienses* 21 (1950), 1:343–56.

30. Crispin's work is edited by Anna S. Abulafia Auctores Britannici Medii Aevi 8 (Oxford: Oxford Univ. Press, 1986). See generally, Arthur Lukyn Williams, *Adversus Judaeos. A Bird's-eye View of Christian Apologiae Until the Renaissance* (Cambridge: Cambridge Univ. Press, 1935).

31. See Rosemarie Potz McGerr, ed., *The Pilgrimage of the Soul* (New York: Garland, 1990).

32. Now York Minster Library MS XVI.A.6; this book was given by Archbishop Thomas Rotherham to his new foundation, Rotherham College.

33. See *Stimulus Amoris Fr. Jacobi Mediolanensis: Canticum Pauperis Fr. Johannis Peck-*

ham. Ed. PP. Collegii S. Bonaventurae. Bibliotheca Franciscana Ascetica Medii Aevi, 4 (Quaracchi, Italy: Collegium S. Bonaventurae, 1905) and B. Distelbrink, _Bonaventurae Scripta: Authentica, Dubia vel Spuria_ (Rome: Istituto Storico Cappuccini, 1975), 194–95.

34. See George F. Reinecke, ed., _John Lydgate, St. Albon and St. Amphibalus_ (New York: Garland, 1989). Though not mentioned by the editor, this manuscript is now probably San Marino, Calif., Huntington Library MS HM 140.

35. Theresa A. Halligan, ed., _The Booke of Gostlye Grace of Mechtild of Hackeborn_ (Toronto: Pontifical Institute, 1979).

36. See L. E. Boyle, "The _Ocula Sacerdotis_ and Some Other Works of William of Pagula," _TRHS_, 5th ser., 5 (1955): 81–110.

37. Xaverio Ochoa and Aloisio Diez, eds., _Raimundus de Pennaforte, Summa de Poenitentia_ (Rome: Commentariarum pro Religiosis, 1975–76).

38. See Joseph E. Gallagher, "The Sources of Caxton's _Ryal Book_ and _Doctrinal of Sapience_," _SP_ 62 (1965): 40.

39. See R. O'Brien, "The _Stimulus Peccatoris_ of William of Rymington," _Citeaux, Commentarii Cisterciensis_ 16 (1965): 278–304.

40. G. Holmstedt, ed., _Speculum Christiani. A Middle English Treatise of the 14th Century_, EETS: o.s., 182 (1933; reprint, Millwood, N. Y.: Kraus, 1971). For a more up-to-date account of this work and its English manuscript tradition, see Vincent Gillespie, "The Evolution of the _Speculum Christiani_," in Minnis, ed., _Latin and Vernacular_, 39–61.

41. Edward H. Weatherly, ed., _Speculum Sacerdotale_, EETS: o.s., 200 (London: Oxford Univ. Press, 1936).

42. Seigfried Wenzel, ed., _Fasciculus Morum: A Fourteenth-Century Preacher's Handbook_ (Philadelphia: Univ. of Pennsylvania Press, 1989).

43. In A. C. Peltier, ed., _S. Bonaventurae Opera Omnia_ (Paris: Augustae Taurinorum, H. Marietti, 1866), 8: 247–346.

44. Useful for some of the titles in this category is G. Dolezalek, _Verzeichnis der Handschriften zum römischen Recht bis 1600_ (Frankfurt-am-Main: Max-Planck Institut für Europäischen Rechtsgeschichte, 1972), 4 vols.

45. This book once belonged to Thomas Hebbeden, (fol.1); it is now Durham Cathedral Library MS C.III.11.

46. A Newton manuscript, now York Minster Library MS XVI.P.5. See _MLGB_, Watson, 113.

47. A Newton manuscript, now York Minster Library MS XVI.P.7. See _MLGB_, Watson, 113.

48. A Newton manuscript, now York Minster Library MS XVI.P.6. See _MLGB_, Watson, 113.

49. A Newton manuscript, now Cambridge, Peterhouse MS no. 36. This large, beautifully written fourteenth-century Italian book had good historiated initials, now mostly cut out, and bears Newton's name as the giver. See James, _Peterhouse_, 54.

50. Possibly a Newton Manuscript, now Cambridge, Gonville and Caius College MS no. 327/527. The book is of thirteenth-century date. See James, _Gonville and Caius_, 1:169–70. The attribution has been made by M. E. S. Walcott, "Mediaeval Libraries," _TRSL_, 2d ser., 9 (1870): 77.

51. See Neil Ker, "Patrick Young's Catalogue of the Manuscripts of Lichfield Cathedral," _MRS_ 2 (1950): 161.

52. A Newton Manuscript, now York Minster Library MS XVI. P.8. See _MLGB_, Watson, 113.

53. Possibly a Newton manuscript, now Gonville and Caius College MS no. 242/

488. See James, *Gonville and Caius*, 1:293–94 and Walcott, 77. This fourteenth-century English book has elegantly flourished initials. Another copy in the same collection, no. 482/478, belonged to William Poteman. This Italian book is of thirteenth-century date. See James, ibid., 2:552–53.

54. A Newton manuscript, possibly now Cambridge, Gonville and Caius College MS no. 118/187. This English manuscript is of fourteenth-century date. See James, *Gonville and Caius*, 1:126.

55. A Newton manuscript, now Cambridge, Peterhouse MS no. 39. This large, Italian book is of fourteenth century date. See James, *Peterhouse*, 56.

56. Possibly a Newton manuscript, now Cambridge, Peterhouse MS no. 34. This Italian book is of fourteenth-century date. See James, *Peterhouse*, 52–3.

57. A Newton manuscript, possibly now Cambridge, Gonville and Caius College MS no. 118/187. This English manuscript is of fourteenth-century date. See James, *Gonville and Caius*, 1:126.

58. Possibly a Newton manuscript, now Cambridge, Gonville and Caius College MS no. 261/665. On this elegantly produced thirteenth-century Italian book, see James, *Gonville and Caius*, 1:315–16.

59. Possibly a Newton manuscript, now Oxford, Bodleian Library MS Laud Misc. 646 (SC 1141). See Walcott, 77.

60. Lloyd and Bernadine Daly, eds., *Summa Britonis: Guillelmi Britonis Expositiones Vocabulorum Biblie* (Padua: Editrice Antenore, 1975).

61. F. Stegmüller, *Repertorium Biblicum Medii Aevi* (Madrid: Istituto Francisco Suárez, 1950–80), 3:5566.

62. A Newton manuscript, now Cambridge, Peterhouse MS no. 144. This large, well-written English book with tables dates from the fourteenth and fifteenth centuries. See James, *Peterhouse*, 171–72.

63. A Newton manuscript, now Cambridge, Peterhouse MS no. 237. This English book dates from the fourteenth and fifteenth centuries. See James, *Peterhouse*, 288–89.

64. See Percival Horton-Smith Hartley and Harold Richard Eldridge, *Johannes de Mirfeld of St. Bartholomew's, Smithfield: His Life and Works* (Cambridge: Cambridge Univ. Press, 1936) and more recently, Fay Marie Getz, "John Mirfeld and the *Breviarium Bartholomei:* The Medical Writings of a Clerk of St. Bartholomew's Hospital in the Later Fourteenth Century," *SSFHMB* 37 (1985): 24–26.

65. G. Kratzmann and E. Gee, eds., *The Dialogues of Creatures Moralysed*, Oxford Medieval and Renaissance Texts (Oxford: Clarendon, 1988).

66. Joseph Gildea, ed., *Remediarium conversorum: A Synthesis in Latin of Moralia in Job by Gregory the Great/Peter of Waltham* (Villanova, Pa.: Villanova Univ. Press; London: Associated Univ. Press, 1984). This work is sometimes confused with the *Pantheologus* of Peter of Cornwall.

67. Christina von Nolcken, *The Middle English Translation of the Rosarium Theologie* (Heidelberg: Winter, 1979).

68. Oxford, Lincoln College MS Lat. 15. See Coxe, *Catalogus Codicum*, 23.

69. A Bishop Thomas Langley book, now Durham Cathedral MS A.I.1.

70. On the Toletan tables, also called Alfonsine Tables after Alfonso X of Castile, see J. D. North, "The Alfonsine Tables in England," in Y. Maeyama and W. G. Saltzer, eds., *Prismata. Festschrift für Willy Hartner* (Wiesbaden: Georg Olms, 1977), 269–300, and North's *Chaucer's Universe* (Oxford: Oxford Univ. Press, 1988), 148–49.

Glossary of Art Historical and Codicological Terms

Acanthus: Long, deeply notched, or lobed leaves wrapped around vines in border decoration.

Anglicana: A literary cursive hand common in fourteenth- and fifteenth-century English books. Its dominant features are a high two-compartment *a* rising above the headline, a looped stem on *d* inclining to the left, a two-compartment *g*, and a long *r*, whose tail descends well below the base line.

Antiphonal: A very large book containing the music and texts of the daily offices sung in the choir. Sometimes called a *cowcher* because it lay on a stand.

Arabesque: A springing or arching vine or tendril used in border decoration.

Arma Christi: The various implements of the Passion, such as the Crown of Thorns and the nails, represented heraldically on a shield or grouped in other ways around the crucified figure of Christ.

Ascender: The vertical strokes of letters like *h, b, l,* rising above the head line.

Austin: English name for the order of Augustinian or White Friars.

Babewyn: A polymorphic or grotesque figure common in fourteenth-century English border decoration.

Baguette: A long, slender or bar-like border element.

Banderole: A ribbon-like frame containing words of a text.

Bar border: A narrow freestanding border that sometimes develops as a tendril put out by an element of an initial letter.

Bas-de-page: A drawing or scene at the bottom of a page, usually unconnected with the art of the border decoration and often of a parodic or "subversive" character.

Bâtarde: A Gothic text hand containing cursive elements, usually inclined sharply to the right and with a low balance and pronounced dagger-shaped descenders of *s* and long *f*.

Beatus initial: The elaborately decorated *B* of the Psalm 1, which begins with "Beatus vir."

Blob: A ball-shaped motif used at the ends of sprays in border decoration.

Breviary: A book containing all the offices for the daily hours of the liturgy for public performance during the four seasons of the liturgical year. Large ones are distinguished from smaller ones called *portoforia*.

Cadel: An elaboration of a capital letter in the form of strap, ribbon or lattice penwork, in which the strokes suggest a woven carpet; cadels often occur in the musical portion of a service book.

Calyx: Cup-shaped leaf whorl around a flower bud in border decoration.

Carpel: The central seed-bearing female organ of a flower.

Carpet page: A form of decoration common in Hiberno-Saxon art in which the ground of an initial is formed of densely woven interlace reminiscent of an oriental carpet.

Cartulary: A collection of various documents usually made by a religious institution recording its property, lands and feudal obligations.

Catchword: A word or words written at the bottom right of the last verso of a manuscript gathering. It comprises the first word or words of the beginning of the next gathering, so that the book may be properly assembled during binding.

Cartouche: A banner-like frame around a catchword.

Chainwork: A form of pen decoration in which a border bar is made from interlinked, chain-like elements.

Champ: Literally "field," a small, colored initial on a broad ground of gold leaf, often with sprays or penwork flourishing at the corners.

Clarea: A medium for binding pigment to parchment, made of eggwhite.

Colophon: An inscription at the end of a text, giving information about the scribe, the place and date of completion of the book, and often incorporating a pious saying, motto, or brief witty poem.

Commendatio animae: Commendation of the soul, prayers to be recited for a dying person, a text contained in psalters and breviaries and often illustrated by a soul lifted to God in a napkin.

Cornerpiece: A large, rectangular motif appearing at the top and bottom corners of bar borders.

Decretals: A collection of canon law drawn from the edicts of Pope Gregory IX (1234) or Pope Boniface VIII (1298).

Descender: The vertical stroke of letters like *p* "descending" below the base line.

Diapering: A geometrical grid-like decorative pattern, usually of diamonds or squares, behind the figures in a miniature, each compartment containing a contrasting color.

Feast of the Relics of the Cathedral: October 19, the day on which the relics of the saints of York Minster were venerated annually and often noted in red in kalendars of York liturgical books.

Filigree: A lace-like pattern of red, blue or violet penwork outlining or surrounding a major initial.

Finial: The elaborated end of a tendril or vine freestanding in a margin.

Floriated initial: An initial whose bows or other compartments contain floral motifs rather than representational scenes.

Flourishing: The penwork decoration of the field and surrounding area of an initial letter with foliate or arabesque penwork often in contrasting colors of red and black, red and blue, or red and violet-purple.

Folio: The recto and verso of a single leaf of a manuscript made by folding a single large sheet of parchment or paper once.

Frogspawn: A cluster of small circular or dot motifs forming part of the penwork outlining or infill of an initial.

Gathering: The folded leaves arranged in groups of six, eight or twelve folios, making pamphlet-like units that when sewn together are sometimes called *quires.*

Girdle book: A folded set of tables or small book of a practical, astrological, or mathematical character carried in a pouch at the girdle or hung by a leather loop on the cover from the girdle.

Gloss: Commentary on a literary, biblical, legal, or other text, which can be marginal, interlinear, or arranged in blocks around the text.

Golden Legend: The *Aurea Legenda,* compiled by Jacob of Voragine between 1255 and 1266, containing the lives of the saints arranged according to the order of their feasts in the church kalendar.

Gradual: A service book of medium-large size containing music for the great feasts.

Guide letters: Small letters or words placed in the margin next to the space —or in the space itself—where a penwork or painted initial is to come, indicating to the artist what he should draw and where. They are usually painted over by the artist or trimmed when the book is bound.

Gutter: The space between the outer rulings around two columns of text on the page.

Heraldic representations of coats of arms on shields: The French names of the heraldic colors mentioned in this book are *or,* gold, *argent,* silver or white, *gules,* red, *azure,* blue, *sable,* black, *vert,* green, *purpure,* purple, ermine and *vaire,* fur patterns in black or blue-gray on white. Among the terms for the charges or stripe-like motifs on the field of a shield are *bar,* a series of horizontal bands; *fess,* a horizontal band; and *bend,* a diagonal band. Objects sometimes appear there as well, such as a wheel or rowel-like shape called a *mullet.*

Historiated initial: An initial containing, usually within a bow, a picture of someone or something.

Horae: Book of hours containing daily offices of the Virgin, primarily for the domestic use of lay people, comprised of the hours of the Virgin, Office for the Dead, penitential Psalms, gradual Psalms, kalendar and litany; other hours and prayers were added. This material was recited by the owner at the canonical hours of the day.

Inhabited initial: An initial containing a figure of some kind.

Illuminated manuscript: A manuscript with border decoration or miniatures within the text containing gold leaf or paint.

Illustrated manuscript: A manuscript with drawings or paintings of representational subjects, often pictorializing events or scenes in the text.

Impaled: A term from heraldry indicating the combining of two families' arms, usually through marriage, with the shield divided vertically and the arms of one family occupying the left or sinister side and the other the right or dexter side.

I/J border: A border made from the elaborated descender of the capital letter *I* or *J* used as a major initial.

Infill: Non-representational decorative work within the bow of an initial letter.

International Gothic Style: Late gothic painting in Europe about 1400 showing a strong admixture of the different decorative styles of Europe, especially Italy, France, and Bohemia. The style contains much naturalistic detail, architectural motifs such as canopies or oratories in margins, and realistic portraits of owners or patrons, scribes, and illuminators.

Kalendar: A listing of the feasts and saints' days of the liturgical year arranged by months beginning in January. The presence of some saints and feasts is locally determined.

Litany: Invocations of the saints arranged in order of martyrs, confessors, virgins and followed by requests for protection against various evils. The litany forms a distinct portion of certain types of service books and often contains saints of local popularity.

Littera magna: Large colored letters.

Littera partita **initial:** An initial in three colors, which uses the white of the paper or parchment as an uncolored area outlined by lobed or dentilated areas of red or blue on each side, sometimes called parted or reserved, or coxcomb initials.

Littera parva: Small colored letters.

Lombardic letters: Blue and red majuscule letters based on the curving forms of uncial script.

Major initial: The initial that indicates an important division in a work, such as the start of a new book.

Maiestas Domini: Christ in Majesty, usually seated on a rainbow.

Man of Sorrows: A devotional image of Christ as a frontal half-length figure with crossed or imploring hands, usually emerging from the tomb-chest.

Mariale: A book combining material about the Virgin Mary and prayers to her.

Medallion: A shield- or escutcheon-shaped frame that contains a vine pattern.

Mise-en-page: The visual organization or layout of a page in a manuscript.

Missal: Book containing masses for feast days and saints' days of the liturgical year. They are comprised of a temporale and sanctorale with the ordinary, preface, and canon of the mass and various votive masses for special occasions.

Monastic use: The liturgical practice of an enclosed order of religious such as Benedictines or Carthusians. Usually the founder of the order is specially commemorated.

Noli me tangere: The phrase "do not touch me," said by Jesus to Mary Magdalene after the Resurrection (John 20.17).

Obit: Record in a kalendar of the death date of a book's owner.

Obituary roll: A parchment roll, sometimes called a prayer roll, often many yards long, made to honor a dead ecclesiastic and sent round to other religious houses for the inscription of prayers.

Office for the Dead: Devotions to honor a dead person recited at vespers, matins, and lauds comprised of readings from the Psalms, the book of Job, and antiphons, versicles, and responses. It occurs in breviaries and sometimes in psalters and *horae* and is illustrated by monks praying over a pall-draped coffin or a scene of a burial.

Oratory: An architectural enclosure representing a small private chapel found in border decoration in the International Gothic Style.

Pamphlet: A group of quires forming a small volume often joined to an unrelated volume.

Paraph: What would today be called a paragraph mark, usually done in red or blue ink by a rubricator in medieval manuscripts.

Paschal verses: Mnemonic verses for the determination of Easter, a "movable" feast based on the lunar cycle.

Polymorph: A figure mixing human and animal parts found in border decoration.

Primer: A term often used to mean a book of hours.

Psalter: The book of Psalms used often by lay people, and in addition to the Psalms including a kalendar, offices and hours of various sorts.

Register: A portion of a border, boxed off from the rest by a vine or geometrical element.

Rinceaux: A spiraling pattern of foliage, often of gold, against a painted ground in a miniature.

Roundel: A circular frame in border decoration containing a decorative or representational image.

Rubricated: A service book containing music, usually on red staves.

Sanctorale: A book containing material about saints and their feasts.

Scroll: A book in a roll form, made of a number of rectangular strips of parchment or paper joined end to end.

Secretary: A script with cursive elements, often used for legal documents. It has considerable contrast between thick and thin strokes, many broken strokes, cusps on the bows of letters, and a single compartment *a*. Some forms can look superficially like *Anglicana*.

Spray: A group of arching tendrils ending in leaves, buds, or flowers, and lying parallel to each other.

Squiggle: A curlicue or corkscrew-like pen elaboration of the end of a spray or tendril.

Stationer: An establishment producing manuscripts and sometimes writing materials like parchment, paper, quills, and inks at retail.

Suffrage: A devotional text honoring a saint, containing beside a picture of the saint in question, an antiphon, versicle, and memorial prayer.

Swag: A penwork motif hanging below a flourished letter and tenuously attached by a single tendril.

Teasel: A spiny pod found in border decoration.

Textura: The formal script of service or high-quality books. Each letter is distinct from the others.

Transi **tomb:** A free standing tomb-chest with a sculptural representation of the dead on the lid, and on the actual chest below a carving of the corpse within rotting and eaten by worms.

Translation: The moving of a saint's relics from one church to another, the day of which is often commemorated in kalendars.

Trefoil: A termination to a vine in the form of three differently colored leaves.

Trellis border: A border in the form of parallel bars with ladder-like rungs of vinework upon which leaf clusters and other decoration are placed.

Use: The liturgical practice characteristic of a given region or locality, *e.g.,* York use. Uses can be monastic or secular.

Vein man: A standing figure with lines drawn to the various veins and instructions in roundels indicating which veins should be bled at what seasons of the year.

Versiculi: Small colored letters, usually the capitals for versicles in the text of a service book.

Vinet: Used in this book to mean an arching or spray-like motif of slender, ivy-like vine.

Zodiac man: A standing figure surrounded by the planets and twelve signs of the zodiac to show the influence of the heavens on human health.

Bibliography

Primary Sources

Arnold, Thomas, ed. *Henry of Huntingdon, Historia Anglorum*. Rolls Series no. 74. Reprint. Millwood, N.Y.: Kraus, 1964.

Assize rolls for Lancashire. *Lancashire Records Society* 47, 49, 1904–5.

Borthwick Institute for Historical Research, York. Also available as *Church Authority and Power in Medieval and Early Modern Britain Microform: The Episcopal Registers 1215–1650, Part One. Registers of the Archbishops of York, 1215–1650*. Brighton, Sussex: Harvester Press, 1983.

    Register 10, Zouche, 1342–52

    Register 11, Thoresby, 1352–73

    Register 12—13, Neville, 1374–88

    Register 14, Arundel, 1388–96

    Register 15, Waldby, 1396–98

    Register 16, Scrope, 1398–1405

    Register 17–18, Bowet, 1407–16, 1416–26

    Register 19, Kemp, 1426–52

    Register 20, Booth, 1452–64

    Register 23, Rotherham, 1480–1500

    Register 25, Savage, 1501–7

Bliss, William Henry, C. Johnson, and Jessie A. Twemlow, eds. *Calendar of Entries in the Papal Registers Relating to Great Britain and Ireland: Papal Letters*. London: H.M. Stationer's Office, 1893–97.

Bond, Edward A., ed. *Chronica Monasterii de Melsa* III. Rolls Series no. 43. 1886. Reprint. Millwood, N. Y.; Kraus, 1967.

Botfield B., ed. *Catalogi Veteres Librorum Ecclesiae Cathedralis Dunelmi*. Surtees Society Vol. 7. London: Surtees Society, 1838.

Catalogue of the Stowe Manuscripts in the British Museum. Vol. 1. London: British Museum, 1895.

Challenor, J., and C. Smith. *Index of Wills Proved in the Prerogative Court of Canterbury 1383–1558, and now Preserved in the Principal Probate Registry, Somerset House, London*. British Record Society Limited, Index Library 10. London, 1893–1895.

Ciaconius, A. *Vitae et res gestae pontificum Romanorum et S. R. E. Cardinalium.* Paris: P. and A. de Rubeis, 1687.

Clay, Charles Travis, ed. *York Minster Fasti.* Yorkshire Archaeological Society Record Series 124. Leeds, 1958.

Clay, J. W., ed. *North Country Wills: Abstracts of Wills at Somerset House and Lambeth Palace, 1383–1558.* Surtees Society Vol. 116. Durham: Surtees Society, 1908.

Collins, Francis C., ed. *Register of the Freemen of the City of York.* Surtees Society Vols. 96, 102. Durham: Surtees Society, 1897.

————. *Index of Wills in the York Registry 1389–1551,* YASRS 6. Worksop, Eng.: Yorkshire Archaeological Soc., 1889.

Constant, Jean Baptiste, ed. *Bullarium Franciscanum.* Rome: Sacrae Congregationis, 1759.

Craster, H. H. E., and M. E. Thornton, eds. *The Chronicle of St. Mary's Abbey, York.* Surtees Society Vol. 148. York: Surtees Society, 1934.

De Ricci, Seymour. *A Census of Medieval and Renaissance Manuscripts in the United States and Canada.* New York: H. W. Wilson, 1935–40.

Dendy, F. W., ed. *Visitations of the North.* Surtees Society Vol. 122. Durham: Surtees Society, 1912.

Dobson, R. B., ed. *York City Chamberlains' Account Rolls 1396–1500.* Surtees Society Vol. 192. Durham: Surtees Society, 1980.

Farrow, M. A. *Index of Wills Proved in the Consistory Court of Norwich 1370–1550.* I. Norfolk Record Society. London, 1943–1945.

Fowler, J. T., ed. *Extracts from the Account Rolls of the Abbey of Durham.* Surtees Society Vol. 99. Durham: Surtees Society, 1898.

Jones, B., ed. *John Le Neve, Fasti Ecclesiae Anglicanae 1300–1541,* Vol. 6, *Northern Province.* London: Athlone, 1963.

Kerhervé, J., Peres, A-F. and Tanguy, B., eds. *Les Biens de la couronne dans la sénéchaussée de Brest et Saint-Renan.* Brest: Institute Culturel de Bretagne, 1984.

Lamaré M., ed. *Inventaire-sommaire des archives départementales antérieures à 1790: Côtes-du-Nord.* Saint-Brieuc, France: Imprimerie et Librairie de Guyon, 1896.

Monsignano, Eliseus, ed. *Bullarium Carmelitanum.* Rome: G. Plachi, 1715.

[Paquelin, Louis], ed. *Sanctae Mechtildis . . . Liber Specialis Gratiae . . . Solesmensium OSB Monachorum Cura et Opera.* Poitiers: H. Oudin Frères, 1877.

Purvis, J. S. *A Mediaeval Act Book with Some Account of Ecclesiastical Jurisdiction at York.* York: Herald Printing Works, 1943.

Raine, James, ed. *Fabric Rolls of York Minster.* Surtees Society Vol. 35. Durham: Surtees Society, 1859.

————. *Historiae Dunelmensis Scriptores Tres, Gaufridus de Coldingham, Robertus de Graystanes, et Willielmus de Chambre.* Surtees Society Vol. 9. London: Surtees Society, 1834.

————. *The Obituary Roll of William Ebchester and John Burnby, Priors of Durham.* Surtees Society Vol. 31. Durham: Surtees Society, 1856.

————. *The Priory of Finchale, The Charters of Endowment, Inventories, and Account Rolls of the Priory of Finchale.* Surtees Society Vol. 6. Durham: Surtees Society, 1837.

————. *Testamenta Eboracensia.* Surtees Society Vols. 4, 30, 45, 53, 79, 106. Durham: Surtees Society, 1836–1902.

————. *Wills and Inventories Illustrative of the History, Manners, Language, Statistics &c. of the Northern Counties of England from the Eleventh Century Downwards.* Reprint. London, 1967.

————. *Yorkshire Fines.* Surtees Society Vol. 94. Durham: Surtees Society, 1897.

Rhymer, Thomas, ed. *Foedera.* London: J. Tonson, 1704–35.

Sellers, Maud, and Joyce W. Percy, eds. *York Memorandum Book.* Surtees Society Vols. 120, 125, 186. Durham: Surtees Society, 1912–73.

Shäfer, Karl H. *Die Ausgaben der apostolischen Kammer unter Johann XXII Nebst den Jahresbilanzen von 1316–1375.* Vatikanische Quellen zur Geschichte der päpstlichen Hof-und Finanzverwaltung. Paderborn, 1911.

Skaife, Robert A., ed. *The Register of the Guild of Corpus Christi.* Surtees Society Vol. 57. Durham: Surtees Society, 1872.

Storey, Robin L., ed. *The Registers of Thomas Langley, Bishop of Durham.* Surtees Society Vols. 64, 166, 169, 170. Durham: Surtees Society, 1956–61.

Theiner, Augustin, ed. Caesar Baronius. *Annales Ecclesiastici.* Paris: Barri-Ducis, 1864–83.

Tillotson, John H., ed. *Monastery and Society in the Late Middle Ages, Selected Account Rolls from Selby Abbey, Yorkshire, 1398–1537.* Woodbridge, Suffolk: Boydell Press, 1988.

Wilson, James, ed. *The Register of the Priory of St. Bees.* Surtees Society Vol. 126. Durham: Surtees Society, 1915.

Wilson, Ronald A., ed. *The First [and Second] Register of Bishop Robert de Stretton 1358–1385: An Abstract of the Contents.* William Salt Archaeological Society, n. s., vols. 8 and 10, pt. 2. London: Harrison, 1905–7.

Secondary Sources

A.J.C. "A Missal of the Use of York." *BMQ* 7 (1932–1933): 107–9.

Abulafia, Anna S., ed. *Gilbert Crispin, Disputatio Judaei cum Christiano.* Auctores Britannici Medii Aevi 8. Oxford: Oxford Univ. Press, 1986.

Adams, William Y. "Celtic Interlace and Coptic Interlace." *Antiquity* 49 (1975): 301–3.

Alexander, J. J. G. *The Decorated Letter.* London: Thames and Hudson, 1978.

————. "An English Illuminator's Work in Some Fourteenth-Century Italian Lawbooks at Durham." *Medieval Art and Architecture at Durham Cathedral.* British Archeological Association Conference Transactions 3 (1980): 149–53.

————. *Medieval Illuminators and Their Methods of Work.* New Haven: Yale Univ. Press, 1992.

————. "Painting and Manuscript Illumination for Royal Patrons in the Later Middle Ages." In *English Court Culture in the Later Middle Ages.* ed. V. J. Scattergood and J. W. Sherborne, 141–62. London: Duckworth, 1983.

————. "Scribes as Artists: The Arabesque Initial in Twelfth-Century English Manuscripts." In *Medieval Scribes, Manuscripts, and Libraries: Essays Presented to N. R. Ker,* ed. M. B. Parkes and Andrew G. Watson, 87–116. London: Scolar, 1978.

————. and Elżbieta Temple. *Illuminated Manuscripts in Oxford College Libraries, the University Archives, and the Taylor Institution.* Oxford: Clarendon, 1985.

Alexander, S. M. "Towards a History of Art Materials—A Survey of Published Technical Literature in the Arts: Part I, From Antiquity to 1599." *Art and Archaeology Technical Abstracts Supplement* 7, no. 3 (1969): 123–48.

Alker, Lisl, and Hugo Alker. *Das Beutelbuch in der bildenden Kunst. Ein beschreibendes Verzeichnis. Zusammengestellt von Lisl und Hugo Alker.* Mainz: Gutenberg, 1966; Supplement. *Gutenberg-Jahrbuch,* (1978) 302–8. Mainz: 1966.

Allen, Hope Emily. "The Desert of Religion: Addendum." *Archiv* n. s. 27, 127 (1911): 388–90.

————. ed. *The English Writings of Richard Rolle.* Oxford: Clarendon, 1931. Reprint. St. Clair Shores, Mich.: Scholarly Press, 1971.

————. *Writings Ascribed to Richard Rolle, Hermit of Hampole, and Materials for His Biography.* MLA Monograph Series 3. Reprint. Millwood, N.Y.: Kraus, 1966.

Allen, P. S. "Bishop Shirwood of Durham and his Library." *EHR* 25 (1910): 445–56.

Allmand, C. T. "The Civil Lawyers." In *Profession, Vocation, and Culture in Later Medieval England: Essays Dedicated to the Memory of A. R. Meyers,* ed. Cecil H. Clough, 155–80. Liverpool: Liverpool Univ. Press, 1982.

Anderson, David, ed. *Sixty Bokes Olde and Newe. Manuscripts and Early Printed Books from Libraries in or near Philadelphia Illustrating Chaucer's Sources, His Works and Their Influence.* Knoxville: Univ. of Tennessee Press, 1986.

Anderson, Marjorie O. *Kings and Kingship in Early Scotland.* Edinburgh: Chatto and Windus, 1973.

————. "The Scottish Materials in the Paris Manuscript, Bibliothèque Nationale Latin 4126." *SHR* 28 (1949): 37–39.

Anon. "A Mediaeval Biography." *BullIHR* 3 (1925–26): 46.

Anon. " 'Rough Register' of Acquisitions of the Department of Manuscripts, British Library 1976–1980." Typescript.

Anon. "A Relic of the Pilgrimage of Grace." *YAJ* 21 (1911): 107–9.

Arnould, Alain and Elisabeth Leedham-Green, eds. *Fifteenth-Century Flemish Manuscripts in Cambridge Collections.* TCBS 10, pt. 2. Cambridge: Cambridge Univ. Press, 1992.

Arnould, E. J. *Étude sur le livre des Saintes Médicines du Duc Henri de Lancastre.* Paris: M. Didier, 1948.

————. ed. *Henry of Lancaster, Le Livre des seyntz Médicines.* Oxford: Blackwell, 1940.

Ashley, Kathleen and Pamela Sheingorn, eds. *Interpreting Cultural Symbols: Saint Anne in Late Medieval Society.* Athens: Univ. of Georgia Press, 1990.

Aston, Margaret. *Lollards and Reformers: Images and Literacy in Late Medieval Religion.* London: Hambledon, 1984.

———. *Thomas Arundel, A Study of Church Life in the Reign of Richard II.* Oxford: Clarendon, 1967.

Atkinson, J. C., ed. *The Coucher Book of Furness Abbey.* Chetham Society, n. s., 9, 11, 14. Manchester: Chetham Society, 1886–1888.

Auden, G. A. "The Guild of Barber Surgeons of the City of York." *PRSM* 21 (1928): 70–76.

Avril, François. "La technique de l'enluminure d'après les textes médiévaux: essai de bibliographie," typescript. Paris: Réunion du Comité de l'Icom pour les laboratoires de Musées et de Sous-Comité de l'Icom pour le traitement des peintures, 1967.

———. "Un Enlumineur ornemaniste parisien de la première moitié du XIVe siècle: Jacobus Mathey (Jacquet Maci?)." *BullM* 129 (1971): 249–64.

Avril, François, and Patricia Danz Stirnemann. *Manuscrits enluminés d'origine insulaire VIIe–XXe Siècle.* Paris: Bibliothèque Nationale, 1987.

Axon, William E. A. "The Symbolism of the 'Five Wounds of Christ.'" *TLCAS* 10 (1892): 67–77.

Babington, Churchill, ed. *Polychronicon Ranulphi Higden Monachi Cestrensis.* Rolls Series no. 41. Reprint. Millwood, N.Y.: Kraus, 1964.

Bachmann, Erich, ed. *Gothic Art in Bohemia: Architecture, Sculpture and Painting.* Oxford: Phaidon, 1977.

Backhouse, Janet. "An Illuminator's Sketchbook." *BLJ* 1 (1975): 3–14.

———. *The Lindisfarne Gospels.* Oxford: Phaidon and British Library, 1981.

———. *The Madresfield Hours: A Fourteenth-Century Manuscript in the Library of Earl Beauchamp.* Oxford: Oxford Univ. Press, 1975.

Baildon, W. P. "Notes on the Religious and Secular Houses of Yorkshire." *YASRS* 81 (1931): 19–94.

Bain, Iain. *Celtic Knotwork.* London: Constable, 1986.

Bainvel, Jean Vincent. *Devotion to the Sacred Heart: The Doctrine and Its History*, translated by E. Leahy. London: Burns and Oates, 1924.

Baker, A. T. "La Vie de Sainte Marie l'Egyptienne." *RLR* 59 (1916–17): 145–400.

Baker, D. C., J. L. Murphy, and L. B. Hall, eds. *The Late Medieval Religious Plays of Bodleian MSS Digby 133 and e Museo 160.* EETS: o.s., 283. Oxford: Oxford Univ. Press, 1982.

Bale, John. *Scriptorum Illustrium Maioris Brytanniae Catalogus.* 1557–59. Reprint. Farnborough, Hants.: Gregg Press, 1971.

Banik, Gerhard. "Discoloration of Green Copper Pigments in Manuscripts and Works of Graphic Art." *Restaurator* 10 (1989): 61–73.

Banks, Doris H. *Medieval Manuscript Bookmaking: A Bibliographic Guide.* Metuchen, N.J.: Scarecrow Press, 1989.

Bänsch, Birgit, and Susanne Linscheid-Burdich. "Theophilus, Schedula diversarum artium: Textauszüge." In *Ornamenta Ecclesiae: Kunst und Kunstler der Romanik*, edited by Anton Legner, 363–84. Cologne: Schnütgen Museum, 1985.

Barber, Peter. "Visual Encyclopedias: The Hereford and Other Mappae Mundi." *The Map Collector* 48 (1989): 2–8.

Barr, C. B. L. "The Minister Library." In *A History of York Minster*, edited by G. E. Aylmer and Reginald Cant, 487–539. Oxford: Clarendon, 1977.

Barratt, Alexandra. "The *De Institutione Inclusarum* of Aelred of Rievaulx and the Carthusian Order." *JTS* 23 (1977): 528–36.

———. trans. *The Herald of God's Loving-Kindness: Books One and Two*. Cistercian Fathers Series 35. Kalamazoo, Mich.: Cistercian Institute, 1991.

Bartlett, J. N. "The Expansion and Decline of York in the Later Middle Ages." *EcHR*, 2d ser., 12 (1959): 17–33.

Bateman, W. *The Five Wounds of Christ*. Manchester: R. and W. Dean, 1814.

Batlle, C. M. *Die "Adhortationes sanctorum patrum" ("verba seniorum") im lateinischen Mittelalter: Überlieferung, Fortleben und Wirkung*. Münster: Aschendorff, 1972.

Baxandall, Michael. *Painting and Experience in Fifteenth-Century Italy: A Primer in the Social History of Pictorial Style*. Oxford: Oxford Univ. Press, 1988.

Bazire, J., and E. Colledge, eds. *The Chastising of God's Children and the Treatise of Perfection of the Sons of God*. Oxford: Blackwell, 1957.

Beadle, Richard, and A. E. B. Owen, eds. *The Findern Manuscript: Cambridge University Library MS Ff.1.6*. London: Scolar Press, 1977.

Bean, John M. W. *The Estates of the Percy Family 1415–1537*. London: Oxford Univ. Press, 1958.

———. "The Percies' Acquisition of Alnwick." *AA*, 4th ser., 32 (1954): 318–19.

———. "Plague, Population, and Economic Decline in England in the Later Middle Ages." *EcHR*, 2d ser., 15 (1963): 423–37.

Beaumont, Richard. *Purdey's: The Guns and the Family*. North Pomfret, Vt.: David and Charles, 1984.

Beer, Ellen. *Beiträge zur oberrheinischen Buchmalerei in der ersten Hälfte des 14. Jahrhunderts, unter besonderer Berücksichtigung der Initialornamentik*. Basel: Birkhäuser, 1959.

Bell, David. *An Index of Authors and Works in Cistercian Libraries in Great Britain*. Cistercian Publications 130. Kalamazoo, Mich.: Medieval Institute, 1992.

———. *The Libraries of the Cistercians, Gilbertines, and Premonstratensians*. Corpus of British Medieval Library Catalogues 3. London: British Library and British Academy, 1992.

Bell, H. E. "The Price of Books in Medieval England." *The Library*, 4th ser., 17 (1936): 312–32.

Bell, Susan Groag. "Medieval Women Book Owners: Arbiters of Lay Piety and Ambassadors of Culture." In *Women and Power in the Middle Ages*, edited by Mary Erler and Maryanne Kowaleski, 149–87. Athens: Univ. of Georgia, 1988.

Belting, Hans. *Das Bild und sein Publikum im Mittelalter. Form und Funktion früher Bildtafeln der Passion.* Berlin: Gebr. Mann, 1981.

Bénédictines du Bouveret. *Colophons du manuscrits occidentaux des origines au XVIe siècle.* Spicilegi Friburgensis Subsidia 2–7. Fribourg, 1965–82.

Bennett, Adelaide. "A Late Thirteenth-Century Psalter-Hours from London. In *England in the Thirteenth Century: Proceedings of the 1984 Harlaxton Symposium,* edited by W. M. Ormrod, 15–30. Woodbridge, Suffolk: Boydell, 1986.

Bennett, Henry Leigh. *Archbishop Thomas Rotherham.* Lincoln: J. W. Ruddock, 1901.

Bennett, Judith M. "Medieval Women, Modern Women: Across the Great Divide." In *Culture and History 1350–1600: Essays on English Communities, Identities, and Writing,* edited by David Aers, 147–75. Detroit: Wayne State Univ. Press, 1992.

Bense, J.-F. *The Anglo-Dutch Relations from Earliest Times to the Death of William the Third.* 's-Gravenhage: Martinus Nijhoff, 1924.

Benson, Larry, ed. *The Riverside Chaucer.* Boston: Houghton Mifflin, 1987.

Beresford, Maurice. *New Towns of the Middle Ages.* London: Lutterworth Press, 1967.

Berkovits, Ilona. *Illuminated Manuscripts in Hungary: XI–XVI Centuries,* translated by Zsuzsanna Horn. Shannon: Irish Univ. Press, 1969.

Berliner, R. *"Arma Christi." MJBK* 6 (1955): 35–152.

Bernards, M. *Speculum Virginum: Geistigkeit und Seelenleben der Frau in Hochmittelalter.* Cologne: Böhlau, 1982.

Bertelli, Carlo. "The *Image of Pity* in Santa Croce in Gerusalemme." In *Essays in the History of Art Presented to Rudolf Wittkower,* edited by D. Fraser et al., 40–55. London: Phaidon, 1967.

Bestul, Thomas H. "Chaucer's *Parson's Tale* and the Late-Medieval Tradition of Religious Meditation." *Speculum* 64 (1989): 600–19.

Bignami-Odier, Jeanne. *Études sur Jean de Roquetaillade (Johannes de Rupescissa).* Paris: J. Vrin, 1952.

Bischoff, Bernhard. "Elementarunterricht und 'Probationes Pennae' in der ersten Hälfte des Mittelalters." *Mittelalterliche Studien* 1, 74–87. Stuttgart: Anton Hiersemann, 1966.

———. "Zur Frühgeschichte des mittelalterlichen Chirographum." *Mittelalterliche Studien* 1. Stuttgart: Anton Hiersemann, 1966.

Blake, J. B. "The Medieval Coal Trade of Northeast England: Some Fourteenth-Century Evidence." *NH* 2 (1967): 1–26.

Blakiston, Herbert E. D. "Some Durham College Rolls." *Collectanea 3,* Vol. 32, 1–76. Oxford: Oxford Historical Soc., 1896.

Blanchard, I. S. W. "Commercial Crisis and Change: Trade and the Industrial Economy of the North-East, 1509–1532. *"NH* 8 (1973): 64–85.

Blanciotti, Bonaventura, ed. *Doctrinale Fidei Ecclesiae Catholicae contra Wiclevistae et Hussitas.* (Thomas Netter). 1757. Reprint. Farnborough, Hants., Eng.: Gregg Press, 1967.

Boase, T. S. R. *The York Psalter*. New York: Thomas Yoseloff, 1962.

Bober, Harry. "The Zodiacal Miniature of the *Très Riches Heures* of the Duke of Berry—Its Sources and Meaning." *JWCI* 11 (1948): 1–34.

Boffey, Julia, and John J. Thompson. "Anthologies and Miscellanies: Production and Choice of Texts." In *Book Production and Publishing in Britain 1375–1475*, edited by Derek Pearsall and Jeremy Griffiths, 292–95. Cambridge: Cambridge Univ. Press, 1989.

Bolton, J. L. *The Medieval English Economy 1150–1500*. Totowa, N.J.: Rowman and Littlefield, 1980.

Bommarito, D. "Il ms 25 della Newberry Library: La tradizione dei ricettari e trattati sui colori nel Medioevo e Rinascimento veneto e toscano." *La Bibliofilia* 87 (1985): 1–38.

Bonetti, Ignazio. *Le Stimate della Passione*. Rovigo, Italy: Istituto padano de Arti Grafiche, 1952.

Bonner, Gerald, et al., eds. *St. Cuthbert: His Cult and His Community to A.D. 1200*. Woodbridge, Suffolk: Boydell Press, 1989.

Bonney, M. *Lordship and the Urban Community: Durham and Its Overlords 1250–1540*. Cambridge: Cambridge Univ. Press, 1990.

Borrodaile, Viola, and Rosamund Borrodaile, eds. and trans. *The Strassburg Manuscript: A Medieval Painters' Handbook*. London, 1966.

Bowers, R. H. "Middle-English Verses on the Appearance of Christ." *Anglia* 70 (1951): 430–33.

———. "Middle English Verses on the Founding of the Carthusian Order." *Speculum* 42 (1967): 710–13.

Boyd, Anne. *Life in a Medieval Monastery: Durham Priory in the Fifteenth Century*. Cambridge, Cambridge Univ. Press, 1987.

Boyle, Leonard E., and Richard H. Rouse. "A Fifteenth-Century List of the Books of Edmund Norton." *Speculum* 50 (1975): 284–88.

———. "The *Oculus Sacerdotis* and Some Other Works of William of Pagula." *TRHS*, 5th ser., 5 (1955): 81–110.

Bradshaw, Henry. "Two Lists of Books in the University Library." In *The Collected Papers of Henry Bradshaw*, edited by J. H. Jenkinson, 25–34. Cambridge: Cambridge Univ. Press, 1889.

Breeze, A. Q. "The Number of Christ's Wounds." *BBCS* 32 (1985): 84–91.

Brewer, D. S., and A. E. B. Owen, eds. *The Thornton Manuscript, Lincoln Cathedral MS 91*. London: Scolar Press, 1975.

Brighton, Christopher. *Lincoln Cathedral Cloister Bosses*. Lincoln, Eng.: Honywood Press, 1985.

Brooke, Christopher. "Reflections on Late Medieval Cults and Devotions." In *Essays in Honor of Edward B. King*, edited by Robert G. Benson and Eric W. Naylor, 33–45. Sewanee, Tenn.: Univ. of the South Press, 1991.

Broomfield, F., ed. Thomas of Chobam. *Summa Confessorum (Analecta Mediaevalia Namurcensia 25)*. Louvain: Éditions Nauwelaerts, 1968.

Brotanek, Rudolf. "Nachlese zu den Hss. der *Epistola Cuthberti* und des *Sterbespruches Bedas*." *Anglia* 64 (1940): 178–79.

Brown, Carleton, ed. *Religious Lyrics of the XVth Century.* Oxford: Clarendon, 1939.

Brown, Carleton, and Rossell Hope Robbins, eds. *Index of Middle English Verse.* New York: Columbia Univ. Press, 1943.

Brown, Sandra. *The Medieval Courts of the York Minster Peculiar.* Borthwick Paper no. 66. York: St. Anthony's Press, 1984.

Brunello, Franco. *L'Arte della Tintura nella storia dell'umanità.* Vicenza: Nieri Pozza, 1968.

————. *De Arte Illuminandi e altri trattati sulla tecnica della miniatura medievale.* Vicenza: Nieri Pozza, 1975.

Brünner, Karl. "Mittelenglische Todesgedichte." *Archiv*, n.s., 67, 167 (1935): 20–35.

Brunskill, Elizabeth. "Missals, Portifers, and Pyes." *BJP* 2 (1974): 1–34.

Bühler, Curt. *The Fifteenth-Century Book.* Philadelphia: Univ. of Pennsylvania Press, 1960.

————. "Prayers and Charms in Certain Middle English Scrolls." *Speculum* 39 (1964): 270–78.

Burke, John. *A Genealogical and Heraldic History of the Extinct and Dormant Baronetcies of England.* London: J. R. Smith, 1844.

Burke, John Bernard. *Burke's Complete Peerage.* London: Burke's Peerage, 1932.

Burrow, J. A. "The Audience of *Piers Plowman.*" *Anglia* 75 (1957): 373–84.

Bursill-Hall, G. L. *A Census of Medieval Latin Grammatical Manuscripts.* Stuttgart: Frommann-Holzboog, 1981.

Byvanck, A. W., and G. J. Hoogewerff. *Noord-Nederlandsche Miniaturen.* The Hague: Martin Nijhoff, 1925.

Cabussut, André. "La dévotion au Nom de Jésus dans l'Église d'Occident." *LVS* 86 (1952): 46–69.

Cadei, Antonio. "Giovannino de Grassi nel Taccuino di Bergamo." *CA* 17 (1970): 17–36.

————. *Studi di miniatura Lombarda: Giovannino de Grassi, Belbello da Pavia.* Rome: Viella, 1984.

Cailhol, Charles. "Sources bibliographiques pour l'étude des pigments utilisés en peinture jusqu'au XVe siècle." *RSSHN:* Histoire de l'Art 20 (1960): 23–53.

Caines, Anthony. "The Pigments and Organic Colours." In *The Book of Kells MS 58 Trinity College Library, Dublin. Commentary*, edited by Peter Fox. Lucerne: Faksimilie-Verlag, 1990.

Caldwell, Robert A. "The Scribe of the Chaucer MS, Cambridge University Library Gg.4.27." *MLQ* 5 (1944): 33–44.

Callmann, Ellen. "Thebiad Studies," *AV* 14 (1975): 3–22.

Camille, Michael. "The Book of Signs: Writing and Visual Difference in Gothic Manuscript Illumination." *WI* 1 (1985): 133–48.

————. "Labouring for the Lord: The Ploughman and the Social Order in the Luttrell Psalter." *AH* 10 (1987): 423–454.

Carné, G. de. "Contrat pour la copie d'un missel au XVe siècle." In *Artistes, Artisans es production artistique en Bretagne au Moyen Âge*, edited by Xavier Barral i Altet et al., 127. Rennes, 1983.

Carruthers, Mary. *The Book of Memory: A Study of Memory in Medieval Culture.* Cambridge: Cambridge Univ. Press, 1990.

Carter, Charles. "The *Arma Christi* in Scotland." *PSAS* 90 (1956–57): 116–29.

Catalogue Général des Manuscrits des Bibliothèques Publiques des Départements, IV Arras-Avranches-Boulogne. Paris: Imprimerie Nationale, 1872.

Chambers, D. S. *Patrons and Artists in the Italian Renaissance.* London: Macmillan, 1970.

Chandler, Paul. "Philippe Ribot. *Dictionnaire de Spiritualité Ascétique et Mystique.* Vol. 13, 537–39. Paris: Beauchesne, 1987.

Chastel, A. "La Véronique." *RA* 40–41 (1978): 71–82.

Chédeville, A. "L'Immigration bretonne dans la royaume de France du XIe au début du XIVe siècle." *AnBr* 81 (1974): 301–43.

Cheetham, Francis. *English Medieval Alabasters.* Oxford: Phaidon, Christie's, 1984.

———. "A Fifteenth-Century English Alabaster Altar-Piece in Norwich Castle Museum." *BM* 125 (1983): 356–59.

Cheney, C. R. *Notaries Public in England in the Thirteenth and Fourteenth Centuries.* Oxford: Clarendon, 1972.

———. "Notaries Public in Italy and England in the Late Middle Ages." *SS* 92 (1980): 173–88.

Chetwynd-Stapylton, H. E. "The Stapletons of Yorkshire." *YAJ* 8 (1883–84): 65–116, 223–58, 381–423, 427–74.

Chevreul, M. E., ed. *Pigments et colorants de l'antiquité et du moyen âge, teinture, peinture, enluminure: études historiques et physico-chimiques.* Paris: CNRS, 1990.

Childs, Wendy R., and John Taylor, eds. *The Anonimalle Chronicle, 1307–1334.* ASRS 147. Leeds: Yorkshire Archaeological Soc., 1991.

Chippindall, W. H. "Tunstall of Thurland Castle." *TCWAAS*, n. s., 28 (1928): 292–313.

Chrimes, Stanley B. *An Introduction to the Administrative History of Mediaeval England.* Oxford: Blackwell, 1966.

Christianson, C. Paul. "A Century of the Manuscript-Book Trade in Late Medieval London." *MH*, n. s., 12 (1984): 143–65.

———. "A Community of Book Artisans in Chaucer's London." *Viator* 20 (1989): 207–18.

———. *A Directory of London Stationers and Book Artisans, 1300–1500.* New York: Bibliographical Soc. of America, 1990.

———. "Early London Bookbinders and Parchmeners." *The Book Collector* 34 (1985): 41–54.

———. "Evidence for the Study of London's Late Medieval Manuscript-Book Trade." In *Book Production and Publishing in Britain, 1375–1475*, edited by Derek Pearsall and Jeremy Griffiths, 87–108. Cambridge: Cambridge Univ. Press, 1989.

————. *Memorials of the Book Trade in Medieval London: The Archives of Old London Bridge.* Cambridge: D. S. Brewer, 1987.

Cipolla, Carlo M. *Literacy and Development in the West.* Harmondsworth, Eng.: Penguin, 1969.

Clanchy, Michael. *From Memory to Written Record. England, 1066–1307.* Cambridge, Mass.: Harvard Univ. Press, 1979.

Clark, Charles W. "The Zodiac Man in Medieval Medical Astrology." *JRMMRA* 3 (1982): 13–38.

Clark, George T. "The West-Riding Poll Tax and Lay-Subsidy Rolls, 2d Richard II." *YAJ* 7 (1882): 187–93.

Clarke, Edwin. "The Early History of the Cerebral Venticles." *TSCPP* 30 (1962): 85–89.

Clarke, Edwin, and Kenneth Dewhurst. *An Illustrated History of Brain Function.* Berkeley: Univ. of California Press, 1972.

Clarke, M. V., and Noel Denholm-Young. "The Kirkstall Chronicle, 1355–1400." Reprinted in *Fourteenth Century Studies by M. V. Clarke,* edited by L. S. Sutherland and M. McKisack, 99–114. Oxford: Clarendon, 1937.

Clay, Rotha Mary. "Further Studies on Medieval Recluses." *JBAA,* 3rd ser., 16 (1953): 75–78.

————. *The Medieval Hospitals of England.* London: Methuen, 1909.

————. "Some Northern Anchorites." *AA,* 4th ser., 33 (1955): 210–12.

Clemens, J. R. "Fifteenth Century English Recipes for the Making of Pigments." *AArc* 34 (1933): 206–10.

Cockshaw, Pierre. "Mentions d'auteurs, de copistes, d'enlumineurs et de libraires dans les comptes généraux de l'État Bourguignon (1384–1419)." *Scriptorium* 23 (1969): 122–44.

Colker, Marvin L. *Trinity College Library Dublin: Descriptive Catalogue of the Mediaeval and Renaissance Latin Manuscripts.* Aldershot, Hampshire: Scolar Press, 1991.

Colledge, Edmund, and J. C. Marler, "Mystical 'Pictures' in the Suso 'Exemplar', MS Strasbourg 2929." *AFP* 54 (1984): 293–354.

————. "South Netherlands Books of Hours Made for England." *Scriptorium* 32 (1978): 55–57.

Colledge, Edmund, and James Walsh, eds. *A Book of Showings to the Anchoress Julian of Norwich.* Studies and Texts 35. Toronto: Pontifical Institute, 1978.

The Color Index. Bradford, Yorkshire: Soc. of Dyers and Colourists, 1976.

Conway-Davies, J. "The Muniments of the Dean and Chapter of Durham." *DUJ* 44 (1951–52): 77–87.

Cook, Robert B. "Wills of Leeds and District." *TSM* 26 (1924): 172–220, 311–49.

Cottineau, L. H. *Répertoire topo-bibliographique des abbayes et prieurés.* Mâcon, France: Protat Frères, 1939.

Couffon, R., and A. Le Bars. *Répertoire des Églises et Chapelles du diocèse de Quimper et de Léon.* Saint-Brieuc: Les Presses Bretonnes, 1959.

Cowan, E. J. "The Scottish Chronicle in the Poppleton Manuscript." *IR* 32 (1961): 3–21.

Cox, D. *The Brotherton Collection, University of Leeds. Its Contents Described with Illustrations of Fifty Books and Manuscripts.* Leeds: Univ. Library, 1986.

Coxe, Henry O. *Catalogus Codicum Manuscriptorum qui in Collegiis Aulisque Oxoniensibus Hodie Adservantur.* Oxford, Clarendon, 1852.

Cremascoli, Giuseppe. "Uguccione da Pisa: Saggio bibliografico." *Aevum* 42 (1968): 123–68.

Crick, Julia C. *The Historia Regum Britannie of Geoffrey of Monmouth, 4: Dissemination and Reception in the Later Middle Ages.* Woodbridge, Suffolk: D. S. Brewer, 1991.

Curwen, John F. "The Castle Dairy, Kendal." *TCWAAS*, n. s., 16 (1916): 101–7.

Dalton, O. M. "Coventry Finger Rings." *PSAL*, 2d ser., 23 (1911): 340–44.

Daly, Lloyd W. *Contributions to a History of Alphabetization in Antiquity and the Middle Ages.* Brussells: Latomus, 1967.

Daly, Lloyd W. and Bernardine Daly, eds. *Guillelmi Britonis Expositiones Vocabulorum Biblie.* Padua: Editrice Antenore, 1975.

Darby, H. C., et al. "The Changing Geographical Distribution of Wealth in England, 1086–1334–1525." *JHG* 5 (1979): 247–262.

Darbyshire, H. Stanley, and George D. Lumb, eds. *The History of Methley.* Thoresby Society Vol. 35. Leeds: Thoresby Society, 1937.

Darwin, Francis D. *The English Mediaeval Recluse.* London: Society for the Promotion of Christian Knowledge, 1944.

Davidson, Clifford. "Northern Spirituality and the Late Medieval Drama of York." In *The Spirituality of Western Christendom,* edited by E. Rozanne Elder, 125–51. Kalamazoo, Mich.: Medieval Institute, 1976.

———. *York Art: A Subject List of Extant and Lost Art Including Items Relevant to Early Drama.* Kalamazoo, Mich.: Medieval Institute, 1978.

Davis, G. R. C. *Medieval Cartularies of Great Britain.* London: Longmans, Green, 1958.

Davis, Norman, ed. *Sir Gawain and the Green Knight.* Oxford: Clarendon, 1968.

Davis, Virginia. "The Rule of St. Paul, the First Hermit, in Late Medieval England." In *Monks, Hermits, and the Ascetic Tradition,* edited by W. J. Sheils, 203–14. Oxford: Blackwell, 1985.

Dawson, Nicholas. "The Percy Tomb at Beverley Minster: The Style of the Sculpture." In *Studies in Medieval Sculpture,* edited by F. H. Thompson, 125–46. London: Society of Antiquaries, 1983.

De Hamel, Christopher F. R. "Reflections on the Trade in Books of Hours at Ghent and Bruges." In *Manuscripts in the Fifty Years after the Invention of Printing,* edited by J. B. Trapp, 29–33. London: Warburg Institute, 1983.

de la Borderie, A. "Notes sur les livres et les bibliothèques au Moyen Âge en Bretagne." *BEC* 23 (1862): 39–53.

de la Mare, Albinia. *Duke Humfrey's Library & the Divinity School, 1488–1988: An Exhibition at the Bodleian Library June–August 1988.* Oxford: Bodleian Library, 1988.

de Mauny, Michel. *Le Pays de Léon*. Rennes: Armor, 1977.

de Rostrenen, Grégoire. *Dictionnaire français-celtique ou français-breton*. Guingamp, France, 1834.

de Saint-Luc, Conen. "Guilers." *BSAF* 43 (1916): 320–29.

Deanesly, Margaret. "Vernacular Books in England in the Fourteenth and Fifteenth Centuries." *MLR* 15 (1920): 349–58.

———, ed. *The Incendium Amoris of Richard Rolle of Hampole*. Reprint. Folcroft Library Edition. Folcroft, Pa., 1974.

Delaissé, L. M. J. "Towards a History of the Mediaeval Book." In *Miscellanea André Combes*. Vol. 2, edited by Antonio Piolanti, 27–39. Rome: Pont. Università Lateranense, 1967–68.

Delisle, Léopold. "Rouleaux des Morts du IXe au XVe siècle." *Annuaire-Bulletin de la Société de l'histoire de France* 135 (1866): 177–279.

Denholm-Young, N. *Handwriting in England and Wales*. Cardiff: Univ. of Wales Press, 1954.

Dennison, Lynda. "An Illuminator of the Queen Mary Psalter Group: The Ancient 6 Master." *AJ* 66 (1986): 287–314.

Derolez, Albert. "Codicologie ou archéologie du livre? Quelques observations sur la leçon inaugurale de M. Albert Gruijs à l'Université catholique de Nimègue." *Scriptorium* 27 (1973): 47–49.

D'Haenens, A. *Europe of the North Sea and the Baltic: The World of the Hanse*. Antwerp: Fonds Mercator, 1984.

Dickens, Arthur G. *The English Reformation*. New York: Peter Bedrick, 1990.

———. *Lollards and Protestants in the Diocese of York*. Oxford: Oxford Univ. Press for Univ. of Hull, 1959.

———. "Secular and Religious Motivation in the Pilgrimage of Grace." In *Studies in Church History* 4, edited by G. J. Cuming, 39–64. Leiden: Brill, 1967.

Dickson, W. "Contents of the Cartulary of Hulne Abbey." *AA*, 1st ser., 3 (1844): 46–47.

Distelbrink, B. *Bonaventurae Scripta: Authentica, Dubia vel Spuria*. Rome: Istituto Stovico Cappucini, 1975.

Dobson, R. Barrie. "Admissions to the Freedom of the City of York in the Later Middle Ages." *EcHR*, 2d ser., 26 (1973): 1–21.

———. "Cathedral Chapters and Cathedral Cities: York, Durham, and Carlisle in the Fifteenth Century." *NH* 19 (1983): 12–44.

———. *Durham Priory, 1400–1450*. Cambridge: Cambridge Univ. Press, 1973.

———. "The Foundation of Perpetual Chantries by the Citizens of Medieval York." In *Studies in Church History* 4, edited by G. J. Cuming, 22–38. Leiden: Brill, 1967.

———. "Mendicant Ideal and Practice in Late Medieval York." In *Archaeological Papers from York Presented to M. W. Barley*, edited by P. V. Addyman and V. E. Black, 109–22. York: York Archaeological Trust, 1984.

———. "The Residentiary Canons of York in the Fifteenth century." *JEH* 30 (1979): 145–73.

————. "Richard Bell, Prior of Durham (1464–1478) and Bishop of Carlisle (1478–1495)." *TCWAAS*, n. s., 65 (1965): 182–221.

————. "York Art." In *The Cambridge Guide to the Arts in Britain*. Vol. 2, *The Middle Ages*, edited by Boris Ford, 109–22. Cambridge: Cambridge Univ. Press, 1988.

Dodwell, C. R., ed. and trans. *Theophilus, The Various Arts. De Diversis Artibus*. Reprint. Oxford: 1986.

Dolezalek, G. *Verzeichnis der Handschriften zum römischen Recht bis 1600*. Frankfurt-am-Main: Max-Planck Institut für Europäische Rechtsgeschichte, 1972.

Donkin, R. A. *The Cistercians: Studies in the Geography of Medieval England and Wales*. Toronto: Pontifical Institute, 1978.

Donovan, Claire. *The de Brailes Hours. Shaping the Book of Hours in Thirteenth-Century Oxford*. London: British Library, 1991.

Doyère, Pierre, ed. and trans. *Gertrude D'Helfta, Oeuvres Spirituelles*. Sources Chrétiennes 139. Paris: Les Éditions du Cerf, 1968.

Doyle, Ian. "Book Production by the Monastic Orders in England (c. 1375–1530): Assessing the Evidence." In *Medieval Book Production: Assessing the Evidence*, edited by Linda Brownrigg, 1–19. Los Altos Hills, Calif.: Red Gull Press, 1990.

————. "Books Connected with the Vere Family and Barking Abbey." *TEAS*, n. s., 25 (1958): 222–43.

————. "The English Provincial Book Trade Before Printing." In *Six Centuries of the Provincial Book Trade In Britain*, edited by P. Isaac, 13–29. Winchester: St. Paul's Bibliographies, 1990.

————. "Reflections on Some Manuscripts of Nicholas Love's *Myrrour of the Blessed Lyf of Jesu Christ*." *LSE*, n. s., 14 (1983): 82–93.

————. "A Text Attributed to Ruusbroec Circulating in England." In *Dr. L. Reypens-Album*, edited by A. Ampe, 153–171. Antwerp: Ruusbroec Genootschap, 1964.

————. "The Work of a Late Fifteenth-Century English Scribe, William Ebesham." *BJRL* 39 (1957): 298–325.

————, ed. *The Vernon Manuscript, A Facsimile of Bodleian Library, Oxford, MS. Eng. Poet. a.1*. Cambridge: Boydell and Brewer, 1986.

Doyle, Ian, and George B. Pace. "Further Texts of Chaucer's Minor Poems." *SB* 28 (1975): 41–46.

Dreves, Guido M., and C. Blume, eds. *Analecta Hymnica Medii Aevi*. Reprint. New York, 1961.

Drobná, Zoroslava. "Kresba problematice bible Boskovské." *Uměni* 13 (1965): 127–38.

Du Boulay, F. R. H. *An Age of Ambition: English Society in the Late Middle Ages*. New York: Viking, 1970.

Duff, E. Gordon. *The English Provincial Printers, Stationers, and Bookbinders to 1557*. Cambridge: Cambridge Univ. Press, 1912.

Duhem, G. *Les églises de France: Morbihan*. Paris: Librairie Letouzey et Ané, 1932.

Dunlop, Louisa. "Pigments and Painting Materials in Fourteenth- and Early Fifteenth-Century Parisian Manuscript Illumination." In *Artistes, artisans et production artistique au moyen âge, 3: Fabrication et consomation de l'oeuvre*, edited by Xavier Barral i Altet, 272–93. Paris: Picard, 1990.

Dumville, David. *Histories and Pseudo-Histories of the Insular Middle Ages*. Aldershot, Hampshire: Variorum, 1990.

Dutschke, C. W., et al. *Guide to Medieval and Renaissance Manuscripts in the Huntington Library*. San Marino, Calif.: Huntington Library, 1989.

Dyer, C. *Standards of Living in the Later Middle Ages: Social Change in England c. 1200–1520*. Cambridge: Cambridge Univ. Press, 1989.

Eaeles, F. C. "On a Fifteenth-Century York Missal Formerly Used in the Church of Broughton-in-Amounderness." *Chetham Miscellanies* 6, n.s., 94. Manchester: Chetham Society, 1935: 1–11.

Ebel, F., et al. *Römisches Rechtsleben im Mittelalter. Miniaturen aus den Handschriften des Corpus Juris Civilis*. Heidelberg: C. F. Müller Juristicher Verlag, 1988.

Eckhardt, Caroline D. *The Prophetia Merlini of Geoffrey of Monmouth: A Fifteenth-Century English Commentary*. Cambridge, Mass.: Medieval Academy of America, 1982.

Edmondson, Joseph. *A Complete Body of Heraldry*. London: T. Spilsbury, 1780.

Egan, Keith J., O. Carm. "Medieval Carmelite Houses, England and Wales." *Carmelus* 16 (1969): 142–226.

Ehrhart, Margaret J. *The Judgment of the Trojan Prince Paris in Medieval Literature*. Philadelphia: Univ. of Pennsylvania Press, 1987.

Eisenhut, Werner, ed. *Dictys Cretensis Ephemeridos Belli Troiani Libri*. Leipzig: Teubner, 1973.

Eisenstein, Elizabeth. *The Printing Press as an Agent of Change: Communications and Cultural Transformations in Early Modern Europe*. Cambridge: Cambridge Univ. Press, 1979.

Eisner, Sigmund, ed. *The Kalendarium of Nicholas of Lynn*. London: Scolar Press, 1980.

Elliott, Alison Goddard. *Roads to Paradise: Reading the Lives of the Early Saints*. Hanover, N.H.: Univ. Press of New England, 1987.

Ellis, Roger. " 'Flores ad Fabricandam . . . Coronam': An Investigation into the Uses of the Revelations of St. Bridget of Sweden in Fifteenth-Century England." *MAe* 51 (1982): 163–86.

Emden, A. B. *A Biographical Register of the University of Cambridge to 1500*. Cambridge: Cambridge Univ. Press, 1963.

———. *A Biographical Register of the University of Oxford to A.D. 1500*. Oxford: Clarendon, 1957–59.

———. "Dominican Confessors and Preachers Licensed by Medieval English Bishops." *AFP* 32 (1962): 180–210.

———. *A Survey of Dominicans in England Based on the Ordination Lists in Episcopal Registers (1268 to 1538)*. Rome: S. Sabina, 1967.

Emery, Richard W. *The Friars in Medieval France, a Catalogue of French Mendicant Convents, 1200–1550*. New York: Columbia Univ. Press, 1962.

England, George, and Alfred W. Pollard, eds. *The Towneley Plays*. EETS: e.s., 71. 1897. Reprint. Millwood, N.Y.: Kraus, 1978.

Erbe, Theodor, ed. *John Mirk, Festial: A Collection of Homilies by Johannes Mirkus (John Mirk)*. EETS: e.s., 96. London, 1905. Reprint. Millwood, N.Y.: Kraus, 1975.

Ernault, Emile. *Glossaire Moyen-Breton*. Reprint. Marseille: Lafitte, 1976.

Esdaile, K. A. "Sculptors and Sculpture in Yorkshire." *YAJ* 35 (1943): 362–88.

Evans, Michael. "An Ilustrated Fragment of Peraldus's *Summa* of Vice: Harleian MS 3244." *JWCI* 45 (1982): 14–68.

Farmer, David Hugh. *The Monk of Farne*. Baltimore: Helicon Press, 1961.

———. *The Oxford Dictionary of the Saints*. Oxford: Clarendon, 1978.

———. ed. "Meditaciones Cuisdam Monachi Apud Farneland Quondam Solitarii." *SA* 41 (1957): 141–245.

Feldbusch, Michael, ed. *Epistola Alexandri ad Aristotelem*. Meisenheim Am Glam: Hain, 1976.

Ferrante, Joan. "The Education of Women in the Middle Ages in Theory, Fact, and Fantasy." In *Beyond their Sex: Learned Women of the European Past*, edited by P. H. Labalme, 9–42. New York: New York Univ. Press, 1980.

Finnegan, Mary Jeremy. *The Women of Helfta, Scholars and Mystics*. Athens: Univ. of Georgia Press, 1991.

Fishwick, H. *The History of the Parish of Lytham in the County of Lancaster*. Chetham Society Vol. 60. Manchester: Chetham Society, 1907.

Fleming, John V. *An Introduction to the Franciscan Literature of the Middle Ages*. Chicago: Franciscan Herald Press, 1977.

Fletcher, J. S. *The Cistercians in Yorkshire*. London: Society for the Promotion of Christian Knowledge, 1919.

Flieder, Françoise. "Mise au point des techniques d'identification des pigments et des liants inclus dans la couche picturale des enluminures de manuscrits." *StC* 13 (1968): 49–86.

Flodr, M. *Skriptorium olomoucké*. Prague, 1960.

Folz, Robert. "St. Oswald roi de Northumbrie, étude d'hagiographie royale." *AnB* 98 (1980): 49–74.

Forshaw, Helen P., ed. *Edmund of Abingdon's Speculum Religiosorum and Speculum Ecclesie*. Auctores Britannici Medii Aevi 3. Oxford: Oxford Univ. Press, 1973.

Fowler, J. T., ed. *Life of St. Cuthbert in English Verse*. Surtees Society Vol. 87. Durham: Surtees Society, 1889.

Fowler, Kenneth. "Les finances et la discipline dans les armées anglaises en France au XIVᵉ siècle." *CV* 4 (1966): 55–84.

———. *The King's Lieutenant: Henry of Grosmont, First Duke of Lancaster, 1310–1361*. London: Elek, 1969.

Fransson, Gustav. *Middle English Surnames of Occupation, 1100–1350*. Lund Studies in English 3. Lund: C. W. K. Gleerup, 1935.

Freise, Eckhard. "Zur Person des Theophilus und seiner monastischen Umwelt." In *Ornamenta Ecclesiae: Kunst und Kunstler der Romanik*, edited by Anton Legner, 357–62. Cologne: Schnütgen Museum, 1985.

French, T. W. "The Tomb of Archbishop Scrope in York Minster." *YAJ* 61 (1989): 95–102.

Frere, Walter Howard. *Bibliotheca Musico-Liturgica. A Descriptive Handlist of the Musical and Latin-Liturgical MSS of the Middle Ages Preserved in the Libraries of Great Britain and Ireland*. Reprint. Hildesheim: G. Olms, 1967.

Frey, E. F. "Saints in Medical History." *CM* 14 (1979): 35–70.

Frick, Bertha M. "Columbia's Giant Encyclopedia: Plimpton ms. no. 263." *CLC* 2.3 (1953): 8–15.

Friedman, John B. "Bald Jonah and the Exegesis of 4 Kings 2.23." *Traditio* 44 (1988): 125–44.

———. "Cluster Analysis and the Manuscript Chronology of William du Stiphel, a Fourteenth-Century Scribe at Durham." *History and Computing* 4 (1992): 14–38.

———. " 'Dies boni et mali, obitus, et contra hec remedium': Remedies for Fortune in Some Late Medieval English Manuscripts." *JEGP* 90 (1991): 311–26.

———. "Cultural Conflicts in Medieval World Maps." In *Implicit Understandings: Observing, Reporting, and Reflecting on the Encounters between Europeans and Other Peoples in the Early Modern Era*, edited by Stuart Schwartz, 64–95. Cambridge: Cambridge Univ. Press, 1994.

———. "Harry the Haywarde and Talbat His Dog: An Illustrated Girdlebook from Worcestershire." In *Art into Life: Collected Papers from the Kresge Art Museum Medieval Symposia*, edited by Carol Fisher and Kathleen Scott, 115–53. East Lansing, Mich.: Michigan State Univ. Press, 1994.

———. " 'He hath a thousand slayn this pestilence': Iconography of the Plague in the Late Middle Ages." In *Social Unrest in the Late Middle Ages*, edited by F. X. Newman, 75–112. Binghamton, New York: MRTS, 1986.

———. "John Siferwas and the Mythological Illustrations in the *Liber Cosmographiae* of John de Foxton." *Speculum* 58 (1983): 391–418.

———. *The Monstrous Races in Medieval Art and Thought*. Cambridge, Mass.: Harvard Univ. Press, 1981.

———. "Richard de Thorpe's Astronomical Kalendar and the Luxury Book Trade at York." *SAC* 7 (1985): 137–60.

———, ed. *John de Foxton's Liber Cosmographiae (1408): An Edition and Codicological Study*. Leiden: Brill, 1988.

Frinta, Mojmir. "The Master of the Gerona *Martyrology* and Bohemian Illumination." *AB* 46 (1964): 283–306.

Fryde, E. B. *Some Business Transactions of the York Merchants: John Goldbeter, William Acastre and Partners, 1336–49*. York: St. Anthony's Press, 1966.

———. *The Wool Accounts of William de la Pole: A Study of Some Aspects of the English Wool Trade at the Start of the Hundred Years' War*. York: St. Anthony's Press, 1964.

Furnivall, Frederick J., ed. *The Minor Poems of the Vernon Manuscript*, Part II, EETS: o.s., 117. 1892. Reprint. Millwood, N.Y.: Kraus, 1987.

————, ed. *Political, Religious, and Love Poems*. EETS: o.s., 15. Oxford, 1965.

Gabriel, Astrik. "Motivations of the Founders of Medieval Colleges." In *Garlandia. Studies in the History of the Mediaeval University*, edited by Astrik L. Gabriel, 211–23. Notre Dame, Ind.: Univ. of Notre Dame Press, 1969.

Gage, John. "Colour in History: Relative and Absolute." *AH* 1 (1978): 104–30.

Galbraith, Vivian Hunter. "Extracts from the *Historia Aurea* and a French 'Brut' (1317–1347)." *EHR* 43 (1928): 203–17.

————. "The *Historia Aurea* of John, Vicar of Tynemouth, and the Sources of the St. Albans Chronicle (1327–1377)." In *Essays in History Presented to Reginald Lane Poole*, edited by H. W. C. Davis, 379–98. Reprint. Freeport, N.Y.: Books for Libraries Press, 1967.

————. "Nationality and Language in Medieval England." *TRHS*, 4th ser., 23 (1941): 113–28.

Gallagher, Joseph E. "The Sources of Caxton's *Ryal Book* and *Doctrinal of Sapience*." *SP* 62 (1965): 40–62.

Garand, M.-C. "Livres de poche médiévaux à Dijon et à Rome." *Scriptorium* 25 (1971): 18–24.

Gardner, Arthur. *Alabaster Tombs of the Pre-Reformation Period in England*. Cambridge: Cambridge Univ. Press, 1940.

Gasparri, Françoise. "L'Enseignement de l'écriture à la fin du moyen âge: À propos du 'Tractatus in omnem modum scribendi,' ms. 76 de l'abbaye de Kremsmünster." *ScrC* 3 (1979): 243–65.

Gaythorpe, S. B. "Richard Esk's Metrical Account of Furness Abbey." *TCWAAS* 53 (1953): 98–109.

Gee, E. A. "The Painted Glass of All Saint's Church, North Street, York." *Archaeologia*, 2d ser., 52, 102 (1969): 151–200.

————. "The Topography of Altars, Chantries, and Shrines in York Minster." *AJ* 64 (1984): 347–48.

Gérard, Alexandre. *Catalogue des livres manuscrits et imprimés composant la bibliothèque de la ville de Boulogne-sur-mer*. Boulogne-sur-mer: Imprimerie de C. Aigne, 1844.

Gerard, John. *The Herball or Generall Historie of Plantes*. London: Islip, Norton, and Whitakers, 1633.

Germer-Durand, Eugène. *Dictionnaire topographique du département du Gard*. Paris: Imprimerie Imperiale, 1869.

Gerth van Wijk, H. L. *A Dictionary of Plant Names*. 1911–16; Reprint. Vaals, Holland: A. Asher, 1971.

Getz, Fay Marie. "John Mirfield and the *Breviarium Bartholomei:* The Medical Writings of a Clerk of St. Bartholomew's Hospital in the Later Fourteenth Century." *SSHMB* 37 (1985): 24–26.

Gibson, William S. *The History of the Monastery Founded at Tynemouth, in the Diocese of Durham*. 2 vols. London: William S. Gibson, 1846–47.

Gildea, Joseph, ed. *Remediarium conversorum: A Synthesis in Latin of Moralia in Job by Gregory the Great/Peter of Waltham*. Villanova, Pa.: Villanova Univ. Press; London: Associated Univ. Press, 1984.

Giles, Phyllis M. "A Handlist of the Bradfer-Lawrence Manuscripts Deposited on Loan at the Fitzwilliam Museum." *TCBS* 6 (1973): 86–99.

Gillespie, Vincent. "The *Cibus Anime*. Book 3: A Guide for Contemplatives?" In *Spiritualität Heute und Gestern: AC 35*, 90–119. Salzburg: Institut für Anglistik und Amerikanistik, 1983.

———. "Cura Pastoralis in Deserto." In *De Cella in Seculum*, edited by Michael Sargent, 161–81. Woodbridge, Suffolk: D. S. Brewer, 1989.

———. "The Evolution of the *Speculum Christiani*." In *Latin and Vernacular. Studies in Late-Medieval Texts and Manuscripts*, edited by A. J. Minnis, 39–61. Cambridge: D. S. Brewer, 1989.

———. "Mystics' Foot: Rolle and Affectivity." In *The Medieval Mystical Tradition in England*, edited by Marion Glasscoe, 199–230. Exeter: Univ. of Exeter, 1982.

———. "Strange Images of Death: The Passion in Later Medieval English Devotional and Mystical Writing." In *Zeit, Tod und Ewigkeit in der Renaissance Literatur*, vol. 3, edited by Erwin A. Stürzl et al., 111–59. *AC*, Salzburg: Institut für Anglistik und Amerikanistik, 1987.

———. "Vernacular Books of Religion." In *BPPB*, 317–44.

Gillett, H. M. *The Story of the Relics of the Passion*. Oxford: Blackwell, 1935.

Gilson, Étienne. "Saint Bonaventure et L'Iconographie de la Passion." *RHF* 1 (1924): 405–24.

Glasser, H. *Artists' Contracts of the Early Renaissance*. New York: Garland, 1977.

Glauning, Otto. "Der Buchbeutel in der Bildenden Kunst." *ABG* 63 (1926): 124–52.

Goldberg, P. J. P. "Mortality and Economic Change in the Diocese of York, 1390–1514." *NH* 24 (1988): 38–55.

———. *Women, Work, and Life Cycle in a Medieval Economy: Women in York and Yorkshire, c. 1300–1520*. New York: Oxford Univ. Press, 1992.

Goldthorp, L. M. "The Franciscans and Dominicans in Yorkshire. Part II. The Black Friars." *YAJ* 32 (1936): 365–428.

Gollancz, Israel, and Magdalene Weale, eds. *The Quatrefoil of Love*. EETS: o.s., 195. London: Oxford Univ. Press, 1935.

Gompf, Ludwig. *Werke und Briefe von Joseph Iscanus*. Leiden: Brill, 1970.

———, ed. *Joseph of Exeter*. Leiden: Brill, 1978.

Gougaud, Louis. *Devotional and Ascetic Practices in the Middle Ages*. London: Burns Oates and Washborne, 1927.

———. "Étude sur les 'Ordines Commendationis Animae'." *EL* 49 (1935): 3–27.

Graesse, Theodor, ed. *Jacobi a Voragine Legenda aurea vulgo historia lombardica dicta*. 1846, Reprint. Osnabrück: Zeller, 1969.

Graff, Harvey J. *Literacy in History: An Interdisciplinary Research Bibliography*. New York: Garland, 1981.

Graham, Rose, ed. *A Picture Book of the Life of Saint Anthony the Abbot. A Reproduction in Full of a Manuscript of the Year 1426 in the Malta Public Library at Valetta*. Oxford: Roxburghe Club, 1937.

Gransden, Antonia. "The Continuations of the *Flores Historiarum* from 1265–1327." *MS* 36 (1974): 472–80.

———. *Historical Writing in England c. 550 to c. 1307*. Ithaca, N.Y.: Cornell Univ. Press, 1974.

———. *Historical Writing in England: c. 1307 to the Early Sixteenth Century*. Ithaca, N.Y.: Cornell Univ. Press, 1982.

Grassi, J. L. "Royal Clerks from the Archdiocese of York in the Fourteenth Century." *NH* 5 (1970): 12–33.

Gray, Douglas. "The Five Wounds of Our Lord." *N&Q* 208 (1963) I, 50–51; II, 82–89; III, 127–34; IV, 163–68.

———. *Themes and Images in the Medieval Religious Lyric*. London: Routledge and Kegan Paul, 1972.

Greenhill, E. *Die Stellung der Handschrift British Museum Arundel 44 in der Überlieferung des Speculum Virginum*. Munich: Hueber, 1966.

Greenslade, S. L. "The Contents of the Library of Durham Cathedral Priory." *TAASDN* 11 (1965): 347–69.

Griffiths, Ralph A. "Local Rivalries and National Politics: The Percies, the Nevilles, and the Duke of Exeter, 1452–55." *Speculum* 43 (1968): 589–632.

Griscom, Acton. *The Historia Regum Britanniae of Geoffrey of Monmouth*. London: Longmans, Green, 1929.

Grissom, Carol A. "Green Earth." In *Artists' Pigments: A Handbook of Their History and Characterization*, edited by Robert L. Feller, 141–67. Washington, D.C.: National Gallery of Art, 1986.

Gruys, A. "Codicology or Archaeology of the Book? A False Dilemma." *Quaerendo* 2 (1972): 87–108.

Guest, John. *Thomas de Rotherham Archbishop of York and His College of Jesus at Rotherham. A Paper Read Before the Rotherham Literary and Scientific Society 18th November, 1867*. Rotherham: A. Gilling, 1869.

Guinochet, Marcel, and Roger de Vilmorin. *Flore de France*. Paris: CNRS, 1975.

Gumbert, J. P. "La Page intelligible: quelques remarques." In *Vocabulaire du livre et de l'écriture au moyen âge*, edited by Olga Weijers, 111–19. Turnhout: Brepols, 1989.

Güntherová, Alzbeta. *Illuminierte handschriften aus der Slowakei*. Artia: Prague, 1962.

Gurney, N. "The Borthwick Institute of Historical Research." *Archives* 7 (1966): 157–62.

Gwynn, Aubrey. "The Date of the B-Text of *Piers Plowman*." *RES* 19, (1943): 1–24.

———, ed. *The Writings of Bishop Patrick, 1074–1084*. Scriptores Latini Hiberniae Vol. 1, Dublin: Dublin Institute for Advanced Studies, 1955.

Haage, B. "Zur Überleiferung des 'Malogranatum.'" *ZDADL* 108 (1979): 407–14.

Hackett, M. B. "William Flete and the *De Remediis Contra Temptaciones*." In *Medieval Studies Presented to Aubrey Gwynn, S.J.*, edited by J. A. Watt et al., 330–48. Dublin: O. Lochlainn, 1961.

Hadcock, R. Neville. "A Map of Mediaeval Northumberland and Durham." *AA*, 4th ser., 16 (1939): 148–218.

Haines, Roy Martin. "A York Priest's Notebook." In *Ecclesia Anglicana: Studies in the English Church of the Late Middle Ages*, 156–79. Toronto: Pontifical Institute, 1989.

Hall, John George. *A History of South Cave*. Hull: E. Ombler, 1892.

Halleux, Robert, and Paul Meyvaert. "Les origines de la Mappa Clavicula." *AHDLMA* 54 (1987): 7–58.

Halligan, Theresa A., ed. *The Booke of Gostlye Grace of Mechtild of Hackeborn*. Toronto: Pontifical Institute, 1979.

Halliwell, J. O., ed. *Early English Miscellanies in Prose and Verse*. 1855. Reprint. New York: AMS, 1966.

Hamand, L. A. *The Ancient Windows of Great Malvern Priory Church*. Reprint. St. Albans, Eng.: Canfield Press, 1978.

Hamburger, Jeffrey. "The Use of Images in the Pastoral Care of Nuns: The case of Heinrich Suso and the Dominicans." *AB* 71 (1989): 20–46.

———. "The Visual and the Visionary: The Image in Late Medieval Monastic Devotions." *Viator* 20 (1989): 161–82.

Hamilton, N. E. S. A., ed. *De Gestis Pontificum Anglorum Libri Quinque*. Rolls Series no. 52. Reprint. Millwood, N.Y.: Kraus, 1967.

Hammer, Jacob. "A Commentary on the *Prophetia Merlini*, (Geoffrey of Monmouth's *Historia Regum Brittaniae*, Book VII)." *Speculum* 10 (1935): 3–30.

———. "Note on a Manuscript of Geoffrey of Monmouth's *Historia Regum Britanniae*." *PQ* 12 (1933): 225–34.

Hammerich, Louis L. *The Beginning of the Strife Between Richard FitzRalph and the Mendicants, with an Edition of His Autobiographical Prayer and His Proposition 'Unusquisque.'* Copenhagen: Levin and Munksgaard, 1938.

Hanawalt, Barbara. "Keepers of the Lights: Late Medieval English Parish Guilds." *JMRS* 14 (1984): 21–37.

Hanna, Ralph. "*Compilatio* and the Wife of Bath: Latin Backgrounds, Ricardian Texts." In *Latin and Vernacular*, edited by A. J. Minnis, 1–11.

Hanning, Robert W. *The Vision of History in Early Britain from Gildas to Geoffrey of Monmouth*. New York: Columbia Univ. Press, 1966.

Haraszti, Zoltan. "Additions to the Rare Book Department." *BPLQ* 9 (1957): 60–61.

Hardwick, C., and H. R. Luard. *A Catalogue of the Manuscripts Preserved in the Library of the University of Cambridge*. Reprint. Millwood, N.Y.: Kraus, 1980.

Hardy, Thomas D. *Descriptive Catalogue of Materials Relating to the History of Great Britain and Ireland*. Rolls Series no. 26. Reprint. Millwood, N.Y.: Kraus, 1967.

Harley, John, and Francis Bickley, eds. *Report on the Manuscripts of the Late Reginald Rawdon Hastings, Esq., of the Manor House, Ashby de la Zouche.* Historical Manuscripts Commission 78. London: Historical Manuscripts Commission, H. M. Stationery Office, 1928.

Harley, R. D. *Artists' Pigments c. 1600–1835.* New York, London: Butterworths, 1970.

Harris, G. L. *King, Parliament and Public Finance in Medieval England to 1369.* Oxford: Clarendon, 1975.

Harris, Kate. "The Origins and Make-up of Cambridge University Library MS Ff.1.6." *TCBS* 8, pt. 3 (1983): 299–333.

———. "Patrons, Buyers and Owners: The Evidence for Ownership and the Rôle of Book Owners in Book Production and the Book Trade." In *BPPB*, 163–99.

Harrsen, Meta. *Medieval and Renaissance Manuscripts in the Pierpont Morgan Library.* Vol. 2, *Central European Manuscripts.* New York: Pierpont Morgan, 1958.

Hartley, P. H. S., and H. R. Aldridge. *Johannes de Mirfeld of St. Bartholomew's, Smithfield: His Life and Works.* Cambridge: Cambridge Univ. Press, 1936.

Hartshorne, Charles Henry. *Feudal and Military Antiquities of Northumberland and the Scottish Borders.* London: Bell and Daldy, 1858.

Hathaway, Neil. "Compilatio: From Plagiarism to Compiling." *Viator* 20 (1989): 19–44.

Haupt, Gottfried. *Die Farbensymbolik in der sakralen Kunst des abendländischen Mittelalters.* Dresden: Dittert, 1941.

Hawkin, Richard York. *A History of the Freemen of the City of York.* York: James L. Burdekin, 1955.

Heath, Peter. *English Parish Clergy on the Eve of the Reformation.* London: Routledge and Kegan Paul, 1969.

Heaton, Herbert. *The Yorkshire Woollen and Worsted Industries.* Oxford: Oxford Univ. Press, 1965.

Hedeman, Anne D. *The Royal Image: Illustrations from the Grandes Chroniques de France, 1274–1422.* Berkeley: Univ. of California Press, 1991.

Heffernan, Thomas. "The Use of the Phrase *Plenus Amoris* in Scribal Colophons." *N&Q* 226 (Dec. 1981): 493–94.

Hegi, Gustav. *Illustrierte Flora von Mittel-Europa.* Berlin: P. Parey, 1979.

Heimann, A. "Trinitas Creator Mundi." *JWCI* 2 (1938): 42–52.

Hendrix, G. "Hugh of St. Cher, O.P., Author of Two Texts Attributed to the Thirteenth-Century Cistercian Gerard of Liège." *Studia Cisterciensia R. P. Edmondo Mikkers Oblata.* Studie Cistercienses 21. Vol. 1 (1950), 343–56.

Hepple, R. B. "Uthred of Boldon." *AA*, 3d ser., 17 (1920): 153–68.

Hewitt, Joseph W. "The Use of Nails in the Crucifixion." *HTR* 25 (1932): 29–45.

Hey, David. *Yorkshire from A.D. 1000.* London and New York: Longman, 1986.

Hildburgh, W. L. "An English Alabaster Carving of St. Michael Weighing a Soul." *BM* 89 (1947): 129–31.

————. "English Alabaster Carvings as Records of the Medieval Religious Drama." *Archaeologia* 93 (1949): 51–101.

Hill, Arthur Du Boulay. "The Wollaton Antiphonale." *TTS* 36 (1932): 42–50.

Hill, Geoffrey. *English Dioceses, a History of Their Limits from the Earliest Times to the Present Day.* London: E. Stock, 1900.

Hindman, Sandra. "The Roles of Author and Artist in the Procedure of Illustrating Late Medieval Texts." In *Text and Image.* ACTA. Vol. 10, edited by David Burchmore, 27–62. Binghamton, N.Y.: Center for Medieval and Early Renaissance Studies, 1983.

Hindman, Sandra, and James D. Farquhar. *Pen to Press: Illustrated Manuscripts and Printed Books in the First Century of Printing.* College Park: Univ. of Maryland Press, 1977.

A History of Northumberland Issued under the Direction of the Northumberland County History Committee. Newcastle: A. Reid Sons, 1893–1940.

Hogg, James. "Mount Grace Charter House and Late Medieval English Spirituality." *Collectanea Cartusiensia* 3. AC 82.3: 18–21. Salzburg: Institut für Anglistik und Amerikanistik, 1980.

————"A Morbid Preoccupation with Mortality? The Carthusian London British Library MS Add. 37049." In *Zeit, Tod und Ewigkeit in der Renaissance Literatur.* Vol. 2, edited by Stürzl et al., 139–89. Salzburg: Institut für Anglistik und Amerikanistik, 1986.

————. "Surviving English Carthusian Remains: Beauvale, Coventry, Mountgrace: Album." *AC* 36 (1976).

————. "Unpublished Texts in the Carthusian Northern Middle English Religious Miscellany British Library MS Add. 37049." In *Essays in Honour of Erwin Stürzl on his Sixtieth Birthday,* edited by James Hogg, 241–84. Salzburg: Institut für Anglistik und Americanistik, 1984.

Holmstedt, G., ed. *Speculum Christiani. A Middle English Treatise of the 14th Century.* EETS: o.s., 182. 1933. Reprint. Millwood, N.Y.: Kraus, 1971.

Höltgren, Karl Josef. "Arbor, Scala und Fons Vitae. Vorformen devotionaler Embleme in einer mittelenglischen Handschrift (B. M. Add. MS 37049)." In *Chaucer und Seine Zeit, Symposion für Walter F. Schirmer,* edited by Arno Esch, 355–91. Tübingen: Max Niemeyer Verlag, 1968.

Holzworth, Jean. " 'Hugutio's Derivationes' and Arnulfus' Commentary on Ovid's *Fasti.*" *TPAPA* 73 (1942): 259–76.

Horstman, Carl, ed. *Nova Legenda Anglie.* Oxford: Clarendon, 1901.

————, ed. *Yorkshire Writers, Richard Rolle of Hampole an English Father of the Church and His Followers.* London: Swan, Sonnenschein, 1895–96.

Hoste, A., and C. H. Talbot, eds. *Aelredi Rivallensis Opera Omnia.* Corpus Christianorum: Continuatio Medievalis 1. Turnhout, Belgium: Brepols, 1971.

Hübner, Walter. "The Desert of Religion." *Archiv,* n. s., 26, 126 (1911): 58–74.

Hudson, Anne. *Lollards and Their Books.* London: Hambledon, 1985.

————. "A New Look at the Lay Folks' Catechism." *Viator* 16 (1985): 243–58.

————. "Some Aspects of Lollard Book Production." In *Schism, Heresy and Religious Protest*, edited by Derek Baker, 147–57. Cambridge: Cambridge Univ. Press, 1972.

Hudson, Douglas R. "Keltic Metalwork and Manuscript Illumination." *Metallurgia* 31 (1945): 283–90.

Hughes, Andrew. *Medieval Manuscripts for Mass and Office*. Toronto: Pontifical Institute, 1982.

Hughes, J. *Une Excursion dans la Commune de Grand-Gallargues*. Nîmes: J. Hughes, 1836.

Hughes, Jonathan. *Pastors and Visionaries: Religion and Secular Life in Late Medieval Yorkshire*. Woodbridge, Suffolk: Boydell Press, 1988.

Hugo, Michel. *Les Tonaries*. Publications de la société français de musicologie. 3d ser., 2. Paris: Société français de Musicologie, 1971.

Humphries, K. W. "Scribes and the Medieval Friars." In *Bibliothekswelt und Kulturgeschichte. Eine internationale Festgabe für Joachim Wieder zum 65. Geburtstag*, edited by Peter Schweigler, 213–220. Munich: Verlag Dokumentation, 1977.

————, ed. *The Friars' Libraries*. Corpus of British Medieval Library Catalogues. London: British Library, 1990.

Hunt, R. W., ed. *Umbrae Codicum Occidentalium* 4. Amsterdam: North-Holland, 1961.

Hunt, Tony. *Plant Names of Medieval England*. Cambridge: Boydell and Brewer, 1989.

Hunter Blair, C. H. "The Armorials of the County Palatine of Durham." *AA*, 4th ser., 4 (1927): 1–67.

Hunter, Joseph. *Hallamshire: The History and Topography of the Parish of Sheffield in the County of York*. London: Virtue, 1875.

Hutchinson, G. Evelyn. "Attitudes Toward Nature in Medieval England: The Alphonso and Bird Psalters." *Isis* 65 (1974): 5–37.

Jackson, Kenneth, et al. *Celtic and Saxon: Studies in the Early British Border*. Cambridge, Cambridge Univ. Press, 1964.

Jacob, E. F. *The Fifteenth Century, 1399–1485*. Oxford: Clarendon, 1961.

Jacob, John. *English Medieval Alabaster Carvings. A Catalogue*. York: City of York Art Gallery, 1954.

James, M. E. "The First Earl of Cumberland (1493–1542) and the Decline of Northern Feudalism." *NH* 1 (1966): 43–69.

James, Mervyn. "Ritual, Drama and Social Body in the Late Medieval English Town." *PP* 98 (1983): 3–29.

James, Montague Rhodes. "An English Medieval Sketch Book, No. 1916 in the Pepysian Library, Magdalene College, Cambridge." *WS* 13 (1924–25): 1–17.

————. "The Anlaby Cartulary." *YAJ* 31 (1934): 337–47.

————. *A Descriptive Catalogue of the Western Manuscripts in the Library of Clare College*. Cambridge: Cambridge Univ. Press, 1905.

————. *A Descriptive Catalogue of the Manuscripts in the Library of Corpus Christi College, Cambridge*. 2 vols. Cambridge: Cambridge Univ. Press, 1912.

———. *A Descriptive Catalogue of the Manuscripts in the Library of Gonville and Caius College:* 3 vols. Cambridge: Cambridge Univ. Press, 1907–14.

———. *A Descriptive Catalogue of the Manuscripts in the Library of Jesus College, Cambridge.* Cambridge: Cambridge Univ. Press, 1895.

———. *A Descriptive Catalogue of the Manuscripts in King's College.* Cambridge: Cambridge Univ. Press, 1895.

———. *A Descriptive Catalogue of the Manuscripts in the Library of Pembroke College, Cambridge.* Cambridge: Cambridge Univ. Press, 1905.

———. *A Descriptive Catalogue of the Manuscripts in the Library of Peterhouse.* Cambridge: Cambridge Univ. Press, 1899.

———. *A Descriptive Catalogue of the Manuscripts in the Library of Sidney Sussex College, Cambridge.* Cambridge: Cambridge Univ. Press, 1895.

———. *A Descriptive Catalogue of the Western Manuscripts in the Library of Trinity College, Cambridge.* 4 vols. Cambridge: Cambridge Univ. Press, 1900–04.

———. *A Descriptive Catalogue of the Manuscripts in the Library of Trinity Hall.* Cambridge: Cambridge Univ. Press, 1907.

———. *A Descriptive Catalogue of the McClean Collection of Manuscripts in the Fitzwilliam Museum, Cambridge.* Cambridge: Cambridge Univ. Press, 1912.

———. *A Descriptive Catalogue of the Western Manuscripts in the Library of Emmanuel College.* Cambridge: Cambridge Univ. Press, 1904.

———. *Lists of Manuscripts Formerly Owned by Dr. John Dee.* Cambridge: Cambridge Univ. Press, 1921.

———. "Points to be Observed in the description and Collation of Manuscripts, particularly Books of Hours." In *A Descriptive Catalogue of the Manuscripts in the Fitzwilliam Museum,* xxiii–xxxviii. Cambridge: Cambridge Univ. Press, 1895.

James, Montague Rhodes, and Claude Jenkins. *A Descriptive Catalogue of the Manuscripts in the Library of Lambeth Palace.* 5 vols. Cambridge: Cambridge Univ. Press 1930–32.

Jancey, Meryl. *Mappa Mundi: The Map of the World in Hereford Cathedral: A Brief Guide.* Hereford: Friends of Hereford Cathedral, 1987.

Jayne, Sears, and Francis R. Johnson, eds. *The Lumley Library: The Catalogue of 1609.* London: British Museum, 1956.

Jeffrey, David L. *The Early English Lyric and Franciscan Spirituality.* Lincoln: Univ. of Nebraska Press, 1975.

Jenni, Ulrike. *Das Skizzenbuch der internationalen Gotik in den Uffizien: der Übergang vom Musterbuch zum Skizzenbuch.* Vienna: Holzhausen, 1976.

Jewell, Helen M. "English Bishops as Educational Benefactors in the Later Fifteenth Century." In *The Church, Politics and Patronage in the Fifteenth Century,* edited by Barrie Dobson, 146–67. Gloucester: Sutton, 1984.

———. "North and South: The Antiquity of the Great Divide." *NH* 27 (1991): 1–25.

Joanne, Paul. *Dictionnaire géographique et administratif de la France.* Paris: Rachette 1894–1905.

Johnston, Alexandra F. "The Plays of the Religious Guilds of York: The Creed Play and the Pater Noster Play." *Speculum* 50 (1975): 55–90.

Johnston, Alexandra F., and Margaret Dorrell. "The Doomsday Pageant of
the York Mercers, 1433." *LSE*, n. s., 5 (1971): 29–34.
———. "The York Mercers and Their Pageant of Doomsday, 1433–1526."
LSE, n. s., 6 (1972): 10–35.
Johnston, Alexandra F., and Margaret Rogerson, eds. *Records of Early English
Drama: York*. Toronto: Pontifical Institute, 1979.
Jolliffe, Peter S. *A Check-List of Middle English Prose Writings of Spiritual Guid-
ance*. Toronto: Pontifical Institute, 1974.
———. "Middle English Translations of the *De Exterioris et Interioris Hominis
Compositione*." *MS* 36 (1974): 259–77.
Joly, N. "Recherches sur la fabrication du tournésol en drapeaux, et sur le
principe colorant du *Chrozophora tinctoria* employé à cette fabrication."
Annales de Chemie et de Physique, 3d ser., 6 (1842): 111–26.
Jones, Joseph R., and John E. Keller, eds., and trans. *The Scholar's Guide:
A Translation of the Twelve-Century Disciplina Clericalis of Pedro Alfonso*.
Toronto: Pontifical Institute, 1969.
Jones, Michael. *Ducal Brittany 1364–1399*. Oxford: Oxford Univ. Press, 1970.
———. "Education in Brittany During the Later Middle Ages: A Survey."
NMS 22 (1978): 58–77.
———. "L'Enseignement en Bretagne à la fin du moyen âge: quelque terrains
de recherche." *MSHAB* 53 (1975–76): 33–49.
———. "L'Histoire du bas moyen âge breton (1200–1500)." *MSHAB* 56
(1979): 207–20.
Jones, W. R. "English Religious Brotherhoods and Medieval Lay Piety." *The
Historian* 36 (1974): 646–59.
Jönsjö, Jan. *Studies on Middle English Nicknames I. Compounds*. Lund Studies in
English 55. Lund: Liber Laromedel/C. W. K. Gleerup, 1979.
Kane, George, and E. Talbot Donaldson, eds. *Piers Plowman: The B. Version*.
London: Athlone Press, 1988.
Kapoor, V. K., et al. "Studies on Some Indian Seed Oils." *Fitoterapia* 57
(1986): 188–90.
Kauffmann, C. M. *Romanesque Manuscripts, 1066–1190*. Oxford: Harvey
Miller, 1975.
Kaufmann, Thomas Da Costa, and Virginia Roehrig Kaufmann. "The Sancti-
fication of Nature: Observations on the Origins of Trompe l'Oeil in
Netherlandish Book Painting of the Fifteenth and Sixteenth Centuries."
JPGMJ 19 (1991): 43–64.
Keiser, George. "Lincoln Cathedral Library MS 91: Life and Milieu of the
Scribe." *SB* 32 (1979): 158–79.
———. "þe Holy Boke Gratia Dei." *Viator* 12 (1981): 289–317.
———. " 'To Knawe God Almyghtyn': Robert Thornton's Devotional Book."
In *Spätmittelalterliche Geistliche Literatur in der Nationalsprache*, edited by
James Hogg, 2, 103–29. Salzburg: Institut für Anglistik und Amerikan-
istik, 1984.
———. "More Light on the Life and Milieu of Robert Thornton." *SB* 36
(1983): 111–19.

———. "Patronage and Piety in Fifteenth-Century England: Margaret, Duchess of Clarence, Symon Wynter and Beinecke MS 317." *YULG* 60 (1985: 32–46.

Kelly, Thomas. *Early Public Libraries: A History of Public Libraries in Great Britain Before 1850.* London: Library Association, 1966.

Kemp, Simon. *Medieval Psychology.* Westport, Conn.: Greenwood Press, 1990.

Ker, Neil. *Medieval Libraries of Great Britain: A List of Surviving Books.* London: Royal Historical Society, 1964.

———. "Medieval Manuscripts from Norwich Cathedral Priory." *TCBS* 1 (1949–53): 1–28.

———. *Medieval Manuscripts in British Libraries.* Vols. 1–3. London, 1969–83.

———. *Pastedowns in Oxford Bindings.* Oxford Bibliographical Society, n. s., 5, Oxford, 1954.

———. "Patrick Young's Catalogue of the Manuscripts of Lichfield Cathedral." *MRS* 2 (1950): 151–68.

———. *Records of All Souls College Library 1437–1600.* Oxford: Oxford Univ. Press, 1971.

Ker, Neil, and Alan J. Piper. *Medieval Manuscripts in British Libraries.* Vol. 4, *Paisley-York.* Oxford: Clarendon, 1992.

Ker, Neil, and Andrew Watson. *Medieval Libraries of Great Britain, Supplement.* London: The British Library, 1987.

Kerby-Fulton, Kathryn. "Hildegard of Bingen and Antimendicant Propaganda." *Traditio* 43 (1987): 386–99.

Kermode, Jennifer I. "The Merchants of Three Northern English Towns." In *Profession, Vocation, and Culture in Later Medieval England: Essays dedicated to the Memory of A. R. Meyers,* edited by Cecil H. Clough, 7–48. Liverpool: Liverpool Univ. Press, 1982.

Kershaw, I. *Bolton Priory: The Economy of a Northern Monastery, 1286–1325.* Oxford: Oxford Univ. Press, 1973.

Kieckhefer, R. "Major Currents in Late Medieval Devotion." In *Christian Spirituality: High Middle Ages and Reformation,* edited by Jill Raitt et al., 75–108. World Spirituality 17, New York: Crossroads, 1987.

King, Archdale A. *Liturgies of the Past.* London: Longmans, Green, 1959.

———. *Liturgies of the Religious Orders.* London: Longmans, Green, 1955.

Kingsford, Charles L. "Two Forfeitures in the Year of Agincourt." *Archaeologia* 70 (1920): 71–100.

Kletzel, Otto. "Studien zur böhmischen Buchmalerei." *MJK* 7 (1993): 1–76.

Kloss, Ernst. *Die Schlesische Buchmalerei des Mittelalters.* Berlin: Deutscher Verein für Kunstwissenschaft, 1942.

Knowles, David. *Saints and Scholars.* Cambridge: Cambridge Univ. Press, 1962.

Knowles, David, and R. Neville Hadcock. *Medieval Religious Houses: England and Wales.* London: Longman, 1971.

Knowles, David, and J. K. S. St. Joseph. *Monastic Sites from the Air.* Cambridge: Cambridge Univ. Press, 1952.

Knowles, John Alder. "A History of the York School of Glass-Painting, VII." *JBSMGP* 3 (1929): 31–42.

König, Eberhard. "Un atelier d'enluminure à Nantes et l'art du temps de Fouquet." *RA* 35 (1977): 64–75.

Korteweg, Anne S., ed. *Kriezels, aubergines en takkenbossen. Randversiering in Noordnederlandse handschriften uit de vijftiende eeuw.* 's-Gravenhage: Rijksmuseum Meermano-Westreenianum/Koninklijke Bibliothek, 1992.

Krása, Josef. *Die Handschriften König Wenzels IV.* Prague: Odeon, 1971.

———. "Olomoucké illuminované rukopisy." *Uměni* 16 (1968): 413–41.

———. *The Travels of Sir John Mandeville: A Manuscript in the British Library.* New York: Braziller, 1983.

Kratzmann, G., and E. Gee, eds. *The Dialogues of Creatures Moralysed.* Oxford Medieval and Renaissance Texts. Oxford: Clarendon, 1988.

Kraus, H. P. *Fifty Mediaeval and Renaissance Manuscripts, Catalogue 88.* New York: H. P. Kraus, n.d.

Krochalis, Jeanne E. "God and Mammon: Prayers and Rents in Princeton MS 126." *PULC* 44 (1983): 209–22.

Kuhn, Charles L. "Herman Scheerre and English Illumination of the Early Fifteenth Century." *AB* 22 (1940): 138–56.

Kühn, Hermann. "Verdigris and Copper Resinate." *StC* 15 (1970): 12–36.

Kühn, Hermann, et al., eds. *Reclams Handbuch der Künstlerischen Techniken, Farbmittel, Buchmalerei, Tafel- und Leinwandmalerei.* Stuttgart: Reclam, 1984.

Kuhnholtz-Lordat, G., and G. Blanchet. *Flore des environs immediats de Montpellier.* Paris: P. Lechevalier, 1948.

Künzle, Pius, ed. *Heinrich Seuses Horologium Sapientiae.* Spicilegium Friburgense 23. Freiburg: Universitätsverlag, 1977.

Kutal, Albert. *Gothic Art in Bohemia and Moravia.* London: Hamlyn, 1972.

Květ, Jan. *Illuminované Rukopisy Královny Rejčky.* Prague: Ceske Akademie ved a Uměni, 1931.

L'Anson, William M. "Coverham Abbey." *YAJ* 25 (1923): 273–301.

Lacroix, Dominique. *Paroisses et communes de France: Dictionnaire d'histoire administrative et demographique.* Paris: CNRS, 1986.

Lagorio, Valerie, and Ritamary Bradley, eds. *The 14th-Century English Mystics: A Comprehensive Annotated Bibliography.* New York: Garland, 1981.

Lapsley, Gaillard T. "The Account Roll of a Fifteenth-Century Iron Master." *EHR* 14 (1899): 509–29.

———. *The County Palatine of Durham.* Harvard Historical Studies 8. New York: Longmans, Green, 1900.

Lawrance, N. A. H., ed. *Fasti Parochiales V: Deanery of Buckrose.* YASRS 143. Leeds: Yorkshire Archaeological Soc., 1983.

Le Gonidec, J. F. M. M. A. *Dictionnaire Breton-français.* 1850. Reprint. Saint-Brieuc, France: Les Presses Bretonnes, 1980.

Leach, Arthur Francis. *Early Yorkshire Schools.* Vol. 2. ASRS 33. Leeds: Yorkshire Archaeological Soc., 1903.

———. "Wykeham's Books at New College." *Collectanea* III. Oxford Historical Society 32. Oxford: Clarendon, 1896, 230.

Legge, W. Heneage. "A Decorated Mediaeval Roll of Prayers." *The Reliquary*, n. s., 10 (1904): 99–112.

Lehmann-Haupt, Hellmut, ed. *The Göttingen Model Book*. 1972. Reprint. Columbia: Univ. of Missouri Press, 1978.

Leonardi, Claudio. "Patricius Hibernorum ep." *ML* 5 (1982): 346.

Leonardi, Corrado. "La vita e l'opera di Uguccione da Pisa decretista." *SG* 4 (1956–57): 37–120.

Leroquais, V. *Les livres d'heures, manuscrits de la Bibliothèque nationale*. Paris: Protat Fréres, 1927–43.

Lewis, Flora. "From Image to Illustration: The Place of Devotional Images in the Book of Hours." In *Iconographie Médiévale: Image, Texte, Contexte*, edited by Gaston Duchet-Suchaux, 29–58. Paris: CNRS, 1990.

———. "The Veronica: Image, Legend and Viewer." In *England in the Thirteenth Century: Proceedings of the 1984 Harlaxton Symposium*, edited by W. H. Ormrod, 100–106. Woodridge, Suffolk: Boydell, 1986.

Lewis, Samuel. *A Topographical Dictionary of England*. London: S. Lewis, 1831.

Lieftinck, Gerard Isaac. *Manuscrits datés conservés dans les Pays-Bas: Catalogue paléographique des manuscrits en écriture latine portant des indications de date*. 2 vols. Amsterdam: North Holland; Leiden: Brill, 1964–88.

Lindberg, Conrad. "The Manuscripts and Versions of the Wycliffite Bible: A Preliminary Survey." *SN* 42 (1970): 333–47.

Little, Andrew G. *Grey Friars in Oxford*. Oxford: Clarendon, 1892.

Littlehales, Henry, ed. *The Prymer or Lay Folk's Prayer* 1895. Reprint. Millwood, N.Y.: Kraus, 1981.

Loeber, E. G. "Tournesol-Lappen." *IPH* (International Association of Paper Historians) *Information* 19, nos. 3–4 (1985): 103–8.

Loengard, Janet S. " 'Legal History and the Medieval Englishwoman' Revisited: Some New Directions." In *Medieval Women and the Sources of Medieval History*, edited by Joel T. Rosenthal, 210–36. Athens: Univ. of Georgia, 1990.

Lomas, R. A. "A Northern Farm at the End of the Middle Ages: Elvethall Manor, Durham 1443/44–1513/14." *NH* 18 (1982): 26–53.

———. "The Priory of Durham and Its Demesnes in the Fourteenth and Fifteenth Centuries." *EcHR*, 2d ser., 31 (1978): 339–53.

Long, C. *Biochemist's Handbook*. London: Spon, 1961.

Loret, H., and A. Barrandon. *Flore de Montpellier*. Montpellier: C. Coulet, 1876.

Lovatt, Roger. "Henry Suso and the Medieval Mystical Tradition in England." In *The Medieval Mystical Tradition in England*, edited by Marion Glasscoe, 47–62. Exeter: Univ. of Exeter, 1982.

Löw, Immanuel. *Zeitschrift . . . und der Flora der Juden*. Vienna: G. Olms: 1924–34.

Lowe, E. A. *Codices Latini Antiquiores*. Oxford: Clarendon, 1935.

Lübbeke, Isolde. *Early German Painting 1350–1550.* London: Sotheby's, 1991.

Lucas, P. J. "The Growth and Development of English Literary Patronage in the Later Middle ages and Early Renaissance." *The Library,* 6th ser., 4 (1982): 219–48.

Lyall, R. J. "Books and Book Owners in Fifteenth-Century Scotland." In *BPPB,* 239–56.

MacCracken, Henry N., ed. *The Minor Poems of John Lydgate.* EETS: e.s., 107. London: Kegan Paul and Henry Frowde, 1911.

Mackie, Peter. "Chaplains in the Diocese of York, 1480–1530: The Testamentary Evidence." *YAJ* 58 (1986): 123–33.

Macray, William D. *Annals of the Bodleian Library, Oxford.* Reprint. Oxford: Clarendon, 1984.

———. *Catalogi Codicum Manuscriptorum Bibliothecae Bodleianae Pars V fasciculus I Viri Ricardi Rawlinson.* Oxford: Clarendon, 1878.

Madan, Falconer. "Hours of the Virgin Mary: Tests for Localization." *BQR* 3 (1920): 40–44.

Madan, Falconer, and H. H. E. Craster, eds. *A Summary Catalogue of Western Manuscripts in the Bodleian Library in Oxford.* Oxford: Clarendon, 1970.

Madan, Falconer, et al. *Catalogue of the Additions to the Manuscripts in the British Museum 1900–1905.* 1905. Reprint. London: British Library, 1969.

Maddicott, J. R. *Thomas of Lancaster, 1307–1322: A Study in the Reign of Edward II.* Oxford: Oxford Univ. Press, 1970.

Malvern, Marjorie M. "An Ernest 'Monyscyon' and 'þinge Delectabyll' Realized Verbally and Visually in a 'Disputacion Betwyx þe Body and Wormes', A Middle English Poem Inspired by Tomb Art and Northern Spirituality." *Viator* 13 (1982): 415–43.

Manion, Margaret M., and Vera F. Vines. *Medieval and Renaissance Illuminated Manuscripts in Australian Collections.* Sydney: Sydney Univ. Press, 1984.

Manly, John M., and Edith Rickert, eds. *The Text of the Canterbury Tales Studied on the Basis of All Known Manuscripts.* Chicago: Univ. of Chicago Press, 1940.

Mann, Colin N. *Petrarch Manuscripts in the British Isles.* Padua: Editrice Antenore, 1975.

Marcett, Mildred. *Uhtred de Boldon, Friar William Jordan and Piers Plowman.* New York: Mildred Marcett, 1938.

Marchant, Ronald A. *The Church under the Law: Justice, Administration and Discipline in the Diocese of York, 1560–1640.* Cambridge: Cambridge Univ. Press, 1969.

Marichal, Robert. "L'Écriture Latine et la civilisation occidentale du Ier au XVIe siècle." In *L'Écriture et la psychologie des peuples,* edited by Marcel Cohen and Jean Sainte Fare Garnot, 233–42. Paris: Armand Colin, 1963.

Marigo, A. *I codici manoscritti delle "Derivationes" di Uguccione Pisano.* Rome: Istituto di Studi Romani, 1936.

Marks, Richard. *The Burrell Collection.* London: Collins, 1983.

———. "The Glazing of Fotheringhay Church and College." *JBAA* 130 (1977): 79–109.

Marks, Richard, and Nigel Morgan. *The Golden Age of English Manuscript Painting, 1200–1500.* New York: Harvey Miller, 1981.

Marks, Richard, and F. Anne Payne. *British Heraldry.* London: British Museum, 1982.

Martin, H. *Cataloque de manuscrits de la bibliothèque de l'arsenal.* Paris: Imprimerie Nationale, 1885.

Martin, Hervé. *Les Ordres mendiants en Bretagne (vers 1230–vers 1530).* Paris: C. Klineksieck, 1975.

Marujol, R. *Le Gard à travers l'histoire.* Nîmes: Assoc. . . . du Gard, 1973.

Más y Guindal, Joaquin. *Plantas Tintóreas, Taniferas y Cauchiferas.* Madrid: Ministerio de Agricultura, 1943.

Masai, F., and Martin Wittek, eds. *Manuscrits Datés Conservés en Belgique, 1401–1440.* Brussels, Éditions Scientifiques E. Story-Scientia, 1968-.

Matějček, Antonin, and Jaroslav Pěsina. *Czech Gothic Painting 1350–1450.* Prague: Melantrich, 1950.

Mathew, Gervase. *The Court of Richard II.* London: John Murray, 1968.

Matthews, C. W. *English Surnames.* New York: Scribners, 1967.

Mazzarella, Bernardine. "St. Bernardine of Siena, A Model Preacher." *FS,* n. s., 4, 25 (1944): 309–27.

McCord, Norman, ed. *Durham History from the Air.* Newcastle-on-Tyne: Graham, 1971.

McCutcheon, K. L. *Yorkshire Fairs and Markets to the End of the Eighteenth Century.* Leeds: Thoresby Society, 1940.

McGerr, Rosemarie Potz, ed. *the Pilgrimage of the Soul.* New York: Garland, 1990.

McKenna, J. W. "Popular Canonization as Political Propaganda: The Cult of Archbishop Scrope." *Speculum* 45 (1970): 608–23.

McKitterick, R. *The Carolingians and the Written Word.* Cambridge: Cambridge Univ. Press, 1989.

———, ed. *The Uses of Literacy in Early Mediaeval Europe.* Cambridge: Cambridge Univ. Press, 1990.

McNamer, Sarah. "Female Authors, Provincial Setting: The Re-Versing of Courtly Love in the Findern Manuscript." *Viator* 22 (1991): 278–310.

McNiven, P. "The Betrayal of Archbishop Scrope." *BJRL* 54 (1971): 173–213.

Meale, Carol M. " '. . . alle the bokes that I have of Latyn, Englisch, and Frensch': Laywomen and Their Books in Late Medieval England." In *Women and Literature in Britain in 1150–1500,* edited by Carol M. Meale, 128–58. Cambridge: Cambridge Univ. Press, 1993.

Meech, Sanford B., and Hope Emily Allen, eds. *The Book of Margery Kempe.* EETS, o.s. 212. London: H. Milford and Oxford Univ. Press, 1940.

Meister, Ferdinand, ed. *Daretis Phrygii De Exidio Troiae Historia.* Leipzig: Teubner, 1873.

Melnikas, A. *The Corpus of the Miniatures in the Manuscripts of Decretum Gratiani.* Rome, 1975.

Mendyk, Stanley G. *Speculum Britanniae: Regional Study, Antiquarianism, and Science in Britain to 1700*. Toronto: Univ. of Toronto Press, 1989.

The Merck Index. 11th ed. Rahway, N.J.: Merck, 1989.

Merrifield, Mary Philadelphia. *Original Treatises Dating from the XIIth to the XVIIIth Centuries on the Arts of Painting*. 1849. Reprint. New York: Dover, 1967.

Michael, Michael A. "English Illuminators c. 1190–1450: A Survey from Documentary Sources." *EMS* 4 (1993): 62–113.

———. "Oxford, Cambridge and London: Towards a Theory for 'Grouping' of English Gothic Manuscripts." *BM* 130 (1988): 107–15.

Miles, M. R. *Image as Insight: Visual Understanding in Western Christianity and Secular Culture*. Boston: Beacon Press, 1985.

Millar, Eric G. "The Egerton Genesis and the M. R. James Memorial Manuscript." *Archaeologia* 87 (1938): 1–5.

———. *English Illuminated Manuscripts from the XIVth to the XVth Centuries*. Paris: G. van Oest, 1928.

———. *The Luttrell Psalter*. London, 1932.

Miller, E. *War in the North: The Anglo-Scottish Wars of the Middle Ages*. Hull: Univ. of Hull Publ., 1960.

Milner White, E., and Frederick Harrison. "A Medieval Hours of York Use." *The Friends of the Minster: Seventeenth Annual Report* (1945): 14–18; 27–29.

Miner, John N. *The Grammar Schools of Medieval England: A. F. Leach in Historiographical Perspective*. Montreal: McGill-Queen's Univ. Press, 1990.

Minnis, A. J., ed. *Late-Medieval Religious Texts and Their Transmission: Essays in Honour of A. I. Doyle*. Cambridge: D. S. Brewer, 1994.

Mitchell, R. J. "English Law Students at Bologna in the Fifteenth Century." *EHR* 51 (1936): 270–87.

Mohler, Ludwig, ed. *Die Einnahmen der apostolichen Kammer*. Padeborn: F. Schoningh, 1931.

Mone, F. J., ed. *Lateinische Hymnen des Mittelalters*. 1853–55. Reprint. Aalen, Germ.: Scientia, 1964.

Moore, Ellen W. *The Fairs of Medieval England: An Introductory Study*. Toronto: Pontifical Institute, 1985.

Moorman, J. R. H. *Church Life in England in the Thirteenth Century*. Cambridge: Cambridge Univ. Press, 1945.

Moran, Jo Ann. "A 'Common Profit' Library in Fifteenth-Century England and Other Books for Chaplains." *Manuscripta* 28 (1984): 17–25.

———. *The Growth of English Schooling 1340–1548: Learning, Literacy, and Laicization in Pre-Reformation York Diocese*. Princeton, N.J.: Princeton Univ. Press, 1985.

Morgan, Nigel. *Early Gothic Manuscripts (1) 1190–1250 and (2) 1250–1285*. London: Harvey Miller, 1982–88.

Morgan, Nigel, and Lucy Freeman Sandler. "Manuscript Illumination of the Thirteenth and Fourteenth Centuries." In *Age of Chivalry: Art in Planta-*

genet England 1200–1400, edited by Jonathan Alexander and Paul Binski, 148–56. London: Royal Academy of Arts, 1987.

Morgan, Paul. "Early Printing and Binding in York, Some New Facts." *BC* 30 (1981): 216–24.

Morrin, M. J. *John Waldeby, OSA, c. 1315–1372, English Augustinian Preacher and Writer.* Studia Augustiniana Historia 2. Rome: Analecta Augustiniana, 1975.

Morris, Richard, ed. *Cursor Mundi.* EETS: o.s., 66. London: Kegan Paul, Trench, Trübner, 1877–92.

————, ed. *Legends of the Holy Rood: Symbols of the Passion and Cross-Poems* EETS: o.s., 46. 1871. Reprint. New York: Greenwood Press, 1969.

Morris, Richard, and Eric Cambridge. "Beverley Minster Before the Early Thirteenth Century." In *Medieval Art and Architecture in the East Riding of Yorkshire*, edited by Christopher Wilson, 9–32. London: British Archaeological Association, 1989.

Mullin, Francis A. *A History of the Work of the Cistercians in Yorkshire 1131–1300.* Washington, D.C.: Catholic Univ. of America Press, 1932.

Munby, A. N. L. *Connoisseurs and Medieval Miniatures 1750–1850.* Oxford: Clarendon, 1972.

Müller, Ellen. "Saintly Virgins: The Veneration of Virgin Saints in Religious Women's Communities." In *Saints and She-Devils: Images of Women in the Fifteenth and Sixteenth Centuries*, edited by Lène Dresen-Coenders, 83–100. London: Rubicon Press, 1987.

Müller, Wolfgang P. *Huguccio: The Life, Works, and Thought of a Twelfth-Century Jurist.* Washington D.C.: Catholic Univ. of America Press, 1994.

————. "Huguccio of Pisa: Canonist, Bishop, and Grammarian?" *Viator* 22 (1991): 121–52.

Musgrove, Frank. *The North of England: A History from Roman Times to the Present.* Oxford: Blackwell, 1990.

Nelson, Allan H. *The Medieval English Stage: Corpus Christi Pageants and Plays.* Chicago: Univ. of Chicago Press, 1974.

Nelson, Philip. "The Byland Trinity Preserved at Ampleforth Abbey." *AmpJ* 23 (1918): 99–102.

————. "English Alabasters of the Embattled Type." *ArcJ* 75 (1918): 310–34.

Neugebauer, O. "Astronomical and Calendrical Data in the *Très Riches Heures.*" In *The Limbourgs and Their Contemporaries*, edited by Millard Meiss, 421–31. New York: Pierpont Morgan Library, 1974.

Nickson, Margaret Annie Eugenie. *The British Library, Guide to the Catalogues and Indexes of the Department of Manuscripts.* London: British Library Board, 1982.

Nordenfalk, Carl. *Celtic and Anglo-Saxon Painting.* New York: Braziller, 1977.

North, J. D. "The Alfonsine Tables in England." In *Prismata. Festschrift für Willy Hartner*, edited by Y. Maeyama and W. G. Saltzer, 269–300. Wiesbaden: Olms, 1977.

————. *Chaucer's Universe.* Oxford: Oxford Univ. Press, 1988.

Oates, J. C. T., and H. L. Pink. "Three Sixteenth-Century Catalogues of the University Library." *TCBS* 1 (1949–53): 310–40.

O'Brien, R. "The *Stimulus Peccatoris* of William of Rymington." *Citeaux, Commentarii Cisterciensis* 16 (1965): 278–304.

O'Connor, B. A. *Henri d'Arci's Vitas Patrum: A Thirteenth Century Anglo-Norman Rimed Translation of the Verba Seniorum.* Washington, D.C.: Catholic Univ. of America Press, 1949.

Oettinger, Karl. "Der Illuminator Nikolaus." *JPK* 45 (1933): 221–38.

Oliver, George. *The History and Antiquities of the Town and Minster of Beverley.* Beverley, Eng.: M. Turner, 1829.

Oliver, Judith. "The Mosan Origins of Johannes von Valkenburg." *WRJ* 40 (1978): 23–37.

———, ed. *Manuscripts Sacred and Secular from the Collections of the Endowment for Biblical Research and Boston University.* Boston: Endowment for Biblical Research, 1985.

Orme, Nicholas. *English Schools in the Middle Ages.* London: Methuen, 1973.

Pächt, Otto. "A Bohemian Martyrology." *BM* 73 (1938): 192–204.

———. "The Illustration of St. Anselm's Prayers and Meditations." *JWCI* 19 (1956): 68–83.

Pächt, Otto, and J. J. G. Alexander. *Illuminated Manuscripts in the Bodleian Library Oxford 3: British, Irish, and Icelandic Schools.* Oxford: Clarendon, 1973.

Page, Christopher. "The Rhymed Office for St. Thomas of Lancaster: Poetry, Politics and Liturgy in Fourteenth-Century England." In *Essays in Memory of Elizabeth Salter,* edited by Derek Pearsall, 134–51. Leeds Studies in English 14. Leeds: Univ. of Leeds School of English, 1983.

Palmer, Barbara. *The Early Art of the West Riding of Yorkshire.* Kalamazoo, Mich.: Medieval Institute, 1990.

Palmer, C. F. R. "The Friars Preachers, or Black Friars of Beverley." *YAJ* 7 (1882): 32–43.

Panofsky, Erwin. " 'Imago Pietatis.' Ein Beitrag zur Typengeschichte des 'Schmerzensmanns' und der 'Maria Mediatrix'." In *Festschrift für Max J. Friedländer zum 60 Geburstage,* edited by Gustav Kirstein, 261–308. Leipzig: E. A. Seemann, 1927.

———. *The Life and Art of Albrecht Dürer.* Princeton, N.J.: Princeton Univ. Press, 1955.

———. *Tomb Sculpture.* London: Thames and Hudson, 1964.

Pantin, William A. *Documents Illustrating the Activities of the General and Provincial Chapters of the English Black Monks, 1215–1540.* London: Royal Historical Soc., 1931–37.

———. *The English Church in the Fourteenth Century.* Cambridge: Cambridge Univ. Press, 1955.

———. "The Monk-Solitary of Farne: A Fourteenth-Century English Mystic." *EHR* 59 (1944): 162–86.

———. *Report on the Muniments of the Dean and Chapter of Durham.* n.p., 1939.

————. "Some Medieval English Treatises on the Origins of Monasticism." In *Medieval Studies Presented to Rose Graham,* edited by Veronica Ruffer and A. J. Taylor, 189–215. Oxford: Oxford Univ. Press, 1950.

Papworth, John W. *An Alphabetical Dictionary of about 50,000 Coats of Arms Belonging to Families in Great Britain and Ireland.* 1857. Reprint. Baltimore: Genealogical Publishing Co., 1965.

Parkes, M. B. *English Cursive Book Hands 1250–1500.* 1969. Reprint. London: Scolar Press, 1979.

————. "The Literacy of the Laity." In *Literature and Western Civilization.* Vol. 2, *The Mediaeval World,* edited by David Daiches and Anthony Thorlby, 555–77. London: Aldus, 1973.

Parkinson, John. *Theatrum Botanicum, The Theater of Plantes or an Universal and Compleate Herball.* London: Thomas Cotes, 1640.

Parks, George B. *The English Traveler in Italy. The Middle Ages (to 1525).* Palo Alto: Stanford Univ. Press, 1954.

Pearsall, Derek, ed. *Piers Plowman by William Langland, an Edition of the C-Text.* Berkeley: Univ. of California Press, 1978.

Pearsall, Derek, and Kathleen Scott. *The Illustrations of Bodleian Library, Oxford, MS Douce 104.* Cambridge: D. S. Brewer, 1992.

Pearson, Karl. *Die Fronika, Ein Beitrag zur Geschichte des Christusbildes im Mittelalters.* Strassburg: K. J. Trübner, 1887.

Peers, C. R. "Finchale Priory." *AA,* 4th ser., 4 (1927): 193–220.

Pelham, R. A. "Medieval Foreign Trade: Eastern Ports." In *An Historical Geography of England Before A.D. 1800,* edited by H. C. Darby, 324–27. 1936. Reprint. Cambridge: Cambridge Univ. Press, 1986.

Peltier, A. C., ed. *S. Bonaventurae Opera Omnia.* Paris: Augustae Taurinorum, H. Marietti, 1866.

Pepler, Conrad. "John Lacy: A Dominican Contemplative." *LS* 5 (1951): 397–400.

Percy, Thomas, ed. *The Regulations and Establishment of the Household of Henry Algernon Percy.* London: A. Brown, 1905.

Perdrizet, P. "De la Véronique et de sainte Véronique." *Seminarium Kondakovianum* 5 (1932): 1–15.

Pernoud, Régine. *Couleurs du moyen âge.* Images du Monde I. Geneva: Éditions Claire Fontaine, 1987.

Perroy, Edouard. "The Anglo-French Negotiations at Bruges 1374–77." *CM* 19, Camden Society, 3d. ser., 80 (1952): v–xix.

Pěsina, Jaroslav. "Desková Malba Katalog Descové Knižní." In *Ceské uměni Gotické 1350–1420,* edited by Frantisek Kavka et al. Prague: Academia Praha, 1970.

Pfaff, R. W. *New Liturgical Feasts in Later Medieval England.* Oxford: Clarendon, 1970.

Pickford, C. E. "An Arthurian Manuscript in the John Rylands Library." *BJRL* 31 (1948): 330–44.

Pieper, Paul. "Zum Werk des Meisters der Heiligen Veronika." In *Festschrift für Gert von der Osten,* edited by Rudolf Hillebrecht, 85–99. Cologne: M. DuMont Schaubert, 1970.

Pinkerton, John. *An Equiry into the History of Scotland.* Edinburgh: Bell and Bradfute, 1814.

Piper, A. J. "The Libraries of the Monks of Durham." In *Medieval Scribes, Manuscripts, and Libraries: Essays Presented to N. R. Ker,* edited by M. B. Parkes and Andrew G. Watson, 213–49. London: Scolar, 1978.

Platt, Colin. *The Abbeys and Priories of Medieval England.* London: Secker and Warburg, 1984.

———. *The English Medieval Town.* London: Secker and Warburg, 1976.

Plimpton, G. A. *The Education of Chaucer.* London: Oxford Univ. Press, 1935.

Plummer, John. " 'Use' and 'Beyond Use'." In *Time Sanctified: The Book of Hours in Medieval Art and Life,* edited by Roger S. Wieck et al., 149–56. Baltimore: Walters Art Gallery, 1988.

———, ed. *The Hours of Catherine of Cleves.* New York: George Braziller, 1966.

Pollard, A. J. *North-Eastern England During the Wars of the Roses: Lay Society, War, and Politics 1450–1500.* Oxford: Clarendon, 1990.

Poncelet, A. *Catalogus Codicum Hagiographicorum Latinorum Bibliothecae Vaticanae.* Brussels: Apud Socios Bollandianos, 1910.

Post, George E. *Flora of Syria, Palestine, and Sinai.* Beirut: Amer. Univ. of Beirut Press, 1933.

Postan, M. M. "The Economic and Political Relations in England and the Hanse (1400 to 1475)." In *Studies in English Trade in the Fifteenth Century,* edited by E. Power and M. M. Postan, 91–153. 1933. Reprint. London: Routledge and Kegan Paul, 1966.

Powicke, F. M. *The Medieval Books of Merton College.* Oxford: Clarendon, 1931.

Prain, D. "The Genus *Chrozophora.*" *Kew Bulletin* (1918): 103–9.

Prior, E. S., and Arthur Gardner. *An Account of Medieval Figure Sculpture in England.* Cambridge: Cambridge Univ. Press, 1912.

Pugh, T. B. "The Magnates, Knights and Gentry." In *Fifteenth-Century England, 1399–1509: Studies in Politics and History,* edited by Stanley B. Chrimes et al., 86–128. Manchester: Manchester Univ. Press, 1972.

Purvis, J. S. *The Archives of the York Diocesan Registry.* 1952. Reprint. London, 1967.

———. "The Archives of York." In *Studies in Church History* 4, edited by G. J. Cuming, 1–14. Leiden: Brill, 1967.

———. *Notarial Signs from the York Archiepiscopal Records.* London: St. Anthony's Press, 1957.

Radcliffe-Smith, A. "Chrozophora A. Juss." In *Flora of Turkey and the East Aegean Islands,* edited by P. H. Davis, 567–69. Edinburgh: Edinburgh Univ. Press, 1982.

Raine, Angelo. *Mediaeval York.* London: John Murray, 1955.

Raine, James. *Saint Cuthbert.* Durham: G. Andrews, 1828.

Ramsay, Nigel. "La production et exportation des albâtres anglais médiévaux." In *Artistes, artisans, et production artistique on moyen âge, 3: Fabrication et consomation de l'oeuvre,* edited by Xavier Barral i Altet, 609–19. Paris: Picard, 1990.

Raynaud, Gaston, ed. *Oeuvres complètes de l'Eustache Deschamps.* Paris: SATF, 1894.

Reaney, P. H. *A Dictionary of British Surnames.* London: Routledge and Kegan Paul, 1977.

Reeves, Marjorie. *The Influence of Prophecy in the Later Middle Ages. A Study in Joachimism.* Oxford: Clarendon, 1969.

Reinecke, George F., ed. *John Lydgate, St. Albon and St. Amphibalus.* New York: Garland, 1989.

Renesse, Jean Louis. *Dictionnaire de Figures Héraldiques.* Brussels: Société belge de Librairie, 1892–1903.

Revell, Peter. *Fifteenth-Century English Prayers and Meditations: A Descriptive List of Manuscripts in the British Library.* New York: Garland, 1975.

Reybekiel, W. A. *Fons Vitae.* Bremen, 1934.

Reynolds, Susan. *An Introduction to the History of English Medieval Towns.* Oxford and New York: Clarendon, 1982.

Richard of Saint Victor. *De Laudibus Beatae Mariae Virginis.* In *B. Alberti Magni Opera Omnia,* vol. 36, edited by A. and E. Borgnet. Paris: Vivès, 1898.

Rickert, Margaret. *Painting in Britain: The Middle Ages.* Harmondsworth, Eng.: Penguin, 1965.

———. *The Reconstructed Carmelite Missal.* London: Faber and Faber, 1952.

———. "The So-Called Beaufort Hours and York Psalter." *BM* 104 (1962): 238–46.

Riederer, Josef. "Pigment-untersuchung bei Buchmalereien." *Restaurator* 5 (1981): 151–55.

Riessner, C. *Die "Magnae Derivationes" des Uguccione da Pisa und ihre Bedeutung für die romanische Philologie.* Rome: Edizioni di Storia e Letteratura, 1965.

Riley, Marjorie A. "The Foundation of Chantries in the Counties of Nottingham and York, 1350–1400." *YAJ* 33 (1937): 122–65.

Ringböm, S. "Devotional Images and Imaginative Devotions: Notes on the Place of Art in Late Medieval Piety." *GBA,* 6th ser., 73 (1969): 159–70.

Ritchie, C. I. A. *The Ecclesiastical Courts of York.* Arbroath, Eng.: Herald Press, 1956.

Robbins, Rossell Hope. "The Arma Christi Rolls." *MLR* 34 (1939): 415–21.

———. "Private Prayers in Middle English Verse." *SP* 36 (1939): 466–75.

Robinson, J. Armitage, and M. R. James. *The Manuscripts of Westminster Abbey.* Cambridge: Cambridge Univ. Press, 1909.

Robinson, J. W. "The Late Medieval Cult of Jesus and the Mystery Plays." *PMLA* 80 (1965): 508–14.

Robinson, Pamela R. *Catalogue of Dated and Datable Manuscripts c. 737–1600 in Cambridge Libraries.* 2 vols. Cambridge: D. S. Brewer, 1988.

Robson, Thomas. *The British Herald.* Sunderland, Eng.: Thomas Robson, 1830.

Rodes, R. E., Jr. *Ecclesiastical Administration in Medieval England: The Anglo*

Saxons to the Reformation. Notre Dame, Ind.: Univ. of Notre Dame Press, 1977.

Rogers, Nicholas. "The Boulogne Hours: An Addition to York Art." *The EDAM Newsletter* 6 (1984): 35–41.

———. "Fitzwilliam Museum MS 3-1979: A Bury St. Edmunds Book of Hours and the Origins of the Bury Style." In *England in the Fifteenth Century: Proceedings of the 1986 Harlaxton Symposium,* edited by Daniel Williams, 229–43. Woodbridge, Suffolk: Boydell Press, 1987.

Rollason, Lynda. "English Alabasters in the Fifteenth Century." In *England in the Fifteenth Century: Proceedings of the 1986 Harlaxton Symposium,* edited by Daniel Williams, 245–254. Woodbridge, Suffolk: Boydell Press, 1987.

Roosen-Runge, Heinz. *Farbgebung und Technik frühmittelalterlicher Buchmalerei. Studien zu den Traktaten "Mappae Clavicula" und "Heraclius."* Munich: Deutscher Verlag, 1967.

Roosen-Runge, Heinz, and A. E. A. Werner. "The Pictorial Technique of the Lindisfarne Gospels." In *Evangeliorum Quattuor Codex Lindisfarnensis,* edited by T. D. Kendrick et al. Olten and New York: Urs Graf and Philip C. Duschenes, 1960.

Rosenthal, Constance L. *The Vitae Patrum in Old and Middle English Literature.* Philadelphia: Univ. of Pennsylvania Press, 1936.

Rosenthal, Joel T. "Aristocratic Cultural Patronage and Book Bequests, 1350–1500." *BJRL* 64 (1981–82): 522–48.

———. *Late Medieval England 1377–1485: A Bibliography of Historical Scholarship 1975–1989.* Kalamazoo, Mich.: Medieval Institute, 1992.

———. "The Fifteenth-Century Episcopate: Careers and Bequests." In *Sanctity and Secularity: The Church and the World,* edited by Derek Baker, 117–27. Oxford: Blackwell, 1973.

———. *The Purchase of Paradise: Gift Giving and the Aristocracy, 1307–1485.* London: Routledge and Kegan Paul, 1972.

Rosenzweig, L. *Dictionnaire topographique du département du Morbihan.* Paris: Imprimerie Nationale, 1870.

Ross, Thomas W. "Five Fifteenth-Century 'Emblem' Verses from Brit. Mus. Addit. Ms. 37049." *Speculum* 32 (1957): 274–82.

Rouse, Richard H., and Mary A. Rouse. "The Commercial Production of Manuscript Books, Late-Thirteenth-Century and Early-Fourteenth-Century Paris." In *Medieval Book Production: Assessing the Evidence,* edited by Linda Brownrigg, 103–15. Los Altos Hills, Calif.: Red Gull Press, 1990.

———. *Preachers, Florilegia and Sermons: Studies on the Manipulus Florum of Thomas of Ireland.* Studies and Texts 47. Toronto: Pontifical Institute, 1979.

Routh, Pauline, " 'Full of Imageis': The Ripon Alabasters." *YAJ* 57 (1985): 93–100.

———. "A Gift and Its Giver: John Walker and the East Window of Holy Trinity, Goodramgate, York." *YAJ* 58 (1986): 109–21.

———. *Medieval Effigial Alabaster Tombs in Yorkshire.* Ipswich, Eng.: Boydell Press, 1976.

————. *The Sheriff Hutton Alabaster: A Re-assessment.* Wakefield, Yorkshire: Rosalba Press, 1981.

Routh, Pauline, and Richard Knowles. *The Medieval Monuments of Harewood.* Wakefield, Yorkshire: Wakefield Historical Soc., 1983.

Rowntree, C. B. *A Carthusian World View: Bodleian MS e Museo 160. AC* 35.9. Salzburg: Institut für Anglistik und Amerikanistik, 1990.

Royster, James Finch. "A Middle English Treatise on the Ten Commandments." *SP* 6 (1910): 6–7.

Rubin, M. "*Corpus Christi* Fraternities and Late Medieval Piety." In *Voluntary Religion,* edited by W. J. Sheils and D. Wood, 97–109. Oxford: Blackwell, 1986.

Rud, Thomas. *Codicum Manuscriptorum Ecclesiae Cathedralis Dunelmensis Catalogus Classicus,* edited by J. Raine. Durham: G. Andrews, 1825.

Ruggiers, Paul, ed. *The Canterbury Tales: A Facsimile and Transcription of the Hengwrt Manuscript.* Norman: Univ. of Oklahoma Press, 1979.

Rushforth, Gordon M. *Medieval Christian Imagery.* Oxford: Clarendon, 1936.

Russell, Josiah Cox. *British Medieval Population.* Albuquerque: Univ. of New Mexico Press, 1948.

Sackur, Ernst, ed. *Sibyllinische Texte und Forschungen.* Halle: M. Niemayer, 1898.

Saenger, Paul. "Books of Hours and the Reading Habits of the Later Middle Ages." *ScrC* 9 (1985): 238–69.

————. *A Catalogue of the Pre-1500 Western Manuscript Books at the Newberry Library.* Chicago: Univ. of Chicago Press, 1989.

St. John Hope. W. H. "On the Early Workings of Alabaster in England. " In *Illustrated Catalogue of the Exhibition of English Medieval Alabaster Work,* edited by W. H. St. John Hope and Edward Prior, 1–15. Oxford: Horace Hart, 1913.

————. "Inventory of the Parish Church of St. Mary, Scarborough, 1434; and that of the White Friars or Carmelites of Newcastle-on-Tyne, 1538." *Archaeologia* 51, pt. i (1888): 61–72.

————. "On the Whitefriars or Carmelites of Hulne, Northumberland." *ArcJ* 47 (1890): 105–29.

Salmon, John. "St. Christopher in English Medieval Art and Life." *JBAA,* n. s., 2, 41 (1936): 76–115.

Salter, Elizabeth. "Ludolphus of Saxony and His English Translators." *MAe* 33 (1964): 26–35.

————. *Nicholas Love's Myrrour of the Blessed Lyf of Jesu Christ.* Analecta Cartusiana 10. Salzburg: Institut für Anglistik und Amerikanistik, 1974.

Samaran, Charles, et al. *Catalogue des manuscrits en écriture latine datés.* Paris, 1962.

Samaran, Charles, and André Vernet. "Les Livres de Thomas Basin (1412–1490)." In *Hommages à André Boutemy,* edited by Guy Cambier, 324–39. Collections Latomus 145. Brussels, 1976.

Sandler, Lucy Freeman. *Gothic Manuscripts 1285–1385.* Oxford: Harvey Miller, 1986.

————. "Notes for the Illuminator: The Case of the *Omne Bonum*." *AB* 71 (1989): 551–64.

————. "Omne bonum: *Compilatio* and *Ordinatio* in an English Illustrated Encyclopedia of the Fourteenth Century." In *Medieval Book Production: Assessing the Evidence,* edited by Linda Brownrigg, 183–200. Los Altos Hills, Calif.: Red Gull Press, 1990.

————. *The Peterborough Psalter in Brussels and Other Fenland Manuscripts.* London: Harvey Miller, 1974.

————. "Reflections on the Construction of Hybrids in English Gothic Marginal Illustration." In *Art the Ape of Nature: Essays in Honor of H. W. Janson,* edited by Moshe Barasch et al., 51–65. New York and Englewood Cliffs, N.J: Abrams and Prentice-Hall, 1981.

Sargent, Michael. "Bonaventura English: A Survey of the Middle English Prose Translations of Early Franciscan Literature." *Spätmittelalterliche Geistliche Literatur in der Nationalsprache* 2. *Analecta Cartusiana* 106 (1984): 145–76.

————. *James Grenehalgh as Textural Critic. AC* 85. Salzburg: Institut für Anglistik und Amerikanistik, 1984.

————. *Nicholas Love's Mirror of the Blessed Life of Jesus Christ: A Critical Edition.* New York: Garland, 1993.

————. "The Transmission of the English Carthusians of Some Late Medieval Spiritual Writings." *JEH* 27 (1976): 225–40.

Scammell, G. V. "English Merchant Shipping at the End of the Middle Ages: Some East Coast Evidence." *EcHR,* 2d ser., 13 (1961): 327–41.

Scammell, Jean. "The Origin and Limitations of the Liberty of Durham." *EHR* 81 (1966): 449–73.

Scarisbrick, J. J. *The Reformation and the English People.* Oxford: Blackwell, 1984.

Schildhauer, Johannes. *The Hansa: History and Culture.* Translated by K. Vanovitch. N.p.: Dorset Press, 1988.

Schiller, Gertrud. *Ikonographie der christlichen kunst.* Gütersloh: Güterslohen Verlagshaus G. Mohn, 1966–76.

Schmidt, Gerhardt. "Malerei bis 1450: Tafelmalerei-Wandmalerei-Buchmalerei." In *Gotik in Böhmen,* edited by Karl M. Swoboda, 167–321. Munich: Prestel-Verlag, 1969.

Schmitt, F. S., ed. *Sancti Anselmi Cantuariensis Archiepiscopi opera omnia.* Edinburgh: T. Nelson, 1938–61.

Schneyer, J. B. *Repertorium der lateinischen Sermones des Mittelalters für die Zeit von 1150–1350.* Münster: Aschendorff, 1969–80.

Schofield, R. S. "The Geographical Distribution of Wealth in England, 1334–1649." *EcHR,* 2d ser., 18 (1965): 483–510.

Schottlander, Rudolf, ed. *Francesco Petrarcha De remediis utriusque Fortunae.* Munich: Fink, 1988.

Schrader, C. R. "A Handlist of Extant Manuscripts Containing the *De Re Militari* of Favius Vegetius Renatus." *Scriptorium* 33 (1979): 280–305.

Scott, E. J. L. *Index to the Sloane Manuscripts in the British Museum.* Reprint. London: Trustees of the British Museum, 1971.

Scott, Kathleen. "*Caveat Lector:* Ownership and Standardization in the Illustration of Fifteenth-Century English Manuscripts." *EMS* 1 (1989): 19–63.

———. "Design, Decoration, and Illustration." In *BPPB*, 31–64.

———. *Later Gothic Manuscripts.* London: Harvey Miller, forthcoming.

———. "Lydgate's Lives of Saints Edmund and Fremund: A Newly-Located Manuscript in Arundel Castle." *Viator* 13 (1982): 335–66.

Scott-Fleming, Sonia. *The Analysis of Pen Flourishing in Thirteenth-Century Manuscripts.* Leiden: Brill, 1989.

Seaton, Ethel. *Sir Richard Roos c. 1410–1482, Lancastrian Poet.* London: Rupert Hart-Davis, 1961.

Sessions, William K., and Margaret E. Sessions. *Printing in York from the 1490's to the Present Day.* York: William Sessions, 1976.

Seymour, M. C. "The English Manuscripts of *Mandeville's Travels.*" *TEBS* 4, pt. 5 (1966): 169–210.

Shäfer, Karl H. *Die Ausgaben unter Benedikt XII, Klemens VI, und Innocenz VI.* Paderborn: F. Schoningh, 1914.

Shailor, Barbara. *Catalogue of Medieval and Renaissance Manuscripts in the Beinecke Rare Book Room and Manuscript Library, Yale University: Vol. II, MSS 251–500.* Binghamton, N.Y.: MRTS, 1987.

———. *The Medieval Book, Illustrated from the Beinecke Rare Book and Manuscript Library.* Toronto: Univ. of Toronto Press and Medieval Academy of America, 1991.

Sheehan, Michael. *The Will in Medieval England from the Conversion of the Anglo-Saxons to the End of the Thirteenth Century.* Toronto: Pontifical Institute, 1963.

Sheingorn, Pamela. "The Bosom of Abraham Trinity: A Late Medieval All Saints Image." In *England in the Fifteenth Century: Proceedings of the 1986 Harlaxton Symposium,* edited by Daniel Williams, 273–95. Woodbridge, Suffolk: Boydell Press, 1987.

Silvia, Daniel S. "Some Fifteenth-Century Manuscripts of the Canterbury Tales." In *Chaucer and Middle English Studies in Honour of Rossell Hope Robbins,* edited by Beryl Rowland, 153–63. Kent, Ohio: Kent State Univ. Press, 1974.

Simmons, T. F., and H. E. Nolloth, eds. *Archbishop Thoresby's The Lay Folks Catechism.* EETS: o.s., 118. 1901. Reprint. Millwood, N.Y.: Kraus, 1975.

Simpson, Amanda. *The Connections Between English and Bohemian Painting During the Second Half of the Fourteenth Century.* New York: Garland, 1984.

Sinclair, K. V. *Descriptive Catalogue of the Medieval and Renaissance Western Manuscripts in Australia.* Sydney: Wentworth, 1969.

———. *Medieval and Renaissance Treasures of the Ballerat Art Gallery, The Crouch Manuscripts.* Sydney: Wentworth, 1968.

Skene, William F. *Chronicles of the Picts and Chronicles of the Scots.* Edinburgh: H. M. General Register House, 1867.

Smailes, A. E. *North England.* London: Nelson, 1968.

Smalley, Beryl. *English Friars and Antiquity in the Early Fourteenth Century.* Oxford: Blackwell, 1960.

————. "Which William of Nottingham?" *MRS* 3 (1954): 200–38.

Smeyers, M., and B. Cardon. "Brabant of Parijs: Aantekeningen bij een handschrift met vrome legenden, afkomstig uit het kartuizerklooster te Zelem bij Diest." *Handschriften uit Dieste Kerken en Kloosters.* Diest: Vrienden van hed Stodelijk Museum en Archief Diest: 1983.

Smith, Cyril S., and John G. Hawthorne, eds. and trans. *Mappae Clavicula: A Little Key to the World of Medieval Techniques,* 1–128. In *TAPS,* n. s., 64.4. Philadelphia: Amer. Philosophical Soc., 1974.

Smith, David M. *A Guide to the Archive Collections in the Borthwick Institute of Historical Research.* York: The Borthwick Institute, 1973, and Supplement, 1980.

Smith, Julie A. "An Image of a Preaching Bishop in Late Medieval England: The 1498 Woodcut Portrait of Bishop John Alcock." *Viator* 21 (1990): 301–22.

Smith, William. "The Fifteenth-Century Manuscript *Horae* in the Parochial Library of Steeple Ashton." *Manuscripta* 25 (1981): 151–63.

Snape, M. G. "Some Evidence of Lollard Activity in the Diocese of Durham in the Early Fifteenth Century." *AA,* 4th ser., 39 (1961): 355–61.

Snape, R. H. *English Monastic Finances in the Later Middle Ages.* Cambridge: Cambridge Univ. Press, 1926.

Somerville, Robert. "The Cowcher Books of the Duchy of Lancaster." *EHR* 51 (1936): 598–615.

————. *The History of the Duchy of Lancaster.* London: Chancellor and Council of the Duchy of Lancaster, 1953.

Sotheby's Auction Catalogue, Tuesday, 25th March, 1975.

Spalding, M. C. *The Middle English Charters of Christ.* Bryn Mawr, Pa.: Bryn Mawr College, 1914.

Sparrow-Simpson, W. "On the Measure of the Wound in the Side of the Redeemer, Worn Anciently as a Charm." *JBAA* 30 (1874): 52–61.

————. "On the Pilgrimage to Bromholm in Norfolk." *JBAA* 30 (1874): 357–74.

Springer, P. " 'Trinitäts-Creator-Annus:' Beiträge zur mittelalterlichen Trinitäts ikonographie." *WRJ* 38 (1976): 17–46.

Spufford, Margaret. "Wills and Their Scribes." *LPS* 8 (1972): 55–57.

Stahl, E. C. *Die Legende vom heiligen Riesen Christophorus in der Graphik des 15, und 16, Jahrhunderts.* Munich: J. J. Lentner, 1920.

Stanley, M. "The Geographical Distribution of Wealth in Medieval England." *JHG* 6 (1980): 315–20.

Staring, Adrian. "Notes on a List of Carmelite Houses in Medieval France." *Carmelus* 11 (1964): 150–60.

Steel, J. P., ed. *Subsidy: Being the Account of a Fifteenth and Tenth Collected 6th Edward III.* Kendal: T. Wilson, 1912.

Stegmüller, F. *Repertorium Biblicum Medii Aevi.* Madrid: Instituto Francisco Suárez, 1950–80.

Steinberg, S. H. "Medieval Writing-Masters." *The Library,* 4th ser., 22 (1941): 1–24.

Stenton, Doris. *The English Woman in History.* London: Allen and Unwin, 1957.

Stenton, F. M. *Anglo-Saxon England.* Oxford: Clarendon, 1943.

Stirnemann, Patricia, and Marie-Thérèse Gousset. "Marques, Mots. Pratiques: Leur Significations et leurs liens dans le Travail des Enlumineurs." In *Vocabulaire du Livre et de l'écriture au moyen âge,* edited by Olga Weijers, 35–55. Turnhout: Brepols, 1989.

Stohlmann, Jürgen, ed. *Anonymi Historia Troyana Daretis Frigii.* Düsseldorf: Henn, 1968.

Stones, Lionel. "English Chroniclers and the Affairs of Scotland, 1286–1296." In *The Writing of History in the Middle Ages: Essays Presented to Richard William Southern,* edited by R. H. C. Davis et al., 323–48. Oxford: Clarendon, 1981.

Storey, Robin L. "The Chantries of Cumberland and Westmorland." *TCWAAS,* n. s., 60 (1960) 66–96; 62 (1962): 145–70.

———. *Diocesan Administration in Fifteenth-Century England.* York: St. Anthony's Press, 1972.

———. *The End of the House of Lancaster.* London: Barrie and Rockliff, 1966.

———. "The North of England." In *Fifteenth-Century England, 1399–1509: Studies in Politics and History,* edited by Stanley B. Chrimes et al., 129–44. Manchester: Manchester Univ. Press, 1972.

———. *Thomas Langley and the Bishopric of Durham, 1406–1437.* London: Soc. for the Promotion of Christian Knowledge, 1961.

Straub, Rolf E., ed. " 'De Clarea' in der Burgerbibliothek Berne. Eine Anleitung für Buchmalerei aus dem Hochmittelalter." *Jahresbericht 1964,* 89–114. Zurich: Schweizerisches Institut für Kunstwissenschaft, 1965.

Streeter, B. H. *The Chained Library.* London: Macmillan, 1931.

Stubblebine, James H. "Segna di Buonaventura and the Image of the Man of Sorrows." *Gesta* 8 (1969): 3–13.

Suntrup, Rudolf. "*Te igitur*—Initialen und Kanonbilder in mittelalterlichen Sakramentarschriften." In *Text und Bild, Aspekte des Zusammen-wirkens Zweier Künste in Mittelalter und früher Neuzeit,* edited by Christel Meier and Uwe Ruberg, 278–382. Wiesbaden: Reichert, 1980.

Surtees, Robert. *The History and Antiquities of the County Palatine of Durahm.* London: Surtees Society, 1816–40.

Swan, G. A. "Isolation, Structure, and Synthesis of Hermidin, a Chromogen from Mercurialis perennis L." *Journal of the Chemical Society, Perkin Transactions* 1 (1985): 1757–1766.

Swanson, Heather. *Medieval Artisans: An Urban Class in Late Medieval England.* Oxford: Blackwell, 1989.

Szirmai, J. A. "The Girdle-book of the Museum Meermanno-Westreenianum." *Quaerendo* 18 (1988): 17–34.

Szittya, Penn. *The Antifraternal Tradition in Medieval Literature.* Princeton, N.J.: Princeton Univ. Press, 1986.

Szövérffy, J. *Latin Hymns.* Typologie des Sources du Moyen Âge Occidental 55. Turnhout, Belgium: Brepols, 1989.

Talbot, C. H. "A List of Cistercian Manuscripts in Great Britain." *Traditio* 8 (1952): 402–18.

Talbot, C. H., and E. A. Hammond. *The Medical Practitioners in Medieval England.* London: Wellcome Historical Medical Library, 1965.

Tanguy, Bernard. *Les noms de lieux bretons I. Toponymie descriptive.* Rennes: CRDP, 1975.

Tarvers, Josephine Koster. " 'Thys ys my mystrys boke': English Women as Readers and Writers in Late Medieval England." In *The Uses of Manuscripts in Literary Studies: Essays in Memory of Judson Boyce Allen,* edited by Charlotte Morse et al., 305–27. Kalamzoo, Mich.: Medieval Institute, 1992.

Tate, George. *History of the Borough, Castle and Barony of Alnwick.* Alnwick: H. H. Blair, 1867–69.

Tatlock, J. S. P. "Geoffrey of Monmouth and the Date of *Regnum Scotorum.*" *Speculum* 9 (1934): 135–39.

Taylor, John. *English Historical Literature in the Fourteenth Century.* Oxford: Clarendon, 1987.

——. *The Kirkstall Abbey Chronicles.* Leeds: Thoresby Soc., 1952.

——. *Medieval Historical Writing in Yorkshire.* Borthwick Papers no. 19. York: St. Anthony's Press, 1961.

——. *The Universal Chronicle of Ranulf Higden.* Oxford: Clarendon, 1966.

Taylor, Rupert. *The Political Prophecy in England.* New York: Columbia Univ. Press, 1911.

Thomas, Marcel. *The Golden Age: Manuscript Painting at the Time of Jean, Duke of Berry.* New York: Braziller, 1979.

Thomas, Marcel, and Françoise Flieder. "La composition des parchemins pourprés démystifiée par la chromatographie en phase gazeuse." In *La Vie mystérieuse des chefs-d'oeuvre: La science au service de l'art,* edited by Madeleine Hours, 232–33. Paris: Denöel/Gonthier, 1980.

Thomspon, A. Hamilton. "The Chapel of St. Mary and the Holy Angels, Otherwise Known as St. Sepulchre's Chapel, at York, pt. ii." *YAJ* 36 (1945): 214–48.

——. "The Pestilences of the Fourteenth Century in the Diocese of York." *ArcJ* 71 (1914): 97–154.

——. "The Registers of the Archdeaconry of Richmond, 1361–1442." *YAJ* 25 (1920): 129–268.

——. "The Register of the Archdeacons of Richmond, 1442–1477, pt. i." *YAJ* 30 (1931): 1–132.

——. "Thomas Langley, Bishop of Durham, 1406–1437." *DUJ* 38 (1945): 1–16.

Thompson, Daniel Varney, Jr. "Artificial Vermillion in the Middle Ages." *Technical Studies in the Field of the Fine Arts* 2 (1933): 62–70.

———. "The *De Clarea* of the So-Called 'Anonymous Bernensis.' " *Technical Studies in the Field of the Fine Arts* 1 (1932): 8–19, 69–81.

———. "*Liber de coloribus Illuminatorum siue Pictorum* from Sloane MS. no. 1754." *Speculum* 1 (1926): 280–307.

———. *The Materials and Techniques of Medieval Painting.* Reprint. New York, 1957.

Thompson, Daniel Varney, Jr., and George Heard Hamilton, eds. *An Anonymous Fourteenth-Century Treatise De Arte Illuminandi.* New Haven: Yale Univ. Press, 1933.

Thompson, E. Margaret. *The Carthusian Order in England.* London: Macmillan, 1930. Reprint. New York, n.d.

Thompson, H. S. *Flowering Plants of the Riviera.* London: Longmans, 1914.

Thompson, John J. *Robert Thornton and the London Thornton Manuscript.* Cambridge: D. S. Brewer, 1987.

Thomson, R. M. *Catalogue of the Manuscripts of Lincoln Cathedral Chapter Library.* Cambridge: D. S. Brewer, 1989.

———. "William of Malmsbury as Historian and Man of Letters." *JEH* 29 (1978): 387–413.

Thomson, S. Harrison. *The Writings of Robert Grosseteste Bishop of Lincoln, 1235–1253.* 1940. Reprint. Millwood, N.Y.: Kraus, 1971.

Thorp, Nigel. *The Glory of the Page, Medieval & Renaissance Illuminated Manuscripts from Glasgow University Library.* London: Harvey Miller, 1987.

Thrupp, Sylvia. *The Merchant Class of Medieval London, 1300–1500.* Reprint. Ann Arbor: Univ. of Michigan Press, 1989.

Todd, John M. "Saint Bega: Cult, Fact and Legend." *TCWAAS* 80 (1980): 23–35.

Tolkien, J. R. R. "Chaucer as a Philologist: *The Reeve's Tale.*" *Transactions of the Philological Society* (1934): 1–70.

Tout, T. F. *Chapters in the Administrative History of Mediaeval England: The Wardrobe, The Chamber and the Small Seals.* Manchester: Manchester Univ. Press, 1920–33.

Trevelyan, W. C. "The Copy of an Indenture Preserved Amongst the Records of University College, Oxford, dated 1404. Between Walter Bishop of Durham and the Master of That College." *AA,* 1st ser., 2 (1832): 99.

Trost, V. "Tinte und Farben. Zum Erhaltungszustand der Manesseschen Liederhandschrift." In *Codex Manesse Die Grosse Heidelburger Leiderhandschrift. Texte. Bilder. Sachen,* edited by E. Miller et al., 440–45. Heidelberg: Braus, 1988.

Tuck, J. A. "Northumbrian Society in the Fourteenth Century." *NH* 6 (1971): 22–39.

Turner, Derek H. *English Book Illustration 966–1846. 1: Illuminated Manuscripts.* London: British Museum, 1965.

——. "The Wyndham Payne Crucifixion." *BLJ* 2 (1976): 8–26.

Turner, Derek H., et al., eds. *The Benedictines in Britain.* London: Braziller, 1980.

Turner, Ralph V. "The *Miles Literatus* in Twelfth- and Thirteenth-Century England: How Rare a Phenomenon?" *AHR* 83 (1978): 928–45.

Turville-Petre, Thorlac. "Some Medieval English Manuscripts in the North-East Midlands." In *Manuscripts and Readers in Fifteenth Century England,* edited by Derek Pearsall, 125–141. Woodbridge, Suffolk: D. S. Brewer, 1983.

Tutin, Thomas G., et al., eds. *Flora Europaea.* Cambridge: Cambridge Univ. Press, 1968.

Vale, M. G. A. *Piety, Charity and Literacy among the Yorkshire Gentry, 1370–1480.* Borthwick Paper no. 50. York: St. Anthony's Press, 1976.

Valleé, François. *Grand Dictionnaire français-breton.* Rennes: CRDP: 1931.

van Dijk, S. "Books of Hours." Vol. 4. Bodleian Library typescript.

van den Gheyn, J. *Album belge de paléographie: Recueil de spécimens d'écritures d'auteurs et de manuscrits belges.* Brussels: Jette, 1908.

van de Woestijne, P., ed. *La Périégèse de Priscien.* Bruges: Rijksuniversiteit te Gent, 1953.

Verger, Jacques. "Le recrutement géographique des universités françaises au début du XVe siècle d'après les *Suppliques* de 1403." *MAHEFR* 82 (1970): 855–902.

Voigts, Linda E., "Scientific and Medical Books." In *BPPB,* 345–402.

Voigts, Linda E., and Robert P. Hudson, "A drynke þat men callen dwale to make a man to slepe whyle men kerven him. A Surgical Anesthetic from Late Medieval England." In *Health, Disease and Healing in Medieval Culture,* edited by Sheila Campbell, et al., 34–56. New York: St. Martin's Press, 1992.

von Dobschütz, E. *Christusbilder: Untersuchungen zur christliche Legende.* Leipzig: J. C. Hinrichs, 1899.

von Nolcken, Christina. *The Middle English Translation of the Rosarium Theologie.* Heidelberg: Winter, 1979.

von Schlosser, Julius. "Die Bilderhandschriften Königs Wenzel 1." *JKSAK* 14 (1893): 214–317.

Wackernagel, Martin. *The World of the Florentine Renaissance Artist.* Translated by A. Luchs. Princeton, N.J.: Princeton Univ. Press, 1981.

Wade, Benjamin. *Yorkshire Ruined Abbeys.* London: E. J. Burrow, 1938.

Wadell, Maj-Britt. *Fons Pietatis. Eine ikonographische Studie.* Göteborg: Akademisk Avhandling, 1969.

Wagner, A. R. *Heralds and Heraldry in the Middle Ages.* London: Oxford Univ. Press, 1956.

Waites, Bryan. "Medieval Iron Working in Northeast Yorkshire." *Geography* 49 (1964): 33–43.

——. "The Monastic Settlement of North-East Yorkshire." *YAJ* 140 (1961): 478–95.

Walcott, Mackenzie E. S. "Medieval Libraries." *TRSL,* 2d ser., 9 (1870): 68–86.

Walker, Thomas Alfred. *A Biographical Register of Peterhouse Men.* Cambridge: Cambridge Univ. Press, 1927–29.

Wallert, A. "Alchemy and Medieval Art Technology." In *Alchemy Revisited: Proceedings of the International Conference on the History of Alchemy at the University of Gröningen 17–19 April 1989,* edited by Z. R. W. M. von Martels, 154–61. Leiden: Brill, 1990.

———. *"Chrozophora tinctoria Juss.* Problems in Identifying an Illumination Colorant." *Restaurator* 11 (1990): 141–55.

Walne, Peter. *English Wills.* Richmond, Va.: Virginia State Library Publ., 1964.

Walsh, Katherine. *A Fourteenth-Century Scholar and Primate: Richard FitzRalph in Oxford, Avignon and Armagh.* Oxford: Clarendon, 1981.

Ward, B. "The Desert Myth: Reflections on the Desert Ideal in Early Cistercian Monasticism." In *One Yet Two: Monastic Tradition East and West,* edited by Basil Pennington, 183–99. Kalamazoo, Mich.: Medieval Institute, 1976.

Ward, H. L. D. *Catalogue of Romances in the Department of Manuscripts in the British Museum.* 1883. Reprint. London: British Library, 1961.

Warner, G. F., and J. P. Gilson. *Catalogue of Western Manuscripts in the Old Royal and King's Collections.* Vol. 1. London: British Museum, 1921.

Warren. Ann K. *Anchorites and Their Patrons in Medieval England.* Berkeley: Univ. of California Press, 1985.

Watson, Andrew. *Catalogue of Dated and Datable Manuscripts c. 700–1600 in the British Library.* London and New York: Clarendon, 1979.

———. *Catalogue of Dated and Datable Manuscripts c. 435–1600 in Oxford Libraries.* Oxford: The British Library, 1984.

———. *The Manuscripts of Henry Savile of Banke.* London: Bibliographical Society, 1969.

Watson, Andrew, and R. J. Roberts. *John Dee's Library Catalogue.* London: Bibliographical Society, 1990.

Watson, Nicholas. *Richard Rolle and the Invention of Authority.* Cambridge: Cambridge Univ. Press, 1991.

Weatherly, Edward H., ed. *Speculum Sacerdotale* EETS: o.s., 200. London: Oxford Univ. Press, 1936.

Wenzel, Seigfried. *Preachers, Poets and the Early English Lyric.* Princeton, N.J.: Princeton Univ. Press, 1986.

———, ed. *Fasciculus Morum: A Fourteenth-Century Preacher's Handbook.* Philadelphia: Univ. of Pennsylvania Press, 1989.

Werner, Martin. *Insular Art: An Annotated Bibliography.* Boston: G. K. Hall, 1984.

Western Manuscripts and Miniatures, Sotheby's Catalogue, Tuesday, 24, June, 1986.

Westlake, Herbert Francis. *Parish Guilds of Mediaeval England.* New York: Macmillan, 1919.

Whaite, H. C. *St. Christopher in English Mediaeval Wallpainting.* London: University College, 1929.

White, Eileen. *The St. Christopher and St. George Guild of York.* Borthwick Paper no. 72. York: St. Anthony's Press, 1987.

Wichgraf, Wiltrud. "Suso's 'Horologium Sapientiae' in England. Nach Handschriften des 15. Jahrhunderts." *Anglia* 53 (1929): 123–33, 269–87; 54 (1930): 351–52.

Wieck, Roger S. *Late Medieval and Renaissance Illuminated Manuscripts, 1350–1525, in the Houghton Library.* Cambridge, Mass.: Harvard College Library, 1983.

Wightman. W. E. *The Lacy Family in England and Normandy, 1066–1194.* Oxford: Clarendon, 1966.

Williams, Arthur Lukyn. *Adversus Judaeos. A Bird's-Eye View of Christian Apologiae until the Rennaissance.* Cambridge: Cambridge Univ. Press, 1935.

Williams, Charles A. "Oriental Affinities of the Legend of the Hairy Anchorite, Part I: Pre-Christian." *UISLL* 10 (1925): 187–242.

———. "Oriental Affinities of the Legend of the Hairy Anchorite, Part II: Christian." *UISLL* 11 (1926): 429–509.

———. "The German Legends of the Hairy Anchorite," *UISLL,* 18 (1935): 1–140.

Williams, E. A. "A Bibliography of Giraldus Cambrensis." *NLWJ* 12 (1961): 97–140.

Williamson, Joan B. "Paris B.N. MS fr. 1175: A Collaboration Between Author and Artist." In *Text and Image,* ACTA Vol. 10, edited by David Burchmore, 77–92. Binghamton, N.Y.: Center for Medieval and Early Renaissance Studies, 1983.

Willis, John Christopher. *A Dictionary of the Flowering Plants and Ferns.* Cambridge: Cambridge Univ. Press, 1957.

Willmot, G. F. "A Discovery at York." *MJ* 57 (1957): 35–36.

Wilmart, André. *Auteurs spirituels et textes dévots du moyen âge latin.* 1932. Reprint. Paris: Études Augustiniennes, 1971.

———. "Le 'Jubilus' sur le nom de Jésus dit de Saint Bernard." *EL* (1943): 1–285.

———. "La Tradition des prières de Saint Anselm: tables et notes." *RB* 36 (1924): 52–71.

Wilson, Adrian, and Joyce Lancaster Wilson. *A Medieval Mirror: Speculum Humanae Salvationis, 1324–1500.* Berkeley: Univ. of California Press, 1984.

Wiseman, Peter. "Julius Caesar and the Hereford World Map." *HT* 37 (1987): 53–57.

Witty, F. J. "Early Indexing Techniques: A Study of Several Book Indexes of the Fourteenth, Fifteenth, and Early Sixteenth Centuries." *LQ* 35 (1965): 141–48.

Wood-Legh, K. L. *Perpetual Chantries in Britain.* Cambridge: Cambridge Univ. Press, 1965.

Woolley, R. M., ed. *The Gilbertine Rite.* London: Henry Bradshaw Soc., 1921.

Wordsworth, Christopher, ed. *Horae Eboracenses: The Prymer or Hours of the Blessed Virgin Mary, According to the Use of the Illustrious Church of York.* Surtees Society Vol. 132. Durham: Surtees Society, 1920.

———. "Yorkshire Pardons and Indulgences." *YAJ* 16 (1902): 399–418.

Wormald, Francis. "Decorated Initials in English MSS. from 900 to 1100." *Archaeologia* 91 (1945): 107–135.

———. *The Miniatures in the Gospels of St. Augustine (Corpus Christi College, Ms 286).* Cambridge: Cambridge Univ. Press, 1954.

———. "Some Popular Miniatures and Their Rich Relations." In *Miscellanea Pro Arte. Zur Vollendung des 60. Lebensjahres am 13 Januar 1965,* edited by Joseph Hoster and Peter Bloch, 279–85. Düsseldorf: Schriften Pro Arte Medii Aevi, 1965.

Wormald, Francis, and P. M. Giles. *A Descriptive Catalogue of the Additional Illuminated Manuscripts in the Fitzwilliam Museum Acquired between 1895 and 1979 (Excluding the McClean Collection).* Cambridge: Cambridge Univ. Press, 1982.

Xiberta, Bartholomaeus Maria. *De Scriptoribus Scholasticis Saeculi XIV ex Ordine Carmelitarum.* Louvain: Bureaux de la Revue, 1931.

Young, John, and P. Henderson Aitken. *A Catalogue of the Manuscripts in the Library of the Hunterian Museum in the University of Glasgow.* Glasgow: J. Maclehose, 1908.

Zanghieri, Pietro. *Flora Italica.* Padua: CEDAM, 1976.

Zeeman, Elizabeth Salter. "Nicholas Love A Fifteenth-Century Translator." *RES* n. s., 6, 22 (1955): 113–127.

Zehnder, Frank Günther. "Salve sancta facies. Zu Christusbildern in der Kölner gotischen Malerei." *MSKB* 3 (1986): 41–44.

Zell, Michael L. "Fifteenth- and Sixteenth-Century Wills as Historical Sources." *Archives* 14 (1979): 67–74.

Zohary, Michael. *Flora Palaestina.* Jerusalem: Academy of Sciences and Humanities, 1972.

Zuriel, S. et al. "Controlling Weeds in Peanuts with Dinitramine." *Phytoparasitica* 4.2 (August 1976): 151.

Dissertations and Conference Papers

Bartle, R. H. "A Study of Private Book Collections in England Between c. 1200 and the Early Years of the Sixteenth Century, with Special Reference to Books Belonging to Ecclesiastical Dignitaries." B.Litt. thesis, Oxford Univ. 1956.

Candon, Mary Patrick. "An Edition of the 15th-Century Middle English Translation of Gerard of Liège's *De Doctrina Cordis.*" Ph.D. diss., Fordham Univ. 1963.

Cavanaugh, Susan H. "A Study of Books Privately Owned in England 1300–1450." Ph.D. diss., Univ. of Pennsylvania, 1980.

Dasef, David. "The Lawyers of the York Curia. 1400–1435." M.A. thesis, Univ. of York, 1977.

Doyle, A. I. "Dating the Development of the Style of Penwork Flourishing of Initials in Later Fourteenth-Century England." Lecture given at Comte-International de Paléographie Latine, Vatican City, Sept. 1990.

———. "A Survey of the Origins and Circulation of Theological Writings in English in the 14th, 15th and Early 16th Centuries with Special Consideration of the Part of the Clergy Therein." Ph.D. diss., Cambridge Univ., 1953.

Dunlop, L. J. V. "The Use of Color in Parisian Manuscript Illumination c. 1320–1420 with Special Reference to the Availability of Pigments and their Commerce at that Period." Ph.D. diss., Univ. of Manchester, 1988.

Esposito, Lisa. "Orationes Excerpte de Diversis Tractatibus quos Composuit Beatus Ricardus Heremita ad Honorem Nominis Ihesu, Edited from Cambridge University Library MS Kk.6.20." Ph.D. diss., Univ. of York, 1982.

Markow, Deborah. "The Iconography of the Soul in Medieval Art." Ph.D. diss., New York Univ. 1983.

Mellick. H. "A Study of Texts and Drawings in B.M. Additional MS 37049." Ph.D. diss., Centre for Medieval Studies, Univ. of York, 1972.

Michael, Michael A. "The Artists of the Walter de Milemete Treatise." Ph.D. diss., Univ. of London, 1987.

Moran, Jo Ann H. "Educational Development and Social Change in York Diocese from the Fourteenth Century to 1548." Ph.D. diss., Brandeis Univ., 1975.

Orr, Michael. "Bohemian Influences on English Manuscripts from around 1400." Paper presented at the Twenty-first International Congress on Medieval Studies, Kalamazoo, Mich. May 9, 1986.

———. "The Work of a Foreign-Trained Artist in the Hours of Elizabeth the Queen." Paper presented at the Twenty-seventh International Congress of Medieval Studies, Kalamazoo, Mich. May 7, 1992.

Pearman, Sara Jane. "the Iconographic Development of the Cruciform Throne of Grace from the Twelfth Century to the Sixteenth Century." Ph.D. diss., Case Western Reserve Univ. 1974.

Rogers, Nicholas J. "Books of Hours Produced in the Low Countries for the English Market in the Fifteenth Century." M.Litt. thesis, Cambridge Univ. 1982.

Index

Index